Gardening
Month by Month
in
New England

Alison Beck

Lone Pine Publishing

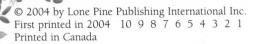

The Distributor: Lone Pine Publishing
1808 B Street NW, Suite 140
Auburn, WA, USA 98001

Website: www.lonepinepublishing.com

National Library of Canada Cataloguing in Publication

Beck, Alison, 1971–
        Gardening month by month in New England / Alison Beck.

ISBN 1–55105–377–2

        1. Gardening—New England. I. Title.

SB453.2.N3B42 2004   635'.0974   C2003–907159–6

Front cover photographs (clockwise from top right): by Tamara Eder, 'Rosemary Harkness'; *by Tim Matheson*, coreopsis; *by Tamara Eder*, poppy, blanket flower, *Heliopsis*, sunflower, marsh marigold, poppy; *by Tim Matheson*, daylily.

The photographs in this book are reproduced with the generous permission of their copy-right holders.

All other photos: All-American Selections 99c, 120–21; Sandra Bit 81a, 113a; Don Doucette 15b, 23b, 39c, 147b; Elliot Engley 31b&d, 33a&b; Jen Fafard 123c, 125b&c, 127a&b, 129c, 131c, 132–33, 151b; Derek Fell 4–5, 5a, 6–7, 35b, 43b, 65c, 75b, 81c, 87b, 93c, 129a, 137b; Erika Flatt 115a&d; Anne Gordon 137c; Saxon Holt 143c, 148; Duncan Kelbaugh 7b&c, 35a, 51b, 57b, 67b, 75a, 83b, 101c, 117a, 147c; Linda Kershaw 36–37; Colin Laroque 96–97; Dawn Loewen 117b; Heather Markham 21a; Marilynn McAra 51c; Steve Nikkila 131a; Kim Patrick O'Leary 29b, 53b; Allison Penko 27a, 113c, 139c, 143a; Laura Peters 19c, 31a, 79a, 119c, 147a, 149d, 151a&c, 152, 153b, 155b,c&d; RBG/Chris Graham 39b; Robert Ritchie 59a, 137a; Peter Thompstone 45b, 141a; Don Williamson 135b, 144–45.

Frost date charts: data from *Climatography of the U.S.* No. 20, Supplement No. 1, provided online by the Victory Seeds Company. **Hardiness zones map:** based on USDA Hardiness Zones Map. **Climate normals and extremes:** data from the Northeast Regional Climate Center at Cornell University.

This book is not intended as a 'how-to' guide for eating garden plants. No plant or plant extract should be consumed unless you are certain of its identity and toxicity and of your potential for allergic reactions.

PC: 01

INTRODUCTION

Despite its challenges, New England is an enviable place to garden. The summers are warm, but often not hot enough to cause heat stress in plants. The winters are cold, ensuring good dormancy and flowering. The coldest areas receive plenty of protective snow. The soil, though often sandy and rocky, supports a huge variety of popular plants.

Geographically, New England is a diverse and varied region. Nothern areas are characterized by forests, rivers, lakes, mountains and a shorter growing season. The climate of coastal areas is tempered by their proximity to the salty air and strong winds of the Atlantic. Inland, deep valleys and rolling foothills provide shelter from cold winter storms that blow in from both the north and the coast.

The USDA hardiness zone map places New England in zones 3 to 7. Possible lows range from –40° to 20° F. While it's useful to know this when selecting plants for your garden, this designation is just a starting point for determining the hardiness of any given plant. The soil conditions and climatic factors such as precipitation and length of growing season equally influence how successfully plants will grow.

New England's climate is indeed excellent for growing many plants, but it can still be challenging. Some research and experimentation are required to get the best results from your garden. Lack of consistent snowcover, cycles of freezing and thawing in winter, high heat and humidity in summer and too much or too little rain are all climatic challenges New England gardeners face. Learning what to expect and when to expect it as well as what plants are best suited to your garden are key elements to gardening.

One of the first steps in knowing what will grow well in your garden is knowing what grows naturally in your region. Native plants

loosestrife

and those that naturalize, occurring in places like wilderness areas or vacant lots, give you an indication of what will also thrive in your garden. Look also at other gardens. The variety of plant material and designs displayed in New England gardens is a testament to the broad selection gardeners here have to choose from.

Free-form English-style cottage gardens, cool, moist woodland gardens, Zen-like Japanese gardens and formal knot gardens—all garden styles you will find in New England. These gardens reflect the skill and enthusiasm of their gardeners and the diversity of the situations in which they garden.

Where we garden varies almost as much as what we garden. Apartment and condo dwellers enjoy container gardening; rural gardeners may till the same soil that many generations of their ancestors did; urban gardeners benefit from living in older neighborhoods with deep topsoil or face the challenge of a new suburban garden with thin, poor quality

Shirley poppies

soil. Whatever the situation, beautiful, successful gardens are possible in every situation.

During the growing season, adequate precipitation can make the difference between gardening success or failure. In a good year, regular rainfall takes care of all our watering needs and only hanging baskets and plants beneath the overhang of the house need to be watered. In a bad year, it seems as if it will never stop raining or that it will never rain again. Although rainfall is fairly dependable, droughts

gazanias

seaside garden (*above*); mini alpine garden (*below*)

naturalistic water feature (*below*)

in mid- and late summer and deluges in spring and fall can occur. As with all the factors that influence our gardens, we must be prepared to make the most of what nature offers us and try to take up the slack where it lets off.

The last frost in spring typically occurs between late April and late May and the first frost of fall between mid-September and late October. The growing season, as defined by these two occurrences, ranges from 100 to 200 days, depending on the year and where you live in the region.

Though soil type and climate can limit our plant selections, it is possible to garden for plants that aren't hardy or that don't like your soil. Planning an entire garden around these more difficult plants results in a lot of extra work, but a small area set aside for just a few such plants is part of the adventure of gardening. Hedges block the wind, trees give shade, raised beds of acidic or moist soil can be built. Know your garden and what it supports, but don't be limited by it. Warmer microclimates exist in almost every garden, regardless of your hardiness zone. They serve to expand the variety of plants your garden will support, so it's worth it to identify where they are in your yard.

The purpose of this book is to give you ideas and to help you plan what should be done and when. Garden tasks are listed in the month they should be completed, and general ideas that can be applied in a variety of months are also included. There is also space for you to write in your own thoughts and ideas.

Climate data and frost and hardiness zone maps are included as general guides to the weather patterns across New England. Most climate statistics shown here were

New England greenery

collected at local or regional airports and may not represent the actual weather in every part of a particular town or city.

The information in this book is general. If you need more detailed information on a topic, refer to the resources listed at the back of the book. Your local library is also an excellent place to search for the information you need. Gardening courses

golden marguerite

a secret garden

crocuses herald the coming of spring

hot peppers

are offered through colleges, continuing education programs, gardening societies and through Master Gardener programs. You can tackle even the most daunting garden task once you are prepared and well informed.

Whether you live in a downtown apartment or condo, a small suburban bungalow or a large country house with several acres of land, you can garden. Beautiful gardens are possible in any location. This monthly guide should answer some of your specific questions about the wonderful gardening possibilities in New England. Add your particular experiences with such factors as unusual weather conditions, when plants sprout and first flower and the birds and insects that appear in your garden. By keeping track of your gardening activities in this book, you will create your own custom-made gardening guide.

Above all else, enjoy your New England garden!

NEW ENGLAND CLIMATE NORMALS 1971–2000

(Climate data from the Northeast Regional Climate Center at Cornell University.)

	CATEGORY	JAN	FEB	MAR	APR	MAY	JUN	JUL	AUG	SEP	OCT	NOV	DEC	YEAR
PRESQUE ISLE, ME	DAILY MAXIMUM (°F)	20.7	25	35.6	48.3	64.3	73.2	77.2	75.6	65.9	52.9	38.3	25.9	50.2
	DAILY MINIMUM (°F)	1.2	4.7	16.2	29	40.6	49.8	55.1	53.1	44.6	34.9	24.7	9.3	30.3
	SNOWFALL (IN)	21.3	18	16.7	6.8	0.2	0	0	0	0.1	0.6	7.4	17.7	88.8
	PRECIPITATION (IN)**	2.55	1.68	2.12	2.35	3.44	3.43	3.71	3.94	3.44	3.28	2.77	2.56	35.27
BANGOR, ME*	DAILY MAXIMUM (°F)	27.6	30.9	40.2	52.6	65.4	74.4	79.6	78.1	69.1	57.3	44.8	33.1	54.4
	DAILY MINIMUM (°F)	8.3	11.4	22.1	33.2	43.6	53.3	58.7	57.2	48.5	38.2	29.3	15.8	35
	SNOWFALL (IN)	N/A	15.8	N/A	N/A	N/A	N/A	N/A	N/A	N/A	N/A	N/A	N/A	N/A
	PRECIPITATION (IN)	3.34	2.54	3.44	3.32	3.4	3.41	3.24	2.99	3.39	3.48	3.69	3.33	39.57
PORTLAND, ME*	DAILY MAXIMUM (°F)	30.9	34.1	42.2	52.8	63.3	72.8	78.8	77.3	68.9	57.9	47.1	36.4	55.2
	DAILY MINIMUM (°F)	12.5	15.6	25.2	34.7	44.2	52.9	58.6	57.2	48.5	37.4	29.5	18.7	36.3
	SNOWFALL (IN)	20.5	12.7	13	3.2	0	0	0	0	0	0.1	3.2	13.6	66.3
	PRECIPITATION (IN)	4.09	3.14	4.14	4.26	3.82	3.28	3.32	3.05	3.37	4.4	4.72	4.24	45.83
CONCORD, NH*	DAILY MAXIMUM (°F)	30.6	34.1	43.8	56.9	69.6	77.9	82.9	80.8	72.1	60.5	47.6	35.6	57.7
	DAILY MINIMUM (°F)	9.7	12.6	22.7	32.2	42.4	51.8	57.1	55.6	46.6	35.1	27.6	16.2	34.1
	SNOWFALL (IN)	18.9	13	11.6	3.1	0	0	0	0	0	0	4.7	13.4	64.7
	PRECIPITATION (IN)	2.97	2.36	3.04	3.07	3.33	3.1	3.37	3.21	3.16	3.46	3.57	2.96	37.6
BURLINGTON, VT	DAILY MAXIMUM (°F)	26.7	29	39.6	53.3	67.8	76.5	81.4	78.4	68.9	56.4	44	32.3	54.5
	DAILY MINIMUM (°F)	9.3	10.9	21.8	33.6	45.2	54.7	59.8	58.1	49.9	38.9	30.3	17.3	35.8
	SNOWFALL (IN)	21.4	15.7	15.6	6.2	0	0	0	0	0	0.3	7.3	17.3	83.8
	PRECIPITATION (IN)	2.22	1.67	2.32	2.88	3.32	3.43	3.97	4.01	3.83	3.12	3.06	2.22	36.05
BOSTON, MA*	DAILY MAXIMUM (°F)	36.5	38.7	46.3	56.1	66.7	76.6	82.2	80.1	72.5	61.8	51.8	41.7	59.3
	DAILY MINIMUM (°F)	22.1	24.2	31.5	40.5	50.2	59.4	65.5	64.5	56.8	46.4	37.9	27.8	43.9
	SNOWFALL (IN)	13.4	11.2	8.1	1.1	0	0	0	0	0	0	1.4	6.7	41.9
	PRECIPITATION (IN)	3.92	3.3	3.85	3.6	3.24	3.22	3.06	3.37	3.47	3.79	3.98	3.73	42.53

*weather data collected at local airport **equivalent to rainfall

NEW ENGLAND CLIMATE NORMALS 1971–2000
(Climate data from the Northeast Regional Climate Center at Cornell University.)

BEDFORD, MA

CATEGORY	JAN	FEB	MAR	APR	MAY	JUN	JUL	AUG	SEP	OCT	NOV	DEC	YEAR
DAILY MAXIMUM (°F)	35	38	46.8	58	69.4	77.5	82.7	80.7	72.4	61.7	50.7	39.6	59.4
DAILY MINIMUM (°F)	15.7	18.2	26.6	35.8	45.8	54.7	60.3	58.9	50.2	39	31.2	21.5	38.2
SNOWFALL (IN)	15.6	11.6	9.4	2.8	0.3	0	0	0	0	0.1	3.2	10.2	53.2
PRECIPITATION (IN)	4.24	3.33	4.21	3.99	3.76	3.61	3.83	3.54	3.84	4.14	4.39	4.07	46.95

GRT. BARRINGTON, MA

CATEGORY	JAN	FEB	MAR	APR	MAY	JUN	JUL	AUG	SEP	OCT	NOV	DEC	YEAR
DAILY MAXIMUM (°F)	31.6	33.9	43.4	56	68.2	76.4	81.2	79	70.8	59.5	47.9	36.4	57
DAILY MINIMUM (°F)	10.5	12.3	22	31.9	42.7	51.6	55.9	53.9	45.6	34	27.5	17.3	33.8
SNOWFALL (IN)	N/A	N/A	N/A	N/A	0.4	0	0	0	0	0.5	3.8	N/A	N/A
PRECIPITATION (IN)	3.7	3.03	3.6	3.85	5	4.18	4.16	4.63	4.07	4	4.12	3.64	47.98

BRIDGEPORT, CT*

CATEGORY	JAN	FEB	MAR	APR	MAY	JUN	JUL	AUG	SEP	OCT	NOV	DEC	YEAR
DAILY MAXIMUM (°F)	36.9	38.8	46.9	57	67.4	76.4	81.9	80.7	73.6	63.1	52.6	42.1	59.8
DAILY MINIMUM (°F)	22.9	24.9	32	40.7	50.6	59.6	66	65.4	57.7	46.3	37.5	28	44.3
SNOWFALL (IN)	8.5	7.2	4.3	0.9	0	0	0	0	0	0	0.7	3.6	25.2
PRECIPITATION (IN)	3.73	2.92	4.15	3.99	4.03	3.57	3.77	3.75	3.58	3.54	3.65	3.47	44.15

HARTFORD, CT*

CATEGORY	JAN	FEB	MAR	APR	MAY	JUN	JUL	AUG	SEP	OCT	NOV	DEC	YEAR
DAILY MAXIMUM (°F)	35.5	38.4	47.1	58.5	70.1	78.6	83.8	81.9	74.1	62.8	51.5	40.3	60.2
DAILY MINIMUM (°F)	16.3	19.2	27.3	37.6	47.8	57.4	63.4	61.2	51.4	39.8	32.3	22.2	39.7
SNOWFALL (IN)	N/A	5.1	3.2	0.6	0	0	0	0	0	0.4	3.1	N/A	
PRECIPITATION (IN)	3.66	2.65	3.61	3.82	3.99	3.83	3.93	3.83	3.83	3.91	3.79	3.44	44.29

WINDSOR LOCKS, CT*

CATEGORY	JAN	FEB	MAR	APR	MAY	JUN	JUL	AUG	SEP	OCT	NOV	DEC	YEAR
DAILY MAXIMUM (°F)	34.1	37.7	47.7	59.9	71.7	80	84.9	82.5	74.3	63.1	50.9	39	60.5
DAILY MINIMUM (°F)	17.2	19.9	28.3	37.9	48.1	57	62.4	60.7	52.1	40.6	32.6	22.6	40
SNOWFALL (IN)	14.4	11.2	7.9	1.5	0.1	0	0	0	0	0.1	2.5	8.4	46.1
PRECIPITATION (IN)	3.84	2.96	3.88	3.86	4.39	3.85	3.67	3.98	4.13	3.94	4.06	3.6	46.16

PROVIDENCE, RI*

CATEGORY	JAN	FEB	MAR	APR	MAY	JUN	JUL	AUG	SEP	OCT	NOV	DEC	YEAR
DAILY MAXIMUM (°F)	37.1	39.3	47.7	58.1	68.5	77.3	82.6	80.9	73.4	62.9	52.4	42.1	60.2
DAILY MINIMUM (°F)	20.3	22.5	30	39.1	48.8	57.9	64.1	62.8	54.5	43.1	35.1	25.6	42
SNOWFALL (IN)	11.4	9.4	5.2	0.7	0.3	0	0	0	0	0.1	1.4	5.8	34.3
PRECIPITATION (IN)	4.37	3.45	4.43	4.16	3.66	3.38	3.17	3.9	3.7	3.69	4.4	4.14	46.45

NEW ENGLAND CLIMATE EXTREMES 1971–2000
(Climate data from the Northeast Regional Climate Center at Cornell University.)

PRESQUE ISLE, ME

MAXIMUM (°F)	99 IN AUGUST 1935
MINIMUM (°F)	-37 IN FEBRUARY 1955
MONTHLY RAINFALL (IN)	9.4 IN SEPTEMBER 1999
DAILY RAINFALL (IN)	4.47 IN SEPTEMBER 1954
MONTHLY SNOWFALL (IN)	49.5 IN DECEMBER 1972
DAILY SNOWFALL (IN)	25 IN MARCH 1931

BANGOR, ME

MAXIMUM (°F)	97 IN SEPTEMBER 2002
MINIMUM (°F)	-30 IN FEBRUARY 1962
MONTHLY RAINFALL (IN)	11.61 IN NOVEMBER 1983
DAILY RAINFALL (IN)	5.98 IN SEPTEMBER 1954
MONTHLY SNOWFALL (IN)	62.5 IN FEBRUARY 1969
DAILY SNOWFALL (IN)	25.5 IN DECEMBER 1962

PORTLAND, ME

MAXIMUM (°F)	103 IN AUGUST 1975
MINIMUM (°F)	-26 IN JANUARY 1971
MONTHLY RAINFALL (IN)	15.22 IN AUGUST 1991
DAILY RAINFALL (IN)	9.62 IN OCTOBER 1996
MONTHLY SNOWFALL (IN)	62.4 IN JANUARY 1979
DAILY SNOWFALL (IN)	30.2 IN JANUARY 1945

CONCORD, NH

MAXIMUM (°F)	102 IN JULY 1966
MINIMUM (°F)	-37 IN FEBRUARY 1943
MONTHLY RAINFALL (IN)	10.72 IN MARCH 1937
DAILY RAINFALL (IN)	7.3 IN MARCH 1937
MONTHLY SNOWFALL (IN)	49.8 IN FEBRUARY 1969
DAILY SNOWFALL (IN)	20.1 IN DECEMBER 1969

BURLINGTON, VT

MAXIMUM (°F)	102 IN JULY 1966
MINIMUM (°F)	-33 IN JANUARY 1984
MONTHLY RAINFALL (IN)	11.54 IN AUGUST 1955
DAILY RAINFALL (IN)	4.45 IN JUNE 1942
MONTHLY SNOWFALL (IN)	58.5 IN DECEMBER 1970
DAILY SNOWFALL (IN)	17.4 IN JANUARY 2003

BOSTON, MA

MAXIMUM (°F)	103 IN JULY 1926
MINIMUM (°F)	-18 IN FEBRUARY 1934
MONTHLY RAINFALL (IN)	17.09 IN AUGUST 1955
DAILY RAINFALL (IN)	7.06 IN AUGUST 1955
MONTHLY SNOWFALL (IN)	42.3 IN JANUARY 1945
DAILY SNOWFALL (IN)	23.6 IN FEBRUARY 2003

BEDFORD, MA

MAXIMUM (°F)	101 IN AUGUST 1975
MINIMUM (°F)	-19 IN JANUARY 1984
MONTHLY RAINFALL (IN)	13.24 IN JANUARY 1979
DAILY RAINFALL (IN)	7.83 IN OCTOBER 1996
MONTHLY SNOWFALL (IN)	61 IN FEBRUARY 1969
DAILY SNOWFALL (IN)	21 IN MARCH 1960

GRT. BARRINGTON, MA

MAXIMUM (°F)	99 IN JULY 1988
MINIMUM (°F)	-27 IN JANUARY 1994
MONTHLY RAINFALL (IN)	12.82 IN MAY 1984
DAILY RAINFALL (IN)	5.83 IN SEPTEMBER 1999
MONTHLY SNOWFALL (IN)	58 IN JANUARY 1996
DAILY SNOWFALL (IN)	18 IN MARCH 1993

BRIDGEPORT, CT

MAXIMUM (°F)	103 IN JULY 1957
MINIMUM (°F)	-7 IN JANUARY 1984
MONTHLY RAINFALL (IN)	17.7 IN JUNE 1972
DAILY RAINFALL (IN)	6.18 IN JUNE 1972
MONTHLY SNOWFALL (IN)	29.8 IN JANUARY 1965
DAILY SNOWFALL (IN)	17 IN FEBRUARY 2003

HARTFORD, CT

MAXIMUM (°F)	103 IN AUGUST 2001
MINIMUM (°F)	-24 IN FEBRUARY 1943
MONTHLY RAINFALL (IN)	14.59 IN SEPTEMBER 1938
DAILY RAINFALL (IN)	6.1 IN SEPTEMBER 1938
MONTHLY SNOWFALL (IN)	35.9 IN DECEMBER 1945
DAILY SNOWFALL (IN)	17.7 IN DECEMBER 1945

WINDSOR LOCKS, CT

MAXIMUM (°F)	102 IN JULY 1966
MINIMUM (°F)	-26 IN JANUARY 1961
MONTHLY RAINFALL (IN)	21.29 IN AUGUST 1955
DAILY RAINFALL (IN)	7.7 IN AUGUST 1955
MONTHLY SNOWFALL (IN)	43.3 IN MARCH 1956
DAILY SNOWFALL (IN)	16.3 IN FEBRUARY 2001

PROVIDENCE, RI

MAXIMUM (°F)	104 IN AUGUST 1975
MINIMUM (°F)	-13 IN JANUARY 1976
MONTHLY RAINFALL (IN)	12.74 IN APRIL 1983
DAILY RAINFALL (IN)	6.31 IN AUGUST 1979
MONTHLY SNOWFALL (IN)	37.8 IN JANUARY 1978
DAILY SNOWFALL (IN)	25 IN JANUARY 1979

NEW ENGLAND STATES AVERAGE FROST DATES, 2004

Spring frost occurs 10% of the time after given date.
Fall frost occurs 10% of the time before the given date.

Connecticut	Last Spring	First Fall
Danbury	May 15	Sept 15
Falls Village	June 3	Sept 12
Hartford	May 12	Sept 23
Mt. Carmel	May 14	Sept 24
Norwalk (Gas Plant)	May 8	Oct 2
Storrs	May 14	Sept 24
West Thompson	June 4	Sept 13

Maine	Last Spring	First Fall
Augusta	May 12	Sept 22
Bar Harbor	May 17	Oct 3
Lewiston	May 10	Oct 3
Portland	May 25	Sept 18
Presque Isle	June 6	Sept 4
Ripogenus	May 31	Sept 12
Rumford	June 1	Sept 13

Massachusetts	Last Spring	First Fall
Boston	May 3	Oct 5
Greenfield	May 26	Sept 16
Haverhill	May 2	Oct 6
Hyannis	May 26	Sept 25
New Bedford	April 20	Oct 22
Rochester	May 22	Sept 24
Springfield	April 29	Sept 29

New Hampshire	Last Spring	First Fall
Bethlehem	June 9	Sept 9
Concord	June 9	Sept 8
Hanover	May 30	Sept 18
Keene	June 4	Sept 11
Lakeport	May 21	Sept 30
Mt. Washington	July 29	Aug 2
Nashua	June 2	Sept 12

Rhode Island	Last Spring	First Fall
Block Island	April 20	Oct 29
Kingston	May 23	Sept 17

Vermont	Last Spring	First Fall
Bellows Falls	May 28	Sept 21
Burlington	May 25	Sept 19
Chelsea	June 23	Aug 27
Dorset	June 14	Sept 2
Montpelier	June 3	Sept 8
Newport	June 6	Sept 10

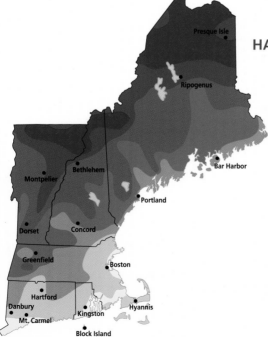

HARDINESS ZONES MAP

Average Annual Minimum Temperature

Zone	Temp (°F)
3b	-30 to -35
4a	-25 to -30
4b	-20 to -25
5a	-15 to -20
5b	-10 to -15
6a	-5 to -10
6b	0 to -5
7a	5 to 0

JANUARY

*Now is the time for planning and
dreaming of the distant summer
and the garden yet to be.*

JANUARY

1

2

*Avoid using chemical de-icers because they are
harmful to lawns and garden plants, and they
add to the salt problem in areas affected by
salt-laden wind and spray.*

3

4

*Instead of recycling your Christmas tree,
cut it up and use the branches
as a mulch to shelter low-growing shrubs
and groundcovers.*

5

6

7

One of the flowers you might dream of adding to
your garden in spring is the beautiful hybrid tea
'Loving Memory' (*left*). This zone 5 rose will flourish
in many New England gardens. Cotoneaster (*right*)

In most years, the garden is blanketed in snow in January, but some New England gardens are just as likely to be bare and exposed to fluctuations in temperature. South-facing walls are always warmer than other areas of the garden. Snow melts most quickly here, leaving plants vulnerable to the stressful cycles of heat and cold. A thick fall mulch proves to be extremely valuable in a snowless area.

THINGS TO DO

January is one of the hardest months for the garden and the easiest for the gardener.

The ice storms and freezing rain that commonly occur during our winters can damage plants, though in warmer weather they should spring back to normal. Annual pruning promotes a compact form that resists ice damage.

Don't forget to top up your bird-feeders regularly. Feeding the birds encourages them to keep visiting in summer when they will help keep your insect pest populations under control.

Snow is the garden's best friend. Pile clean snow on snowless garden beds to insulate them against the wind and cold. Some people refer to this as 'snow farming.'

JANUARY

8

9

Avoid placing houseplants in hot or cold drafts.

10

11

Order gardening and seed catalogs to look through even if you don't start your own seeds.

Ice fishers: save a bag of smelt or tommy cod in the freezer. Put one fish next to each potato eye next spring for a great natural fertilizer.

12

13

14

Begonias (*left*) can be brought indoors in fall and kept as houseplants in a sunny location through the winter. Peony-flowered poppies (*top and bottom right*); Iceland poppies (*center right*)

Gently brush snow off the branches of evergreens such as cedars, but leave any ice that forms to melt naturally. The weight of the snow or ice can permanently bend flexible branches, but more damage is done trying to remove ice than is done through its weight.

Choose and order seeds for early starting. Sort through the seeds you have, test them for viability and throw out any that don't germinate or that you won't grow. Trade seeds with gardening friends.

Get lawn mowers and other power tools serviced now. They will be ready for use in spring, and you may get a better price before the spring rush.

Annual poppy seeds are easy to collect and share. Pick seedheads when they are dry, and shake the fine seed on open ground from August to December for flowers next year.

To test older seeds for viability, place 10 seeds between two layers of moist paper towel and put them in a sealed container. Keep the paper evenly dampened but not too wet. Seeds may rot if the paper towel is too moist. Check each day to see if the seeds have sprouted. If fewer than half the seeds have sprouted after two weeks, buy new ones.

JANUARY

*Reduce watering of houseplants because
most need less water during winter.*

*For a rustic bird treat, spread peanut butter
around pine cones, roll them in bird seed and
then hang them around the yard.*

The datura (*left*) is an elegant, exotic-looking plant
that produces large, showy, scented flowers. Daturas
must be brought indoors in the winter or left to die
with the annuals. *From top right:* rex begonia; coleus
with spider plant; pothos

Clean the foliage of your houseplants. When light levels are low, it is important for plants to be able to use whatever light is available. As a bonus, you might help reduce insect populations because their eggs will likely be wiped off along with the dust.

Check houseplants regularly for common indoor pests such as whiteflies, scale insects, spider mites and mealybugs.

GARDEN DESIGN

As you look out your windows at the frozen yard, think about what could make your garden look attractive in winter. Features such as birdbaths, ponds, benches, decks and winding pathways improve the look and function of your garden year-round. Persistent fruit or seedheads, unusual bark and branch patterns, evergreens and colorfully stemmed shrubs also provide winter interest.

Most indoor plants will benefit from increased humidity levels. Place pots on a tray of pebbles. If you add water to the pebbles when needed, you will increase the humidity through evaporation but prevent water-logged roots.

JANUARY

January is a great time for garden planning.
In winter, the bones of the garden are
laid bare, so you can take a good look
at its overall structure.

Give pot-bound houseplants a boost—and
make them look better too—by repotting them
into larger pots every year or two.

Rosehips (*left*), spiral topiary, the bright berries
of viburnum (*top left and right*), the winged
seeds of amur maple (*center right*), and the
curving branches of Japanese maple (*bottom
right*) add interest to the garden in winter.

Plants that add variety to a winter garden:

- Clematis (*Clematis*): fuzzy seed-heads
- Corkscrew Hazel (*Corylus*): twisted and contorted branches
- Cotoneaster (*Cotoneaster*): persistent red berries
- Dogwood (*Cornus*): red, purple or yellow stems
- Highbush Cranberry (*Viburnum trilobum*): bright red berries
- Maple (*Acer ginnala*, *A. palmatum*): attractive bark and branching patterns
- Shrub Rose (*Rosa*): brightly colored hips
- Topiary: sculpted trees, many species, in spiral, pompom and clipped standard shapes
- Weeping trees such as Peatree (*Caragana*), Birch (*Betula*), Mulberry (*Morus*): striking form
- White cedar (*Thuja*), False Cypress (*Chamaecyparis*) or Juniper (*Juniperus*): evergreen branches
- Winged Euonymus (*Euonymus alatus*): corky ridges on the branches

JANUARY

*Imagine the garden you'd like to have,
and keep this notebook and your diagrams
at hand so you can jot down ideas
as they come to you.*

*The gorgeous blue of Colorado spruce is a
surface pigment that may get weathered away
during winter. June's flush of growth brings
new steel blue needles.*

Woody evergreens,
such as white cedar
(*left*), upright juniper
(*top right*) and white
spruce (*far right*), add
interesting texture and
rich green color to a
sometimes monotonous
winter landscape.

PROBLEM AREAS
IN THE GARDEN

Keep track of these potential problem areas in your garden:

- windswept areas: perhaps a tree, shrub or hedge could be added next summer to provide shelter
- snowfree areas: places where the snow is always quick to melt are poor choices for very tender plants, which benefit most from the protection of the snow
- snowbound areas: places where the snow is slowest to melt provide the most protection to plants but stay frozen longest in spring, making them poor locations for spring-flowering plants
- waterlogged areas: places where water pools or is slow to drain during extended wet periods are best reserved for plants that tolerate their roots being wet
- dry areas: places that rarely get wet and drain quickly when they do should be used for drought-tolerant plants.

Spruce are widely grown, and new varieties are available almost every gardening season. They are well suited to cold winters, and some, such as the Colorado blue spruce (*left*), provide wonderful blue-green color against brilliant white snow.

FEBRUARY

The longer days and occasional warm
spells turn our thoughts to the
upcoming gardening season.

FEBRUARY

1

2

Keep a birdfeeder stocked with niger (thistle seed) all winter and goldfinches may stick around. Siskins and redpolls like them, too.

3

4

Keep an eye out for low spots and puddles in garden beds. 'Wet feet' kills more perennials than extreme cold in winter. Raise these areas next spring for better drainage.

5

6

7

Colorful little crabapples often remain on the branches of the tree through winter, a reminder of the beautiful blossoms to come in spring (*left and top right*). Flowering crabapple trees in spring (*bottom right*)

Groundhog Day is a teaser for New England gardeners. By February we all want winter to be over soon, but more often than not, the cold and snow stay around. Gardening can get under way, however. Finish ordering plants and seeds from catalogs and gather other supplies for indoor seeding, such as containers, soil, amendments and lights.

THINGS TO DO

February is another month with few tasks, but preparations can be made now that will keep things moving smoothly once the season kicks into high gear.

Check shrubs and trees for storm-damaged branches, and remove them using proper pruning techniques.

Cut branches of flowering shrubs, such as forsythia, crabapple and cherry, to bring indoors. Placed in a bright location in a vase of water, they will begin to flower, giving you a taste of spring in winter.

FEBRUARY

8

Three excellent houseplants for low light areas are spider plant (Chlorophytum), compact Janet Craig dracaena (Dracaena) and umbrella tree (Schefflera).

9

Continue to check for insect pests on your houseplants.

10

Thoroughly clean empty planters, containers and seed trays to get them ready for spring planting.

11

12

13

Don't forget your fish out there in the cold! Keep a small hole in the pond ice open to let gases out and oxygen in. A small pump on the bottom of the pond aimed upwards keeps a spot open all winter.

14

Dianthus (*left*), browallia (*top right*), lady's mantle (*far right*) and begonia (*near right*) are plants you can start from seed in February.

Some slower growing annual and perennial flowers should be started in late February:

- Amethyst Flower (*Browallia*)
- Baby's Breath (*Gypsophila*)
- Begonia (*Begonia*)
- Bellflower (*Campanula*)
- Dusty Miller (*Senecio*)
- Geranium (*Pelargonium*)
- Lady's Mantle (*Alchemilla*)
- Pansy (*Viola*)
- Pinks (*Dianthus*)

Starting plants from seed is a great way to propagate a large number of plants at a relatively low cost. You can grow plants you can't find at any garden center and get a jump-start on the growing season.

FEBRUARY

15

16

Pond lovers, bring your hobby inside for winter with an aquarium. Start small (and less expensive) goldfish and koi inside to put in your pond when they get big.

17

18

Check to see if any of the tubers or bulbs you are storing indoors have started sprouting. Pot them and keep them in a bright location once they do.

19

20

21

Many varieties of dahlia (*left*) can be started from seed in March for transplanting after the danger of frost has passed. Calamondin (*top left*); fresh herbs growing in a greenhouse in winter (*center right*); seed tray, pots, soil and spray mister for indoor seeding (*bottom right*)

STARTING SEEDS

To start seeds, you'll need
- pots, trays or peat pots
- sterile seed-starting mix
- plastic bags or tray covers to keep the seedbed humid
- spray bottle or watering can with sprinkler attachment
- heat mat (optional)

Seedlings will be weak and floppy if they don't get enough light. Consider purchasing a fluorescent or other grow light (*above*) to provide extra illumination for them.

Styrofoam meat trays make economical seed-starting trays. Seeds sprinkled on moist perlite and covered with plastic wrap germinate quickly. Lift wrap when seed leaves form (one to two weeks) and transplant.

Tips for growing healthy seedlings:
- Transplant seedlings to individual containers once they have three or four true leaves to prevent crowding.
- Space plants so that the leaves do not overshadow those of neighboring plants.
- Grow seedlings in moderate temperatures away from direct heat.
- Provide air circulation with a small fan to keep foliar diseases from starting.
- Don't fertilize young seedlings until the seed leaves (the first leaves to appear) have begun to shrivel; then use a weak fertilizer once a week.

22

23

As the days get longer, indoor plants may start to show signs of new growth. Increase watering and apply a weak fertilizer (1/4 strength) only after they begin to grow.

24

25

Do most of your indoor seeding in March and April so that you'll have sturdy transplants ready by the time the last frost has come and gone in spring (late April to late May). For guidance, see the seed-starting notices in March, April and May.

26

27

29

Calathea plants (*left*) offer strikingly exotic foliage and prefer moist, partially shaded conditions.

SEED STARTING TIPS

- Moisten the soil before you fill the containers.
- Firm the soil down in the containers, but don't pack it too tightly.
- Leave seeds that require light for germination uncovered.
- Plant large seeds individually by poking a hole in the soil with the tip of a pen or pencil and then dropping the seed in the hole.
- Spread small seeds evenly across the soil surface, then lightly cover with more soil mix.
- To spread small seeds, place them in the crease of a folded piece of paper and gently tap the bottom of the fold to roll them onto the soil (*top right*).
- Mix very tiny seeds, like those of begonia, with very fine sand before planting to spread them out more evenly.
- Plant only one type of seed in each container. Some seeds will germinate before others, and it is difficult to keep both seeds and seedlings happy in the same container.
- Cover pots or trays of seeds with clear plastic to keep them moist (*right*).
- Seeds do not need bright, direct light to germinate and can be kept in an out-of-the-way place until they begin to sprout.
- After germination, and once seedlings start to emerge, moisten the soil with a hand-held spray mister when it begins to dry out.
- Keep seedlings in a bright location to reduce stretching, and remove plastic cover.

To prevent seedlings from damping-off, always use a sterile soil mix, thoroughly clean containers before using them, maintain good air circulation around seedlings and keep the soil moist, not soggy.

FEBRUARY

Envision the garden you want rather than the one you have by designing your own layout (*example below*). Garden design can be as simple as planting a container to display on your patio or deck, or as complex as creating beds and borders or building shelters, walkways or a pond (*opposite page*).

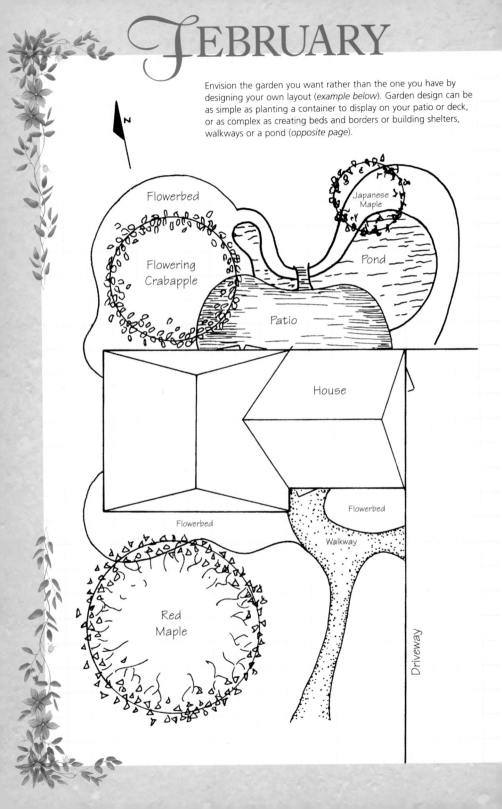

Flowerbed

Japanese Maple

Flowering Crabapple

Pond

Patio

House

Flowerbed

Flowerbed

Walkway

Red Maple

Driveway

GARDEN PLANNING

Using graph paper, plot out the existing yard and house:

- Put in trees, shrubs and other solid structural elements. If you remember where the flowerbeds are, add those as well. Garden beds can be added later if you're not sure. Make copies and use them to keep track of your plans.
- Create a master plan and then sub-plans so you can keep track of the changes you'd like to make each year.
- Make another plan of just your vegetable garden, if you have one, so you can plan and keep track of crop rotations.

MARCH

Expect the unexpected in March. Our gardens
can be under a blanket of snow one day
and showing the first signs of spring the next.

MARCH

1

2

Prune any growth that was damaged over winter off your trees and shrubs (see p. 58).

3

The single most important thing you can do when planting is to make sure you have the right plant in the right location. Consider the mature size of the plant and its cultural requirements.

4

5

6

When pruning larger limbs, look for the branch collar (ring of bark at the base) and prune just outside the collar to ensure proper healing. Leave the pruned area exposed to dry and heal—do not apply tree paint or tar.

7

When designing your garden, consider planting a fast-growing, drought-tolerant elder (*left and near right*). The elder's showy foliage adds color and texture to a landscape, and its edible berries can be made into jelly or wine, or left for the birds.

Early warm spells lure us out to see what's sprouting. Catkins and pussy willows begin to swell, hellebores open from beneath the melting snow and snowdrops begin the long parade of spring bulbs. Just when we think winter is over, a late snowfall blankets the garden and we go back to planning.

THINGS TO DO

The first few tasks of spring get us out in the garden in March.

Days can be warm enough so that some plants start sprouting. Keep snow piled on beds or top up mulches to protect tender plants from the freezing nights.

Prune red-twig dogwoods (*above*) anytime after snowmelt, but wait to prune spring-bloomers like the native pagoda dogwood (*top*) until they finish blooming.

MARCH

8

SEEDS TO START INDOORS NOW
leeks, onions

9

As the snow melts, start clearing up the debris in your yard, such as leaves, sticks, garbage and animal droppings.

10

Prune late-flowering shrubs (July or later) and shrubs grown for colorful young growth (see p. 58 for tips).

11

12

13

14

As soon as the snow begins to melt in spring, the leaves of the bergenia become visible and are quickly followed by its pretty magenta flowers (*left*). Spirea (*top right*); hardy kiwi (*center right*); big-leaf hydrangea (*bottom right*). Bigleaf hydrangeas should be given a sheltered spot and winter mulch.

Keep off your lawn when it is frozen, bare of snow and/or very wet to avoid damaging the grass or compacting the soil.

Apply horticultural oil (also called dormant oil), used to control overwintering insects, to trees, shrubs and vines, before the buds swell. Follow the directions carefully to avoid harming plants and beneficial insects.

Plants to prune in spring:

- Butterfly Bush (*Buddleia davidii*)
- Golden or Purple-leafed Elder (*Sambucus*)
- Hardy Kiwi (*Actinidia arguta*)
- Hydrangea (*Hydrangea*)
- Japanese Spirea (*Spirea japonica*)
- Potentilla (*Potentilla*)
- Red-twig Dogwood (*Cornus* spp.)
- Spirea (*Spiraea*)

MARCH

15

16

Traditional maple-tapping season starts now and continues for a month or so. Twenty taps, one or two per mature sugar maple tree, will yield a gallon or more of delicious syrup per season.

SEEDS TO START INDOORS NOW
alyssum, candytuft, cosmos, delphinium, foxglove, impatiens, salvia, sweet william

17

18

More houseplants will start growing in response to longer days; increase watering and fertilize sparingly.

19

20

21

Bigleaf (or *macrophylla*) hydrangea (*left*) is a popular shrub that needs a protected site and moist soil. If planted early enough in spring, clematis (*top left*) flowers the first summer; a lush sunken garden (*bottom right*)

PLANTING IN SPRING

Early spring is prime planting time. Trees, shrubs, vines and perennials often establish most quickly if planted just as they are about to break dormancy. Plan now what you will want to move, divide and plant as soon as you can work the ground in April.

Avoid using horticultural oil on blue-needled evergreens, such as blue spruce (*above*). The treatment takes the blue off the existing needles, though the new needles will be blue.

MARCH

22

SEEDS TO START INDOORS NOW
*carnation, lobelia, feverfew,
chrysanthemum*

23

*Before doing any digging, call your utility
companies to locate any buried wires,
cables or pipes. Doing so prevents injury
and saves time and money.*

24

*Don't plant vigorous spreaders in rock
gardens with tiny alpine plants or large
shrubs right next to walkways. Choose the
plant that best fits the location.*

25

26

27

*To keep hand pruners sharp, use a round file
on the bevelled edge of the blade only.
Four or five strokes should do the job.*

28

Rhododendrons (*left*) thrive in sheltered locations and
must be planted in moist, fertile, acidic and well-drained
soil to do well. Rhododendrons are sensitive to high
pH, salinity and extreme winter exposure,
and will not grow well if these
conditions are present. Flowering
quince (*top right*); goat's beard
(*bottom right*)

A few things to keep in mind when planting your garden:

- Never work with your soil when it is very wet or very dry.

- Avoid planting during the hottest, sunniest part of the day. Choose an overcast day, or plant early or late in the day.

- Prepare your soil before you plant to avoid damaging roots later.

- Get your new plants into the ground as soon as possible when you get them home. Roots can get hot and dry out quickly in containers. Keep plants in a shady spot if you must wait to plant them.

- Plants are happiest when planted at the same depth they have always grown at. Trees, in particular, can be killed by too deep a planting.

- Remove containers before planting. Plastic and fiber pots restrict root growth and prevent plants from becoming established.

- Plants should be well watered when they are newly planted. Watering deeply and infrequently will encourage the strongest root growth.

- Check the root zone before watering. The soil surface may appear dry when the roots are still moist.

MARCH

29

30

If a plant needs well-drained soil and full sun to thrive, it will be healthiest and best able to fight off problems in those conditions. Work with your plants' natural tendencies.

31

The splendid yellow shrub rose 'Morden Sunrise' (*below*) works well in cold and mild climates. Flower color intensifies in cooler temperatures and becomes softer and paler in hot weather.

Harden annuals and perennials off before planting them by gradually exposing them to longer periods of time outside. Doing so gives your plants time to adapt to outdoor weather conditions and reduces the chance of transplant shock. Hardening off allows plants to adapt to outdoor conditions and reduces transplant shock. Hardy perennials can be planted by late April and annuals by late May.

Remove only dead and damaged branches when planting trees or shrubs, and let the plant establish itself for at least one year before you begin any formative pruning. Plants need all the branches and leaves they have when they are trying to get established.

Trees less than 5' tall do not need staking unless they are in a very windy location. Unstaked trees develop stronger root systems.

planting a balled-and-burlapped tree

planting a bare-root tree

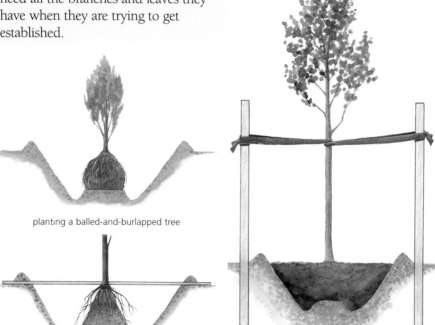

staking a tree properly

APRIL

*Cool, wet weather prevails, but the garden
continues to awaken, sprout and flower.
Spring is almost here.*

APRIL

1

aster, celery, pepper, petunia, pinks, snapdragon, zinnia

2

Plant trees, shrubs and vines once the soil can be worked.

3

Check your power tools, such as the lawn mower, and have them serviced if you didn't do it over winter.

4

5

6

7

The columbine (*left*) is a beautiful flower that some say resembles a bird in flight. Its jewel-like colors herald the coming of summer. *Opposite page, clockwise from top left:* primroses; tulips; Bethlehem sage (*Pulmonaria saccharata* 'Mrs. Moon'), all early bloomers

Frequent and early trips to the garden center give you an opportunity to buy spring-flowering plants and those in limited supply. Regular trips through the season allow you to see what's in bloom at different times so you can create a garden of long-lasting floral displays.

Though winter seems to have passed for most gardeners, it doesn't yet feel warm enough to be spring. Old snowbanks take forever to melt. Fog, rain and even a late spring flurry hold off the warmer weather. Green shoots emerge and call us to the garden, but only the truly devoted venture forth. The rest of us feel assured that warm days are just around the corner and that the tidying can wait just a bit longer.

APRIL

8

9

Pull back mulch from sprouting plants, but keep mulch or a sheet handy to cover plants up when frost is expected.

10

11

Clean up the garden. Rake debris off lawns and prune back old perennial growth.

12

13

14

Consider planting daylilies (*left*) this spring. Though each bloom lasts only a day, these hardy perennials are easy going, prolific and versatile, and come in an almost infinite variety of forms, sizes and colors. Magnolia (*top right*); Juniper bonsai (*bottom right*)

THINGS TO DO

Gear up for raking, digging, planting and pruning. We begin the hard work that will let us sit back and enjoy the garden once summer arrives.

Bring garden tools out of storage and examine them for rust or other damage. Clean and sharpen them if you didn't before you put them away in fall.

Store any plants you have purchased or started indoors in as bright a location as possible. You may begin to harden them off by placing them outdoors for a short period on warmer days.

Avoid working your soil until it has thawed and dried out a bit. It's dry enough when you can make a soil ball that will crumble apart again when squeezed.

Seeds sown directly into the garden may take longer to germinate than those planted indoors, but the resulting plants will be stronger.

Ever considered creating your own bonsai? It's a great activity for a rainy day. The best plant to start with is a one- or two-gallon potted Japanese garden juniper. Prune away excess branches to reveal the twisted trunk structure: instant bonsai. Get a textbook for a detailed how-to.

APRIL

15

16

SEEDS TO START INDOORS NOW
coleus, dwarf dahlia, herbs, lavatera,
marigold, tomato

17

18

19

20

Divide perennials that bloom in summer or
later, such as asters, daylilies and sedums, as
soon as plants exhibit spring growth.

21

Clematis such as C. 'Gravetye Beauty' (*left*) are popular
perennial vines with beautiful, showy flowers in
many shapes and sizes. By planting a variety of them,
you can have clematis in bloom from spring to fall.
Opposite page, clockwise from top left: C. 'Hagley
Hybrid'; C. integrifolia; C. viticella 'Etoile Violette'

Remove mulch from perennials and trim back and clear away any of last year's growth. Cover them again when a hard frost is expected.

Clear away any of the annuals or vegetables that didn't make it to the compost pile last fall.

By the end of the month, you will have an idea of what has been damaged or killed back over winter, and you can begin trimming or removing plants as needed.

Cool, wet spring weather can cause drought-loving plants to rot. Improve soil drainage through the addition of organic matter and by raising bed height.

Dwarf Alberta spruce doesn't like hot sun and may burn or get spider mites if planted in a sheltered, south-facing location. Plant it in a breezy, partly shaded spot.

*A*PRIL

22

SEEDS TO START INDOORS NOW
*vegetables in the cabbage family,
hollyhocks, lettuce*

23

Repot houseplants if needed.

24

*Branched twigs make great natural supports
for leaning houseplants such as
umbrella tree, dracaena and jade plant.
They blend in perfectly and work
for outdoor flowers, too.*

25

26

27

28

You can depend on aubretia (*left*) to put
on a great floral show in spring. *Opposite
page, clockwise from top right:*
pruning with long-handled
loppers; pompom juniper;
formally pruned yew hedge
and white cedar

PRUNING

Prune trees and shrubs to maintain their health and attractive shape, increase the quality and yield of fruit, control and direct growth and create interesting plant forms.

Once you learn how to prune plants correctly, it is an enjoyable garden task. There are many good books available on the topic of pruning. Two are listed at the back of this book. If you are unsure about pruning, take a pruning course, often offered by garden centers, botanical gardens and adult education programs.

Start pruning when your shrubs are young. That way it's an easy task, and you'll learn as the plant grows how it responds to your pruning.

APRIL

Opposite page, clockwise from top left: climbing rose with support; espalier; proper hand pruner orientation

PRUNING TIPS

- Prune at the right time of year. Trees and shrubs that flower before June, usually on the previous year's wood, should be pruned after they have flowered. Trees and shrubs that flower after June, usually on new growth, can be pruned in spring.

- Use the correct tool for the size of branch to be removed: hand pruners for growth up to ¾" in diameter; long-handled loppers for growth up to 1½" in diameter; or a pruning saw for growth up to about 6" in diameter.

- Always use clean and sharp tools.

- Always use hand pruners or loppers with the blade side towards the plant and the hook towards the part to be removed.

thinning cuts

Thin trees and shrubs to promote the growth of younger, healthier branches. Doing so rejuvenates a plant. Thinning out longer branches will control size and shape.

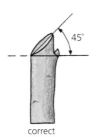

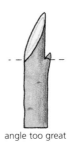

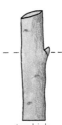

| correct | too low | angle too great | too high |

When pruning, avoid the following:

- Don't leave stubs. Whether you are cutting off a large branch or deadheading a lilac, always cut back to a joint. Branches should be removed to the branch collar, and smaller growth should be cut back to a bud or branch union. There is no absolute set angle for pruning. Each plant should be pruned according to its individual needs.

- Never use pruning paint or paste. Trees have a natural ability to create a barrier between living and dead wood. Painting over a cut impairs this ability.

- Never try to remove a tree or large branch by yourself. Have someone help you, or hire a professional to do it.

- Don't top trees. It's bad for their health and makes them look ugly.

Always hire an ISA (International Society of Arboriculture) certified professional to remove branches on trees growing near power lines or other hazardous areas, especially if they could damage a building, fence or car if they were to fall. Branches and trees are usually much heavier than anticipated and can do a lot of damage if they fall in the wrong place.

MAY

The promise of spring is fulfilled with
the sprouting and blooming of May, and
winter becomes a distant memory.

MAY

1

2

*Move or divide any perennials that didn't
have enough space last summer.*

3

4

*Start new garden beds or expand
and improve old ones.*

5

6

*Time to clean your pond. Drain the water,
keeping fish in a large cooler of pond water;
hand pick, flush and pump out leaves and
debris; divide lilies and other plants; install the
pump; refill the pond and return your fish.*

7

The Japanese anemone or windflower (*left*) is
an attractive plant at all stages. Some varieties
bloom in spring while others reserve their lovely
display for fall. Saucer magnolia (*top right*) flowers
in mid- to late spring; the combination of tulips and
pansies (*bottom right*) makes an interesting color
and height contrast in a spring flowerbed.

May weather is unpredictable, one year warm and sunny and the next cold and wet. In a typical May, bulbs are blooming, peonies poke up their red and green spears and spring-flowering trees like magnolia and crabapple burst forth in a riot of color. Even the most devoted lawn lover knows that spring is truly here when the first dandelion of spring, tucked up against a south wall, opens its fuzzy face to the sun.

THINGS TO DO

A new gardening season awaits, one where we haven't forgotten to weed or water, where all our plants are properly spaced and well staked and where no insects have chewed any leaves. Now is the time to finish tidying up the garden, prepare the garden beds and get the planting done.

MAY

8

9

SEEDS TO START INDOORS NOW
snapdragons, cleome (spiderflower)

10

11

Begin to harden off any houseplants you plan to move outdoors for summer.

Work compost into your garden beds and fork them over, removing weeds as you go, to prepare them for planting later in the month.

12

13

14

A traditional garden favorite, sweet peas (*left*) are easy to grow from seed in spring. They sprout quickly and have sweetly scented blooms that can be cut often for fragrant indoor bouquets. Phlox (*top left*), cabbage (*top right*) and love-in-a-mist (*center right*) can be planted before the last spring frost; raised cutting garden (*bottom left*)

You can sow many seeds and plants early if you use row covers to warm up your vegetable beds.

Many plants prefer to grow in cool weather and can be started outside well before the last frost. These seeds can be planted as soon as the soil can be worked:

- Bachelor's Buttons (*Centaurea cyanus*)
- Cabbage (*Brassica oleracea*)
- Calendula (*Calendula officinalis*)
- California Poppy (*Eschscholzia californica*)
- Godetia (*Clarkia amoena*)
- Kale (*Brassica napus*)
- Love-in-a-Mist (*Nigella damascena*)
- Peas (*Pisum sativum*)
- Phlox (*Phlox drummondii*)
- Poppy (*Papaver rhoeas*)
- Potato (*Solanum tuberosum*)
- Rocket Larkspur (*Consolida ajacis*)
- Spinach (*Spinacea oleracea*)
- Sweet Pea (*Lathyrus odoratus*)
- Swiss Chard (*Beta vulgaris*)

MAY

15

16

SEEDS TO START INDOORS NOW
cucumbers, squash, pumpkins, melons

Continue to harden off your early-started seedlings and purchased plants so they will be ready to plant outside as soon as the weather is warm enough.

17

18

When planning your vegetable garden, consider planting extra to donate to a local food bank or homeless shelter. Even if you just end up with extra zucchini and tomatoes, they can be put to good use.

Wait until this late date to seed heat-loving plants indoors to ensure vigorous transplants and warm soil and weather.

19

20

21

Plant a sunny spring flower such as doronicum (*left*) with tulips and forget-me-nots to create a cheerful May display.

It is possible to have a healthy, attractive organic lawn. Grass is an extremely competitive plant, capable of fighting off invasions by weeds, pests and diseases without the use of chemicals. Watering with compost tea encourages a healthy lawn.

Accept that grass will not grow everywhere. Grass requires plenty of sun and regular moisture. Many trees and buildings provide too much shade and don't allow enough water to get to the soil for grass to grow successfully. Use mulch or other groundcovers in areas where you have trouble growing grass. When selecting trees to plant in the lawn, choose ones that will provide only light shade and that will tolerate sharing a limited water supply with the grass, or have a grass-free zone extending from the base of the tree to the dripline.

Lawns need very little water to remain green. Watering deeply and infrequently will encourage deep roots that are not easily damaged during periods of drought. Generally, 1" of water a week keeps grass green. Deeper topsoil (6" or more) with higher organic content needs less watering, if any.

The last frost in New England falls between late April and late May, depending on the year and where you garden. In a warm year, when the nights stay above freezing earlier than expected, you can try a few tender plants, such as tomatoes. If there are no more frosts, you will gain several weeks on the growing season. In a cool year you may have to wait until the end of May or the beginning of June before planting to give the soil more time to warm before planting tender heat-lovers such as squash, peppers and beans (*left*).

MAY

22

23

Leave several strong stems of asparagus uncut per plant to ensure future strength.

24

25

De-thatch lawns in spring if the thatch layer is deeper than 3/4". Hardware stores carry simple attachments to make your lawnmower a de-thatching aid.

26

27

To restore bare spots in your lawn, loosen turf, sprinkle grass seed and cover lightly with compost.

28

With their wide variety of leaf shapes, sizes and colors, hostas (*left*) are a popular addition to shaded New England gardens.

TURFGRASS

Turfgrass aficionados are having a hard time these days. Many cities have banned pesticide use on lawns, and summer water bans leave turf dry and crisp during hot spells. Alternative groundcovers and xeriscapes are being hailed as the way of the future, but there are positives to turfgrasses that make them worth keeping. Lawns efficiently filter pollutants out of run-off water, prevent soil erosion, retain moisture, cool the air and resist drought.

Although lawns require a layer of thatch to improve wear tolerance, reduce compaction and insulate against weather extremes, too thick a thatch layer can prevent water absorption, make the grass susceptible to heat, drought and cold and encourage pests and diseases.

May-blooming flowers (*clockwise from top left*): some irises bloom in early spring; forget-me-nots flower in spring, set seed and go dormant; rockcress and creeping phlox flowers attract bees and butterflies in spring and look exceptional in rock gardens.

MAY

29

30

31

Finish planting your vegetable garden now.
All crops including heat lovers (e.g., beans,
squash, tomatoes, peppers) are safe
to sow or transplant.

Euphorbia (*below*), rockcress (*top right*) and bergenia
(*bottom right*) are easy-to-grow, reliable bloomers
and perfect for beginner gardeners.

Here are some tips for maintaining a healthy, organic lawn:

- Aerate your lawn in spring, after active growth begins, to relieve compaction and allow water and air to move freely through the soil.
- Feed the soil, not the plants. Organic fertilizers or compost will encourage a healthy population of soil microbes. These work with roots to provide plants with nutrients and to fight off attacks by pests and diseases. Raise low pH to about 7.0 by adding lime in fall or spring. This helps control weeds, which prefer acidic (sour) soil. Apply an organic fertilizer in late spring after you aerate the lawn and in fall just as the grass goes dormant.
- Keep lawn mowed to a height of 2–3". The remaining leaf blade shades the ground, reducing moisture loss and keeping roots cooler. Mowing less often keeps grass healthier and bettter able to out-compete weeds.

- Grass clippings should be left on the lawn to return their nutrients to the soil and add organic matter. Mowing your lawn once a week or as often as needed during the vigorous growing season will ensure that the clippings decompose quickly.
- Healthy grass out-competes most weeds. Remove weeds by hand. If you must use chemicals, apply them only to the weeds. Chemical herbicides disrupt the balance of soil microbes and are not necessary to have a healthy lawn.

JUNE

The long, warm days
of summer are with us, and the
garden flourishes.

JUNE

1

Finish planting tender transplants such as pumpkins, tomatoes, begonias and coleus.

2

Remove dead flowers from plants growing in tubs, window-boxes and hanging baskets. Deadheading encourages more flowering and keeps displays looking tidy.

3

Heat-loving plants such as beans and marigolds germinate quickly in warm soil. Direct sow early in June.

4

5

6

Deepen and define bed edges with an edger, hoe and grass shears.

7

Cranesbill geraniums (*left*) are charming late-spring perennials with attractive foliage. The leaves of some varieties emit a lemon-mint scent. *Clockwise from top left:* moonbean coreopsis and black-eyed Susan; daylilies and phlox; masses of daylilies serve as a screen.

I n June, the grass is green, flower-beds are filling, and perennials, trees and shrubs are blooming. We watch as seeds germinate and leaves unfold. The fear of frost is behind us, and the soil is warm enough for even the most tender plants. Rain is usually plentiful in June, but in a dry year, newly planted annuals and perennials may need supplemental watering until they become established.

THINGS TO DO

June is the month to finish up the planting and begin general garden maintenance.

Stake plants (peonies, delphiniums) before they fill in if you haven't already done so.

Apply mulch to shrub, perennial and vegetable beds. Doing so will shade the roots and reduce the amount of water the plants will require in drier areas.

Goldfish actively graze algae off rocks. They do not need extra food, which pollutes the water and makes it cloudy with floating algae.

JUNE

*Prune early-flowering shrubs that have
finished flowering to encourage the
development of young shoots that will
bear flowers the following year.*

*Identify the insects you find in your
garden. You may be surprised to find
out how many are beneficial.*

Despite the delicate look of its satiny flowers,
godetia (*left*) enjoys cooler summer weather.
Opposite page, clockwise from top left: bee
balm; black-eyed Susans mixed with
purple coneflower; purple coneflower;
artemisia

Perennials to pinch back in June:

- Artemisia (*Artemisia* spp.)
- Bee Balm (*Monarda didyma*)
- Black-eyed Susan (*Rudbeckia* spp.)
- Catmint (*Nepeta* hybrids)
- Purple Coneflower (*Echinacea purpurea*)
- Shasta Daisy (*Leucanthemum* hybrids)

Pinch late-flowering perennials back lightly to encourage bushier growth and more flowers.

Set up a feeder for ruby-throated hummingbirds. To make nectar, dissolve one part white sugar in four parts boiling water and let cool. Remember to clean your hummingbird feeder, all other feeders and birdbaths weekly by dipping them in a mild bleach solution, rinsing and refilling.

JUNE

15

16

Timely weeding pays. Ten minutes spent pulling tiny new weeds can prevent an hour's worth of work later on when those same weeds mature.

17

18

Keep soil moist around transplants until they become established.

19

20

For a dense, smooth surface on pines, shear the candles (new shoots) back by one half to two thirds while still tender. Thinning pruning creates a more natural look and can be done anytime.

21

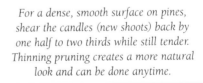

Coreopsis (*left*) enlivens a summer garden with its bright yellow, continuous blooms. Shear back in late summer for more flowers in fall. *Opposite page, clockwise from top right:* abutilon trained into a tree form; formal containers with vinca, bacopa, verbena and other annuals; nasturtiums, daisies, geraniums, asparagus ferns and bacopa in a terra-cotta pot.

CONTAINER GARDENING

Most plants can be grown in containers. Annuals, perennials, vegetables, shrubs and even trees can be adapted to container culture. There are many advantages to gardening in containers:

- They work well in small spaces. Even apartment dwellers with small balconies can enjoy the pleasures of gardening with planters on the balcony.
- They are mobile. Containers can be moved around to take advantage of light or shade and can even be moved into a sheltered location for winter.
- They are easier to reach. Container plantings allow people in wheelchairs or with back problems to garden without having to do a lot of bending.
- They are useful for extending the season. You can get an early start without the transplant shock that many plants suffer when moved outdoors. You can also protect plants from an early frost in fall.

*Put trailing plants near the edge of
a container to spill out, and bushy and
upright plants in the middle where they will
give height and depth to the planting.*

*Consider mixing different plants together in
a container. You can create contrasts of
color, texture and habit and give a small
garden an inviting appearance.*

*Mugo pine and dwarf Alberta spruce
are two winter-hardy evergreen shrubs that
will survive container life year-round.*

The flowers of *Salvia farinacea* 'Victoria' (*left*) are a
beautiful deep violet blue. They look stunning planted
with yellow or orange flowers such as nasturtiums,
coreopsis, California poppies or marigolds. *Opposite
page, clockwise from top left:* lettuce in a unique tub
planter; decks improved by vibrant containers;
marigolds, sweet potato vine and begonias in planters;
terracotta pot filled with petunias, dahlias and ornamental millet

Gardeners can get over a month's head start on the gardening season by using containers. Tomatoes, pumpkins and watermelons can be started from seed in late April. Planted into large containers, they can be moved outside during warm days and brought back in at night as needed in April and May. This prevents the stretching that many early-started plants suffer from if kept indoors for too long before being planted into the garden.

Many houseplants enjoy spending the summer outside in a shady location. The brighter a location you need to provide for your plant indoors, the better it will do outdoors. Avoid putting plants in direct sun because when you bring them back indoors at summer's end, they will have a hard time adjusting to the lower intensity of light.

JUNE

29   30

Keep an eye open for the early signs of pest and disease problems. They are easiest to deal with when they are just beginning.

Though considered old-fashioned or boring by some gardeners, petunias (*left*) are versatile and dependable annuals that bloom continuously in any sunny location. New varieties of this flower seem to appear every spring in garden centers. Spirea (*top right*) by water feature

Water gardens can be created in containers. Many ready-made container gardens are available, or you can create your own. Garden centers have lots of water garden supplies, and many water plants will grow as well in a large tub as they will in a pond.

Most perennials, shrubs or trees will require more winter protection in containers than they would if grown in the ground. Because the roots are above ground level, they are exposed to the winter wind and cycles of freezing and thawing. Protect container-grown plants by insulating the inside of the container. Thin sheets of foam insulation can be purchased and fitted around the inside of the pot before the soil is added. Containers can also be moved to sheltered locations. Garden sheds and unheated garages work well to protect plants from the cold and wind of winter.

A very natural look for informal ponds can be achieved by covering the rubber liner with beach rock and pebble (*right*). This also provides plenty of surface area for bacteria to colonize, which keep the water clear by consuming excess nutrients.

JULY

The hot, sunny days of July encourage us
to sit back, relax and enjoy all the hard work
we've put into our gardens.

JULY

1

2

Deadhead repeat-blooming annuals and perennials regularly to keep them looking their best.

3

4

Cut flowers to use in fresh arrangements indoors.

Faded green areas on dense evergreens in warm spots usually means spider mites are on the attack. Spraying the area with a mild dish soap and water solution should eliminate them.

5

6

7

The hardy shrub rose 'Bonica' (*left*) blooms profusely all summer, producing medium pink roses on a 4–5' wide bush. A riot of phlox, daylilies, yarrow, ageratum and snapdragons (*top right*); backyard garden with arbor, deck, pond and mixed plantings (*bottom right*).

Flowerbeds have filled in; green tomatoes form on the vine. The season's transplants are established and need less frequent watering. By July, the days are long and warm. The garden appears to grow before your eyes. Some spring-blooming perennials become dormant while others thrive, filling in the spaces left by the earlier bloomers.

THINGS TO DO

Though droughts are uncommon in most of New England, rainfall can be irregular during July and August.

Water deeply, but no more than once a week during dry spells. Water early in the day to minimize potential disease and reduce water lost through evaporation.

Rocky ground and thin soil are two of the biggest complaints of New England gardeners. Mulch with compost to gradually boost your soil's organic content and its water and nutrient retention.

Top up water gardens regularly if levels drop because of evaporation.

Thin vegetable crops such as beets, carrots and turnips. Crowded plants lead to poor crops.

Train new shoots of climbing vines such as morning glory and sweet peas to their supports.

JULY

8

9

Weed regularly to keep beds tidy.

10

Turn the compost pile, and when the compost is ready, add it to your flowerbeds and vegetable garden.

11

Fluff compacted mulch and cultivate bare soil areas to break the crust that forms in hot, dry weather. Doing so will allow air and water to get to plant roots.

12

13

14

Annual clary sage (*left*) loves sun, and its brilliantly colored bracts attract butterflies and hummingbirds to the flowers. Plant it among other sun-loving annuals and perennials where its whites, pinks and purples will provide bright bursts of color.
Opposite page, clockwise from top left: zinnias; statice; candytuft

You can use an organic fertilizer on container plants and on garden plants if compost is scarce.

Sawfly larvae may attack your spruce, pine, mountain ash and currant plants. To eliminate them easily, spray a solution of mild dish soap and water on affected areas.

Pick zucchini when they are small. They are tender and tasty, and you are less likely to wind up with boxes full of foot-long zucchini to leave on unsuspecting neighbors' front doorsteps. Consider donating extra vegetables to a homeless shelter or food bank, where they will be much appreciated.

Plan to replace fading flowers and vegetables by sowing seeds for a fall display or crop. Peas, bush beans, annual candytuft and lobelia are often finished fruiting or blooming by mid- to late summer, leaving holes in the garden that can be filled by new plants. Seeds for replacement plants can be direct sown or started indoors.

JULY

15

16

Top mulch up if it is getting thin in places in your garden. Mulch protects roots, holds in moisture and helps keep weeds at bay.

17

18

Tie plants to their stakes as they grow.

Organic treatment for ant hills: loosen the soil and pour boiling water into them to avoid using toxic pesticides or gasoline.

19

20

Heliopsis (*left*), a native prairie perennial, is easy to grow and tolerates poor conditions, but it thrives in full sun and fertile, moist soil. Its name means 'resembling the sun' and its sunny blooms make long-lasting cut flowers. *Opposite page:* Use a mixture of annuals and perennials to decorate garden rooms (*top left*), escort visitors along a garden path (*top right*) or create a garden view (*bottom right*).

21

An important factor in ensuring the survival of a plant in your garden is where you plant it. Find out what the best growing conditions are for your new plant to thrive, and then plant it where these conditions exist in your yard. For example, a shrub that needs full sun will never do well in a north-facing location.

PLANT PROBLEMS

Problems such as chewed leaves, mildews and nutrient deficiencies tend to become noticeable in July when plants finish their first flush of growth and turn their attention to flowering and fruiting.

Such problems can be minimized if you develop a good problem-management program. Though it may seem complicated, problem management is a simple process that relies on correct and timely identification of the problem and then using the least environmentally harmful method to deal with it.

JULY

22

23

Trim or shear back early-flowering perennials when they have finished blooming.

24

25

Trim hedges regularly to keep them looking tidy and lush.

26

27

'Cupcake' (*left*) is a delightful miniature rose with a classic hybrid tea shape. It produces an abundance of blooms and is disease resistant. Like all hybrid roses, it needs special winter protection. *Opposite page, clockwise from top left:* a birdbath in a shade garden; a swallowtail on cherry blossoms; a natural creek provides ongoing moisture to ferns

28

Garden problems fall into three basic categories:

- pests, such as aphids, mites, caterpillars, mice and deer
- diseases, caused by bacteria, fungi and viruses
- physiological problems, caused by nutrient deficiencies, too much or too little water, incorrect light levels and severe exposure.

Choose healthy plants bred for disease and pest resistance and suited to the conditions of your garden.

Vegetable gardens may get raided by deer and raccoons. A safe, low-voltage electric fence is the best protection. Put wires at 6", 12" and 40". See your farm supply dealer for advice and supplies.

Prevention is the most important aspect of problem management. A healthy garden is resistant to problems and develops a natural balance between beneficial and detrimental organisms.

JULY

29

30

The natural pesticide pyrethrin is derived from certain species of chrysanthemums.

31

Coleus (*below*) is a versatile plant widely grown as an indoor houseplant and outdoors in the garden. Ladybug (*top right*), a beneficial insect that feasts on aphids; Dahlberg daisies (*bottom right*)

PEST MANAGEMENT

Correct identification of problems is the key to solving them. Just because an insect is on a plant doesn't mean it's doing any harm.

Chemical pest control should always be the last alternative. There are many alternatives that pose no danger to gardeners or their families and pets.

- Cultural controls are the day-to-day gardening techniques you use to keep your garden healthy. Weeding, mulching, adding lots of organic matter to soil and growing problem-resistant cultivars are a few techniques you can use to keep gardens healthy.
- Physical controls are the hands-on part of problem solving. Picking insects off leaves, removing diseased foliage and creating barriers to stop rabbits from getting into the vegetable patch are examples of physical controls.
- Biological controls use natural and introduced populations of predators that prey on pests. Birds, snakes, frogs, spiders, some insects and even bacteria naturally feed on some problem insects. Soil microbes work with plant roots to increase their resistance to disease.

The pesticide industry has responded to consumer demand for effective, environmentally safe pest control products. Natural pesticides are made from plant, animal, bacterial or mineral sources. They are effective in small quantities and decompose quickly in the environment. These products help reduce our reliance on synthetic pesticides.

AUGUST

Though the warm weather continues,
the ripening fruit, vegetables and seeds are
signs that summer is nearing its end.

AUGUST

1

2

Reduce fertilizer applications to allow perennials, shrubs and trees ample time to harden off before the cold weather.

3

4

Continue to water during dry spells. Plants shouldn't need deep watering more than once a week at this time of the year.

5

6

Raccoons catching goldfish in ponds can be a problem. Ponds at least 8' wide by 2' deep are resistant. Give fish a hiding place, such as a flagstone suspended on rocks high enough to swim under—they'll love it.

7

Calendula (*left*) is an easy flower to grow from seed. It blooms quickly in spring and all summer long, even tolerating light frost. It can be used as a culinary herb as well. *Opposite page, from top:* geraniums; ripening apples; petunias

The warm days of July blend into August, but the nights are cooler and if it hasn't been too dry, many plants respond with a renewed display of color.

THINGS TO DO

The garden seems to take care of itself in August. We gardeners putter about, tying up floppy hollyhock spikes, picking vegetables and pulling an odd weed, but the frenzy of early summer is over and we take the time just to sit and enjoy the results of our labors.

Continue to deadhead perennials and annuals to keep the blooms coming.

Remove worn-out annuals and vegetables, and replace them with new ones from the nursery or those you started last month. Shearing some annuals and perennials back will encourage new growth, giving them a fresh look for fall.

Keep an eye open for pests that may be planning to hibernate in the debris around your plants or the bark of your trees. Taking care of a few insects now may keep several generations out of your garden next summer.

Pick apples as soon as they are ready, being careful not to bruise the fruit.

8

9

Seed areas of the lawn that are thin
or dead. Keep the seed well watered, if
necessary, while it germinates.

10

11

Depending on the size of your perennials,
you can divide them using a shovel or
pitchfork (for large plants), a sharp knife
(for small plants) or your hands
(for easily divided plants).

A few drops of mineral oil on new corn silk
safely discourages corn earworm.

12

13

14

The French marigold (*left*) is just
one variety of this popular
annual. All marigolds are low-
maintenance plants that stand up
well to heat, wind and rain.

PLANT PROPAGATION

Now is a good time to divide some perennials and to note which of your plants will need dividing next spring. Look for these signs that perennials need dividing:

- The center of the plant has died.
- The plant is not flowering as profusely as it did in previous years.
- The plant is encroaching on the growing space of others.

August is a good time to propagate plants. Taking cuttings and gathering seed are great ways to increase your plant collection and to share some of your favorite plants with friends and family.

Plants such as Siberian bugloss (*top left*), anemone (*top right*), evening primrose (*center*) and liatris (*right*) are good plants to divide if you're just starting your perennial collection. They recover and fill in quickly when divided.

15

16

Gradually move houseplants that have been summering outdoors into shadier locations so they will be prepared for the lower light levels indoors. Make sure they aren't infested with bugs; the pests will be harder to control once the plants are indoors.

17

18

Turn the layers of the compost pile and continue to add garden soil, kitchen scraps and garden debris that isn't diseased or infested with insects.

19

20

Remove the top 4" or so from Brussels sprouts stems to force larger heads to develop.

21

Verbena (*left*) works well in full sun and can be used as a groundcover, in beds, along borders or in containers. *Opposite page, clockwise from top left:* basket-of-gold, sedum and aster are easy to propagate from stem cuttings.

Perennials, trees, shrubs and tender perennials that are treated as annuals can all be started from cuttings. This method is an excellent way to propagate varieties and cultivars that you really like but that are slow or difficult to start from seed or that don't produce viable seed.

There is some debate over what size cuttings should be. Some claim that smaller cuttings are more likely to root and will root more quickly. Others claim that larger cuttings develop more roots and become established more quickly once planted. Try different sizes and see what works best for you.

The easiest cuttings to take from woody plants such as trees, shrubs and vines are called semi-ripe, semi-mature or semi-hardwood cuttings. They are taken from mature new growth that has not yet become completely woody, usually in late summer or early fall.

AUGUST

Continue watering newly planted perennials, trees and shrubs if dry weather occurs. Water deeply to encourage root growth.

Avoid pruning rust-prone plants such as mountain ash and crabapple in late summer and fall because many rusts are releasing spores now.

A quick, effective, organic method to eliminate sidewalk weeds is to pour scalding water on them.

You won't need to collect seed from borage (*left*) because these plants self-seed profusely and will no doubt turn up in your garden next spring. *Opposite page, clockwise from top left:* larkspur; nasturtiums with creeping Jenny; zinnias

You'll save money over the years by collecting seeds of annual plants. Choose plants that are not hybrids or the seeds will probably not come true to type and may not germinate at all. A few plants easy to collect from are listed below:

- Calendula (*Calendula officinalis*)
- Coriander (*Coriandrum sativum*)
- Dill (*Anethum graveolens*)
- Fennel (*Foeniculum vulgare*)
- Larkspur (*Consolida ajacis*)
- Marigold (*Tagetes* spp.)
- Nasturtium (*Tropaeolum majus*)
- Poppy (*Papaver rhoeas*)
- Zinnia (*Zinnia elegans*)

Always make cuttings just below a leaf node, the point where the leaves are attached to the stem.

Many gardeners enjoy the hobby of collecting and planting seed. You need to know a few basic things before you begin:

- Know your plant. Correctly identify the plant and learn about its life cycle. You will need to know when it flowers, when the seeds are likely to ripen and how the plant disperses its seeds in order to collect them.
- Find out if there are special requirements for starting the seeds. For example, do they need a hot or cold period to germinate?

29

30

Find a source of straw for mulching and decorating now because it can be harder to find later in fall.

31

Nasturtiums (*below*) are versatile annuals. Their edible flowers and foliage are attractive additions to baskets and containers as well as to salads. Even the seedpods can be pickled and used as a substitute for capers. *Opposite page, clockwise from top left:* golden clematis flowers and seedheads; Oriental poppy; Hens and Chickens poppy seedpod

When collecting seeds, consider the following:

- Collect seeds once they are ripe but before they are shed from the parent plant.
- Remove capsules, heads or pods as they begin to dry and remove the seeds later, once they are completely dry.
- Place a paper bag over a seed-head as it matures and loosely tie it in place to collect seeds as they are shed.
- Dry seeds after they've been collected. Place them on a paper-lined tray and leave them in a warm, dry location for one to three weeks.
- Separate seeds from the other plant parts before storing.
- Store seeds in air-tight containers in a cool, frost-free location.

Don't collect seeds or plants from the wild because harvesting from natural areas is severely depleting many plant populations. Many species and populations of wild plants are protected, and it is illegal to collect their seeds.

Collecting and saving seeds is a time-honored tradition. Early settlers brought seeds with them when they came to North America and saved them carefully each fall for the following spring.

SEPTEMBER

*Though we cling tenaciously to any
summer weather that lingers, there's
no denying that fall is upon us.*

SEPTEMBER

1

2

Time to stop fertilizing, but consider topdressing your garden with compost. Start gathering your leaves and garden waste from this season to make new compost.

3

4

Plant colorful fall ornamentals, such as chrysanthemums, flowering cabbage and flowering kale, available in fall at most garden centers.

5

6

Weak, declining flowering crab, mountain ash or apple trees may have borers in the trunk at ground level. Look for small holes and 'sawdust.' Squirt an organic remedy into holes because borers kill young trees.

7

Goldenrod (*left*), amaranthus (*top right*), strawflower (*center right*) and love-in-a-mist (*bottom right*) can be harvested now for dried flower arrangements.

Fall in New England is glorious. Leaves begin to change color, seedheads nod in the breeze and brightly colored berries and fruit adorn many trees and shrubs. There is a slight chance of frost in some gardens before the end of September, but on a warm after-noon summer can seem endless. Many annuals are undamaged by early frosts and continue to bloom until the first hard freeze.

THINGS TO DO

Having enjoyed another summer gar-den, your big fall clean up begins.

Take advantage of end-of-season sales. Many garden centers are getting rid of trees, shrubs and perennials at reduced prices. There is still plenty of time for the roots to become established before the ground freezes. Do not buy plants that are excessively root bound.

Consider starting some herb seeds now. You can plant them in pots and keep them in a bright window so you'll have fresh herbs to add to soups and salads over winter. Moving herb plants in from outdoors is also possible, but the plants often have a difficult time adapting to the lower light levels indoors.

SEPTEMBER

8

9

Dig up tuberous tender plants such as begonias for drying and storing over winter before the first frost. Wait to dig up dahlias until the first frost hits the leaves.

10

11

Though the garden may be getting lots of rain now, make sure to water beds under the overhangs of the house. Soil must be kept moist right up to hard freeze.

12

13

14

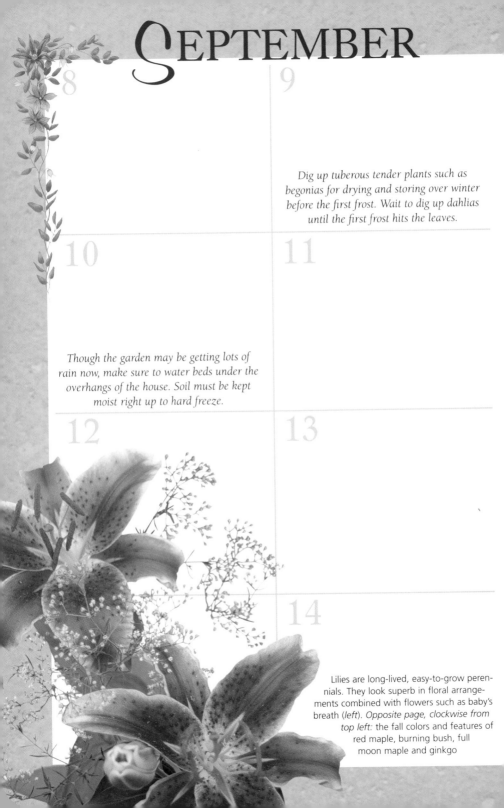

Lilies are long-lived, easy-to-grow perennials. They look superb in floral arrangements combined with flowers such as baby's breath (*left*). *Opposite page, clockwise from top left:* the fall colors and features of red maple, burning bush, full moon maple and ginkgo

If you've let your weeds get out of hand over summer, be sure to pull them up before they set seed to avoid having even more weeds popping up in the garden next summer.

Cool fall weather is ideal for sowing grass seed and repairing thin patches in the lawn. Get seeding done by October 1.

Enjoying the stunning fall colors is an annual ritual in New England. Bright reds, golds, bronzes and coppers seem to give warmth to a cool day. The display doesn't have to be reserved for a walk in the park. Include trees and shrubs with good fall color, such as the ones listed here, in your garden:

- Maple (*Acer*)
- Burning Bush (*Euonymus alatus*)
- Boston Ivy (*Parthenocissus tricuspidata*)
- Cotoneaster (*Cotoneaster*)
- Witch-hazel (*Hamamelis*)

September

15

16

Set up birdfeeders and begin to feed the birds if you didn't do so all summer.

17

18

Move tender container plants into a sheltered location or cover with a sheet when frost is expected. This strategy will allow you to enjoy them for longer.

To grow oak or horse chestnut, plant newly fallen nuts 3" deep in a garden bed along the house, water and mulch them over. They survive winter best in a sheltered spot.

19

20

The cheery golden marguerite daisy (*below*) forms a tidy mound that works wonderfully in both formal and informal garden settings. *Opposite page, clockwise from top left:* Asiatic lilies; black-eyed Susan; alliums

21

Begin to plant bulbs for a great display next spring. Tulips, daffodils, crocuses, scillas, muscaris and alliums are just a few of the bulbs whose flowers will welcome you back into the garden next year.

Spring-flowering perennials such as primroses and candytuft will be a delightful sight come April and May and can be planted now.

For vivacious color from summer through fall, a continuously blooming perennial such as black-eyed Susan can't be beat.

SEPTEMBER

22

23

When planting bulbs, you may want to add a little bonemeal to the soil to encourage root development.

24

25

Check houseplants for insect pests before moving them back indoors for winter.

Press fall leaves at their peak in layers of newsprint for dried arrangements all winter.

26

27

28

Echinacea purpurea (*left*), commonly called purple coneflower and used as a popular herbal cold remedy, is a long-blooming, drought-resistant perennial. Its distinctively cone-shaped flowers look good in fresh and dried floral arrangements. *Opposite page:* Ponds, fruiting trees and tall flowering perennials such as bee balm, coneflower and yarrow attract wildlife to your yard.

If your backyard borders a woodland, dispose of your brush in small piles just out of sight to provide wildlife with shelter as the piles slowly rot away.

CREATING WILDLIFE HABITAT

The rapid rate of urban sprawl has led to the relentless expansion of large cities and a loss of habitat for wildlife. Our gardens can easily restore some of the space, shelter, food and water that wildlife needs. Here are a few tips for attracting wildlife to your garden:

- Make sure at least some of the plants in your garden are locally native. Birds and small animals are used to eating native plants, so they'll visit a garden that has them. When selecting non-native plants for your yard, choose those that wildlife might also find appealing, such as shrubs that bear fruit.
- Provide a source of water. A pond with a shallow side or a birdbath will offer water for drinking and bathing. Frogs and toads eat a wide variety of insect pests and will happily take up residence in or near a ground-level water feature.

- A variety of birdfeeders and seed will encourage different species of birds to visit your garden. Some birds will visit an elevated feeder, but others prefer a feeder set at or near ground level. Fill your feeders regularly but especially when birds' natural food supplies may be low (e.g., winter, early spring). They will appreciate an extra, reliable food source.

SEPTEMBER

*Pull out annual plants and vegetables
as they fade or are killed by frost.*

Zinnias (*below*) are easy annuals to grow, come in a rainbow of colors and make long-lasting cut flowers for floral arrangements. *Opposite page, clockwise from top left:* sunflower; monarda with butterfly; birdfeeder; maple tree

- Butterflies, hummingbirds and a wide variety of predatory insects will be attracted if you include lots of pollen-producing plants in your garden. Plants such as goldenrod, comfrey, bee balm, salvia, Joe-Pye weed, black-eyed Susan, catmint, purple coneflower, coreopsis, hollyhock and yarrow will attract pollen lovers.

- Shelter is the final aspect to keeping your resident wildlife happy. Patches of dense shrubs, tall grasses and mature trees provide shelter. As well, you can leave a small pile of twiggy brush in an out-of-the-way place. Nature stores and many garden centers sell toad houses and birdhouses.

Inevitably squirrels and chipmunks will try to get at your birdfeeders. Instead of trying to get rid of them, why not leave peanuts and seeds out for them as well? Place them near a tree, where they can easily get at them. If you have a large spruce tree, they will eat the seeds out of the cones. Leave cones out with the other food offerings. The little cone scales that are left when they are done can be composted for the garden or used to prevent slipping on icy walks and driveways.

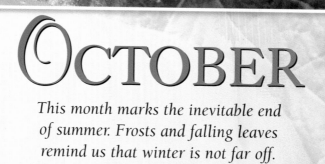

OCTOBER

*This month marks the inevitable end
of summer. Frosts and falling leaves
remind us that winter is not far off.*

OCTOBER

1

2

Try to get bulbs planted by mid month so they can grow their new roots this fall for good spring performance.

3

4

Lawn mowing comes to an end soon. Leave the grass neat, but not too short, for the winter.

Last chance to divide and plant perennials that need 4–6 weeks to settle in before winter begins.

5

6

Collect newly fallen Austrian, Scots and white pine cones to dry for Christmas decorating.

7

If the first frost hasn't yet arrived and your apples are still on the tree (*left*), now is the time to harvest them. However, some varieties taste better after the first frost. *Opposite page, clockwise from top:* colorful fall foliage; a bountiful harvest of carrots; endearing teddy bear sunflowers

The garden may still be vigorous early in the month, but by Halloween, only the hardy bloomers may still be going strong. Though we may wake up some mornings to a frost-dusted world, it is more likey that we will be enduring the inevitable wet weather. Enjoy any warm weather. Jumping into raked up piles of leaves is a pleasure that need not be reserved for the young.

THINGS TO DO
October is the time to finish tidying up and putting the garden to bed for another year.

Harvest any remaining vegetables. Soft fruit such as tomatoes and zucchini should be harvested before the first frost, but cool weather vegetables such as carrots, cabbage, Brussels sprouts and turnips can wait a while longer because they are frost hardy.

Unless your plants have been afflicted with some sort of disease, you can leave faded perennial growth in place and clean it up in spring. The stems will collect leaves and snow, protecting the roots and crown of the plant over the winter.

OCTOBER

8

9

Continue to tidy up dead plant material.
Most can be composted, but diseased
material is better thrown out.

10

11

Start mulching the garden, but avoid
covering plants completely until the ground
has frozen. Doing so prevents plants from
rotting and deters small rodents from digging
down and feasting on plant roots and crowns.

12

13

Collect and freeze berry-laden mountain
ash and cranberry branch tips to feed the
birds all winter.

14

The serviceberry (*left*) is a small tree that bears white
flowers in spring, edible red berries in summer and
lovely orange-red foliage in fall. It requires little
maintenance and does quite well near water.

Fall is a great time to improve your soil. Amendments added now can be worked in lightly. By planting time next spring, the amendments will have been further worked in by the actions of worms and soil microorganisms and by the freezing and thawing that takes place over winter.

Local farmers' markets are often the best places to find a wide variety of seasonal vegetables and flowers (*above and below*).

Things to do with your fall leaves: add them to the compost pile; gather them into their own compost pile to decompose into leaf mold; rototill them into your vegetable garden; or mow them over and then pile them onto flowerbeds. Whole leaves can become matted together, encouraging fungal disease.

Don't let your goldfish pond freeze solid with ice. Remove the larger falls pump, and place a small pump on the bottom of the pond aimed upwards to keep an open spot for gases to escape all winter. Check the hole periodically to ensure it stays open.

OCTOBER

15

16

Continue to water trees and shrubs
until the ground freezes up. Apply an organic
anti-desiccant to newly planted evergreens
to reduce winter moisture loss.

17

18

Faded annuals and vegetables can be
pulled up and added to the compost pile.

19

20

Poppy seedheads make great eyes
for your jack o'lantern.

21

Honeysuckle vine (*left*) flowers from summer to fall
frost. Prune in spring to cut back dead growth as new
leaves emerge. Fall harvest (*top left*); composting (*far
right*); ripe tomato (*bottom right*)

COMPOSTING

One of the best additives for any type of soil is compost. Compost can be purchased at most garden centers, and many communities now have composting programs. You can easily make compost in your own garden. Though garden refuse and vegetable scraps from your kitchen left in a pile will eventually decompose, it is possible to produce compost more quickly. Here are a few suggestions for creating compost:

- Compost decomposes most quickly when there is a balance between brown and green materials. There should be more brown matter, such as chopped straw or shredded leaves, than green matter, such as vegetable scraps and grass clippings.
- Layer the brown and the green matter, and mix in some garden soil or previously finished compost. This step introduces decomposer organisms to the pile.

OCTOBER

As outdoor gardening winds down,
try starting bulbs such as paperwhites
(narcissus) indoors. Fragrant white blooms
should emerge in a few weeks.

Cure pumpkins and winter squash
(acorn, buttercup, hubbard, etc.)
in a cool, frost-free location before
storing for winter.

Fertilize deciduous trees and shrubs
after leaf drop.

Yarrow's showy, flat-topped flowerheads
(*left*) provide months of continuous color
in summer, and the seedheads persist
into winter. Stone steps through a
mixed tree and shrub planting (*top left*).

- Compost won't decompose properly if it is too wet or too dry. Keep the pile covered during heavy rain and sprinkle it with water if it is too dry. The correct level of moisture can best be described as that of a wrung-out sponge.
- To aerate the pile, use a garden fork to poke holes in it or turn it regularly. Use a thermometer with a long probe attached, similar to a large meat thermometer, to check the temperature in your pile. When the temperature reaches 160° F, give the pile a turn.
- Finished compost is dark in color and light in texture. When you can no longer recognize what went into the compost, it is ready for use.
- Compost can be mixed into garden soil or spread on the surface as a mulch.

Images of fall: juicy clusters of vine-ripened grapes (*top right*) and tasty corn on the cob fresh from the garden (*above*). Many gardeners find fruiting plants to be decorative as well as useful.

OCTOBER

29

30

If you don't have the time or the inclination to fuss over your compost, you can just leave it in a pile and it will eventually decompose with no added assistance from you.

31

Sunflowers (*below*) are synonymous with fall for many gardeners. Their bold yellow, seed-filled flowerheads celebrate the harvest season and provide treats for the birds. Canada serviceberry (*top right*) and viburnum (*center right*) both bear berries in fall. The fruit attracts birds and can be used to make jellies, pies and wine.

Before adding specific nutrients to your soil, you should get a soil test done. Simple kits to test for pH and major nutrients are available at garden centers. More thorough tests can be done; consult your local cooperative extension for information. These tests will tell you what the pH is, the comparative levels of sand, silt, clay and organic matter and the quantities of all required nutrients. They will also tell you what amendments to add and in what quantities to improve your soil.

Adding amendments to your soil will alter its condition, depending on what's required:

- Compost can be mixed into a clay soil to loosen the structure and allow water to penetrate.
- Elemental sulfur, peat moss or pine needles added on a regular basis can make soil under rhododendrons more acidic.
- Calcitic or dolomitic limestone, hydrated lime, quicklime or wood ashes can be added to an acidic soil to make it more alkaline.

Sunflowers (*above*) and other cut flowers can be found in abundance in farmers' markets. Use them for fresh or dried table arrangements, or flower pressing for winter crafts.

NOVEMBER

Branches lie bare, dry flowerheads sway in the breeze and excited birds pick brightly colored fruit from frost-covered branches.

NOVEMBER

1

2

After raking and once the lawn is dormant, apply an organic fertilizer. If you haven't needed to mow in a couple of weeks, it is probably sufficiently dormant.

3

4

If you have healthy willows, dogwoods, Virginia creeper or evergreens, cut a few branches to use in Christmas wreaths. Store in a cool place until needed.

5

6

Thinning pruning of shrubs can continue up until hard freeze. There's more time now than during the spring rush.

7

Compact, bushy and cold-hardy to zone 2b, the 'Champlain Explorer' rose (*left*) produces abundant clusters of velvety red roses almost all summer long and is resistant to black-spot and powdery mildew.

Despite the inevitable frosts, a few stragglers always hang on. Flowers like pansies keep blooming, even under a light blanket of snow, until the ground starts to freeze. A fall of wet snow draws children into the garden, happy to build a snowman on the lawn.

THINGS TO DO

Garden tasks this month involve tucking the garden in for winter.

Harvest any remaining vegetables. Root vegetables, such as carrots, parsnips and turnips, and green vegetables, such as cabbages and broccoli, store well in a cool place, and their flavor is often improved after a touch of frost.

The garden can be quite beautiful in November, especially when persistent fruit becomes more visible on branches (*below*), after a light dusting of snow or frost (*right*) or dripping with rain.

NOVEMBER

8

9

Clear away tools, hoses and garden furniture
before the snow flies so they won't be
damaged by the cold and wet weather.

10

11

Mound mulch around the bases of semi-
hardy shrubs once the ground freezes
to protect the roots and stem bases
from temperature fluctuations.

12

13

To leave your potentillas and spireas neat
and set for spring growth, shear them
to about half their size, then thin out
8–10 older stems to the ground.

14

The beautiful hybrid tea rose 'Rosemary
Harkness' (*left*) produces fragrant orange-
yellow double blooms from summer to
autumn. Like other tender hybrid teas,
it should be protected from any
harsh winter weather. The richly
colored rosettes of ornamental kale
(*top right*) are reminiscent of roses
(*top left*); strawberry (*center right*);
coastal woodland (*bottom right*)

Prepare hybrid tea and other semi-hardy roses for winter before the ground freezes. Mound dirt up over the base and cover with mulch, or surround the plant with loose, quick-drying material, such as sawdust, shredded leaves or peat moss, and cover with a wooden box. Hold the box in place with a heavy rock on top when you are done.

Avoid completely covering perennials with mulch until the ground freezes. Mound the mulch around them (*above*) and store some extra mulch in a frost-free location to add once they are frozen. If you pile the mulch in the garden, you may find it has also frozen solid when you want to use it.

NOVEMBER

15

16

Be sure to enjoy any remaining warm days before the garden becomes the dream of next summer.

17

18

Fill your birdfeeders regularly. Well-fed birds will continue to visit your garden in summer, feeding on undesirable insects in your garden.

Clean tools thoroughly and wipe them with an oily rag to prevent them from rusting. Sharpen pruners, shovels and spades before storing them for winter.

19

20

Pieris (left); opposite page, clockwise from top left: mountain ash, staghorn sumac, nest spruce and serviceberry

21

Your garden doesn't have to be right on the coast to experience some of the same conditions. The wind can carry the salty air inland far from the coast. If this is a problem in some or all of your garden, consider growing salt and seaside-tolerant plants such as Austrian pine, mountain ash, nest spruce, serviceberry, sumac, thyme, creeping juniper, pinks, common thrift, nasturtiums and geraniums. A walk in a local wilderness area or park can give you lots of ideas for what to include in your own garden.

Now that you've had the chance to observe your garden for a growing season, consider the microclimates and think about how you can put them to good use. Are any areas always quick to dry? Do some stay wet longer than others? What area is the most sheltered? Which is the least sheltered? Cater your plantings to the microclimates of your garden.

NOVEMBER

22

23

Large, heavy perennial clumps can still be moved, but smaller pieces are prone to frost heave and winter kill.

24

25

Anti-dessicant spray can be applied now to newer evergreens in exposed sites to limit the drying that causes winter burn.

26

27

To deter deer from eating your evergreens, plant species they don't like: pine, spruce, juniper, false cypress and rhododendron. Avoid their favorites—yew, eunonymous and cedar.

28

Flowers such as marsh marigolds (*left*), irises (*top left and right*), daylilies (*center right*) and ligularia (*bottom right*) work well in damp areas of the garden because they prefer moist growing conditions.

BOG GARDENING

Turn a damp area into your own little bog garden. Dig out a damp area 14–20" below ground level, line with a piece of punctured pond liner and fill with soil. The area will stay wet but still allow some water to drain away, providing a perfect location to plant moisture-loving perennials. A few to consider are

- Astilbe (*Astilbe* spp. and hybrids)
- Cardinal Flower (*Lobelia* x *speciosa*)
- Daylily (*Hemerocallis* hybrids)
- Doronicum (*Doronicum orientale*)
- Goat's Beard (*Aruncus dioicus*)
- Hosta (*Hosta* hybrids)
- Iris (*Iris ensata*, *I. siberica*)
- Ligularia (*Ligularia dentata*)
- Marsh Marigold (*Caltha palustris*)
- Meadowsweet (*Filipendula rubra* and *ulmaria*)
- Primrose (*Primula japonica*)
- Rodgersia (*Rodgersia aesculifolia* and *pinnata*)

Finish collecting seeds from open-pollinated flowers and vegetables. Stored in a cool, dry place, they will be ready for planting in next year's garden.

Japanese maple (*top left*); bigleaf hydrangea (*top right*); camellia (*center right*); magnolia (*bottom right*)

Rodgersia (*left*) bears bold foliage and fluffy flower plumes in mid- to late summer. It does best in a site sheltered from strong winds and extreme weather. Rodgersia plants prefer moist soil.

New England has a diverse climate, but gardeners in all its regions love trying to grow out-of-zone plants. Northern mountain gardeners might try Japanese maple and saucer magnolia while southern and coastal gardeners may find big leaf hydrangea and even camellias will thrive in a sheltered spot.

If you have a very exposed area in your garden, you can find plants that will do well there, or you can make a planting that will shelter the area. A hedge or group of trees or shrubs will break the wind and provide an attractive feature for your garden.

DECEMBER

Already summer seems far away. Ghostly
forms and dashes of color are all that
remain to inspire us until spring.

DECEMBER

1

2

Light levels are low, so cycle your houseplants from darker to lighter rooms to give each some time by the brightest windows to stay healthy.

3

4

*New England gardeners can have beautiful holly like that seen in warmer climates. Blue holly (*Ilex x meserveae*) thrives in sheltered beds, reaching 5–8' in diameter. Thin-prune it in early December for Christmas decorating.*

5

6

A little wood ash added to your vegetable garden will help, but not too much. Any extra makes a good traction aid for icy driveways.

7

Holly ('Blue Girl' blue holly, *left*) makes an attractive addition to fresh winter arrangements. To keep it looking its best, keep the cut ends consistently moist. *Opposite page, clockwise from top left:* decorative Christmas peppers are ideal for holiday color indoors; Swiss stone pine provides year-round interest; seasonal centerpiece

The garden begins its winter display of colorful and peeling bark, branches with persistent fruit and evergreen boughs. With a bit of luck, snow begins to pile up on garden beds, covering withered perennials and shrubs and clinging to evergreen branches. Winter arrives, hopefully in time for the holidays, leaving only our fond memories of the garden.

THINGS TO DO

Our thoughts turn to indoor gardening though we may still have a few garden tasks to complete before we call it a year.

If rabbits and mice are a problem in your garden, you can protect your trees and shrubs with chicken wire. Wrap it around the plant bases and higher up the tree or shrub than you expect the snow to reach.

Gently brush snow off flexible evergreen branches. Heavy snow can weigh down juniper and white cedar branches enough to permanently bend them.

Check the soil in the beds under the overhangs. Watering to get soil moist before freeze up will keep the plants healthy.

Seasonal centerpiece (*below*) made with evergreen clippings from the yard: white pine, blue spruce, hemlock, cedar, yew, blue holly, balsam fir and false cypress.

DECEMBER

8

9

Move clay and concrete pots and statues into a protected location to prevent them from cracking over winter.

10

11

Reduce watering and cease feeding houseplants.

12

13

Rooting slips of houseplants often works as well in moist potting soil as it does in water, and it eliminates one step.

14

Poinsettias (*left*) add rich color and beauty to our homes during the dark days of December. *Opposite page, clockwise from top left:* dracaena; African violets; *Cattleya* orchid; spider plant

HOUSEPLANT CARE

You don't have to forget gardening completely when the snow begins to fly. All you have to do is turn your attention to indoor gardening. Houseplants clean the air, soften the hard edges of a room and provide color, texture and interest to your home.

Just as you did for the garden outdoors, match your indoor plants to the conditions your home provides. If a room receives little light, try houseplants that require very low light levels. Plants that like humid conditions may do best in your bathroom where showering and the toilet bowl full of water maintain higher moisture levels than in any other room. Low-light-tolerant plants include philodendron, spider plant, cast iron plant and snake plant; bright-light-tolerant plants include cacti, jade plant and goldfish plant.

DECEMBER

15

16

*Most indoor plant pests can be controlled
by wiping leaves with a damp sponge.
More difficult pests can be controlled
with insecticidal soap.*

17

18

*Any herbs you are growing indoors
should be kept in the brightest window
you have to prevent them from becoming
too straggly or dying.*

19

20

Although orchids are reputed to be difficult and
needy, the moth orchid *Phalaenopsis* (*left*) is easy to
grow on a windowsill. There are many thousands of
species of orchids in an amazing array of sizes, shapes,
colors and fragrances. Pearl plant and tiger jaws
(*center right*); Rex begonia (*bottom right*)

21

There are three aspects of interior light to consider: intensity, duration and quality. Intensity is the difference between a south window with full sun and a north window with no direct sunlight. Duration is how long the light lasts in a specific location. An east window will have a shorter duration of light than a south window. Quality refers to the spectrum of the light. Natural light provides a broader spectrum than artificial light.

Watering is a key element to houseplant care. Overwatering can be as much of a problem as under watering. As you did with your garden plants, water thoroughly and infrequently. Let the soil dry out a bit before watering. Some plants are the exception to this rule. Find out what the water requirements of your houseplants are so you will have an idea of how frequently or infrequently you will need to water.

Look for creative ways to display your plants and add beauty to your home. Indoor fountains and moisture-loving plants, such as a peace lily in a vase of water (*top*), are interesting and attractive to look at. They add a decorative touch to a houseplant display.

DECEMBER

22

23

*Dust on plants is more than just an eyesore.
It prevents plants from making full use
of the light they receive. Clean leaves
regularly with a damp cloth or sponge,
or place them in the shower and let
the water stream wash away any dust.*

24

25

*Poinsettias last longest when kept in
a cool bright room with moist soil that isn't
allowed to dry out completely.*

26

27

*Twigs from your garden make an
excellent, natural-looking climbing
structure for potted vines.*

28

Chinese evergreen (*left*) is one of the easiest houseplants to grow. Succulent and cacti display (*top
right*); snake plant (*bottom right*) is a striking, long-
lived indoor plant

Houseplants generally only need fertilizer when they are actively growing. Always use a weak fertilizer to avoid burning the roots. Never feed plants when they are very dry. Moisten the soil by watering and then feed a couple of days later.

When repotting, go up by only one size at a time. In general the new pot should be no more than 2–4" larger in diameter than the previous pot. If you find your soil drying out too frequently, then you may wish to use a larger pot that will stay moist for longer.

Houseplants are more than just attractive—they clean the air in our homes. Many dangerous and common toxins, such as benzene, formaldehyde and trichloroethylene are absorbed and eliminated by houseplants.

Here are a few easy-to-grow, toxin-absorbing houseplants:

- Bamboo Palm (*Chamaedorea erumpens*)
- Chinese Evergreen (*Aglaonema modestum*)
- Dragon Tree (*Dracaena marginata*)
- English Ivy (*Hedera helix*)
- Gerbera Daisy (*Gerbera jamesonii*)
- Peace Lily (*Spathiphyllum* 'Mauna Loa')
- Pot Mum (*Chrysanthemum morifolium*)
- Snake Plant (*Sansevieria trifasciata*)
- Spider Plant (*Chlorophytum comosum*)
- Weeping Fig (*Ficus benjamina*)

DECEMBER

29

30

Plants can be grouped together in large containers to more easily meet the needs of the plants. Cacti can be planted together in a gritty soil mix and placed in a dry, bright location. Moisture- and humidity-loving plants can be planted in a large terrarium where moisture levels remain higher.

31

A bouquet of cheerful gerberas (*below*) will brighten a drab winter day and remind you of summer, when these flowers were growing in your garden. *Clockwise from top left:* bromeliad; burro's tail; amarylis; aloe

Keep in mind that many common houseplants dislike the dry winter air in our homes. Most will thrive in cooler, moister conditions than the typical home provides. Always turn thermostats down at night and create moist conditions by sitting pots on pebble trays. Water in the pebble tray can evaporate but won't soak excessively into the soil of the pot because the pebbles hold it above the water.

There's nothing like treating yourself to a seasonal flowering plant when you're feeling the doldrums of winter. Many beautiful varieties are available. Watch for some of the more exotic plants from South America and Australia at grocery stores and florist shops.

RESOURCES

All resources cited were accurate at the time of publication. Please note that addresses, phone numbers and web sites/emails may change over time.

BOOKS

Armitage, Allan M. 2000. *Armitage's Garden Perennials*. Timber Press, Portland OR.

Brickell, C., T.J. Cole and J.D. Zuk, eds. 1996. *Reader's Digest A–Z Encyclopedia of Garden Plants*. The Reader's Digest Association Ltd., Montreal, PQ.

Brickell, Christopher and David Joyce. 1996. *Eyewitness Garden Handbook: Pruning and Training*. Dorling Kindersley, London, England.

Bubel, Nancy. 1988. *The New Seed Starter's Handbook*. Rodale Press, Emmaus, PA.

Courtier, Jane and Graham Clarke. 1997. *Indoor Plants: The Essential Guide to Choosing and Caring for Houseplants*. Reader's Digest, Westmount, PQ.

Dirr, Michael A. 1997. *Dirr's Hardy Trees and Shrubs*. Timber Press, Portland, OR.

Ellis, B.W. and F.M. Bradley, eds. 1996. *The Organic Gardener's Handbook of Natural Insect and Disease Control*. Rodale Press, Emmaus, PA.

Heintzelman, Donald S. 2001. *The Complete Backyard Birdwatcher's Home Companion*. Ragged Mountain Press, Camden, ME.

Hill, Lewis. 1991. *Secrets of Plant Propagation*. Storey Communications Inc., Pownal, VT.

McHoy, Peter. 2002. *Houseplants*. Hermes House, New York, NY.

McVicar, Jekka. 1997. *Jekka's Complete Herb Book*. Raincoast Books, Vancouver, BC.

Merilees, Bill. 1989. *Attracting Backyard Wildlife: A Guide for Nature Lovers*. Voyageur Press, Stillwater, MN.

Robinson, Peter. 1997. *Complete Guide to Water Gardening*. Reader's Digest, Westmount, PQ.

Thompson, P. 1992. *Creative Propagation: A Grower's Guide*. Timber Press, Portland, OR.

ONLINE RESOURCES

Attracting wildlife to your yard.com. How to make your backyard inviting to compatible and beneficial creatures. www.attracting wildlife-to-your-garden.com

Backyard Gardener. Offers gardening information, a newsletter, articles and online shopping. www.backyardgardener.com

Boston Gardens.com. Articles, events, trivia and a list of local gardening experts who will speak on an array of gardening topics specific to Massachusetts. www.bostongardens.com

Butterfly Website. Learn about the fascinating world of butterflies. www.butterflywebsite.com

Connecticut Botanical Society. Native plant advocates share their knowledge regarding gardening with native plant material. www.ct-botanical-society.org/garden/

Cooperative Extension at the University of Rhode Island. Attend the latest courses and receive the most current horticultural information. www.uri.edu/ce/index1.html or www.uri.edu/ce/factsheets/index.htm

Evergreen Foundation. A national environmental organization that provides tools to transform residential and commercial spaces into healthy outdoor spaces. www.evergreen.ca/en/index.html

Garden Time Online. Lists over 1000 free online gardening resources for the state of Vermont. www.gardentimeonline.com/Vermont.html

Gardening in Vermont from Vermont Living. Learn the secret to gardening success in Vermont. www.vtliving.com/gardening/

Gardening in Western Massachusetts. A comprehensive list of W. MA nurseries and growers, garden clubs and Master Gardener Association information. http://webpages.charter.net/gcking/Orgs.htm

Hill Gardens of Maine. A Palermo nursery dedicated to providing interesting and useful information on a wide range of gardening subjects. www.hillgardens.com

Home and Garden. A garden design and outdoor living guide for New Hampshire. www.homeandgardennh.com/Garden Resource_ContentIndex.asp

Maine MemoriesGarden Design. Nancy and David Funk from Kennebunkport, Maine share their gardening knowledge. www.mainememories.com/Garden01.htm

Master Composter Rhode Island. State information, resources and contact information for your composting needs. www.mastercomposter.com/local/rdisland.html

New England School of Gardening. The NESG at Tower Hill Botanic Garden provides an extensive schedule of programs, including workshops, lectures and demonstrations. **www.towerhillbg.org/thwebclwdem.html**

New England Wild Flower Society. Promotes conservation of North American native plants through education, research, horticulture, habitat preservation and advocacy. **www.newfs.org/**

North American Native Plant Society. Dedicated to the study, conservation and restoration of native plants. **www.nanps.org/index.shtml**

People, Places and Plants Magazine. An independent gardening magazine produced in New England and the mid-Atlantic region for local gardeners. **www.ppplants.com**

Turf Resource Center and The Lawn Institute. The latest data regarding turfgrass. **www.TurfGrassSod.org**

University of Maine Cooperative Extension. Why and how you should become a Maine Master Gardener. **www.ume.maine.edu/MGMAINE/**

University of Massachusetts Extension. Links to a range of sites on natural resources and environmental conservation, gardening and the departments of cooperative extension at several New England universities. **www.umassextension.org/topics/gardening.html**

University of New Hampshire Cooperative Extension. Master Gardener program information. **www.ceinfo.unh.edu/agmastgd.htm**

University of Rhode Island Cooperative Extension. An invitation to extend your gardening knowledge while becoming a URI Master Gardener. **www.uri.edu/ce/ceec/mastergardener.html**

Virtual Gardener. An online magazine based on organic principles. **www.beseen.net/virtualgardener/**

Worm's Way. A great online resource for a variety of gardening questions. **www.wormsway.com**

Yankee Gardener. Gardening topics, activities and products. **www.yankeegardener.com**

SOIL-TESTING FACILITIES
Connecticut
Soil Nutrient Analysis Laboratory
6 Sherman Place, Unit-5102
Storrs, CT 06269-5102
860-486-4274

Soil Testing Lab
2019 Hillside Road
Storrs, CT 06269
860-486-2928

Maine
Maine Soil Testing Service
5722 Deering Hall, University of Maine
Department of Plant, Soil and Environmental Sciences
Room 407
Orono, ME 04469-5722
207-581-2934

Woods End Research Lab, Inc.
1850 Old Rome Road
PO Box 297
Mt. Vernon, ME 04352
207-293-2457

Massachusetts
Soil and Plant Tissue Testing Laboratory
West Experiment Station
University of Massachusetts
Amherst, MA 01003-8020 or 8021
413-545-2311
email: soiltesting@hotmail.com
www.umass.edu/plsoils/soiltest

New Hampshire
University of NH Analytical Services Lab
Spaulding Life Sciences Center
Rooms G-54 and 55
38 College Road
Durham, NH 03824
603-862-3210 or 3212
email: Soil.Testing@unh.edu
www.ceinfo.unh.edu/Agriculture/Documents/SoilTest.htm

Rhode Island
Soil Test Coordinator
Cooperative Extension Education Center
University of Rhode Island
Kingston, RI 02881
800-448-1011

Vermont
Agricultural and Environmental Testing Laboratory
219 Hills Building, University of Vermont
Burlington, VT 05405
802-656-3030 or 800-244-6402
email: ecarr@zoo.uvm.edu
www.pss.uvm.edu/ag_testing/

HORTICULTURAL SOCIETIES
Federated Garden Clubs of Connecticut
PO Box 854
Branford, CT 06405
203-488-5528
www.ctgardenclubs.org

Federated Garden Clubs of Vermont
35 Randall Street
St. Johnsbury, VT 05819
802-748-2963
email: cfrey35@charter.net

Garden Club Federation of Massachusetts
219 Washington Street
Wellesley Hills, MA 02181
781-237-0336
www.gcfm.org

New Hampshire Federation of Garden Clubs
10 Surrey Coach Lane
Bow, NH 03304
603-225-8804
email: suissmiss@mailstation.com
www.nhfgc.org

Rhode Island Federation of Garden Clubs
PO Box 1063
Bristol, RI 02809-1063
email: rifgc@cox.net
www.nebgprovidence.org/federation.html

The Garden Club Federation of Maine
6 Old Cottage Lane
Eliot, ME 03903
207-748-3430
email: kennebus@comcast.net or statemember-
ship@mainegardenclubs.com
www.mainegardenclubs.com

The New England Wild Flower Society
180 Hemenway Road
Framingham, MA 01701
508-877-7630 or 508-877-3658
www.newfs.org/

GARDENS TO VISIT

Connecticut
Caprilands Herb Farm
Silver Street
Coventry, CT 06238
860-742-7244
www.caprilands.com

Denison Pequotsepos Nature Center
Pequotsepos Road
Mystic, CT
860-536-9248

Elizabeth Park Rose Garden
Prospect at Asylum Avenue
West Hartford, CT
860-242-0017
www.elizabethpark.org

Glebe House Museum and Gertrude Jekyll Garden
Hollow Road
Woodbury, CT
203-263-2855
www.nationalgeographic.com/books/9805/
glebehouse.html

Sundial Gardens
Higganum, CT 06441
860-345-4290
www.sundialgardens.com

Twombly Nursery and Display Gardens
163 Barn Hill Road
Monroe, CT 06468
203-261-2133
www.twomblynursery.com

Maine
Deering Oaks Rose Circle
Deering and Forest Avenue
Portland, ME
207-874-8300

Leighton Sculpture Garden
24 Parker Point Road
Blue Hill, ME
207-879-0427, 207-774-1822 or 207-374-5001

McLaughlin Garden and Horticultural Center
97 Main Street
South Paris, ME
207-743-8820
www.mclaughlingarden.org

Merryspring
End of Conway Road, just off US Rte. 1 at
Camden/Rockport town line
Camden, ME
207-236-2239
www.merryspring.org

R.P. Coffin Wildflower Reservation
Chopps Point Road
Woolwich, ME

Massachusetts
Arnold Arboretum at Harvard University
125 Arborway
Jamaica Plain, MA
617-524-1718
www.arboretum.harvard.edu/

Garden in the Woods
180 Hemenway Road
North Framingham, MA
508-877-7630
www.newfs.org/garden.htm#top

Magic Wings Butterfly Conservatory and Gardens
281 Greenfield Road (Routes 5 & 10)
South Deerfield, MA
413-665-2805
www.magicwings.net/gardens.htm

Mount Holyoke College Botanic Garden
Mount Holyoke College
50 College Street
South Hadley, MA
413-538-2116
www.mtholyoke.edu/offices/botan

"What are you talking about?" Canidy asked.

"I'm not suggesting you will, or ever could, accomplish your objective," Matuszek replied. "But I am suggesting, more accurately, *saying*, that there is another means by which you may accomplish your mission without embarking on the impossible task of entering Canaris's lair."

"I'm all ears," Canidy said. "But understand our skepticism. We're supposed to—as you indicated—obtain something located in Germany, but you tell us we can accomplish that without going to Germany?"

"Better. Not only do you not have to go to Germany, but you can acquire what you need here in Poland. Still quite hazardous, but not certain death. And you may give the Allies a strategic advantage for decades to come."

Matuszek's response raised several obvious questions. But before Canidy could pose any of them, a piercing whistle preceded an explosion that catapulted all ten men several feet into the air and propelled them against the corrugated metal walls of the office.

PRAISE FOR PETER KIRSANOW

"Peter Kirsanow delivers a crafty, edge-of-your-seat story in crackling prose and pulsating action."

—Barry Lancet on *Second Strike*

"Kirsanow . . . rarely misses an opportunity to maximize suspense." —*Publishers Weekly* on *Second Strike*

W. E. B. GRIFFIN

THE DEVIL'S WEAPONS

PETER KIRSANOW

G. P. PUTNAM'S SONS
NEW YORK

PUTNAM
— EST. 1838 —

G. P. PUTNAM'S SONS
Publishers Since 1838
An imprint of Penguin Random House LLC
penguinrandomhouse.com

The Library of Congress has catalogued
the G. P. Putnam's Sons hardcover edition as follows:

Names: Kirsanow, Peter N., author.
Title: W. E. B. Griffin the devil's weapons / Peter Kirsanow.
Description: New York : G. P. Putnam's Sons, [2022] |
Series: Men at war ; vol 8
Identifiers: LCCN 2022043919 (print) | LCCN 2022043920 (ebook) |
ISBN 9780593422281 (hardcover) | ISBN 9780593422298 (ebook)
Subjects: LCGFT: Novels.
Classification: LCC PS3611.I769845 W43 2022 (print) |
LCC PS3611.I769845 (ebook) | DDC 813/.6--dc23/eng/20220928
LC record available at https://lccn.loc.gov/2022043919
LC ebook record available at https://lccn.loc.gov/2022043920

First G. P. Putnam's Sons hardcover edition / December 2022
First G. P. Putnam's Sons premium edition / October 2023
G. P. Putnam's Sons premium edition ISBN: 9780593422304

Printed in the United States of America
3   5   7   9   10   8   6   4   2

W. E. B. GRIFFIN
THE DEVIL'S WEAPONS

CHAPTER 1

It was the peculiar smell that he remembered most.

Not the hideous scenes, the horrific sounds, or the paralyzing cold. Not the terrified faces, or even the bodies mangled beyond recognition.

It was the smell. Utterly unlike anything he'd experienced in his nearly forty-one years on Earth. It was almost a tactile sensation, damp and suffocating. The product of blood and urine and intestines; rotting flesh and pulverized organs. It seemed to have lined his nostrils, penetrated his skin.

As he trod carefully through the woods, trying to orient himself while remaining alert for patrols, he recited the names of his four contacts and the three passwords assigned for each. The passwords had been given to him just once, hurriedly and in a hushed tone. He hoped he'd heard correctly. If he hadn't, he'd be dead within seconds of uttering the error.

There was little risk of his forgetting the names and passwords, no matter how tense the circumstances. Dr. Sebastian Kapsky had a prodigious memory capable of re-

*taining and retrieving the most complex equations ever
generated by the human brain. Equations that could affect
or alter history. Memory wasn't the issue. Rather it was
whether what his brain retrieved when he spoke to the contacts was actually what was spoken to him by his seatmate,
Bronislaw Haller.*

Katyn, Soviet Union
1430, 23 April 1940

Bronisław Haller was a jeweler from Białystok. He and
Kapsky had been rounded up by Red Army soldiers
within days of the Soviet invasion of Poland, ostensibly
for "administrative processing"—at least that's what
they'd gleaned from the statements from the *praporsh-
chiks* taking their names before herding them onto transports. A lumbering open-bed lorry transferred them to
the Ostashkov Camp in Katyn Forest, where they would
be funneled into concrete bunkers along with thousands
of other men—mainly soldiers and policemen—but
also a fair number of municipal officials, clergy, and academics.

From the moment they clambered aboard the lorry
and sat next to each other, Haller had been anxious.
More than anxious; his face was covered with a look that
ranged between apprehension and dread. Within seconds
of sitting next to Kapsky, Haller leaned near and whispered, "Find your opportunity, friend, and run. Don't
hesitate. You'll only get one chance. Run and run fast."

Kapsky was startled. None of the detainees had spoken a word since they'd been marched toward the transports. Haller recognized the indecision on Kapsky's face. "Listen to me, friend. This isn't going to be random questioning, temporary detainment." Haller nodded toward two Russians dressed in civilian clothes standing apart from the Red Army soldiers. "That is NKVD. They do not send NKVD to verify names and addresses. They send NKVD for one thing: to kill."

Kapsky glanced toward the two civilians. Each wore dismissive, contemptuous expressions as they surveyed the Poles arrayed on the lorries. It was as if they were looking at something that would soon be irrelevant, like spoiled food being hauled to a dumpster. Kapsky leaned toward Haller. "Run where?"

"Anywhere. Just run. You'll know where to go later, but you must go."

Kapsky looked back at the NKVD officers, then leaned closer to Haller. "You lead. I'll follow."

A sardonic look came over Haller's face. "Obviously, you were not paying attention when I came aboard." He moved his long coat aside and gestured toward his legs. They were encased in a latticework of metal braces. "I've not run since I was eighteen years old." He shook his head. "I have no chance. But you may have one. And I can help."

A Soviet soldier closed the lorry's tailgate. One of the NKVD officers motioned for the driver to drive. As he waved his arm, the seams of his overcoat parted, revealing a Tokarev semiautomatic. The lorry lurched forward slowly.

Kapsky asked, "What do you mean you can help?"

Haller said, "You don't have much time, and few opportunities." He glanced about the bed of the vehicle and reached into his pocket. Most of the passengers were watching the Soviet troops lining the lorry's path. He withdrew a small cloth purse and pressed it into Kapsky's hand. Kapsky inspected it quizzically before opening it. Inside were several dozen *złoty*.

Kapsky snorted. "What am I supposed to do with this?"

"Train fare."

Kapsky handed the purse back. "No disrespect, but that is no help. I will get nowhere near a train." He waved at the scores of troops escorting the caravan of lorries. "They will seize the purse as soon as we get to our destination."

"No. They will not."

Kapsky squinted. "Why not?"

"Because you will give them something much more valuable. Something that will make them ignore your train fare."

"I have nothing of value."

"But I do. And I will give it to you in return for an oath."

Kapsky struggled not to appear impatient. "Oath? Is this a child's game? No riddles, please. Tell me what you want from me."

"Go to my family. Keep them safe."

Kapsky inspected Haller's face. It was a practical face. The face of a man with few illusions. A man who assessed

Kapsky in scant minutes and judged him up to the task. Or perhaps the only one who would consider performing it.

Nonetheless, Kapsky gestured toward the escort vehicles on either side of the convoy carrying scores of Red Army troops. "Seriously? You ask the impossible."

Haller drew closer. "I did not say it would be easy, but it *is* possible. With money all things are possible. Indeed, probable."

"A few *złoty*?"

"More than a few. More than train fare. Much more."

"Show me."

"I cannot at this time."

Kapsky turned away sharply and scanned the muddy road ahead. It was lined on each side by tall pine, the tops enshrouded in depressing gray mist. It produced a sense of foreboding. Haller was silent for several seconds, then leaned forward. "I have several grams of uncut precious stones. Their value is considerable. Very considerable. You may use some to secure your release, the remainder to see to my family's safety."

Kapsky returned his gaze to Haller's face. He scanned it skeptically for several seconds. "Show them to me."

A sheepish look came over Haller's face. "I cannot." He paused, then added hurriedly, "But understand, I do have them with me."

Kapsky continued examining Haller's face. It looked as if it were imploring him to understand what Haller was saying. After a few seconds, Kapsky blinked and sat erect. "You have them with you . . ."

"In a manner of speaking, yes."

". . . *Within* you."

Haller nodded. "Undetectable, yet retrievable."

Kapsky gazed toward the tops of the pines, then at the guards brandishing Soviet submachine guns. "How do you know that I won't simply abscond with the remaining stones after bribing the guards?"

"I do not."

Kapsky said, "We have no options . . ."

"We always have options, friend, always."

Kapsky stared at the floor of the lorry for nearly a minute. "How do I find them, your family?"

"They're in a hamlet outside Białystok. The address is in the purse."

Kapsky nodded and said nothing. They rode in silence for several minutes. Then Kapsky asked, "And when I find them, your family, what should I tell them about you?"

Haller smiled. "Tell them I escaped but had to take a different route, a longer route. It will take a while for me to arrive. Tell them I will join them when circumstances permit."

Kapsky understood. It was the response of a man who believed he was doomed.

CHAPTER 2

The humidity in Washington, D.C., was oppressive even in late April. It was compounded by Professor Aubrey Sloane's unfortunate choice in clothing. Originally from New Hampshire and now a lecturer at Cornell, his wardrobe consisted primarily of clothing suitable for New England. For his meeting today with Secretary of War Henry Stimson he'd worn his best suit—pure wool. Though it breathed well, it nonetheless caused him to perspire, which in turn caused him to itch. Consequently, he was about to enter the most important meeting of his life miserable and distracted.

He was astounded that he'd even secured the meeting. Obscure associate professors of physics didn't score meetings with the secretary of war—especially one as formidable as Stimson—unless the secretary had collected information validating the purpose of the meeting.

Sloane's purpose was to warn Stimson that the United

States of America, and much of the world, might soon be in peril.

Sloane walked slowly up the steps of the Munitions Building trying not to exert himself and precipitate a flood of perspiration. His footfalls echoed throughout the cavernous halls until he came to the tall wooden door of the Office of the Secretary of War.

Upon his entry, the sternly efficient receptionist sitting behind a massive oak desk startled him by immediately addressing him by name. "Please have a seat, Professor Sloane." She gestured to the wooden chairs arranged along the wall of the anteroom. "The secretary will receive you presently."

Sloane proceeded to the chair closest to the entrance. But before he could sit, a buzzer sounded on the receptionist's desk and she said, "The secretary is ready for you."

Sloane straightened and walked through the wooden gate next to the desk and knocked twice on the door to the office before entering. Secretary of War Henry Stimson, seated at the desk, was sifting through a sheaf of documents. Another man Sloane didn't recognize was seated in one of the two chairs opposite Stimson's desk. He had the countenance of a bulldog, a taciturn expression. He said nothing.

Stimson glanced at Sloane, tilted his head toward a seat, and returned his attention to the papers. Sloane sat in the chair for a full minute before Stimson placed the papers neatly on the corner of the desk and said, "Thank you for coming to see me, Professor."

"Thank *you*, sir."

"There have been a few scientists and mathematicians who advised us that there have been some rather profound developments in certain academic quarters of Europe. No one provided much by way of specifics, other than the developments could be rather transformative." Stimson nodded toward the bulldog. "Professor, this is Colonel Donovan. He, in fact, is the person who first alerted me to these transformative issues. When I related your message, he advised that I should, indeed, meet you face-to-face. And he insisted on being present."

Sloane nodded at Donovan, who was dressed in civilian clothes. Donovan remained expressionless.

"I gather the purpose of your visit has something to do with these developments."

"Yes, it does. It relates to an individual who is integral to what you referred to as 'transformative' scientific developments. He is one of a small group of kindred spirits. These are rather gifted physicists who I met two years ago at a conference in London. They had common, in fact parallel, pursuits in a field known as quantum mechanics. Since that conference we've been collaborating by correspondence, occasionally with Fermi of the University of Chicago, Niels Bohr of the University of Copenhagen, and Robert Goddard. They are the most renowned—"

"I know who they are, Professor. They are rather well known. Please continue."

"Yes, well, the individual of whom I speak was the key, the most integral, member of the collaboration. He was the man who initiated the joint correspondence among the group, developed the foundational theories, and produced the 'transformative' applications . . ."

". . . and?"

". . . and we haven't heard from him in nearly a month. Nothing. No cables. No letters. Even after the invasion of his country last September by the Red Army, he kept up regular correspondence without interruption—two, three times per week. He was prodigious. Then, suddenly, nothing."

The man introduced as Colonel Donovan had an intense expression on his face. Sloane could see muscles protruding like cables beneath his jawline.

"What do you think happened?"

"I don't know," Sloane whispered. "But with the Nazis to the west and the Soviets to the east . . ."

"You're concerned, obviously, that some harm has come to him," Stimson said. "But it's more than that, isn't it? This isn't just about looking out for a friend or colleague."

Sloane appeared anguished. "Mr. Secretary, I know nearly nothing of international affairs, war, or diplomacy, but I'm wholly capable of making reasonable deductions.

"I read the newspapers and see the Movietone reels in the theaters like everyone else, and it seems only a matter of time before we're drawn into the war in Europe. Heck, we're already assisting Great Britain logistically and with matériel." Sloane halted abruptly, raising his palms plaintively. "I don't mean to be speaking out of school, I just . . ."

"No apologies necessary, Professor. I think I understand where you're going with this." Stimson looked at Donovan.

"The Germans are quite proud of their array of modern weaponry—superweapons, they call them. We've been watching the development keenly. Although they pose no threat to us at the moment, Mr. Churchill is obsessed with them." Donovan paused and withdrew a cigar from his breast pocket. "Your colleague . . . I assume his work would be of utmost interest to the Germans?"

"Not just to Hitler, but to Stalin as well."

"And to America, I suppose?"

"The potential strategic value of his work is unparalleled. Not only did he work with the likes of Bohr and Goddard, but before the war he also worked with Walter Riedel and Wernher von Braun. He is intimately familiar with the science behind the German rocket programs. Clearly, they would not want those revealed. But it goes even beyond that. I do not say this lightly. Bohr, Fermi, and the rest of us are knowledgeable about discrete components, but this individual is the glue. He is knowledgeable about *all*. Moreover, he has multidisciplinary proficiency. He is gifted, and not just in one subject. Although it remains hypothetical, the matters upon which we've been working have extraordinary implications, and he is the one among our cohort who is most capable of turning theory into reality."

Donovan exchanged a knowing look with Stimson, leaving Sloane to suspect that the two may have heard something similar from other sources. Donovan shook his head as if he were hoping Sloane would have dispelled or downplayed what these sources had said.

"What do you propose be done, Professor Sloane?"

"Keep him out of the hands of the Russians and Germans. If we're too late for that, *rescue* him from the Russians and Germans."

Donovan glanced at Stimson, who nodded almost imperceptibly.

"What's your colleague's name?"

"Sebastian Kapsky."

"You know what I think of these kinds of operations, Bill. The kind MI6 performs," Stimson said after Sloane had left to take the train back to New York. "This isn't what civilized nations do."

Colonel William "Wild Bill" Donovan didn't need a reminder. Stimson was old-school. Civilized nations, *gentlemen*, didn't engage in clandestine operations on another nation's soil unless they were at war. And even then, there were rules, conventions.

"Henry, we *are* at war. Maybe not formally. But we're assisting the Brits, we've got aviators in Indochina. The professor's right, it's inevitable and you know it. Churchill's been hounding the President for months, and you know that the President won't be able to withstand that man's relentlessness."

"I cannot go to the President and ask that he send troops to Poland, even if it's a small tactical force. Both the Nazis and the Soviets would declare war," Stimson said.

Donovan inclined his massive bulldog head forward, a fullback about to plunge into a defensive line. "You've seen the reports, Henry. Hell, you have access to more reports than I do. Britain can't hold out much longer, even without the Germans deploying these 'superweapons' Hitler keeps going on about." Donovan jabbed his meaty index finger on Stimson's desktop. "That's a strategic disaster for us, even if we're not at war. And that's even without whatever superweapon Sloane's talking about. If either Hitler or Stalin get the type of capability Sloane implies, we won't have a chance in hell. The mere *threat* of its deployment will cause us to cave. We'd have to."

Stimson was taken aback. He'd never imagined Donovan was capable of even entertaining any result other than success, victory.

"You don't know that, Bill. This is all theoretical. Sloane even said so. Even if it got off the drawing board, it would be several years—as much as a decade or two—before it would become a reality. By then, the war in Europe will be long over."

Donovan remained adamant. Stabbing the desk again, he said, "You cannot take that chance. Right now it might be just a bunch of numbers and hieroglyphs on a chalkboard, but what if Hitler's math wizzes can turn those equations into reality a lot faster than we think? You heard Sloane. Hell, you heard that white-haired guy from Princeton, Eisenstein . . ."

"Einstein."

". . . You heard him, too. What if Hitler's people—or Stalin's—get it off the chalkboard with this Kapsky's help?"

Stimson, who'd been secretary of war under Presidents William Howard Taft and Franklin Delano Roosevelt, struck a pose familiar only to his closest friends. It was a pose of deliberation and concern, a patrician pose. Nearly a full minute passed. He nodded to himself, then looked at Donovan. "What do you propose?"

"We don't need a large force, just one or two men. With adequate support, as needed."

Stimson shook his head. "That codicil is what worries me. 'Support, as needed.' That almost inevitably means an escalation."

"No, it wouldn't. I'm not talking about military support. Not artillery, not aircraft. Just logistical support."

Stimson shook his head again. "One or two men— with some undefined logistical support—to find one man somewhere in Europe? In the middle of a two-front war?"

"Put that way, it *does* sound absurd. But it can be done." Donovan's bulldog head remained inclined toward Stimson. His eyes, though plaintive, were locked in.

A rare, wan smile creased Stimson's face. "And who is the remarkable man who would achieve this? You must already have someone in mind."

"I do."

"Who, then?"

"You don't know him."

"I sure as hell will if you expect me to approve this."

Donovan straightened from his incline. "I haven't really decided yet. But I'm thinking of some Rangers."

"Why these particular fellows? What qualifies them for a task like this?"

"They're somewhat reckless, yet deliberate."

As he spoke he was considering another option. Someone who didn't stay in the lanes. Borderline reckless, even brazen, but dependable and effective. A young major by the name of Dick Canidy.

CHAPTER 3

They first brought the doomed, one by one, into a dark concrete chamber the size of a large conference room. Two guards armed with PPSh-41 submachine guns would stand next to the exit as a *praporshchik* conducted a perfunctory final interrogation of the prisoner. The questions were anodyne: name, place of birth, current residence, occupation, immediate relatives. Any valuables that hadn't already been confiscated would be placed in a large bin near the entrance.

Due to the noise from massive exhaust fans in the adjacent room, both the interrogator and the prisoner had to shout their questions and answers. Accordingly, the interrogators would change every hour so that their voices wouldn't become hoarse.

The questioning lasted little more than a minute; the answers were not recorded in a journal or ledger. When done, one of the guards would escort the prisoner through a door opposite the entrance and into a larger concrete chamber for execution.

And so it was that Sebastian Kapsky was led by two guards into the antechamber, where he stood under a caged lightbulb, blinking against its harsh light at the *praporshchik* who would pose the last questions Kapsky would ever hear. One of the guards retreated to the side of the entrance while the other patted Kapsky down, retrieving a brown leather billfold from his right back pocket. Opening it, the guard found several *złoty*, and a University of Lviv identification card bearing a photo of the smiling professor of theoretical physics, room 201, Galician Sejm. Grinning, the guard held up the billfold, opening it to display the currency that they would momentarily distribute among themselves after the prisoner was questioned.

The interrogator nodded, then examined the clipboard that he held in his left hand, tracking his right index finger to the next name on the list.

"Name?"

"Sebastian Kapsky."

"Date and place of birth?"

"January 7, 1902, Kraków."

"Current address?"

"Hell."

The interrogator looked up sharply, unamused.

"Immediate family?"

"All deceased. Your compatriots saw to that."

"Occupation?"

"Professor. Lviv University."

"Do you have anything to declare?"

"You are a horse's ass."

The interrogator looked at the guard standing next to Kapsky, who winced as the guard delivered a blow to Kapsky's left kidney.

The interrogator's eyes narrowed as he studied the clipboard. Kapsky noticed his finger sliding back and forth as if he were checking Kapsky's name against a second list. After several moments he looked up, his head tilted slightly to the side.

"Your name again?"

"Sebastian Kapsky."

A glimmer of excitement shone in the interrogator's eyes. "Professor Sebastian Andrejz Kapsky?"

"Yes."

The interrogator spun on his heel, hurriedly proceeded to the door to the larger chamber, and disappeared. Kapsky heard him speaking rapidly to someone inside, his tone subservient. He reappeared momentarily and beckoned Kapsky to the larger chamber. The guard standing next to Kapsky flipped Kapsky's billfold to the other guard, grabbed Kapsky's right arm, and pushed him past the interrogator into the larger chamber and withdrew, closing the door behind him.

The larger chamber had a concrete floor that sloped toward a drain over which hung a water hose. The room smelled of gunpowder, blood, and disinfectant. As in the antechamber, a single lightbulb encaged in steel wire provided illumination. Standing beneath the bulb was a hulking figure built like a heavyweight prizefighter. He looked as if he could absorb multiple powerful blows to the face without flinching. He was encased from head to toe in rubberized gear: overalls, a trench coat, boots, and goggles. A sleek Walther .25 ACP was in his right hand.

He was NKVD Commandant Vasily Mikhailovich Blokhin, the most prolific executioner in the history of mankind. Stalin's chief assassin. Everyone in Ostashkov, including Kapsky, knew his reputation. It was tattooed on their minds. To this point, he had killed more than 5,500 prisoners—each with a single shot from the Walther to the back of the head. It was a seemingly incomprehensible figure, one not remotely approached by many whole armies.

Blokhin's prodigious kills preceded his arrival at Katyn Forest. They included the famous as well as the obscure. Among his victims were many of those convicted during the Moscow Show Trials, even Mikhail Tukhachevsy, marshal of the Soviet Union, and Genrikh Yagoda, former head of the NKVD itself. It was said that when Blokhin died, half the population of hell would pursue him throughout eternity and half the population of heaven would be cheering for his capture.

Blokhin stared impassively at Kapsky for several seconds before speaking—his voice impossibly deep and guttural.

"You are Sebastian Kapsky." It wasn't a question.

"I am."

"Professor Sebastian Kapsky, the mathematician."

"Indeed, I am."

"From Lviv University."

Kapsky nodded.

Something resembling a smile crossed Blokhin's face. It projected greed and success.

"You are most fortunate, Professor. You will not be sharing the fate of your comrades this day. A very important figure wishes to see you. Apparently, you have significant value."

Kapsky permitted himself a smile. "May I ask who this important person to whom I owe my life is?"

"Lavrentiy Beria, Professor Kapsky. My superior. The head of the NKVD."

Kapsky nodded. His smile disappeared. "The most feared man in the Soviet Union, perhaps the world."

"He *may* be the most feared man in the world. But he is the *second* most feared man in the Soviet Union, Professor. He reports, after all, to Joseph Vissarionovich Stalin."

"What, may I ask, would someone like Beria want with me?" Kapsky asked.

Blokhin shrugged. "I do not have the details, only that you are of extreme importance. And apparently not just to Comrade Beria. I was told finding you was of some urgency. We are in a competition. It seems Admiral Canaris also has instructed his people that locating you is of prime importance."

"I'm afraid I'm unfamiliar with this Mr. Canaris," Kapsky said.

"Chief of the Abwehr-German military intelligence. The genius spy."

Kapsky nodded, impressed with his own apparent

fame. "A competition? Between the signatories to Molotov-Ribbentrop? I confess I do not understand."

Blokhin waved him off. "We will leave for Moscow in the morning. I am to deliver you to Beria personally. In the meantime, you may spend the night in the officer's quarters."

Kapsky smiled appreciatively. "I am very hungry also."

"Of course, Professor. You will be fed, provided a change of clothes, and will be—"

The interrogator burst into the chamber, a panicked expression on his face. He strode rapidly toward a startled Blokhin and without a word displayed Kapsky's open billfold to his superior. An irritated Blokhin blinked as he adjusted his focus upon the billfold's contents, the task made more difficult by the interrogator's trembling hand. Blokhin grasped the interrogator's hand to steady it and a moment later a look of terror covered the executioner's face. Blokhin recognized the professor's photo ID. He knew the face; he'd seen it yesterday, as the lorries brought in the prisoners. He remembered it because of the owner's distinctive shock of jet-black hair that combined with deep green eyes that made him appear almost spectral. He remembered thinking that the face belonged to an uncommonly inquisitive individual because the eyes darted about, scanning the surroundings as if he were calculating multiple probabilities—the best odds for escape. A futile calculation.

But the face was not that of the stooped man standing before him.

Blokhin looked up abruptly. "You are not Kapsky?"

Alarmed, he looked down at the photo ID and then back up again. "You are *not* Kapsky."

Sebastian Kapsky was long gone. Bronislaw Haller, meticulous, nervous jeweler from the outskirts of Białystok, smiled and began to shake his head just as a single 6.35-millimeter round, fired in rage by the most prolific killer in creation, penetrated his forehead.

CHAPTER 4

He behaved as if they weren't watching him, inspecting him: Nonchalant. Indifferent.

His eyesight was good, but peripheral vision could be deceptive. Nonetheless, he determined that the tall blonde on the left was the most attractive—and most interested—of the four women huddled together on the periphery of the field.

Each was subtle. No staring, only furtive, coy glances and whispered assessments, probably of his physique.

Lieutenant (junior grade) Richard Canidy had attended MIT on a Navy scholarship, graduating with honors in 1938 with a B.S. in aeronautical engineering. He'd already logged 350 hours of flying time by then and was approached by General Claire Chennault to fly P-40B fighters, defending Burma Road supply lines against the Japanese in China.

He hated exercise for the sake of exercise. Physical exertion, he believed, should be directed toward a purpose other than improving one's physique. Otherwise, it was mere vanity. Vanity wasn't manly. It wasn't productive. It was the indulgence of those who otherwise were failures.

Canidy knew that he had a naturally superior build. It was primarily a matter of heredity. The males on both sides of his family were tall, lean, and naturally well muscled. He'd inherited all of those characteristics. He appreciated all of those characteristics. He would never, however, concede vanity because of those characteristics.

Canidy, nonetheless, was competitive to the point of irrationality. Although he disdained exercise, he hated being second best even more, and despite being blessed with a splendid physique he determined that his friend Eric Fulmar's was even better. Not much more, and perhaps not even discernible to the casual observer, but enough to ignite Canidy's competitive instincts.

So three weeks ago he'd embarked on a punishing regime of running, calisthenics, and weight training. He'd performed the latter in strict privacy; *normal* people didn't indulge in such pursuits. It was the province of wrestlers and circus performers. But he'd experimented with it at the suggestion of a friend—a former Annapolis football player—and was impressed at the results after just a few sessions.

So he persisted.

The women ostensibly were watching the baseball game on the diamond next to the football field on which Canidy was finishing up a set of fifty-yard sprints. There were no items on his agenda for the rest of the day or evening. He'd given some thought to meeting Fulmar at the St. Regis Hotel for a drink and taking advantage of whatever opportunities presented themselves. But he decided to explore the more immediate opportunities that had presented themselves on the bleachers along the first base line.

While catching his breath from the sprints, he considered what approach to use. Separating one woman from a group was not a task for amateurs. And while Canidy certainly was no amateur, even skilled players often floundered.

He'd already taken the first step—determining which one to separate. The blonde. Although it was a close call, really a matter of personal preference. She was tied with the raven-haired one for most attractive. Although something about the raven-haired girl suggested greater long-term erotic potential, the blonde had already displayed the most interest. Canidy didn't want to work at it. He preferred to go with the best short-term odds.

His calculus, however, was momentarily scrambled when he noticed the brunette casually stroke her left thigh while giving him a sidelong glance. The gesture was crafted to look innocent rather than purposeful, but a man like Canidy knew better. Still, after a slight hesitation, he decided to stick with the blonde.

Severing the blonde from the group would require finesse and tact so as not to alienate the rest. In these circumstances, females were more loyal to one another than males were. Males understood it was every man for himself; let the best man win and no hard feelings.

Women, however, were far less likely to break off from the group if the pursuing male had offended or hurt the feelings of one of its members.

The scoreboard noted that it was the bottom of the eighth inning, one out. The game would be over soon. Canidy didn't have the luxury of finesse and tact. He'd ratchet the Canidy charm machine to ten and employ a full-on frontal assault.

Canidy began striding toward the group. It was a relaxed stride, projecting confidence. He was the big dog.

Before he got to where the women were seated, he noticed a man with a bulldog countenance standing in the parking lot behind the bleachers. He wore a suit with no tie. Next to him was an Army major in uniform.

Canidy recognized the man in the suit immediately. He was Colonel William "Wild Bill" Donovan, winner of the Medal of Honor, the DSM, and DSC, among other awards. He was without question the most remarkable man Canidy had ever known. The fact that Donovan even knew him amazed Canidy.

The sight of Donovan caused Canidy to forget the women in the stands. He immediately changed course and approached the legend. Canidy saluted the major and turned to Donovan and said, "Sir."

Donovan, whose seemingly limitless achievements included being a star athlete, looked Canidy's physique up and down and remarked, "Impressive as far as it goes, Dick. But it's what you can do with it that counts."

"No argument there, sir."

"I'm here because I think you *can* do something with

it. And, far more important, do something with your mind."

"Yes, sir."

"You're not my first choice." Donovan's reputation for bluntness was well deserved. "But you are, at least, my second choice." Donovan put up his hand to signal he meant no insult. "I'm in the process of selecting a team for an operation in Europe. It's a risky operation. Very risky. Extraordinarily difficult. Men will die. And the likelihood of success is, well, quite limited."

Canidy glanced at the colonel, who looked as if he were gazing upon a dead man.

"You're my second choice because the first choice consists of a group of highly proficient men who've seen extensive ground combat and have proven themselves uniquely gifted and resourceful. Nonetheless, the odds are that this group of men will all be killed before completing the operation."

"And as always, sir, you have a backup plan."

"Yes."

"And I'm that backup plan."

"Precisely."

"Sir, why me?"

"Because you're an unconventional, reckless SOB."

Canidy could barely suppress a smile. He'd never felt more flattered than at that moment. Wild Bill Donovan had called *him* a reckless SOB.

Canidy straightened. "Sir, with permission, what's the operation?"

"Too soon, Canidy. Need-to-know only."

"Respectfully, then why tell me anything at all?"

"Because we need to begin training now, regardless of whether you're ever needed. If the primary team fails, we'll need you to go at a moment's notice. Planning and training need to be done beforehand. That training will necessarily be rigorous. More intensive and demanding than anything you've been through."

Candidy nodded pensively. "Who else will be on my team?"

"So far, just you. And it may end up being *only* you. Although I have someone in mind to assist, I may leave *that* selection to you."

"Just one other person?"

"Perhaps."

"*My* choice?"

"Not entirely. He'll need to meet my approval. But I have a feeling we'd both choose the same man."

Candidy grinned. He suspected they would. "When do we get at it, sir?"

"Right now."

CHAPTER 5

Professor Sebastian Kapsky was trapped between the two largest armies in the world. And the deadliest elements of those armies were aggressively searching for him.

He'd narrowly evaded capture by the Soviets twice and the Germans once. In each instance, the cost of such evasion was the lives of Polish patriots and even some Russian peasants who had provided him shelter and sustenance. They included the four Home Army guides toward whom Haller had directed him. He'd never have gotten more than two or three kilometers from Katyn without them. They'd adroitly guided him from just outside Katyn to Hrodna by train and foot.

Kapsky had secreted himself among the corpses conveyed in large flatbed trucks to the outlying trenches of Katyn Forest. He lay inert, feigning death as best he could. Although the ride was short in time and distance, it felt interminable. The suffocating stench of rotting flesh and congealed blood permeated his clothing and made him nauseated, but he'd willed himself not to react, to remain absolutely still until an opportunity to jump off and sprint to the woods presented itself.

He waited for a dense growth of shrubs in which he could conceal himself. But none appeared. The closer they drew to the burial site the more anxious he grew. He imagined being dumped with the other bodies into a trench and being covered with earth by a bulldozer.

He knew he couldn't wait for optimal cover to present itself. It might never come. So when the truck slowed to round a bend, he rolled off the other corpses into a ditch and remained prone until all of the trucks disappeared from view. Then he sprang to his feet and ran due west as fast and as long as he could. When he could run no more he hunched over, hands on knees, and gulped air until he could run some more. He repeated the pattern until nightfall, when he reached Varniken Forest. He then followed Haller's instructions meticulously and walked northwest until he came to Svetly, where he encountered the four *Armia Krajowa* who guided him toward the northernmost part of the old border between Poland and the Soviet Union.

The patriots understood the risk when they volunteered to assist him. They'd lost friends and family members in similar pursuits. But the price was invariably brutal. Women, children, even grandchildren were slaughtered during interrogation or to coerce cooperation. A tiny hamlet of twenty-three, consisting of just four families, was machine-gunned by a Soviet platoon because their lieutenant believed the residents were hiding Kapsky. They were not. The *burmister* of the village of Grajewo was disemboweled in the public square because the SS Totenkopf-Standarte believed he had harbored Kapsky. He had, but months before the arrival of the Wehrmacht, and Kapsky had long since fled.

Scores of patriots had assisted Kapsky in ways large and small. They didn't know the specific reason why the Germans and Soviets were looking for him, they simply knew that if evil was searching for Kapsky, it was important to keep him alive and away from such evil. It was the Sikorski standard.

A few patriots had an inkling of his importance to the enemy. He was a scholar, a mathematician. It didn't take much imagination to deduce that he possessed knowledge that could provide a military advantage—possibly a strategic one—to whomever captured him. But the urgency of the search was breathtaking. It was almost as if Poland's conquest and occupation were secondary.

Ever since escaping from Ostashkov in Katyn Forest by bribing two guards with a few of Bronislaw Haller's gems, Kapsky stayed on the move, never remaining in one place for more than a few days. He kept part of his promise and delivered the remainder of the jewels to Haller's family. He did not, however, tell Anna, Haller's widow, that he'd be rejoining them. The moment Kapsky gave Anna Haller the jewels, he could tell from her face that she knew her husband of twenty-two years was dead.

She remained stoic and offered him lodging in a small flat above the jewelry shop. Exhausted and needing to orient himself, Kapsky accepted, stating that she'd be rid of him as soon as he was capable of traveling more than a short distance.

The next morning, he was awakened by the sound of voices from the shop. He crept carefully down the steps and observed Anna huddling with another woman who looked remarkably similar. He detected urgency in their voices.

Turning to see him at the bottom of the stairs, Anna dispensed with greetings and introductions and simply said, "You should go. It is not safe."

Kapsky nodded that he understood. Although he didn't need an explanation, Anna provided one. Gesturing toward the other woman, she said, "My sister says the Russians have been asking questions in Mikołajki in the way only Russians can do, if you understand my meaning. They are looking for a Sebastian Kapsky. Mikołajki is only thirty kilometers away. Go north to Ryn. My sister says word is that there are Americans nearby looking for someone."

Americans.

Kapsky nodded thanks and left, but not before Anna gave him a sack filled with sausage, bread, and cheese. As he made his way out of the city, he heard machine-gun fire far in the distance.

He did not hear any return fire.

CHAPTER 6

Canidy sighted the target ten yards away with the Colt M1911 and fired six .45 ACP rounds in rapid succession. He straightened and considered his aim, tilting his head slightly to the right. Three shots had hit the bull's-eye and the three others were grouped in a tight semicircle slightly to the right. Not bad. Indeed, pretty good. But he was still dropping his shoulder and pulling off to the right.

The M1911 was his personal weapon. He'd bought it from Ithaca Gun during a trip to visit two Tri-Delt sorority sisters at Cornell, neither of whom knew about the other.

The weapon's weight and balance suited him. More important, he had grown to rely on it. Over the last several months, he'd trained with a variety of weapons, several hours per day: on stationary targets and moving targets; on firing ranges and in combat simulations. He estimated that during that span of time he'd fired more than fifty thousand rounds—most from the M1911, but also from a Smith & Wesson M1917 revolver, an M1 Garand, and a Winchester 90 sniper rifle. That didn't include the Thompson submachine gun that he enjoyed firing just for the hell of it.

But the M1911 was his weapon of choice.

Canidy raised his pistol and fired the last two rounds. He straightened again to consider the results.

"Still pulling off."

Canidy turned to see Colonel Donovan standing behind him. Canidy waited expectantly for a few seconds and then asked, "Well, sir, aren't you going to tell me to slap in another magazine and go again?"

Donovan said nothing. He merely pursed his lips and stared as if contemplating what to say and how to say it. Donovan had devised the training regimen that Canidy had endured for the last few months. It was part preparation and part torture. Donovan had adapted it from the innovative regimen developed by Lieutenant Colonel Robert Laycock of the British No. 8 Commando Unit. Donovan had been clandestinely provided the details of the training by Lieutenant Commander Ian Fleming. It was unlike any military training that preceded it, premised on an expectation that the individual soldier would at some point be required to perform as a self-contained one-man unit—as a guerrilla, a saboteur, a spy—fully capable of creating havoc in any theater under any conditions. Speed, stealth, adaptability, and sheer ruthlessness were the primary and essential qualities of such men.

The concept was abhorred by most in the traditional military hierarchy. Some, including civilian oversight, had gone so far as to lobby against the creation of any such force. Civilized nations, they maintained, didn't employ such tactics. Stimson was one such man. He'd been appalled when Donovan broached the concept with him. "The United States," Stimson responded indignantly, "does not employ pirates and assassins."

Donovan was undaunted. He embarked on an intense campaign to persuade both Stimson and Roosevelt that such a force was not just necessary, but imperative. The world was changing. *Warfare* was changing. The United States owed its very existence, in part, to similar tactical innovations. Now it was the Brits, those that had been defeated by such innovations, who were at the cutting edge.

To achieve the objective of standing up such a unit, Donovan attacked Stimson's flank. First, working through Laycock, Archibald Stirling, known as the Phantom Major, and Fleming, they'd prevailed upon PM Churchill to broach the concept with President Roosevelt.

Donovan knew Churchill could convince Roosevelt of almost anything. It didn't take long before Roosevelt raised the idea of a "commando" force with Stimson. Stimson, as expected, resisted at first. But also, as expected, after a few nominal protestations, he conceded.

Donovan, with occasional guidance from Fleming— who had a penchant for cloak, dagger, and dramatics— devised the tortuous training program Canidy had been going through for several months. Fifteen hours a day, seven days a week. In the field and in the classroom. Physical and mental. Canidy was drilled in every form of weapons combat imaginable: knives, guns, explosives, even poisons. Hours of hand-to-hand techniques, mental agility drills, sleep deprivation, and interrogation/torture resistance. Donovan fully expected the exhaustive regimen to purge Canidy of his conceit and impertinence, to sober his daredevil rebelliousness.

It had the opposite effect.

Canidy increasingly behaved as if he were invincible. He developed more of a swagger, an even bigger ego than before. By pushing Canidy's limits appreciably beyond that of other fighting men, Donovan had produced an elite, albeit somewhat overconfident, warrior.

And, though Donovan hadn't expected it, it was precisely what Donovan intended. But now all of the effort may have been wasted, at least that's what Stimson thought. The patrician was logical to a fault. Donovan, however, thought it was only a temporary setback, a delay.

Though Donovan was blunt and without pretense, he hesitated before giving Canidy the news. Canidy, after all, had put himself through weeks of hell in preparation for an operation that now would be scrubbed.

"Dick, you've performed admirably, done everything I've asked," Donovan began.

Canidy, nobody's fool, anticipated what Donovan hesitated to say before he said it. ". . . But the mission is off. Over."

Donovan, never at a loss for words, couldn't summon even a word of affirmation. He nodded almost imperceptibly. A dejected Canidy lowered the M1911, his arm hanging limply at his side. He forced a rakish smile. "The women of America thank you, sir. I'll now be returning to the playing field."

Though Donovan returned a fleeting smile, his expression quickly turned grave. "Just learned that a squad led by Staff Sergeant McTear was shredded by machine-gun fire from Soviet T-34. 7.62-millimeter DT machine guns. Not the easiest way to go."

A rare look of seriousness covered Canidy's face. "The entire squad?"

Donovan nodded. "Signals picked up a transmission from the *Armia Krajowa* confirming same." He nodded again. "That's a nasty weapon."

Canidy straightened, jocularity gone. "Sir, what do you need me to do?"

"The secretary has told us to stand down. The *Armia Krajowa* intercepted a message sent by the Soviet tank commander identifying—misidentifying—our men as Polish guerrillas—Home Army."

Canidy said, "So the Russians . . ."

". . . and probably the Germans . . ."

"Don't know we're involved."

"Right," Donovan said. "If they knew it, surely Hitler would declare war. Probably Stalin, too."

"Jesus . . ."

". . . had nothing to do with it."

"We got lucky." Donovan stopped himself. "What I mean is . . ."

"I understand what you mean, sir," Canidy offered. "It sure wasn't lucky for McTear and his men, *but* it was lucky for us Adolf and Uncle Joe don't know it was us."

Donovan looked down and kicked the dirt. He appeared hesitant at first. At least, the first time Canidy had seen it.

Donovan looked up, his face a mixture of frustration and contrition. "The President has ordered us to stand down. He thinks we dodged a bullet and doesn't want to tempt fate right now. Churchill's been pressing him to go beyond lend-lease, to commit troops. He's resisted thus far, but this could have thrown us in with both feet. We'll probably get in eventually, but the President doesn't want to be forced into it. If we get in, it has to be on our timetable."

Canidy's jaw tightened. "Hell, sir." He caught himself. "Sir, we're knee-deep already. What was I doing in Indochina?"

"A full-fledged war against the Nazis and Soviets is a whole 'nother ball game, Dick."

Canidy shook his head. Months of pain and discipline and nothing to show for it. He didn't even know what he'd been trained for, other than an operation in Europe. An important mission, unquestionably. He could tell simply by Donovan's behavior. Nonetheless . . .

Canidy transferred the M1911 to his left hand and extended his right hand to Donovan. "All things considered, sir, it's been an honor just to be considered for—whatever this was going to be."

Donovan shook Canidy's hand. "This isn't over, Dick. The original mission remains incomplete. And it can't stay that way. If what I've learned about the objective is accurate, it simply *can't* remain incomplete. Not for long."

Donovan kept pumping Canidy's hand absentmindedly before releasing it. "Stay close. We may need you."

"You know where I'll be, sir."

Donovan smiled. "Where you headed, Dick?"

"With permission, sir, I plan on getting drunk and getting laid. The order of those occurrences doesn't particularly matter."

Donovan turned to walk back to his vehicle. Canidy took a few steps in the opposite direction before turning around and calling after the legend. "Sir, can you at least tell me what the hell this is all about?"

Donovan turned, a somber expression on his face. "Even if I could, you'd never believe it."

At precisely the same moment Donovan was entering his vehicle, SS Obersturmführer Konrad Maurer was entering 76 Tirpitzufer, headquarters of the Wehrmacht. He did so with a mixture of curiosity and trepidation, for he was going to see the genius, Vice Admiral Wilhelm Franz Canaris, chief of the Abwehr. Hitler's inner circle sported a number of formidable men, but none more so than the head of all German military intelligence.

Not that Maurer was easily intimidated. At six six, 240 pounds, with ice-blue eyes and hair so blond it was almost white, the well-muscled veteran of Fall Gelb and the Battle of Sedan was a menacing figure to most everyone he encountered. Among the badges decorating his chest were the Knight's Cross, Iron Cross (2nd Class), and the Infantry Assault Badge.

But no medal could shield him from Canaris's penetrating gaze. It was unnerving. Even Guderian, legendary commander of the Panzertruppe bearing his name, was said to look askance.

The Oberstleutnant in the antechamber to Canaris's office looked up from his paperwork and glanced at the wall clock to his right as Maurer entered at 4:57 p.m., only three minutes before his meeting with the chief. Unacceptable. All visitors were to arrive precisely five minutes before their respective appointments. No exceptions. The Oberstleutnant pointedly recorded Maurer's name and arrival time in a ledger. Ten seconds before 5:00, the Oberstleutnant pressed a buzzer to alert Canaris of the visitor's arrival, then rose from his chair and opened the office door at exactly 5:00.

Maurer entered and stood at attention in front of Canaris's desk. Without looking up from his papers, the chief gestured for Maurer to take a seat in one of the three high-backed leather chairs that formed a semicircle around the desk. After a moment Canaris raised his gaze to Maurer. His thick white eyebrows formed a canopy over his eyes that appeared to look through and beyond whatever they were directed at.

"What have you got?"

"A report from Eighth Army staff under Generaloberst Blaskowitz, if accurate, is very unusual, Herr Admiral. It appears a patrol near Mikołajki captured several members of the Polskie Państwo Podziemne."

"Of what possible interest could this be to me?"

"Herr Admiral, it appears the Soviet tank group killed

several members of the Resistance. But on closer inspection, it's doubtful they actually were members of the Resistance."

Canaris slapped the top of his desk sharply in disgust. "SS. Again, the SS. They continue to bring dishonor upon us. They do not act as soldiers. They act as terrorists. I've expressed my concerns to OKW Keitel numerous times."

Maurer paused to ensure Canaris was finished before responding somewhat defensively. "Herr Admiral, it does not appear that it was the SS. This occurred in an area occupied by the Soviets. All indications are that it was indeed fire from a T-34 tank that killed these men . . ."

Canaris frowned. "I assume there is a reason I should be interested in this minor skirmish in Soviet-occupied territory?"

"The initial assumption was, indeed, that the dead were Polish underground. They were dressed accordingly and were carrying weapons that appeared to have been salvaged from battles with the Red Army. But they carried no identification whatsoever."

Canaris shrugged. "That's standard practice for the Resistance. Accordingly, when captured there are no identifying documents or other indices allowing the captors to trace back to the guerrillas' relatives."

Maurer nodded respectfully. "True, Mein Herr. But the appearances of these men were PPP to a fault. Nothing was amiss that would arouse suspicion."

"And that was what was suspicious," Canaris said flatly.

"Yes, Herr Admiral. So, therefore, the Russians examined the bodies in minute detail—more out of curiosity than suspicion. Until they came upon a faint discoloration on one of the dead men. Really, it was serendipitous. A *starshina* with tinea noticed what he believed was the same condition on the forearm of one of the bodies. It was faded, barely detectable, but he advised the others not to touch it.

"When he looked more closely he determined that it wasn't, in fact, tinea, but a tattoo of an eagle, barely discernible, as if the owner had done his best to scrub it, hide it."

Canaris's eyes narrowed. "And what did the Russians deduce from this?"

"Herr Admiral, we do not believe the Russians deduced anything. But one of the troops in question made casual mention of it and it eventually made its way to Blaskowitz's people.

"*They* gave it considerable deliberation. And they concluded the deceased was an American."

Canaris nodded slowly. "American." He rose from his chair, lost in thought. *"American,"* he repeated. He looked at Maurer. "And our intelligence suggests the Soviets have not yet concluded this man is American?"

"Herr Admiral, the Russians are brutes. There is no evidence they have come to that conclusion."

"The Soviets may be brutes, but they are extremely clever brutes."

"Clever, Herr Admiral? Respectfully, we got the better of them with Molotov-Ribbentrop, by far."

Canaris shook his head sharply. "That's what the politicians and the newspapers and the scholars say. We took all of the major cities—Warsaw, Kraków, Łódź, Danzig. But look at what problems they cause. We are tied down in every one of the great cities, battling constant resistance, committing massacres by the day. Whereas the brutes, as you call them, immediately consolidated their position. Staging elections and granting Soviet citizenship to legitimize their gains. We, on the other hand, have engaged in extermination. Look at Warsaw. The Soviets will hold on to their gains long after the war. Mark my words."

Maurer listened, but said nothing. He heard whispers that Canaris was at odds with much of the Führer's agenda. A less prudent man might utter some concurrence to ingratiate himself with his superior. But such a man could easily find himself in prison or before a firing squad, the subject an entrapment to smoke out those disloyal to the Führer.

"If these men were Americans, Maurer, why do you think they were there?"

"Herr Admiral, I suspect they were there to foment or help the Resistance. Perhaps they are Polish Americans?"

"Sensible conclusion, but no, Maurer. They were there to find someone. To extract him."

"Who, Herr Admiral?"

"A man I need you to find before anyone else does."

CHAPTER 7

The hayloft in the barn made it tolerable. In fact, border-line comfortable. It was dry, clean, and it wasn't infested with rodents.

Kapsky was nearing his limit. He'd been constantly on the move, trying to evade Red Army patrols. When he could, he slept in barns, sheds, and abandoned buildings. More often, he slept in the woods.

Fortunately, he had plenty of provisions. The gems that Haller had given him for his own use had yielded a generous sum of currency. He frequently was tempted to use the money to purchase lodging for a night or two, but he thought that might alert those who were searching for him.

Originally, he planned to move northward toward Danzig, eight to ten kilometers per day, reasoning that with a slow, deliberate pace he'd be less likely to make mistakes leading to detection. But even that pace proved difficult to sustain. Soviets seemed to be everywhere, and he had yet to encounter many Home Army personnel.

He never used rail or any form of motorized transportation. Red Army checkpoints were ubiquitous, and NKVD, posing as ordinary citizens, were known to ride buses, trollies, and trains looking for members of the underground and their collaborators.

Kapsky rose from a bed of hay he'd crafted for himself and gathered the bag that carried the few possessions—necessities—he'd acquired. It was almost dawn. He wanted to get moving before the owner of the barn began his day.

He oriented himself as he peeked out the barn door at the surrounding countryside. Other than the farmhouse and a copse of trees to the north, nothing but fields in every direction. It was completely silent. The stars were receding in brightness as the eastern horizon began to glow. He walked northward at a casual pace, hoping as he did every morning that this would be the day someone would deliver him from purgatory. Someone who could provide passage to the coast, perhaps even to England. Although he conceded it was mere fantasy, he used it to motivate himself and to ward off feelings of despair. But what if someone *could* actually help him? What if he encountered someone from the Home Army, Sikorski's tourists? Why *couldn't* it happen? And why stop at England? After all, it was under siege. Why not America?

Engrossed in escapism as he approached the copse of trees, he almost didn't discern the movement in its periphery a few meters away. Startled, the professor, who had never struck anyone in his life, seized a knife from the outer pocket of his bag and ran toward a figure emerging from the copse. *Strike before being struck. Take no chances. Eliminate the threat, silence the spy.*

Kapsky was on the figure in seconds. They crashed to the ground, Kapsky on top, knife raised.

And in the twilight before dawn, he saw that the person he was about to kill was a girl—probably eleven or twelve years old—her face contorted in terror. Her mouth was agape as if she were attempting to scream, but no sounds emerged. Her body was rigid, anticipating the thrust of the knife, the piercing pain from the blade.

Kapsky rolled off her in horror. His chest heaved as he tried to suck air into his lungs and compose himself, but his heart continued beating so rapidly it felt as if it would burst from his chest. It was several seconds before he gathered himself to speak. To his astonishment, the girl, already more composed than he, spoke first.

"You are the professor?" Fear remained in her voice.

"Who are you?"

"It is not important."

"It is to me. Who are you?"

"My name is Lara. I saw you enter the barn yesterday."

Kapsky stared at her in bewilderment. He'd been extraordinarily careful that no one would see him enter the barn. He hadn't seen the girl, but she'd seen *him*. As if she read his mind, she assured, "No one else saw you. So do not worry."

"Why did you ask if I'm the professor?"

"My uncles, Bogdan and Janusz, said the Russians

were looking for someone—a professor. I have never seen you before. You are not from here. And you slept in the barn. It makes sense."

Kapsky blinked in bewilderment. The girl had regained her composure more quickly than he. "What are you doing here at this ungodly hour? Why aren't you at home?"

"This is my duty. I keep watch from four to eight."

"Watch for what? For whom?"

"For Home Army. Uncle Bogdan is the commander. Uncle Janusz is intelligence. Everyone does something. We all have a job."

"And your job was to look for me?"

"No. It is to watch for the Russians. But when I saw you I could tell you are hiding. You are not from here. Since the Russians are looking for a professor, I figured you must be that person."

Lara is going to go far, Kapsky thought, *provided she survives the war.* "Lara, I am going in the direction of Danzig," he said, pointing northward. "Do you know if there are Russians there?"

Lara shook her head. "If you do not know the area, they will get you. You do not *look* like you are from here. You will die. I am sure of it. But my uncles can help you. They are smarter and stronger than the Russians. You must come with me."

Lara rose and began walking. Kapsky got up and found himself obeying her command. She was not even as old as the shoes he was wearing, but she carried herself like a field marshal. And, just maybe, she could keep him alive.

CHAPTER 8

Every time Canidy entered the ornate lobby of the Willard Hotel he imagined himself as Errol Flynn or Basil Rathbone. He suspected most men who entered did the same and most women imagined they were Vivien Leigh. It wasn't merely the hotel's ornateness, it was also its proximity to the White House and the fact that there was a fair probability that on any given occasion a Flynn, Rathbone, or other star would be lounging in the foyer with a Macallan or Dewar's just presented by a member of the waitstaff.

Unbeknownst to Canidy—although it would have delighted him—was that several of the people in the lobby *had* suspected he might be a star of the silver screen, though they couldn't quite recall the motion picture in which he'd appeared. Nonetheless, they were relatively certain that he was a hero of some sort. Someone daring and dashing who had recently saved the day.

No one in the lobby, including Canidy, noticed the man who *was* one of the most daring individuals in American history. A man who had saved the day on multiple occasions and for which his country had awarded him its highest honors for heroism. As opposed to Canidy, he didn't look the part. He appeared unremarkable, save for a face that suggested unshakable tenacity, a suggestion that was, if anything, understated.

Donovan sensed Canidy possessed many of the same qualities. His swagger was partially that of a young man who hadn't yet suffered many setbacks or defeats, but it was mostly that of a man who had a realistic appreciation that his gifts and abilities were well above those of most. Donovan sensed Canidy's potential in the way a champion boxer senses that the upstart ducking into the ring might just be the heir apparent, but not before he had his face rearranged a few more times.

Canidy hadn't noticed Donovan sitting in the far corner opposite the reception desk. Donovan, however, had noticed the likely purpose for Canidy's visit to the hotel—an attractive brunette of about thirty-five who had deftly removed her wedding ring and deposited it into the side pocket of her handbag a few moments after Canidy had appeared at the entrance. Donovan suspected it wasn't the first time she'd practiced the maneuver.

Donovan watched as Canidy kissed the woman on the left cheek at the same time her right hand momentarily disappeared behind Canidy's back somewhere below the waist. Clearly, not their first or even their second encounter.

Canidy was no neophyte. Donovan suspected Canidy knew the woman was married. Donovan disapproved, but understood better than most that men who were inclined to take the greatest risks the nation asked of its citizens didn't limit such risks to death and dismemberment. Donovan was, however, disappointed in Canidy's lack of judgment. Donovan recognized the woman as the wife of a member of the House Appropriations Committee—a preening jackass who had fought any increases in the armed services budget after Neville Chamberlain had summarily declared "peace in our time." Although the cuckold was no longer in a position to affect military appropriations, he retained several influential connections on Capitol Hill and was just the type of jackass who would seek retribution against Canidy by sticking it to the military as a whole.

Nonetheless, Donovan believed Canidy's attributes made him the optimal spy, especially because the requirements of the occupation were evolving. Donovan believed traditional spycraft was gradually becoming much more physical: intelligence plus direct action. The Brits incorporated both in its MI6 and SAS operations. Donovan was fast doing the same with OSS. And Canidy was his prototype.

Canidy noticed Donovan sitting to the right in a plush high-backed chair. Donovan saw a look on Canidy's face that ranged between embarrassment and contrition—a child disappointing a parent. Canidy immediately, albeit smoothly, disengaged from the woman and approached Donovan, stopping a few feet in front of his chair.

"Sir. I didn't see you there."

"Obviously," Donovan said. "Don't let me interrupt, son. Clearly, you have business to which you should attend."

Canidy wore a rare, flustered look. "Sir . . ."

"I'm not your priest or your father. Nor am I your immediate commanding officer, son."

Canidy became even more chagrined. He felt like an undisciplined flake standing before one of the most serious men in the country. He looked at his watch: 2:44 p.m. "Sir, I just got your message to meet here at five o'clock as soon as I got back from—"

"Son, I said no explanations, please. Take care of your business. Meet me here in . . ." Donovan glanced at his watch. "Two hours and fifteen minutes."

Canidy glanced back at the woman, who wore a look between impatience and irritation. She was a married woman with a schedule that didn't accommodate interruptions. "Sir, I'll be back in thirty seconds."

Canidy crossed the lobby and spoke to the woman briefly. She appeared alarmed and walked briskly out of the hotel. Canidy returned, swaggering once again.

Donovan asked, "Everything buttoned up?"

Canidy nodded. "Apologies, sir, but I told her you were a private detective hired by her husband and that I promised to double your fee if you agreed to tell your client that his wife was as pure as Caesar's."

Not bad, Donovan thought. He gestured to the seat next to him and signaled to the waiter by raising his glass of Macallan. The waiter approached expectantly.

Donovan looked to Canidy. "What are you drinking?"

"Thank you, but nothing for me, sir."

"Feigned abstemiousness is a wasted effort on me, Canidy." Donovan nodded to the waiter, who retreated.

"Dick, we're in a real fix," Donovan said. "I asked you here because we need to move on a critical matter immediately. No time whatsoever to waste. If you volunteer for this, you will leave immediately."

"Whatever you need, sir. You know that."

"I do. But you don't know what I need."

"Respectfully, sir, but I do. You just told me you need me immediately on a critical matter. Not to sound like a kid whose coach just told him he's the starting quarterback in the title game, but being picked for a critical job by a man awarded the MOH makes it a no-brainer. I'm in, whatever it is."

Donovan took a sip of his whisky. "We put you through some godawful training a while back, mental and physical. We've never done anything like that before. Running, push-ups, chin-ups, and sit-ups for hours. Hand-to-hand combat, incessant marksmanship drills . . ."

"Brutal, but it took. I keep it up when I can."

"Good, because you'll need all of it and more. What we're asking of you is the closest thing to a death sentence the War Department can issue. No margin for error. Even if you commit *no* errors it's still likely you won't come back. You need to understand that."

Canidy said nothing.

"We decided that because of the nature of this run, we'll only use volunteers."

"There's someone else besides me?"

"Possibly."

"How many more?"

"Only one. Logistics precludes more than two."

"You say that neither of us is coming back?" Canidy asked.

"That's not what *I'm* saying. That's what *math* says. I chose you because I think you have the best chance of beating the math and getting the results we need."

Canidy smiled sardonically. "Sir, you're not making this very appealing."

"I'm not trying to. If I'm going to ask you to do this, you need to go in with your eyes open. No illusions."

"What are you asking me to do?"

Donovan placed his glass on the table next to him and rose from his chair. "Let's go for a walk." Canidy thought to remind Donovan of the order he'd just placed with the waiter, but said nothing and followed Donovan as he proceeded out of the main entrance of the Willard, past the bell stand, and left onto Pennsylvania Avenue. Donovan said nothing until they reached the intersection of 14th Street.

"The Abwehr has ears and eyes in the damnedest places. Beria, too. We're not nearly as sophisticated as they, but we're catching up. Slowly."

Donovan paused as two men walked past. When they were outside earshot, he resumed. "Do you remember the operation for which you were trained about a year and a half ago?"

"You may recall, sir, I was never told what the operation was."

"The President initially opposed that operation because he didn't want any complications that could drag us into war. That concern is, obviously, moot now. So the operation is back on—with even greater urgency." Donovan paused again to permit a woman to pass. "Frankly, with due respect to the President, it was a mistake to cancel it. In the meantime, the conditions for its execution have become exponentially worse."

"Eight men were killed the last time the operation was attempted," Canidy observed. "How, then, sir, are two men supposed to execute under much worse conditions?"

"War is not easy. War is not fair."

Canidy simply shrugged. "What do you need me to do?"

"Extract someone trapped somewhere between the Germans and the Russians."

"*Somewhere* between the Russians and the Germans?" Canidy asked incredulously.

"Maybe even *among* them. In Poland. But where in Poland . . . we have no idea."

"Well, that certainly narrows it down." Canidy exhaled. "Do we know who we are extracting?"

"Professor Sebastian Kapsky. He had been rounded up by the Soviets shortly after they invaded and transported eastward. He was in one of the internment facilities in Katyn Forest. There had been reports he escaped and is still alive, but we haven't gotten anything definitive. We assume—hope—he made it to Poland and he's being sheltered by Polish Resistance. Sikorski's tourists are known to operate in the eastern Soviet Union. But just before Molotov-Ribbentrop fell apart, the NKVD and Gestapo held a conference in which it was decided they'd jointly eradicate all resistance fighters. That didn't change after the pact was dissolved. Now they're trying to eradicate all resistance fighters *and* each other. It's possible that Kapsky may be in the middle of it. Both the Germans and Russians are scouring the area for him.

"Now, with Operation Barbarossa, the Germans bombed the hell out of Soviet-occupied Poland, followed by an artillery barrage beyond the scope of anything seen in warfare. And *then* millions of German troops swarmed Soviet positions. The scale of the fighting is downright biblical.

"The Germans have pushed the Russians back toward their border and now control most of the area from which we last received reports—more accurately, rumors—that Kapsky was last seen. The area is still the subject of ferocious fighting between the Nazis and Soviets, though the Germans are advancing incrementally. It's an area where before Barbarossa, the *Armia Krajowa*—Home Army—was very active."

"*Was* very active? Not anymore?" Canidy asked.

"Once Barbarossa began, reliable reports have been few and far between. The *Armia* is tenacious and clever, but they are overwhelmed by the sheer firepower of the Wehrmacht. Plus, the Germans are plenty clever themselves—and vicious.

"When the Soviets controlled the area they got information from partisans by interrogating them with a gun to their heads. Literally. Make no mistake, that produced results. But the toughest partisans still held out. So the Soviets then would point their weapons at the wives, sons, daughters—even grandchildren—of the partisans. That produced even greater compliance—maybe up to ninety-five percent. Outstanding for any intelligence operation.

"The Germans were no less vicious, but they got nearly one hundred percent compliance because they were just a bit cleverer."

Canidy understood. "Not just the stick. Carrot and stick."

Donovan nodded. "When German interrogators identified a high-level member of the Resistance who possessed lots of information, they'd first try to bribe him—provide him with promises that he and his family would be unharmed. As you might expect, few patriots would betray their country for an executory deal. The interrogator would then offer things of value—currency, jewelry, paintings, or even land seized from other Poles, often Jews. Again, a few would take it, but a substantial number would not.

"The Germans then would threaten the lives of family members of resistance fighters. The Germans, you see, understood the psychology of choice of graduated alternatives. When presented with a binary choice—betrayal or death—two bad choices, a sizable number chose death. Even if it meant family also."

"But when presented with multiple choices," Canidy said, "including one that's ostensibly good—at least materially good—a certain percentage will yield."

"Unfortunately, it only takes one."

The pair stopped at F Street, waiting for vehicular traffic to pass. Both shielded their eyes against the sun reflecting off the windows of the office building across the street.

Canidy asked, "So, we think somebody gave the Nazis information as to Kapsky's whereabouts, or general whereabouts?"

"We really don't know jack," Donovan responded. "We think, we hope, Kapsky's still alive, and preferably under the protection of the *Armia*," he said as they crossed New York Avenue. "The operating assumption is that Kapsky's in an area formerly held by the Soviets exclusively and now the subject of contention between the Wehrmacht and the Red Army. It's a race and we're behind. Every hour that passes vastly increases the probability that either the Nazis or the Soviets will capture him. They've had a head start and they control the area. Hell, one of them may have captured him while we've been talking."

Donovan's response produced a look on Canidy's face between skepticism and disbelief. "Sir, hundreds of thousands have been killed in that area. Poles, Germans, Russians, Ukrainians, hell—sheep, cows, and pigs, too. Now, I'd like to think I'm as optimistic as the next guy, but it doesn't sound like an environment conducive to a mathematician's survival."

The pair crossed H Street. Donovan stopped and turned to Canidy. The bulldog face that had seen and cheated death countless times looked even more sober than usual. "Look, Dick, here's the operation in broad strokes: You go to Sweden. From there a vessel will take you and several British Commandos from Lieutenant Colonel Robert Laycock's special service brigade across the Baltic to the Elblag vicinity. The Commandos have some experience at this type of operation and the *Armia* know the territory. Your insertion point will be in the no-man's-land between the Wehrmacht and the Red Army somewhere east of Danzig, hopefully during a lull in fighting. From there you'll make your way to wherever our sources say Kapsky may be. After you find him, you extract him by going to the same extraction point and returning by boat to Sweden."

Canidy gazed at Donovan for several seconds without expression. Donovan returned the look, aware of the implausibility of the operation he'd just described. Implausibility invited, at a minimum, a skeptical eye roll, an ironic chuckle. But no one, not even the President and definitely not an irreverent Dick Canidy, dared laugh at any utterance by Wild Bill Donovan. No one recognized that better than Donovan himself. After a moment, Canidy rubbed his forehead, exhaled, and said, "Two questions, sir."

"Fire away."

"When do I leave?"

"Immediately. There's a Lodestar 18 waiting at Langley Field. Everything you need will be on board."

"Sir, when we first spoke about this more than a year ago you said there might be someone else on the operation, someone we'd both choose."

Donovan nodded curtly. "I did."

"Is that still operative?"

Donovan stopped walking and squared against Canidy, who did the same. Wild Bill's enormous right hand grasped Canidy's and pumped it once. "Fulmar's waiting for you at the plane."

CHAPTER 9

Giżycko, Poland
1429, 4 March 1942

The building was made of twelve-foot-thick concrete walls, with a flat roof consisting of six-inch steel beams, all painted black. The engineers claimed it could sustain a direct hit from a Schwerer Gustav. A typical Russian exaggeration, but not by much: it had been strafed by Jagdgeschwader 77s on multiple occasions without suffering more than a few pockmarks; it had even been struck by a fifty-kilogram iron bomb with little effect. It was likely the safest place in eastern Poland, which was not saying very much.

The interior consisted of a four-hundred-square-foot room containing a ten-foot-by-ten-foot iron table with two cushionless iron chairs on either side. Illumination was provided by a dozen painfully bright lights. The only other feature in the room was a single gunmetal-gray filing cabinet.

Major Taras Gromov, the sole occupant of the room,

sat impassively on the chair facing the entrance. The two NKVD guards who had ushered him in a short time ago remained unsettled by his appearance. Physically, he wasn't particularly remarkable. He appeared to be a fit male in his early thirties, above-average height. But he appeared . . . predatory. Both in his eyes and in his carriage. As if his only purpose in life was to locate prey and kill it, quickly, unceremoniously, without any increase in his heart rate. Then on to the next victim.

The guards' instincts were accurate. Gromov was uncommonly proficient at killing, both in war and otherwise. He killed with guns, knives, and his hands. He was a soldier and an assassin. He was relentless. And he would kill again.

And that was why he was sitting in a concrete tomb. He'd been directed by Moscow, the fourth floor of the Lubyanka itself. He'd arrived thirty minutes before the appointed time. Even a killer as formidable as Gromov didn't dare be late.

At precisely 3:00 p.m. he heard the metallic groan of the metal door opening, and a stocky guard wielding a PPSh-41 submachine gun entered tentatively, scanned the room, and withdrew. Seconds later he heard several footsteps—someone moving at a casual, indifferent pace; someone unconcerned with punctuality. Yet he was precisely on time.

Gromov rose as Aleksander Belyanov, chief of the Otdel KontrRazvedki, the dread OKRNKVD, entered and stood tall and regal for several seconds, examining Gromov as if evaluating a racehorse for a wager. Gromov stood instantly and saluted. The guard withdrew and shut the iron door.

Belyanov regarded Gromov coolly for several seconds before approaching the iron table and gesturing for Gromov to sit. Gromov nodded deferentially. No one would presume to take a seat before a man who reported only to Lavrentiy Beria took his.

Belyanov sat, leaned back, and crossed his legs—hands folded in his lap. Gromov sat inclined forward.

"Your number of kills?" Belyanov's voice was cool and indifferent.

"I have not kept a tally."

"Of course you have."

"Several," Gromov replied.

"Precision, Comrade Gromov."

"Eighty-eight."

"Dyachenko has 179. Ilyin has 212."

"They are snipers. They kill from afar."

"And you kill with your hands. So what is the difference?"

"In my case, the target can fight back."

"Maybe you are just not as smart as Dyachenko and Ilyin. Maybe your brain is not as big."

"Maybe, Comrade Belyanov, their balls aren't as big."

Belyanov's face remained expressionless. "The kills were all during war?"

"Mostly."

"Any children?"

"No."

"Women?"

"Not yet."

Belyanov examined Gromov. The killer was surprisingly urbane. Yet the file in the Lubyanka said he had no formal education. Before the war he'd been a railyard worker, a common laborer from Novosibirsk Oblast, albeit with uncommon physical strength and endurance. His commander during the Ukrainian famine reported that Gromov had killed two kulaks with no more than a single blow to the head of each.

"What is your opinion of the war, Gromov?"

Belyanov saw a familiar flicker of suspicion in Gromov's eyes. Like everyone in the Soviet Union who valued his life, he gave the proper response. "We will defend the Motherland with our dying honor and prevail against the Nazi regime."

Belyanov waved his hand dismissively. "Speak plainly, Gromov. This is not a loyalty test and you will not end up in a camp or in the bowels of the Lubyanka."

Gromov looked skeptically at Belyanov for a second or two, but no more. "We will defeat the Nazis because no army can overcome our natural defenses: land and cold. But it will not end there. At some point soon we will have to confront our ultimate enemy—the Americans."

Belyanov didn't try to disguise his surprise. The brute Gromov was more perceptive than ninety percent of the general staff. No wonder his reputation had reached Cathedral Square.

"Explain, Gromov."

Another look of caution flashed across Gromov's face, but he replied without reservation. "Germany is our present enemy because of Hitler's treachery. They have the most powerful fighting force in history. But history proves no fighting force can vanquish the Motherland. America, however . . ."

". . . is our ally," Belyanov interjected.

". . . is our long-term enemy. Our natural enemy. They're capitalists and exploiters of the proletariat, oppressors of the people. Inevitably, we will be at war with them. And that war will be cataclysmic."

Belyanov stared for several seconds as if Gromov was Rasputin reincarnated. This was no ordinary killer. He was calculating; more than that, he seemed uncommonly knowledgeable.

"That is an interesting observation, Gromov. I believe, therefore, the task I am about to describe will make perfect sense to you. It involves a mathematician . . ."

Gromov scowled. "Killing a mathematician will not be particularly difficult. Literally any soldier could—"

"You're not to kill him, Gromov, although it is likely you will need to kill several people along the way. Our last report is that the mathematician is in an area straddling our front line and that of the Wehrmacht. Our information is very good."

"Where does it come from?"

"Multiple sources."

"Specifically . . . ?"

Belyanov scowled. "Be careful, Gromov. Do not test me. Be assured that the sources are real and that some are in places that would astonish you. Indeed, they would astonish both our allies as well as our adversaries."

Gromov responded respectfully, but wasn't cowed. "The probability of apprehending this mathematician is dependent on the speed and accuracy of these sources."

"That is not your concern, Gromov. Your task is to first find the mathematician, secure him, and bring him to Moscow."

"He must be an uncommonly important mathematician."

Belyanov said, "Important enough that if we fail to find him, we may not just lose the war, we will lose the future. It is imperative we find him."

Gromov sat silently for a few moments. "I can do that."

Belyanov leaned forward. "Do that, Gromov, and the Order of Lenin is yours."

CHAPTER 10

The Polish partisan was a small, wiry man with intelligent gray eyes. Maurer would translate that intelligence into deceitfulness.

The partisan wore a ragged cloth coat and baggy pants that smelled of manure. The panzer group had captured him after surrounding his band of nine or ten *Armia*—a number uncertain because a few of them had managed to escape into the thick underbrush on the opposite bank of the shallow Nogat River. Despite being cornered by several panzers and a dozen soldiers on foot, the wily partisan had tried to conceal himself in the marsh into which the runoff from a nearby farm drained—a runoff composed in large part of cow dung.

The partisan sat on a rickety wooden chair on the other side of a small table within the small farmhouse where he'd been captured. He provided no resistance to the German troops, dropping his rifle and raising his arms immediately upon being told he had no means of escape and he'd be ripped to shreds by panzer machine-gun fire if he attempted to flee across the river.

Two German soldiers had escorted the partisan to the farmhouse at Maurer's direction several hours earlier. The man had been denied food and drink and use of the outhouse toilet. He sat nervously at the kitchen table waiting, likely for something bad. He wasn't a pessimist by nature. Experience had made him so. Everything seemed to go wrong for him in the war. First, the Germans had destroyed his village, then they'd slaughtered most of his family, and the previous evening they'd killed every member of his unit save for the two who had escaped into the river and—he assessed—had made it to the opposite bank to blend into the thick forest cover.

He expected to die, but hoped he wouldn't. The two soldiers flanking him betrayed nothing. No hint of what was to come, no clue as to his fate. Strangely, they, too, seemed anxious, apprehensive, as if whomever they were waiting for was as likely to kill them as the partisan. Their anxiousness frightened him.

The partisan glanced furtively about the room, hoping the guards didn't notice. He looked for items that could be used as a weapon and any means by which he could escape. It was largely an exercise to occupy his mind, to distract his imagination from whatever was to come. He saw nothing that might be employed as a weapon, and he was certain any escape attempt would be futile.

There came a barely audible footfall from the front

porch, followed by the creak of the battered wooden front door. Then clearly audible footfalls and an intake of breath from the guards as they straightened to attention. Seconds later, the partisan saw a man nearly twice his size appear in the doorframe of the entrance to the room. He was a full head taller than the two guards, with boulder-like shoulders tapering to a small waist. His hair appeared white, but not from age. He appeared no older than his late twenties, perhaps thirty. But his arctic blue eyes projected the cynicism of someone much older. They were skeptical eyes, exceptionally intelligent. Eyes that couldn't be fooled.

SS Obersturmführer Konrad Maurer pulled a small wooden chair from the corner of the room and placed it a few feet from the partisan. It appeared it might not bear the giant's weight, but he descended into it without concern—as if he expected the chair wouldn't dare fail—and leaned forward until his face was no more than a foot from the partisan's.

The partisan withdrew his head sharply, an involuntary reaction. He looked askance, not wanting to provoke the giant with what might be perceived as an insolent look.

Maurer stared calmly at the partisan for several moments, saying nothing. Then, still staring, he softly said to the guards, "Get him."

The guard to the partisan's right immediately left the room and walked out the front door and disappeared. Barely twenty seconds later he reappeared holding a frightened man by the arm. He was Janusz, the partisan's only brother, who he'd assumed had escaped into the woods across the river. He was only a year older than the partisan, but appeared haggard and emaciated from the months of battling the Wehrmacht under unforgiving conditions. The guard pushed Janusz to within two meters of Maurer, who, without uttering a word, casually withdrew his Walther and fired three rounds into Janusz's left temple, causing him to pitch and collapse onto the floor.

The partisan's chest heaved in terror and he soiled himself. Maurer calmly slid his chair back several inches and resumed staring at the Pole. For nearly a half minute the only sounds in the room were the partisan's rapid breathing accompanied by a reedy wailing sound.

Maurer watched dispassionately, then turned to the guard, nodded, and the guard disappeared through the door once again. Maurer continued staring at the Pole, whose hands were shaking violently. Moments later the guard returned with a terrified young man in his late teens. He was tall, handsome, and robust, with more than a slight resemblance to the partisan.

Upon seeing the young man, the partisan's intake of breath was so sharp and abrupt that he began choking for several seconds. Maurer waited patiently as the Pole labored to catch his breath. His eyes wide with terror, he struggled to speak, but the only sounds he produced were a strangled wail.

Maurer leaned forward slightly. "What did you say?"

The partisan's chest continued to heave rapidly as he struggled to make intelligible sounds. Blood that had sprayed on his face from his brother's gunshot wounds formed bubbles around his mouth as he exhaled. "Please . . ." Terror rendered the word nearly unintelligible.

Maurer nodded. "You are eager to tell me everything I need to know. Yes?"

The partisan nodded frantically.

"You will do so truthfully and withhold nothing?"

Again the partisan nodded, so vigorously that his skull appeared as if it might become detached from his neck. "What do you want to know? If I have information, it is yours. Please. What do you want to know? Tell me."

"Very simple. I am looking for a man."

"Who?"

"His name is Sebastian Kapsky."

The partisan appeared confused. His eyes darted about the room as his mind desperately tried to recall anyone by that name.

"I do not know the name. I do not know anyone with this name."

"I am certain that you do," Maurer said evenly. "I am certain that he is under the protection of the *Armia*."

"I do not know the name. Please. I am being truthful. Who is he? Where is he from?"

"Think harder."

"I am telling you, I do not know anyone with that name. Who is he? Where is he supposed to be?"

"Think *much* harder."

Tears welled in the partisan's eyes, which grew wider

when Maurer began to raise the Walther resting on his right thigh.

"I do not know the name. I do not know anyone by that name. You cannot punish me—punish my family—because I do not know someone."

"In fact, I can and will." Maurer shifted slightly in the direction of the young man. "Strong and fit," Maurer said and nodded. "He looks able to kill many Germans in the coming months. Who knows? Perhaps he will kill me or someone close to me."

"Where was this Kapsky last? What did he do?"

Maurer turned back to the partisan. "You see, that is the problem. Despite our prodigious intelligence apparatus, I confess I have no idea where he may be, other than somewhere between Katyn and Danzig. Many of your countrymen have died because they refused to give us a location." Maurer cocked his head slightly to his left. "Perhaps they did not know where he was. Like you."

"I tell you I do not know. Though I do not want to betray anyone, I would tell you his location to spare a life, especially that of a friend or family member." The partisan's voice cracked. "Tell me, what can I do to help you?"

Maurer shook his head in resignation. "Apparently nothing."

"Wait," the man pleaded. "Wait. Tell me something about this Kapsky. What does he look like? What did he do?"

Maurer shook his head again. "I've never seen the man. I do not have a photograph or sketch. I am told only that he is tall and lean, with black hair and green eyes. For what it is worth, the eyes are said to somehow make him appear exceptionally intelligent."

The partisan waited for Maurer to continue, but he did not. The description didn't register with the partisan, making him even more nervous. He feared if he provided nothing of value the young man would be shot. He temporized. "What did he do?"

"To my knowledge, he has not done anything yet. The concern is what he may do sometime in the future."

A genuine look of puzzlement covered the partisan's face. Maurer noticed.

"I am told he is, in fact, very bright. Accordingly, his eyes are not lying. He has the ability, apparently, to cause great harm with his intelligence."

Maurer noticed the partisan's eyes dart about as if trying to retrieve something from the recesses of his brain. He was connecting pieces of information, drawing inferences. He looked up at Maurer.

"He is very smart? Such as an academic? A professor?"

"That is correct."

The partisan's eyes grew wide and bright. Maurer saw a flicker of recognition and then excitement. "I know such a man," the partisan said rapidly. "Rather, I do not *know* him, but I know *of* him. He was a professor before the war—maybe even since it has begun." The partisan nodded as if affirming to himself the accuracy of his recollection. "Yes, he was an academic at the University of Lviv. A mathematician, I think . . ."

Maurer watched as the partisan dredged every piece of

information he could recall about the mathematician from the depths of his brain. He held nothing back. The information was his son's—and his—salvation. The more he could provide, the greater his interrogator's appreciation. "He is tall and lanky. He came to the *Armia* in 1940 or 1941, late spring, I believe. A child brought him. It was said he came from Katyn. No one believed him. Rather, I did not believe him. *No one* came from Katyn. Katyn is a furnace. Katyn is a pit.

"I believe I even saw this person myself south of Pinsk." He paused again to refresh his memory. "Yes, I *did* see him. I remember now. He said he had been hiding, he needed to go to Danzig. Commander Matuszek gave orders to assist. Matuszek clearly thought the man was important. We could not readily spare men to escort someone to Danzig unless that person was very important."

A flicker of relief played on the partisan's face. He was providing value. *He* was valuable. By extension, his *loved ones* were valuable. He scoured his memory for anything he could provide regarding the professor.

Maurer nodded. "Go on. What else?"

"Several men volunteered to escort the man as far as Bydgoszcz, along the Vistula," the partisan continued. "We could not spare men to escort him all the way to Danzig. That was a journey of some distance. There and back would take too long. But, as I recall, four of our men were to accompany the mathematician about sixty kilometers southeast of Bydgoszcz. There, he would be handed off to others that would take him to Danzig."

"Very good. Helpful." Maurer nodded. "If you know, how long ago did this happen?"

"It was several days ago."

"Do you know whether they have reached Bydgoszcz yet?"

"I have not been told. Bydgoszcz is approximately one hundred fifty kilometers north of where *Armia* first encountered this professor. Wehrmacht controls much of the area. Patrols are everywhere. Travel is difficult. If they have not been killed or captured, they may reach Toruń in a few days. They are probably near Włocławek now. Maybe a kilometer or two north of there."

"To be clear, how many escorts?"

"I understand that there are three. Maybe no more than two." The partisan took a deep breath. "Is that helpful?"

Maurer nodded. "Very much so. I am grateful beyond measure." He leaned forward slightly and patted the partisan's knee. "Thank you."

The partisan exhaled.

Maurer rose from his chair. He shot the partisan twice in the head and the young man once in the chest.

CHAPTER 11

The flight was long, loud, and bumpy. Within two hours of takeoff both Major Richard Canidy and Lieutenant Eric Fulmar were beginning to get hoarse over the noise of the engines.

Lean, energetic, and exuding boundless confidence, First Lieutenant Eric Fulmar, Army Infantry, spoke German fluently and five other languages at least passably. As far as Canidy was concerned, there was no one better with whom to infiltrate German-held territory. With his blond hair and blue eyes he *looked* quintessentially German; not difficult, given that his father was, in fact, German.

When not ribbing each other, both Canidy and Fulmar wore skeptical expressions, not uncommon for men in their position. It was the ribbing common among siblings, although they weren't biologically related. Indeed, Fulmar, with his Germanic blond hair and blue eyes, was an Aryan contrast to Canidy—they'd known each other ever since Fulmar's mother had sent him to St. Paul's School in Cedar Rapids, Iowa, over which a Reverend George Crater Canidy, Ph.D., D.D., presided. Fulmar's father was a German citizen and his mother an American actress. When his father returned to Germany, his mother sent him to St. Paul's, where he and Canidy engaged in all manner of youthful escapades. Those escapades formed the foundation of both friendship and the daredevil temperaments that Donovan prized in his operatives.

It was a full three hours into the flight before either of them spoke of the mission. Fulmar spoke first.

"Who the hell did we piss off to draw this assignment?"

"You're looking at this the wrong way," Canidy said. "We're the best and the brightest, the United States military's prime weapons. No one else has a rat's chance of pulling this off. You should be flattered."

"Well, I suppose that's one way of looking at it," Fulmar conceded. "A slightly more realistic way of looking at it is that we're the most expendable specimens in the U.S. military. And probably the dumbest, too." He took a sip of water from a canteen to lubricate his throat before continuing. "You know me, Dick. I generally look at the bright side. I'm an optimist about most things. But no matter how many times I turn this around, I come to the conclusion that this is a major train wreck. Someone must really have it in for us, because we're cooked, my friend. We're not coming back."

Canidy shrugged. "I'm not so sure."

"Not so sure? Were you paying the slightest bit of attention when Donovan gave you the particulars? Or did your ego get in the way? Wild Bill comes to you with all those medals flapping on his chest and tells you he has an operation that only you and the idiot Fulmar can execute. And with your trademark humility, you say, 'You're right, sir, only Fulmar and I can vanquish the Hun and save the damsel in distress. Where do I sign?'"

"It's not a damsel."

"And how is that relevant? Just so I'm clear, did he explain to you exactly *where* we're going?"

"He did."

"He told you about the Germans and the Russians and how we'll be right in the middle, looking for one man among hundreds of thousands of men trying to tear each other to pieces?"

"He did."

"And he told you that the highly specialized troops who he'd sent in before haven't been seen or heard from since?"

"He did."

"Yet you saluted and said, 'I can't wait to die, sir.'"

"I did. And you did, too."

"Hell, *someone* needs to make sure you don't lose this war for us."

"You came because of the layover in Sweden. You thought you might get a chance to bag a Teutonic goddess."

"Nordic."

"There's a difference?"

Fulmar smiled.

The plane began pitching violently for thirty seconds that seemed like thirty minutes as it approached the Scandinavian landmass. Fulmar waited until the noise of the turbulence subsided before speaking again.

"What do you know about our escorts?"

"Not much," Canidy said. "They're Swedish, or something, and have been helping the Brits infiltrate into Poland and Germany. We'll be accompanied by some of those Brits, who will help us get into Poland. That's the easy part. Once in Poland we'll be in the maw of the Wehrmacht, as well as the Red Army, and on our own."

"Right in the middle of the heaviest expenditure of firepower in human history," Fulmar noted. "Should be quite a show. If we live to see even five seconds of it."

Canidy smiled sardonically and nodded. "I confess I'm a little nervous about this. But you're right. When Donovan asks, what the *hell* are you supposed to say? The man has been in situations like the one we're about to go into and came out of them with a rack of hardware. Not just *any* medals. Hell, even if you didn't know about the medals, that face is a face you don't say no to. You feel like a coward for hesitating even a second before responding in the affirmative."

"I was awed that he even thought about someone like me." Fulmar chuckled. "But you know what really went through my mind? Sure, his medals and all. But what kept going through my head was this picture of him sitting in some damn room in the White House drinking brandy with the President, tobacco smoke swirling around his head, saying, 'You know, that Fulmar's a pussy. He rejected the mission.' The President of the United States is told by the toughest SOB in North America that I'm a pussy."

"Well, you are."

"And I had this thought that somehow that description would make it into the history books because there would be a stenographer there taking down everything they were saying because, well, it's the *White House* . . . it's history. And then that transcript would leak to the press and the headlines would say 'Donovan Declares Fulmar a Pussy.'"

Canidy looked askance at Fulmar. "Right. That's *exactly* what would have happened. So much for your Teutonic rationalism."

"*And* that I'm half Kraut. Shouldn't have been trusted in the first place."

Canidy and Fulmar felt the aircraft begin its descent. Reality intruded. The operation would begin shortly.

Fulmar said, "They're going in steep. Maybe Luftwaffe in the area."

The craft broke the cloud deck and Canidy and Fulmar could see the coastline of Sweden as they crossed the North Sea.

"Not maybe. Definitely. We're coming in over the southern tier of Norway, just northwest of Denmark. We're lucky that most of the Luftwaffe is occupied with bombing the hell out of Mr. Churchill six hundred miles southwest of here. We're supposed to be landing at a club airfield east of Visby on Gotland Island. Probably no more than an old cow pasture. So it'll be a little bumpy."

The aircraft banked to the south. Farmland appeared below—a few random edifices dotted the landscape. Not a landing strip in sight.

"This should be fun," Canidy said. "Hold on."

The aircraft descended abruptly, touching down on what appeared to Canidy to be nothing more than a strip of grass without any markings whatsoever. Nonetheless, it was surprisingly smooth.

The plane taxied to a stop a half kilometer from touchdown. Canidy and Fulmar saw three vehicles speeding toward them across the pasture. The pair deplaned, the door closing behind them just as the vehicles came to a halt thirty meters away. Canidy waved to the cockpit and the plane resumed taxiing.

The three vehicles stopped a few feet from the two Americans. A large man sporting a beret and a bushy handlebar mustache emerged from the lead vehicle and strode toward the pair with his hand extended.

"Sergeant Conor McDermott," he said with a Highland brogue as he pumped Canidy's hand, then Fulmar's. "We best get going into the vehicles and out of the open. Damn Gerry planes appear at the damnedest times."

Canidy and Fulmar climbed into the back of the lead vehicle, McDermott seated in the front passenger seat next to a freckled redheaded driver whose face resembled that of a greyhound. McDermott gestured toward the greyhound. "This is Corporal Colin Spivey. We and the lads in the trail cars, Corporal Mark Trent and Corporal

Alain Colby, are your escorts to northern Poland—well, some say Prussia. Have you been briefed on the itinerary?"

"The basic outlines," Canidy replied. "I'm Canidy and this is Eric Fulmar."

"Where is the remainder of your gear?" McDermott said.

"What are you talking about?" Canidy asked.

"Your gear. Those devices the famous Research and Development branch of your OSS keeps cooking up—silent pistols, K&L pills—all manner of gadgets that Mr. Donovan has your laboratory people create."

"I suppose he thinks this assignment is different than the others. No occasion for gadgets. We do, however, have our most valuable weapons—the most effective devices in the OSS lab."

"And what would those be, or can't you say?"

"Cigarettes, my friend. Wild Bill says they're the most important item OSS operatives can carry. Universal currency. And of the highest denomination."

McDermott again shook Canidy's hand and then Fulmar's. "We'll take these vehicles until we get within a kilometer or so of the Baltic coastline. The terrain becomes a little rough in vehicles like this, so we'll go by foot until we reach the shore. A boat is tied off at a small dock there. Our skipper—quite experienced at these matters—will take us across the Strait to northern Poland."

"That's consistent with our brief," Canidy said and nodded.

"Unlikely that we'll encounter any Gerries between here and the Polish coast, but those bastards don't exactly announce their intentions, so keep your eyes open. They're downright hateful bastards, but very clever."

"How many times have you done this?" Fulmar asked.

McDermott grinned. "A little nervous, are we? No worries, mate. So are we, despite the fact that we've made this trip about a half-dozen times. It helps to be nervous. Keeps you alert and alive. Never *ever* let your guard down or underestimate the Germans. They don't miss anything, believe me. One small error in judgment—only one—and you're dead."

Canidy said, "We were told you'd be providing our supplies."

"Quite right." McDermott nodded. "Weapons and such are on the boat. The quartermaster acquired them from your people in London. I must say I was a bit surprised at your choices."

"I don't understand," Canidy said. "M1911 is a good weapon, by my lights, the best of its kind. Why would you be surprised?"

"I don't fault the quality of your choice, old man. Splendid weapon. Just the model. I would think that for an operation in enemy-held territory, you might want to 'blend in,' as it were. Use German weapons—perhaps a Luger or Walther."

"If it gets to the point where we're close enough to the Germans that they notice the make of our weapons, we're dead anyway. I don't speak German, and"—Canidy jabbed his thumb toward Fulmar—"I doubt even his German would fool them for long."

They drove in silence on dirt and gravel roads for half

an hour. Canidy could smell the salt water in the air twenty minutes before they reached the ocean. McDermott raised his voice over the din of the vehicles.

"The owner of the vessel has conveyed us across the Baltic several times, sometimes from Gotland, other occasions from the mainland. Knows the best routes to avoid the Germans and will be our guide for the first ten kilometers or so after we make landfall."

Canidy raised his head abruptly. "Whoa. Hold it right there. That wasn't part of the brief. I don't like last-minute changes and I don't want some sailor guiding me on land. That was supposed to be your job. Besides, I don't want anyone who can't consistently hit a target from at least thirty yards anywhere near us."

"Sorry, mate," McDermott said with a tone of finality. "The captain calls the shots. If you want to go to Poland, you've got to obey the captain. End of discussion."

"Great," Canidy said. "We're not even in the water and already this is turning into a cock-up."

"Look, mate," McDermott responded in a sympathetic tone, "I had the same reaction the first time the captain conveyed us across the Strait. But no one is better at navigating the Strait, avoiding the Germans, or, for that matter, killing the Gerries. Bloody deadeye. Never seen a better shot."

They rode in silence for several minutes before cresting a hill, the Baltic appearing before them no more than a kilometer away. The caravan maneuvered another three-quarters of a kilometer around a series of large boulders toward a cove hidden within a thick grove of silver birches. A thirty-foot vessel was moored next to a pinewood dock where a tall figure stood, fists on hips, scanning the sea. The captain wore a battered cap, baggy gray trousers, and a yellow slicker.

McDermott looked at his watch. "Damn, twenty minutes late. The captain is notoriously punctual. Insanely so. We're going to catch hell."

They walked the remaining quarter kilometer, came to a halt adjacent to the dock, and the occupants gathered their gear and proceeded toward the vessel, McDermott and Canidy in the lead.

"Apologies, Captain," McDermott called out over the sound of the waves lapping against the dock. "The plane was a few minutes late."

The tall figure turned and stood imperiously, fists still on hips. As Canidy drew near, he was struck by the mesmerizing quality of the piercing pale blue eyes staring at him from beneath the cap's visor. They conveyed an almost regal aloofness. He thrust his hand toward the captain, more a peace offering than a salutation.

The captain grasped Canidy's hand and respectfully removed the cap, releasing an avalanche of blond hair that fell in cascades to the small of her back.

"Kristin Thorisdottir."

Both Canidy and Fulmar came to a complete halt—their British escorts looked on, grinning broadly at their comrades, gauging whether they were more stunned by the fact that the captain was female or that her looks were otherworldly. Each had had similar experiences upon first meeting their skipper.

Canidy's brain, although not unacquainted with such female beauty, took several seconds to absorb the vision. Captain Thorisdottir was at least his height. Although the contours of her figure were hidden under the baggy pants and slicker, it was obvious she was slender and fit. Canidy concluded she had the longest hair, longest neck, and longest legs he'd ever seen on a woman.

Realizing he hadn't responded, Canidy said, "Major Dick Canidy, U.S. Army Air Force." Canidy turned vacantly to his right to introduce Fulmar, who had appeared on Canidy's left and introduced himself instead.

"Lieutenant Eric Fulmar. Sergeant McDermott informed us that you'd be taking us across the sea to Poland and then escorting us into the interior. Thank you." Fulmar winced at his imitation of a lovestruck thirteen-year-old boy.

Thorisdottir turned to the sea and pointed southwest. "Admiral Donitz's wolfpack has been sinking many Liberty ships. There have been reports of U-boat patrols there. Approximately thirty kilometers offshore. Primarily in the afternoon and evening."

"Is that unusual?" Fulmar asked.

"Reports, no. Fishermen report mermaids also." Thorisdottir squinted at the sea. "*Reports* are as plentiful as mosquitoes. U-boats are more like mermaids. I'm skeptical, but of course we must be vigilant."

"I understand. But if there are, indeed, mermaids, how do you evade them?"

"Pray." Thorisdottir waved them toward her boat. "It is best to depart sooner rather than later. Please board now."

As they boarded with their weapons and gear, Thorisdottir walked along the pier conducting one last inspection. Fulmar turned to McDermott. "Now I know why you Brits invaded Iceland. It had nothing to do with sealanes and shipping. I'm impressed at your initiative and strategic vision."

"Thanks, mate. But strategic vision won't count for much if one of those German mermaids happens along."

Thorisdottir was the last to board, casting off the line and settling into the cabin. The motor rumbled to life and they pushed from the dock.

Canidy and the Brits sat aft while Fulmar sat on a bench next to the captain. "How long will it take to reach the Polish coast?"

"If the weather cooperates, approximately five hours. Provided, of course, we encounter no hostile vessels requiring evasive maneuvers."

"How many times have you made this trip?"

"At least once a week over the last year and a half," Thorisdottir replied, her gaze fixed on the horizon.

"*Why* do you make the trip?"

"I have my reasons, Lieutenant Fulmar."

There was a brief silence. Thorisdottir asked, "Why are *you* making the trip? This is not an ordinary exercise, especially for an American."

"All I can say is that I was asked to make the trip and I agreed," Fulmar responded.

"You had options?"

Fulmar chuckled. "I'm not sure that under the circumstances I truly had options. But I suppose, theoretically, I could have chosen not to do this."

Thorisdottir considered Fulmar's reply for several moments. "Your superiors chose you because you possess certain unique skills or you are particularly talented and trustworthy, or, perhaps, both."

Fulmar didn't respond. He could think of no good reason to disabuse her of the notion he was an exceptional individual.

The wind picked up, as did the waves, although both remained relatively modest. Fulmar scanned the cabin. It was unremarkable save for the absence of any charts or maps. "Do you usually take the same route?" he asked.

"The route depends on the circumstances, Lieutenant Fulmar."

"I ask because I don't see any navigational guides."

"They're not much use to me, Lieutenant Fulmar." Thorisdottir shrugged. "My father taught me to sail. He fished the North Atlantic, the Norwegian Sea, and the Greenland Sea for nearly thirty years. You're not a true seaman until you master waters such as those. He had little use for charts. He said one must sail by instinct."

Fulmar considered that for a moment. "No disrespect, but that seems a little imprecise for this operation. Especially when we're near shore. If we're sailing by instinct, how do we know there won't be German troops where we make landfall?"

Thorisdottir smiled. The effect was electric. "I have several locations for docking that have proven relatively secure. There are no guarantees, of course. But for this occasion, the best option is a narrow channel east of the Gulf of Danzig. It was a canal that once connected to the Vistula before being abandoned half a century ago. No one goes there now. It is overgrown and infested with flies and mosquitoes. There is still a small dock around a bend approximately four hundred meters inside the mouth. It's a bit tricky sometimes, but it's a good place for our purposes."

Fulmar nodded. "And from there?"

"I will guide you to a small place a few kilometers from there. Southeast. It is near the place the man you are seeking was last reported to be. Rumors, actually."

"Why you?" Fulmar asked. "McDermott has done this before. Why not leave it to him?"

Thorisdottir nodded. "Perhaps, but the problem is that the geography changes constantly. By that I mean who controls the area, Wehrmacht or *Armia*, the number of troops, so on and so forth.

"I make the trip regularly. Sergeant McDermott and his men last made the trip over a month ago. I do not have to tell you that may as well be millennia when it comes to troop deployment. A satisfactory infiltration point a week ago may now be overrun with German infantry."

"Still, why accompany us into the interior? Once you've safely gotten us into the country, we can take it from there."

Thorisdottir remained silent for several seconds. Then, "I have my reasons, Lieutenant."

They sailed in silence for a few minutes, then Canidy called out, "Lieutenant Fulmar, would you join us aft?"

Fulmar nodded to Thorisdottir and proceeded to the rear, taking a seat between McDermott and Canidy.

"You look to be making a fair amount of progress up there with our Viking princess," Canidy observed. "I should note, however, that I haven't yet thrown my hat in the ring, at which point you don't have a prayer."

"Go ahead, Dick." Fulmar grinned. "Give it your best shot. She's not easily impressed, as opposed to your usual collection of desperate housewives and widows."

"It's not a fair competition. Look at you and look at me. No comparison. Ask McDermott."

McDermott laughed, waving his hands. "Leave me out of it, lads. If you want my opinion, neither of you have a chance in hell. If you don't want to be shot down, leave the woman alone and just focus on the operation."

"You're saying *I* don't have a chance?" Canidy scoffed. "Look at Fulmar. Now look at me. It's no contest."

McDermott nodded with mock earnestness. "Fine specimens indeed. The both of you. Handsome as fairy-tale princes."

Canidy shook his head. "I'm not sure that description applies to Fulmar."

"It doesn't really matter, my friend. She doesn't care."

"What are you talking about?" Fulmar asked.

"She doesn't really care what you look like, lads."

Canidy and Fulmar appeared puzzled. "What the hell are you talking about?" Canidy asked.

"She only cares about the operation," McDermott said. "She's obsessed with defeating the Nazis. Wouldn't be surprised if she swore an oath of celibacy until they're beaten. Most important, she's a damn fine sailor. This is our fifth trip with her, Canidy. I wouldn't put my men in jeopardy if I had the slightest doubt about her."

As if for emphasis, McDermott rubbed his bushy mustache. "And let me tell you, she's pretty nifty with a carbine, too. I saw her plug an Oberstleutnant straight in the center of his chest at forty meters."

"We all get lucky," Canidy said.

McDermott raised an eyebrow. "Every soldier I've served with would rather have someone beside him who can't shoot very well but is lucky as opposed to someone who can shoot the eye of a hawk but has bad luck."

"Speaking of lucky"—Canidy waved his hand at Fulmar—"that would be this guy. Not only does he know how beautiful she is, she doesn't care how ugly *he* is. He wouldn't stand a chance otherwise."

The men were startled by a loud voice from the bow. "Gentlemen," Thorisdottir shouted over her shoulder. "In fairness, you should know that God often blesses those who have bad eyesight with the gift of exceptional hearing." She paused so they'd be appropriately mortified. "You should also know that we're only a short distance from waters that contain the occasional German vessel. I suggest you cover yourself with the canvas in the rear of the boat until further notice."

CHAPTER 12

The chilled night air seared Jan Kalinowski's lungs as he ran as hard as he could through the forest. His legs faltered every few steps as he drew closer to his limits of endurance.

Tymon was already dead. Or at the very least, severely incapacitated. He hadn't been able to keep up and had been overtaken before they'd reached the stream over half a kilometer back. Kalinowski hadn't seen Tymon go down. He hadn't dared lose a step by glancing back. But he'd heard it: the sound of an impact on flesh, then a piercing shriek.

Kalinowski tried to listen for pursuing footsteps, but the sound of his own on the twigs and pine needles of the forest floor prevented distinguishing quarry from predator. So he kept running, hoping to put distance between himself and his pursuer.

He struggled up a small ridge, slipping and stumbling

as he ascended. Just as he reached the crest, a half-moon emerged briefly from behind a cloud, revealing a dense tree line approximately three hundred meters down the opposite slope. If he could reach the tree line before being overtaken, he'd have a chance. He could see another bank of clouds moving swiftly toward the moon, and he'd soon be enveloped in the safety of near complete darkness.

Just two hundred meters.

He scrambled down the sheer slope toward the tree line. He lost control of his acceleration down the hill and fell—tumbling and rolling—but regained his footing, barely losing a step.

As he continued to sprint as fast as he could, he now heard sounds behind him. Footfalls. Panting. The sound of the Russian. *Gaining* on him.

When he approached to within one hundred meters of the tree line, the sounds behind him seemed to drift to his right—still to his rear but veering away at a slant. The moonlight continued to illuminate the landscape, but the clouds were approaching and would provide cover within seconds. When he was within fifty meters of the forest the sounds of pursuit faded to silence, but Kalinowski continued to run toward the trees as fast as he could. The moonlight faded almost simultaneously with his entry into the woods, causing him to slow his pace slightly in order to gain his bearings in the gloom.

His breathing was shallow and ragged, mixing once again with the sound of twigs and pine needles snapping underfoot.

Moments later Jan Kalinowski came to an abrupt stop. A few meters in front of him was his pursuer. He'd passed Kalinowski on his right flank and, improbably, had circled in front of him.

Kalinowski fixed on him with an expression of disbelief. He estimated that the pursuer was approximately five eleven, maybe 170 pounds. Not a particularly imposing physical presence. But he had wolf eyes. Predatory. He wasn't even breathing very hard. And he held an NR-40 combat knife at his side, likely covered with Tymon's blood. Kalinowski held his hands chest high, palms facing his pursuer.

"Please, I don't know any more than what we told you," Kalinowski said between strangled gasps for air. "It's the truth."

"Then why did you run?" Taras Gromov asked.

"The Germans killed many of us looking for the same man. They executed several men outside Hajnówka to make us talk."

"I am not German," Gromov said.

"But you are looking for Sebastian Kapsky?"

"I am," Gromov confirmed. "I am not, however, looking to kill anyone. I require only information."

"Believe me, if I had any information about Sebastian Kapsky, I would give it to you. But I have none. That is the truth. I have no reason to lie."

"Perhaps," Gromov conceded. "Tell me, where are you from?"

Kalinowski looked perplexed. "I am a Pole."

Gromov shook his head. "What region?"

"Near Danzig, east of the Vistula."

"And you have family, yes?"

Kalinowski nodded.

"Then, clearly, you would lie to protect your family. Because you know the Germans are also searching for Kapsky. And if the Germans suspect you are withholding information, your family would be executed."

Kalinowski said nothing.

"I believe you know nothing about Kapsky." Gromov approached Kalinowski slowly. "Tell me what you *do* know."

Kalinowski's eyes darted about as he scoured his brain for anything that Gromov might deem useful. Gromov took a few steps closer, causing Kalinowski's anxiety to spike.

"The SS officer looking for Kapsky. He has been in several places looking for him. I know wherever he goes he leaves corpses. Is that of use?"

Gromov recognized that Kalinowski had no information directly pertaining to Kapsky. He was desperately trying to placate Gromov. Nonetheless, information about Germans searching for Kapsky was not without value. They had more extensive networks in western and northern Poland than the Soviets. If they were searching in a particular area, it might be because their informants had relayed Kapsky's probable whereabouts, areas in which Gromov might concentrate his own efforts.

Gromov pointed the blade at Kalinowski. "Go on."

"The name of the officer asking the questions is Maurer, Obersturmführer Maurer. Earlier this week he was in

Kazubski interrogating villagers and captured *Armia*. When he does not get satisfactory answers, he kills. I understand he has killed many."

"What questions was he asking, specifically?" Gromov asked.

"That I do not know, but he was asking for the whereabouts of Sebastian—"

"Yes. I know. Do you know where Maurer is?"

"No. But I understand that he's been moving in an easterly direction. As the Wehrmacht pushes eastward, he follows. But there are rumors that he does not confine himself to German-held territory."

"Tell me about the rumors."

"I have not heard much," Kalinowski said. "But it has been reported to Commander Matuszek that he occasionally infiltrated behind Red Army lines."

"Do you know how he does this?" Gromov asked.

"No. But he is said not to be the kind of man who simply blends in. He's said to be quite large and distinguishable."

"You are suggesting he has assistance from Soviet troops or officers?"

"I am not suggesting anything," Kalinowski said wearily. "I am simply repeating what I have heard, to tell you all that I know about Kapsky."

"And since then?" Gromov asked.

"I do not know. He was, however, traveling in a southeast direction."

Gromov closed to within two feet of the Pole, who flinched. "You have been helpful. I can use the informa-

tion you have provided," Gromov said to a relieved Kalinowski. "But I believe, however, that you would be
similarly helpful to the Germans." Gromov thrust the
NR-40 under the Pole's jaw, through his tongue, and
into the roof of his mouth.

CHAPTER 13

Baltic Sea
0545, 1 July 1943

Thorisdottir guided her boat expertly around a sandbar and into a narrow channel filled with muddy water and moss. Canidy stood slightly behind her. He could see smoke rising approximately thirty-five kilometers to the west.

"I thought we were landing near Danzig," he said to Thorisdottir.

"This is as close to Danzig as we dare go. The Nazis have been executing non-Germans there. Hundreds. Maybe thousands. German troops saturate the area within a ten-kilometer radius of the city. In fact, this may be too close. But this is the only place where we have a chance of going undetected."

"I understand you to say we are going to an area to the east of Danzig?"

"Correct," Thorisdottir acknowledged. "I know Mc-

Dermott. I don't know who you are. I am not going to tell you anything until I know I can trust you."

They traveled nearly a quarter kilometer down the channel, the banks of which were lined with thick rows of trees and shrubs, until it began to bend westward. A small wooden pier extended from the eastern bank. Thorisdottir cut off the motor and allowed the vessel to drift slowly toward the pier.

Fulmar, McDermott, and his men slung their gear over their shoulders and climbed onto the dock. Canidy watched Thorisdottir tie off the boat and sling a Gevarm 1938 over her shoulder.

"What's the weapon for?" Canidy asked.

"What do you think? I am taking you inland to the last place the person you are seeking was reported to be. Jan, an *Armia* partisan, should be there. He may have information, he may have Kapsky, but he may also be dead. And there is more than a remote possibility we'll encounter German troops on the way. The area is infested with them."

"Look," Canidy said, "you've already done more than enough. McDermott can get us there. That's why he's here. You've done everything you were asked."

"Not nearly," Thorisdottir said. "Besides, McDermott has been here four times, yes. But I've been here dozens. And more recently. The battlefield is, how you say? Fluid. It changes weekly, if not daily. It is not the same as it was last time McDermott was here."

Canidy pointed to the rifle. "All due respect, what do you plan to do with this?"

"Kill Germans if it becomes necessary," Thorisdottir said matter-of-factly. She cocked her head to the right. "I sense you are restraining yourself from laughing. An understandable reaction. But I will wager that if we encounter a German patrol, I will be much more effective than you in eliminating the threat."

Canidy replied, "The idea is to *avoid* Germans. How effective are you at that, given—"

"Given that I am a mere sailor? Again, I suspect more effective than you." Thorisdottir turned to face him directly. "How many German patrols have you evaded in the last year, Mr. Canidy?"

Canidy smiled. "Lead the way, ma'am."

Thorisdottir motioned to get everyone's attention and beckoned them toward her. The six men formed a semicircle before her.

"My understanding is that the latest information from the *Armia* is that the person you are looking for was last seen twenty kilometers southeast of Danzig. It is also my understanding that you recognize that the information may not be timely or otherwise reliable."

Canidy and McDermott nodded their concurrence.

"Before we proceed further, it is imperative that we all understand certain matters. I have been briefed by Sergeant McDermott on the essential timing and logistics of your operation, but it's important to acknowledge that the timing contained in the plans may not conform to reality. First, it is probable that this individual . . . I am sorry, what is the person's name?"

McDermott looked at Canidy, unsure whether the information should be disclosed to Thorisdottir. Canidy nodded assurance.

"Sebastian Kapsky," McDermott said.

"It is probable—very probable—that Mr. Kapsky has been killed or captured by the Germans. Second, if he is alive, it is very probable he is not remotely near the area last reported. Not only is information in this area notoriously unreliable, even reliable information remains so only briefly. Circumstances shift with a blink of an eye—and not merely from day to day, but hour to hour and minute to minute."

Thorisdottir swept her left hand in an arc. "This area is not just *occupied* by the Germans, they have taken a unique interest in it. By virtue of the large ethnic German population that inhabited this region before the war, Hitler believes this to be not merely occupied territory, but German territory and Germany itself. It is, after all, Prussia.

"I will guide you near Koszwały, which is ten kilometers south. From there, you are on your own. Although my boat is well concealed, the probability of its discovery increases with the passage of every hour, so I will take the vessel back to the sea and return in twenty-four hours after I leave you at Koszwały."

"How long will you wait for us?" Canidy asked.

"Not long."

"The plan was that the extraction vessel would not leave sooner than seventy-two hours after our initial insertion," Canidy said. "You were informed of this, right?"

"I'm afraid, Major Canidy, that such precision works only on chalkboards," Thorisdottir replied. "I will wait as long as I deem it prudent. But it is likely to be very brief—a few hours at best. That is simply acknowledging reality. So endeavor to return to the insertion point in a timely fashion."

Canidy glanced at McDermott and nodded.

Thorisdottir continued. "Please discard any German weaponry you are presently carrying. It marks you for immediate execution if you are captured." She looked disapprovingly and pointed at Sergeant McDermott. "*You* should know better."

McDermott gestured toward Canidy. "He doesn't speak German. I thought if he was carrying German armaments, he'd be presumed German."

"Anyone wearing civilian clothing bearing German arms will be presumed to have taken said arms from dead Germans. You'll be shot on sight. If you are fortunate. Besides, if the Germans don't shoot you, *Armia* snipers will unquestionably do so, then gut you and feed your intestines to swine."

Canidy nodded agreement and turned to the others. "I'm carrying only my M1911." He turned toward Thorisdottir. "Okay if I stick it into my belt and cover it with my shirt?"

"It would be much more satisfactory, Major Canidy, if you carried no firearms whatsoever."

"Not going to happen," Canidy said with a shake of his head.

"I thought not," Thorisdottir conceded.

Canidy said to the other men, "Put all weapons other than pistols back on the boat." He turned toward Thorisdottir. "Okay?"

Thorisdottir nodded. "I can conceal them if I am stopped—there is a compartment below."

Canidy examined his M1911. "Men, sidearms only. Place all other weapons back on the boat." As they complied, he turned to Thorisdottir and pointed to the Gevarm. "What about you?"

"Probabilities and captain's privilege, Major Canidy. I will be accompanying you only a short distance, in which we are unlikely to encounter Germans. But if we do, I'm going to kill them."

Canidy inspected her face and concluded that was precisely what she would do. "Let's get moving," Thorisdottir said. "If Kapsky is as important as they say, we're not going to be the only ones looking for him. And whoever else *is* looking for him probably has gotten a pretty good head start on us. We need to play catch-up and fast. Otherwise, we'll lose the war, and if by chance we were to win this war, we'll lose the future."

Thorisdottir walked wearily but briskly through the woods. Canidy, Fulmar, McDermott, and McDermott's men falling into a single line behind her.

CHAPTER 14

Donovan studied the desk in the Oval Office as he waited silently for the President to sign several documents that his aide, Harry Hopkins, handed him.

Donovan liked the desk. It was large, heavy, and practical. It lacked the pompous ornateness of the desks favored by many cabinet secretaries and bureaucrats. Much of Franklin Delano Roosevelt's New Deal agenda was signed into law on the desk. Although Donovan strenuously opposed much of the legislation, he understood that history demanded ceremonial signings, and the desk was perfectly suited for ceremony. Nonetheless, Donovan thought the *Resolute* desk was probably better suited for ceremony. It had a backstory fit for Presidential furniture. Located in the President's office on the second floor of the White House residence, it was an ornately carved gift from Britain's Queen Victoria in 1880. It had been crafted from oak taken from the HMS *Resolute*, a British research ship that had been locked in ice in the Arctic until rescued by an American whaler and returned to England. It was a symbol of the enduring bond between the two countries.

The President seemed forever to be signing something at the desk, and this occasion was no different. Donovan had grown accustomed to waiting patiently for Roosevelt to scan the documents placed before him by Hopkins or Hopkins's aide, Laurence Duggan, sign them with a flourish, and expel a stream of blue smoke from his cigarette. Donovan would know the President had signed the final document when he tapped it with his pen after signing it with the flourish—as he'd just done. He handed the stack of documents to his aide, who nodded to Donovan and left the room.

Roosevelt removed the cigarette holder from his mouth and asked, "What do we know so far, Bill?"

"Very little," Donovan replied. "The last concrete information we have is that our two men arrived in Sweden and immediately departed the airport in the company of Churchill's men. They were to travel to the southern coast of Gotland, where they were to be conveyed by boat across the Baltic to the northeast coast of Poland. If all is proceeding without any hitches, we can assume they've made landfall by now."

A blue haze surrounded the President's head. "Just so you know, I informed Marshall," he said. "He thinks the probabilities of success are near zero. And the odds of our men's survival even less."

Donovan shifted in his seat. "Mr. President . . ."

Roosevelt waved him off. "Yes, I know, Bill. You object to my telling him anything about the operation. But for God's sake, he's the U.S. Army chief of staff. I can't possibly leave him ignorant about something like this. In his position, he'd find out eventually, whether the mission was a failure or success. And then I'd have an Army chief of staff who would no longer trust a single thing I say or do. That is, if he didn't resign."

"No argument there, sir. It's simply a matter of timing, that's all."

"Don't you think I know that, Bill? How would you react if I told you about an operation only at its conclusion that it was a success or failure? An operation over which you have ostensibly command authority?" Roosevelt held up his hand to forestall Donovan's reply. "You wouldn't simply tender your resignation on parchment in a dignified, soldierly fashion. You'd storm in here, smash the coffee table, and throw the pieces through the window. And rightly so."

"*Marshall* wouldn't do that," Donovan replied.

"The effect would be the same. I'd lose the confidence of half my staff," Roosevelt said. "In fact, Bill, you and I need to consider how we tell Eisenhower, Gerow, and MacArthur."

Donovan raised his eyebrows. "Eisenhower and Gerow I understand. But why the hell MacArthur? He's on the other side of the world, for God's sake."

Roosevelt looked at his old friend with mock incredulity. "Are you suggesting I leave that immense ego in the dark? Hell, immediately upon finding out about the operation he'd declare his candidacy for President." Roosevelt pointed his cigarette holder at Donovan. "And you, you son of a bitch—you'd vote for him. You share the exact same politics."

Donovan remained taciturn save for a slight crinkling of his eyes that betrayed his amusement. "The odds of success of the operation are not good. This is the biggest test of the OSS thus far. A unique operation combining intelligence and direct action. This will be a template for Special Operations going forward. The fewer that know, the better. And not merely from the standpoint of security. Failure will have its own effect on morale," Donovan observed.

Roosevelt grunted. "Hell, Bill, morale will be the least of our concerns if we don't succeed. If Hitler or our good friend Uncle Joe wins this race—"

"Mr. President . . ." Donovan interrupted. "We'll make sure no matter what happens, neither Hitler nor Stalin gain access to that information."

Roosevelt looked askance at Donovan. "I don't like the sound of that, Bill. I understand what you're saying, but I just don't like the sound of it."

"Believe me, sir, neither do I. I'm not advocating anything other than preventing those two from acquiring strategic superiority."

Donovan noticed Roosevelt looking past him to the entrance to the Oval Office. Glancing over his left shoulder, Donovan saw Harry Hopkins standing in the doorway, pointing at his watch.

"Yes, Harry, in a moment," Roosevelt said. Hopkins

turned and left. Roosevelt looked at Donovan. "I'm scheduled to spend more of your money in ways you won't approve." He smiled. "But before I do, tell me where we are with this."

"The short answer, Mr. President, is that we don't know. And we likely won't know for several days. Any information we get before our team is extracted will come from Commander Ian Fleming, who is in sporadic communication with the British Special Operations executive.

"What we know right now, Mr. President, is this: Our two men and four Brits made contact with a boat captain who is to convey them to the Polish coast—"

Roosevelt interrupted. "A boat captain," he repeated.

"Yes, sir," Donovan replied. "A civilian boat. Anything else would have been detected and blown out of the water."

"Who is this captain? Who would volunteer for something this risky?" Roosevelt smiled. "Are we sure he's sane?"

"She, Mr. President."

"She?"

"Yes, sir. She was recommended by Ian Fleming as being highly competent and reliable. And as a woman, Fleming believes she may be given a pass if interdicted by the Germans."

"What do *we* believe?" Roosevelt asked.

"Frankly, Mr. President, we have little upon which to base a belief. We're new to this and do not have assets readily available, so we must rely on the Brit's judgment."

"Do we know anything about this person?"

"According to Fleming, she's done several runs for British secret service. All successful."

"She's British?"

"She's from Iceland, sir."

"I don't know, Bill," Roosevelt said skeptically. "Why would she have a dog in this fight?"

"Fleming vouches for her. It seems her father, also a fisherman, was killed early on by the Germans."

Roosevelt nodded. "What about her mother? Siblings?"

Donovan hesitated. "She has one sibling, sir. Our information is that her mother is still alive. She's German. More precisely, she's German on one side and Russian on the other, but born in Germany."

Roosevelt removed the cigarette holder from his mouth. "My lord, Bill, you approved this?"

"The mother left Germany shortly after the Great War. Fleming reports that she was appalled by Hitler's ascent to power. That hatred of Hitler was conveyed to the daughter even before the father was killed."

Roosevelt motioned with the cigarette holder. "Go on."

"They were scheduled to land in Poland a short time ago. They should be on their way south to make contact with *Armia* near Kapsky's last reported location. Once they make contact with Kapsky, they will return to the vessel and take him to Gotland."

"Rather straightforward."

"I wish, sir. We estimate that there are over two hundred thousand German troops in the immediate area.

And we have to presume they consider Kapsky to be as valuable as we do . . ."

"Splendid," Roosevelt said sarcastically.

". . . and Uncle Joe has large numbers of troops nearby also. The question is whether Stalin is fighting for Polish land, or fighting to get Kapsky."

Roosevelt sat silently for nearly thirty seconds. "Bill, what percentage do you place on our team's getting out alive?"

Donovan rubbed the back of his neck. "Optimistically? Twenty-five percent."

Roosevelt closed his eyes. "What about extracting Kapsky alive?"

"Half that."

CHAPTER 15

Northern Poland
1242, 1 July 1943

Canidy was impressed with the speed with which they traveled. More impressive was the fact that they'd encountered no German troops. Thorisdottir had guided them expertly through brush, across streams, and around open fields to the sparsely wooded highland area that overlooked a small village consisting of approximately twenty edifices approximately a third of a kilometer away. Two Kübelwagens were parked next to what appeared to be a mechanic's garage. No German soldiers were in sight. No villagers, either.

Thorisdottir knelt on the grass and motioned for the others to do the same. Canidy took a position next to Thorisdottir, who pointed toward the village. "The last time I made this journey this was an *Armia* waystation. Armaments are hidden in the cellars of several of the buildings. Residents provide whatever other supplies they can."

"Would Kapsky be here?"

"Clearly not at the moment. Otherwise, I'd expect some commotion with the Kübelwagens next to the garage. But it's likely the Resistance would eventually bring him here on the way to the coast. Our last information was that he wasn't far from here."

Canidy saw at least a dozen figures dressed in what appeared to be German military uniforms emerge from the garage. Each of them was carrying a firearm.

"They look serious."

A civilian emerged from the garage, followed by two more Germans holding rifles trained at his back. Canidy could hear angry shouts that sounded German. They came from a German soldier who appeared to be an officer. He was jabbing a finger into the civilian's chest as he shouted. Remarkably, the civilian appeared to shout back.

Canidy turned to Thorisdottir. "*Armia?*"

"I don't know, but he's either crazy or incredibly brave."

"Maybe both," Canidy said. "Do you think they're asking about our friend?"

"I can't distinguish the words," Thorisdottir replied. "It could be they're asking about the location of *Armia* or accusing him of harboring *Armia*. The person doing the questioning is SS."

Fulmar and McDermott crept next to Canidy. The shouting seemed to increase in volume and intensity. The civilian continued to give as good as he got.

Fulmar said, "This is not good. He's looking for our guy. Something's about to happen."

"That's not our man, not our fight," Canidy observed.

"How can you be so certain from this distance?" McDermott asked, squinting toward the scene.

"If it were our guy, they wouldn't be shouting at him. They'd treat him like precious cargo, bundle him up in one of those vehicles, and be happily off to see the Führer. Besides, from here it looks like the guy's hair is thinning. It sure doesn't look like a—what is it? 'A thick shock of black hair.'"

The shouting below only seemed to grow louder with each passing second. The Pole's gestures grew increasingly agitated as well. The officer appeared to throw up his hands in exasperation and turned to his men to issue commands. Several broke off from the rest and trotted toward the dwellings, where, moments later, they ushered the inhabitants outside.

Fulmar pointed at the scene. "What's going on here?" It was less a question than a statement of trepidation.

Roughly two dozen civilians were herded into the square, where the Pole was shouting guttural Polish phrases that were unmistakably profanity. The officer issued another command and one of the German soldiers raised his rifle and shot a male villager in the chest. Anguished screams wafted through the valley as a female member knelt next to the body, sobbing.

The officer turned sharply toward the Pole and angrily asked another question. More unmistakable profanity issued in torrents from the Pole's mouth. Again, the officer turned and shouted commands. And, again, one of his men shot another male villager in the chest.

"Jesus," McDermott whispered.

"Stay calm," Canidy said.

Before the officer turned to face the Pole again, the man leapt forward, seized the sidearm holstered at the officer's hip, and shot him twice in the back. The Pole pivoted and managed to squeeze off several more rounds, felling two Germans before being riddled with fire from the other troops. When the echoes of the gunfire subsided, they were replaced by the sobbing and wailing of the village citizens. Canidy glanced at Thorisdottir, whose gaze was riveted to the scene below, the muscles in her jaws tensing and contracting.

"What do you think that was about," Fulmar said. It was not a question.

"Yep," Canidy acknowledged. "It's pretty clear we're not the only ones looking for the good professor."

"No one can be that important," McDermott said.

Canidy noticed a wispy swirl of dust approaching the village rapidly from the south. As it drew near the square, Canidy could see that it was a German Horch 108 convertible staff car with two soldiers in the front and a single officer to the rear. As it came to a halt in the square, the soldiers in the square stood at attention and saluted. The officer stood and returned the salute before stepping from the vehicle. Even from a distance, he cut an impressive figure. He towered over the troops. His peaked visor cap added to the disparity. As the officer moved imperiously among the troops, Canidy instinctively sensed that he was searching for something of exceptional importance.

Canidy's concentration on the German officer was broken by Thorisdottir's voice. He had caught only the word "now." He turned toward her. "I'm sorry," Canidy said. "What were you saying?"

"I said the show is over. This is where I leave you. Apparently, Jan is either late or dead. Either way, he is not here. Continue proceeding south and you will encounter *Armia* near Pszczółki. McDermott should be able to take it from there."

Canidy nodded, reluctant to see her go for more reasons than one.

Thorisdottir examined her watch. "It is now 1312 hours. I will return to where we docked in twenty-four hours."

"And you won't wait long if we're late," Canidy added.

Thorisdottir nodded.

"Thank you," Canidy said. He couldn't think of anything clever to say. "Good luck."

"Luck is for gnomes and idiots," Thorisdottir said dismissively before descending the slope and vanishing into the forest.

Canidy turned to McDermott. "You're the tour guide now. Take it from here."

McDermott pointed southwest. "We'll take a wide westerly arc around the village before proceeding south again. It's mainly farmland and woods. We have fairly decent cover if we need it all the way to south of Pszczółki."

"How long do you estimate it will take before we get there?"

McDermott cocked his head to the side as he performed a mental calculation. "Ten to eleven hours, maybe less if we get going right away."

Canidy said, "Ten hours, then, because we're not going until we're fairly certain the Germans won't detect our movement. This will be tight."

Canidy watched the activity in the village. The troops had lined up the residents, including children, in a single row. The attitude of their bodies conveyed obedience and fear. The tall officer, flanked by two troops, walked down the line, stopping to question each resident. Most remained absolutely still. A few shook their heads, presumably in response to a question posed by the giant. Canidy watched the officer closely. He wasn't conducting a perfunctory interrogation. He appeared to pose multiple questions to each resident. Even the children.

Canidy understood that he was watching his rival in the hunt for Sebastian Kapsky.

CHAPTER 16

Taras Gromov peered through the 6x30 binoculars at the towering German officer as he strode down the line of civilians, questioning each. Gromov had witnessed scenes like this before. They rarely had a pleasant ending, and something about the officer suggested that the ending in this case could be horrific.

The assassin raised his binoculars to the surrounding countryside and conducted a slow sweep of the hills on the opposite side of the valley. Nothing but tall grass punctuated by an occasional tree. His sweep was interrupted by an anguished cry from the village. He returned his gaze to the square and saw one of the villagers on his knees in front of the tall officer. It was unclear whether he had been struck or was simply begging for mercy.

Less than an hour ago Gromov had received information from his contact in Pszczółki that Kapsky was in the vicinity. The contact emphasized that he couldn't vouch for the timeliness of the information, but all indications were that it was fairly recent. More important, the contact conveyed two messages from Belyanov. First, the Americans had dispatched a team to secure Kapsky. The contact didn't know how many were on the team, but NKVD concluded that by now they should have entered Poland from the north coast after crossing the Baltic from Sweden. Gromov didn't doubt the accuracy of the information, but wondered about its provenance. He knew the NKVD had placed informants within Allied governments, but this information was unusually detailed.

The second message was unequivocal. Acquire Kapsky, or, failing that, be sure that neither the Germans nor the Americans acquire Kapsky.

Gromov understood the latter message to be quite plain. Belyanov was not suggesting Gromov simply thwart the German and American efforts to acquire Kapsky. Rather, Belyanov would rather that Gromov kill Kapsky than allow him to fall into the hands of anyone else. Gromov had few illusions as to why he was chosen for this assignment. He was a proficient killer, and that is what Belyanov—and Beria—expected him to be. If, however, he could secure Kapsky and return him to the Kremlin—so much the better. But doing so was not the imperative.

Gromov watched the German officer methodically go down the line of villagers, conducting examinations. The Russian concluded the officer was likely among those that would have to be eliminated. It was clear he was exacting and would leave no stone unturned in his efforts to secure Kapsky.

Gromov studied his appearance as well as his movements and methods. Had Gromov raised his binoculars across the valley and slightly to the north he would have seen Canidy, directed by McDermott, lead his team in a wide westerly arc around the village, on their way south.

CHAPTER 17

Northern Poland
1545, 1 July 1943

They'd traveled for the last two hours in near silence, not uttering more than a few words among them. Each was stunned by the horrific scenes from the village. The sheer brutality was beyond anything any of them had ever witnessed. Gratuitous cruelty such as that demanded retribution. And each member of Canidy's team silently vowed that when the opportunity presented itself, he'd exact that retribution.

It was a slow slog. Not because of the terrain, which was relatively manageable despite brush and mud, but because the area was saturated with Germans. They were in panzers and trucks and cars and planes. They were in the tiny villages that dotted the landscape as well as on the roads and in the fields. Canidy's team seemed to be dropping to the ground or hiding behind foliage every few minutes.

Nonetheless, they were making progress, moving in a

general southeast direction, even with the many detours occasioned by German presence.

Canidy calculated that they were proceeding at roughly two to three kilometers an hour. While the Germans seemed omnipresent, there had been no signs of *Armia*. McDermott assured them that was to be expected. The last time he had been in the region, *Armia* had not been operating in the area, and it was likely that since then the Germans had further consolidated their positions. Moreover, the Resistance was not likely to announce their presence. After all, the Germans were forever laying traps for them. But McDermott assured Canidy that they would be in contact soon.

Canidy glanced frequently at his watch. It had been several hours since they'd left the boat, and he had no doubt that Thorisdottir would be as precise as possible in her departure, Kapsky on board or not. His team had been moving almost without pause, no stops for rest or sleep, eating small bites of food from their rucksacks while walking through brush and tall grass.

When they came to another shallow stream—there seemed to be one every half kilometer—Canidy motioned for his team to stop and gather around. They dropped to one knee in a semicircle.

Canidy looked to McDermott. "How much farther?"

"No more than a couple of kilometers."

"Okay, we barely have time at our present pace to go another two kilometers and return to the dock on time. In fact, we're at about the halfway point now. We can't afford to pause for any distractions, like the scene at the village, or any detours whatsoever. We're all a little tired, but we have to be careful our pace doesn't slow. Otherwise we won't make it back on time. And let's hope we don't run into any Germans."

Fulmar asked, "What happens if we *do* run into Germans?"

"We can't. Simple as that. We can't afford any delays. We have to do whatever we can to avoid them, not be detected. If we get pinned down by fire or have to remain concealed or immobile for more than thirty minutes, we're going to have a very hard time meeting Thorisdottir's time frame. And I don't think any of us doubts that she means it."

"Hell, if we encounter German fire we're done for anyway," Fulmar said, holding up his M1911. "Their Kar98k rifles against these? We're done for."

"We can't let it get to that," Canidy said. "Let's be disciplined. Let's be smart."

"Even so, all of this assumes that Kapsky is waiting for us wrapped up in a big red ribbon, ready to go," Fulmar said. "Like you said, we can't really afford *any* slowdowns and expect to be back at the dock on time. I don't know what Thorisdottir means by 'not long,' but my guess is it's measured in minutes, not hours."

Canidy nodded. "Right. We're going to have to pick up the pace. But be smart. No mistakes."

Canidy began to rise when he was startled to see a figure dressed in loose gray cotton clothing carrying a carbine standing behind McDermott. The figure held a finger to his lips and smiled. Seeing Canidy's expression, the other members of the team turned in the direction of his gaze and saw the figure also. He was a boy. No more than fifteen or sixteen, but with the face of someone who had lived a lifetime.

"American?" he asked.

Canidy nodded. "American and British."

"We were expecting you. Well, maybe not *you*, but someone."

"*Armia*?" Canidy asked.

The boy nodded. "Commander Matuszek has been expecting Americans to arrive for some time. He received word from your OSS through Czech Resistance. We've been watching you for the last two hours. You are very fortunate to have avoided German patrols. One such patrol almost intercepted you an hour ago. We could not warn you without alerting them to your presence. That was—how you say?—a close shave."

"Where is your Commander Matuszek?" Canidy asked.

"Not far. Do not worry. I heard your discussion—we will be there in less than fifteen minutes."

Canidy inspected the boy for a moment. "What's your name?"

"Emil."

"How the hell old are you?"

"Twelve years. I will be thirteen in a few weeks."

"Emil, how the hell do you know we aren't Germans dressed as civilians?"

Emil smiled. "Because I would be dead by now."

Canidy shook his head. "You've been watching us how long?"

"At least two hours, maybe more. Since you crossed the creek just before the railroad tracks, and"—he pointed to McDermott—"the one with the big mustache fell on his face."

Canidy grinned. "Emil, after you take us to Commander Matuszek, I may have a job for you."

"You must make your request to the commander," Emil informed him. "What kind of job is it?"

"Get us back to our boat before it leaves without us. Otherwise, based on what we've seen so far, we're dead."

CHAPTER 18

Northern Poland
1630, 1 July 1943

Gromov's contact was a small, thin man with wiry hair and teeth stained brown from nearly incessant smoking. His eyes were rheumy and his skin was sallow. He was standing, as directed, next to a barn with faded red paint and had the look of someone resigned to a miserable fate. He did not have the look of someone who should be entrusted with highly sensitive information audaciously procured for the NKVD by its mole within the White House from a source trusted by the United States President himself. When he saw Gromov emerge from the woods at precisely the time he was told, he began to twitch noticeably.

Gromov approached slowly so as not to frighten the man any further. "You know who I am?"

"Yes."

"What do you have for me?"

"Americans are looking for a professor. The professor is nearby."

The man stared with rheumy eyes bulging, as if he expected to be struck for his statement.

Gromov asked, "Is there nothing else? I know that already."

"Americans are here now. They will leave by boat."

Gromov shook his head in disgust. Having a source in the highest levels of the United States government was of scant value if the information gleaned was so unremarkable.

"You must be sure the Americans do not leave," the man added.

Gromov was skeptical the man was conveying the directive accurately. "Do you mean the Americans must not leave with a certain individual?"

The man stared blankly.

Irritated, Gromov restated the question. "I'm to kill the Americans *regardless* of whether they have located the person they're seeking? Is that what Belyanov said?"

The man continued to stare, now with a look of panic and confusion. Gromov turned sharply in disgust and began walking away, when he heard the man make an indiscernible croaking noise. Gromov spun toward the man again.

"Did you say something?"

The man nodded and said, "Before they return to the coast. You are to kill them before they reach water."

"No matter what?"

"That is my understanding. They are not to reach the sea."

Gromov, having scant confidence in the man, pressed. "Is this directive from Belyanov?"

Again, the infuriating vacant stare.

"*Belyanov*," Gromov repeated. "The directive is from Belyanov himself?"

"I do not know what you are saying."

"*Aleksandr Belyanov*, you idiot," Gromov snapped. "Is that who told you this?"

"I don't know."

Gromov restrained himself from seizing the man's throat and crushing his trachea. It wasn't his fault he was stupid. And it wasn't his fault NKVD had entrusted a simpleton to convey instructions. Belyanov had a reputation for intelligence and precision. He left little room for misapprehension. Clearly, he'd entrusted the message to this simpleton because the message was unambiguous. The message, Gromov concluded, was the Americans were to be eliminated with all deliberate speed.

"When did you receive the message?" Gromov asked.

"Today, I believe."

"You believe?" Gromov shook his head. "Who gave it to you?"

"I do not know him."

"Describe him."

"He was short and thin. A sharp nose." The man paused to refresh his recollection.

Gromov placed a few *złoty* in the man's breast pocket

to aid his recollection. "With a beard and round spectacles?" Gromov asked.

"Yes!" the man replied excitedly, as if relieved to know he hadn't hallucinated the encounter. "He was as you described. He was very short. He would come barely to your shoulder and he had a very sharp and straight nose. A very thin nose. And a beard—very, very neat; very neat. His spectacles had gold-wired rims like a watchmaker might wear. He spoke very slowly and quietly, and he gave me a goral and"—the man rifled through his pockets, retrieved two photographs, and thrust them toward Gromov—"these photographs, I believe, of the Americans." The man squinted to jog the last morsel of information from his brain, unsuccessfully. "I do not know the man's name, the one who gave me the directive."

"I do," Gromov said flatly.

He was Colonel Yevgeni Goncharov, former battalion political officer and NKVD assassin, without a unique portfolio. He was there to ensure that no witnesses remained alive who could confirm that someone connected to the Soviet military had anything to do with the assassination of American and British troops. No witnesses whatsoever.

CHAPTER 19

Northern Poland
1647, 1 July 1943

Emil's estimate of their arrival time at Commander Matuszek's encampment was disrupted by a column of panzers and troop carriers. Although the procession seemed interminable, in fact, it passed in less than ten minutes.

When the last panzer had passed, Emil motioned for the others to remain concealed in the tall grass. No more than five minutes later several German infantry troops passed by them—a common German tactic to intercept enemy troops who would emerge from concealment after a German column had passed.

Shortly thereafter, they arrived at the *Armia* encampment—located at a deserted farmhouse and barn obscured by an overgrowth of trees, wheat, and weeds. There was no sign of Commander Matuszek or any *Armia* as they approached the rotting edifices.

Emil held up his hand to signal Canidy and the others to stop approximately fifty meters from the front porch of the farmhouse. Several seconds later, several score of ghostlike figures brandishing firearms rose out of the tall grass like corpses from a graveyard, their weapons trained on the Americans and Brits.

A man who Canidy immediately identified as Commander Matuszek emerged from the front door of the farmhouse. He didn't look like someone who was commanding an outgunned, outmanned, untrained group of civilians fighting the most powerful military force in history. Instead, he looked as if he had stepped out of a painting of a sixteenth-century pirate captain, and he had the swagger of a Viking raider.

He was missing his right eye, gnarled flesh surrounding the uncovered cavity where it had once been. His left eye regarded them with disdain bordering on contempt for a full ten seconds before he strode forward, stopping several feet away with his fists on his hips.

"It's clear God loves Americans and British because you are too stupid to survive long without his favor." Matuszek turned to his right and spat. "It is your choice if you wish to commit suicide by exposing yourself as you have, almost completely oblivious to the multitude of German convoys and patrols in this area. If you wish to operate so recklessly that *your* discovery and death are assured, I have no quarrel with you. But where your idiocy threatens brave Poles, that is a matter altogether different. Irresponsible. Inexcusable."

Matuszek strode even closer, his proximity to Canidy and McDermott making them both uncomfortable. He pointed his finger at McDermott's chest. "You in particular have no excuse for your carelessness. This is not, as the frivolous Americans like to say, 'your first dance.' We have seen you here before. You may be an outstanding operative by British standards, but by our standards, you are a liability. Churchill may think he's helping us, but all you are doing is alerting the Germans to our presence. My troops have saved your life at least twice. Yes, *twice*. Not that you would know."

Matuszek shifted his ire to Canidy. "So the Americans have arrived, finally. The cowboys. The saviors. Do you expect us to be impressed? Genuflect at your feet? I'm not sure what is worse, the evil of the Nazis and Soviets, or the ineptitude of the British and Americans. All of you contribute in your own way to Polish death and suffering."

"Commander Matuszek," Canidy said, his tone contrite, "we didn't mean—"

A young man jogged up to Matuszek, addressed him in a low voice, and then backed away. Matuszek said, "I'm advised that the Germans once again have snipers in the area. They are quite clever. Their sights may be obstructed by the trees and tall grass, but it is not advisable to afford them a stationary target." He turned toward the farmhouse and said, "Follow me."

As they followed Matuszek toward the dwelling, Emil sidled up to Canidy. "Commander Matuszek lost nearly two dozen men in the last day, including his father," he said, to explain the commander's belligerence. "We killed many Germans, but that will not bring back our dead."

Matuszek pointed to the steps and the warped wood of the porch. "Be careful."

The commander entered the farmhouse door with Canidy and his men. The front room was a large kitchen with a long wooden table surrounded by enough chairs to accommodate the group. Everyone remained standing, Matuszek once again with his fists on his hips.

"You are looking for a professor, am I correct?"

"We are," Canidy answered. "His name is Sebastian Kapsky."

"Why are you looking for him?"

"Because I was asked to look for him. *Find* him," Canidy said.

"Asked?" Matuszek scoffed. "Do American superior officers no longer issue orders?"

Canidy felt strangely defensive, as if the integrity of the U.S. military was being questioned. "The operation was deemed extremely high-risk, with a high probability that the personnel charged with executing it wouldn't be coming back. So our government looked for volunteers. We were given the option of taking it or rejecting it."

Matuszek shook his head disdainfully. "Only the very, very stupid volunteer."

"Guilty," Canidy conceded.

"Your governments must have a great deal of confidence in you to select you for something so risky. You must have a demonstrated competence."

Canidy shrugged. "I don't know about that. But we're the ones they asked. Maybe they thought we're the only ones dumb enough to accept this assignment."

"Maybe it is a mixture of both," Matuszek said.

"Look, Commander," Canidy said. "No disrespect.

I'd like nothing better than to engage in idle banter with you all day, but we're on the clock. We need to secure Kapsky and then find our way back to the extraction point as fast as possible. We don't have any margin for error. In fact, we're probably a little behind schedule if you factor in one or two surprises or delays on our return trip. We need Kapsky and we need him now. Do you have him or do you know where we can find him?"

Matuszek stroked his chin. "Why are your governments so keen on securing him? Of the millions of Poles under the thumb of the Nazis, why is he so important that they'd send their best to possibly die in order to find him?"

Canidy was becoming impatient and irritated. "Hell if I know. He's important, okay? That's all I know. I don't give a damn about anything else."

"Poles are being massacred by the thousands every day. No one is coming to save *them*. No secret expeditionary forces. No armies. You only came to get Kapsky. Because he is useful to *your* governments. Not because he could help save his own countrymen."

"Commander, all due respect—I don't have time to discuss national interest or political motivation. We need Kapsky now. *Right now*. And then we need to sprint the hell out of here. Are you going to help or be a pain in the ass?"

"I can't help you," Matuszek replied.

"Jesus!" Fulmar erupted. "Why are you wasting our time?"

Matuszek turned to Fulmar. "Wasting *your* time? You

are wasting *my* time. *I* have a war to fight. *You* are playing hide-and-seek."

Canidy spoke calmly, trying to lower the temperature. "Commander, look, I understand you've had a rough time with the Germans. We aren't trying to make things any rougher. We just want to complete our assignment, okay?"

"If I could help you, I would," Matuszek responded. "But that is not within my control."

"Whose control is it?"

"God's," Matuszek informed them dryly. "Kapsky is dead."

Canidy blinked several times before staring at Matuszek for several seconds. "Dead? You're sure?"

Matuszek nodded slowly.

"You're sure," Canidy repeated. "Sebastian Kapsky is dead. Sebastian Kapsky, professor of theoretical physics at the University of Lviv."

"Yes. He is dead. Single shot to the chest."

"How can you be so sure?"

"Unfortunately," Matuszek said, "I have seen the body."

Fulmar pressed, unwilling to believe the expedition was for nothing. "How do you know it was Kapsky's body? Did you know him? Did he tell you he was Kapsky before he died?"

Matuszek asked, "Have you ever seen him? A photo?"

Canidy said, "I have seen a drawing of him. We weren't allowed to bring it with us for operational security, but I memorized it. He was recognizable. I'd know him on sight. He had a distinctive shock of hair. I was told it was black. I was also told he had distinctive green eyes."

Matuszek walked to the door. "Come with me."

They followed Matuszek, along with Emil, out of the farmhouse and to the right. They were escorted immediately by four rough-looking *Armia*, each carrying a Poln M29.

They walked silently and alertly through the tall grass for approximately half a kilometer before coming to a shallow, muddy stream bisected by a cluster of large, smooth boulders. Canidy could see someone sitting in the stream with his back resting against the rocks. Two corpses were lying nearby on the bank. Matuszek stepped into the water—it was no more than a foot deep—and approached the person resting against the boulders. The others followed.

When he closed to within a few feet of the body, Matuszek gestured as if displaying a piece of fine art. The others gathered around the scene as if at a wake.

Canidy examined the corpse closely for a full minute. There was an entry wound in the chest—fairly large-caliber. Rimless spectacles—the type in fashion among academics—stuck out of the breast pocket of the tweed waistcoat.

Atop the corpse's skull was a thick shock of black hair, the most distinctive feature from the drawing shown to him by Donovan. And the eyes—though lifeless—were vivid green, just as described. Unmistakable. Professor Sebastian Kapsky was, indeed, dead. But at least he'd killed the two who had killed him.

Canidy turned to Matuszek and said, "That's him. That's Kapsky. Jesus."

Canidy raised his voice slightly and confirmed it to the rest. "The operation is over. All that's left is getting back to the boat."

There was a round of sighs and expletives from the squad. Fulmar said, "We should at least check his pockets. See if there's anything useful."

Canidy nodded and did as Fulmar suggested. He found nothing in Kapsky's pants pockets except a small tin containing four L&M cigarettes. Canidy ran his hands over the corpse's torso and inserted his fingers into an inside breast pocket that contained the rimless spectacles, retrieving a slim 3x5 leather notebook. He thumbed through the pages, then handed it to Fulmar. "What do you make of that?"

Fulmar scanned the contents, his brow furrowed. "Equations of some kind, I guess. Way beyond me." Fulmar turned to McDermott and the rest of the squad. "Any of you go beyond long division in school?" Fulmar glanced at the contents again and then passed the notebook to the other members. Not expecting to decipher its contents, each examined it perfunctorily before handing it to Canidy, who handed it to Matuszek. "Any ideas?"

"I suggest you take it with you and have your mathematicians examine it. Perhaps it is what your governments sent you here for."

Canidy asked, "How long has he been here?"

"At least a few hours. We couldn't move or bury the

corpse because there were still lots of Germans around. We think they propped him up like this as bait, a common trick to lure us into the open. So we watched and waited until they left. We'll make sure he has a proper burial in due time."

Canidy put the notebook in his shirt pocket, looked at his watch, and curtly announced to the squad, "Time to go."

Canidy turned to Matuszek and said, "We need a favor. Can we borrow Emil? He offered to guide us back to our boat if you approved."

"Yes. Frankly, if I let you go without a guide, the Germans will have you within an hour. It was only by sheer luck that you arrived here without encountering them."

Canidy extended his hand to Matuszek, who grasped it. "You should know that there has been an SS officer and his detail in this area the last several days," Matuszek said. "Based upon what we've heard from villagers, I suspect he was searching for Kapsky also. He was in the vicinity in the last twenty-four hours."

"A big man? Tall?" Canidy asked.

"That's him. With white hair."

"I couldn't really see his hair, but we saw an SS officer terrifying villagers several kilometers from here. Seems like a real sweetheart."

"He's a monster—mentally as well as physically. He's established quite a reputation here recently."

"Do you think he was responsible for killing Kapsky?"

"I do not know, but I would be surprised if it was without his knowledge and approval."

"Why would he *kill* Kapsky?" Fulmar asked.

"Because the professor is so important to his enemies that the Americans and the British would dispatch soldiers on a suicide mission to secure him," Matuszek replied. "Plainly, to keep him out of your hands."

"Maybe," Fulmar said skeptically. "But if they know the professor was that important to us, he must be equally as valuable to them—"

Canidy interrupted. "We can speculate later. Right now, we need to move."

Matuszek gestured for Emil to escort the squad, and Canidy grasped Matuszek's hand once more. "Thanks for your help. Good luck to you and your men."

"Luck is better spent on you. My men and I are unlikely to survive the war, no matter how much luck we have."

Canidy motioned the squad forward. He took a last look at Matuszek. He wanted to remember the face. And then he directed Emil to the point.

Emil led the squad so deftly through the forest and tall grass that McDermott was pleased to have been demoted. The boy had memorized the recent locations of German sniper teams as well as the usual routes for German convoys and patrols. Although they couldn't afford to stop more than a few times for breaks and orientation, at their present pace they would arrive at the dock with about thirty minutes to spare.

Fulmar, walking alongside Canidy, nodded ahead to

Emil and asked in a low voice, "What were you doing at that age?"

"Riding my bike, collecting bottle caps and baseball cards."

Fulmar shook his head. "What do you think he'll be like—after all he's experienced—when he becomes a man?"

"He *is* a man. Tell me there isn't a part of you that isn't a little in awe of him."

"Good-looking kid, too. Hell, Canidy, in a couple more years you'll have stiff competition for the ladies."

"If he makes it," Canidy said soberly. "Care to give odds as to whether he sees fifteen?"

Emil held up his left hand, signaling for the squad to halt. He listened for a few moments and then made downward movements with the same hand as he dropped through the knee-high grass onto the ground. The squad did the same.

They remained motionless and listened for nearly a minute. They heard nothing but sporadic bird chirps until there was a barely perceptible sound of a cautious footfall on vegetation. A scant five seconds later they saw an infantry squad pass through the tall grass less than twenty meters from their position. The squad leader carried an MP 40 submachine gun. Several feet behind him was a Stabsgefreiter carrying an MG 42 machine gun. An assistant gunner carrying a light load of ammunition trailed him. He was followed by several riflemen armed with Karabiner 98s. All wore black uniforms. They looked experienced, competent, and lethal.

The Germans moved slowly past them, training their weapons from left to right as they scanned their surroundings. They disappeared from view in less than a minute, but the squad remained prone for several minutes thereafter just to be sure the patrol wasn't trailed or didn't double back. Emil was the first to rise and gave the others a signal to do the same.

"It is best we move more quickly to place distance between us and that patrol," Emil advised. "They are quite smart. They run patterns to entrap hidden *Armia*. We are fortunate we heard them before we saw them or we would be dead."

Emil began walking silently but swiftly north, followed by the squad. They didn't have much time.

CHAPTER 20

Taras Gromov saw the same German patrol five minutes later. He was even more fortunate to evade them than the squad, for he hadn't been alerted by a stray noise. Rather, he saw a momentary glint of light reflected off the barrel of the squad leader's MP 40 when he briefly emerged from the shade. Gromov reacted the same way as the squad, waiting a sufficient interval for the German patrol to pass before he resumed tracking his quarry.

Gromov's primary target was no more. He'd surveilled the Americans and British as they first met with the *Armia* commander. He followed at a distance when they went to the stream and watched as they inspected the corpse resting against the boulder. He'd instantly recognized it as Professor Kapsky. As opposed to Canidy, he hadn't needed to assess the corpse against his memory or an oral description given by his superiors.

Rather, Gromov simply withdrew the photo of the professor given to him by way of Belyanov, a photo forwarded by Vasily Blokhin from Katyn to the Lubyanka.

It wasn't difficult for Gromov to surmise that Blokhin didn't come into possession of the photo due to his intelligence or cleverness, but because he'd been outwitted. Kapsky must have switched identities with someone at Katyn, given that person his papers, and somehow escaped. Quite simply, Blokhin had been tricked. But this wasn't any ordinary error. This error was on a titanic scale. Judging simply from the fact that the Americans, British, Germans, and Soviets all had been searching for this professor in the midst of one of the biggest military engagements in history, the escape of Sebastian Kapsky clearly was of extreme strategic significance.

For any other Soviet citizen, errors of far less significance would result in summary execution. Not so Vasily Blokhin. He had been Lavrentiy Beria's most prolific and reliable executioner. In Joseph Stalin's Union of Soviet Socialist Republics, an individual such as Blokhin had a unique and nearly indispensable status. He wasn't merely an assassin, a surgical instrument like Gromov; Blokhin was an executioner on an industrial scale. As such, he was too valuable to Beria—and to Stalin—to suffer permanently for the blunder.

Belyanov, on the other hand, wouldn't give Gromov similar latitude; his errors wouldn't lightly be forgiven. He needed to execute his assignment without a flaw: the American and British soldiers must be killed. Gromov estimated he had no more than two or three hours to complete the task, more than enough time if it weren't for the presence of Germans in the area.

Gromov observed that the squad was moving quite briskly. The boy leading them clearly knew what paths were quickest and what areas to avoid. Nonetheless, Gromov was closing on them incrementally. He needed to find a spot that afforded a view of the entire squad and permitted a quick series of shots. An interval of even a second between shots would provide one or more of them the ability to disperse and seek cover. He'd given some thought to closing the distance completely and killing them with his NR-40, but concluded that seven were too many, especially since the tall one who seemed to be in command appeared as if he might be a challenge.

Gromov pulled from the scope and gauged their distance. He estimated that it would take him approximately five to seven seconds to shoot all of them. The boy was farthest from cover. Gromov determined he should shoot the man farthest to the rear who was closest to cover and then proceed forward. By doing so he should be able to hit them all—with the possible exception of the boy—before they could get to cover. It was immaterial whether he hit the boy; Belyanov hadn't known of his existence before he directed all of the squad be eliminated anyway, so there was no need to waste precious rounds on him.

Gromov steadied himself, sighted the man to the rear, exhaled, and squeezed the trigger. Corporals Spivey and Trent collapsed to the ground before the rest of the squad even heard the report from Gromov's weapon.

Canidy glanced to the rear just in time to see Corporal Colby's skull explode into fragments. The corpses of Spivey and Trent had already fallen to the ground before his mind registered that they were under attack. He turned forward and instinctively fired several rounds in the general direction of the report. Simultaneously, Fulmar and Emil began firing several rounds in the same direction as they dropped to the ground for cover.

McDermott was a fraction of a second too late. A round skimmed his left shoulder, inches from his heart, propelling a jet of red mist into the air above his head just before a second round struck his right arm. He dropped to the ground grimacing in agony, but held on to his Enfield.

Canidy raised his head slightly to see where the fire was coming from but saw nothing but tall grass. He ducked when he heard the air snap inches above his heard. "Stay down. He's somewhere in the grass. On my signal . . ." Canidy's voice was drowned out by the sound of machine-gun fire coming from somewhere at the bottom of the slope to their left. It was directed not at them, but toward the sniper. Two panzers emerged from the woods to the left, firing devastating bursts of 7.92-millimeter rounds in the sniper's direction and scything all of the vegetation and saplings in a five-thousand-square-foot swath at the base of the hill. Hundreds of jets of dirt erupted into the air as a haze of blue smoke wafted over the devastation.

"I don't think they see us," Fulmar shouted over the echoes of machine-gun fire. "They're directing their fire at the sniper, who must be a pile of ground beef right now."

Canidy looked back at McDermott. "Can you move?"

Still grimacing, McDermott nodded. "Sniper got my boys."

A sustained burst of panzer machine-gun fire began ascending the slope. "They know we're somewhere on the slope," Canidy shouted over the din. "They'll just saturate it with fire. We have a better chance if we spread out and move over there." He pointed toward the woods to their right. "On my signal sprint like hell—McDermott on the right, then Fulmar, me, and Emil." Everyone nodded concurrence.

Canidy seized a momentary lull in the fire to shout, "Move!"

The squad immediately sprinted for the woods, spreading from one another as they did so. The panzer machine-gun fire roared back to life, strafing the ground thirty meters to their rear and closing rapidly. Fulmar was the first to reach the woods, followed by Emil, and then McDermott. Canidy reached the tree line last. The machine-gun fire ceased seconds after they disappeared into the woods. All kept running for another thirty to forty meters before slowing to a jog, shoulders hunched as they panted from exertion and adrenaline.

"Keep moving," Canidy commanded. "Anyone hit?"

Before anyone could answer, Canidy saw that McDermott's right sleeve was shredded and soaked in blood. McDermott caught Canidy's gaze. "It's okay. I caught one on my upper arm. It looks worse than it is. It's really just a nick."

"Like hell," Canidy said. "Look at your shoulder. The blood's dripping from your wrist. Once we clear some distance between us and the panzers, we're going to need to take care of that."

They moved rapidly through the woods, Emil taking the lead. Even though the sniper must have been atomized by the panzer fire, they kept their heads on swivels, looking for other sources of danger.

A half kilometer later the woods became denser, but Emil seemed well familiar with the area. He motioned in a northwesterly direction and minutes later they encountered what appeared to be a dried-up creekbed that allowed them to move without being hindered by the dense, thorny undergrowth covering the forest floor. They traveled along the creekbed for another kilometer before Canidy raised his hand.

"We'll stop here for a few minutes, orient, rest, and take care of McDermott's arm."

Canidy looked to Emil. Anticipating the question, Emil said, "At best, another nineteen, twenty hours."

Canidy nodded and turned to Fulmar. "This has turned out to be a class A screwup. No professor. Three Brits dead and one who will be out of commission for a long time."

"If you're expecting an argument or reassurance from me, Dick, you'll be disappointed. When he was trying to convince me to volunteer for this, Donovan told me this would be a 'low-probability' operation. I didn't know if he meant there was a low probability we'd accomplish our objective or a low probability we'd survive. Turns out it wasn't either/or. It was both."

Candidy leaned close to Fulmar. "Look at McDermott," he whispered. "He's seen his last action. That arm's shot. He won't be able to even lift a weapon with it. Oh, sure, he'll give 'em hell for suggesting he handle logistics or some such, but you can already see it in his eyes."

Fulmar looked at McDermott, whose arm was being dressed by Emil. His face betrayed not the slightest bit of pain, but he couldn't mask the resignation. The unmistakable millennia-old look of a warrior who knew that, for him, the war was over.

McDermott glared at the two. "Don't give me those pitiful looks, you shits," he hissed. "I know what you're thinking and I'm telling you right now, you don't know anything about it. You Yanks can afford to put someone like me to pasture. You've got a dozen more to take his place. We Brits don't have that luxury."

Candidy smiled. "All that assumes we meet the lovely Miss Thorisdottir's timetable. If we don't, all of us will be *buried* in a pasture."

Emil secured a bandage made from cloth torn from the leg of his trousers around McDermott's arm.

"Done," Emil said.

Candidy looked at his watch. "Absolutely no time to waste. Let's move. *Now.*"

CHAPTER 21

Four kilometers southeast, Gromov finished wrapping his left thigh with cloth from his left sleeve. He hadn't realized he was bleeding until he'd run more than a kilometer from the site of the panzer attack. Adrenaline had obscured the pain until he was out of immediate danger from machine-gun fire.

The wound was minor, at least by his standards. He hadn't found any shrapnel lodged in the tissue. Nothing like his last wound, a six-inch-long gash inflicted by a kulak with a rusted sickle.

Gromov was more concerned about any wounds that might be inflicted by order of Belyanov.

Gromov had killed three of the squad; of that he was certain. But unless the panzers had struck the rest, they had escaped, including their apparent commander. He'd reasoned, however, that there was a fair probability that the barrage from the 7.92-millimeter guns had finished the job. He could plausibly report to Belyanov that the squad had been eliminated. Besides, in the context of a massive, sprawling, chaotic war, there would be no way of disproving the assertion.

But his failure to secure the professor was another matter. Realistically, there was nothing he could have done to affect the outcome. He'd been dispatched too late. And neither the Germans, British, nor Americans had secured him, either.

Gromov concluded that the assignment, while not a success, also wasn't a failure. A rationalization to be sure, but when dealing with men such as Belyanov, the quality of rationalizations often was the difference between life and death. *Belyanov* might accept the rationalization, but *he* had to report to Beria. If Beria wasn't satisfied with the rationalization, Gromov would be summoned to the Lubyanka and, like countless others, wouldn't emerge. At least not in any recognizable form.

Gromov had, however, a more immediate concern. He was a lone Red Army soldier deep within German-occupied Poland in the midst of a raging battle involving hundreds of thousands of combatants. He'd have plenty of time to perfect his excuses for Belyanov. Right now, he needed to find his way back to relative safety. As was common, the NKVD had provided only for his entry into Poland, not for his exit. He was on his own, his only resources the M91 slung over his right shoulder, the NR-40 strapped to his left hip, and his wits.

CHAPTER 22

Maurer was reasonably pleased with himself.

Canaris had charged him with finding Professor Sebastian Kapsky before anyone else. Maurer had done just that. More precisely, soldiers under his command had discovered a body fitting his description and had advised Maurer, who had gone to the site and had seen the corpse sitting peculiarly against a boulder in the midst of a stream, two dead soldiers lying nearby. True, Kapsky was dead when he found him. But Maurer had found him before the Russians, Americans, and British.

The whole matter was as inconsequential as it was peculiar. Yet another corpse in the woods. Maurer had matched the corpse against the meticulously detailed description given to him by the genius Canaris and then, before returning to his Schutzstaffel, gave orders to have all three bodies carried to a field hospital south of Danzig.

He expected to be recalled to Berlin and given an assignment more relevant to the war effort. Something befitting his talents. He'd operated long enough in Poland. He'd been efficient—bordering on brilliant—and that brilliance was best suited for strategy, not mere tactics. Berlin, not Danzig. Although Berlin appreciated his talents, until now he'd been used as a laborer wielding a sledgehammer, not a surgeon wielding a scalpel. But he'd demonstrated over the last several months that he was meant to lead, not merely execute.

Sitting in this cramped, makeshift office in a converted railroad depot on the outskirts of the godforsaken city of Danzig, he was scanning a stack of communiques from Berlin when his Unteroffizier knocked twice on the open door and saluted.

"Herr Maurer, Oberbannführer Frantz to see you."

The Unteroffizier stepped outside, and a small, thin, severe-looking man appeared in the doorway. He was a contrast to Maurer in nearly every way. Whereas Maurer was large and muscular, Frantz was short and slim. While Maurer had the handsome features of a stage actor, Frantz had the face of a bookkeeper; and while Maurer was direct, Frantz was duplicitous.

Maurer hated him. But Canaris respected him, so Maurer feigned the same.

Maurer motioned to the chair opposite his desk. "Please sit, Herr Frantz."

Frantz took a few steps into the room but remained standing, his hands clasped behind his back. He looked disapprovingly about the cramped office for several seconds before addressing Maurer.

"I am to provide a full report to Admiral Canaris regarding your assignment involving the professor." Frantz tilted his chin upward. "What do you have?"

Maurer was both irritated and puzzled. He'd immediately conveyed a thorough report to Berlin upon returning from the forest where the professor's body had been found. He'd described the body, location, and time of discovery. There was nothing more to report. Frantz was purposefully trying to aggravate Maurer.

"It is, Herr Frantz, as set forth in my report." Maurer's tone was both deferential and inquisitive. He sensed that Frantz was somehow baiting him to make a misstep or error that could be reported, with the requisite amount of disdain, to Canaris.

"Your report is noticeably deficient in several aspects, Maurer. That is why I am here." Frantz gazed slowly about the cramped quarters. "That you do not recognize its manifest deficiencies is somewhat concerning."

You little shit, thought Maurer. *Without that badge of rank and Canaris's protection, you'd be pissing in your boots if you addressed me like that. I've got ten times more accomplishments than you in this war and you know it. You owe your position to your impressive proficiency in licking boots.*

"Apologies," Maurer said respectfully. "What deficiencies would those be?"

Frantz's upper lip curled in disdain. "Most glaringly,

Maurer, you failed to explain why you did not capture the professor *alive*."

"Herr Frantz, Admiral Canaris commanded that I find Professor Sebastian Kapsky before anyone else. I did so. He was dead when I found him."

"Then, obviously, you were not the first to find him. Someone else must have gotten to him first and killed him."

Maurer was slightly thrown off balance. Yes, someone had killed Kapsky. But there was no evidence that Kapsky had yielded anything of value to that person.

"Herr Frantz, we found the professor in the stream, dead. Judging by the condition of the corpse, he had expired a short time before we discovered him. Clearly, if someone desired that he provide information, they would have *captured*, not killed, him."

"Do you know what killed him?"

"A chest wound."

"Do you know *who* killed him?"

Maurer hesitated. "Clearly it was either our troops or *Armia*. Stray fire."

"You do not *know* that," Frantz hissed.

"Herr Frantz, I am well familiar with this area. It is an area of heavy conflict and often intense fire. The only plausible explanations are stray fire from our troops or *Armia*." Regaining his footing, Maurer paused for emphasis. "Given that Kapsky was a professor, it is plain that whatever value he possessed was the provision of information, unique information, likely complex, that could not be conveyed in mere minutes or seconds. And definitely not information that could be comprehended and conveyed by a mere foot soldier."

Maurer knew that what he was saying made perfect sense. More important, Frantz knew it also.

But Frantz remained unplacated, nonetheless. "All assumptions," he said. "Your job is not to make assumptions. Your job is to execute. This is not acceptable."

Although Maurer nodded deferentially, he doubted Canaris felt the same way as Frantz. In the first instance, Canaris understood the remote probability of locating a lone individual during an ongoing conflict, especially one as large and intense as the current one. He would also appreciate the possibility, if not the probability, that such an individual might become a casualty. And he would know that an individual who possessed information so valuable that Admiral Canaris himself believed the Americans were searching for him—well, such information could not be conveyed in mere minutes, or even hours.

The look on Frantz's face told Maurer he'd scored. But someone like Frantz didn't easily concede.

"Admiral Canaris dispatched you to acquire and deliver Kapsky. You did not deliver Kapsky. You failed."

Maurer's face remained passive as he scrutinized every detail on Frantz's face. He wanted to sear it into his memory so that when he eventually rearranged that face he'd be able to measure the damage inflicted.

The two saluted before Frantz spun curtly and walked out of the office.

Soon, you little shit, thought the big man. *Very soon.*

CHAPTER 23

They moved at a surprisingly brisk pace considering Mc-
Dermott's pain. Emil had led them along the dry creekbed for at least a kilometer before veering northeast
through dense brush that slowed them a bit. But even
so, their pace was much faster than their trip from the
boat. The last hour of their journey was uneventful,
save for an encounter with a massive herd of deer that
became confused when startled and nearly stampeded
them before changing direction. Other than that, and
the occasional chirp of a bird, or snap of dry twig underfoot, there was barely a sound.

Candy saw the boat first. He could tell by the barely
perceptible ripple in the surrounding water that it had
just arrived. Seconds later Fulmar let out a muted cheer.
McDermott simply smiled in relief.

Thorisdottir gave a curt wave from the foredeck,
which they all returned, including Emil, who was in-

stantly enraptured. "A woman," he said with a note of surprise. "From here, she appears quite attractive."

"Just wait until you get closer," Canidy said. "You sure you don't want to come along? The war is going to go on with or without you."

"Once again, thank you for the offer. But it will go on *with* me." He grinned expansively. "Perhaps one day you will read about me. Like Sikorski, or perhaps even Kościuszko."

Canidy grasped Emil's hand. "I'll be reading the papers." He shook Emil's hand once. "Stay smart."

Fulmar and McDermott each clapped Emil on a shoulder. "Give 'em hell, kid," Fulmar said.

Emil gave a slight nod of acknowledgment, turned, and within seconds disappeared into the brush. Canidy turned back to the boat, where Thorisdottir was standing imperiously with fists on hips. "Been waiting long?" he asked.

"Actually, no," she replied with an inflection conveying mild astonishment. "You're several minutes ahead of schedule. Come aboard." As Canidy, Fulmar, and McDermott climbed onto the dock, a second figure emerged from the cabin and stood next to Thorisdottir, causing a stutter in the gait of each of the men. The two figures were identical in every respect but clothing. Each was approximately six feet tall with ice-blue eyes and blond hair to the waist. But while Kristin was clothed in formless weather gear, the second figure wore shorts that displayed toned legs that caused Fulmar to mutter, "Incredible."

"This is Katla," Kristin informed them. "She is my twin sister," she added superfluously.

The effect on the warriors was electric, causing each to take extra care in boarding, lest their distraction cause them to plummet into the canal. Once they were securely on deck, Katla extended her hand to each, in the case of McDermott with considerable gentleness. Her broad smile was an inviting contrast to the taciturn Kristin.

"Katla is an able seaman. I asked her to join me because there was an increased number of Admiral Dönitz's vessels in, and Reichsmarschall Göring's planes over, the Baltic on my return to Gotland after dropping you off. This ordinarily does not pose a problem, but given your presence on the vessel, I determined it best to have assistance."

"Makes sense to me," Fulmar said and nodded appreciatively. "Good decision."

Kristin added, "Endeavor not to stare, gentlemen. Katla has perfect vision and can perceive leers from one hundred meters. In addition, she is quite strong."

Despite their fatigue all the men laughed, albeit a bit self-consciously. Canidy noticed Fulmar's enraptured look and nudged him back to reality. "We're ready to shove off whenever you are," he informed Kristin.

Kristin scanned the bank. "Where are the rest? Your three mates?" She suspected she knew the answer, but wanted confirmation before departing.

Canidy replied simply, "They won't be making the return trip."

Kristin nodded and said to Katla, "Let's go." Then

she said to the men, "Until we're clear of the canal and at least a kilometer offshore, it is best if you go below."

Canidy didn't argue, although he thought two stunning women sailing a boat on the Baltic might generate at least as much attention as a crew of three men and a couple of women.

They reached the sea in less than ten minutes without event. Canidy knew they'd done so because of the pitch and swale of the boat, the water choppy if not rough. He could hear the wind whistling above deck.

He felt anxious. Not so much because of the rough sea or the increased German patrols, but because of the failure of the operation. Nothing he could have done would have changed the outcome. He had made no mistakes, but Wild Bill Donovan had chosen him out of hundreds of thousands of other candidates to execute the rendition of Sebastian Kapsky to the government of the United States of America, and that wouldn't happen. The reasons it wouldn't happen were immaterial. Canidy was coming home empty-handed. Worse, Kapsky was dead. Whatever made him important to the U.S. government, it was now unattainable and there would be a notation in his file—if he was fortunate, it would be a mere footnote or asterisk—that said, in essence, "Failed Operation." It was not a notation seen in the files of those who had advanced from obscurity to respect or even notoriety. History was being written. The world was at war and Canidy wouldn't even be a footnote, or, if he was, it would say "Failed."

Fulmar had similar thoughts. "What do you put the

odds that we get debriefed by Donovan himself?" he asked Canidy.

"Zero to none. Maybe less," Canidy replied. "No one likes to be around failure. You don't want the stench to rub off on you—seep into your clothes."

"To be fair," Fulmar noted, "it wasn't our fault. It wasn't really a failure."

"You're welcome to tell that to Wild Bill," Canidy said. "Personally, I'm determined to say as little about this operation as possible. I just hope we get another opportunity to distinguish ourselves."

"Based on the German firepower we saw on display, this war isn't ending anytime soon, Dick. There will be other opportunities," Fulmar assured. "Right now I'm contemplating the opportunities presented by the lovely and talented Thorisdottir sisters. Not so much Kristin— she's a hard case. But Katla . . ."

Canidy said, "We're in the middle of the Baltic, infested with German ships and probably U-boats, and you're thinking about some damn women?"

"Hell, why do you think I'm thinking about some 'damn women'? Better than thinking about a torpedo from a German U-boat or strafing from a Messerschmitt."

Canidy looked to McDermott. "How does it feel?" he asked.

"A bit of pain, to be sure. I'll manage."

"Stiff upper lip and all that," Fulmar said.

"I'll ask the Thorisdottir twins if they might have something to ease the journey," Canidy said and winked.

Canidy began to climb the stairs to the deck, stopping when he saw Kristin standing at the top with her fists on her hips. Again.

"You'll find some spirits in the chest next to the bunk," she informed. "I recommend Luksusowa vodka applied to the wound and Mortlach whisky for consumption."

Canidy grinned appreciatively. "Splendid recommendation, Captain Thorisdottir. You seem to have a passing familiarity with the medical arts."

"More than a passing familiarity, Major. One cannot sail the Baltic and the North Sea without intimate knowledge of salves, potions, and medicinal applications."

Kristin turned and disappeared. Canidy winked at Fulmar, who had already retrieved the Luksusowa vodka and the Mortlach whisky. He removed the cork from the Mortlach and took a healthy slug before handing it to McDermott, who did the same. "Our captain has excellent taste," he said. Then he took two more long swallows, belched ceremoniously, and offered the bottle to Canidy, who declined.

"You need more painkillers than I do," Canidy said.

McDermott returned the bottle to his lips, gulped, and belched again. "Already feeling no pain," he said. "How much more satisfying it would be if we had the professor—simply to celebrate?"

Canidy pulled the small notebook from his pocket and held it in front of him. "We don't have the professor, but we didn't come away completely empty-handed."

"Hate to be the pessimist," Fulmar said. "But I doubt that whatever caused the President of the United States to send us into German-occupied territory could be captured in a small notebook like that. Besides, what's to say the Germans didn't already take a much bigger notebook off the corpse?"

Canidy thumbed through the pages of the notebook. Nothing but hieroglyphics. He retrieved the bottle of Mortlach from McDermott and took a healthy gulp.

It did little to stem his growing sense of foreboding.

CHAPTER 24

As he approached the stream from the north with a team of six men, Maurer could see Sebastian Kapsky's corpse still resting against the boulder. From fifty meters, it truly appeared to be a naturalist in repose, taking a break from a hike. A slender ray of sunshine shone directly over his head, as if blessed from above.

As he drew nearer, Maurer saw signs of spreading decay not apparent during the previous inspection. Exposed flesh was flecked with brown and gray splotches. The eyes were essentially gone—probably consumed by birds and insects, leaving hollow sockets that appeared to stare intently at Maurer and his detail.

As they closed to within a few feet, the stench of decaying flesh prompted Maurer to withdraw a kerchief from his pocket and place it over his nose and mouth while he inspected the remains. Save for that decay, the corpse was not appreciably different than it was when he had first seen it.

Maurer had returned before the detail he'd dispatched had retrieved the corpse because Frantz had angered him. He'd insisted that Maurer had been negligent in handling Kapsky's remains. The little man made it abundantly plain his disdain at Maurer was personal and that he would emphasize said negligence to Canaris. Men like Frantz, thought Maurer, took pleasure in destroying men like Maurer. Little men who needed to redress some childhood injury sustained from superior specimens such as him.

Maurer had also returned because he feared he had, indeed, been negligent. His initial examination of the corpse had been standard. After confirming cause of death, his men had rifled through the clothing, doing a perfunctory pat-down. Since the directive had been to return a live Professor Sebastian Kapsky to Canaris, and since that wouldn't be feasible, Maurer reasonably assumed that nothing remained of his mission. Maurer was a soldier, not a detective.

The stench of decaying flesh caused Maurer to retreat a few steps and wave two of his men forward. "Search his clothing thoroughly. Pockets, sleeves, socks, undergarments."

The men held their breath as they rifled through Kapsky's clothing, pausing every fifteen to twenty seconds to turn away and catch their breath.

Nothing.

"Remove the clothing," Maurer commanded.

Less than a minute later, Maurer examined Kapsky's mottled flesh, the extremities covered with scores of slugs. The chest wound was a garish multicolored cavity infested with small flies and maggots. No tattoos. No diagrams or codes written on the flesh.

"Search all cavities."

One of the two unfortunates signaled to the other to turn the corpse onto its stomach. As they examined the alimentary canal, both retched. They then turned the body over and examined the nose, mouth, and throat, yielding nothing. Both turned to Maurer and shrugged.

"Hold the mouth open once more," Maurer directed.

One of the soldiers grasped Kapsky's head and pulled the jaw downward as far as he could. Maurer held his breath and leaned toward the corpse. The oral cavity was dark, but he could see that the decomposition of the tongue was more advanced than the rest of the body and the gums appeared to be receding from the teeth. He picked up a twig from the bank and used it as a probe, pushing the tongue from side to side, then lifting it to inspect underneath.

Maurer withdrew so he could exhale and catch his breath. He motioned for the soldier holding Kapsky's head to open the mouth wider.

Maurer took another deep breath and leaned inward.

Using the twig, he depressed the tongue to the floor of the mouth. "Flashlight," he said to no one in particular. One of the men dutifully provided a flashlight that Maurer turned on and shined inside the oral cavity. He could barely see what appeared to be a foreign object lodged in the throat, protruding slightly above the floor of the mouth. Maurer attempted to snag the object by inserting the twig inside the mouth and scraping it forward along the floor of the mouth without success. After three attempts to pull the object upward and outward, Maurer adjusted his tactics, using the twig to push the object deeper down Kapsky's throat. When the object disappeared from view, he turned to his men. "Knife."

One of the men handed Maurer a bayonet.

"Hold the skull firmly," he instructed. Maurer made a deep incision just above Kapsky's sternum and sliced upward to the chin, releasing an overpowering stench in the process. He rose and stepped back to inhale a lungful of clean air before bending over once again and pulling the sides of Kapsky's throat open to remove what appeared to be a slender scroll of waxy paper. Maurer seized it between his thumb and forefinger and carefully withdrew it from the cavity.

Maurer took several steps back from the corpse and exhaled before holding the scroll before his face and turning it at several angles in order to examine it thoroughly. It was surprisingly large and appeared to be sealed with some type of gummy substance. The wax paper exhibited little, if any, corrosion or damage, but Maurer rolled it gently between his fingers to ensure that it wouldn't flake or tear if he removed the gum and unrolled it. As he did so, he glanced at his men. They were watching him with a mixture of curiosity and apprehension, feelings Maurer shared, although he'd never before projected anything but supreme confidence to his men.

Accordingly, they were somewhat surprised when he asked, "What do you think this is?" and "Why was it in Kapsky's throat?"

No one responded.

"Quite peculiar," Maurer observed. "Did he attempt to swallow this or was it shoved down his throat?"

Unteroffizier Becker, who nearly matched Maurer in size, observed, "Herr Maurer, he was shot in the chest with a medium- to large-caliber weapon at range. It strikes me as unlikely that whoever shot him shoved the scroll in his mouth after he was dead. It seems more likely Kapsky was attempting to swallow it in order to hide it."

"Yes." Maurer nodded slowly. "My thought also. But quite large to swallow. Either way, most peculiar, don't you think?" He continued to slowly roll the cylinder between his thumb and forefinger, considering whether he should open it or present it to Canaris's forensics team to reduce the chances it might be damaged upon inspection. Curiosity prevailed over caution. Holding the scroll in his left hand, he used the nail of his right index finger to gently slice and scrape the gummy substance from the scroll.

It took nearly a minute to peel the substance off the waxy paper without damaging it. He unwrapped the scroll gingerly and held it with one hand at the top and the other at the bottom as if he were a page or town crier reading a proclamation.

The scroll was covered with small, densely packed symbols that appeared to Maurer's untrained eye to be mathematical equations or formulae. The multiple lines were in black ink save for the last two, which were in red and underscored.

Maurer studied the document for more than a minute and then looked up, his expression pensive. After several seconds, Becker asked timidly, "Herr Maurer, do you understand it? What is it?"

Maurer didn't reply, his gaze remaining intense.

Becker repeated the question. Maurer looked past him into the woods. "I cannot say for certain. I am a soldier, not a mathematician. But as a soldier, considering the obsessive pursuit by the major powers, my instincts say it is an instrument for civilizational dominance," he replied. "Or civilizational destruction."

CHAPTER 25

London, England
1806, 7 August 1943

The carnage was almost incomprehensible. Hundreds of thousands had perished in Europe from enemy fire, disease, or starvation. More than even in the Great War.

The reports across his desk were horrific, but he didn't have need of the reports. He could tell from the mangled bodies stacked on the lorries that the world, let alone Britain, was witnessing human suffering on a scale once unimaginable even to the most alarmist members of Parliament.

Churchill knew, however, that the British people were resolute. They would fight the Nazis until the last man perished in the Highlands of Scotland. Hitler's Wehrmacht had inflicted grievous wounds on the island and its people. And yet Great Britain remained standing, and aside from a few backbenchers who wet their trousers every time they heard the drone of an airplane engine, the people were steeled for the fight. Churchill's primary concern was with his allies. In the east, Stalin was treacherous, a man never to be trusted. But he could be relied upon to send millions of his countrymen into the Eastern Front meat grinder without flinching. The worst mistake Hitler had made thus far wasn't declaring war on the United States, it was breaching Molotov-Ribbentrop and engaging the Soviet Union in war on their land. Was the man that ignorant of history? Of simple geography?

Stalin wasn't Churchill's problem. It was his English-speaking cousin to the west. Roosevelt was smart and savvy, but he was also political. Perhaps more so than anyone Churchill had ever met. More Machiavelli than Disraeli. FDR calculated the political implications of everything from the Allied invasion of the European continent to the cost of lanyards for MacArthur's binoculars. That made him more difficult to manipulate than Stalin, who was wholly unconstrained by politics. In the Soviet Union Stalin *was* politics. Nothing distracted him from concentrating on Hitler.

Churchill exerted enormous effort to keep Roosevelt's concentration on Hitler as opposed to Hirohito or domestic political opposition. One of the more successful techniques in maintaining FDR's concentration on Hitler was to remind the President of not just the consequences of defeat in discrete battles in the European theater, but the consequences of a postwar Europe with *either* a German *or* Soviet hegemony.

Intelligence from MI9 often proved to persuade Roosevelt better than almost anything else. It had to be deployed deftly and not overplayed, but after Roosevelt devoured the information, he usually came to the same policy conclusions as Churchill. The latest piece of information came from Commander Ian Fleming, who sometimes trafficked in hyperbole, but more often than not possessed nuggets of intelligence that were not only useful but valuable.

Churchill enjoyed listening to Fleming's briefings, which occasionally sounded like mystery novels reaching a climax.

Last night, Stewart Menzies, chief of the Security Intelligence Service, lately referred to as MI6, sent a message to Whitehall requesting a meeting to discuss certain information Fleming had obtained from British OSS operations in Berlin. According to Menzies's boss, the information was potentially of strategic significance. A source alleged to be in the office of Chief of German Intelligence Wilhelm Canaris claimed that the Germans were in possession of information that could tilt the strategic balance of the war, as well as the postwar world, decidedly in Hitler's favor.

The claim sounded fantastic to Churchill. He had a difficult time believing that *anything* of value could be pried loose from the office of the Genius, let alone anything of strategic significance. But Churchill knew history better than any other world leader. And he knew that entire empires had vanished because leaders had discounted certain information as implausible.

Moreover, despite Fleming's theatrics and occasional hyperbole, his intel was usually spot-on. And Churchill valued both theatrics and accuracy. So Churchill had summoned MI6 and Fleming to Whitehall.

There was a perfunctory knock—two raps—and Churchill's security opened the door to the War Room to announce the arrival of Stewart Menzies and Naval Intelligence Officer Fleming. Churchill, sitting in a high-backed leather chair at the head of the horseshoe-shaped table, a massive color map of continental Europe directly behind him, opened his mouth slightly in surprise. He hadn't been expecting Menzies, whose appearance signaled something of great importance was afoot. Moreover, Churchill hadn't known Menzies to work with Commander Fleming in the past. The combination caused Churchill's expression to shift from mild surprise to consternation.

Menzies entered the room with his usual Eton aplomb, followed by Fleming, who sported civilian clothing with his trademark bow tie. Menzies nodded toward the prime minister. "Good day, sir. My sincerest apologies for the intrusion on my part. I hope you'll forgive me, but I'd learnt from Rear Admiral Godfrey that Commander Fleming had secured an appointment with you. And since MI6 was integral to obtaining the information Commander Fleming wishes to share, I insisted on coming along."

Churchill's jowls quaked. The rivalries within British military and military intelligence were almost as pitched as the animosity between Britain and its enemies. Churchill, however, did little to quell the rivalries. He believed competition produced better outcomes. Churchill waved an unlit cigar toward the chairs to his left on the horseshoe. Menzies sat nearest to Churchill, Fleming to Menzies's left.

"This must be a matter of some importance for you to be pried from your codebreaking, Stewart," Churchill observed. "I don't think I've seen you concerned with anything else in more than a year. *I'm* concerned that you're going to inform me that Hitler and Stalin have kissed and made up."

Menzies flashed a patrician smile. "We've been making splendid progress on the Gerry codes, sir. Some of our finest chaps are on them. Including Gaither—you may recall his father at Sandhurst."

Churchill nodded. "I am just as interested in the Germans' capabilities in deciphering *our* conversations, Stewart. Please remember that. If Hitler catches wind of our plans for one General Bernard Law Montgomery, we'll have quite a problem on our hands."

Menzies smiled again. "We may have a greater problem with Ike."

"True." Churchill turned to Fleming, who appeared somewhat agitated, unusual for a man who normally appeared unflappable, even serene. "Well, Commander, I've been told very little about the matter, but I gather you believe this is of some grave importance. Please do not tell me those infernal engineers Hitler keeps entombed in those tunnels in Bavaria have developed a better panzer."

Fleming pointed to the cigarette holder peeking from his breast pocket. "May I, sir?"

"Hell, why don't we all?" Churchill proffered the tip of his cigar to Fleming, who produced a match, lit it, and placed it under Churchill's cigar until it glowed. He then lit a cigar withdrawn by Menzies from the inside of his suit coat. Fleming then retrieved the cigarette holder from his pocket and lit the cigarette. The entire stoking ceremony consumed nearly a full minute, then each of the three men leaned back in their respective chairs simultaneously.

Fleming said, "Sir, we've obtained information which, I'm afraid, may compel the mounting of an operation in German-held territory to confirm."

"Why must we *confirm* the information?" Churchill asked. "That sounds like the information is mere rumor. I'm quite disinclined to authorize an operation in German-held territory to confirm a mere rumor."

"Sir, to be more precise, the existence of the information needn't be confirmed," Fleming explained. "Rather, it is more to confirm that the information is what it purports to be."

Churchill scowled. "Well, *that* clears it up."

"It is a matter of whether the information may plausibly be what our informant claims it is, sir," Menzies explained. "If it is what he thinks it is, it would be worth moving heaven and earth to obtain it—which is nearly what we would be required to do, given that it is presently in the custody of Canaris."

"What does he think the information is?"

Menzies said, "As I understand it, he's unsure but believes it may be a blueprint for a new superweapon.

One that would be two to three generations beyond anything the Germans or anyone else presently have. Something that, if developed, would provide Hitler with an insuperable advantage."

Fleming nodded in agreement. Churchill puffed his cigar while examining the faces of the two intelligence officers. "Let's start from the beginning, shall we, Commander Fleming? Perhaps with an explanation of who the informant is and why we should consider him credible?"

"He is a clerk in Canaris's office, sir."

Churchill removed the cigar from his mouth, incredulous. "A clerk in Canaris's office? The office of the Genius has been so compromised? Why haven't I heard of this before and why aren't we three steps ahead of Guderian, Rommel, and Keitel at all times?"

"Sir, the term 'informant' may be somewhat misleading," Fleming explained. "He is not a regular asset. Indeed, this is the first time we have ever gotten information from him. As we understand it, he works in cartography now, but before the war he was some sort of engineer for Krupp, and from what we gather, a fairly adept one.

"A short time ago, information came into the Abwehr that created a bit of a stir. Not immediately, mind you, but after some analysis. It seems as if some SS officer had obtained a document containing certain formulae—equations and such. Seventy-six Tirpitzufer, normally so tight the air within is the same as it was last year, was buzzing at first, primarily because of internal politics. One of Canaris's closest lieutenants, a chap by the name of Frantz, seems to have rapidly lost favor at the same time the SS officer became a Canaris favorite—precisely because of something to do with the information.

"The information was on a document obtained by the SS officer. The document purportedly came from Professor Sebastian Kapsky."

Churchill straightened slightly and turned to Fleming. "Kapsky? The chap you identified as the target for extraction?"

"That's correct, sir," Fleming replied. "The mathematician. You and President Roosevelt authorized a mission to extract him from occupied Poland. He was killed before the team could acquire him."

"What makes them think it came from Kapsky?"

"Frankly, sir, we can't answer that specifically. But circumstances strongly indicate it came from him."

"I need specifics, Commander," Churchill said.

"The informant says the SS officer who acquired the document is a bit of a climber—a self-promoter. He said nothing directly, mind you, but gave a hint about his involvement in highly consequential matters—as if the fate of the Fatherland hinged upon his deeds. The matter of the document was one of those consequential matters to which he alluded, however vaguely. Rumor had it in headquarters that this SS officer had been charged with finding Kapsky and that the document came from Kapsky himself."

Churchill waved his cigar dismissively. "Rumors."

"Yes, sir, rumors. But more than that. The informant relates that immediately after the Obersturmführer presented the document to Canaris, several mathematicians and physicists were immediately summoned to Tirpit-zufer to decipher the document. They determined it was produced by Kapsky, although they were unclear about its conclusions."

Churchill appeared surprised. "They don't know what it means?"

"Sir, our people—that is, our scientists—concede that Kapsky was of a different order," Menzies interjected. "In the category of a Newton, or a Tesla, or Einstein. Without him, his theories and equations could take a generation or two to confirm and put into use. They know that Kapsky was working on the matters contained on the document and they have familiarity with it, but it will take them time to understand it completely. That said, the informant says they were acting like toddlers unwrapping presents at Christmas, even though part, or even most, of it was encrypted."

Churchill's brow furrowed with worry. "I've never seen scientists or mathematicians excited."

"Precisely, Prime Minister," Fleming said.

Fleming and Menzies watched Churchill's face turn dark as he puffed on his cigar, contemplating the implications and options. "How voluminous is the Kapsky document?"

"Our understanding—the informant's understanding—is that the entire document consists of one scroll of paper," Fleming responded.

"A scroll of paper?" Churchill asked. "How could something so purportedly consequential be contained on one scroll of paper?"

"The handwriting is said to be rather small," Menzies explained.

"Still," Churchill scoffed. "The Germans think the fate of the world may be decided by the contents of a scroll of paper?"

"More than the outcome of the war, sir. Hegemony for the foreseeable future," Menzies said.

"Even if we were to acquire the document, it's been in the possession of the Germans for some time. Even if we dispatched agents in the next five minutes to acquire it, they've had an insuperable head start."

"True," Menzies conceded. "Unavoidable, sir."

"Could this informant get it for us, or make a copy? A transcription?"

"He is not trained for such things, Prime Minister. Not remotely. And it is impossible to leave the Tirpitz-zufer without being thoroughly searched each and every time you do so."

"Could he memorize portions and record them after he leaves the building?"

"Much too complex. The problem is that we can't afford even the slightest error, and this is a supremely complicated formula or equation, as we understand it. Quite long."

"Who is this individual?" Churchill asked.

"Kurt Bauer," Menzies replied. "Thirty-five. From just south of Mainz."

"How did we recruit him?"

"We didn't, sir," Fleming answered. "He made contact with a Czech Resistance fighter and began transmitting information through him nearly a year ago, sporadically. Nothing of much use to us, until now."

"Do we have any idea why he would take the risk of contacting us? Could this be a German misdirection operation?"

"Although we never discount that possibility, sir, we've assessed it as unlikely. The Czechs tell us that Bauer's maternal grandmother and several of his cousins were taken into custody by the Geheime Staatspolizei before the Anschluss. They haven't been seen or heard from since then. It's believed they've been killed, sir."

"Why were they arrested?" Churchill asked. "What was their offense?"

"We understand his grandmother and the cousins in question were Jews," Menzies said. "We understand Bauer was quite close to his grandmother. We suspect that may have some bearing on his motivation."

"I see," Churchill said. "Nonetheless, quite curious that Bauer would be permitted anywhere near Canaris's office. They never miss such matters."

Fleming grinned. "Ah, yes, Mr. Prime Minister. We conducted a thorough amount of research on this chap to ascertain his bona fides to determine whether we were being set up for some form of disinformation operation. And as you know, there exists in Germany a remarkably vibrant black market in false identities, manufactured personal histories. These operations are enormously sophisticated, given both the consequences if a true identity is revealed, as well as the fact that the Nazis are astonishingly proficient at rooting out such frauds.

"It seems Bauer did not attempt to hide the fact that his grandmother and cousins were Jewish. One Czech told us that what he did was kill both the person that had reported them to the Gestapo as well as the Gestapo Kriminaldirektor to whom he had made such a report. Then he went to the Gestapo Kriminaldirektor's superior to confirm that his relatives had been taken into custody, claiming that it was *he* who had turned in his relatives. The Gestapo Kriminaldirektor's superior was sufficiently impressed with Bauer's fealty to the Reich that a year later he recommended him to a position with the Abwehr, where he's performed with proficiency ever since."

"Quite clever," Churchill said.

The room fell silent for several seconds while Churchill puffed on his cigar.

"Gentlemen, you've come to me for approval of this operation rather than simply execute it on your own authority, not because this promises to be an unusually difficult operation behind enemy lines, but because you have prudently concluded that this is the type of operation that suggests consultation with the American President."

"That is your prerogative, sir," Menzies said superfluously.

"It would be politic for me to do so, obviously, and I shall. But am I correct that some functionary in cubicle 14A of your establishment has concluded that certain American assistance is advisable?"

"That is correct, sir," Menzies and Fleming said in unison. "The assistance, if I may," Fleming added, "consists not of matériel or logistics, but of personnel." Fleming glanced collegially at Menzies, who nodded. Fleming continued. "Any logistical assistance Mr. Roosevelt—through Messrs. Eisenhower and Donovan—may choose to provide, is, naturally, very much appreciated. But after some deliberation with our Lieutenant Colonel Laycock, as well as Major Stirling, we've concluded that the odds of success of any operation along the lines contemplated would be enhanced by the participation of two Americans in particular—a Major Canidy and a Lieutenant Fulmar, who come fairly recommended by one of our best and most experienced men."

"I see," Churchill said. "Is it expected that we will command the operation?"

Fleming and Menzies glanced at each other. As senior, Menzies spoke.

"Sir, we understand the trials you've had managing a certain general—indisputably a talented general—in both North Africa and Italy. We do not wish to replicate that trial for you. However, whomever is leading the operation is less important, we believe, than the talent of the individuals taking part in such operations. And we've identified, sir, Canidy and Fulmar as two highly talented—and might I say—somewhat daring individuals of the sort that would improve the probability of the operation's success considerably."

Churchill smiled. "Given that the Special Air Service commends them and based on the description of the objective, I gather they must be quite mad also."

Menzies and Fleming chuckled. "A prerequisite, I'm afraid." Fleming nodded agreement.

Churchill looked pensively toward the ceiling, his jowls quaking as he did so. "Remind me, are they the chaps who accompanied McDermott to Danzig or some such?"

"They are, Mr. Prime Minister," Fleming confirmed. "To be sure, McDermott was accompanying *them*."

Churchill pointed his cigar at Menzies. "Didn't you say we lost men on that operation?"

"True, sir, but it is our opinion that, but for Canidy, we would have lost them all. They faced overwhelming firepower deep in hostile territory, yet managed to evade Gerry patrols across difficult terrain."

Churchill fell silent contemplating the next steps.

"Very well, gentlemen. I shall consult with the Yanks and leave it to you to plan this operation. I confess that in all of my years I've rarely, if ever, encountered one that presented so many self-evident and steep barriers to success; inserting a team into Germany itself and retrieving a document that, based on what I've just heard, must be one of the most tenaciously guarded items in one of the most securely protected environments in all of Europe, if not the world."

Churchill pointed his cigar at Fleming. "I suspect you've already taken the liberty of planning the operation?"

"We have, indeed, developed a series of plans in consultation with the SAS, sir. Quite challenging, as you've just suggested. The one with the greatest promise replicates in large measure the operation McDermott and Canidy ran a while ago to retrieve Professor Kapsky."

"Remind me a bit of the particulars," Churchill said.

"Well, sir, it involved the insertion of the team into Poland by way of the Baltic. We still maintain contact, however sporadic, with elements of the Polish Home Army, who continue to prove quite resourceful. In that operation we had the good fortune of encountering members of the Home Army who provided assistance, primarily in extraction. In the present case, rather than moving southward, we will be moving westward into Germany until reaching the outskirts of Berlin."

"Forgive me, Commander, but this already appears to be a suicide mission," Churchill said.

"Clearly not a holiday jaunt," Fleming agreed. "Nonetheless, we've done a bit of this before—admittedly, with increasing difficulty, but that's the job. We've continued to develop and expand a network of ethnic Poles and Polish émigrés in Germany to guide us to Seventy-six Tirpitzufer. They are even more extensive now than they were during our previous operations."

Churchill smiled at the mention of the audacious operation that resulted in the airlifting of an entire intact V-2 rocket out of Poland. "I confess, that was one of the few delights of this godforsaken war."

Menzies said, "The nightmare, sir, will be the extraction. More so than the insertion. If we can succeed in obtaining the document, the Germans will be on high alert. Every depot and every terminal will be crawling with Gestapo and SS. German civilians will have their heads on a swivel looking for and reporting anyone they do not immediately recognize—and the Germans are unparalleled at this."

Menzies lowered his voice as if he were concerned about being overheard. "We continue to monitor our contact with Admiral Canaris, Mr. Prime Minister. If there is a chance we might be able to get assistance from the admiral, obviously we will do so."

"I wouldn't bank on it, General," Churchill said. "By all means, continue to work on him, but I am increasingly convinced that the rumors of his disaffection with Hitler and Nazism are little more than a counterintelligence operation designed to get us to chase ghosts. They don't call him the Genius for nothing."

"Mr. Prime Minister," Fleming said, "Canaris may have a weak spot. A beautiful young lady who works for Jan Karski."

"Karski? The Polish agent?"

"Yes, sir."

Churchill nodded approvingly. "Can we use her, Commander?"

"We will certainly try, sir."

"We also have access to a number of Austrians and Germans trained by Donovan's OSS, but they are for assisting with extraction, not in turning Canaris. Nonetheless, I would not bank on anything positive from Canaris. He's outwitted us several times before. I'll be damned if he does so again." Churchill slapped his hand on the table. "You'll forgive me, gentlemen, but I have other matters to which I must attend. I will speak with Roosevelt presently. The rest of the details you may provide as necessary."

Menzies and Fleming rose to leave.

"Oh, yes," Churchill added. "Who do you propose to accompany Canidy and Fulmar?"

"McDermott, sir," Fleming replied.

"Wasn't he shot up last time?"

"Indeed, sir. His arm does seem to flop about a bit. But he insists he is just as lethal with the other arm and he does have experience with the Americans. Besides, he understands that, as he put it, if the mission doesn't succeed, Germany may rule the world."

"Hell with all that world-domination drivel," Churchill retorted. "We simply can't afford to make a bad showing in front of the Americans."

CHAPTER 26

"Back to Poland again?" Canidy asked. "Let me tell you, I had my fill the last time. The place is rotten with Germans."

William Donovan nodded. "No argument there. It will be far more challenging than last time. Not only because you will insert into German-occupied territory, but because you will go to Germany itself."

"Say again?"

"You, Fulmar, and McDermott will insert into Poland by way of the Baltic, make contact with the Home Army, who will guide you to German territory, where you will be met by an associate of Jan Karski by the name of Krupa. He and whomever he enlists to assist will take you within a kilometer of the Tirpitzufer. From there, you will be essentially on your own."

"A suicide mission," Canidy said flatly.

"If you choose it to be, it certainly will be so," Donovan said. "Dick, we have far more resources and support than we did last time. Your previous operation was among the first of its kind, not merely intelligence but intelligence combined with special military operations—or, if you will, commando tactics. We still have our fair share of gadgets and spycraft; but now with more blood, sweat, and guts. As the war evolves, the OSS has evolved. That includes a vast number of collaborators in both Germany and Poland. We've developed an extensive network of partners and collaborators in both countries and we have a little more experience than we had then. We've gone from being amateurs to highly sophisticated professionals. And that description includes you and Fulmar."

"Sir, not to be flip or insubordinate, but I've found during the course of this war that flattery often precedes an impossible assignment. I've seen more than my fair share of friends never return from doomsday assignments."

"No argument there," Donovan conceded. "But that's what OSS is all about. Fulmar and McDermott will accompany you, but as opposed to last time, you'll have plentiful and rather sophisticated support—Poles, Czechs, and Austrians who are positioned in the singular goal of acquiring the Kapsky document."

Canidy winced almost imperceptibly upon mention of the name. Ever since Donovan first contacted him about the operation several hours ago he wrestled with the feeling of acute embarrassment bordering on humiliation. *The Kapsky document.* He'd been charged with rescuing the professor but had found him dead. The notebook recovered from Kapsky was still being analyzed, but thus far the scientists charged with deciphering it had concluded that portions of it were, in fact, *indecipherable*, or, perhaps, just plain gibberish. Now it appeared the Germans had somehow acquired another critical document authored by Kapsky. Canidy couldn't help wondering if he'd somehow missed the document when searching Kapsky's body. He'd assumed the Germans had gotten to Kapsky first, but what if they hadn't? What if they'd encountered Kapsky's body after Canidy but had conducted a far more exhaustive search of the remains and found the document? The question had nagged him since Donovan first contacted him. He was determined to rectify the matter.

"Where do we insert, sir?"

"Same place as last time. No sense changing what works."

"*How* do we insert?"

"Again, the same as last time."

"By boat? It wouldn't by any chance be skippered by . . ."

". . . a six-foot Viking goddess." Donovan chuckled. "With her twin as first mate."

Canidy grinned. "One hell of a way to die, sir."

"You'll meet McDermott in Gotland as before. Then cross the Baltic to Poland. As you know, there'll be Messerschmitts everywhere."

"When do we leave?"

"Now. The Germans have had the scroll for some time. Although the most recent intelligence from Bauer indicates that they've yet to decipher the document, it's only a matter of time. When they do, they'll have a head start on us that may be insuperable. So it's imperative that we get it to our analysts immediately, or . . . die trying."

CHAPTER 27

The broad smile through what appeared to be the world's thickest mustache revealed impressively white, if misaligned, teeth.

For a man who was about to embark on an operation that would subject him to a high probability of death, dismemberment, or capture, McDermott appeared remarkably carefree and jovial. He was standing in the same spot and dressed in the same civilian clothes as he'd been when Canidy and Fulmar had first met him. Only, this time he was alone.

Canidy and Fulmar approached him across the tarmac, hands extended. McDermott grasped their hands in turn and shook each vigorously. "I had a suspicion I hadn't seen the last of you two. When Commander Fleming told me about this operation, I thought that if the Yanks were going to send anyone, it would be one or both of you."

"Hell, Conor," Canidy said, "how did you draw the short straw again?"

"I didn't," McDermott said. "When Commander Fleming told me about it, I volunteered before he could even make the request or issue an order. Sounds like it could be a spot of fun, don't you agree?"

"You certainly have a perverse notion of fun, my friend."

McDermott cocked his head. "*I* have a perverse notion of fun? As I recall, on the last suicide mission we had the pleasure of sharing you two seemed absolutely giddy, like a couple of chaps on holiday."

Fulmar laughed. "That was due in large part to our cruise ship captain."

"And now her twin." McDermott laughed. "Those two look like they descended directly from Asgard. A bit—what's the expression you Yanks use?—'out of my league.'"

McDermott's expression sobered slightly. "I must say, however, that when Commander Fleming described the purpose of the operation, I felt almost compelled to volunteer. I feel somewhat responsible for the Gerries getting that document."

Canidy nodded, glancing at Fulmar. "We had a similar reaction. We were *there*. Kapsky was right in front of us. Did we miss something? Was this document there but somehow we overlooked it?"

"I keep playing it over and over in my head," McDermott said absently. "It was a thorough search. Most likely, we just got there too late—after the Germans had already taken it."

"We didn't search body cavities," Canidy said cryptically.

"Who searches the body cavities of a cadaver in the field?" McDermott asked. "I'll tell you who: nobody."

"Except the thorough and precise Germans," Fulmar said.

"Don't pay any attention to him," Canidy advised. "He's half Kraut."

Fulmar examined his watch. "Time to go. We don't have time to waste."

The three got into the Studebaker on the tarmac, McDermott behind the wheel, Fulmar in the passenger seat, and Canidy in the rear. McDermott started the vehicle and drove as if they'd just robbed a bank.

"How's the arm?" Canidy shouted from the back.

"Not as bad as they'd first feared. It looks like a mess and it gets numb from shoulder to wrist at odd times, but it's pretty strong, and I can move it about pretty well. Weaker than the other arm, but not by much."

"Any problem handling weapons?" Fulmar asked.

"None to speak of. I need to concentrate more, but it's manageable."

Canidy could tell through the fabric of McDermott's shirt that the arm was atrophied in comparison to his left arm. Although it gave Canidy pause, he surmised the Brits wouldn't have sent McDermott on such a critical operation unless he was fully up to the task.

They passed the time driving to the coast talking about everything but the operation, as if to do so would jinx it. Although each was optimistic by nature, a light pall hung over them. None had any illusions about the task ahead. Each thought the likelihood that any of them would return alive, let alone retrieve the Kapsky document, was questionable.

But not one of them would give up the second chance for glory.

The boat sported a fresh coat of paint but otherwise was as they'd remembered it, including the Teutonic skipper wearing drab weather gear standing next to it on the dock. She appeared just as serious as Canidy remembered. But looked even better.

As they approached, Canidy asked, "You never thought you'd see us again, did you?"

"I didn't," Kristin Thorisdottir admitted. "But neither did I think it was impossible."

"Where is your sister? I was told she was going to be on board also. Katla?"

Kristin's twin appeared from belowdecks with a smile on her face. "You were told correctly."

"The gang's back together again," Canidy declared.

Kristin Thorisdottir didn't look much different to Canidy from the last time. Her hair was a bit longer and almost white from the sun. It fell in nearly impossible abundance to her waist. Her facial features continued to remind him of a mythical Nordic goddess, albeit one who appeared somewhat weary from tension.

"We will take essentially the same route but with a few pivots. The Germans are more vigilant and more aggressive than they were last time," she informed them as she scanned the horizon from the helm. "The patrols are more frequent. They have less patience. Admiral Dönitz's wolfpack has been losing lots of subs, but the Baltic is still dangerous. They will sink a vessel with little hesitation if they even suspect it may be working for the Allies, and the planes do strafing runs for fun. My advice is to remain belowdecks."

"Thanks," Canidy said, standing next to her as she steered. "Good advice, but I'd like to see what's coming to kill me."

"It won't matter," Kristin said fatalistically. "There is nothing you can do to avoid them. Once they select us as a target, they'll make as many passes as necessary to shred us to pieces. No mercy."

"Still, I don't want to be surprised in my last seconds on Earth. I want to know what's coming."

Kristin smiled. "So you can curse your killers? Damn them all to hell?"

"Never underestimate the martial power of profanity. The best warriors can deploy curses like weapons. Some are single .45-caliber rounds, others are 155-millimeter howitzers."

Kristin continued smiling, sending a charge through Canidy. "I'm told your General Patton downed a Messerschmitt with a well-placed curse between sips of brandy."

"That just *has* to be true."

Kristin turned to face Canidy, her expression clinical. "This trip of yours is more hazardous than the last one, Major Canidy. I don't think you'll be coming back."

"How could you possibly know how hazardous the mission is? You don't know anything about it other than where you're dropping us off and picking us up. Are you always this optimistic?"

Kristin continued looking in Canidy's direction. "I understand, but I'm a simple sailor whose charge is to convey you across the sea along a relatively challenging course. But the purpose of your mission is plain, and I'm sure the Germans are waiting for you, or someone like you."

"With due respect, Miss Thorisdottir," Canidy said with a mixture of curiosity and irritation. "How the hell would you know that? Why in the hell do you think the Germans are waiting for us? The only people on this entire planet who know we're here are the five souls on this boat, three in Britain, and two in the USA. That's it. And the five who aren't on this boat are in charge of making sure the Allies don't lose the war."

Kristin shook her head almost contemptuously. "Because they're not looking specifically for *you*, although if they were it wouldn't surprise me. They're looking for the Allies to send *someone* for the Kapsky material. Whether it's you or someone else, eventually the Allies need to send someone, and the Germans know it."

Canidy took half a step back and examined Kristin for several seconds. She shouldn't know anything about this matter and, in particular, about the Kapsky document. What the hell was going on?

Kristin, sensing his bewilderment, continued. "Don't worry. Your operation has not been compromised," she assured. "Understand that the tiniest bits of information relating to German capabilities and intention are treated like gold by nearly everyone on the entire continent, especially by the various Resistances. Nearly everyone seizes upon any information, no matter how ridiculous or irrelevant, pertaining to Nazi capabilities, movements, or intentions. Sometimes the rumors are mere fantasy, sometimes not. But because lives—sometimes one, sometimes one million—can depend on such information, it travels like lightning. Often your intelligence services and military leadership are the last to know."

"When did you hear about it? From whom?"

"I don't even remember." Kristin shrugged. "Katla heard something from one of Jan Karski's associates about an SS Obersturmführer who has become Admiral Canaris's fair-haired boy."

"What do you know of Karski?"

". . . Polish Resistance. Katla and I have worked with him and his people. Your people know him and his information intimately. It is probably why they initiated the mission, at least in part. Karski's network heard from the SS Obersturmführer's lady friends that he had been bragging about a promotion and his growing influence with the top people in the Abwehr. He did not say much more than that, obviously. You do not get promoted in the Abwehr by talking about intelligence with friends and lovers."

Canidy turned to Fulmar and McDermott, who were engaged in banter with Katla on the foredeck.

"Come here, you should hear this." All of them gathered about Canidy and Kristin.

Canidy said, "Kristin says we should expect a Nazi welcome party when we arrive. It seems the Abwehr has anticipated someone would come for the Kapsky document."

"You're bleedin' kidding me," McDermott said. "How in God's name could that be?"

"They don't know any specifics," Canidy assured. "They simply calculated the probabilities that something as important as the Kapsky document might start rumors and the logical reaction of the Allies would be to get our hands on it." Canidy pointed to Fulmar and McDermott. "They don't know *we're* the ones coming for the document; they don't know *where* we're coming from or *when*." Canidy looked at Kristin.

"That is correct," Kristin confirmed. "Rather, they are on alert. Gestapo probably has been briefed to be even more vigilant. SS is being ever more aggressive— Karski informs that the Oberst who obtained the document has been assigned the responsibility of protecting it. He has been tracking down Karski associates, and doing so rather effectively. He has developed something of a reputation. Not a pleasant individual."

"That doesn't change anything," Canidy said. "But it

does mean that we have absolutely no margin for error. As impossible as this operation seemed before, it just got more impossible."

Fulmar and McDermott began chuckling, then broke out in guffaws, prompting Canidy to do the same. Kristin and Katla looked on with a mixture of puzzlement and bemusement.

"We're both indispensable *and* expendable," Canidy explained between breaths. "We're supposed to save the world from eternal Nazi domination *and* we're on a suicide mission."

"Then I suggest you go below deck before you become prematurely expendable," Kristin said.

"What do you mean?" Canidy asked, chest still heaving.

Kristin pointed to the southwest sky. "German planes."

Everyone turned in the direction to which she was pointing. Low on the horizon approximately four to six kilometers away, four Messerschmitt Bf 109s were approaching.

"If they see five people on a boat this size, they will become suspicious and likely strafe us," Kristin said. "They may strafe us regardless, but there is no sense increasing the probability."

The three men reacted instantly and descended the stairs. Twenty seconds later they could hear the whine of the planes' engines as they flew over the boat, the din indicating that they were probably no more than seventy-five feet overhead. The trio relaxed as the whine receded, but tensed as the sound grew louder again, indicating the planes were spooling up and doubling back. Canidy reflexively gripped a handle on a storage locker. Fulmar and McDermott simply clenched their fists.

The whine grew louder and more piercing than it was on the first pass, indicating the planes were approaching faster and at a lower altitude. Canidy looked at Fulmar and McDermott, who were staring at the stairs leading to the deck. He couldn't summon any witticisms.

Each of them tensed as the whine reached an apex and then relaxed when the sound receded without any strafing fire.

"I don't mind saying that almost made me wet my britches," McDermott confessed. "We're sitting ducks out here."

"It pains me to say this," Canidy said, "but I think the Thorisdottir twins have bigger balls than we do."

"Hell yes," Fulmar agreed.

The three laughed, but ceased abruptly as the whine once again grew louder.

"Aw, hell," McDermott said. "Hell."

The menacing pitch of the whine signaled that the planes were coming in even lower than before. In his mind's eye Canidy saw them at an altitude of about forty feet, low enough that the Thorisdottirs would be able to make eye contact with the pilots before they fired their MG 17s, shredding the five of them with 7.92-millimeter rounds.

The noise grew loud enough to rattle the utensils in the galley and hurt their eardrums, close enough that they could distinguish each plane's engine. They winced, held their breaths, and braced.

Nothing.

Once again, the whine receded. This time it kept receding east until the noise was replaced by the sound of the sea slapping against the boat.

Canidy exhaled silently. "Well, if I had to guess, I'd say they were just trying to get a better look at the Thorisdottirs." He turned to McDermott. "Sorry to say, Mac, but I suspect this won't be the last time we wet our pants on this run. And let's just hope we spare our pants from anything more disgusting."

CHAPTER 28

"Please shut the door behind you, Bill." Donovan nodded to Harry Hopkins and Laurence Duggan as they left the Oval Office. Donovan was mildly surprised. The President rarely closed the door to the office, even when discussing sensitive matters. He was good at picking reliable people, trusted them, and relied on their discretion. The request meant that FDR planned to address a matter of unusual significance.

Donovan shut the door and took a seat in one of the two chairs opposite the President's desk. The CIC was holding his cigarette holder, but the cigarette was unlit.

"Don't look so worried, Bill. I just wanted to check on the status of our—what do you call it?—operation. Churchill's being his usual pain in the ass. His people haven't heard anything from their man. He seemingly expects that our fellows are in constant contact with us, informing us every time they pass wind."

Donovan shook his head. "Mr. President, our men have been instructed that under no circumstance are they to attempt to contact us until they have acquired the Kapsky document, returned to their extraction point, and are well on their way back to Gotland—preferably not until they arrive at RAF East Moor. Indeed, save for a few underground contacts who will guide them, they are to remain silent. Churchill's inquiries to you are because their men have been instructed similarly."

FDR pursed his lips contemplatively. "And if they are in jeopardy?"

"They are on their own, Mr. President."

"In the middle of enemy territory," FDR noted. "A most thorough, efficient, and ruthless enemy."

"We selected them because they are resourceful and highly trained. And that's putting it mildly. Not just training in weapons and tactics, but physical training of a most grueling sort. Modeled, in fact, after the training of Mr. Churchill's most elite soldiers."

Roosevelt snorted. "Yes, he reminds me of it regularly." He lit his cigarette and drew deeply. "The man is Britain's best hope, but he is a prodigious pain in the ass."

Donovan's expression remained unchanged. He knew better than to agree with the President on that point. Roosevelt complained about Churchill incessantly, but he deeply respected, even admired, him. Donovan had long ago concluded that Roosevelt wouldn't look favorably on anyone who concurred with his frequent disparagement of the prime minister.

"I feel compelled to know who these men are, Bill."

"Their names are Dick Canidy and Eric Fulmar. The Brit is a man by the name of McDermott."

"And how long will it take to complete the operation, Bill?"

"If all goes well, Mr. President, they should be able to go to the Abwehr, acquire the Kapsky document, and return to Gotland in less than a week," Donovan replied evenly. "As you know, nothing ever goes according to plan once an op begins. The probability that everything will go according to plan is near zero."

"The Germans are actively searching for them, I gather?"

Donovan nodded. "We presume so, Mr. President, given that they may be in territory currently occupied by their forces. Our preliminary assessment is that they have likely assigned the task to their man Otto Skorzeny."

"Obersturmbannführer Otto Skorzeny. I have heard of him. Quite a character, from what I understand. Considered perhaps the most proficient—Special Operator, I think they call it—in the world. Am I right?"

"Yes, Mr. President. 'Scarface.' Cunning, ruthless, deadly. Six feet four and quite athletic. Very bright. Based on our intelligence, he's never failed a mission.

"The other possible candidate, we believe, is an Obersturmführer Konrad Maurer, Waffen SS. He possesses all of Skorzeny's qualities, save the scar. And he's even taller."

The President waved his cigarette holder, irritated. "What is it with these damn Germans? Sometimes it seems they actually take this Aryan business seriously."

"Dick Canidy is every bit the equal of Skorzeny or Maurer, Mr. President. Tall, big-boned, athletic. Except he has dark hair, close-cropped. Not very Aryan in that regard. But he's versatile and fearless. From flying protection over the Burma Road to thwarting the Germans' use of chemical weapons. Good man. Our best."

"Coming from you, Bill, quite an endorsement. But why Canidy? Don't we already have some unit under Oppenheimer to do such things?"

"Are you referring to the component under the Manhattan Project, Mr. President?"

"Yes, the group assigned to get the information on the German atomic weapons program."

"Operation Alsos," Donovan confirmed. "Under Lieutenant Colonel Boris Pash. It won't become operational until late September and we must get to Kapsky *now*, before anyone else. Besides, Mr. President, Operation Alsos is an intelligence-gathering endeavor, not a rescue operation. Finding and extracting Kapsky could be very bloody; not your standard spy run. Nonetheless, we must make the effort. Heinrich Maier of the Austrian Resistance provided the OSS with drawings of the V-2. For those efforts dozens of others close to the Resistance were executed by the Gestapo.

"*This* is much bigger, far more advanced. Allen Dulles has obtained information from the Swiss that SS Obergruppenführer Hans Kammler has moved all superweapons production, including the V-2, underground. They have conscripted slave labor to work on rocket production. But most of them are idle for the moment."

"Idle? That doesn't sound like the Germans," Roosevelt said.

"They are reserving them, Mr. President, for production of weapons based on the Kapsky document."

"You're not suggesting that the Kapsky weapons, so to speak, are that much more important than the V-2?"

"Yes, sir. That's what I'm suggesting. Dulles believes Kapsky's formulae relate not just to one component, but to both an incendiary device and a rocket to deliver it."

"How is that different from the V-2?"

Donovan exhaled. "Sir, the Germans are struggling to get the V-2 to land in London, barely a thousand miles from the farthest launch site. Dulles says the Kapsky rocket could deliver payload across the Atlantic to the U.S."

Roosevelt froze. It was several seconds before he uttered the words "My God."

"I'm afraid it gets worse, Mr. President. Do you recall your instructions to Secretary Stimson regarding the Manhattan Project?"

"Of course," Roosevelt responded with both anticipation and trepidation.

"Under Operation Alsos we are to acquire as much information as possible about whether the Germans are also developing an atomic program."

"Operation Alsos wasn't to begin until September," Roosevelt said.

"Yes," Donovan said somberly. "Well, it may not need to go forward at all. The Soviets, by way of Dulles, say that the Kapsky information could permit the Germans to deliver an atomic payload."

A large glowing ash fell from the President's cigarette. He did not so much as flinch.

"Apocalyptic," Roosevelt concluded.

"In a manner of speaking."

Roosevelt sighed. "Stalin has been insisting on a conference, purportedly to discuss how to address the world landscape after the war."

"I'd say that's just a bit premature. The outcome of the war could go either way."

"Indeed," the President said. "That's why it's more likely the actual purpose for the conference is to place pressure on Britain and the U.S. to open a Western Front as soon as possible—yesterday, if Stalin had his way. The Red Army is admittedly engaged in titanic battles with the Nazis. The scale is nearly incomprehensible. He needs to alleviate the pressure immediately."

"Mr. President, where does he propose to conduct the meeting? I assume in the U.S., given the obvious."

Roosevelt chuckled amiably. "Given my obvious travel limitations?"

"Given the security implications of having the Big Three in one location at the same time."

"They have proposed Tehran, Iran," Roosevelt said.

"My lord, Mr. President, that is ridiculous. What kind of security is that? Skorzeny would be salivating at such an opportunity."

"I have confidence in our people—the Brits and the

Soviets included—and their ability to secure such a meeting."

"Needless risk, Mr. President."

Roosevelt shrugged indifferently. "The Kapsky document," he declared somewhat theatrically. "It sounds like a religious artifact, some piece of ancient parchment unearthed in the desert and transcribed with a prophecy of Armageddon."

Donovan exhaled uneasily. "Mr. President, that description may be more accurate than any of us care to admit."

CHAPTER 29

Gromov was bewildered by the speed with which he'd been conveyed to the Lubyanka. He'd been resting between assignments in the apartment of a female acquaintance when two NKVD thugs burst in and instructed him to accompany them by order of Aleksandr Belyanov. Gromov, ordinarily imperturbable, was a bit rattled.

Gromov became even more apprehensive when he was instructed to wait in one of the seemingly innumerable white-walled rooms on the lower level. These were not rooms intended for cordial conversations. They were rooms where various alleged enemies of the state were interrogated, often brutally. The macabre joke was that the walls were painted white so cleaning personnel could more easily spot the blood and other organic matter that often speckled the walls and floors. At least he wasn't in the basement, where limbs and intestines covered the floor in quantities sometimes dwarfing that of a slaughterhouse.

Gromov hadn't been seated more than a minute when he heard the unhurried, staccato cadence of Belyanov's heels on the stone floor of the outer corridor. Seconds later the door opened and two soldiers brandishing PPSh-41 submachine guns entered, followed by the chief of the OKRNKVD.

Gromov stood as Belyanov approached to within a few feet, flanked by the two soldiers. Their presence, though not quite unnerving, was troubling to say the least.

Belyanov observed Gromov in silence for several seconds that passed like minutes. He took another step closer, then said, "Twice shy, Comrade Gromov. Twice shy."

Gromov's brow furrowed with incomprehension. "Pardon, sir?"

Belyanov took yet another step forward, again flanked by the two guards.

"You've failed twice."

Gromov grew even more puzzled. "Respectfully, sir, in what sense?"

"Sit."

Gromov hesitated for a moment, glanced at the two guards, then sat. Belyanov remained standing, looming menacingly over Gromov. "You were given an assignment some time ago to acquire Professor Sebastian Kapsky and return him to us. You failed to do so. That was your first failure. A most pronounced one."

Gromov hesitated to defend himself, but concluded that if he didn't the situation would deteriorate rapidly. "Sir, Kapsky was dead before I could get to him, before anyone else could acquire him."

"The objective, Comrade Gromov, was not to secure Kapsky's body. It was to secure what was in his brain. Recall what I told you when we first met: 'If we fail to find him, we may not just lose the war, we will lose the future.'"

Gromov struggled not to respond with the obvious. He'd been dispatched to acquire the man too late. Kapsky had been dead for some time before Gromov had gotten to him. That wasn't Gromov's fault. It was the fault of those who had sent him on the mission in the first place.

"Sir, respectfully, I searched for and located Kapsky as fast as possible. He was dead before I arrived. He was dead before the Americans arrived . . ."

"You did not search the body," Belyanov hissed.

Gromov looked at him quizzically. "But I did, sir. There was nothing of any consequence. Nothing whatsoever."

Gromov could see Belyanov's jaws tighten and his eyes narrow. A recess of the assassin's brain imagined the scores of individuals for whom that image was the last they'd seen before oblivion.

"Nothing," Belyanov repeated. "Nothing?"

"Yes, sir."

"*Absolutely* nothing."

"Absolutely."

"You are certain? Unequivocally certain?"

Gromov felt a pinprick of anxiety just below the solar plexus. He'd searched Kapsky's body. He believed there'd been nothing on the corpse. Yet the tenor of Belyanov's questions obviously telegraphed that something was amiss. But how? Gromov decided it was better to confront the issue directly rather than be defensive.

"Sir, clearly you have information that is contrary to what I'm telling you. What I told you was accurate at the time I encountered Kapsky." Gromov nodded toward the two guards. "Respectfully, sir, no impertinence intended. Are these two permitted to hear this discussion?"

"They are part of my personal detail," Belyanov replied. "They hear everything, and they disclose only on pain of death."

"Then can you tell me what it is I allegedly missed?"

"There's no 'allegedly,' Gromov. I have told you before, we have very good sources. Especially in Washington. And they've informed us of a document's existence.

"You failed to retrieve a document that is now in the possession of the Germans. The Germans are deciphering the document at this moment. They are said to be ecstatic about the acquisition of such document. Indeed, the SS Obersturmführer who acquired the document has been promoted and is now Canaris's most trusted assistant." Belyanov paused. "Beria is furious."

At the mention of the name Gromov's pinprick of anxiety became a dagger. Thousands went to their deaths when Beria was merely irritated. Indeed, thousands perished even when Beria was content.

"Your malfeasance is not limited to failure to secure the Kapsky document," Belyanov continued. "You were instructed to eliminate the Americans. That was your second failure, a most egregious one, since our informants state that the very same Americans have been sent to acquire the document from the Germans."

Gromov refrained from stating that he'd eliminated three of the Americans' party, under impossible conditions, no less. To state such would merely provoke Belyanov.

"You are, however, most fortunate," Belyanov noted. "You will have what most others on this Earth seldom receive—a second chance. Although, under the circumstances, it may seem a punishment. Despite your manifest failures, Beria maintains that you are the best person to rectify the failure. Among other things, you are undoubtedly the most motivated."

Gromov managed to conceal his relief as his confidence returned. Indeed, he *hadn't* failed. He'd done as well as anyone could have under the circumstances. Better. He was an assassin without peer.

"You are commanded to finish the job you were originally given," Belyanov continued. "Get the Kapsky document, kill the Americans."

"Yes, Comrade Belyanov," Gromov said, invigorated.

"We have arranged transport to a small port on Kattegat Bay, Denmark. You will be provided all the details we have en route. We have contacts with the Danish Resistance there and they will provide assistance infiltrating into Germany. From there, you will be alone, but we have arranged a communication network with elements in both Denmark and Germany if we need to contact you. They will provide assistance when feasible and relay any information about the location of the Americans. But you will largely be on your own."

"I work best on my own."

Belyanov's tone became oddly sympathetic. "Gromov, the likelihood is that you'll be killed or captured, but we must do what we can to acquire that document. Beria thinks highly of you. I agree with Beria that you are the best option we have, so the unfortunate responsibility falls to you. But if you succeed, you will be venerated for decades to come."

"Thank you for the honor, sir."

Belyanov stepped back, as did the guards. "A transport is waiting for you."

Gromov rose to leave. Belyanov placed a hand on his shoulder and said, "Remember one thing. No one can know that it was you who killed the Americans. No one at all. Do you understand?"

Gromov nodded. He also understood that he would have to kill many more individuals than just the Americans to accomplish the objective.

CHAPTER 30

Canidy stood beside Kristin in the center cockpit as
Katla, Fulmar, and McDermott sat on a bench astern,
still chattering about the runs by the Messerschmitt
109s, McDermott insisting, and Fulmar disputing, that
a single sustained burst from just one of the aircraft's
MG 131 machine guns would have sunk the *Njord*.
Canidy watched, bemused. It was painfully obvious that
the dispute was for the purpose of impressing Katla, who
gamely entertained their arguments as if they knew
what they were talking about. Kristin, on the other
hand, remained all business. She wore the same fierce
expression as the first time she'd piloted the vessel with
Canidy's team on board. Canidy expected the expression
might simply be due to her concentration on the task.
Whatever the reason, Canidy found it exceptionally seductive.

Kristin pointed ahead a few degrees off the port bow.

Although Canidy hadn't noticed, the shoreline was on the horizon. "There. Approximately twenty degrees. We should be at the canal very soon."

Canidy turned to the rear. "Get your rucks and check your weapons. We'll be ashore soon. There may be enemy nearby this time."

Fulmar and McDermott went belowdecks to retrieve their equipment.

"The liaison from SHAEF has supplied us with generous allotments of fuel, medical equipment, and provisions," Kristin said. "We can sail the Baltic almost indefinitely, remaining as near to the coastline as possible. We have a rather powerful RCA marine console radio—also supplied by SHAEF—that will allow us to pick up your signal when you near the extraction point. We should be able to synchronize our respective arrivals."

Canidy nodded. "All solved, then? It sounds pretty simple until something breaks down. We have a small radio from our Professor Moriarty. Very weak signal, however."

"You strike me as a resourceful man, Major. Katla and I are fairly resourceful also. We'll improvise," Kristin assured.

"I like your confidence and optimism. I'd like to think I share those qualities. But I'm realistic enough to concede that the odds we don't come back alive aren't insubstantial."

"Consider that the United States of America chose you out of millions of soldiers in its armed forces to execute the assignment," Kristin said. "Your country obviously believes you have the greatest probability of succeeding."

"On a relative basis, yes," Canidy agreed. "But on an absolute basis, it's likely we're a little more than condemned men going through exercises on our way to our fates."

A grin creased Kristin's face. "Trying to generate sympathy for yourself, Major?"

Canidy raised his eyebrows. "Not interested in granting a condemned man his final wish?"

Fulmar and McDermott emerged onto the deck carrying their supplies and weapons—a carbine and a handgun. Katla followed and scanned the shoreline. She pointed to a spot ten degrees off the starboard bow. "There's the mouth of the canal. It appears more overgrown than the last time I saw it. Good cover. We will be there in minutes."

Canidy looked at McDermott. "Get the maps out. We'll need them right away."

"You're more anxious than last time," Kristin observed.

"Compared to this time, that was a walk in the park."

"Very fatalistic, Major Canidy."

"*Realistic*, Captain Thorisdottir." Canidy grinned, leaned close to Kristin, and whispered, "Maybe you'd re-reconsider granting a condemned man his last wish."

Kristin turned her face flush with Canidy and said softly, "I'll be here when you get back."

CHAPTER 31

To many, SS Standartenführer Konrad Maurer's stride appeared intimidating, even menacing. His powerful legs encased in highly polished black boots moved like pistons on a locomotive that would stop for nothing.

Maurer knew this. He wasn't trying to look intimidating or menacing, but didn't mind that he did. He enjoyed being feared. And he liked being treated with respect and deference. He was, after all, an SS Standartenführer who reported directly to the Genius. More than that, he was the person who had obtained and delivered perhaps the most consequential intelligence find of the war. It was likely that even the Führer was aware of that fact.

Maurer entered the antechamber to Vice Admiral Canaris's office and greeted the normally dour Oberstleutnant sitting at the desk. Maurer's newly enhanced status prompted the officer to acknowledge him with a measure of respect given only the Rommels, Guderians, and von Rundstedts. He pressed a buzzer, rose from his chair, and opened Canaris's office door.

Canaris stood next to a credenza adjacent to his desk with a sheaf of documents in his hands. He looked worried. Upon Maurer's entry, he placed the documents on the credenza, pointed to them, and said, "Problems, Maurer. Your great success spawns problems."

"I am afraid I do not understand, Herr Admiral."

Canaris moved to his desk chair and sat. He gestured for Maurer to sit in one of the high-backed leather chairs on the other side of the desk. After Maurer was seated, Canaris explained, "The Americans and the Russians know about the Kapsky document. They know we have it, and they are working to decipher it and employ it to the detriment of the Wehrmacht."

Maurer was somewhat surprised. "How do they know we have the document? And how do *we* know they know we have it?"

"The Americans, British, and Soviets all were searching for Kapsky as we were. All believed acquiring him held strategic significance. Naturally, their resistance networks would be alert to anything pertaining to Kapsky. We have intelligence leaks like any army in wartime."

"Yes, Herr Admiral. But how do we *know* they know?"

"Quite simply, because they have intelligence leaks also. It seems the Americans learned of the Kapsky document from a spy in Germany. In this building, perhaps. The Soviets appear to have a spy in the *American* government who relayed the information to the NKVD.

And *we* have a spy within the NKVD who relayed all of this information to us."

Maurer shook his head. Canaris continued.

"The Americans and the Soviets have each dispatched teams to acquire the document. We must conclude they are on their respective paths here at this very moment."

Maurer's face bore an expression that was a mix of skepticism and arrogance. "A worthless endeavor. Futile. They will sacrifice soldiers to obtain something that is under impenetrable guard and cannot otherwise be produced? The document never leaves the room. Everyone who enters is searched both upon entry and departure and only the most trusted are permitted entry. They are observed the entire time they are in the room to ensure no copies are made and ingested. The document script is far too long and complex to be memorized and the mathematicians analyzing the document are under twenty-four-hour surveillance."

"All true," Canaris agreed. "A suicide mission. Nonetheless, they are making the attempt, which is an indication of the importance they attach to the document."

"A document they have never seen."

"Yes. But they know who produced it. That is sufficient."

"And the fact they would even make the attempt tells us they believe they have a chance of obtaining it, however slight."

Canaris leaned forward in his chair. "Stalin will sacrifice tens of thousands to achieve a low-probability outcome. Lives are meaningless to him. But the Americans and British would not sacrifice lives for a futility."

Maurer grasped Canaris's point. "You believe obtaining the document may *not* be impossible. Neither the Americans nor Soviets have assistance of which we are unaware . . ."

"Just as we know both the Americans and Soviets are attempting to acquire the document, *they* must know something about a security vulnerability relating to the document. They must be receiving assistance from within this building."

"And you would like me to investigate and eliminate such vulnerabilities, Herr Admiral?"

Canaris shook his head. "I have already directed Hauptman Fischer toward such task. He and his men are conducting a thorough review of all individuals who are even remotely aware of the document and the security surrounding it. What I would like you to do, Standartenführer Maurer, is to go on the offensive. Find and destroy the men sent by the Americans and Soviets to acquire the document."

Canaris detected a rare uncertainty in Maurer's expression. "Do not be concerned that you will be intruding on the purview of the Gestapo. Himmler is aware of this. The Führer has been briefed and concurs."

Maurer struggled to conceal his exhilaration. The *Führer* concurs. The Führer himself concurs that SS Standartenführer Maurer—not Himmler, not the Gestapo—should lead the effort to safeguard the Fatherland's most precious strategic document. A document Maurer himself had obtained.

"It shall be done, Herr Admiral," Maurer said boldly. "What additional intelligence do we have regarding the efforts of the Americans and Soviets?"

". . . Don't forget the British," Canaris admonished lightly. "I must remind myself not to do the same. Churchill is perhaps the greatest thorn in the Führer's side, but we—many of us—have a tendency to merely include the British with the Americans, as if they are one.

"The intelligence we have is sparing, Maurer, but useful," Canaris continued. "Our source in the Lubyanka relates that the American team consists of three extremely well-trained, highly resourceful individuals. Two are Americans, one is an Englishman. The Americans are Major Richard Canidy and Lieutenant Eric Fulmar. The Englishman is a Sergeant Conor McDermott."

"Just three men, Herr Admiral? Are they serious?"

"Very much so, Maurer. Their assignment comes from and was fashioned by the most proficient unconventional warfare strategists the British and Americans have." Canaris nodded. "It is, I grant you, difficult to believe that three men could be expected to penetrate behind our lines into this building, obtain the Kapsky document, and successfully return to safety. Yet our informant in the Lubyanka relates that the Soviets are attempting to do the same thing with just *one* man, Major Taras Gromov. By all accounts a prolific assassin. Quite deadly."

Maurer's warrior instincts bristled upon hearing the description. *Maurer* was extremely well trained. *Maurer* was quite deadly. "I will destroy them, Herr Admiral," Maurer assured confidently.

"But to destroy them we must locate them, isolate them. And, preferably, well before they approach this building. Certainly the American team will be entering Poland from the Baltic, near Danzig. We surmise that a relay of resistance fighters familiar with the area between there and here will guide them. We have cartographers plotting the most likely routes of approach. They will provide you with their estimates and I will provide you with any reports we receive from our informants among the relevant resistance groups."

"Americans are sloppy, Herr Admiral," Maurer said. "They can be clever, but they tend to be cavalier and sloppy."

"Perhaps, Maurer," Canaris said. "But their cleverness can overcome their imprecision. Admittedly, their task is a near impossibility. But you should treat them as you would a force far more formidable. That also pertains to Gromov. It says something about him that the Soviets deem it sufficient to send a single man."

"I shall destroy him also," Maurer assured with a hint of irritation in his voice. *He* was more dangerous, more formidable, more competent than any of these four men. He'd proven just how dangerous, formidable, competent he was by obtaining the Kapsky document.

Now he would demonstrate how ruthless he could be.

CHAPTER 32

Major Dick Canidy liked to play the percentages. Except this time the percentages were that the three of them would never set foot on the Thorisdottirs' boat again. Nonetheless, he remained determined to do so.

Kristin had conveyed them to the same spot as before, but the place looked unfamiliar. The foliage was even denser than before and the canal water was dirty and rancid from the detritus of war.

Armed with an OSS compass and a map, they began moving westward with a sinking feeling that they were embarking on an impossibility. But a short time into the journey, a phantom appeared out of the brush.

And each of them beamed with joy.

It was Emil, only a short time later no longer a boy, if he'd ever been one. He was almost as tall as Canidy, with broad shoulders and a serious face that was taciturn, almost hostile, until he broke out into a grin. "You men look lost, once again," he taunted. "Need some help?"

Canidy clapped him on the shoulder. "You Polack son of a bitch. Dammit, you look good. Looks like you had a growth spurt. How in the hell did you know that we'd be here?"

"I did not. Commander Matuszek sent me to the area. We all have areas. We are assigned to harass the enemy. An OSS contact told Matuszek to look for men to take into Germany. I have been in the area for several days and saw your boat as it approached the coastline. It looked familiar, and truthfully, I was tired so I watched for the next half hour until it came to the dock."

"It's damn good to see you." Canidy shook Emil's shoulder. "Damn good."

Fulmar and McDermott each clapped Emil on the back.

"You're still in the fight," Fulmar said. "I will admit I was worried when I left you. After what we went through to get back to the coast . . . Honestly, I thought you'd have a hard time getting back to Matuszek. A boy among panzers. Thought you were likely dead. Boy, was I wrong."

"Yes, but not by much," Emil said. "I think I lost count of the number of times I should have been dead. What is the expression Americans use? I believe I am living on borrowed time."

"We're on our way west," Canidy said. "Any advice?"

"Yes," Emil said emphatically. "Do *not* go west. You will die if you go west."

"Orders," Canidy explained.

Emil shook his head in disgust. "Your orders will get you killed. I will wager you last twelve hours, no more."

Fulmar smiled sardonically. "Your previous experience didn't inspire a whole lot of faith in us?"

Emil shook his head once more. "It has nothing to do with you. It has to do with reality. Hundreds of thousands have died between here and the German border. You likely will be among them—not because of anything you do or do not do. But because of the fury of the war."

Canidy shrugged. "You're probably right, but we're on our way."

Emil asked, "Do you have any idea where you're going? How you're going to get there?"

"We do," Canidy replied with a hint of sarcasm. "We have all the good stuff. Maps, compasses . . ."

"Guides? Transportation?"

"We have the names of contacts along the way. They'll assist with transportation," Canidy replied.

"No, they will not," Emil countered. "The ones who can be trusted and who know what they are doing are probably dead. Those that can be trusted but *don't* know what they are doing will *get* you dead. The rest cannot be trusted. And they, of course, will make *sure* you're dead."

"You're a real ray of sunshine, Emil," Canidy said, but there was a hint of concession in his voice. "Do you have any suggestions?"

"My suggestion is *do not go*. But if you must, get the

best guide you can find. He may prolong your lives a day or two more than would otherwise be the case."

Canidy sighed. "Can you recommend anyone who fits that description? The best guide we can find?"

"Me," Emil said bluntly. "I'm the best. We will survive a day or two longer, then we will all die."

Canidy, Fulmar, and McDermott glanced at one another. Canidy nodded. "Okay, Emil. We vote to live another day or two. Hopefully, you're wrong."

Emil said, "I am not wrong. But before I can lead you I must speak to Commander Matuszek."

"Of course," Canidy said. "We understand. We don't want you to get in trouble. How long will it take to reach him?"

"He's not far from here. To the south. I should be able to get to his position and back before the end of the day."

"All right," Canidy said. "But we're going with you. We can't afford to wait in one place an entire day for you to get back."

Emil turned southward and began walking. "Follow me."

They advanced in a column. Emil, followed by Canidy, then McDermott, with Fulmar bringing up the rear. Emil moved cautiously but at a brisk pace. Canidy didn't recognize the terrain and surmised they were moving along a different path than they had last time. "What's the German presence like now?"

"Worse than before," Emil replied. "Because we have had a few successes now and then they have been retaliating quite viciously. They were never merciful, but now they allow no quarter whatsoever." Emil paused. "I believe the American saying is 'they take no prisoners.'"

They walked silently for no more than a quarter hour before they heard the rumble of heavy vehicles. Canidy, Fulmar, and McDermott simultaneously felt a spike of anxiety, recalling their encounter with a panzer column.

The four sensed a subtle vibration of the earth, Emil motioning for them to stop and lower themselves to the ground.

They lay flat amid the foliage as the vibrations increased and the rumbling grew louder. Less than thirty seconds later a German truck carrying approximately a dozen sullen but alert-looking German troops drove slowly past over uneven ground flattened somewhat by the tracks of previous heavy vehicles. The troops had the unmistakable appearance of the battle-hardened—a forward pitch to their torsos and a distant, almost vacant look to their eyes, one that conveyed both fatalism and determination.

The four remained prone for nearly a minute after the transport passed. Emil was the first to get up, but immediately sank back to the ground as the rumble of another approaching vehicle grew louder.

"At this rate," Canidy hissed, "we'll get to Tirpitzufer around 1950."

Moments later a Panzerkampfwagen IV appeared, moving at ten kilometers per hour with a soldier in its turret wearing headphones.

The four lay prone for nearly a minute after the panzer

passed, waiting for another vehicle or patrol. None came. They rose in unison and continued southward at a brisk pace, Canidy walking alongside Emil.

"How have you folks in the *Armia* been faring?" Canidy asked. "You and Matuszek's men?"

"About as well as could be expected. We are outmanned and outgunned, but our spirits are good, considering," Emil replied. "The Germans, despite having every military advantage imaginable, are showing signs of fatigue and perhaps even hesitancy. We have, of course, heard about their setbacks in Stalingrad and now in Kursk. Yet we are doing self-defeating things."

They came to a clearing that revealed a mammoth abandoned facility that Canidy speculated had once been a metalworks plant of some kind. The ground surrounding the building was pocked with shallow depressions from mortar and artillery fire. The structures appeared lifeless until they approached to within fifty feet, whereupon they were surrounded by more than thirty men and women that seemed to materialize from the debris strewn throughout the site.

A small woman with one arm approached Emil. She held a Tokarev in her remaining hand and scanned Canidy, Fulmar, and McDermott wearily. Emil said to them, "Stay here."

After a brief, hushed, but highly animated discussion, Emil returned and said, "We lost forty-three while I was gone—as I said, Germans are no longer taking prisoners, literally. She says Matuszek has taken some men on a retaliation patrol. He should be back shortly."

"Can you afford to lose that many?" Fulmar asked.

"We cannot afford to lose anyone," Emil replied matter-of-factly.

"How frequently does this happen?" Canidy asked.

"Recently, almost daily. A few days ago, my friend Roman was killed. Today, my closest friend Milo is among the dead."

Canidy scrutinized Emil's face for any traces of emotion. He detected none.

"Follow me," Emil said.

He led them through the skeletal remains and rubble of the enormous facility, to what appeared to have once been an office of some sort. Three of its walls remained intact. The fourth was riddled with holes from machine-gun fire. There were several chairs and a ten-by-four metal table covered in dust in the center of the room. A filing cabinet lay on its side in the corner.

"Wait here," Emil instructed. "I need to see if any of my other mates were killed while I was gone."

Emil disappeared and the three stood in the dusty office examining the surroundings.

"How long do you think you could put up with conditions like this?" Fulmar asked.

"It's his country," Canidy said. "I suspect he'll put up with it as long as it takes."

"Or as long as he can," McDermott added. "Emil's taller than the last time we saw him, but he's a lot thinner, too. Handsome lad, but I couldn't help notice the scars and fresh cuts on his neck and arms. He's had some scrapes since we last saw him."

An elderly man who couldn't have been more than five feet tall emerged from the gloom of the plant carrying an M29 between the crook of his right arm and his waist. He smiled—revealing only upper and lower molars—and motioned with his left hand to put down their weapons. The three hesitated for a moment until they understood. As soon as they placed their handguns on the dirt floor, Matuszek, surrounded by Emil and four other men carrying rifles, also emerged from the gloom.

Matuszek stopped a few feet from them and gazed upon them with an expression of disgust. "You look no different from the last time we met. I must say, I'm impressed by your bravery and absolutely astonished by your stupidity."

Matuszek thrust out his meaty right hand to be shaken first by Canidy, then Fulmar, and then McDermott. Then he withdrew two steps to look them up and down once more. "I suppose you will do," the hardened resistance commander said. "If someone has to be sacrificed, it may as well be three expendable idiots."

Canidy squinted. "What makes you think we're being sacrificed?"

"You're on a futile assignment and everyone knows you're on a futile assignment. You are doomed, my friends." Matuszek smiled as he predicted their demise.

Canidy, although pleased to see the grizzled resistance commander, became more irritated. "What the hell do you mean we're doomed?"

"You are in search of the worst-kept secret in all of

Europe, my friends," Matuszek replied. He put up a hand to ward off the obvious question. "Understand, we do not know *specifically* the terms of your mission. We know that it has something to do with a certain highly critical item in possession of the Germans. We further suspect that you are to obtain such item. An item in the custody of Canaris."

The perplexed look worn by the three prompted Matuszek to add, "You cannot penetrate Germany to your target. No matter how determined and talented you may be. You will be captured, and if you are fortunate, you will be killed immediately rather than suffer interrogation by the Gestapo or SS."

The three stared blankly at Matuszek. After several seconds of silence, Canidy asked, "How in hell do you *think* you know what you are talking about?"

"There is no leak in your Office of Strategic Services, old friend," Matuszek assured. "Do not worry about that. It is simple deduction. General Donovan communicates with us, as necessary, through numerous levels of intermediaries. We have heard he needs logistical help with an extremely important operation, an operation into Germany itself. Something that—shall we say— audacious would necessarily involve something of extreme importance and would have to be executed by men daring to the point of suicidal idiocy in order to obtain—"

"No need for flattery," Canidy said.

"So, here you are," Matuszek continued. "My old dear dog, now deceased three years, could deduce why you are here and that you will not be successful. It is not an improbable mission. It is an impossible mission. But the item is of such critical importance that Mr. Donovan has convinced your President that an effort must be made to obtain it. Or, more accurately, Mr. Donovan, with the indispensable assistance of Mr. Churchill, has convinced your President that history demands the risk be taken."

"At least we're making history," Canidy said amiably.

"Yes. Although your names will be lost—nothing more than anonymous heroes about whom literature is written to inspire the next generation of cannon fodder."

Canidy smiled. "So you are saying Emil can help us commit suicide?"

Matuszek smiled in return. "If you choose to commit suicide, that is your affair. Emil can assist, if he wishes, but he has more important things to do than that. You may have noted that the Germans are trying to conquer the world, and are doing a passable impression of doing so." Matuszek glanced at his four men, who smiled. "I suspect you prefer not to enter Germany and be torn to pieces—as you undoubtedly would in short order—if there were another means by which to accomplish your objective."

Canidy, Fulmar, and McDermott exchanged intrigued looks.

"What are you talking about?" Canidy asked.

"I'm not suggesting you will, or ever could, accomplish your objective," Matuszek replied. "But I am suggesting, more accurately, *saying*, that there is another means by which you may accomplish your mission without embarking on the impossible task of entering Canaris's lair."

"I'm all ears," Canidy said. "But understand our skepticism. We're supposed to—as you indicated—obtain something located in Germany, but you tell us we can accomplish that without going to Germany?"

"Better. Not only do you not have to go to Germany, but you can acquire what you need here in Poland. Still quite hazardous, but not certain death. And you may give the Allies a strategic advantage for decades to come."

Matuszek's response raised several obvious questions. But before Canidy could pose any of them, a piercing whistle preceded an explosion that catapulted all ten men several feet into the air and propelled them against the corrugated metal walls of the office.

Sztum, Poland

Daria Bacior appeared uniquely out of place in Nazi-occupied Poland. She had none of the outward manifestations of someone who had witnessed monstrous atrocities, suffered prolonged bouts of hunger and thirst, and had desperately hidden from the enemy in conditions that were best described as feral.

Somehow, years into the most horrific conflict in human history, Daria Bacior retained the appearance and bearing of a nineteenth-century czarina. She was tall, redheaded, and strikingly beautiful, with an intelligent, erudite-looking countenance unblemished by lines or scars. Her clothing was neat and clean, and she managed somehow to project an utter lack of consternation regarding the madness that surrounded her. She looked, in a word, innocent.

It was a façade.

Daria was, in fact, quite beautiful, but she was a cunning and determined agent of the Home Army. She had not killed any of the enemy, but her actions had resulted in the deaths of hundreds of German soldiers, the destruction of hundreds of metric tons of enemy equipment, and the obliteration of nearly a half-dozen enemy installations.

Daria's most notable contribution to the resistance effort was something to which, despite her intelligence and cunning, she had been entirely oblivious for weeks. Several weeks ago, she'd had the feeling she was being watched. Not by the Germans, but by someone else. A few times she thought she'd glimpsed someone watching her from behind a tree or edifice, but upon closer inspection saw no one there. Then she did see someone; tall, lanky, haggard, with worn clothing. He didn't look like a soldier or partisan. He didn't look like a shopkeeper or farmer.

He'd appear at odd times—just for a moment—before disappearing. Daria thought perhaps her imagination was playing tricks on her.

Then two weeks ago, the apparition appeared before her as she walked to the run-down barn just outside of Sztum, south of Danzig, where she'd often made contact with *Armia*.

The apparition said, "I need assistance getting to the coast."

His voice was low, neutral, and unthreatening. He looked intelligent and sincere. And worn to the bone.

Nonetheless, Daria kept walking. She hadn't survived this long in Nazi-occupied Poland by being naïve. Still, she felt a pang of remorse for not at least listening for an explanation. She told her *Armia* contact about the encounter, who waved it off as inconsequential.

The next day the apparition appeared again, this time closer to the barn. He appeared calm, and once again, unthreatening.

"I need help and I believe you can provide it."

Daria continued to walk without varying her pace. If an informant was watching the encounter, it would appear natural.

"I do not know you."

"Yes," the apparition acknowledged. "That is a problem. I understand. All I can say to assure you is that I am not a collaborator or spy. I am a Pole in need of help."

"And I am a Pole with no resources," Daria said warily.

"I will be grateful for anything you could do to help me get to the coast. Anywhere on the coast."

Daria said nothing and kept walking at the same pace. The apparition followed silently several meters behind. They walked for another minute until Daria entered the barn. The apparition continued past the barn, walked for another minute, then doubled back, surveyed his surroundings, and ducked into the barn. Daria was waiting just inside, a man brandishing a Poln M29 at her side.

"Do not move or you will be shot where you stand," Daria said coldly. The apparition did as he was told. A second man approached the apparition from the rear and searched him for weapons. After a few seconds he withdrew.

"Will you help?" the apparition asked.

"Who are you?" Daria asked.

"I escaped Katyn some time ago."

"I asked who you are, not where you are from."

"My name is Sebastian Kapsky."

Daria stepped backward and examined the apparition's face. "Repeat yourself."

"My name is Sebastian Kapsky."

Daria stared at him for several seconds. "Professor Sebastian Kapsky?"

"That is correct."

"You are a liar. Professor Sebastian Kapsky is dead."

The apparition smiled wanly. "Believe me, I am very much relieved that you and others believe so. Were it otherwise, I would not have a prayer of getting to the coast."

"The Germans were looking for Kapsky for quite some time. An SS Obersturmführer ravaged much of our region, interrogating scores of people and murdering dozens in the process. He did not locate Kapsky, but the Home Army eventually did. Rather, they located his corpse. That was the end of it." Daria glanced at the man holding the rifle. "I do not know what your intentions are, but I do not trust you. At my command or at the slightest provocation, Markus will be pleased to kill you."

The apparition raised his hands, palms toward Daria. "I have absolutely no intention of doing you or anyone associated with you harm. I have been moving about for over three years attempting to evade capture after escaping Katyn. Home Army assisted me when they could—often at the cost of their lives. The German patrols near the coast have been so numerous that I've not been able to penetrate. But then, among the multitude of corpses strewn throughout my travels, there was one that presented an opportunity—a ghoulish one, but such is war. I estimate the poor soul had been dead no more than a few hours, for there was no discernible decomposition. And it looked enough like me that he could have been a brother if not a twin. So I devised a scheme whereby I dressed the corpse in my clothes and left telltales that I hoped would convince the Germans to conclude that the corpse *was* me. And, therefore, they would discontinue their active search. It appears to have been successful. The SS Obersturmführer who led the German effort to capture me, and his men, seem to have left the area."

Daria scrutinized the apparition's face for several moments before turning to Markus, who tilted his head and shrugged, signaling he thought the story at least plausible.

Daria's eyes narrowed. "If you are indeed Kapsky you must understand that many Poles—perhaps more than a hundred—have died because of you. The SS Obersturmführer—an animal—who led the search for you executed many Poles to extract information concerning your location. Many, many more were tortured and disfigured because of you." Daria bit off the end of the sentence and spat. "Including my younger brother, Karol. He can no longer see. His eyes were gouged out."

Tears welled in the apparition's eyes and his face contorted with anguish. Daria immediately regretted her statement but could not summon an apology.

The apparition cast his eyes to the straw on the floor. "Many have been sacrificed because of me. I know. I know that. More acutely than even you, I wager. Please believe me when I say to you that I have many times considered surrendering myself. But I made a calculation. Perhaps an erroneous one. Undoubtedly one with which you would vehemently disagree. The calculation was that many more Poles—perhaps millions—might perish if the Nazis captured me and forced me to help them. And not just Poles, millions upon millions of others as well."

The apparition composed himself and looked at Daria. "I have given thought to killing myself, but I cannot do it. I suppose if I were captured, I might do so, but as long as there is a chance I might escape, I do not have the capacity to take my own life. I am sorry."

Daria and Markus once again exchanged looks. This time Markus's gesture was more emphatic. The phantom's story seemed not just plausible, but probable. Who would make up such a story? And for what purpose?

Daria silently scrutinized the apparition, debating the merits and consequences of assisting him. If he was a Nazi agent, rendering assistance could expose the entire network of resistance agents and Home Army fighters to the Germans, resulting in their likely extermination.

Were she just to ignore him—and if his story were true—she might be providing the Germans a significant tactical, if not strategic, advantage. She decided to assist him . . . cautiously.

"You may stay here—it is relatively safe—until I am able to find a more secure location for you. I will ensure that you are given provisions." Daria turned to Markus but continued to address the apparition. "Should you provide the slightest impetus for doing so, Markus is authorized to shoot you—in the foot or in the head—whatever he deems appropriate for the circumstances.

"I will send word to one of our more resourceful *Armia* commanders about your existence. If he concurs, and only if he concurs entirely, we will convey you to him. He may be able to get you to the coast and secure transfer for you." Daria shook her head and sighed. "You understand the risks to all of us with this course of action," Daria said. "You better merit such risk."

"I am grateful and owe you a debt," the apparition responded with a slight bow.

"Your gratitude is immaterial to me," Daria said coldly. "You better be worth it or we'll find and kill you."

CHAPTER 33

Canidy lay on the floor of the office, desperately trying to suck air into his lungs. The explosion from the 7.5-centimeter KwK L/24 had created a temporary vacuum while also knocking the wind out of everyone in the room. Canidy's eyes grew wide as he inhaled against the lack of oxygen, his body feeling as if he were entombed in concrete. When the first rush of air did enter his lungs, he then felt as if he were drowning. He stabilized his breathing within seconds, only to be overcome by a sensation suggesting nearly every bone in his body had been pulverized. Mercifully, the sensation lasted only seconds, after which he looked about to see what had happened to the others. They all appeared to be alive and grappling with the same sensations he was experiencing. He could see Matuszek's mouth moving but could hear nothing except a shrill ringing that seemed to come from within his skull.

Canidy rose to one knee, fell and rose again, before bracing himself and struggling to his feet. As he stood, he heard Matuszek's voice pierce through the ringing.

"*Move now.* As fast as you're able." He pointed behind Canidy to where a moment earlier there had been a wall.

Canidy shouted at Fulmar and McDermott to move, but they were already sprinting to the cavity in the edifice toward the woods beyond. Matuszek and his men, save one, did the same. The one who didn't no longer had legs for locomotion.

A second explosion blew all of them off their feet and sprawling onto the soft carpet of pine needles blanketing the forest floor. Once again, Canidy and the rest fought to suck air into their lungs as their eyes darted about, struggling to regain their bearings and reacquire their weapons. A blanket of dirt and debris rained upon them as they once again secured their weapons and started running as hard and as fast as they could from the source of the mayhem.

A fraction of a second later yet another explosion staggered but did not upend them as they ran. A random burst of MG 34 machine-gun fire followed them, to no effect other than to cause them to run even harder and farther.

The next shell exploded forty meters and at a seventy-degree angle to their right—indicating that rather than aiming for them, the Germans were simply saturating the area with fire.

Still, they kept running.

They ran until the fire was well behind them.

"Infernal panzers everywhere," Matuszek said between gasps for air. "They fire because they can, not because they have a particular target in mind. They just want to destroy."

Canidy said, "I thought the Wehrmacht was under orders to conserve fuel and ammunition."

Matuszek shook his head dismissively. "No, that is just German precision. They still like to shoot things up as often as they can." Matuszek said to his men, "All but Emil return to camp." His men vanished into the woods in seconds.

They continued moving away from the fire for ten minutes, when Canidy stopped and turned to Matuszek.

"Finish telling me how we save the world without getting ourselves annihilated in the process."

"Frankly, my friend, almost anything has a higher probability of success than infiltrating Germany and absconding with a document in the highly protective custody of the SS. An insane task."

"Insane tasks are what we do."

"Perhaps, but at least give yourselves a possibility, if not a probability, of success."

"You have our attention," Canidy said as they continued to thread through the woods.

"The item you are seeking, the one in Canaris's possession, is a document obtained by the SS from a deceased Polish mathematician."

Canidy said nothing.

"You need not confirm," Matuszek continued. "It may, however, interest you that reports of the deceased

Polish mathematician's demise may have been premature."

Canidy stopped walking, which caused the others to stop also. "What in hell do you mean, *'reports of the deceased mathematician's demise'*? You were there. You saw his rotting corpse. That corpse wasn't coming back to life in this world."

"Perhaps not that corpse, my friend," Matuszek conceded. "But did it occur to you that maybe we were all wrong and the corpse was not that of the mathematician?"

Canidy, Fulmar, and McDermott stared at Matuszek in silence.

"You took us to the corpse. We determined it was Professor Sebastian Kapsky. And evidently the Germans did, too," Canidy said.

"The document in Canaris's possession allegedly came from the corpse," Fulmar added.

"Yes," Matuszek acknowledged. "All true. Note that I said 'perhaps.'"

"Look," Canidy said, "'perhaps' doesn't cut it. We're on an assignment. From the little Donovan has chosen to tell us, it's a pretty damn important one; suicide missions usually aren't about something trivial.

"Now, believe me, I'd rather be on a mission that had a reasonable likelihood of success, while permitting me to get laid in the process. Unless you have something concrete, we're doing precisely what Donovan told us to do."

Matuszek shook his head again. "War is never about

certainty. Success and survival depends upon choosing the most viable option. And having a spot of luck. I cannot guarantee anything, but I have been fighting for ages and have lost many men. I've lost fewer over time with the benefit of experience. That experience tells me that there is a way to actually accomplish your seemingly impossible task and survive the mission."

"Well, stop beating around the bush," Fulmar said. "What the hell are you talking about? What have you got?"

"Professor Sebastian Kapsky may not be dead after all."

The looks on the faces of Canidy, Fulmar, and McDermott were of derision. Canidy's also betrayed contempt.

"He was doing a pretty good imitation of being dead when we saw him," Canidy said.

"*Someone* was doing a pretty good imitation of being dead," Matuszek agreed. "But there is reason to suspect that person may not have been Kapsky."

"This is absolutely nuts," Fulmar said. "Everyone saw him. We saw him. You saw him. And your troops saw him. Apparently, the Germans saw him and came to the same conclusion. *One* case of mistaken identity I get. But *everyone* making the same mistake reduces the probability that it is, in fact, a mistake to near zero."

"Besides," Canidy said, "the clincher is the document. Our intelligence sources maintain it was retrieved by the SS from *inside* one of Kapsky's body cavities. Apparently, the vaunted SS discipline couldn't prevent someone from squawking about it. On top of that, the genius Canaris and the rest of the infallible *Übermenschen* are sure as hell acting like they discovered Kapsky's Holy Grail."

"Misjudgments, errors, mistakes—they are all inescapable components of war," Matuszek said. "I have made more than my share, regretfully. And scores have paid the price for my missteps. Many have died because of my mistakes. I live with it only because I know I used all of my faculties to make the best judgments I could possibly make."

Canidy stopped walking and turned to face Matuszek. The others stopped also. "Look. *You* live with *your* mistakes. Don't expect us to make mistakes of our own. Hell, we don't even know what the hell you're talking about."

Matuszek pointed ahead. "Keep walking. The last thing you need is another panzer surprise."

"We're on our way to Germany, pal," Canidy said. "We'd be immensely grateful if you loaned us Emil to help us get there. The guy is a damn genius. Donovan gave us a task and we're gonna execute it or die trying."

"You will die trying. That's almost a certainty." Matuszek pointed in a southeasterly direction. "Keep moving while I tell you a brief story. Then if you like, you can take Emil—if he volunteers. I will not order it but will allow it." Matuszek halted abruptly, causing everyone to freeze in their tracks. They listened for a full minute before Matuszek resumed walking and the others followed suit.

"A short time ago one of our most reliable operatives had an encounter with an individual with a rather peculiar story. This individual had been observing our person for some time and apparently concluded she was neither careless nor a collaborator. She, in turn, judged him to be sober and truthful."

"Skip the background," Canidy said curtly. "Get to the point."

"The individual identified himself as Dr. Sebastian Kapsky."

Canidy stopped walking again and faced Matuszek. "You've really disappointed me. Everything about you to this point said 'tough, sober, competent.' Now you're telling us ghost stories." Canidy shook his head and resumed walking. "Telling ghost stories or stories you want us to believe. Stories *you* want to believe."

Matuszek nodded. "Skepticism and cynicism are good qualities in a commander, in a leader. It's more likely to keep you and those in your command alive."

"Damn right," Canidy concurred. "And it keeps you in the good graces of the man who gave you an assignment. In our case, a *very* serious man who has earned just about every citation known to a fighting man. Not someone to be trifled with. He gives you an assignment. You execute it. That simple."

Matuszek seized Canidy by the arm, startling him.

"Do not be an idiot, Major. I know of Donovan and his reputation. It's well earned. And I know how Donovan and men of his caliber think." Matuszek dropped Canidy's arm and closed to within inches of Canidy's face—their chests nearly bumping. With his jaw jutting forward, the resistance commander vaguely resembled Donovan himself. "Donovan chose you because he *expects* you will not blindly follow orders, but, rather, use your judgment; to improvise and change direction when the occasion demands." Matuszek poked Canidy hard in the chest for emphasis. "*Think*. That's why you are on this mission. *Think*."

Canidy swatted Matuszek's finger away. "I *think* you're nuts. Look, we have a short time frame to get this done. The longer the mission lasts, the greater chance it fails, that we end up dead or in a German POW camp." Canidy pointed to the rear. "Hell, we nearly got our butts blasted less than twenty minutes ago. We don't have the time or luxury to improvise. We have time to take one route, into Germany and to the Abwehr. We don't have time to go anywhere else. We have to commit to one destination and one destination only."

Fulmar came to within a few feet of the two. "Dick, my vote is to find the guy claiming to be Kapsky."

Canidy stepped back from Matuszek and examined his friend quizzically. "What the hell are you talking about?"

"Pretty simple, really. If we go into Germany, we're not getting the document, we're getting dead. Plain and simple. Sure, we can make a valiant effort, but in the end we're dead and no document.

"If we go to wherever the guy claiming to be Kapsky is, we may still get killed. But we have a better chance of staying alive."

Canidy looked incredulous. "We *may* have a better chance of staying alive, but no document. And we go back to Donovan empty-handed, telling him we went in the *opposite* direction from his instructions?"

Fulmar shook his head. "Matuszek's right. Donovan is the king of improvisation and adaptability. He *expects* that from *us*. Think about it, Dick: What's better, a document allegedly prepared by Kapsky, or the man himself?"

"Presuming he's Kapsky. Whom everyone has seen dead."

"I'm afraid I'm with Eric," McDermott said. "I'm not trying to avoid going to Tirpitzufer, although I have no desire to commit suicide. It seems to me, however, that the very implausibility of Kapsky being alive makes it that much more likely this bloke who claims to be Kapsky is, in fact, Kapsky. What benefit would anyone gain from claiming to be a math professor who everyone thinks is dead? And by everyone, I mean the tiny handful of people who even know who he is. Rather odd, wouldn't you say?"

Fulmar nodded emphatically. "McDermott's got a point, Dick. A guy who needs help doesn't say, 'Hey, my name is Kapsky. You don't know me, but I'm dead and I do math. Can you help?'"

A faint smile crossed Canidy's face and he turned to Emil. "Okay. Let's go. Lead the way."

Puzzled, Fulmar asked, "What?"

"We're going to find the guy who claims to be Kapsky," Canidy said.

"You changed your mind that quickly?"

"What can I say? You guys are very persuasive," Canidy explained.

A look of realization crossed Fulmar's face. "You just wanted buy-in from the rest of us, didn't you?" Fulmar said. It was a conclusion, not a question.

"Damn right. If we're going to disobey Wild Bill Donovan's orders, I sure as hell don't want anyone to say it was *my* idea."

CHAPTER 34

There were Germans everywhere. Dour, uncompromising faces. The lamps along the pier illuminated their forms. They looked as if they would kill without provocation.

They were stationed at equidistant points along the pier and along the dock, rifles slung over their shoulders. In disciplined German fashion, they looked straight ahead. Unflinching.

But Gromov knew they were alert and could see everything. At least everything that was illuminated. He quietly slid off the dinghy and into the water nearly fifty meters from shore. He swam slowly toward the underside of the pier, careful not to make a sound. Once there, he grasped one of the struts supporting the boardwalk and waited in the gloom.

Less than ten minutes later he saw a shadow under the pier approximately thirty meters to the left. Its outline was that of a man, but beyond that he could discern nothing. It remained stationary for about a minute, as if observing him, before it began closing the distance between them. It took nearly a minute, the figure's pace slow, to minimize the possibility of any splashes or other noises.

When the figure drew to within three meters, he stopped, grasping a strut for support. Even in the gloom Gromov discerned the figure was a large, heavy man with thick, short blond hair. A Norseman.

"Magnus Nielsen," the Norseman whispered.

"Gromov."

Nielsen pointed behind Gromov, where the pier extended for another one hundred twenty meters. "Go there," Nielsen whispered.

They proceeded under the boardwalk, pulling themselves slowly from strut to strut to minimize splashes. It took several minutes to reach the end of the pier, where a small black raft sat, a middle-aged woman in the bow. Nielsen slowly and quietly hoisted himself onto the raft, followed by Gromov.

"Bridgette," the woman said.

"Gromov."

Bridgette began paddling slowly away from the pier. Gromov was certain they'd be detected by one of the German sentries, but they were facing toward the sea, oblivious to the raft's presence behind them. A minute later Nielsen grabbed another oar and began paddling also, quickening their pace. They proceeded at a forty-five-degree angle away from the pier and toward the rocky shoreline, saying nothing the entire time.

When they reached the shore, Nielsen secured the raft by looping a rope around one of the rocks and all three scrambled off the raft and into the adjacent woods. Nielsen led them to a small clearing with an abandoned, crumbling water well.

Nielsen stopped and turned to Gromov. "I have excellent news for you, Gromov," he said. "Your suicide mission is aborted. You have new orders."

Gromov blinked at Nielsen uncomprehendingly.

"You need not continue to Tirpitzufer," Nielsen continued. "Not that you had any realistic hope of getting there anyway. An associate of Jan Kubis forwarded a communique earlier this morning. You are being redirected to Poland."

Gromov frowned. "I have orders, Nielsen. You are to escort me to Forst Grunewald next to Tirpitzufer. This is an assignment of paramount importance." Gromov placed his hand on the rubberized holster containing his Tokarev TT-33. The gesture wasn't lost on Nielsen, who raised his hands to his chest, palms outward.

"What I'm telling you is that your orders have changed, Gromov. As have mine. Good fortune for us both."

"Who changed the order?"

Nielsen looked perplexed. "I do not know *who* changed them. I only know that they were changed."

"Who *gave* them?"

"Belyanov," Bridgette said.

Gromov looked at Bridgette. Her face was difficult to make out in the dark. Gromov reached into a waterproof pouch hanging from his belt, produced a book of matches, struck one on the box, and held it near Bridgette's face. She could tell that Gromov was surprised by her appearance.

"I was considered fairly pretty twenty years ago, Gromov."

Gromov didn't respond. Although she had a few lines across her forehead and around the corners of her eyes, Bridgette was astonishingly attractive. Indeed, Gromov found that the age lines added to her appeal.

"I am the leader of our cell," Bridgette explained. "We received a communication that originated from Czech Resistance only a few hours ago that you are not to go to Tirpitzufer."

"And these orders came from Belyanov?"

Bridgette shrugged. "That is what we were told. I do not know Belyanov. I only know that Belyanov, whoever he is, gave the order. The order was conveyed through Czech Resistance mere hours ago."

Gromov was both irritated and perplexed. He had made this journey to occupied Denmark to execute a mission that, if successful, would both vindicate and glorify him. He had no illusions about its difficulty. But as Belyanov had stated, a successful execution would nearly beatify him.

"What is this of Poland?" Gromov asked, his voice dripping with skepticism. "What am I to do there?"

"You are to execute your mission, Gromov," Bridgette replied matter-of-factly.

"My mission is to obtain a certain document in the Abwehr," Gromov said, not disclosing the additional instructions to kill the Americans. "I cannot obtain a document located in Berlin by going to Poland."

"I am merely the messenger." Bridgette shrugged. "Holger Danske was informed by UVOD by way of an *Armia* fighter by the name of Markus Zuchowski that a gentleman who calls himself Kapsky is under their protection."

Gromov stood silently, arms slack at his sides for several moments. "Dr. Sebastian Kapsky is dead."

Bridgette shrugged once more, indifferent. "Perhaps so. But apparently your Belyanov suspects he is alive and instructs that you locate and secure this Kapsky. As soon as possible. Apparently, Belyanov believes others are, or soon will be, searching for Kapsky also. He also instructs that the remainder of your orders, whatever those might be, remain unchanged."

Gromov stood contemplatively for several moments. "Did Belyanov by any chance state precisely how I am to get to Poland and locate Kapsky? I haven't the slightest idea how to get there. I did not plan for this." Frustrated, Gromov waved toward Nielsen. "Is Magnus supposed to guide me there? Did Belyanov provide any guidance whatsoever?"

Bridgette smiled sympathetically. "Magnus is big and beautiful," she noted. "But he has his limitations. I will take you to Markus Zuchowski. From there you may execute your mission."

Gromov's jaw tightened. "It must be at least a thousand kilometers from here."

"Approximately," Bridgette conceded. "Thus, I suspect you should want to get on your way without a moment to waste." She observed the look of consternation on Gromov's face. "You should be pleased, Mr. Gromov. Your original mission was a death sentence. Now, at the very least, you have a prospect of survival." Bridgette drew closer to Gromov and inspected his face. "But mere survival, though welcome, is not sufficient for you, is it, Mr. Gromov? You have the look of someone who wishes to be a hero. Not that you aren't already. But you wish to be spoken about in worshipful tones. In awe. Preferably on national holidays. Am I correct?"

The killer Gromov, whose face was normally rigid and taciturn, looked down at Bridgette and, despite his best efforts, grinned. She'd accurately taken the measure of the assassin within mere minutes of meeting him.

"I am Russian," he said and shrugged.

"You need men to respect you and women to crave you," she said in a mockingly seductive voice. "You want martial hymns to be written about you, sung reverently on national holidays."

The assassin concluded that he liked this woman. Although she was Danish and more than a decade older than he, she seemed to understand him almost immediately, intuitively. Oddly, as opposed to every other woman he'd known, she didn't seem intimidated by him. Neither was she afraid. He sensed she was a kindred spirit; a killer like he, though by circumstance and necessity rather than nature and preference.

Bridgette, eyes still holding Gromov's, said, "Magnus, go back to the shore and send the signal."

For a big man, Magnus moved with surprising speed and agility. He was out of sight within mere moments.

"We've already arranged for a Kriegsmarine Schnellboot to take us to a location off the coast of Poland."

Gromov raised his eyebrows. "A Schnellboot?"

"Yes. It even flies a Reichskriegsflagge."

"How did you manage that?"

Bridgette smiled. "We stole it."

"You stole a vessel with six-thousand-horsepower Daimler-Benz engines? Were the Germans deaf?"

"Ours is a bit smaller, but it can travel over forty knots per hour. We had assistance from the Office of Strategic Services."

"Americans."

"Yes." Bridgette nodded. "They are quite resourceful."

"I have heard."

"The Schnellboot will take us to a location off the Polish coast. From there we will travel inland to Markus's location. We have documents that show we are Sanitätsdienst Heer, so if we encounter Wehrmacht patrols we should be given passage, although we should avoid them at all costs. It should not take much time at all."

"Unless we encounter the Gestapo," Gromov said. "I doubt they will be fooled by your papers."

"We're unlikely to encounter Gestapo south of Danzig, where we are going," Bridgette said with another smile. "Besides, if we do, you look like you can handle the situation, Mr. Gromov."

Bridgette turned and began walking toward the coastline. "Come with me. Let's get started."

Gromov inspected Bridgette's figure approvingly as he followed. He was going from an apparent suicide mission to one that might merit the Order of Lenin, and present other intriguing possibilities.

CHAPTER 35

A single low-wattage lamp illuminated Standartenführer Maurer's desk as he sat with fists clenched and read the Eastern Front intelligence summary. The report, in typical Germanic tradition, was precise and exhaustive. The bulk of the summary pertained to the mammoth battle of Kursk, but three-quarters of the way through was an obscure reference to something that had been resolved some time ago. A Polish collaborator located approximately fifty kilometers south of Danzig had noted a drunken *Armia*'s casual reference to a ghost—a lunatic, really—who had the ability to change the world. The ghost claimed that he was thought to be dead and fervently wished to remain so. Supposedly, he was under the protection of the *Armia*.

No location was attached to the ghost/lunatic. Indeed, there was no other information in the report except for the lunatic's last name: Kapsky.

Maurer reread the passage. Then he stared at it, thinking. He'd verified Kapsky's death some time ago. More important, he'd retrieved a document from the corpse. The question wasn't whether Kapsky was dead. That was inarguable. The question was why would a drunken partisan—presumably some illiterate farmer—claim that Kapsky was alive? What benefit would possibly be derived from the claim? How would he even know who Kapsky was? Neither he nor whomever he was bragging to would have any idea who Kapsky was.

Maurer rose from his desk and walked to the map table at the center of the room. The area from which the report came was not far from the location where Kapsky's corpse had been found. Though navigating the area was treacherous, it was no more so than any war zone and, for the enemy, considerably less than an attempt to enter Germany.

Maurer placed an index finger at a point approximately thirty kilometers south of Danzig and traced it upward toward the Baltic near Danzig. Then he traced a line from Danzig to Tirpitzufer. He stared pensively at the map for a full minute.

Canaris had charged him with seeking and destroying the elements the Americans and Soviets had dispatched to acquire the Kapsky document. Toward that end, Maurer had been reviewing all Gestapo and Wehrmacht reports for any suspected Allied forays into Germany. There were precious few, most of which were from the west. Maurer suspected any intrusions would likely come from Denmark and perhaps western Poland, the former originating in the North Sea and the latter in the Baltic. He'd already dispatched one team to Danzig and another to Copenhagen in anticipation of such Allied forays. Indeed, he was slated to join his Danzig team the day after next.

SS Standartenführer Konrad Maurer slowly paced the length of his office, turned and paced in the other direction. He repeated the trek several times before deciding to play a hunch, something the regimented officer rarely did.

Napoleon played hunches, Frederick the Great played hunches. And when they did so, they conquered entire continents. Konrad Maurer would play a hunch.

He picked up the receiver of the heavy black telephone on his desk and began speaking without salutations to the Unterscharführer who had immediately picked up.

"Expedite all arrangements for Danzig. I will leave immediately."

CHAPTER 36

They walked quietly yet briskly through the woods, Emil on point, followed by Matuszek, Canidy, Fulmar, and McDermott. The accidental brush with the panzers only hours ago still had each of them on edge, keeping them alert despite creeping fatigue. Emil had informed them at the outset that they were approximately forty kilometers from Daria Bacior's location. Canidy estimated they'd already traveled nearly ten. At their present pace, with a few rest stops, they could arrive in a day or so. Canidy caught glimpses of gray through the canopy of leaves. Although the forest remained dark, the sun would be up soon. Canidy was uncertain whether he preferred darkness or light. The former made it easier to conceal themselves but also increased the risk they'd stumble upon a German patrol. The latter increased the probability they'd be seen, but improved their odds of sighting Germans.

Barely two seconds after that thought sparked across the synapses of his brain, he emphatically concluded he preferred neither. The furious fusillade of machine-gun fire that ripped the bark off the trees adjacent to their column demonstrated that they'd both failed to conceal themselves and failed to avoid a German patrol.

All five dove to the forest floor as the fire continued to strafe and denude surrounding trees and saplings. Canidy scanned the area immediately around him and determined that none of them had been shot. They were spread in a fifteen-foot semicircle, Emil at the top of the arc, with Canidy and Fulmar to his left and Matuszek and McDermott to his right. Approximately forty meters in front of them he could see the fire from the weapon but nothing else.

"How many?" Canidy shouted above the din.

Matuszek said, "MG 42 machine-gun fire. I cannot see them, but an MG 42 means an eight- to ten-man *gruppe*."

Matuszek was drowned out by another furious spray of rounds barely three feet off the ground. *These guys sure aren't rookies*, Canidy thought.

Canidy was startled to see Emil stand and sprint in a crouch, looping to the right until he disappeared into the trees and darkness. Instinctively, Canidy rose and sprinted to the left. As he did so, Matuszek, Fulmar, and McDermott laid down suppressing fire, which was met with not just MG 42 fire, but scores of rounds from enemy rifles, one of which seared a shallow but painful gash into the same arm McDermott had wounded on the previous operation.

"Fire discipline!" Fulmar shouted. "That buzzsaw's got more rounds than we do."

"Hell, I can't shoot what I can't see," McDermott said, ignoring the sting in his arm.

Canidy hurdled logs and dodged saplings as he sprinted around the enemy's right flank to their rear. He prayed the din from the machine-gun fire drowned the noise of the snapped twigs and brush in his wake. He caught a flash of muzzle fire to his right and determined he was now approximately forty meters to the right and ten meters behind the enemy's position. He slowed to a walk and crept toward the fire spitting from the MG 42. When he drew to within twenty meters he dropped to the moist ground and began crawling toward the MG 42 placement as fire from Matuszek, Fulmar, and McDermott sliced the air overhead.

Just as Canidy sighted the Unteroffizier next to the MG 42, Emil flew from the brush at the opposite end of the German fire line, rifle slung across his back and an FS blade in his extended right hand. Before the Germans even knew he was upon them, Emil raked the knife across the trachea of the Gefreiter manning the MG 42 with such fury he nearly decapitated him. Canidy sighted the first German who had begun to react to Emil's attack and sent a .40-06 round through the German's right temple at the same time Emil thrust the FS into the abdomen of the soldier to the Gefreiter's left.

Canidy shifted his sight slightly to the left and fired two rounds at a bespectacled German who was just beginning to seize the MG 42 from his fallen compatriot.

The first round missed, but the second round turned his face into a sickening mass of pulverized bone, blood, and brain tissue. With another slight shift to the left with his M1911, Canidy smoothly sighted and fired two rounds at a young German who appeared to be paralyzed by the ferocity of Emil's attack. Both rounds struck the young soldier squarely in the chest, propelling him backward as his Kar98k flew from his grasp.

Canidy rapidly searched for the remaining German troops. Two were lying facedown in the loamy soil behind a rotting log, apparently shot by some combination of Matuszek, Fulmar, and McDermott. The last German Canidy sighted was on his knees, Emil standing behind him with his left arm around the German's skull, holding the FS raised high overhead. Emil plunged the blade deep into the German's thoracic cavity, prompting a geyser of blood to erupt from the wound.

Canidy noted the look on Emil's face: disciplined, stoic. Another day at the office.

The echoes of gunfire were quickly absorbed by the forest. Canidy lay still, listening for any signs of German reinforcements, a task made difficult by the ringing in his ears. After a few moments, he rose and moved swiftly toward Emil and the carnage surrounding him. Matuszek, Fulmar, and McDermott arrived seconds later, weapons at low-ready.

Matuszek poked and prodded the corpses, turning one over on its back. He pointed the rifle at the insignia on the corpse's uniform. "Waffen SS. Not regular army. Himmler's assassins."

Canidy said, "Well, we made quite a racket. They probably heard it all the way back in Berchtesgaden. Let's get out of here before their friends come looking for them."

"Hell, which way should we go?" Fulmar asked. "These guys were in our path. There are probably more in that direction."

"Well, we'll shift slightly eastward, then continue to proceed south," Emil said in the tone of someone who had just come from a tedious meeting. "These troops were likely attached to the Totenkopf regiment outside Tczew." He rubbed a trickle of German blood from his cheek. "They were probably off their assigned patrol and decided to bivouac here for the night."

Canidy massaged the back of his neck with his free hand. "I hope you're right, Emil. And you probably are. But after getting a shot of adrenaline like that, I can't help but wonder why the SS is wandering around a backwoods place like this."

"Hell, Dick, it's war," McDermott said. "They could say the same thing about us."

"Right," Canidy said. "That's exactly right. We *are* wandering around the backwoods. But we've got a very specific reason for doing so.

"What's *their* reason?"

CHAPTER 37

Taras Gromov had a feeling of growing urgency.

Gromov detested feelings of urgency. He rarely had them. Gromov was usually the one who sparked anxiety, fear, and terror in others. The closest he came to feeling anything akin to urgency was a feeling of irritation.

Belyanov, by way of Czech Resistance and Bridgette, had conveyed that others were searching for Kapsky. Presumably, those "others" were the same individuals who had searched for Kapsky before—the ones Gromov was to eliminate. Belyanov didn't say where such individuals were or from where they had begun their mission. But since Belyanov knew they were already searching for Kapsky when he conveyed the message to Bridgette, those individuals already had a head start. Moreover, Gromov had first been going in a direction that took him *away* from Kapsky. Whereas the Americans, presumably, had been heading toward Kapsky from the very start.

Thankfully, they were making swift progress, primarily because of Bridgette's prodigious knowledge and talent. They'd traversed the Baltic to the Polish north coast without encountering a single German vessel. When she pointed out their expected landfall on a map, he'd protested, stating that it wasn't anywhere near Danzig, requiring them to make too much of the journey by land, thus vastly increasing the probabilities of an encounter with German troops. But so far, they'd avoided any such contact.

Gromov was thankful for Bridgette's proficiency. Without her, it would have been difficult if not impossible for him to even remotely make the progress he was making. He liked her. And he was attracted to her. Her attractiveness was not merely a consequence of intelligence and proficiency. Nor was it her face, which was the first feature he'd noticed. Though her clothing was rather utilitarian, he was able to discern that her face and intelligence were not the only impressive assets she possessed.

Her personality also suited him, another fact that made him struggle with his calculation that he most likely would have to kill her. He considered all of the reasons why he wouldn't have to do so, but thus far hadn't been able to persuade himself that there was an alternative. Nonetheless, he didn't have to kill her yet, and there was still time for circumstances to change. Besides, killing her would make navigating Poland very difficult.

Bridgette led him swiftly past several hamlets, all of which bore some scars of war. They remained on the outskirts, reducing the likelihood of encountering Germans or meddlesome villagers. At one point they rode, unbeknownst to the driver, in the bed of a rickety vegetable truck.

"You cannot tell who is friend or foe most of the time," she said. "Best to stay out of range and, as much as possible, avoid 'interactions.'"

"Forgive me for asking," Gromov said. "But how do you know where you are going?"

"Czechs, Poles, Danes . . . The resistance network necessarily has scores of people like me—couriers, guides, informants, and even spies and saboteurs. We are not confined to one country. We travel throughout occupied Europe. I've traveled here several times since September 1, 1939. I've had the privilege of meeting Władysław Sikorski, premier in exile. Women are better at this than men. Men are conspicuous. Men are suspicious. The Germans trust no one, but sometimes women can pass where men cannot."

They walked cautiously along a dry creekbed in a sparsely populated area southwest of Danzig. They were careful not to stumble upon the unexploded ordnance strewn throughout the fields. Trees denuded of leaves, and in some cases bark, were evidence of what not long ago had been a seemingly limitless battlefield.

"Do you have an estimate of how much farther?" Gromov asked.

"Impossible to say. Much depends on whether we must make detours and whether and by how much we must change our route to avoid Germans. If we stay on this route, we should reach Markus's general location in somewhat under forty-eight hours."

"Unacceptable," Gromov said.

"Irrelevant," Bridgette said. "It is what it is. Who are you going to complain to?"

"There must be some way to speed our journey."

"Not without considerable risk," Bridgette informed. "We would need to rely on strangers and the happenstance of a passing vehicle. The Germans are devilishly clever. They send ordinary vehicles about the countryside driven by SS in civilian clothing. We have heard reports of resistance agents seeking rides from these vehicles, only to be executed by the drivers."

"So we walk?"

"So we walk," Bridgette confirmed. "Unless you see your mother driving a Kubuś down the road, and even then, I would insist that you hold your pistol to her temple as she drove." Bridgette touched her index finger to his left temple. Gromov seized her wrist reflexively and bent her hand away from him. He immediately released his grip, embarrassed by his reaction.

Bridgette stood mere inches from him and examined his face. "Gromov, I pity your station in life. It is clear that you are an assassin, a killer, and I suspect a very good one. Otherwise you would not have been sent by someone such as Belyanov. Because you are a very good assassin, that is all that you will do for as long as you live. Killers do not become cobblers, except in absurdly long Russian stories."

Gromov scanned Bridgette's face in turn. He detected no artifice, only despair for him.

They were startled by the sound of an approaching motorcycle somewhere beyond the curve of the nearby dirt road. They flattened themselves into the creekbed just as they heard the vehicle—a BMW with sidecar— shift and come to an idle a mere five meters above their position. Her face buried in the loose red dirt of the creekbed, Bridgette shifted her head to see two German soldiers scanning the area. They appeared not to have yet seen Bridgette or Gromov.

Before Bridgette could take her next breath, she watched as Gromov charged furiously up the slope and slammed his body against the rider and passenger, caus- ing both to fly off the vehicle onto the road, with Gro- mov falling atop the passenger.

Gromov validated Bridgette's assessment of him with a display of savagery exceeding anything she'd witnessed in three years of war. Gromov thrust the three middle fingers of his right hand into the passenger's throat, crushing his trachea, then with both hands immediately grasped the driver's head and twisted it so forcefully that Bridgette could hear the vertebrae snap.

Without a pause, Gromov turned back to the passen- ger, whose desperate gasps for air could be heard even over the idling motorcycle engine. Using the edge of his fist as a bludgeon, Gromov brutally pounded the pas- senger's face for what seemed to Bridgette to be nearly half a minute.

The elapsed time between the vehicle stopping above the canal bed and the last breath of the passenger was no more than forty-five seconds. Even before Bridgette began walking up the slope, Gromov was dragging the motorcycle off the road and down to the canal bed. Within a few seconds, he'd done the same with the two bodies.

Gromov then turned to her. "We must move quickly—and not use the canal bed. We cannot lose more time." He turned and began walking briskly toward an adjacent tree line half a kilometer from the canal bed.

Bridgette followed, disturbed that she was unable to suppress an overwhelming swell of desire toward the assassin.

CHAPTER 38

For several hours Canidy's team moved swiftly but warily over the countryside toward Sztum before stopping in a cornfield near a small farmhouse to reorient.

"How much farther, Emil?"

"Ten, fifteen kilometers. Just a little east of Sztum."

"We'll stop here for a few minutes," Canidy said. "Get our bearings, think." He rattled his small rucksack and looked hopefully at Matuszek. "Any chance the farmer can spare any decent food?"

"None of them can," Matuszek replied, "but they will. We must be careful. The Germans will kill them if they find out . . ."

"Also," Emil added, "these farmers are very suspicious. The Germans have killed a number of them; torched their crops if they assist *Armia*. Sometimes the Germans send troops dressed like civilians to see how the farmers react. I do not know how often this happens, but it doesn't have to be very frequent. If the farmer provides assistance, the Nazis will make a not-very-pleasant example of him. If he is fortunate, maybe a chicken or two is taken. Sometimes something much worse happens. A very effective method of keeping people in line. The uncertainty of retribution is much worse than certainty."

"Do they know you?" Canidy asked Matuszek.

He shook his head. "They may know of me, or the rumor of me, but it is unlikely that they've ever seen me." He pointed to Emil. "I would not be surprised, however, if they know of this fellow."

Canidy looked at Emil and grinned. "That's obvious. Based on what I saw back there, I suspect his legend has spread far and wide throughout the countryside."

Emil's expression remained taciturn, but Matuszek smiled. "In fact, that is not much of an exaggeration. I myself have heard tales told by old men and young women. In desperate times, people need heroes. Regrettably, heroes do not survive long in this theater," Matuszek said. "If the SS find him, they will execute him, most likely in a village square, where attendance is mandatory."

"Do they know who he is?" Fulmar asked.

"They are Germans," Matuszek said. "They have extraordinarily detailed files on much of the *Armia*."

Canidy said, "We need rations. We're low as it is, and we've got a way to go. We shouldn't arrive hungry, if we're fortunate enough to arrive at all. If it *is* Kapsky, we're going to have to move him quickly before we draw a crowd and the Germans are alerted."

"I will go," Emil volunteered.

"We'll all go," Canidy said. "But you make the contact. We'll stay out of sight so as not to alarm the farmer." Canidy pulled up his M1911. "Let's go." The five threaded through the cornfield to remain unobserved until they came to within thirty meters of the farmhouse. It was the size of a small cottage. Through the window closest to them they could see the kitchen. They watched for a full minute but saw no movement.

"I am going in," Emil said. He crossed to the front porch with his rifle at the ready. The door appeared to be ajar, so he pushed it open with his right foot, raised the rifle to his shoulder, and proceeded inside. The rest of the team waited for a signal that they could enter. They waited for more than thirty seconds before Canidy decided to go in. He was followed by the rest, each brandishing their weapons at the ready.

The first thing Canidy noticed was the smell—something akin to rotting meat. It took only a few seconds for him to discover the source: a man's torso lying atop dried blood on the kitchen floor. No head, no legs, just arms spread at odd angles. From the maggots visible at the neckline, Canidy surmised the remains were several days old.

Emil appeared from a hallway that led to a small dining area. "Two more bodies are back there," he informed while cocking his head over his right shoulder. "I cannot tell if they are male or female. They appear, however, to have been adults."

Canidy's face was drawn into something between a scowl and a grimace. To no one in particular, he asked,

"What do you think? Interrogation? Retribution? Making an example?"

"Probably all three," Matuszek replied.

Candidy shook his head, partly from disgust and partly in anger. "What does this have to do with war? These are civilians. There's no sign they were combatants."

"I wish I were carrying a camera right now instead of this rifle," McDermott said.

"Cameras can't kill Germans," Matuszek said.

Fulmar blinked several times as if trying to recall something. Then he placed his M1 on a nearby table, reached into his left front pocket, and pulled out a cigar cylinder. The others watched as he unscrewed the cylinder and pulled out not a cigar, but another cylindrical object slightly larger than his index finger.

"Peculiar time for a smoke, lad," McDermott said.

Fulmar pulled both ends of the cylinder, which extended another two inches, revealing a rectangular lens at the center. "I'm disappointed you don't have one of these," Fulmar said to McDermott. "I would have expected that your man Fleming would have insisted you carry one. He's big into gadgets, isn't he?"

"What is that supposed to be?" McDermott asked.

Candidy laughed as if remembering a joke from the past. "It's a camera," he informed. "It supposedly can take a photograph at close range. At least, that's what Donovan told us. We haven't tried it." Candidy patted his breast pocket. "I have one, too, but completely forgot about it. Donovan had some technicians at the Office gin these up. I think the idea was we could at least take a photograph of the Kapsky document if for some reason we couldn't actually abscond with it or if the document was later destroyed. I don't think any of us actually thought it could work."

"What good is a photograph of a massacred farm family?" Emil asked.

"Accountability," Canidy replied. "To have a record of what happened. The Office is compiling evidence for after the war."

"I do not understand," Emil said.

"I can't say I do, either," Canidy conceded. "But Donovan sees things five to ten years ahead of most. He insists it's important to have a record of events."

"He is a historian, this Donovan?"

"He's a lot of things, including being twelve steps ahead of almost everybody else."

"Where is the . . . flashbulb?" Matuszek asked. "It is so small it does not appear capable of producing a photograph. Where is the film?"

Canidy shrugged. "Hell if I know. They give this stuff to us, show us how to use it, and we don't ask questions. It either works or it doesn't. We'll find out eventually."

Fulmar manipulated a metal lever on the right end of the cylinder, aimed the lens at the remains on the floor, and then flipped it downward. He waited, as if expecting something to happen. Nothing did.

"When does it take the photograph?" Emil asked.

Fulmar smiled sheepishly and returned the device to his pocket. "I think it just did, but I don't really know."

"Let's look for some food," Canidy said. "Something we can take with us."

"I saw a basket of bread on a shelf next to the stove in the next room," McDermott said. "I'll go get it."

The rest rummaged around the small edifice but found little. They gathered next to the front door and took inventory: at most a day's worth of stale bread for the five and a roll of hard sausage. Canidy shrugged. "It is what it is. Let's get out of here."

They ate as they walked, rifles slung over their shoulders. Although it wasn't much, the food was enough fuel for the day—buoyed by the prospect of a more substantial meal once they reached their destination.

They were grateful that most of their path was relatively desolate. It was evident that most of whatever meager population had once inhabited the area had evacuated or been destroyed during Barbarossa. Hamlets and farmland were covered with craters, scorch marks, and makeshift cemeteries. Emil deftly guided them around a minefield, a detour that added another hour to their journey. After a few hours, the topography changed from plains to low, rolling hills but remained relatively desolate. Canidy could see a road a half kilometer to the east. There appeared to be a dry creek or canal bed parallel to the road.

"Does that take us where we need to go?" he asked Emil.

"Generally speaking," Emil acknowledged. "I know what you're thinking. Why not walk along there? Riverbeds are usually good for cover and navigation. But not one like that. It's too exposed to traffic on the road above. Better to stay amid the fields. Slower progress, but better coverage."

"Time," whispered Canidy, "is not our friend."

CHAPTER 39

Maurer had replicated the scene numerous times over the last few years. It had proven highly effective: Petrify the citizenry to elicit information. Break their will. Make even the toughest cower and submit.

Five SS Panzer IVs sat in a precise line in front of a small fountain in the village square, where Maurer sat imperiously in the rear seat of his Horch Kfz, its top down. His visor was drawn low over his forehead, just above his sunglasses. He sat motionless the entire time it took his troops to roust the residents from their dwellings and herd them into the square, where they first gawked at the panzers and then at the menacing figure in the car.

The crowd consisted of women, old men, and children of all ages. As in most such villages, most of the older boys and men were either dead or fighting somewhere. Any men or teenage boys that did remain were the first to be placed in the center of the square. They would be made to kneel with their hands clasped behind their backs. Those that were slow to do so or who outright refused would be shot at the first refusal. Thereafter, obedience was almost always universal. The men knelt for nearly an hour as the SS searched the village and rounded up the remainder. Spouses and children saw husbands, fathers, uncles, and brothers added to the queue. All remained absolutely silent, as if any noise, any utterances, might prompt violence from the SS guards.

The longer they knelt, the more some began to falter. One of the older men fell onto his face. An SS guard strode quickly to his position and struck him in the back of the head with the butt of his rifle. When the man righted himself, his face was smeared with blood from his broken nose. He appeared more dazed than frightened. An Unterfeldwebel faced the semicircle of assembled villagers grasping a Walther P38 in his right hand, which hung at his side. He spoke casually, without raising his voice.

"We are seeking Sebastian Kapsky. He is somewhere in this village. We know that. We know someone is harboring him. We do not wish to visit any harm on any of you or your village. We seek only Kapsky."

Maurer sat quietly and comfortably in his command car, allowing his subordinates to conduct the investigation and interrogation. He understood that his silence made his presence that much more ominous.

The Unterfeldwebel strode behind the line of kneeling men for several seconds, saying nothing. Then he stopped behind a middle-aged man, the left side of whose face was disfigured. Maurer watched the Unterfeldwebel lean forward, whisper something into the man's ear, and discharge his Walther P38 inches from the man's head. Screams and cries erupted from the crowd as the man winced from the weapon's sharp report.

The Unterfeldwebel walked to the end of the line and repeated the maneuver with a boy of twelve. More screams and cries from the crowd. The boy, however, refused to flinch and continued to gaze forward with a look of defiance. A moment later the Unterfeldwebel discharged the weapon into the back of the boy's skull, the round causing his face to explode outward. The body fell forward to the horrified shrieks of his mother and three younger siblings.

Maurer remained expressionless and motionless. Through his sunglasses he could see the villagers with pleading expressions, willing him to put an end to the nightmare. They understood the Unterfeldwebel was operating at the will of the Standartenführer and could do nothing without his approval.

The Unterfeldwebel moved behind an old man kneeling next in line. "Kapsky," the Unterfeldwebel said to the crowd, "he is here among you. Deliver Professor Sebastian Kapsky now." A gurgle of cries and whimpers issued from the crowd. Not of protest, but of resignation. Maurer could hear nothing intelligible. The Unterfeldwebel placed the muzzle of the weapon against the base of the old man's skull. The man closed his eyes; an oddly serene look covered his face.

"The mathematician Kapsky," the Unterfeldwebel said, standing with his free hand on his hip. "Give him to me." He waited no more than two seconds before discharging his weapon. A single, piercing shriek came from somewhere in the crowd. The man fell forward. Maurer remained motionless, though behind his sunglasses his eyes scanned the villagers' faces for reaction, anything that might betray knowledge of Kapsky's whereabouts. All he saw was anguish. All he heard was sobbing.

The Unterfeldwebel took a step to the right, free hand still on his hip, and placed the muzzle of his Walther to the back of another grandfatherly-looking man. Wails of desperation rose from the crowd.

"Kapsky. Produce him."

Maurer rose to his feet and slowly stood erect in the back of the command car, giving the crowd a look at his impressive physical presence. The crowd fell silent and the Unterfeldwebel let the Walther fall to his side.

An Unteroffizier opened the rear door of the vehicle in anticipation. Maurer stood for several moments, his hands clasped behind his back, expressionless. Then he descended onto the square and strode casually—chin tilted upward and black boots gleaming—to the line of kneeling men, stopping within five feet of the man at the center.

There wasn't a sound. There wasn't a person whose eyes weren't riveted to the SS Standartenführer.

Maurer scanned the crowd. He addressed them in a conversational voice, several leaning forward, straining to hear.

"Perhaps Kapsky is not here. Perhaps he was not here. That is immaterial." Maurer paused and again scanned the crowd. He could sense their tension. "Whether Kapsky is here, whether he *was* here, does not concern me," he repeated. "Unterfeldwebel Dietz has demanded production. We know that if he is not here, he is nearby. And we know that someone here knows his location. *Armia* knows his location. Therefore, someone in this village knows his location. Or knows who can produce him.

"Tell me now and no one else will be harmed." Maurer paused and surveyed the assemblage as if assessing whom to execute. "Fail to tell me and be assured, starting in sixty seconds, we will execute one of you every thirty seconds until Kapsky's location or his presentment is secured."

Maurer looked up to each of the machine gunners in the row of five panzers. Almost in unison they pulled the bolts on their MG 34 machine guns. Then he nodded almost imperceptibly to Unterfeldwebel Dietz, who snapped to rigid attention, awaiting Maurer's signal to blow the grandfather's brain tissue through the front of his skull.

A teenage girl fell to her knees wailing. She was joined by a chorus of other women, a few of whom shouted "Please" to the gathered to confess anything they might know about a Sebastian Kapsky's whereabouts. The kneeling grandfather began shouting curses, entreaties, and obscenities at Unterfeldwebel Dietz, alternately pleading for his life and daring him to shoot.

The bedlam continued for nearly a full minute before

a tall, middle-aged woman with striking red hair raised her hands above her head to attract the attention of the crowd, which became silent. She turned to Maurer and asked, "Is this Kapsky a tall man with green eyes and a bolt of thick black hair at his forehead?"

Maurer eyed the woman for a moment and replied, "He is."

"He was near Sztum a week ago."

A hint of a smile, something resembling gratitude, covered Maurer's face. "Splendid," he said softly. Then he turned to Dietz and nodded once. Dietz discharged his weapon into the neck of the grandfather kneeling before him, cleanly severing his skull from his spine.

The villagers erupted in a cacophony of horror. A frail elderly woman collapsed to the ground. Maurer pointed at the fresh corpse. "This is what happens when you withhold information, even for a second. The rest of you have been spared only because information ultimately was provided." Maurer faced the redheaded woman. "But be assured, if the information is false or even merely flawed, I will back."

Maurer returned to the rear seat of his vehicle and commanded the driver to proceed to Sztum. The five panzers roared to life and followed in a single line, leaving the grieving villagers huddled over the dead bodies, praying that Kapsky was indeed in Sztum. The woman with the striking red hair watched as the Germans receded into the distance. Then she turned to the villagers and waved her arms over her head to get their attention.

It didn't take long. After several seconds they grew quiet and focused on her in anticipation.

"Andrej?" she called loudly.

A short, stocky bald man with a scarred face and pronounced limp separated from the crowd. "Here."

"Get on your motorcycle and go as fast as you can to Malbork. Tell my sister Daria that the SS devil is on his way to Sztum in search of Kapsky. It is only a matter of time before he learns Kapsky is not there and the devil will then kill as many as necessary to learn that Kapsky is with Daria in Malbork. She must move. She will know what to do."

Andrej disappeared into a nearby alley and within seconds the crowd heard the roar of a motorcycle and saw a cloud of dust waft from the alleyway. After a moment, their heads turned back to the redhead in anticipation. She addressed them in a powerful, commanding voice.

"We must all leave at once," she instructed. "Gather only necessities for a day's journey and then disperse. It is best to go east, but whatever direction you choose go *now*. I pray you have good fortune."

"But we are doomed," a woman cried. "We cannot outrun the SS. It is useless."

The redhead shook her head firmly. "You are not doomed. Unless you remain here. Once you have placed some distance between yourself and this place, they will not know where you are from. They won't remember your individual faces. But if you remain here, they will return and they will execute every last one of those they find."

CHAPTER 40

"Not much farther," Emil said, pointing to a narrow pass between two wooded hills. "Just a couple of kilometers beyond that gap."

Emil's comment spurred them to pick up their pace.

"Hell, if Kapsky's not there we're really screwed," Canidy reminded them. "We must be hundreds of miles from where we're supposed to be."

Fulmar said, "We'll know soon enough. Fingers crossed. If we chose right, we'll get a medal and maybe a pat on the back from Donovan. If we chose wrong, the consequences—"

"Better not to think about it," Canidy interjected. He pointed to the hill on the right. "Emil, can we see the town from the top of that hill?"

"Much of it," Emil replied, anticipating Canidy's question. "If there are any Germans there, we should be able to spot them."

Minutes later Canidy determined Emil was right. Kneeling at the crest of the hill, they had an excellent view of most of the edifices and roads in the town. Better yet, there was no evidence of German soldiers.

"Where's your *Armia* contact?" Canidy asked Matuszek.

Matuszek turned to Emil. "Same place as before?"

Emil nodded and pointed to one of the larger structures on the western perimeter of the town. "Markus likes that barn over there."

Canidy pointed to the trees to their right. "The trees go all the way to the back of the barn. If we stay just inside the tree line, we'll be able to reach the back door without being seen. I don't see anybody, but if we encounter any Germans, we need to kill them as quietly as possible, find Kapsky, and get the hell out of here as fast as humanly possible."

Canidy rose and began descending the hill, followed by Fulmar, Matuszek, McDermott, and Emil. Staying within the tree line, they were at the back door three minutes later. Canidy listened for any sign the structure was occupied.

Hearing nothing, he nodded to the others, who were holding their weapons at low-ready, and pushed the door open slowly. He expected a creak, but it was silent. Matuszek placed a hand on Canidy's shoulder and moved in front of him. "Better I go first."

Matuszek stood outside and called softly, "Markus? Markus Zuchowski, you lazy sack of shit. Are you asleep?"

The door opened wide to reveal a beaming Markus Zuchowski. Matuszek clapped him on the shoulder and gazed toward Canidy, Fulmar, and McDermott. "Don't shoot them. They're Americans and a Brit. We're here for Kapsky."

Markus frowned. "Daria took him. We received word just a short time ago from her sister that an SS Standartenführer is searching for him. *Seriously* searching for him. Daria had recently moved him to just south of Malbork. Now they'll have to move again shortly."

"Where did you say?" Canidy asked.

"Malbork. The Pomerelia region. The biggest castle in the world is there." Markus pointed to what appeared to be radio equipment in the loft. "She also sent word of her destination to the OSS contact stationed in the Baltic."

Matuszek pointed to Canidy and Fulmar. "These men are OSS."

"That was fast," Markus said and whistled.

"We were dispatched days ago," Canidy explained. "You sure it's Kapsky?"

Markus shrugged. "He claims to be a mathematician everyone is searching for. I do not know. He seems intelligent. Unusual green eyes."

Canidy exhaled audibly. "Kapsky. At least it looks like we made the right choice not going to Germany," he said. "For now."

"By any chance, is the SS officer you mentioned Konrad Maurer?" Matuszek asked.

Markus nodded. "It sounded like his methods."

"How far to Malbork?" Canidy asked.

"Fifteen, twenty kilometers north," Matuszek said. "Not far, but not easy." He turned to Markus. "I recall there is a house we kept there . . ."

"That's where she is headed," Markus affirmed.

"We are—how you say—in business," Matuszek told Canidy. "It is SS Totenkopf area. Very treacherous. But we have smart, tough fighters there."

Canidy looked at Fulmar and punched him on the shoulder. "Odds are we still get killed, but if we make it at least there, probably won't be a court-martial."

CHAPTER 41

Donovan and Stimson waited for the President in the Map Room, Donovan with a scowl and Stimson with a faint patrician air of disapproval. Neither approved of the Map Room for a meeting such as this. It was too large and airy. The acoustics were not suited for a highly sensitive discussion, but FDR hated being confined to the Oval Office and insisted on a change of scenery.

The President entered the room, assisted by Laurence Duggan, who stationed him at the head of the long map table, both Donovan and Stimson to his right.

FDR had a mischievous look in his eyes.

"I've discovered a nearly foolproof way of winning the war and winning it quickly," the President said. "It is quite simple, really. Keep Georgie Patton thinking he is about to be relieved of command. Every time he gets in trouble with Ike or Marshall, or *thinks* he's in trouble with Ike or Marshall, he commits himself to proving to the world—no, not just to the world, but to posterity, to the scribes who will write the history of this epic engagement—that he is the greatest fighting general that this country has ever produced." The President leaned forward as if disclosing a confidence. "And frankly, though I abhor his politics, he *is* the finest fighter we've ever produced. Would that we had two more like him. One more in the European theater and one in the Pacific—though I would expect there would be a titanic clash of egos with Doug MacArthur." The President chuckled at the prospect. "Wager as to which ego will prevail?" He examined the two men before him. "And here we have the two most humorless men who have ever provided counsel to an American President in time of war."

The President removed his cigarette holder from the corner of his mouth. "By God, gentlemen, lighten up. We only have a worldwide war to win. It's not as if we must structure myriad Potemkin villages to confront an economic crisis. War, after all, is something one can understand and address in a rational manner."

Stimson and Donovan remained still.

"All right, gentlemen, we shall remain dour in accordance with your wishes," Roosevelt conceded. "Now, what is it that demands that two men of your elevated status convey information to the commander in chief? Only bad news, am I right? A debacle?" There was a gleam in the President's eyes. He enjoyed projecting flippancy at serious moments.

"Mr. President," the secretary of war said. "There appears to be good news regarding the Kapsky operation. He is in the protective custody of the *Armia* somewhere in northern Poland."

Roosevelt looked exuberant. "Outstanding. He was thought to be deceased, was he not? A remarkable, unexpected development. But what is the likelihood he will remain secure?"

"We understand he is being guarded by several *Armia* troops, and the Germans are completely unaware of his whereabouts in an area east or southeast of Sztum."

FDR laughed and slapped his leg. "War is a cascade of the unexpected. And sometimes it's even good news. We certainly can use it." He paused thoughtfully, then asked, "What of our men who we sent to retrieve the Kapsky document in Germany? I was given to understand the likelihood of their success was nearly nil, as was the likelihood of survival."

Donovan shook his head. "We did not expect to hear from them unless and until the operation had been executed, Mr. President. The assumption must be that they are now somewhere in Germany . . ."

"Or captured. Or dead," Roosevelt concluded.

"There is a good probability of either, yes, sir," Donovan said. "There has been no update regarding their status from our contacts among the resistance groups."

"Are your British counterparts aware of this development?"

"Not to our knowledge, Mr. President," Donovan replied. "We wanted, of course, to inform you first."

"Yes. I will inform the prime minister," Roosevelt

said. "He will insist, I'm sure, upon a joint extraction effort." Roosevelt tilted his head back and gazed at the ceiling for a moment. "Is one even feasible?"

Donovan's face assumed a look of bulldog determination. "Mr. President, the Office has many capabilities. We are designed for innovation."

"You are saying, Bill, that you will do your best. I understand. What about our various resistance contacts?"

"They're quite admirable, Mr. President. They can provide assistance, of course. But an extraction operation would be an enormous challenge. Our best bet would be a joint American/Brit operation with the help of local resistance intelligence."

Laurence Duggan appeared at the entrance to the room. The three looked at him expectantly.

"Mr. President, excuse me. Mr. Hopkins asked that I remind you of the meeting with the speaker. He's waiting outside the Oval Office. Shall I send him here instead?"

Roosevelt appeared irritated. "Yes, please do. In five minutes."

Duggan retreated and Roosevelt looked to Stimson and Donovan. "Gentlemen, domestic policy matters await. Thank you both for the smashing news of Kapsky." Stimson and Donovan took this as their signal to depart, and stood. "I trust your judgment regarding this extraction. Your best estimate as to how long that may take?"

Stimson looked at Donovan and then back to the President. "Ten to fourteen days, sir."

"I understand you're starting from scratch again, Bill," Roosevelt said. "I won't hold you to it. I know that you and your people will do their best." Roosevelt looked down for a moment and then back up. "Any hope for the men we sent to retrieve the document?"

Donovan wore his usual look of determination.

"They were extremely resourceful men. That's precisely why they were selected for this operation."

Donovan's use of tense was not lost on the President.

CHAPTER 42

The five ate voraciously.

Markus had taken up a collection of food from the locals. He didn't tell them the purpose; they assumed it was for the Resistance and gave what they could. Individually, they could spare little, but cumulatively it amounted to a feast for Canidy and his men.

"What the hell is this stuff?" Fulmar asked, pointing to the object in his hand. "It's incredible."

"Pierogies," Matuszek answered. He pointed to a large pot in the middle of their semicircle. "And that's bigos. Don't ask what's in it. But it will give you energy for the next few days."

"Meats, vegetables, and kraut," Emil informed them, dipping a hard roll into the stew. "Very cheap but very filling."

"Hell yes," Canidy mumbled, nodding in agreement as he chewed ravenously. "A pot of this and we can march on Berlin." Canidy pointed to the pierogies. "Everybody, grab as many handfuls as you can and put them in your rucks. We don't know when we'll eat next." Canidy turned to Markus. "You say fifteen to twenty kilometers to Malbork?"

"Closer to twenty. Somewhat wooded. Fairly flat."

Canidy then looked to Emil. "Do you know how to get us there?"

Emil, chewing vigorously, nodded until he was able to swallow. "I've not been there before, but I know how to get there."

"Do I have your permission to take him?" Canidy asked Matuszek.

"I am coming also," Matuszek said. "My men are in capable hands in my absence. It is best to have an old peasant along to communicate with the locals."

"The more the merrier. As long as we can stay out of sight of the Wehrmacht," Canidy said. "Emil, any estimate on how long it will take?"

"Provided we are not delayed by the Germans, less than a day by foot."

Canidy washed down the bigos with a long drink of water. "Okay. Markus, how secure is this place?"

"No place is secure, but we have used it since the invasion with no problem."

"Good. We haven't slept or rested in a long time. Don't know the next time we can. We'll get a few hours' sleep here and then push on. If we do find Kapsky it will likely be another push to the coast without rest." Canidy looked about the barn. "Find your spot. I'll take first watch. Then Fulmar, McDermott, Matuszek, and Emil."

Markus shook his head. "All of you rest. I will stand watch."

"Outstanding," Canidy said. "Thanks. Okay, get some rest. We move when I wake up."

CHAPTER 43

The large office on the fourth floor of the Lubyanka was utterly silent. No footsteps of aides hurrying to discharge commands, no chattering of typewriters producing reports and orders. When the large oak door leading to Aleksandr Belyanov's office was closed, it was understood he demanded not necessarily silence, but quiet.

The door, however, had been shut for nearly an hour, and before he'd closed it Belyanov had appeared uneasy, even apprehensive. No one dared disturb him.

Belyanov sat rigidly at the desk staring at the decrypted message and assessing how to convey the contents to Beria. Beria was precise. Beria was exacting. Beria punished mistakes, however slight.

This was a massive mistake.

Contrary to what Belyanov had told Beria, the Americans were not oblivious to the possibility that Kapsky was alive. In fact, his likely survival was known to the highest levels of American government. Belyanov had previously informed Beria that the Americans were unaware of Kapsky's existence, that they'd futilely directed their efforts at acquiring a Kapsky *document* in the custody of the Abwehr. In fact, they now were focused on acquiring *Kapsky*.

Belyanov had assumed Gromov had a head start, that the Danish Resistance had turned Gromov in the right direction. Belyanov had conveyed that assumption to Beria, who had been pleased. Now Belyanov had to inform Beria that, at the very least, the Americans were aware Kapsky was alive and were, or soon would be, sending a team to secure him. Beria famously did not like corrections or amendments to previous reports. He expected reports to be right the first time.

The last Belyanov had heard from the Danes was that they'd made contact with Gromov. Since then, nothing. Gromov could be dead or wounded. He could be detained. Gromov didn't realize he was in a race against the Americans. The last he knew, the Americans believed Kapsky was dead.

Belyanov rose from his chair to give Beria the news, hesitated, then sat back down. He stared straight ahead as he tapped his index finger on his desk, thinking. He desperately did not want to tell Beria that they'd made a mistake, that the Americans were aware Kapsky was alive and they would try to rescue him. He wanted to present Beria a report of a spectacular accomplishment. Why tell Beria of a mere *assumption* that might not yield negative consequences? Why not wait to see how it plays out?

After all, Gromov still had a head start on the Americans, and Gromov was exceptionally proficient.

Belyanov continued to tap the desk with his index finger. He concluded, quite rationally, that there was no need to inform Beria that the Americans would be dispatching someone to acquire Kapsky. That was a contingency, not a result. Instead, Belyanov would send a communique to the Danes to relay a message to the woman guiding Gromov: Tell Gromov the Americans were coming for Kapsky. Expedite the operation to acquire Kapsky. And all other orders, including those pertaining to the competition, remained unchanged.

No need to trouble Beria with a minor wrinkle. No need to aggravate him with every contingency. Belyanov was determined to present the boss with only one report: success. And he was determined not to share the fate of the untold masses who entered the Lubyanka in the morning, never to be seen alive again.

Maurer sat patiently in the rear of the command car as it drove over the pockmarked dirt road, a light coating of dust covering his clothing and sunglasses. The engines of the trailing panzers masked the sound of the BMW motorcycle with sidecar that approached from behind until it pulled parallel with his door. The Oberschütze in the sidecar saluted and tendered a folded piece of paper. Maurer retrieved the document, returned the salute, and opened the message; it stated that Soviet NKVD has been informed that the Americans believe that Dr.

Sebastian Kapsky was alive and in the custody of the Home Army in Poland. They were dispatching soldiers to acquire him.

Maurer folded the message, tore it into small strips, and let it flutter from his hand into the wind. So it was now a race among the Germans, Soviets, and Americans. No doubt the British were somewhere in the mix. No matter. The race was being run on German-occupied land. And the German entrant in the race had five SS panzers with two MG 34 machine guns and a 75-millimeter cannon. More important, the German entrant was SS Standartenführer Konrad Maurer.

CHAPTER 44

They'd seen the dust in the distance, kilometers away. To be seen from a distance, the volume of dust must have been generated by large vehicles. They were moving slowly. But not as slowly as Gromov.

Gromov liked Bridgette. She was intelligent, capable, and attractive. But she was slowing him down, and that aggravated him.

Nonetheless, he needed her. She had contacts and resources that were helpful. Had it not been for her, Gromov would probably still be in Germany on a futile mission that likely would have ended in his death. So he was grateful. But in Gromov's world, gratitude had limits. It did not supplant duty or efficiency.

"You are tired and hungry," Gromov said.

"You are not?"

"That is irrelevant."

"Not so, my dear Major Gromov. We must execute

the assignment. We need your strength and wits. I am merely your guide."

"A rather exceptional one," Gromov said, despite his irritation with their pace. He was sincere. Absent Bridgette's knowledge of the area—the terrain, distances, and locations of German forces—Gromov wouldn't have made nearly the progress he had.

There was even a fair probability that he would've been killed or captured by now. Nonetheless, they needed to move faster.

"You're tired and hungry," Gromov repeated. "Perhaps a short rest is in order. I can forage to replenish our provisions."

Bridgette dismissed the suggestion with a curt shake of her head. "I can walk faster, Major Gromov. I do not mean to slow you down." She pointed to low hills approximately two kilometers to the southeast. "Besides, just beyond those hills should be our destination. Czech Resistance informs that there are partisans there who are quartering Sebastian Kapsky. The partisans likely can provide some food, and far more quickly than if we forage."

Gromov felt a spark of anticipation. Throughout their journey he'd been anxious that someone would get to Kapsky before he did. The anxiety wore on him. He needed to *see* his objective, know that he could discharge the mission. Especially since Belyanov had judged that he'd been "twice shy."

He would not get a third chance.

He noticed that despite being tired and hungry,

Bridgette had picked up her pace. In fact, to his surprise, he'd fallen several steps behind. He accelerated to draw abreast. "You are quite a good soldier," he said sincerely. "Many Russian women make fine troops . . ."

". . . but Western women do not?" Bridgette finished.

"I suspect they do," Gromov said. "I've not had occasion to observe it until now. You are exceptionally resourceful and dutiful. Thank you."

Bridgette smiled and nodded. "I do my best." She pointed northeast. "But thanks may be premature." Gromov looked where she was pointing. The dust cloud was approaching far more rapidly than either of them had calculated. Though obscured by the dust, Gromov determined that the cloud was produced by at least half a dozen vehicles.

"It is somewhat difficult to tell from here, but I suspect they are several armored vehicles," Bridgette opined. "Panzers, with a motorcycle at the rear."

The spark of anticipation Gromov had felt reverted to anxiety. He was not a believer in happenstance. The competition for Kapsky was about to become pitched.

The Germans were on their way.

They moved almost at double time, Emil in the lead and Canidy nearly abreast. They'd slept far less than any of them had anticipated, nervous energy compelling them to get to Kapsky as quickly as possible.

"I haven't seen much evidence of German occupation in this area," Canidy said to Emil.

Emil shook his head. "We must not be complacent. We are skirting the western edge of the Reichskommissariat Ostland. A few kilometers farther west is an SS nightmare. I am taking a slightly longer route to avoid the area with densest German occupation."

"Hell of a childhood you've had there, Emil."

"The SS Totenkopf are present throughout this area. The Einsatzkommandos are notorious; frankly, merciless. They have slaughtered thousands upon thousands of innocents. The very fact that there is resistance in the face of such terror is extraordinary."

"It would be normal, even natural, to capitulate, hoping one day to be liberated," Canidy agreed. "In the meantime, just keep your head down."

"Some, out of terror, desperation, or calculation, do capitulate. They inform, collaborate. But relatively few, given the circumstances. Poles do not bend to tyranny. But all it takes is a few."

"With Russians on one side and Germans on another, you've plenty of experience with tyranny."

"That is—how you say?—an understatement." Emil pointed north. "There is a camp near Stutthof, only a few kilometers from here. It is difficult to get near because of the dense SS presence. Also, it is surrounded by electrified barbed-wire fences.

"There are dozens of barracks there housing government officials, religious leaders, scholars—but mainly Jews, Jews of every kind: shopkeepers, farmers, teachers, craftsmen. Ordinary people who have committed no offense.

"It is a place of evil."

"Evil? That's not a distinguishing feature in a war zone, Emil," Canidy noted.

"It is in this case. The prisoners there are not combatants. They are not soldiers. They are mere civilians—men, women, and children. Innocents. They are being slaughtered in great numbers."

"We've heard about camps like that. Count Raczyński gave a speech to the League of Nations about them. But without actually seeing them, lots of people just have a hard time believing anyone could do that—even the Nazis."

"Believe it. The SS has constructed chambers that emit gases, poisonous gases. Hundreds at a time are herded into these chambers. The victims are gassed to death and then placed in a large crematorium and incinerated. Some say the stench can be smelled over ten kilometers away.

"Those not immediately gassed upon their arrival at the camp eventually die of starvation or disease. I have not seen this with my own eyes, but my compatriot Milo, the one who was killed yesterday, saw the camp and described it to me. I have heard whispers from others, also."

"We understand there are at least half a dozen such places."

"More. There are at least half a dozen much smaller related or—what is the term?—*satellite* camps in the Danzig area. Larger ones are scattered throughout Poland. Evil."

"If we make it out of this place, first thing we do is let

OSS know the location, although something like that—if it's even remotely as you describe, well, *it must* be known to the Allies."

Emil pointed west. "We are getting close to Malbork. It is a short distance in that direction. Remain alert. There are numerous hamlets between here and there. More populated than where we have been traveling. There are probably a few checkpoints. We will try to remain within cover of forest where possible, but we will be exposed from time to time."

"How much longer?" Fulmar asked.

"I have not gone to that location before. But I estimate just a few more hours if we are not forced to make large detours."

Fulmar made a snorting noise. Canidy turned to see what prompted it. "What?"

"Just thinking about our orders."

Canidy nodded acknowledgment. "Right now we'd be on a wild-goose chase in Germany looking for some damn piece of paper."

Fulmar shook his head. "No, we'd be dead. Now we may be within a few miles of Kapsky himself. If we can come back with Kapsky . . ."

"Let's not get ahead of ourselves. We're on the most dangerous territory on the planet." Canidy smiled. "But, hell yes, if we come back with Kapsky, Donovan will owe us drinks until doomsday."

CHAPTER 45

Bridgette pointed to a small white barn as they stood on the hill overlooking the village.

"That must be it. Kapsky's location. It appears deserted."

She fell silent as she and Gromov watched the cloud of dust approach the outskirts of the village. A car followed by five panzers.

"It appears we are not Kapsky's only visitors," Gromov said.

"What should we do?"

"We have only one option. Get Kapsky before the Germans," Gromov replied. "Let us hope they do not know Kapsky is in the barn. While they search for him it presents an opportunity for us to retrieve him and escape—hopefully unnoticed."

Bridgette pointed toward the vehicles. "We should do it now. It appears they are rounding up villagers for interrogation. It is only a matter of time before someone talks."

"Do they know about Kapsky?"

"I do not think so. Our contact and her assistant should be the only ones. But we cannot be certain no one else has seen a stranger in the area."

"The SS will suspect any stranger might be Kapsky," Gromov said.

"They must."

"Let's go," Gromov said abruptly.

"Where?"

"We have no choice. We cannot wait. We must get to the barn and get Kapsky before they do."

They descended the hill at a brisk pace, losing sight of the German column as they did so. They wove among the trees at a trot until coming to within fifty meters of the barn.

"What is your contact's name?"

"Daria," Bridgette replied. "Only she and her assistant Markus should be in the barn."

Gromov advanced rapidly, Tokarev at the ready and Bridgette trailing a few meters behind. Opening a side entrance, he blinked to adjust to the gloom and scanned the barn, locating a man he assumed was Markus in a loft-like area next to radio equipment. Upon seeing Gromov, the man's face registered alarm and he began to lunge for his rifle resting against a wooden beam. Before he could reach it, Bridgette yelled, "Markus, I am Danish Resistance. Bridgette."

Markus seized the rifle but remained still save for the rapid blinking of his eyes.

"Danish Resistance," Bridgette repeated. She pointed to Gromov. "Major Taras Gromov. Red Army. We are here for Kapsky. We are here to help. We are here to get him to safety."

Markus held his rifle on the pair as he descended the stairs. Gromov held his pistol over his head.

"Markus," Gromov said. "A column of panzers just arrived. They are in the square. They are surely looking for Kapsky. He must leave immediately. We can escort him to safety."

Markus continued to hold his weapon on the pair as he approached. "A column of panzers arrives in the village at the same time you enter my barn," Markus said slowly.

Gromov nodded. "Yes. We concede. Too coincidental. You are right to be suspicious. Any soldier would." He gestured toward Bridgette. "Bridgette is Danish Resistance. Your people, as I understand it, have communicated with her before. We are here to secure Dr. Sebastian Kapsky. You have no time to waste before the Germans smash through the door with their panzers."

Markus stared at Bridgette. "You received the message."

"Yes."

Markus lowered his weapon. "Kapsky is not here. We received word that the Germans were on their way so Daria took him elsewhere."

"My job is to get him out of occupied Poland, Markus. I can do that, but I need to know where he is."

"There is no need," Markus replied.

"There certainly is," Gromov said. "You know their methods. They will come in here and extract the information from you no matter how much you resist. Painfully. They will get Kapsky."

Markus shook his head. "What I mean is a team of Americans, *Armia*, and a British soldier were here. They are already on their way to collect Kapsky and remove him from Nazi-occupied territory. They left some time ago on foot. Provided they've not been intercepted, they are probably within a few hours of Malbork."

Gromov became rigid and bit the inside of his lower lip to keep from cursing. The Americans. They were supposed to have gone to Germany. They were ahead of him.

"That is excellent news," Gromov lied. "How long of a journey on foot?"

Markus shrugged. "It depends on how many Germans they must avoid. The area is saturated with SS. But they have an outstanding guide."

"An estimate?" Gromov asked.

"Not far. A few hours from here. They left a couple of hours ago."

Gromov struggled not to show his frustration. He turned to Bridgette. "Do you know how to get to Malbork?"

"Are you thinking of going there? For what purpose?"

"They may not get there. Or, if they do, they may need assistance. Our orders are to get Kapsky out of harm's way. I cannot tell my superiors I deferred to the

Americans and British, that I heard from a man I never met before that the Americans were on their way. What if they are not successful? What if they do not even get to Malbork?"

"You heard Markus. They are far ahead of you. They will be gone by the time you get there."

Markus said, "Stay adjacent to the paved road that leads you north. It is in that general direction."

"We cannot go on the road."

"Yes, but you can stay near it."

"It is futile," Bridgette said. "You cannot catch up. You are only imperiling yourself."

Gromov stared at the straw on the floor for several seconds and then looked up. "Thank you for your help, Markus. You must leave *now*. When the Germans find you with the equipment upstairs, you will be dead." He turned to Bridgette. "We also must leave now."

"Where are you going?"

"South of Malbork."

Bridgette rolled her eyes. "Impossible."

Gromov grasped her right arm with his free hand, pulled her toward the barn door, and peered outside. No Germans.

"I'm going to be moving quickly and quietly. You must run as fast as you possibly can to follow me."

Without uttering another word, Gromov bolted from the door toward the tree line forty meters away. Then he paused to allow Bridgette to join him. He put his finger to his lips and then began moving rapidly through the trees and brush for several minutes, navigating in the direction of the village square. Bridgette followed close behind.

As they drew near the square, their pace slowed and they moved quietly and cautiously. They halted just within the tree line and watched as German soldiers herded dozens of villagers into the east side of the square at gunpoint.

On the opposite side of the square an imposing figure stood in the rear of a Horch command car. Arrayed behind the car was a row of five panzers, their MG 34 machine guns trained on the villagers. Behind the line of panzers sat a Zündapp KS 750, a driver and passenger seated in their respective seats.

Gromov assessed the scene for scant seconds before telling Bridgette, "Watch me and act appropriately."

Then he inserted his sidearm into his belt, withdrew his NR-40, and sprinted from behind toward the motorcycle. Both driver and rider were oblivious to his presence until he wrapped his free arm around first the driver and then the passenger and sliced their necks to the bone. He pulled each of their bodies from their respective seats, dragged them to the ground, and mounted the motorcycle. He waited no more than a heartbeat as Bridgette climbed into the sidecar. Then he kick-started the vehicle and sped from the square onto the northbound road recommended by Markus.

Startled, the German troops in the square took several seconds to realize that the motorcycle was being stolen. By then, the vehicle was nearly two hundred meters down the road and obscured by thick clouds of dust.

They began firing haphazardly to no effect until a disgusted Maurer ordered them to cease.

Gromov didn't throttle down until they were more than a kilometer from the village. Even then, he stayed at more than sixty kilometers per hour.

Bridgette's chest was still heaving from exertion and exhilaration.

"What will you do if we encounter a German patrol?" she shouted over the din.

"Drive past them as if there is nothing wrong and hope for the best."

"What if they try to stop us?"

"Then I will kill them, too."

CHAPTER 46

It was more a small cluster of dwellings—barely two dozen—than a village or town.

The house in which Kapsky purportedly was hiding was as described by Markus: a small one-story wood-and-brick affair consisting of, at most, four rooms situated at the north edge of the village.

The last two kilometers of the journey had become increasingly treacherous. Emil was right. The SS seemed to be everywhere. Whoever had decided to move Kapsky here, Canidy thought, had made a mistake. There had to be a better place than this to hide. Or maybe it was sheer genius. Very few would suspect someone wanted by the SS would pick a place crawling with them in which to hide.

The five observed the house from inside the ruins of what appeared to have been a general store that had been struck by a mortar some time ago. The shattered piles of bricks, blocks, and mortar provided outstanding cover. They had not spied any sign of civilian activity since they'd arrived a quarter of an hour ago, but a Totenkopf squad had patrolled within seventy-five meters of their position, eventually passing out of sight.

"I'm going in with Matuszek. Daria knows him," Canidy said. "The rest of you remain here and provide cover and keep watch." He pointed to a window on the right. "Watch that window. If Kapsky's there, I'll signal and you be ready to move."

"Then what?" Emil asked.

"Simple. Then we bring him out and we make our way back to the canal."

"What if a patrol stumbles upon us?"

Canidy shrugged. "Use your head. Avoid them if you can. Kill them if you must. But *quietly*."

Canidy looked about before he and Matuszek rose from the rubble and jogged to the front of the dwelling. For a moment Canidy felt foolish. What was he supposed to do, knock on the door and then ask for Sebastian Kapsky? Absurd. But after a short deliberation, that's precisely what he did: two quick raps at the door, his free hand gripping the pistol at his waist. The door opened immediately and a redheaded woman pulled them inside and shut the door. She embraced Matuszek heartily.

"Roch, it is good to see you," she said, grasping his wrists.

Startled by how swiftly the woman had opened the door, Canidy asked, "How did you know who was at the door? There are Germans everywhere."

"I have been watching you for several minutes. You really are not very good at concealing yourselves." She pointed out the window. "See for yourself."

Canidy peered out the window and was appalled to find that he could see the scalps of Fulmar, Emil, and McDermott above the rubble. He had to look very closely, but they were visible nonetheless.

Matuszek wasted no time. "Daria, is Dr. Sebastian Kapsky here with you? We are here to get him to safety."

Daria hesitated, examining Canidy.

"This is Major Canidy of the United States Office of Strategic Services. He has been dispatched by the highest levels of the United States government to secure a document from Dr. Kapsky. I was able to convince him he might be able to secure Dr. Kapsky himself. I trust him."

"SS are everywhere," Daria said.

"Yes, we know."

"I received a message from my sister Ilsa to move Dr. Kapsky immediately," Daria continued. "An SS officer is searching for Dr. Kapsky. His name is Maurer. He has something of a reputation. He was on his way to our previous location, so we came here, a place we've used before—but that was before the Germans seemed to triple in number. Especially Totenkopf. I am afraid it is only a matter of time before Maurer arrives or we are discovered by the Totenkopf. So we will need to move him once again. Clearly, Dr. Kapsky is a priority for them."

"He's a priority for us, too," Canidy said. "Is he here?"

"He is in the cellar," Daria replied.

"No, I'm right behind you," Kapsky said.

Canidy saw a tall, thin man with intelligent green eyes and a shock of black hair across his forehead. He looked like the descriptions Donovan had given him. He looked haggard and ill.

"Dr. Kapsky, I'm Major Canidy. This is Commander Matuszek. We are here to escort you to safety."

"How, may I ask?"

"By any means necessary."

Kapsky, though worn, appeared amused. "I assume you are singularly capable of doing so, otherwise your government wouldn't have chosen you from literally millions of candidates to conduct this operation."

"Capable or expendable, it's unclear which."

Kapsky asked, "You two are to perform this task? Again, how, if I may ask?"

"Before I answer that, answer this: Our original assignment was to retrieve or find you. We did. At least we found your corpse. Along with a notebook containing indecipherable equations. Apparently, the equations are so complex and advanced that it's taking forever to understand. Our next assignment was to retrieve another document created by you: yet more mathematical equations, which document is in the possession of the Abwehr. Two questions: How are you here and what's on that document?"

"You need to verify that I am Dr. Sebastian Kapsky?"

"The last one was dead."

"The corpse you encountered was a decoy. I had subtly spread information of my whereabouts. Then I found a corpse—unfortunately not a difficult task in Poland these days—and placed it where you found it. I had the rather macabre good fortune of finding a corpse roughly my dimensions and appearance. I dressed him in my clothing. But I could not be certain, of course, that those searching for me would necessarily conclude it was me as opposed to some other unfortunate. So for good measure, I crafted both a notebook and a document—a scroll—containing an encrypted series of equations that related to matters the scientific establishment, and, therefore, intelligence services, knew I was working on. The notebook, I estimated, was sure to be found. But the addition of the scroll was in order to be certain to convince the finder they'd found something of extraordinary value. I inserted the scroll into the corpse's mouth to give the appearance that I was trying to destroy it—to keep it out of hostile hands—before I was killed, to convey the impression it was of utmost importance."

"Perhaps too clever," Matuszek said. "We did not see it. It seems you may have shoved it too far down the corpse's throat. Not to worry, however, the meticulous Germans found it and have it in their possession."

"And both you and the Germans abandoned the search for me. You see, I needed the *certainty* that the Germans would cease looking. Both the scroll and notebook contain very complex but ultimately counterfeit equations that scientists would initially conclude pertain to an advanced rocket propulsion as well as a crude atomic device. I expressed the equations in code to slow them down, so it would take considerable time to determine that the equations are infeasible. I would, therefore, have sufficient time before they concluded the same—sufficient to make my escape.

"I do, however, have a notebook with genuine work in it," Kapsky said, patting the right side of his shirt. "Right here. It contains the salient corpus of my work. Taped to my side. Be sure to take it if I do not survive."

"You can bet on it." Canidy walked to the side of the window and waved, alerting the rest. "Dr. Kapsky, it's time to move. If you have anything else that's essential, get it now. I suggest it weigh no more than five to ten pounds total."

"I have no possessions."

"Good." Canidy turned to Daria. "Ma'am, you're welcome to come, but I can't guarantee your safety. My priority is Dr. Kapsky."

"I will remain here. I am a Pole. I will be all right." She grinned. "I have outwitted and bedeviled the Nazis for several years. Why stop now?"

Kapsky kissed Daria on the cheek. "Thank you for everything. Good luck to you. I will see you after the war."

All of them fell silent upon hearing the rumble of a motor vehicle. Canidy stood to one side of the window and looked out. A truck carrying six German soldiers in its open bed passed slowly in front of the house and out of view. The rumble continued for another thirty seconds before fading.

Canidy eyed Kapsky and Matuszek. "On three."

Matuszek and Kapsky both asked, "What?"

Canidy smiled. "We move out after I count to three. Fast."

Before he could begin counting, a German foot patrol emerged from the direction in which the truck had disappeared. From his spot next to the window, Canidy counted eight. He felt the hairs on his arms stand on end as the patrol moved slowly past the rubble where the others were hiding. Canidy signaled to Matuszek to be ready to move, but by the time Matuszek moved to the other side of the window the patrol was receding to the east. Within a minute they were out of sight.

Canidy didn't move. Matuszek frowned. "Dick? Let's go."

Canidy held up a hand. "This isn't going to work."

Puzzled, Matuszek asked, "What do you mean, 'This isn't going to work'?"

"Just that. There are far too many Germans in the area. Too high a risk."

"What are you saying?" Kapsky asked. "That we stay here?"

"No," Canidy replied, thinking as he spoke. "*I* am staying here. *You* are leaving. With Matuszek."

Matuszek looked bewildered. "What?"

"There are too many Germans. We don't stand a prayer of avoiding them much longer. My job is to deliver Kapsky from this hellhole safely. The best way of doing that is to make the Germans think Kapsky is alive and here."

Matuszek and Daria looked perplexed. Kapsky smiled,

anticipating what Canidy was about to say. "A live decoy instead of a dead one."

"Precisely," Canidy said. "Matuszek, you and Dr. Kapsky are going to join the rest of our group and get the hell out of here. Get him to the canal and Kristin's boat. From now on, I am Dr. Sebastian Kapsky, although immeasurably better looking."

Matuszek and Daria stared at Canidy, perplexed. Kapsky continued to smile.

"Pretty simple, really. If a dead decoy could keep Dr. Kapsky alive for so long, a live, moving decoy should do the trick even better. The Germans will be looking for me, a moving target. More specifically, a target moving in a different direction than the real Kapsky."

"You cannot survive," Matuszek said somberly, with a hint of anger. "You do not know the area. You will be caught or killed. Perhaps both."

"We'll see," Canidy said cavalierly. "If Daria just points me in the right direction, I'll take them on a hell of a wild-goose chase and take some pressure off you guys." He extended his hand, shaking first Kapsky's and then Matuszek's. "Now go."

Matuszek glanced out the window. "Clear. Follow me."

Matuszek opened the door and ran toward the rubble, Kapsky just a few feet behind.

Fulmar, McDermott, and Emil provided cover. Upon reaching the rubble Matuszek squatted next to Fulmar. "He's not coming. He's acting as a decoy for Dr. Kapsky here." Kapsky nodded his introduction to Fulmar.

"That's so . . ." Fulmar restrained himself. This was, after all, Dick Canidy. *Nothing* was unexpected. Without a pause, he extended his hand toward Kapsky. "Dr. Kapsky, Eric Fulmar. By order of the President of the United States of America, we are taking you to safety."

Standing next to the window, Canidy watched as Emil led them out of sight.

"You must have a large meal before you go," Daria said. "You do not know when you will eat again. I have latkes already made."

"Thanks. I'll take them with me, if you don't mind."

Daria went into the small kitchen and began wrapping latkes in wax paper. Canidy asked, "How did you know to move Kapsky?"

"My sister Ilsa sent word that the SS was searching for him and were on their way to Sztum."

"What about Markus? We met him in the barn there. Why didn't he go with you?"

"Markus is originally from there."

"If the SS locates him, he's dead."

Daria nodded solemnly. "Yes." A moment later she smiled mischievously. "Markus is quite resourceful, however."

"As is Kapsky," Canidy observed.

Daria placed the wax paper–wrapped latkes in a cloth bag and handed it to Canidy. "Quite resourceful," she agreed. "He escaped from Katyn using his wits."

"Katyn? The place the Nazi's chief liar, Reichsminister

Joseph Goebbels, claims the Red Army supposedly executed thousands of Polish officials and intellectuals?"

"We in the *Armia* heard stories," Daria explained. "More than stories, we saw thousands upon thousands of intelligentsia—doctors, academics, administrators—rounded up by the Red Army and sent to Katyn Forest, where we suspected something terrible was occurring. The Soviets, of course, denied they were executed. But Dr. Kapsky was there. He *saw* it, the executions. And now he's escaped."

Canidy stared at her. "So the Red Army—the Soviets actually did this? It's not just Nazi propaganda? The *Soviets* killed Poles?"

Daria nodded. "Kapsky confirmed it. Bodies stacked in shallow graves. He saw it himself. A credible witness. Not a Nazi propagandist or Soviet *propagandist*. Thousands, maybe tens of thousands, executed. Most of them, he says, by one man with a handgun."

Canidy rubbed the back of his neck and exhaled. He doubted OSS—or any Allied service—had actual verification of this information. Canidy knew little of diplomacy or the compromises Allies made, the fictions that were tolerated, to forge and sustain coalitions. But he knew intuitively that what he'd just heard from Daria, if accurate, had the potential to significantly disrupt the relationship between the U.S. and the USSR, as well as the conduct of the war. The Katyn fiction would be blown wide open.

"Daria, is this common knowledge among Home Army? Among Poles in general?"

She shook her head. "In war one hears lots of things and lots of people hear things. But the only person who was *there* is Dr. Kapsky. He is the only live witness who is not Red Army. Be assured, if anyone had actual proof of it, *Armia* would have known. The knowledge would have spread like wildfire."

Candy sat on a wooden stool and pondered the implications. He understood instinctively he now had two missions: draw the Germans away from Kapsky, and get home alive in case the first objective wasn't met. *Someone* had to convey the Katyn Forest information to the Allies.

Daria scrutinized Candy's face and understood. "You didn't believe you were going to evade the SS, did you? You were only planning to distract them for a while so that Dr. Kapsky could escape."

Candy shook his head distractedly. "I'm not sure what I was thinking."

"But now you cannot simply sacrifice yourself because you must convey the Katyn information to your superiors, correct?"

Candy exhaled. "Something like that."

"Sacrificing yourself for a worthy objective is noble, but sometimes much easier than ensuring that an objective is actually met. The former is heroic, but the latter is responsible. It is easier to be a heroic martyr than a responsible one."

Candy chuckled wryly. "A responsible martyr would have been sure to have a guide get him back to the boat. I just dispatched mine. I have a general idea how to get there, but now I have to be *sure* to get back."

"Where do you need to go?"

"All I know is it's a canal on the Baltic near Danzig."

Daria said, "I can guide you to Danzig. It will be quite hazardous. But I do not believe I am familiar with this canal. Where near Danzig is it located?"

Canidy chuckled again. "I suppose I should have paid closer attention. I depended upon McDermott and Emil. I have a decent recollection, but I can't ask you to do this. It's tantamount to a death sentence."

"Be assured, I'm aware of the risk. Living in Poland under the Nazis is nearly—" Daria stopped abruptly and looked out the window. A German patrol was approaching the house. As she quickly proceeded to the kitchen, she looked over her shoulder at Canidy and said, "Come with me. *Now*."

CHAPTER 47

Gromov pulled the motorcycle off the road and into a dense grove of pear trees. They had encountered no German patrols, but he didn't want to press their luck. According to Markus's directions they were nearing Malbork and the likelihood of running into Germans increased every minute.

Bridgette pointed to a depression several meters into the grove. Gromov wordlessly guided the vehicle into it and cut off the engine. They dismounted, stepped back, examined the area from the road, and satisfied themselves that the bike was invisible.

They could hear the rumble of heavy vehicles to the north, in the direction Markus had given them. Both felt pinpricks of nervousness. Both assumed the Germans in Sztum had radioed ahead that someone—likely *Armia*—had killed two of their men and escaped northward.

"This area is not familiar to me," Bridgette said. "I've never been here."

Gromov chuckled. "As difficult as it may be to believe, I didn't expect you to know all of Europe."

"I'm afraid I will just slow you down."

"I could move a lot more quickly on my own," Gromov conceded. "But after acquiring Kapsky I need help getting him to safety. My original instructions were to acquire the Kapsky document and return to Kattegat, where your people would ensure that I get back to Soviet territory."

"I can help you there," Bridgette said. "We will proceed in a northwesterly direction until we near the coast. We'll have vessels near Mikoszewo and Krynica Morska that can take us to Kattegat. Not Schnellboots, but serviceable. I have used one before. We may have to wait for them, but they are reliable."

"Please tell me again how my original assignment was a death sentence as opposed to this one."

They proceeded quietly but briskly through the woods for nearly a quarter hour, the rumbling of the heavy equipment to the northwest gradually growing louder. Both were startled by a prolonged burst of machine-gun fire to the rear. Instantly, they dropped to the ground and remained silent. Another short burst of fire sounded. Then nothing except the rumbling to the north.

"Someone found the motorcycle," Gromov concluded.

"That was too fast," Bridgette said. "This area must be saturated with Germans."

"They're taking precautions. They don't know precisely when the motorcycle was abandoned, so they are strafing the area just in case."

"Do you mean they know the motorcycle was stolen?"

"That's exactly what I mean. That wasn't random. A patrol—or patrols—is searching for us."

They remained prone for a minute, listening for signs of nearby German presence, before rising and continuing northward. The woods quickly began thinning and the rumbling grew louder. They could see glimpses of movement approximately half a kilometer north.

Gromov stopped and dropped to a knee, Bridgette coming alongside and doing the same. A German armored column was proceeding from west to east. Panzers and troop carriers. Gromov could see neither the head nor the rear of the column.

Bridgette pointed toward the vehicles. "I see rooftops down that slope on the other side of the column. That must be where Kapsky is."

Gromov's jaws clenched. "A stupid place to hide. Germans everywhere."

"Perhaps not so stupid. Who would think to look for him in a place like this? Anyone would expect he would hide in a place where there would *not* be Germans."

"Stupid," Gromov insisted.

"Not stupid. Difficult," Bridgette said. "For us."

Gromov said nothing.

* * *

The cellar Daria had directed him to was small, dank, and dark, with a musty smell. No lights.

Canidy had caught a glimpse of some small wooden shelves lined with jars before Daria had shut the trapdoor behind him after he'd descended a short ladder. He heard something scurrying about the dirt floor around him. Too small to be rats, he convinced himself. Likely mice. He balled his fists and bit his lower lip.

He heard a voice overhead, guttural, imperative, unmistakably German. Then he heard Daria's voice, even and calm. Although he didn't understand what was being said, he knew the issue: "Have you seen someone named Sebastian Kapsky? I do not know such a man. Have you seen anyone more recently? No. Is there anyone else here? No."

Footfalls heavier than Daria's traversed the floor above. Not many. The house was small, not much to search, not many places to hide. Canidy estimated three men above. Maybe more waiting outside.

He withdrew his M1911 and aimed at the trapdoor, his grip tight. There was another German imperative sentence followed by a three-word question. He could hear no response and assumed Daria shook her head either yes or no. Then silence.

He sensed something small run over his right boot, yet somehow resisted the urge to shake his foot. Only good trigger discipline prevented him from involuntarily discharging his firearm.

The voices above became somewhat indistinct. He strained to listen, but was unable to discern what was being said. The inflection of the German soldier's voice was that of a question. Canidy couldn't discern Daria's reply, but the tone of the German's voice became skeptical, then insistent, then urgent. There were a few seconds of silence, then the German's voice became loud enough to startle a swarm of small, unseen creatures whose scurrying movements Canidy could hear around him. The grip on his pistol remained steady as he bit harder on his lip in an effort not to be distracted. He could hear himself breathing: short, ragged, and shallow. He strained to hear any sounds whatsoever from above for the next thirty seconds. Nothing. Not movement, not voices. Then he heard the sound of heels moving rapidly and purposely on wood. He held his breath, but the noise was *receding*. The Germans were leaving.

Canidy continued to train his pistol on the trapdoor. He heard nothing for nearly a minute, then the sound of light footsteps, the steps of someone small.

Then silence for nearly three minutes that seemed to Canidy far longer.

The trapdoor opened and Daria's face appeared from above. Canidy lowered his weapon slowly, then looked about the floor of the cellar for whatever had been scurrying about, but they had disappeared. There appeared to be a transmitter in the corner on the opposite wall. Other than that, he saw nothing but dirt and dust. Not even small tools. He looked back up at Daria, who appeared calm and relaxed.

"They are gone. For now," she informed him. "I think I persuaded them that I know nothing about a Sebastian Kapsky."

Canidy lowered the M1911 and began to ascend the short ladder to the kitchen. He got no farther than the first rung when he heard a rap on the front door and saw Daria's eyes grow wide. Canidy froze for a moment before descending again, brandishing his pistol at low-ready. *A return visit is never a good sign*, he thought.

Daria's face disappeared as she lowered the trapdoor. Canidy heard her cross to the door, then silence. *The Germans were not convinced*, he thought. *They're on to her.* He must have made a noise when the unseen creatures caused him to flinch.

Canidy backed into the corner farthest from the trapdoor and dropped to a knee, the weapon held steady on the trapdoor. He strained to hear the muffled voices from above, prepared to hear commands, shouts. But he heard nothing for several maddening seconds. The next sound Canidy heard was indistinct, but it was not Daria's voice. Though he didn't understand German, he strained to discern what he could from the voice's inflection and tone. It was, however, too low. So low that Canidy could hear the pronounced pulse of blood in his ears.

He thought he heard movement from above, but it was so subtle it may have been his imagination. Then he heard the sound of a door closing. It, however, was distinct. It wasn't his imagination. The footsteps, heavier than Daria's, drew closer to the trapdoor, then stopped.

Canidy glanced about the gloom of the tiny cellar for anything behind which he could conceal himself. There was nothing of use. He determined he'd simply empty his weapon when the trapdoor opened.

He dropped to one knee to get a better angle on the opening. He was a sitting duck, but he'd take as many as he could with him. *A cellar in Poland*, he thought. *A damn rodent-infested cellar in Poland.*

He sensed the presence of someone directly overhead and restrained himself from firing through the trapdoor. There was a confusing mix of heavy footfalls and light. Then silence.

The next sound he heard was Daria's voice posing a question. He strained but couldn't discern what she was saying. After a pause, she spoke again, too soft to comprehend.

Move out of the way, Daria, Canidy thought. *Get out of the line of fire.*

Daria spoke again but was interrupted by a male voice—strong, confident, and commanding. He recognized the voice.

The trapdoor opened slowly. Canidy blinked at the light streaming from above, the dust wafting upward toward the opening. He braced for the target to appear. Instead he heard a voice say, "Do not fire your weapon. It is I, Emil."

Canidy exhaled and lowered the weapon, perplexed but relieved. Light streamed into the cellar as the trapdoor opened slowly. Though his gaze was riveted on the aperture, his peripheral vision nonetheless registered that whatever creatures had scurried about him on the floor remained hidden.

Emil's face and torso appeared overhead, Daria behind him over his left shoulder. Canidy exhaled forcefully, relieved yet perplexed. Before he could ask why Emil had returned, a loud knock on the front door caused the young warrior to leap to the cellar floor, Daria closing the trapdoor behind him.

CHAPTER 48

Standartenführer Konrad Maurer's command car proceeded along the same northwest road Gromov and Bridgette had traveled hours earlier. The five panzers trailed close behind, now with far less machine-gun ammunition, a significant amount of which had been expended in Sztum.

No matter. They were in German-held territory. Besides, they would soon replenish their supply at the depots at their destination.

Nonetheless, Maurer was frustrated, even anxious. Despite his having executed dozens of their compatriots, the peasants in Sztum refused to disclose any information pertaining to Dr. Sebastian Kapsky. They were either uncommonly brave or, more likely, remarkably stupid. Either way, they steadfastly refused to cooperate. Maurer was fortunate to stumble upon the partisan in the barn on the outskirts of the village. He, too, had been obstinate—impressively so—refusing to speak despite the methodical excision of each of his fingers and all but two of his toes. The peasant had nearly bled to death without yielding any information regarding Kapsky before one of Maurer's men discovered notes next to a radio in the loft. They were a handwritten transcription, a confirmation from someone that he or she had arrived safely in Malbork with "the ghost." Maurer felt blessed to have adversaries who were such simpletons.

Despite his frustration, Maurer remained confident. Although he suspected the theft of the motorcycle might be attributable to one of his opponents in the contest for Kapsky, he was still in control.

The entire area was controlled by the Wehrmacht. Even if the Americans and Soviets acquired Kapsky, they would still have to navigate through scores of kilometers of territory over which the Germans held dominion. Maurer would ultimately win the race to secure Kapsky. He was more talented than his adversaries. Because of his prowess, Maurer had come to the attention of the Führer himself. He was *that* talented. He would succeed. He had to succeed.

Canidy and Emil squatted in the recess of the cellar farthest from the trapdoor and listened intently to the sounds upstairs. Daria had opened the front door to a German who identified himself as SS Untersturmführer Lange. His voice sounded gruff and impatient.

Canidy whispered to Emil, "Can you make out what he's saying?"

"Something about whether she's seen any strangers in the area. He says one of his men reports he saw someone come to the door a few minutes ago. Daria says no. He sounds skeptical."

Both Canidy and Emil strained to hear the conversation, which was obscured by the rumble of a lorry passing nearby. For several moments they heard no voices and hoped that the Untersturmführer had satisfied his curiosity and departed. Each of their chests tightened, however, upon hearing what sounded like a door closing and the tap of boots walking slowly across the floor above.

Canidy cursed quietly, motioned for Emil to stay where he was, and moved to the ladder. He paused at its base and listened for what seemed like a minute before he heard the SS officer give a command in German that ended in the only word Canidy recognized: *Keller*.

Canidy cursed again to himself, stuck his pistol in his waistband, and quickly, but quietly, ascended the ladder to just below the trapdoor. As he did the door began to open, with the SS officer leaning forward, preparing to peer inside.

Canidy thrust his right hand upward, seized the officer's service tunic, and pulled downward as hard as he could. The German crashed on top of the American to the cellar floor, Canidy maintaining his grip on the tunic with his right hand while viciously punching the officer with his left. Blood from the German's mouth and nose splattered across Canidy's face, getting into his eyes, but he continued to rain blows down on the man's head. Desperate, the German bucked violently upward, throwing Canidy off him. Emil, however, leapt on him immediately, driving him back to the earth floor and giving Canidy a second to recover and wrap his right arm around the German's head, twisting it viciously clockwise and then counterclockwise. The crack of the man's cervical vertebrae was loud enough to startle Emil, who stared in wonderment as the man's hands maintained a stubborn grip on Canidy's shirt. Canidy withdrew his trench knife from under his shirt and thrust it into the left temple of the German, whose arms and torso twitched for several seconds before ceasing altogether.

Canidy, chest heaving from the exertion, forcefully pulled away the man's hands, which maintained a grip on Canidy's shirt. He then pulled the knife from the man's skull and wiped the blood onto the man's trousers. Noticing a shadow on the cellar's floor, Canidy looked up to see Daria peering down with a rueful look on her face. He understood what she was thinking: how to dispose of the corpse of an SS officer in densely occupied territory and explain to inquiring Nazis what happened to such officer, who was last seen approaching her door.

Canidy rose to one knee, his heart pounding more from adrenaline than exertion. As he caught his breath, Emil, reading his mind, said, "He appears to be about seventy-five kilograms. That is enough dead weight to make disposing of the corpse difficult, but manageable. But that is the easy part. Daria is in trouble."

Canidy stood erect, still breathing hard. "First things first. Why the hell did you come back?"

"Fulmar, through Commander Matuszek, directed that I return to guide you, to assist you both in being a decoy and in evading the Germans. Almost immediately after we left here they concluded that since you don't know the country as I do, your career as a decoy would be a rather short one, resulting in your certain death and Kapsky's eventual capture."

Canidy smiled wryly. "Yeah, that's probably right. Didn't give that as much thought as I should have. I sometimes tend to . . ."

". . . have a great deal of—how do you Americans say it?—hubris? Is that the right word?"

Canidy pursed his lips. "Yeah, that's as good as any. Now, back to matters at hand. You go upstairs and check to see what is going on outside. Let me know if there are any Germans nearby. Then I'll carry this guy upstairs . . ."

"Forgive me, Major Canidy, but I fear you may be, once again, engaging in a bit of hubris. I'll give you a hand taking him upstairs when I get back from checking outside."

Emil scaled the ladder and disappeared. Canidy bent over and grasped the corpse by his belt buckle and collar. Then he bent his knees and hoisted him over his right shoulder. *Hubris.*

Emil returned and peered down from the kitchen. "There are no patrols in sight. Daria suggests we bury the body in the thicket behind the house. I agree. It's about ten meters from the back. We will not be seen from the street." Emil pointed to the body over Canidy's shoulder. "Wait, I'll help you."

"Get back. There's not enough room. It's easier if I do it. Keep watching out the window. We can't afford any surprises."

Emil's face disappeared from overhead as Canidy tested the first rung of the ladder to see if it could bear his weight combined with that of the corpse. He then proceeded tentatively up the next seven steps, until the corpse was level with the floor above, and dumped the body onto the floor. He disciplined himself to take shallow breaths so Emil wouldn't notice his exhaustion.

Daria pointed to the kitchen door leading to the back of the house. "The thicket is about ten to fifteen meters to the rear. There are picks and shovels in the little shed on the left side of the door."

Emil returned from the front room and grasped the corpse's ankles. "No activity out front. We can move the body now."

Canidy gripped the corpse's armpits as Daria held the door open. After Canidy and Emil dumped the body among the shrubs, they used the implements in the shed to dig a grave in the soft earth of the thicket.

Although Daria kept watch out the front window, they paused every thirty seconds or so to listen for any sounds of Germans approaching. Barely fifteen minutes later they lowered the body into the ground, and covered it with earth overlaid with branches and leaves arranged as naturally as possible.

They returned inside and met Daria in the kitchen.

"Emil's going to guide me on my wild-goose chase," Canidy informed. "You need to come with us."

Daria smiled but shook her head. "I understand the risks," she said. "An SS officer goes missing, so they will search every house. Soon they will determine that he was last seen approaching this one. So I will receive special attention. But I have gotten this far by my wits. I will remain here."

"Your wits won't save you this time, Daria," Canidy replied. "Not when they see the earth behind the house."

"A risk, to be sure," Daria conceded. "But if I go with you, you will appear more conspicuous, and I will slow you down."

"Maybe, but not by much," Canidy said. "Come with us."

Daria shook her head with finality. "I am afraid not. The two of you need to be as nimble as possible so you can distract the Germans long enough for Kapsky to get to safety. Once they capture you, the charade is over."

"Then at least leave on your own."

"A Polish woman on her own in a Totenkopf zone? I stand a better chance here."

Canidy and Emil were reluctant to leave her behind, but they didn't argue. They knew she was right.

Daria said, "Go out the back door and through the thicket. The woods clear a half kilometer from here and you will see a gravel road in front of an old coal plant. That road will eventually turn into a larger one bordered most of the way by woodlands, and that will eventually take you to Danzig—at least the general direction of Danzig. I will wait a suitable period after you have left and seek a German officer, resort to my well-worn acting skills, and inform him I saw someone bearing a strong resemblance to their description of 'Dr. Kapstein' proceeding along the road. That," Daria emphasized, "will be where your wild-goose chase begins in earnest."

Daria gave each of them a brief hug. "Remember," she added, "I will be giving the Germans a fairly accurate description of both of you. In the process, I may also gain some credibility, thereby diverting attention from my backyard."

Canidy nodded. "You *have* to give them a good description in order for the charade to be successful."

". . . Therefore, do not travel on the road, otherwise they will capture you too readily. Stay in the woods next to the road. You must prolong the chase, divert them from your friends and the real Dr. Kapsky."

"That's the plan. He escapes, we escape, and you're 'left alone.'"

As they said their goodbyes, Canidy suspected that at least two prongs of the plan would never be met.

CHAPTER 49

Gromov and Bridgette lay on a bluff overlooking the village. One house matched the description that the man in the barn had given them for Kapsky's hiding spot. As they watched, a redheaded woman emerged. She walked unhurriedly less than a kilometer to a store that appeared to have been converted to temporary German Army headquarters. The roof of the store supported a large antennae array and numerous telephone lines, presumably for dispatching orders to the many German Kampfgruppen in the region.

Gromov pointed to the house. "Watch the house for any sign of activity," he instructed Bridgette. "I will watch the headquarters."

Mere minutes after the redhead had entered the headquarters, three Kübelwagens carrying approximately a dozen troops sped in a northwesterly direction from the adjacent lot. A Panzerwagen ADGZ trailed them.

Barely a minute later the redhead left the building and proceeded back toward the house. Gromov believed he detected a spring in her step.

Gromov surveyed the immediate area for the best path toward the Kapsky house. There were no good ones. He told Bridgette, "We will proceed west along the ridge until we are perpendicular to the house." He pointed to the piles of rubble near the home. "Then we'll go down the ridge to those ruins. From the ruins across to the house. That should give us adequate concealment eighty-five percent of the way."

"Then?" Bridgette asked.

"Then we take Kapsky to safety."

"Obviously," Bridgette said. "But by what path? Your original orders were to acquire the Kapsky document and return it to the Soviet Union. But we are now in Poland. I do not know how to guide you to the Soviet Union from here."

"As long as we can get around the German-Russian front, we should be able to get to the Soviet Union."

Gromov rose and proceeded along the ridge with Bridgette behind him. There were no German troops visible in the area. Within minutes, they were crouching in the rubble across from the Kapsky house. They could see movement behind the curtain of the front window. It appeared to be only one person.

Gromov scanned the area for any German presence before he and Bridgette crossed quickly over to the house. Gromov rapped on the door, watching the surrounding area nervously.

Daria opened the door within seconds with a quizzical expression on her face. If anyone, she had been expecting Germans.

Gromov wasted no time. "I am Major Taras Gromov, Red Army. I understand from your man in Sztum that Dr. Sebastian Kapsky is hiding here. I am here to take him to safety."

Daria's face registered caution, then both mirth and confusion. After a second she said, "Come in. Quickly."

Gromov and Bridgette stepped inside and Daria closed the door. Bridgette introduced herself. "I am Bridgette Nørgaard. Danish Resistance. I am assisting Major Gromov."

Daria smiled, shaking her head in wonderment. "This has been a most eventful day. Bridgette, I am Daria. We have spoken at least once before, by radio. And we have exchanged messages. It's good to finally meet you."

Bridgette gave Daria a brief hug, then stepped back. "Markus told us you were here with Dr. Kapsky. He also mentioned that a team of Americans, assisted by a British soldier and *Armia*, were on their way here also."

Daria said nothing.

"So, is Dr. Kapsky here?" Gromov asked.

Daria inspected the two visitors. "Dr. Kapsky is not here."

"Where is he?" Bridgette asked. "Is he with the Americans?"

Daria took several seconds to answer. "I do not know."

"*Was* he here?" Gromov asked.

Daria said nothing.

"Daria," Bridgette said, her voice sympathetic. "Major Gromov and I can get him to safety, but we need to know where he is. I understand you need to be careful. But time is critical."

Daria rubbed her hands against her sides nervously. "He is safe," she replied.

"Where?" Gromov asked. "Is he with the Americans?"

"We can help," Bridgette added.

"I should not say," Daria said. "You are Resistance. You know how it is. The more people who know, the greater the risk."

"But we can *help*," Gromov restated. "Even if he is with the Americans."

Daria said nothing.

"He is with the Americans, then," Gromov said. "Yes?"

"Please," Daria said. "He is safe. That is all I can say."

Gromov's face tightened. "My orders are to ensure Dr. Kapsky's safety, including providing assistance to the Americans," he lied. "We—Soviets, Poles, and Americans—we have a common enemy. The area is controlled by the Germans. Kapsky—and the Americans—need all the help they can get."

Bridgette touched Daria's shoulder gently. "Please. Help Dr. Kapsky. Help us."

Daria exhaled sharply. "The fewer people with knowledge, the less the risk," she said, as if reciting a mantra. "That is the discipline. Again, Bridgette, as Resistance, you know that."

"Yes, but not always. Sometimes we must exercise our best judgment," Bridgette replied. "Under the present circumstances, the best judgment is to do that which provides Dr. Kapsky the most resources, the best opportunity to escape." Bridgette grasped Daria's hands. "The odds for Dr. Kapsky were poor to begin with. We are deep in Nazi-occupied territory. They are formidable and they are vicious. They also are thorough and leave absolutely nothing to chance. Dr. Kapsky's chances improved only slightly with *Armia* assistance. Major Gromov can improve it much more. I have seen him perform. He is an exceptional soldier. He can provide the difference between Dr. Kapsky escaping and his being caught or killed. Please help."

Daria's eyes began to water as she rubbed her sides more vigorously. Gromov stepped closer and put his left hand gently on her shoulder. Daria looked up and held his eyes, which conveyed patience and sympathy. She nodded and then looked down at the floor. After several seconds she said softly, "I cannot."

Gromov emitted what sounded to Bridgette like something between a growl and a roar before his right fist crashed squarely against Daria's face, catapulting her backward more than five feet and onto the floor. Blood gushed from her mouth and nose, which was flattened nearly flush against the rest of her face.

Frozen in horror, Bridgette watched as Gromov leapt on top of Daria and struck her two more times on her right cheek, causing her eyes to roll about in their sockets.

Gromov seized a handful of Daria's hair and slammed

the back of her head against the wooden floor. Then he placed his face inches from hers and hissed, "Where is Kapsky? Where are the Americans? Tell me or I will rip your lungs out of your chest."

Bridgette seized Gromov's shoulder from behind and tried to pull him off Daria, to no effect. She then wrapped her arm around his neck and yanked backward, prompting Gromov to spin about and push her with such force that she was propelled back against the front door nearly ten feet away, the breath knocked from her lungs.

Gromov withdrew his NR-40 from his waistband and placed the tip against Daria's left cheek, just below the eye socket. The sensation prompted her to regain her senses and become rigid with terror. He placed his face inches from hers. "Now you are no longer pretty, Daria, but at least you can still function. Tell me where Kapsky went. Tell me his path or I will first cut out your left eye, and then your right."

Bridgette, air knocked out of her lungs, tried to regain her bearings. Seeing Gromov draw the blade toward Daria's eye, she attempted to scream, but nothing emerged.

Daria coughed up drops of blood and spoke softly, the words indistinct. Gromov placed his ear closer but couldn't make out the words. Daria paused to catch her breath, then spoke again. Once more, too low and garbled for Gromov to discern.

As he bent closer, Gromov felt his pistol being withdrawn from his waistband from the rear but was unable to react in time to prevent Bridgette from leveling the weapon dead on his torso. He rose from his crouch and turned to face Bridgette, who appeared both stunned and frightened. She began to speak, but before she uttered even a syllable, Gromov slashed her trachea to the spine with a powerful backhanded swing of his knife, causing her to involuntarily discharge a 7.62-millimeter round that grazed the right side of his rib cage.

Bridgette collapsed to the floor as if she were a marionette whose strings had been cut. She convulsed once as blood gurgled from her throat and pooled about her head. Then she lay still, lifeless eyes locked on her executioner.

Gromov knelt next to Daria, who was attempting to speak but was struggling to get enough air to do so. He put his ear close to her mouth. She spoke, but he couldn't make out any of the words. She paused to gather her strength, took a deep breath, and in a strangled voice told Gromov the precise direction that Kapsky had taken, as well as what time he'd left, and that he was escorted—guarded—by Fulmar, Matuszek, and McDermott. She took a last breath, said something barely intelligible, and then became rigid.

Gromov rose and moved toward Bridgette's body to retrieve his sidearm. Before he could do so the front door burst open and an Obergefreiter and two Soldaten entered with weapons trained on him.

"Hände hoch!"

With a look of resignation, Gromov complied by placing his hands on top of his head. As the soldiers approached to restrain him Gromov reached into a leather sheath sewn into the back collar of his shirt and pulled out a serrated dagger. He shifted his wrist and swung the dagger forward over his head as if chopping wood. Gromov impaled the German's forehead, penetrating through the cranium and into the soldier's left eye socket. A jet of warm blood burst from the socket as Gromov pulled the dagger from the soldier's skull and he collapsed to his knees. Gromov squatted and plunged the blade into the second soldier's inner left thigh, slicing a deep gash upward from the soldier's knee to his groin, severing the femoral artery.

The third soldier reflexively squeezed the trigger of his weapon, trained on the spot where Gromov had been standing a fraction of a second earlier. The bullet discharged nearly a foot over the kneeling assassin's head and slammed without effect into the wall behind him.

Gromov catapulted himself forward from his crouch and hurled himself, dagger extended, toward the remaining German. The blade drove into the soldier's throat just beneath the Adam's apple, penetrating under his chin, through the floor of his mouth, and impaling his tongue against his palate. The soldier fell to the floor next to the other two, twitching briefly before becoming still.

Gromov exhaled and composed himself. He took a momentary mental inventory of the state of affairs. He needed to leave immediately. But he felt a spark of excitement coupled with optimism. Finally, Kapsky was within reach. It was a matter of catching up to him and disposing of his escorts, a task Gromov could discharge as effectively as he'd disposed of the Germans now lying on the floor.

Gromov went to the door and surveyed the perimeter of the house for German troops. For the moment it was clear. He began walking northwest, consistent with the splendid directions Daria had just given him.

They were precisely the same misdirections she had provided the Germans who had sped away from head-quarters in the three Kübelwagens twenty minutes ago.

CHAPTER 50

Canidy saw the ghostly headlights in the distance before Emil. They were moving slowly, too slowly for a mere transport. Both almost immediately concluded that whoever was behind the lights was looking for them.

They had traveled mostly on the sides of the road, near the brush. The area was predominately rural, and vehicular traffic was nearly nonexistent. Whenever they'd get a hint that a vehicle was approaching, they would resume their practice of traveling inside the tree line, out of sight.

"They are about three kilometers away," Emil estimated. "Moving very slowly. It is very hard to estimate from this distance, but I would say they are moving at no more than fifteen kilometers an hour."

Canidy kept watching the lights. "No doubt, they're looking for us," he said. "More accurately, they're looking for Kapsky. No other reason to be out here. Daria's little misdirection worked."

"For now," Emil said. "We need to string them along somehow. The longer we can do so, the more likely the real Kapsky can get to the boat. I wager those headlights belong to Kübelwagens. They have decent speed and maneuverability. And they usually carry about three, four troops each."

Canidy squinted in the direction of the vehicles. "What's that last one?"

Emil stopped walking and stared at the convoy for several seconds. "Again, if I had to wager, I'd say a panzer. Light."

Canidy spat, exasperated. "What's with these Germans and their damn panzers? Don't they ever go anywhere without them?" Canidy stopped and gauged the distance to the lights. "They'll overtake us in no more than ten minutes. Probably a good idea for us to start walking in the woods again, just in case."

"At some point, if they do not find us, will they not conclude they should search elsewhere?" Emil asked.

"Maybe. Let's hope that we can string them along for a while. Long enough for Fulmar to put more distance between us."

"How do you plan to, as you say, 'string them along'?"

Canidy smiled sardonically. "Very carefully. But we may have to take overt action so they don't become discouraged or suspicious and start looking in areas where the *real* Kapsky happens to be."

"Overt action?"

"What kind of weaponry do you think our friends back there are carrying?"

"Kübelwagens are for transport. They typically do not have mounted weapons, although on occasion one may have a mounted MG 34. The troops will have standard-issue Karabiners."

"And the panzer?"

Emil stopped again to look back at the procession in the distance. "As I say, it looks rather on the small side. Likely a Panzer ADGZ."

"Flamethrowers?"

Emil smiled slyly. "You did not enjoy your previous encounter with panzers?"

"I've had better days than that."

"Panzer ADGZs are light. They have MG 13s."

"Not my favorites," Canidy said. "But okay. If they get close enough, we can hit them with harassing fire. Let them know we're here. Keep them interested."

"Somewhat risky," Emil said without a hint of trepidation.

"That's why they pay us the big bucks, son."

Emil looked a bit confused, but understood Canidy was using an American colloquialism. He pointed back to the vehicle lights.

Canidy watched as the vehicles drew closer. "Yep. They're picking up speed. Let's get into the woods."

The pair stepped off the road and waded into the bordering vegetation a few feet into the tree line, deep enough to be invisible. They lay on the ground, peering through the vegetation, with their weapons trained on the road.

They watched in silence as the vehicles came down the road toward their position. "When they get close enough, take a few harassing shots to cause them to track us. Shoot two to three rounds and keep your head down to avoid return fire. Then move laterally and back—left and backward—to get out of here."

Emil nodded, then noticing movement behind the Kübelwagens, pointed, and said, "Look there. Your favorite German vehicles."

Approximately one-half kilometer behind the Kübelwagens and Panzer ADGZ was the outline of a car trailed by several larger armored vehicles. They were closing rapidly.

"Panzer IVs. The real thing," Emil observed.

"Machine guns and flamethrowers?"

"Yes. Just like our previous panzer encounter."

"And, all things considered, I was having a pretty good day until now."

As the procession drew nearer, Canidy discerned what appeared to be a Horch 108 command car trailed by the five massive panzers. The same configuration Canidy had observed on the first expedition.

"Let's move back farther into the woods. That's a lot of firepower coming toward us. Don't shoot unless I do."

Canidy and Emil rose and retreated at a slight incline another forty meters into the woods, then dropped to the ground.

"I do not have a clear line of sight," Emil informed him. "Too many trees in front."

"We don't need to hit them," Canidy said. "We just need to get their attention. Daria told them Dr. Kapsky went in this direction. We want to make them think that maybe they're getting close."

"I'm afraid we will only convince them we are idiots. Why would Kapsky—or his escorts—fire on a *panzer* column. Will they not think it is a diversion?"

"Nobody thinks while under fire, not even armored troops. They react. The natural reaction is to think the guy they're looking for is the guy shooting at them. And the beauty of that is that they won't fire back because they need Kapsky alive."

"Very well," Emil replied. "Although I'm not completely convinced."

Canidy chuckled wryly. "Tell you the truth, neither am I."

The rattle of the vehicles grew louder and Canidy could feel the earth vibrate. When the procession was parallel with Canidy and Emil's position it came to a halt. Three Kübelwagens, five panzers, and a German command car.

Emil turned to Canidy with a look of concern. "They could not have seen us down the road, could they?"

Canidy didn't respond. His gaze was fixed on the figure in the rear seat of the car. He—more accurately, his silhouette—was recognizable even in twilight.

Emil examined the figure. "It is he," he said to himself.

Konrad Maurer rose slowly from his seat, stood in the rear of the vehicle, and scanned the woods where Canidy and Emil lay with their pistols extended before them. Although in the gloom they couldn't see Maurer's face, the slow, deliberate turn of his head conveyed prescience—a sense that something or someone was concealed in the forest.

Maurer got out of the car and paced the perimeter of the road, seemingly staring directly at Canidy and Emil. He raised a gloved hand over his head and brought it forward, signaling all gunners to aim at the woods.

Canidy's chest seized with terror as the panzer turrets instantly swiveled in unison ninety degrees.

"Feuer!"

Both Canidy and Emil dug their heads into the soil as five MG 34 machine guns sprayed a prolonged burst of 7.92-millimeter rounds into the forest, causing a blizzard of leaves, branches, and pine needles to fall atop the two. The forest quickly absorbed the roar of the guns. Maurer stood silent and immobile, listening. He raised his hand again and again ordered the guns to fire. More debris rained down on Canidy and Emil, but they were unharmed.

Maurer stepped closer to the perimeter of the woods and peered in Canidy's direction. Canidy, M1911 before him, prepared to fire. The probabilities indicated they would not survive another burst. At least he would take Maurer out of the equation.

Maurer stepped back slowly and returned to his vehicle. He took a last look in Canidy's direction before climbing into the backseat and motioning for the procession to continue forward.

Canidy and Emil waited until the caravan was half a kilometer down the road before rising from the ground.

"Panzers," Canidy spat. "Never ran into them flying P-40Bs. Wouldn't bother me if I never ran into them again. If it weren't for all of that firepower, that SS sonuvabitch would have a bullet in his big Prussian forehead right now."

Emil brushed soil from the front of his trousers. "You should be happy. Your—how you say?—wild-goose chase is working. They are searching for us, not Dr. Kapsky. Commander Matuszek should get him to the boat soon."

"I'm not so sure," Canidy said. "I don't know why they were firing in this direction, but it couldn't be because they thought Kapsky was here. They don't want to kill Kapsky, so they wouldn't fire if they had a realistic expectation that Kapsky might get hit."

Canidy and Emil turned and walked into the woods, the American vowing to put as much distance as possible between himself and motorized armor.

CHAPTER 51

They proceeded two abreast. Fulmar and Matuszek in front, Kapsky and McDermott to the rear. They remained, as usual, within the tree line adjacent to the single-lane road.

Fulmar was pleased with their progress and good fortune in not encountering any patrols. The countryside was bleak, riddled with artillery craters and damaged abandoned buildings. There were, however, a fair number of tiny hamlets with small clusters of undamaged buildings. Matuszek made sure they circumvented them and remained out of sight, explaining that they were nearing an area in which a large percentage of the residents were ethnic Germans. More precisely, Prussians, whose allegiances weren't necessarily certain.

They'd consumed most of the latkes, but Fulmar wasn't concerned about the food supply. Even the abandoned or nonworking farms had patches of crops that insisted on growing regardless of neglect.

Fulmar's primary concern was his watch. They had approximately twelve hours to get to the canal and the Thorisdottirs' boat. Fulmar calculated that at their present pace they should be able to get there on time, but barely. They couldn't afford slowdowns or delays. Matuszek seemed to know every road, village, and German outpost in northern Poland—but he was concerned whether Kapsky could keep up this pace.

Kapsky had shown no signs of fatigue in the first hours after they'd left Daria's house. Indeed, Fulmar nearly completely forgot that the professor purportedly had some type of illness or condition. Fulmar hadn't asked about it and Kapsky hadn't talked about it. In Fulmar's estimation, the professor looked pretty good— especially for an academic. Fulmar had assumed that sitting behind a desk or in a laboratory or wherever professors sat, Kapsky would be physically frail and somewhat hunched—the stereotype of an intellectual with little regard for his physique. Kapsky, however, had an athlete's build. Lean and sinewy, likely due—at least in part—to having been constantly on the move for the last forty months. He was a good-looking guy with an interesting face, especially his eyes—intelligent and peculiarly green.

But in the last couple of hours, Fulmar sensed that Kapsky was struggling to keep up. He hadn't faltered— in fact, he'd kept up with the rest. But his strides were shorter and he was breathing through his mouth, a sign that he was challenged by their pace.

Fulmar couldn't afford to stop the team for any appreciable period to rest. Although they were making good time, they had to anticipate and account for contingencies such as German patrols or roadblocks. Fulmar was reluctant to test the radio in his ruck. It was another contraption minted by the OSS lab. Although it seemed to work when they tested it before they'd embarked on the operation, Fulmar remained skeptical about its effectiveness in the field. More important, Fulmar was concerned that if he used it, the Germans might be able to detect it. Although they'd been assured by the lab boys that detection was unlikely, he didn't want to risk it. The lab boys were in the lab; he was in the field—an unforgiving field. So he determined that he'd reserve use of the radio until they were within a few kilometers of the dock. He'd keep it off until then, hoping that Kristin and Katla weren't trying to reach him with important information—such as the dock was swarming with SS.

Matuszek drew next to Fulmar and nudged him with an elbow. He quietly asked, "Do you think he can keep this pace?"

"He doesn't have a choice."

Matuszek nodded. "We should move a little more quickly so we will have—how do you Americans say—a cushion. So far, he's kept up well, but he appears quite fatigued."

"He's a tough son of a bitch for a professor. Hell, all that time evading Nazis probably made him as hard as your best Home Army troops. But Canidy and I were told he could be ill. They were concerned he might even die before he could provide whatever information he possesses. Don't know what it may be. Hell, they briefed us on everything—even speculative stuff—but I'm not sure how much longer he can go at this pace, let alone a faster one."

As if to punctuate Fulmar's statement, Kapsky began coughing—a strained sound unlike a mere cough produced by dust or other ambient cause.

"You okay, Professor?" Fulmar asked over his shoulder.

"I am fine."

"You sure as hell don't sound like it. Look, tell me when you need a break, okay? You're the reason we're on this excursion through the delightful war-torn fields of Poland. We want to keep you in good shape, so say the word and we'll take five."

"Thank you. But that will not be necessary."

Fulmar detected the faint rumble of a motor vehicle somewhere on the road behind them. To this point the only traffic they'd encountered was an iron-and-wood cart driven by an old man and pulled by two oxen.

Fulmar signaled for the team to move farther within the tree line. He knelt and the others did the same. Thirty seconds later they spotted a flat-nosed truck pulling a twelve-foot trailer with a canvas tarp covering the bed. It was moving at about thirty kilometers an hour. Some type of farm vehicle, Fulmar thought, one of only three vehicles they'd encountered on the trip. Not Wehrmacht. Nonetheless, they would remain concealed until it passed before resuming their journey.

Matuszek had other plans. He rose and was at the tree line and in the middle of the road before Fulmar could register a protest. Alarmed, Fulmar whispered, "What the hell is he doing?"

Matuszek raised his rifle with both hands over his head and the truck slowed and came to a halt fifteen feet in front of him. Matuszek walked to the driver's side of the cab. Fulmar and McDermott watched with weapons trained on the front windshield. The look on the driver's face appeared to range from fear to concern to delight.

"Commander! Is it you? Commander Matuszek, no? I recognize you from the posters in Tczew Square. It is you, yes?"

Fulmar and McDermott looked at each other with expressions of disbelief. Fulmar shook his head. "Unbelievable. We're traveling with Clark Gable."

"Yes, it is I, *kolega*," Matuszek confirmed. "Are you traveling much farther down the road?"

"You call this a road? I'm sure to break an axle on this horrible excuse for a road. The Germans have ruined it with their heavy transports."

Matuszek tilted his head toward the trailer. "What are you hauling back there?"

"What else? Potatoes. That is all that I can grow anymore. And I am lucky to be able to grow that."

"How much farther are you going?"

"Another twenty kilometers, if my axles don't break and the motor does not stop. To Borkowo. Just south of Danzig. Do you know it?"

Matuszek shook his head. "I do not think so."

"I do not like going there. Lots of German troops. They sometimes give you a hard time. And the people in the region—they were Poles before the war, now they claim to be Germans."

"Not many," Matuszek said.

"Perhaps not. But still, *too* many."

Matuszek inspected the trailer. "I would like to ask a favor, *kolega*."

"Of course. Anything I can do for Commander Matuszek. Wait until I tell the old goats back in Czarlin. What can I do?"

"I need a ride. Not all the way to Borkowo, but as close as we can get."

The smile on the driver's face turned to apprehension.

"It is a risk, I understand," Matuszek conceded. "But it is most important. I have an appointment, a deadline to meet nearby Borkowo. At foot speed I may make it or I may not. But I cannot be late under any circumstances."

The driver appeared contrite. "Commander, please understand. I do not want to appear reluctant, but I am just a farmer. I am not Home Army. I am not trained. If the Germans stop us—if they see me with you—we will be shot dead. My children will be without their father. They are already without their mother."

"Yes. We have all lost loved ones," Matuszek acknowledged. "I am sorry about your wife. I ask for this favor because I have no other options and it is a matter of great importance that I get there."

The driver rubbed his bald pate and exhaled. "Obviously, I cannot refuse a request for help from Commander Matuszek. Please do not misunderstand. I am not brave, but neither am I a coward. I am just worried for my children. If the Nazis learn I have helped you, they may kill my children also."

"That is a risk," Matuszek acknowledged.

The driver nodded vigorously, part in agreement and part to steel his resolve. "My children will be proud when I tell them I assisted Commander Matuszek. They will look upon me as a *hero*."

Matuszek smiled. "Perhaps you should not tell them for a while."

"Yes. Of course. That would be foolish." The driver waved toward the other side of the cab. "Please, Commander, get in."

"Perhaps I should ride in the back, under the tarpaulin, out of sight."

The driver looked momentarily surprised, then relieved. "Yes, of course. If you do not mind. That would be most shrewd, Commander Matuszek. Very smart. But a bit uncomfortable. The potatoes are fresh. Hard as rocks."

"No matter," Matuszek replied. "My friends and I are used to tough conditions."

The driver frowned, confused.

Matuszek pointed to Fulmar, McDermott, and Kapsky, who had emerged from the woods. "These are my traveling companions . . . What is your name, *kolega*?"

"Mikołaj."

"These men are very important friends, Mikołaj. I tell you that because I trust you and because it is true. I cannot tell you their names. It is that important. It is not because I do not respect you. It is to protect your life. The less you know, the less risk for you, us, and your children." Matuszek could see Mikołaj's grip tighten on the steering wheel. Matuszek understood. This was a potentially fatal undertaking for the driver, one that also could have consequences for his family. But this was Nazi-occupied Poland. Ordinary people were forced to make life-and-death decisions regularly, often by the hour.

The driver loosened his grip on the wheel and smiled genuinely, without bravado. "This will be an adventure that I will tell my grandchildren about. I drove Commander Matuszek and other very important people past the Nazis."

Mikołaj got out of the vehicle and looked down each end of the road before untying the tarp, revealing a mound of brown potatoes, more than Fulmar had ever seen in his life.

Mikołaj said to Matuszek, "You are welcome to ride on top. Just climb on top of the baseboard. I am afraid it will be most uncomfortable. I will put the cover over you when you are settled."

"Thanks," Fulmar said.

Mikołaj turned toward Fulmar, startled. "You are American?" he asked in English.

Fulmar said nothing.

Mikołaj stroked his chin. He turned to Matuszek and spoke in Polish. "Clearly, this is something extraordinary, is it not? I *truly* am helping something important."

"When this is all done, we'll send you a postcard," Fulmar said.

Fulmar stepped onto the rear bumper and climbed on top of the mound of potatoes, which rolled and shifted beneath him. He gained his balance and thrust out his hand to assist Kapsky aboard, followed by McDermott and Matuszek. Each staked out a corner of the truck bed and dug into the surface of the load to secure themselves.

Matuszek checked to see if everyone was secure and then said to Mikołaj, "You can pull the cover over us. We're ready to go anytime you are. Just before we get to Borkowo, stop and let us know."

The driver did as requested, climbed back into the cab, and slowly eased the truck forward so as not to up-end his new passengers, each of whom were trying to maintain a balance among the oblong-shaped vegetables.

Fulmar resigned himself to an uncomfortable journey, but at least Kapsky didn't have to walk and, barring any mishaps, they'd arrive at the dock on time. But mishaps, Fulmar knew, were the currency of war.

A quarter-kilometer north, Frederick Hahn watched with curiosity and anticipation. The farmer had survived the war, indeed thrived, by conveying useful information to those that presently controlled the country. He had waved amiably toward the group before they'd boarded the truck. Trying to convey nonchalance, they'd waved back.

CHAPTER 52

Canidy and Emil continued to walk north through the woods. Canidy muttering curses about panzers from time to time. He was a pilot. A damn good one. One that had bedeviled the Japanese along the Burma Road. He should be destroying panzers from above, he told himself, not acting as their target on the ground.

Not long after the encounter with the panzers, the woods began to thin.

"Emil, are my instincts right? We're no longer going northwest but moving due north?"

"That is correct. Toward Danzig."

They crested a shallow slope, and through the thinning trees could see below the glimpses of civilization: dozens of houses, stores, at least two warehouses, and a small plant of some kind.

And on the west side of the plant, lined up north to

south, was a precise row of Kübelwagens, a precise row of panzers, and a command car.

Canidy cursed loudly.

"I did not expect this," Emil said somberly. "They were moving away from us and away from Kapsky in a westerly direction. They must have turned north somewhere and looped around. I confess my knowledge of this area is lacking."

"Don't worry about it," Canidy said. "Not your fault. They're the ones who screwed up. Based on what they know, they should have kept going west." Canidy stopped and squinted at the command car in the distance. "Got to give that giant son of a bitch credit. He's very thorough. And he's no dummy."

"He is still not on Fulmar's trail, however, Fulmar's group is moving northwest."

"True. But now the big Nazi's not heading *away* from them, either." Canidy pointed to the scores of villagers who were being herded into a lot on the south end of the village. "We've seen this play before. Let's hope none of those poor folks down there happened to see Fulmar's team on their way to Danzig, because that SS SOB will sure get it out of them."

Emil said, "In order to avoid them, we will need to skirt the perimeter of the town, staying in the woods. That will add two or three kilometers, at least another hour, to our trip to the canal. We will need to move very fast to get there in time."

Canidy eyed the scene unfolding in the factory lot. He

estimated more than a hundred villagers were already gathered, with more streaming in at gunpoint.

"Emil," Canidy said somberly, "give me your best estimate as to whether we have enough time to get to the boat if we go around the village. Don't sugarcoat it."

Emil sighed heavily. "We can get there, but everything must fall in our favor. No detours, no delays from trying to avoid or hide from German troops."

"So fifty-fifty?"

"More likely, forty-sixty," Emil replied.

Canidy peered at the scene in the parking lot. Dozens of adult males were being forced to line up on their knees. The big SOB with the gleaming boots had disembarked from his command car and was striding slowly down the line with his hands clasped behind his back. "That's not quite the odds I was hoping for. But it actually makes things much clearer, much easier."

Emil grinned. "It certainly does, doesn't it."

"If it's unlikely I'm going to get to the boat even under the best of circumstances, I may as well increase the chances Fulmar's team gets there. After all, my job is to get Kapsky out of Poland, not necessarily get *myself* out of Poland. I'll have to figure that out later. If I get a chance."

Canidy reached into his ruck and withdrew what looked like a black baseball. "They're going to start executing people down there any minute. We have to assume someone saw something or knows something and is going to talk. I'm going to see if I can buy Fulmar a little more time."

Canidy moved cautiously down the slope, closer to the factory. Emil followed. The trees and brush continued to thin the closer they got to the factory, but were replaced with tall grass that provided good cover, permitting them to approach undetected to within fifty meters of the factory lot. Canidy stopped, knelt, and motioned for Emil to do the same.

Canidy observed the interrogation of the men kneeling in the lot for a minute before turning to Emil and whispering, "Emil, I'm going to distract these guys with some harassing fire. Maybe they'll even chase us. Obviously, they've got a fair amount of firepower. Even if they can't see us, they can saturate the area with those MG 34s on top of the panzers. We got lucky once before—"

Emil interrupted, "How you say—'I am in.'"

Canidy suppressed a chuckle. It struck him that he was kneeling next to probably the toughest adolescent on the planet.

"Seriously, Emil, I knew you'd say that. But you've done your job and more. Spectacularly well. We've provided the misdirection Fulmar's team needed. Since it's unlikely I can get to the boat, I don't need your guidance anymore. There's nothing more for you to do but accept my thanks and that of Wild Bill Donovan for a job well done. So get the hell out of here."

"No."

"Emil . . ."

"I report to Commander Matuszek. He ordered me to guide you to the boat. I will do as he ordered."

Canidy shook his head. "I don't—"

Emil interrupted, pointing to the black baseball. "What is that?"

"A toy from Professor Moriarty and the boys in Donovan's lab. It's a T-13. Affectionately called a Beano. I've got three of them. It's a wonder one of them hasn't gone off already."

"A bomb?"

"Something like that." Canidy took another Beano from his ruck and handed it to Emil. "When I say 'Go,' throw that thing at the Germans farthest from the villagers. Preferably near those Kübelwagens. Then move laterally with me to the left. Fast, so we're not where they'll probably return fire, especially those panzers. When we've moved about one hundred yards—meters—we'll hit them with some harassing fire. It's harder for them to tell where that's coming from. Let's keep drawing them away from a northwesterly direction. Give Fulmar's team more of a cushion to get to the boat."

When Canidy returned his attention to the factory lot he saw that the big SS officer with the gleaming boots had a Walther P38 in his right hand. Someone was about to be shot. Canidy nudged Emil. "No time to waste. Pick your spot now. Ready?"

Emil nodded.

"Go."

Canidy rose from a crouch and threw the Beano at the closest Kübelwagen. Emil then threw his at the German troops farthest from the line of kneeling villagers. Canidy's Beano exploded against the passenger door of the vehicle, propelling it a foot in the air and causing it to burst into flames. Emil's Beano fell a few feet in front of the line of panzers without effect. A dud.

Canidy and Emil sprinted to their left, the tall grass providing cover. Within seconds, hundreds of rounds of machine-gun fire were shredding all vegetation within a hundred-foot radius of the spot the two had just left.

The roar of the machine-gun fire caused them to sprint even harder. A second later the fire was replaced by several deafening explosions caused by the shells from the panzers' cannons.

The machine-gun fire resumed, but this time tracking westward and closing behind them, contrary to Canidy's expectations. Canidy dove to the ground followed by Emil a scant second before scores of 7.92-millimeter rounds caught up with their position and scythed the grass a mere foot over their heads. They remained prone as the fire tracked in front of their position, then returned back to their original position. As it did so the pair rose and began sprinting west through the tall grass once again.

The sound of machine-gun fire was replaced by the shouts of German soldiers. Although Canidy didn't understand precisely *what* they were saying, he could tell the shouts weren't *receding*. The Germans were giving chase.

Canidy cursed. He'd hoped to draw the Germans away from the direction Fulmar's team was proceeding, but not to be so close on Canidy's heels. The pair had no options other than to keep running and hope to elude their pursuers.

Canidy's legs quickly grew heavy from the strain of sprinting against the tall grass. Though younger, Emil was feeling the same. Another half kilometer and they wouldn't be able to go much farther.

Canidy broke to his left—southward—and back up the slope toward the forest. Emil followed. Their chests heaved, trying to inhale as much oxygen as possible as they struggled up the slope against the tall grass.

As they moved farther up the slope, the shouts of the Germans began to fade. Canidy slipped on the incline and fell, followed by Emil. Both popped up immediately and resumed climbing toward the sanctuary of the forest only a hundred meters away, the shouts of the pursuing Germans falling yet farther behind.

The fading shouts, however, were replaced by the growing din from a panzer that was moving across the lot to join the uphill pursuit. The sound of the infernal machine caused Canidy to momentarily forget the pain in his legs and lungs. He and Emil mowed rapidly through the grass to the crest of the slope and continued running into the forest, slowing only after they were more than two hundred meters within. Only then did Canidy slow enough to turn and look behind them. Although the foliage partially obscured his view, he could see no movement.

Canidy came to a halt, listening. No shouts, no snap of branches or twigs broken underfoot. He asked Emil standing next to him, trying to catch his breath, "See anything? Hear anything?"

Panting, Emil simply shook his head.

Canidy took several more breaths before speaking again. "Well, that sure didn't accomplish anything. Amateur hour. The idea was to continue to misdirect them from Fulmar."

Emil shook his head. "No, sir. As you said, the idea was to give Fulmar's team more of a cushion. I think you've done that. Even if they figure out which direction Fulmar's team is actually going, they've been delayed."

". . . But almost got ourselves killed in the process," Canidy said. "Even if we've given Fulmar a cushion, I've probably aggravated the big Nazi with the shiny boots enough that he's going to take it out on the poor SOBs from the town."

"He was going to do that anyway. You know that."

Canidy stood erect and stared at the young soldier. "How old are you *really*, Emil?"

Emil smiled and pointed westward.

CHAPTER 53

When Gromov first heard the explosions and gunfire he ducked from the road into the woods and waited. The sounds were coming from the general direction in which the redheaded woman said Kapsky was going. It didn't seem to be very far away, so he remained still for several minutes, trying to glean more information from the noise.

When the noise abated, he resumed moving in Kapsky's direction. Through the trees in the distance he caught a glimpse of a figure he thought he'd seen before. One of the Americans; one of the Americans he was commanded to kill. He couldn't be certain, but it made sense. The Americans were escorting Kapsky. A person unknown to Gromov was with the American, but Kapsky was nowhere to be seen.

The two figures disappeared from view, concealed by trees and distance. Gromov moved stealthily in pursuit, a task made difficult by the underbrush that both slowed him and made noise when he passed. But Gromov was encouraged. He was on the right path and not far from his target.

Colonel Yevgeni Goncharov cursed several times under his breath. He wasn't one for the wilderness. He much preferred operating in urban environments, as would any civilized person—even assassins.

His shoes were caked with mud, his clothes were torn by thorns, and he sported welts from numerous insect bites. It had not been a pleasant trek. Nonetheless, he remained well within range of his assignment. Gromov had impressed him with his brutality and efficiency. He had little doubt Gromov would discharge his orders. Based on what Goncharov had witnessed thus far, the Americans didn't have a chance. Unfortunately for Gromov, neither did he.

CHAPTER 54

The ride was loud and uncomfortable. Fulmar felt nearly every bump acutely, and there was an uncommonly large number of bumps. Each bump was accompanied by a shifting of the load of potatoes on which they rode, creating a sensation akin to an amusement park ride. Nonetheless, Fulmar was pleased. They were moving far faster than they would be had they remained on foot, and Kapsky didn't have to exhaust himself trying to get to the boat.

The tarp covering the bed of the truck was moldy and smelled accordingly, and Fulmar could feel bugs crawling over him. Annoying, but inconsequential as far as he was concerned.

Fulmar sensed the truck slowing and presently heard the squeaking of brakes. The truck sputtered and came to an abrupt halt. They weren't anywhere near the canal, Fulmar thought. They hadn't been traveling long enough. Maybe a stubborn farm animal in the road? A fallen limb?

Fulmar became rigid and held his breath when he heard the unmistakable inflection of a German imperative sentence. Then a question, accusatory in tone.

Fulmar remained still and tried to listen to the specific words being spoken. At the same time he slowly withdrew his M1911 and held it in his right hand. Although he couldn't see the rest of the team beneath the darkness of the tarp, he suspected they were doing something similar.

Fulmar strained to hear an exchange between the driver and the German speaker. The only discernible word was the German word for potato: *"Kartoffel."* Then he could hear nothing until a bayonet pierced the tarp inches from his face, then withdrew. Then another thrust that narrowly missed his right shoulder. Followed by another and another. Fulmar strained against the urge to fire his weapon. He feared the others might not resist doing the same. He didn't have to fear long. Thankfully, the bayoneting ceased within seconds.

More unintelligible chatter from outside. Then he heard the ignition of the engine and felt the stutter of the truck as the clutch was being released, followed by a slow acceleration.

Fulmar was just beginning to exhale when the truck stopped abruptly, causing the potatoes to shift beneath him. He strained to hear what was happening outside, but it was unintelligible before falling silent. Fulmar surmised the Germans remained suspicious—second-guessing themselves. He prepared to fire at the first figure he saw when the tarp was pulled back.

Suddenly Fulmar heard shouting, Polish mixed with German. Angry, impatient, profane.

Fulmar was astonished. It was Mikołaj berating the Germans. Though Fulmar could understand only the German, he easily concluded that Mikołaj was feigning outrage at being stopped not once, but twice, for reasons unworthy of his time. These frivolous, moronic guards were keeping him from business. *Real* business, not the make-believe plays these idiots were engaged in. Little boys playing soldier. No, he had real work to do and these marionettes were keeping him from doing it.

Fulmar expected the tirade to cease with the sound of a gunshot to the driver's chest. Instead, he heard the sound of contrition. After a few utterances in an apologetic tone, the truck lurched forward again and slowly began to pick up speed.

Only then did Fulmar notice a spider crawling on his chin toward his mouth. He started, nearly discharging his pistol, the trigger of which he had begun to squeeze. He swiped the spider from his face and exhaled.

Fulmar estimated that the truck had traveled nearly ten kilometers.

The noise from the engines was moderating when he heard an anguished groan a couple of feet from him. Although he couldn't see him, Fulmar knew it must have come from McDermott, who was the closest to him.

"McDermott, can you hear me?"

"Yes. They got my arm. Again."

"With the bayonet?"

"Yes. My bad arm. The forearm. I need to tie it off."

Fulmar could hear the strain in his voice. "Can you wait a few minutes?"

"Do I have any options?"

"Just wait enough time so we're pretty sure we're clear of the checkpoint."

"I'll have to manage . . ."

"Hell, I don't know how to let our driver know until we come to a stop. We're trapped back here."

"Not to worry, it feels no worse than when it was shot."

Fulmar ground his teeth. He respected McDermott's stoicism, but if the wound was remotely like the previous one, it needed to be dressed immediately or McDermott wouldn't last long.

Fulmar needed the driver to stop the truck, but first he needed to get the driver's attention. He couldn't see or hear whether there were Germans nearby. Riding in the bed of a noisy truck covered by a tarp left him with few options. He held his breath, hoped for the best, and fired his pistol once. The truck kept moving. He fired again and the truck began to slow and came to a halt moments later.

From outside, Fulmar heard Mikołaj shout a question.

"What is the problem?"

"Are we clear?" Fulmar asked.

"We better be, otherwise we're all dead. We are

between Pszczółki and Borkowo. We are in a wooded area."

"One of my men needs help," Fulmar said. "He was stabbed with a bayonet."

"One moment."

Mikołaj untied the ropes that secured the tarp and pulled it back. Fulmar blinked against the light, looked about, and saw the others do the same. McDermott was doing his best not to grimace, but the strain was evident on his face.

All four descended awkwardly from the load of potatoes and gathered at the side of the road. McDermott's right arm dangled limply and blood was dripping off his hand and onto the ground.

Fulmar said, "Let's get off the road and go into the trees in case someone comes down the road." He turned to Mikołaj. "Thanks for the lift. We've made outstanding progress."

Mikołaj looked confused. "What do you mean? You are leaving? But I will drive you as far as you need to go."

"You've already taken a hell of a risk," Fulmar said.

"That is nothing." Mikołaj nodded toward McDermott. "He is tough. But he is in tremendous pain. He is also . . ."

"Conspicuous?" Fulmar added.

"Conspicuous, yes. Blood everywhere. Also"— Mikołaj pointed to Kapsky—"he does not look well. I am uncertain he can get to the canal."

Fulmar examined Kapsky in the light of day. Mikołaj was right. Kapsky's face was colorless and he appeared exhausted. The ride atop the potatoes surely hadn't done him any favors, but Fulmar wasn't sure Kapsky had the strength to walk—and if necessary run—the remaining distance to the dock.

"Okay," Fulmar said. "We ride as far as we can. But first, let's patch up McDermott."

Mikołaj waited in the cab of the truck as Fulmar, McDermott, Kapsky, and Matuszek proceeded to the woods bordering the road. Movement appeared to increase the blood flow from McDermott's wound, so Fulmar guided him toward the nearest fallen tree and had him sit. Fulmar knelt next to McDermott and gently peeled back the Scot's sleeve to reveal a gash in the forearm deep enough to see glimpses of ulnar bone. "We need to tie this off or he's going to start getting light-headed fast, maybe pass out. Especially if he has to exert himself."

Matuszek handed Fulmar strips of cotton and iodine from his rucksack. "Here, use these. God knows where that bayonet's been."

Fulmar applied the iodine and dressed the wound as well as he could. McDermott grimaced but remained silent throughout.

"I'm not going to be of much use from here on," McDermott said. "Dead weight. The smart thing for you to do is cut me loose at the first sign of me slowing you down, because I'm not going to get any better between here and the boat. If I do get back, this time they *will* put me to pasture. The arm's done."

"Shut the hell up," Fulmar snapped. "You might not make it back, but the rest of us might not, either. I don't want to hear any of this heroic self-sacrifice crap from you, McDermott. We're dragging you across the finish line, no matter how much you bitch about it. You can take your sweet time dying later."

Fulmar secured the wrap around McDermott's arm. The Scot flexed the arm painfully and nodded appreciation. The wrap was fully soaked with blood within seconds.

"Commander, what's your best estimate for how much longer it will take before we get to the boat?"

"We're approaching Danzig. This area has one of the highest concentrations of Germans in Poland. Depending on how far our potato farmer can drive us and assuming we do not have to make excessive detours around Germans, we should get to the boat in between fourteen hundred and fifteen hundred hours."

Fulmar shifted to Kapsky. "Professor, no disrespect, but you look like crap. How are you feeling?"

Kapsky smiled gamely. "Your assessment is correct. I look and feel like crap. But I've been evading the Germans without an escort for more than three years. I can do so for another couple of hours."

"What about Canidy?" McDermott asked.

"We will have to play it by ear." Fulmar shrugged. "He's somewhere out there. Likely well behind us. Knowing Dick, he's probably making things as difficult for the Germans as possible, which means he's probably *really* far behind us."

"If he's alive, Emil will get him to the boat," Matuszek said firmly.

"I have no doubt, Commander," Fulmar agreed. "But my first responsibility is to make sure that Dr. Kapsky gets out of Poland safely. My orders couldn't be clearer. Everything, *everything* else is secondary. And if you know my boss, you'd know that *everything* is to be sacrificed to that objective."

"I do not wish to burden all of you, cause you to make such sacrifices," Kapsky said quietly. "I did not expect a party to come to my rescue."

"We weren't responding to your request, Professor," Fulmar said. "We're executing my boss's command. So don't worry about it." Fulmar rose. "All right, we're wasting time. We have a load of potatoes waiting for us."

McDermott rose and the others turned and walked back to the truck.

Fulmar stopped instantly and signaled for the others to do the same just as the driver issued a shrill whistle from the road.

CHAPTER 55

Moscow, Soviet Union
0800, 15 August 1943

Belyanov was adept at intimidation. The mere fact of being chief of OKRNKVD was sufficient to intimidate all but a handful of individuals in the entire Soviet Union. But he was about to enter a meeting with the two individuals whose titles and reputations were more fearsome than his own: head of People's Commissariat for Internal Affairs Lavrentiy Beria and. . . . premier of the Union of Soviet Socialist Republics, Joseph Vissarionovich Stalin himself.

Like most in the Soviet Union, Belyanov had spent a good portion of his lifetime developing a thick skin, a veneer of stoicism. He conveyed toughness and confidence to nearly all. Stalin and Beria, however, were the two most frightening people in the Soviet Union, and Belyanov was suitably anxious about meeting with them.

The aide opened the large, highly polished oak double doors to the room. Stalin was seated at the end of a long marble table, Beria to his immediate left. They were illuminated by bright rays of sunshine beaming through the tall windows to Belyanov's right. The rays sparkled off a mammoth chandelier hanging over the center of the table.

Belyanov felt his chest tighten and his throat constrict. He stood awkwardly for what seemed to be a full minute, but in reality was no more than five seconds, during which Stalin and Beria inspected him like a laboratory specimen.

"Enter, Belyanov," Beria commanded. "Sit."

Belyanov hesitated, unsure whether to sit at the end of the table opposite Stalin, or move closer, perhaps next to Beria. He decided to do neither and took a seat across from Beria and to Stalin's right.

Stalin and Beria stared at Belyanov, the only sound in the room the ticking of an ornate grandfather clock near the entrance. He sat rigidly with his hands folded in his lap like a schoolboy waiting to be scolded by his teacher. He was relieved when Beria finally spoke.

"What is the status of the Kapsky matter, Belyanov?"

"Major Gromov remains in pursuit. The last information we received is that he is closing on Professor Kapsky southeast of Danzig."

"When does he expect to acquire Kapsky?"

"Unknown. My information does not come from Gromov but from Colonel Goncharov."

"Goncharov, I assume, is to ensure that there are no witnesses to Gromov acquiring Kapsky or any matters ancillary thereto?"

"Correct."

"Goncharov reports a high probability of success?"

"Yes."

"What percentage?"

A charge of anxiety coursed through Belyanov. Goncharov hadn't provided any probability.

"Ninety percent," he lied.

Beria's eyes seemed to bore through him as if he could mine Belyanov's brain for details and accuracy. Belyanov dared not glance at Stalin.

"Under ordinary circumstances, Belyanov, ninety percent would be sufficient. These are not ordinary circumstances," Beria informed. "The acquisition of Professor Kapsky was originally an imperative for our own short- and long-term strategic interests. Those interests, although of extreme importance, are joined by another interest of equal importance. An interest that must be met urgently.

"As you know, Dr. Kapsky escaped from Katyn Forest. Do you appreciate the significance of that fact, Belyanov?"

Belyanov nodded. "Should the Americans and British acquire Kapsky, and thus acquire *proof* of Katyn Forest, it will complicate matters with the Western Allies, particularly Mr. Roosevelt."

"The Germans only discovered the graves barely four months ago. They have been trying to propagandize it to drive a wedge between the Western Allies and the Motherland. To this point the story seems so fantastical that neither the Americans nor the British believe it. After all, it comes from the Nazis, from Hitler. But if a credible source, someone other than the Nazis, were to confirm the story, that might cause the Americans and British to rethink opening a Western Front against Hitler, a front the Motherland desperately needs. Katyn Forest is the difference between fighting a Hitler whose energies are fully directed at the Motherland or fighting a Hitler who must be concerned with two fronts. We have been encouraging, persuading, whipping, and prodding Churchill and Roosevelt to open a Western Front against the Wehrmacht for quite some time. Churchill presently demurs that he is barely surviving the Battle of Britain and Roosevelt is occupied with the Japanese. They make pleasant noises about opening a Western Front and we believe they will do so—but if the reality of Katyn Forest was ever confirmed it would complicate things drastically. We cannot permit such complications, Belyanov."

In his periphery, Belyanov watched Stalin's expression. Nothing. Only an intensity that caused Belyanov's stomach to burn. His decision not to inform Beria that the Americans had taken custody of Kapsky would prove fatal if they escaped. But if Belyanov informed them now, they'd be outraged at being kept in the dark. He rationalized that it didn't matter; they'd be outraged that the Americans had Kapsky, regardless of when he informed them of such.

"Gromov is proficient. He will acquire Kapsky," Belyanov assured.

Stalin shifted in his seat to face Belyanov, whose

throat and jaw tightened. Both Belyanov *and* Beria sat frozen.

"Belyanov, Kapsky must be acquired," Stalin said coldly. "You understand me, yes?"

Belyanov nodded and consciously tried to sound confident. "Yes."

"However, as you know, that is insufficient. Nothing whatsoever must be left to chance. Anyone with whom Kapsky may have had contact—specifically, the Americans—cannot be permitted to survive. I assume Gromov understands that?"

"He does."

Stalin leveled his gaze directly at Belyanov's eyes. "Good. Is there anything that I should know?"

Belyanov's chest constricted. "No. I shall report immediately upon the mission's conclusion."

"No, you will not, Belyanov," Stalin corrected. "You will report on the mission's *successful* conclusion. Which, I expect, is imminent?"

"It is and I will."

Stalin sat utterly motionless and stared at Belyanov. The chief of OKRNKVD had an unblemished record. He'd served loyally and well. He'd received nothing but accolades over the course of his career. And he understood his life had absolutely no value to the men staring at him as though he were a worm underfoot.

"Leave us," Beria said. "Report to me the successful conclusion of the operation."

Belyanov rose and awkwardly walked the length of the room to the large oak doors.

CHAPTER 56

The quartet lay silently among the brush at the edge of the woods and watched a dozen German troops surrounding the potato truck as an Oberfeldwebel questioned Mikołaj, who repeated his act of appearing irritated that he'd been stopped. The act had worked at the previous checkpoint, but this Oberfeldwebel didn't appear to be impressed with the performance. Indeed, to Fulmar's ear the tone of the Oberfeldwebel's question was between skeptical and hostile.

One German was lying on the ground inspecting the truck's undercarriage. One was rifling through the truck's cab. And two were climbing onto the truck's bed, half of which remained covered by the tarpaulin.

The two on the bed repeated the checkpoint guard's maneuver of stabbing the tarp and the uncovered potatoes with the bayonets. Mikołaj protested vehemently.

Part of it was an act, but part was genuine: his crop was being destroyed.

The Oberfeldwebel's questioning grew in intensity. Whatever Mikołaj was saying, it wasn't satisfactory.

"Let's hope those guys on the bed don't notice the blood from McDermott's wound on any of the potatoes," Fulmar whispered to Matuszek.

"This isn't routine or happenstance. The Germans must have been alerted to something, perhaps by that farmer we saw in the distance. He keeps asking about passengers. Mikołaj insists the only passengers are his potatoes, which the troops are destroying."

"They've gone over the truck thoroughly," Fulmar said. "But they're not leaving."

Matuszek agreed. "The Oberfeldwebel doesn't seem to be in a hurry to be on his way. He's waiting for something to happen."

"How much farther to the canal?"

"You mean by foot?"

Fulmar nodded.

"If we leave in the next ten minutes, between eight to ten hours, depending upon how much evasive action we need to take."

"That's cutting it really close. Too close. I don't think our ride will leave us—at least not right away. But we need to get going right away to be sure."

The Oberfeldwebel was walking casually around the truck, inspecting it for the third time. His men were now arrayed in front of the truck, blocking the roadway. Fulmar could see no other vehicles up or down the road.

"This isn't good," Fulmar said. "They're in no hurry to leave and we need to get moving—whether or not that's by truck or on foot." Fulmar glanced at Kapsky, who was lying just behind them. "Also, the professor's not looking any better. I'm not sure he can travel very far by foot. We may have to force the issue."

"We only have two guns," Matuszek replied. "Mc-Dermott may have the will, but his arm is useless."

"Believe me, I prefer not to have to engage. But we're fast running out of options."

"Taking on that many Germans isn't much of an option."

"I can take two or three before they can react. I'm sure you can do the same. Plus, it'll take the remainder several seconds to even figure out where the fire's coming from."

Matuszek shook his head. "I am used to being outnumbered and outgunned, but these are not favorable odds. Let's wait a few more minutes."

Fulmar examined the scene in front of him. He counted the number of German troops again to be sure. Twelve, including the Oberfeldwebel. All but the Oberfeldwebel carried Karabiners. Half were now in front of the truck with the Oberfeldwebel and the driver. The remainder were walking about the truck, continuing to inspect.

Fulmar glanced back at Kapsky again. The professor wasn't even watching the scene. His head was resting on his folded arms, eyes closed, as if trying to conserve strength. McDermott was watching the scene in front of them with his jaw clenched, grimacing in pain.

"They have more rifles," Matuszek whispered, driving his argument home.

"No good options," Fulmar agreed. "But we're being forced into taking one. These guys look like they're in no hurry to leave, like they're just passing the time waiting for something to happen. But we can't afford to wait."

"They have a big firepower advantage. If we engage them now, they will probably win. Even if *we* win, how long will the fight last? What if one or two get away and alert others?"

Fulmar withdrew his M1911 and extended it before him, sighting the Oberfeldwebel. He held the sight for two seconds before moving to the soldier to the Oberfeldwebel's immediate right and then to his left. At least three of the soldiers were hidden from view on the opposite side of the truck bed. He calculated that he would be able to hit two or three before the rest could get to cover.

Fulmar expelled a lungful of air, cursed, and rested the butt of the pistol on the ground. "We need that truck," he concluded.

"They've checked the truck already," Matuszek observed, perplexed. "What are they doing? What are they waiting for?"

Fulmar nodded to the road behind the truck. "Maybe that."

Matuszek followed Fulmar's line of vision to see several vehicles engulfed in a swirl of dust approaching rapidly from the rear. Within moments, a command car and four Kübelwagens came to a halt immediately behind the truck. The passenger in the rear of the command car got out and strode imperiously toward the Oberfeldwebel and the truck driver. Fulmar recognized his bearing in an instant. Six foot five, at least 250 pounds, gleaming black boots, the hair exposed under his peaked visor cap so blond it was almost white. The monster who terrorized villagers into confessing. The one who executed women and children to coerce cooperation. For once he was without his precious panzers.

Konrad Maurer ignored the salutes from the soldiers surrounding the truck and walked slowly toward the driver until he was barely two feet away. The Oberfeldwebel moved deferentially several steps back.

Maurer towered over the driver in silence. Then he craned his neck about, slowly scanning the surrounding countryside before staring down at the driver once more.

"Where are they?" he asked quietly.

The driver blinked several times, a confused expression on his face. "What do you mean?"

Before the driver's mouth had even closed, Maurer's gloved right hand struck the man on the right side of his head with enough force to cause his legs to quake.

"Do not waste my time or I will have you disemboweled. They are nearby. I will ask only once more. Where are they?"

Staggered, the driver tested his jaw with his right hand before vomiting, barely missing Maurer's gleaming boots. Fulmar could see a sneer of disgust cross Maurer's face as he withdrew his Walther from his holster and placed it against the driver's temple.

"You were conveying four men in this wretched piece of machinery. I know that, so do not try to be clever. Polish potato farmers are not clever.

"I assume you do not know these men. Indeed, you could *not* know, having only just encountered them. They mean nothing to you. You provide assistance to them only out of your hatred for us Germans. To be frank, I care nothing about them, either. I care only for the one among them who is a professor."

Maurer pressed the barrel of the pistol against the driver's temple. "Do you know this professor? No. But you know who I am, correct? You have heard of me? Perhaps even seen me. You know how I proceed with such matters. So save yourself. Where did you drop your passengers? Tell me where and you can be on your way with your precious potatoes. In fact, I will *purchase* them from you at double—no, triple—your standard price."

The driver looked terrified but said nothing. Maurer waited several more seconds.

"You are an old fool," Maurer said resignedly. "It appears you prefer to die. Is it because you believe it is the honorable thing to do? Where is the honor in dying for men you do not even know? They would not do the same for you, believe me. You are just a potato farmer. A stupid Polish potato farmer. You will provide them with precious transportation and, in return, they let you die."

Maurer turned the barrel of the weapon so that it was parallel to the driver's temple. The SS Standartenführer tilted his head upward and shouted, "Professor Kapsky! You are nearby. I know it. You do not want any more to die because of you. This man *will* die if you do not come out and surrender. Should you surrender, this man will be treated well, extremely well, because you are extremely valuable to the Reich. You will have every comfort provided, every need fulfilled. You will become wealthy. You will be celebrated.

"Now you are exhausted. Already, many have died because of you. *This man* will die because of you if you do not surrender."

Maurer fell silent and scanned the woods where the quartet remained prone. Then he discharged the pistol next to Mikołaj's temple, the muzzle flash scorching the skin, and the shock collapsing him to his knees.

Fulmar flinched but restrained himself from firing. He glimpsed Kapsky, who had an anguished look on his face, tears pouring from his eyes. Fulmar put a finger to his lips and shook his head sharply.

"Son of a bitch," Fulmar whispered to Matuszek. "Kapsky can't take much more of this. He's going to break. Crawl back there and put a hand over his mouth. Don't let him make a *sound*."

Matuszek did just that. Kapsky nodded that he understood, but Matuszek's hand remained clamped firmly across Kapsky's mouth.

Maurer reached down, pulled Mikołaj upright by the back of his collar, and steadied him on his feet. "We shall repeat the performance, Professor Kapsky," Maurer shouted, "but this time the bullet will enter your friend's temple and exit out the other side of his skull, taking large amounts of brain matter along with it. Think about that for a moment, Professor. That image will be seared into your brain for the remainder of your life." Maurer paused and again scanned the woods, listening for a response.

Fulmar braced for the SS officer to fire his weapon, looking behind him to be sure that Matuszek had a firm grip over Kapsky's mouth. Then he cursed furiously.

Standing over Matuszek and Kapsky, mere feet behind, were four black-clad German troops, Karabiners trained on Fulmar, McDermott, Matuszek, and Kapsky.

"Hände hoch," one of the Germans ordered.

McDermott swore loudly, the volume magnified by the pain in his arm.

Fulmar, McDermott, and Matuszek each complied, McDermott with a continuing string of profanities. The Obergefreiter motioned with his rifle for the four to stand. "Hands over your heads." He motioned with his rifle in Maurer's direction. "Move."

The four complied, walking slowly through the woods toward the road, Fulmar grinding his teeth and McDermott continuing to issue profanities.

When Fulmar emerged onto the road he saw a smile of superiority on Maurer's face.

"So," the Standartenführer said smugly. "My performance so riveted you fools that my men could approach undetected. A simple ruse and you idiots are mesmerized. Just as I'd expected. Only Americans could be so stupid."

"I'm British," McDermott growled through the arm pain.

"Nearly as bad," Maurer said dismissively. He examined Matuszek's face. "Am I mistaken or is this Commander Matuszek himself? Hero of the *Armia*?" Maurer grinned expansively. "Kapsky and Matuszek; Canaris will be pleased. The *Führer* will be pleased." Maurer examined Kapsky. "Professor Kapsky. It is a pleasure to finally meet you. Much of my time these last three years has been occupied trying to find you. I must say, you do not appear to be well. Do not be concerned. You will receive the finest care and sustenance as soon as we convey you to our post in Danzig. That will not be long. We will convey you there presently and then, after treatment and all the food you can eat, to Seventy-six Tirpitzufer." Maurer scrutinized the twelve soldiers and the Kübelwagens. "Oberfeldwebel, take your men and tell them we have Kapsky and to prepare for treatment."

Maurer watched as they departed. He then gestured toward Mikołaj. "I am certain you observed from your place in the woods that this man, despite being threatened with his life, refused to disclose your whereabouts. A mere potato farmer. Most courageous, especially given that he does not appear to have any connection to you. Motivated, perhaps, out of patriotism. In a sense, quite admirable."

Maurer raised his Walther and shot Mikołaj twice in the face. Kapsky emitted a strangulated wail.

"Admirable," Maurer continued, "but ultimately useless. The rest of you will not be shot, at least not by me. You shall be prisoners and interrogated. Again, not by me, but by experts in extracting information. This, of course, does not apply to Professor Kapsky, who shall have only exemplary treatment as long as he cooperates."

Maurer stopped speaking and stared at Fulmar, whose expression had gone from anger and consternation to amusement. Maurer took several steps toward him until he was at arm's length.

"You have quite a curious look on your face for someone who has just been captured by enemy forces and has just witnessed someone executed. Do you find your predicament amusing?"

Fulmar broke into a grin. "I find *you* amusing."

Maurer cocked his head back slightly, perplexed. No one, especially prisoners, found him amusing. Intimidating or frightening, perhaps. But he was anything but amusing. Amusing suggested that he might be an object of ridicule. Maurer was nothing of the sort. He fired several rounds into the engine of the potato truck.

"How am I amusing . . . Fulmar, is it not?"

Although Fulmar was taken aback by Maurer's knowledge of his name, he betrayed no emotion. "You're obviously impressed with yourself. In my experience, individuals with such high regard for themselves usually crash and burn spectacularly, because they're oblivious to their deficiencies and don't make provision for them."

Maurer stood ramrod straight and made a show of looking down on Fulmar. "Deficiencies, Fulmar? It strikes me as ironic—no, humorous—that a prisoner in custody would remark about the deficiencies of his captor. After all, *your* manifest deficiencies resulted in your team being captured by me. I dispatched soldiers to circle behind your position well before I arrived on the scene and you were so riveted by my little performance with the idiot potato farmer that you were oblivious to their presence. A mere schoolboy ruse was sufficient to capture you."

Fulmar shrugged. "I'll concede that. But your deficiencies will ultimately lead to your defeat."

Maurer smirked. "Precisely which deficiencies are those?"

"Lack of self-awareness."

"A tautology. Would you care to be more specific?"

"Not really." A jocular smile crossed Fulmar's face. "I don't want to give you any clues as to how we're going to beat you."

Maurer threw his head back and laughed uproariously. "You're quite the comedian, Fulmar. I shall enjoy your interrogation."

"I will say this," Fulmar offered. "You do have an utter lack of irony."

Maurer raised his eyebrows. "Really? How so?"

"You're pretty impressed, obviously, with your cleverness, your wits. You outsmarted us. But it's always the guy that thinks he's so smart that gets outsmarted in the end."

Maurer laughed again and drew closer. "Did it occur to you that in this play, *you* are the character that gets outsmarted in the end?"

Maurer turned abruptly and addressed the officer who had halted Mikołaj's truck. "Leutnant, take your men back up the road and conduct a thorough sweep of the area between here and the factory. There is another American somewhere in the vicinity. He is to be found and captured. Kill him only if you have no option." The officer immediately directed his men into their vehicles and departed, dust in their wake.

Fulmar remained composed despite his bewilderment that Maurer seemed to have infallible intelligence. Intelligence that suggested the highest levels of the U.S. government may have been compromised.

Maurer turned back to Fulmar with a self-satisfied smirk. "Throughout this war I have been baffled by the ineptitude of you Americans. You have an abundance of resources and a sizable population. One would think you could produce a more effective opposition. Perhaps, in the end, there is no remedy for stupidity."

Maurer stepped back from Fulmar and addressed Kapsky. "Professor, it is my privilege to convey you to Berlin, where I'm sure you will thoroughly enjoy the comforts and privileges afforded you there. But first, we will take care of your immediate needs: food, medical care, rest. There is a factory not far from here that we have converted into a fine medical facility. We will convey you there, where you will receive the necessary medical attention and sustenance. Once the medical personnel declare you fit for travel, you will be taken to Tirpitzufer, Berlin—most likely by rail, but perhaps by air. There is an airstrip east of Danzig."

Maurer stopped and looked at Fulmar, who was shaking his head. "Do you have commentary, Lieutenant Fulmar?"

"No, but I have a wager."

"I rather enjoy gambling. What is your wager?"

"You won't get to Tirpitzufer," Fulmar said. "There is a man in Washington, D.C., who will make sure of it."

"Would that be your head of Office of Strategic Services?" Maurer asked with a smirk. "I rather doubt it."

Fulmar, concealing his astonishment, said nothing.

Maurer motioned to the Kübelwagens. "Get into the vehicles, please. We are done wasting time."

Maurer stepped into his car and signaled for his driver to proceed. The driver looped around the Kübelwagens and proceeded to the front. Maurer's troops directed Fulmar and McDermott into the vehicle directly behind Maurer's; Kapsky and Matuszek were directed to the third vehicle in the caravan. The remainder followed in the fourth vehicle.

Maurer signaled his driver, who led the caravan back in the direction of the factory. Fulmar's mind was racing, evaluating options for escape. They had no viable means to do so while moving. Perhaps if they came to a stop he could overpower the driver, but the other troops would easily assume control merely by brandishing their weapons. Fulmar was reluctant to concede that they had few, if any, options. But he was also a realist. An opportunity might present itself at some point. He had to be prepared to seize it immediately. Even so, he couldn't rely on McDermott for assistance. The man's right arm was useless and he was in extreme pain. Matuszek was the only person on whom he could plausibly rely, and he was in another vehicle. Coordination would be impossible. Any escape attempt would likely result in one of them—and perhaps everyone but Kapsky—being killed.

Waiting until they arrived at the factory was not much more satisfactory. Presumably there would be a greater troop presence there, and Maurer—if he hadn't done so already in anticipation of capturing Kapsky—would likely order the construction of a field prison or convert part of the facility into one.

No good options. The worst option, however, was to do nothing. Kapsky would be in the custody of the SS and Fulmar had no illusions that they wouldn't gain his "cooperation." That would have potentially catastrophic implications.

Fulmar concluded that under no circumstances could Kapsky remain in German custody. He glanced back at the vehicle in which Kapsky and Matuszek were riding, the soldier in the front passenger seat giving Fulmar a disapproving look. Kapsky's appearance remained the same— weak and distraught—maybe too weak to exert enough energy to flee even if they could engineer an escape.

Matuszek, on the other hand, wore a determined, defiant look that telegraphed willingness to take on the Germans at the best opportunity. Matuszek knew the odds as well or better than anybody. But, Fulmar surmised, Matuszek calculated that this might be his last opportunity to strike a blow against the enemy.

Fulmar turned and faced forward again, looking at Maurer sitting almost regally in his command car: the conquering hero of the Reich, and, Fulmar conceded, justifiably so. The acquisition of Kapsky and the knowledge he possessed purportedly had world-changing implications, and so it would have momentous implications for Maurer's career. The soulless bastard needed killing, and Fulmar tried his best to conjure a way to do so.

As he did, he noticed Maurer barking at his driver as he pointed forward. Fulmar looked past the lead vehicle and saw what appeared to be a small cloud of black smoke approximately a kilometer ahead. The lead vehicle slowed as the convoy approached the source of the smoke, which to Fulmar appeared to have the heaviness and thickness of an oil fire. From a distance it seemed to shroud the entire width of the road and extend into the woods on each side.

The convoy slowed as it got closer. Fulmar could smell the heavy odor of hot oil. Nothing beyond the curtain of black smoke, which rose to at least twenty feet, was visible, and the stench was nearly overwhelming.

When they came to within fifty meters of the smoke curtain, Fulmar could make out the source of the smoke—an overturned Kübelwagen that had caught fire. Fulmar couldn't discern any passengers, but concluded they had to be seriously injured or dead.

Fulmar saw Maurer stand in the rear of his car, surveying the scene, his head moving from right to left. There was no room on either side of the vehicle for the convoy to pass. The fire would have to be extinguished and the obstruction removed for the convoy to pass.

Maurer stepped from the rear of his car and onto the dirt road to inspect the obstruction more closely. The soldiers on the passenger side of each of the Kübelwagens also got out in anticipation of executing whatever command Maurer was about to issue. As they did so, the top of his driver's skull was sheared off by a round coming from somewhere in the woods to Fulmar's right. Before the driver's body slumped limply against the door, Fulmar felt warm blood spray across his face from the head of *his* driver, who also fell against the driver's-side door.

Fulmar reacted instantly, lunging toward the German in the front passenger seat, who was stunned by what he had just seen. Fulmar grasped the side of the German's head and jacked it backward over the rear of his seat with such force that the snap of his cervical vertebrae could be heard by McDermott, who had already relieved the man of his Karabiner 19 and was beginning to sight the German in the passenger seat in the rear vehicle. Before McDermott, face contorted in pain, could acquire the target and squeeze the trigger, the German's body shuddered twice from two shots to his torso, and fell against the vehicle's driver, who was being strangled from behind by Matuszek, whose face remained beet red from exertion even after the driver collapsed limply against the rear of his seat.

Fulmar reached forward instantly and seized the sidearm of the passenger-side German and began to train it on SS Standartenführer Maurer standing along the edge of the woods. But Maurer was not alone.

Fulmar smiled, then laughed, then hooted. Standing behind Maurer was Major Richard Canidy, USAAF, with his combat knife against Maurer's trachea and a vicious look on his face.

Fulmar scrambled out of the Kübelwagen and approached Canidy and Maurer. On the other side of the road, Emil emerged from the woods carrying his rifle. He looked, as usual, calm—as if he'd been on a butterfly expedition in the woods.

As Fulmar drew within a few meters of Canidy, he could hear him interrogating Maurer, who shook his head—carefully, to avoid slicing his neck on the blade.

"Are there any more checkpoints heading northwest along the road? Have they been alerted to us?" Canidy asked.

"Surely you don't expect a response."

"Surely I do."

"You'll not get one," Maurer said coolly. "You have no recourse."

"My recourse is to slit your throat and watch your face as the blood drains from your body."

"If you were a Russian, that might persuade me," Maurer said, keeping his head and neck as still as possible, "but you are an American. You cannot and will not do anything even remotely approaching that threat."

Canidy's jaws tightened. "No one, other than the men you see here, will know." Canidy tilted his head toward Commander Matuszek. "You see that man over there? You know who he is? You know precisely what he's capable of and what he'd love to do to you. Scores of his troops are dead or mutilated because of you. Scores more Polish civilians. I'll just hand the blade over to him."

Maurer forced a relatively convincing chuckle. "You are not dealing with an ignorant foot soldier. I know a bit about the American military and its strictures. You cannot avoid accountability by simply looking away while another performs a violation of one of your codes."

Candidy began to respond when Kapsky rushed toward Maurer and struck him in the face with his open hand, drawing a bead of blood from the German's left nostril.

"Professor Kapsky is uniquely motivated to elicit the information from you," Candidy said. "And he's a civilian. I'll defer to him."

Maurer swallowed carefully so his Adam's apple wouldn't make contact with the blade. "Be my guest. Place the burden on a poor civilian. A pathetic display, Major Canidy. I was given to understand that you were somewhat of—what do you Americans refer to it as?—a cowboy. That is why you were selected for this extraordinarily challenging mission. Your superiors believed you had the talent and courage to do it. Clearly you have neither."

Canidy's wrist tensed involuntarily, and the blade nicked the underside of Maurer's chin, a smear of blood oozing from the incision. Fulmar's eyes locked on Canidy and he shook his head sharply once.

Everyone's head but Maurer's turned upon hearing the sound of an engine somewhere behind the curtain of black smoke. A vehicle was approaching at high speed.

Canidy heard the vehicle brake and skid to a halt. Emil immediately raised his rifle to his shoulder and aimed toward the curtain. Fulmar bent down, withdrew the sidearm of the driver of one of the Kübelwagens, and also raised it toward the smoke. There was silence for at least ten seconds and then Canidy heard shouts in German from behind the curtain. In a low voice Matuszek said, "They are asking Maurer if he's here and if he can hear them."

The shouting continued for a few more seconds. Canidy's team remained utterly still. Seconds ticked by in silence. Suddenly, Maurer erupted with shouts for help. Canidy reflexively dragged the blade of the knife across Maurer's trachea, slicing nearly to his spine.

Canidy stepped back from the gush of blood, dropping Maurer's lifeless body to the ground as shouts came from the other side of the curtain. Without hesitation Emil sprinted into the woods with his rifle held low. Less than a minute later Canidy's team heard a series of shots, a slight pause, and another series. Then silence.

Moments later there was a rustle in the woods and Emil appeared, a passive expression on his face. Yet another day at the office. Canidy, Fulmar, Matuszek, and McDermott all nodded their appreciation toward the young soldier.

Fulmar said, "Okay. We've handled the immediate problem, but we've got a ways to go. An unknown number of checkpoints, and the possibility that we won't get to the canal on the Thorisdottirs' timetable." He looked at Sebastian Kapsky, whose face was drawn and sallow. "Professor, we need to move now. Can you walk?"

"I will have to."

"That won't work," Canidy said. "Our job is to get you out alive. Due respect, Professor, you look like hell."

Kapsky nodded. "I've heard that before. I feel worse."

Fulmar stated what was obvious to everyone: "No way can we walk, evade Germans, and get to the boat on time—or even within a reasonable proximity of the Thorisdottirs' window."

"Give it to me straight, no bull, Professor. We need to go fifteen to twenty kilometers to the canal in about five hours. The good news is the terrain from here to the Baltic is mostly pretty flat. The bad news is we need to be prepared to run if we encounter unfriendlies. Now, can you do that?"

Kapsky straightened and said, "I think—"

"Sorry," Canidy interrupted. "I don't care what the hell you think. Can you *do* it? Yes or no?"

"I do not know."

"Honest answer," Canidy said.

"Dick," Fulmar said. "Let's at least start moving. We'll know whether or not the professor can get to the canal when we do or don't get there. In the meantime, we're wasting precious minutes."

Canidy's face tensed with frustration. "Hell, you're right. Let's get moving. We don't have any options. We either get there or we don't. But we can't stand around here playing Hamlet."

Canidy put his hand on Kapsky's shoulder. "Professor, this is your last and only opportunity to get the hell out of here. You've evaded the Germans longer than anyone could have expected. You can do it again. One last push. One last push, then freedom."

Kapsky nodded. "Thank you. Thanks to all of you. I

will do my best in honor of those who have perished to protect me or simply because of me. I owe all of you my best effort." Kapsky shuddered as if chilled. "But I must eat soon. I need fuel."

"We all do," Canidy acknowledged. "Anybody got any crumbs in their rucks?"

"All out," McDermott said.

The rest grumbled and shook their heads.

"Okay. Let's get moving, then. First order of business is rustling up something edible. We'll all need some calories if we're going to hump fifteen kilometers."

McDermott, jaws clenched from pain, piped up. "There were some blackberry bushes where we were lying in the woods"—he pointed to Maurer's corpse—"watching that SOB. It's on our way. There's probably some other fruits in the woods along the way."

"And don't forget," Matuszek added, "there's a whole truckload of potatoes back there, too."

Canidy stared blankly at Matuszek as he stuffed the Walther in his waistband. "Yum."

"We better get going," Fulmar said. "We can discuss our options on the way. Walk."

They turned and began walking back down the road. Canidy stopped abruptly. "No," he said sharply. "We'll ride."

The rest looked at him, confused.

"We'll ride," he repeated.

"What the hell are you talking about?" McDermott asked. "Ride *what* exactly? The potato truck again? Under the tarp? You, Fulmar, and I don't speak Polish and our sweet little SS Standartenführer shot the truck up, if you recall. It won't operate."

Canidy shook his head and pointed to Maurer's command car. "Would be a shame to waste an exquisite specimen such as that."

Everyone looked at the car and then back to Canidy. Fulmar said, "Dick, you don't look like you're suffering from battle fatigue or anything, but all due respect, you're nuts. We might as well put a siren on it with flashing lights, drive right to the nearest German field headquarters, and turn ourselves in."

Canidy squinted as he pondered the command vehicle. "I'll grant you it's not without risk, but we might just be able to pull it off with a bit of discipline."

Canidy walked toward the vehicle, the others following.

"Dick," McDermott said. "Do I need to point out that if we come to a checkpoint and they see us in this we'll get machine-gunned before we even have a chance to brake or stop?"

"No one would dare impede, let alone machine-gun, an SS Standartenführer and his staff," Canidy replied.

Fulmar shook his head. "I don't believe this. We're going to play Halloween?"

"Damn right. We're going to change clothes with these guys and drive as far as we can." Canidy patted Kapsky on the shoulder. "This guy's game, and I respect that. But the odds of us getting him to the boat on foot aren't good. He can barely walk now. And"—Canidy faced Kapsky—"to be honest and respectful, the wear and tear may be too much for you, too, right?"

Kapsky said nothing.

"We have no good options, gentlemen," Canidy said. "But this is the better one."

Thumbing his shirt, Fulmar noted what the others were thinking. "Even if we do this, we can't ride in an open command car looking like this . . ."

"Exactly right," Canidy acknowledged. "So start getting undressed."

"Whoa." Fulmar put a hand up. "Hold it, Dick. You're actually serious? We're supposed to . . . ?"

"Getting a little squeamish, Eric? I'll grant you, I'm not a big fan of wearing a dead man's clothes, but we can't very well ride around in a topless SS command car looking like Home Army rejects."

"There's blood on some of them," McDermott said. "Bullet holes."

"What do you expect? We're getting them at no charge." Canidy pointed to Maurer's corpse. "That's mine. I think I can pull off SS Standartenführer."

Canidy bent down and began removing Maurer's uniform. The others reluctantly chose subjects similar in size and began doing the same. Matuszek said, "We are six. The car can fit six, but it will appear peculiar."

Canidy asked, "What do you suggest?"

"It will look more natural if two ride in front and three in back," Matuszek replied. "I suggest I sit in the front passenger seat, since I'm most familiar with the area and the route to the canal. Fulmar drives, since he speaks

German and is most likely to have to speak if we are stopped, although I doubt anyone would dare stop a car conveying an SS Standartenführer.

"Major, you obviously should sit in the rear center seat flanked on the right by your loyal adjutant McDermott so that his wounded arm is better concealed against the door, and to the left by the professor"—Matuszek glanced at Kapsky—"who appears to have assumed the rank of Stabsgefreiter."

Matuszek came over to Emil. "You have performed well, son. Your services will no longer be needed here. Report back to Porucznik Kutylowski. Tell him I said you shall be promoted upon my return and you deserve a leave."

Emil slung his rifle over his shoulder, straightened, and saluted Matuszek, who returned the salute. Canidy, Fulmar, and McDermott did the same. Canidy began clapping, and Fulmar and McDermott followed suit.

"See you in hell, Emil," Canidy said with a grin.

Emil laughed. "See you in hell, Major." Then he waded into the woods and disappeared.

"I hope to see him again one day," Canidy said.

"I hope you do, too," Matuszek said as he pulled the trousers from a German corpse. "The probabilities, however, are not good."

Canidy removed his shirt and dabbed at the fresh blood from the throat wound on the collar of Maurer's shirt. Thankfully, it blended sufficiently with the shirt collar that it would be visible only from a short distance.

Although Maurer was a bigger man, his clothes fit Canidy surprisingly well. Canidy struggled, however, to pull the boots on, never having worn footgear that rose above the knee. Canidy checked Maurer's Walther and made sure he had spare ammunition. He saved the visor cap for last, letting it sit low on his brow. When he was done dressing, he examined himself in the car's sideview mirror.

He looked the part.

Fulmar, McDermott, and Matuszek didn't look bad, either. The clothing was a bit loose on each, but not noticeably so. Kapsky's uniform, however, was visibly ill-fitting. The sleeves were too short and the pants and shirt were baggy. Canidy hoped that the mismatch wouldn't be visible while seated in the vehicle.

They placed most of their own clothing they'd removed in the trunk of the vehicle. Fulmar fingered the bullet hole in the shoulder of his uniform. "What do we do about these?"

Canidy shrugged. "If we get stopped, we say nothing. What checkpoint guard is going to question the staff of an SS Standartenführer?"

"A petrified Soldat who wants to appear alert and thorough in the eyes of such Standartenführer," Fulmar responded.

"You say what should be obvious. We were in a fight," Canidy said to Fulmar. "Then I'll act impatient and ask the Soldat what the hell does he *think* happened?"

"But you don't speak German."

"Even better. I'll let you, my subordinate, do the talking for me. Just be sure to act highly offended."

CHAPTER 57

Donovan sat at the end of the bar at the Old Ebbitt Grill farthest from the 15th Street NW entrance, sipping Macallan. The restaurant and bar, usually filled with White House and Treasury staffers, was sparsely populated. He recognized an assistant secretary of state sitting with a woman not his wife at a table on the other side of the room. Secretary of the Interior Harold Ickes and Secretary of Labor Frances Perkins were engaged in conversation at the other end of the room. When Henry Stimson walked in the door, they rose to greet him. After short salutations, Stimson came to the bar and sat next to Donovan.

"Hell, Bill," Stimson said. "I know you're not a big fan of their politics, but for goodness' sakes, you could at least acknowledge them."

"I don't see them going out of their way to acknowledge me," Donovan said dismissively.

"Of course not. You scare the hell out of them. They think you eat small children for breakfast."

Donovan took a sip of Macallan. "Not this morning."

"What do you hear from Commander Fleming?"

Donovan took another sip of whisky and shook his head. "They haven't heard a thing since the operation began, either. None of their contacts have sighted Canidy, Fulmar, or McDermott anywhere in Germany. We know from the boat captain that they were dropped off as scheduled at the designated spot near Danzig, but after that it's been radio silence."

"They have a radio?"

"Figure of speech. But, as a matter of fact, yes. A tiny contraption put together by our mad scientists. Not much range. Doubt it even works."

Donovan stopped talking as the bartender approached.

"Water, Mr. Secretary?"

"Thank you, Bert."

"Christ's sake," Donovan said as the bartender retreated. "At least order something with some flavor."

"What conclusions, if any, do you draw from the silence?" Stimson asked.

Donovan shook his head. "The logical one. These men were sent to perform a near impossible task. In Germany."

Stimson clapped Donovan on the back. "You can't blame yourself over this, Bill. Everyone knew what was at stake. Everyone knew the risks. Those men had absolutely no illusions about what they volunteered to do."

"They didn't volunteer."

"Of course they did, Bill. No one ordered them to go."

Donovan took another sip of Macallan and looked at Stimson. "Come on, Henry. The head of the Office of Strategic Services asks you to go on an operation of extreme importance to the Allied effort, an operation that few beyond Roosevelt and Churchill have been briefed on. Seriously, that's an order. No one would refuse that."

"And they didn't." The bartender placed a glass of water before Stimson and retreated. "Did Fleming say *anything* whatsoever about the operation?"

"The last time they heard from their man was when he was in Gotland. Shortly thereafter, he was to meet Canidy and Fulmar and they were all to cross the Baltic into Poland. The Brits are as much in the dark as we are. None of their resistance contacts reported seeing Canidy, Fulmar, or McDermott. We don't know if they even made it into Germany. They disappeared shortly after making landfall."

"I expect you assume the worst."

Donovan pinched the bridge of his nose. "There's nothing else to expect, logically. Canidy and Fulmar are the best. I assume if Churchill sent him, McDermott was their best, or at least one of their best."

"What are our options, Bill?"

"We have no option other than pray that the Nazis can't figure out what the Kapsky document is about. And if they do figure out what it's all about, pray some more."

CHAPTER 58

Gromov was growing increasingly anxious.

Despite moving through the countryside at a trot, he feared he was getting no closer to the Americans and Kapsky. Worse, he believed that for a considerable period of time he had been moving in the wrong direction.

The redheaded woman had misled him, causing him to pursue the Americans at nearly a forty-five-degree angle from what he now believed was their actual path. Thankfully, he had heard the gunfire through the forest and followed his instincts, threading through the woods until coming upon some type of factory in a valley where German troops were guarding civilians. The smell of gunpowder was still in the air, and from his vantage point atop the hill he could see rapidly moving vehicles in the distance.

He knew he had to take a chance. He circumnavigated the factory and followed the path of the vehicles. More anxiety. Even assuming he was now following the right path, he couldn't make up the distance on foot. He had no visual contact with the Americans.

Thankfully, he encountered a boy of about twelve riding a bicycle on the same road taken by the vehicles. Gromov flagged the boy, who, upon discerning Gromov was armed, prudently turned around and began pedaling in the opposite direction.

Gromov surprised himself by not shooting him. Instead he sprinted after him, overtaking the frightened adolescent and pulling him to a halt. Then he tendered twenty *złoty* for the bicycle, which the relieved boy happily exchanged.

Gromov pedaled at a brisk pace for more than an hour, encountering only a farmer driving an empty ox-drawn cart. Yet more anxiety.

Then he heard gunfire again. Hopeful, he began pedaling faster, only to have the bike's chain snap, rendering it useless. The assassin cursed to himself repeatedly as he dismounted and began jogging down the road until he heard another round of gunfire, this time much closer. Above the treetops there appeared to be a plume of black smoke.

He ducked into the adjacent woods and proceeded quietly and cautiously toward the sound of the gunfire, silently praying that his instincts would be confirmed. With each moment, the window of opportunity for acquiring Kapsky was closing, and he'd yet to even *see* the man.

He paused to orient himself, to listen for more sounds, when there was a sound of movement—subtle, barely audible. Perhaps an animal.

Perhaps not. He dropped to the ground and lay still.

Less than a half minute later Gromov saw the tall

young scout he had seen leading the Americans previously. He was weaving expertly through the trees, making hardly any noise.

Gromov's tension eased and was replaced by anticipation. This wasn't coincidence. The appearance of the scout meant the Americans—and Kapsky—were nearby. But where?

Gromov remained still, tracking the scout until he vanished amid the foliage. The scout was moving in the wrong direction—the direction of the factory—and no one was following. The gunfire Gromov had heard a short time ago had come from the opposite direction—northwest. Northwest was where the Americans would go to get out of the country.

The assassin counted slowly to one hundred. He wanted to rise, but disciplined himself to keep still for another count of one hundred. Then he rose and continued in the direction from which he'd heard the gunfire. He moved slowly and quietly, looking behind him every few seconds to ensure the scout hadn't doubled back.

It took only a few minutes. He could see breaks of light between the trees, indicating he was coming to a clearing, maybe a road. He slowed his pace yet further, moving from tree to tree, pausing for a moment before proceeding onward.

He saw a dirt road twenty meters ahead. He crouched with his weapon at the ready and crept toward the edge of the woods. He saw nothing to the right—southeast. But approximately a quarter-kilometer to the left—northwest—was the unmistakable scene of combat. There were bodies on the ground, vehicles strewn haphazardly. Maybe an ambush. He observed the scene for a moment before approaching. He saw no movement. Whoever was responsible had moved on.

A peculiar scene. Kübelwagens, dead bodies stripped of their outer garments, a few random civilian garments strewn about nearby.

One body appeared familiar. The assassin took a closer look. The corpse was that of a large, tall man, throat cut to the bone. The hair was so blond it was almost white.

Not an ambush, Gromov thought. If it had been an ambush it would be more likely that the SS officer would have been shot.

Gromov inspected the immediate vicinity for clues. The most obvious was the absence of a command car. An SS Standartenführer did not travel in a Kübelwagen with the troops. The tire tracks in the dirt showed that a vehicle had turned about and headed northwest.

Gromov reflected as his mind's eye re-created the events that resulted in the macabre scene. The Americans had overpowered the Germans, stripped them, donned their uniforms, and departed in the command car.

It wouldn't work. The Germans would identify them as impostors and kill them at the next checkpoint. And if Kapsky was also wearing a German uniform, it would be unlikely German soldiers would know his importance, and would kill him, too.

They had a head start, but not by much. Gromov inspected the remaining Kübelwagen. The keys were in the ignition. He got in, started the engine, and drove as fast as it would go after the Americans.

CHAPTER 59

The sense of optimism bordering on exhilaration the team had felt when they drove off in the German vehicle lasted no more than twenty minutes. They'd traveled primarily through countryside dotted with a farm or two until they came to a nameless cluster of dwellings near Suchy Dąb, where they were compelled to come to a halt because of the seemingly endless procession of panzers crossing the road.

A large, empty, open-bed truck was in front of them, so the procession and the Gefreiter directing traffic at least fifteen meters away were not close enough to afford close inspection.

"Dick," Fulmar said. "Just remember, look smug and arrogant. In other words, be yourself. If one of these jackboots has the nerve to come over, I'll do all the talking."

Canidy thought he could see the tail of the procession

less than a quarter of a kilometer to their right. But on closer inspection determined the procession was endless.

The Gefreiter directing traffic finally seemed to take interest in the car, glancing over every few seconds with a puzzled look on his face. He was short, stocky, with a pug face, and looked like a busybody. He waved over a Soldat standing on the other side of the convoy to take over for him and began walking past the truck toward the command car with a curious, somewhat irritated expression on his face.

Everyone in the command car except Canidy tensed upon his approach. The Gefreiter didn't appear cowed or intimidated by the presence of an SS Standartenführer.

Fulmar, speaking High German, changed that in an instant.

"You have the temerity to leave your post when this convoy is crawling along at a timid pace in the midst of a combat zone? What kind of incompetent fool are you to both slow the progression of a fighting column as well as that of SS Standartenführer Maurer?"

Stunned, the portly Gefreiter stopped abruptly.

"Come here, you incompetent idiot," Fulmar shouted. "Now!"

The Gefreiter obeyed instantly, if reluctantly, the attitude of his body shifting from dominance to almost canine submission.

"What are you waiting for?" Fulmar hissed.

The Gefreiter looked horrified, unsure of what to do.

"Name and unit. Commanding officer," Fulmar demanded.

The Gefreiter stuttered before beginning to respond. Fulmar cut him off. "Where is your salute? You have the audacity to address the Standartenführer without a salute? Particularly after this incompetent display?"

The Gefreiter began to salute, stopped abruptly, then stood at attention and began to salute again. Fulmar cut him off.

"Get out of here."

The Gefreiter spun abruptly and began to retreat.

"Wait. What is your company commander's name?"

The Gefreiter spun about to face Fulmar. "Hauptmann Hans Meyer."

"He will hear directly from Admiral Canaris and will be made to account for your incompetence and impudence. Now, expedite that column. *Move*."

The Gefreiter saluted and spun on his heels, scrambling toward his previous post. A trail vehicle and convoy came into view over the northern horizon. Each of the car's occupants cursed silently. It would be some time before they could move.

"That came way too naturally for you," Canidy observed of Fulmar's performance, adding, "That's our one free pass. We're lucky we encountered the one blithering idiot in all the Wehrmacht. That won't happen again."

"With any luck, it shouldn't," Matuszek said, pointing northwest to wisps of smoke in the distance. "That's Danzig ahead. We should go on for a bit more, then proceed the rest of the way by foot."

"This doesn't look familiar," Canidy said.

"That's because, if you recall, the first time we were

here we proceeded from the canal in a more westerly direction before turning south," McDermott explained in a strained voice.

Canidy turned and looked closely at McDermott, whose face was crimson with pain. His eyes were shot red and he was perspiring heavily. The sleeve covering his wounded arm was soaked with blood.

"McDermott, how are you hanging in there?" Canidy asked.

Instead of an oral response, McDermott nodded, causing Canidy to conclude that, in fact, the Scot was barely hanging in there.

Canidy looked to the right. The trail vehicle seemed barely closer over the horizon. Each of the car's occupants silently cursed. It would be some time before they could move. Canidy hoped the idiot traffic cop wouldn't suddenly have an epiphany regarding McDermott's appearance. If he did, he was probably too intimidated to say anything. But it would be a while before they could move. Maybe enough time for him to begin thinking straight and summon the courage to say something.

Canidy passed the time performing mental calculations on how long it would take to get to the canal, but conceded to himself that without more precise knowledge of their whereabouts, any such calculations were little more than wild guesses. He hesitated to ask Matuszek, whose estimate would be far more accurate but, he feared, much longer.

Not one of the passengers spoke the entire time it took the column to pass. McDermott's breathing was becoming more audible and ragged. When the final vehicle passed before them, every occupant of the command car moved his feet as if engaging the clutch to put the vehicle into gear.

No more than a minute after they had begun moving again, Canidy couldn't wait any longer. "Commander, what's your estimate of when we'll reach the canal?"

"Close. But the roads are poor. Slow. With no delays we should arrive in the next two hours. We will drive for another twenty minutes. The remainder of the trip will be by foot."

Canidy refrained from glancing at McDermott. Everyone in the vehicle, McDermott included, wondered whether McDermott could possibly walk a half hour, a portion of which would no doubt be through dense forest and over challenging terrain.

"How long before we need to ditch the car and go on foot?" Canidy asked.

"At this pace, twenty minutes at the most."

Canidy pursed his lips, thinking. "Maybe we should've ditched our clothes back there instead of bringing them with us. We'll look conspicuous walking in civilian clothes."

"Hell, we'd be conspicuous no matter what," Fulmar said. "Roll with the punches."

Canidy exhaled. "Exactly right. Fourth quarter, ninth inning, championship round. We've made it this far, miraculously. Time to close the deal."

Canidy reached under his seat for the potatoes they'd taken from Mikołaj's truck along the way. He handed one to each of the passengers and was about to take a bite when he noted the potato was covered with numerous, almost microscopic, white grubs.

A torrent of Polish profanities from Matuszek confirmed that Canidy's potato wasn't an anomaly. They'd have to hump on empty stomachs.

CHAPTER 60

The Americans were a little more than a kilometer ahead and oblivious to his presence. Gromov had seen them stop in front of a lengthy German convoy. He'd been a bit surprised to see them so soon—he'd estimated they were at minimum several kilometers ahead of him. The convoy, however, had permitted him to gain significant ground and the ability to calibrate the distance between their vehicle and his.

He was but one against five. More accurately, for combat purposes, four—since Kapsky was not a combatant. Their numerical advantage was offset by their ignorance of his proximity. And by his martial superiority.

Gromov assessed that only three of them posed a challenge. Kapsky clearly was not. And Gromov detected something amiss with the one seated in the rear to the right. The pitch and attitude of his body was that of a wounded man. Of this Gromov was fairly confident, as he'd wounded more than he could recall and could assess the dispositions of the wounded well enough that he could tell even from a distance.

One of them appeared older than the rest, at least from a distance. Probably brave and experienced. War was for the young and strong; which meant middle-aged men who were still in the field were tough and savvy, but they had invariably lost a step. He most likely was an honorable soldier, but no match for Gromov's speed and ferocity.

Gromov concentrated on the driver and the tall one sitting in the middle rear. The latter was the leader. Gromov had observed him the last time. A proficient warrior, although not in Gromov's class. Still, uncommonly talented. Gromov needed to kill him first.

Fulmar slowed the vehicle as the road became increasingly pockmarked and the ride bumpy. Matuszek, as if in response, assured, "Not much farther."

Canidy felt Kapsky jostle against his shoulder and then slump forward. Alarmed, Canidy grasped Kapsky's collar and pulled him upright, his head lolling against the backrest.

"Slow down. We've got a serious problem," Canidy informed. "The professor is unconscious."

Fulmar immediately reduced the vehicle's speed and craned his head around to see for himself. Kapsky's eyes were half closed and appeared vacant, lifeless. "Check his pulse. He looks worse than just unconscious."

Canidy placed two fingers against Kapsky's neck, just beneath the jaw. After several seconds Canidy said, "I can't tell if his heart is even beating."

He quickly grasped Kapsky's left wrist, placing the same two fingers just below the base of the thumb. Canidy clenched his teeth and cursed. "He's barely got a pulse. Stop the car."

Fulmar took his foot off the accelerator and coasted to a halt. Both he and Matuszek turned in their seats to see Kapsky's head slump forward. Canidy placed his hand under Kapsky's nostrils for ten seconds. "Weak, damn it. I can hardly feel a damn thing."

"Slap him," Matuszek instructed. "Listen to me! Slap him hard."

Canidy slapped Kapsky twice across each cheek and immediately checked for a pulse in his right wrist. He cursed again. Then froze. "Wait, I think I have something. It's just that it's weak. Barely there." Canidy's eyes darted about the interior of the vehicle. "Everybody look for something. A field box. A first-aid kit . . ."

"What do you hope to find?" Matuszek asked.

"Hell if I know. Something."

Fulmar waved his hand underneath the driver's seat. Matuszek opened the compartment in the console separating the driver and passenger seats. Both said, "Nothing" simultaneously, but kept running their hands against the dashboard, side door pockets, and under the seats.

Canidy gently propped the professor up against the backrest and kept him upright with his left hand while running his right hand over the back of the front seat. Again, nothing.

"What do you have?" he asked the others. "What do you have?"

Fulmar and Matuszek continued to search. "Still nothing."

Canidy began slapping Kapsky's face several times, but there was no visible response.

"Here!" Fulmar shouted. "Here!"

A canteen in the bottom of the console. He pulled it out, unscrewed the top, and thrust it toward Canidy. "It's full. Throw some water on his face and then get him to drink the rest. It's all we've got."

Canidy tilted Kapsky's head back with his left hand, seized the canteen from Fulmar, and placed the nozzle to the professor's mouth.

"Be sure he doesn't choke," Fulmar cautioned.

Canidy ignored him and poured nearly half the contents of the container into Kapsky's mouth. Then he doused the professor's face with the remainder, drawing his head back from the pungent odor wafting toward him.

Shocked, Canidy said, "Crap."

"What?" Fulmar asked.

Canidy didn't respond. A moment later Kapsky's eyes snapped open and he retched violently, chest heaving.

Canidy continued to hold the professor upright as he hacked and wheezed for a full minute, his eyes darting about wildly.

"Professor, can you make it?" Canidy asked. "How do you feel? Are you able to keep going?"

Kapsky's eyes darted about wildly. Canidy patted his cheek repeatedly. "Professor? Are you with us? Can you hear me?"

Kapsky nodded, a startled expression making him appear frightened but alert. He continued hacking for another minute, then took several deep breaths, trying to compose himself.

Canidy withdrew his left hand from Kapsky's chest. "Listen to me. Do you think you're okay?"

Kapsky nodded vigorously and continued to gasp for air. Canidy looked at Fulmar and Matuszek, whose expressions continued to convey concern. "Based on the evidence," Canidy said, "it appears the previous operator of this vehicle had a fondness for rye."

Fulmar and Matuszek exhaled simultaneously. Kapsky placed a hand on Canidy's shoulder, a gesture of gratitude and assurance. "I am weak. I am very weak. But I will not let you down."

"That's what I want to hear," Canidy said resolutely. "All we need to do is hold out until we get to the boat. There will be food, water, and medicine on board. Just hang on."

"Dick," Fulmar said, "look at McDermott."

Canidy turned to see the Scot slumping against the door, barely conscious. The entire right side of his shirt was soaked with blood.

Canidy winced but said nothing. McDermott's face was drained of color. His eyelids fluttered, but his eyes were motionless and vacant.

Canidy shook his head. "This bandage isn't doing the

trick, even for a tough bastard like him," he said as he bent down, seized the cuff of his left pant leg, and began tearing the fabric. "Got to put a tourniquet on the upper arm or we may lose him."

Canidy placed the strip of cloth from his pant leg around McDermott's upper arm just below the shoulder socket, pulled it as tight as he could, and tied it with a double knot. McDermott remained slumped against the car door.

Canidy shook the canteen and listened. A few dregs left. "I think he might appreciate this more than our good professor." He placed the canteen to McDermott's lips and simply poured. The Scot stirred a bit, and his eyes opened a bit wider.

Fulmar said, "We need to get going or we'll miss the boat, literally."

Canidy nodded and asked Matuszek, "How much farther?"

"We'll need to leave the car in less than a couple kilometers and go by foot the rest of the way."

"How long will it take?"

"Not long. Shorter than last time, because we've traveled farther west before turning northward than when Emil guided you previously."

Canidy examined his watch and then looked at Fulmar. "What time do you have?"

"Fifteen hundred hours. Almost on the dot."

"That's what I show also." Canidy nodded. "Commander, our boat is already at the dock. The Thorisdottirs will give us as much leeway as they can, but our window will close at about seventeen hundred hours. Can you get us there?"

Matuszek looked at Kapsky, and then McDermott. "I do not know."

CHAPTER 61

The anxiety had returned.

More than mere anxiety, something close to panic. The road had veered west, but there had been a north-ward split several kilometers after the convoy. Gromov was uncertain which road the Americans had taken. Both roads, he knew, passed within the woodland areas near Danzig that led to the sea. One went northward, while the other went farther to the west. They might have taken either. The northward road was safer. They'd have to disembark and travel a bit farther by foot to the sea, but the area was more heavily wooded, providing better coverage. The westward road was faster but more treach-erous. It was closer to Danzig, and, as such, concentra-tions of German troops. The probability of encountering those troops was far greater.

Gromov chose to go westward. If it were his decision, that's what he would do. The tall one seemed to share

THE DEVIL'S WEAPONS   433

many of Gromov's qualities. So that's likely what he would do.

Matuszek squinted and pointed to a thicket on the right side of the road. "There."

Fulmar veered off the road and slowed as he drove on the grass and into a grove of apple trees. The car pitched and bounced as he guided it as deep into the woods as it would go, obscuring it from anyone who might pass on the road.

Canidy looked to Kapsky. "Can you walk?"

"I do not know."

"Can you stand?"

"I will try."

Canidy looked at McDermott. "How about you?"

"I *will* walk."

Fulmar got out of the car, went to the rear, and assisted Kapsky. McDermott got out of his side of the vehicle, stood, and tested his legs. He slapped his right thigh and looked at Canidy. "Good enough."

Canidy was the last to get out of the car. He went to the rear and opened the trunk. "All right, everybody. We need to change back into our civilian clothes." He thumbed Maurer's shirt. "If the Thorisdottirs see us approaching in these things, they'll either shoot us or leave. Probably both. Besides, I doubt there are any SS Standartenführers strolling through the woods around here."

They were changed within minutes.

"We're going to have to hump. They'll wait, but not

long. If the radio works as advertised, we might be able to let them know our expected arrival time and to wait, but we shouldn't count on it. Anyway, I think we need to get closer." He pointed at Kapsky and McDermott. "Can you go?"

Both nodded.

"Don't be heroes. If you need help, let us know. Hell, I'd put McDermott over my shoulder if he didn't smell so bad." Canidy patted Matuszek on the back. "Commander, your show. Lead the way and make it quick, please."

They began walking up a slight grade into the woods.

"Hold it," Canidy said. "Eric, let's give the radio a shot right now, see if Moriarty's contraption really works."

Fulmar dug into his ruck and retrieved a leather case no more than six inches in length, eight inches in width, and two inches thick. The others looked on in curiosity as he unzipped it and pulled out a device matching the dimensions of the case.

"*That* is a radio?" Matuszek asked. "It cannot possibly work."

"It's got no W/T transmitter box and doesn't use Morse code, but let's try it," Fulmar said. He pressed a small black button on the right side of the device and it came to life, static crackling softly. Fulmar pressed another button and spoke into the front grid of the device.

"Saint Paul to *Njord*. Come in. Saint Paul to *Njord*."

Fulmar released the button and the soft static returned. All five men listened intently.

Fulmar pressed the button again. "Saint Paul to *Njord*. Come in. Saint Paul to *Njord*." Fulmar released the button again and the static returned. They listened for another ten seconds before Fulmar repeated the exercise. Once again, nothing.

"I don't know if that means Moriarty's contraption doesn't work or the Thorisdottirs aren't there," Canidy said. "But we can't waste time standing around here. Just our luck the damn Nazis are picking it up. Clever bastards. Let's move before they locate us."

CHAPTER 62

Gromov grew increasingly concerned as he continued to drive westward. He'd contemplated doubling back and taking the northerly route but calculated he was already past the point of no return. He drove as fast as the vehicle would go along the bumpy road, feeling slightly nauseated from the persistent jostling. Thankfully, the road was beginning to smooth out a bit. With one hand on the steering wheel, he reached into his ruck on the seat next to him, rummaged about, and pulled out a hard roll. Bread helped settle his stomach, but it did nothing for his nerves. He took a large bite of the roll but stopped chewing almost immediately and slowed the vehicle. He squinted at a spot approximately a kilometer ahead on the right side of the road. Two . . . three . . . four . . . eight German soldiers were gathered near a grove, their evident attention on something they appeared to have found.

Gromov slowed and drove only a bit farther before stopping to focus on the scene ahead. He confirmed; one, two, three, four . . . eight soldiers milling about something he was unable to discern until one of them moved a bit.

Gromov exhaled. It was the command car, somewhat obscured by the trees in the grove. He'd guessed right. They couldn't be too far ahead, but he'd have to move quickly before they reached the sea. He should be able to overtake them: one man could move faster than five.

Gromov drove forward slowly, assessing the scene, judging angles and distances. When he neared to within two hundred meters, the soldiers began gesturing toward the woods. After a few seconds, Gromov could see them nodding in unison and gesturing toward the forest. Seconds later they disappeared into the brush.

Competition, thought Gromov. *They may not know they're pursuing Americans, let alone Kapsky, but they are pursuing something suspicious.*

He got out of the vehicle, placed his Tokarev in his belt, and carried his rifle at low-ready. He walked briskly into the woods—moving northward along a parallel path fifty meters west of the Germans.

Gromov could hear the sounds of the Germans moving through the woods. In reaction, he stepped lightly so as not to reveal his presence. He winced upon hearing a dried twig snap underfoot and paused to see if there was any reaction from the Germans. There was none. Gromov sensed a subtle change in the air quality, the scent of salt water. He estimated the sea was no more than thirty minutes away.

He had less than that to acquire Kapsky.

CHAPTER 63

Canidy looked at his watch for the fourth time since abandoning the command car in the grove. The Thorisdottirs were probably well into the second hour of waiting for them at the dock. He pictured Kristin standing impatiently at the bow with her fists on her hips, listening intently for signs of their approach. She would not leave precisely at 17:00 hours, but neither would she wait longer than she deemed prudent. Canidy didn't know how long that would be, but he didn't want to test it. She made it clear that the German patrol boats along the coast dictated her timing. And Canidy couldn't argue with that. Katla might implore her to wait five or ten minutes longer for them to appear, but that would be the most Kristin would wait. And Canidy couldn't argue with that, either. He'd do the same.

The rest of the team appeared to share Canidy's sense of urgency. Matuszek, guiding them at the point, was advancing at near double time. Behind him McDermott gamely kept pace despite being visibly in pain and demonstrably weakened from loss of blood. Fulmar followed, looking a bit exhausted but otherwise fit and moving well. The professor trailed Fulmar by several meters, struggling to keep up. His breathing was labored and raspy, and his legs were unsteady; Canidy placed an arm around him every thirty to forty meters to keep him upright and moving. It was obvious that if they did make it to the boat, he'd need immediate and intensive medical attention. Canidy admired his grit.

The area was beginning to look familiar to Canidy, but he knew that the woods could play tricks with one's perception. He didn't want to risk going in any but the most optimal direction to get to the boat, but neither did he want to slow down.

Nonetheless, Canidy stage-whispered to Fulmar, "Eric, ask Matuszek to stop for a second." Fulmar, in turn, stage-whispered the request to Matuszek, who halted. All four huddled around Canidy.

"McDermott, you look like crap. You still in the fight?"

Irritated, McDermott said, "I told you, don't worry about me. You worry about yourself, you big shit."

Canidy looked at Matuszek. "Commander, how are we doing on time? Is this the best route?"

"We're closer. This is the direct route. We should see the terminus of the canal any moment. From there, perhaps another fifteen, twenty minutes to the dock."

"Good," Canidy replied. "Because that's all the time we've got." Canidy turned to Kapsky. "Twenty minutes more, Professor. Let me know if you can't go on your own power and we'll carry you. Got it?"

Kapsky nodded.

"How do you feel?"

"I cannot say. My legs and feet are numb."

"I'm not sure what he means," Canidy conceded. "But it's not good. We *have* to get past the next twenty to thirty minutes. You'll be okay if we get to the boat. All right?"

Kapsky, breathing heavily, said, "Let's move."

Immediately, Kapsky stumbled and fell. Canidy helped him up and stooped in front of him. "Get on my back, Professor. Piggyback, like when you were a kid." Kapsky nodded and climbed aboard Canidy's back, wrapping his arms around Canidy's neck and his legs around his waist. Canidy was grateful that he was lighter than he looked.

Mere moments later Matuszek pointed ahead to a canal. Canidy felt a charge.

"Almost there, Professor," Canidy informed. "Keep your fingers crossed."

The sight of the waterway prompted them to move faster despite the fact that the ground was becoming softer and, in some places, muddy. Canidy strained to keep pace with Matuszek and Fulmar. McDermott had fallen slightly behind Canidy but was buoyed by the sight of the water.

The sound of their movement remained minimal—primarily a muted crunch of leaves, even more so because of the soft ground. As a result, the snap of a branch behind them immediately caused Canidy, with Kapsky fastened to his back, to spin around and scrutinize the woods behind them. He remained still, looking from left to right.

Then another sound of indeterminate origin. He dropped Kapsky to his feet. The others also stopped and turned around. They remained still for several seconds without hearing another noise. Canidy turned and signaled to the others to advance. "Professor, I need you to do your best to walk on your own power just in case I need to make a fast move."

Kapsky blinked acknowledgment and followed the others. Canidy brought up the rear.

Gromov moved smoothly and silently through the forest, listening intently for noises made by the German troops.

Gromov was more experienced and was more disciplined. He discerned the subtlest of movements—the crack of a twig, the soft crunch of rotted leaves. He couldn't see through the foliage, but he gauged their presence approximately seventy to eighty meters west of him. They were a complication he didn't need. Given that the Americans were moving northward toward the Baltic, he knew his window would close soon—perhaps in less than twenty minutes. Their escape route was the sea. A boat would rendezvous with them or was already waiting for them. They would have to time their exit to avoid the infernal German maritime patrols, but they would be leaving soon.

Gromov evaluated his options as he threaded through the woods. He concluded he had few. The most methodical option, the one that most reduced his risk of death, was to kill the Germans first, then kill those escorting Kapsky. But he had no effective or timely means by which to kill the Germans without alerting the Americans to his presence. On the other hand, killing Kapsky's escorts first would require him to secure Kapsky and fight the Germans—all while preventing Kapsky from escaping.

He decided to keep moving and simply let the circumstances unfold.

Canidy grew more anxious the closer they got to the dock. He'd heard no suspicious sounds in the last few minutes, but every sound his own team made seemed magnified with each step closer to the dock. He walked with his head turned at nearly a ninety-degree angle to his right so as to see as far to their rear as possible without losing momentum. Were it not for Kapsky, he wouldn't resist the urge to break into a near sprint for the dock.

In front of him Kapsky was slowing. His strides grew shorter and unsteady and his arms were swinging in an exaggerated manner to afford more locomotion than his legs could generate on their own. His labored breathing was the loudest sound in the forest, but nothing could be done about it. He had to keep moving. If the sound gave them away, they'd just have to handle the consequences.

Gromov changed his opinion of the Germans somewhere to his left. Though he had judged them undisciplined, it seemed that was merely a matter of orienting themselves. For the last couple minutes, he heard no sounds whatsoever coming from their direction. They're *concentrating*, he thought. Focusing on their prey as they closed in for the kill.

He stopped for a moment, hoping to catch a telltale sound.

Nothing.

Though anxious to continue his pursuit, he waited a few seconds longer: nothing but the ambient rustle of leaves.

Gromov stared in the direction where the Germans should be, hoping to get a glimpse of fabric or maybe even exposed skin moving between gaps in the leaves and trees.

Still nothing.

He cursed under his breath as the anxiety rose once again.

"I must stop a moment," Kapsky said to Canidy as he sat on the rotting trunk of a fallen tree. "I am sorry. I cannot move as fast as the rest of you. After all of this time evading Germans, I thought I could. But, no."

"Take a blow, Professor," Canidy said, patting him on the shoulder. "But just for a minute. We have no options. We have to make our window, and it's closing quickly."

"Just for a moment," Kapsky repeated between labored breaths.

"Hold up," Canidy stage-whispered to the rest. "Hold up."

The others stopped and turned with sympathetic expressions, save for Fulmar.

"No," Fulmar said sharply, pointing at his wristwatch. "No way. Sorry. We've got to move. Now. *Right* now. We can rest later, on the boat. If there still *is* a boat."

Kapsky nodded and placed his hands on his thighs to lever himself upright. Canidy grasped him under his left armpit to assist, but Kapsky sat back down.

"Let's give it another shot," Canidy said. "We're out of time."

Once again assisted by Canidy, Kapsky catapulted himself up, this time successfully, although unsteadily.

"Eric," Canidy said. "Try Moriarty's radio again."

"That thing's a piece of shit," Eric replied. "Besides, no time. They're either there or they're not. Let's go."

"Try it," Canidy insisted.

Fulmar flashed an aggravated look, but pulled off his ruck, retrieved the device, and tried to transmit. All five men listened intently for a response. There was none. Fulmar shoved the device back in his ruck and said, "Okay. Let's go."

"Now we know if they leave without us, we'll have no means to get them to come back," Canidy said. He placed his hands under Kapsky's arms and lifted. "That's it, Professor, this is the home stretch. You didn't spend three years on the run only to fail ten minutes from the end."

Kapsky exhaled sharply, his jaw tensing with determination. "I will do my best not to slow you down anymore."

"Just a few more minutes, Professor. Just a little farther."

* * *

Gromov heard something he couldn't quite discern except that it wasn't indigenous to the forest. And it came from somewhere ahead of him. Somewhere close. He paused again and scanned the surroundings. Another sound. This time distinctly that of footsteps on litterfall. From somewhere ahead of him but very close. *If I can hear them, they can hear me*, he thought. But he had an advantage over the Germans and Americans. He *knew* someone was close. They did not.

Gromov dropped to one knee and focused on the spot from which the sounds had come. Almost immediately he heard another sound and locked his eyes on the point of origin. Only two heartbeats later he glimpsed a movement of leaves, then branches, then a flash of metal.

Good. Within striking distance. A bit closer and I have them.

Canidy had his right arm around Kapsky's waist, holding him upright as they proceeded at a brisk pace along the canal. Fulmar, at the point, had quickened the pace.

Canidy wasn't sure, but the area seemed to be getting more familiar. He refrained from raising his hopes, but the area appeared to be recognizable. He permitted himself to do the mental calculations he'd avoided earlier. Five, no more than ten minutes, he estimated. Although the banks of the canal had no benchmarks and the docks were nowhere in sight, the air's scent and humidity signaled they were getting much closer to the sea.

"A few more minutes, Professor," he guessed. "We'll be at the dock and on the boat. Then England. Hang in there. You've just about made it."

Gromov's stealth yielded to speed. He feared he'd fallen dangerously behind the Americans and needed to close the gap.

He could easily hear the movement in the forest in front of him now, close enough that he couldn't lose them. The Germans, on the other hand, seemed to have gone off track. Amateurs. He had heard no sounds whatsoever coming from his left flank for several minutes.

Good. Fewer complications. He'd kill the American team, get Kapsky, and proceed eastward out of the woods.

Canidy released his arm from Kapsky's waist and spun around. M1911 held at shoulder level.

The sound was clear. Something or someone was moving behind them. Canidy bet it was the latter. He signaled to Kapsky to get the attention of the rest. Not hearing any footsteps behind him, McDermott had already stopped. He whispered to Fulmar—who whispered to Matuszek—to halt. All faced toward the rear, weapons ready.

For a fraction of a second, Canidy thought he saw movement. He signaled for everyone to drop to the ground, but after everyone complied, they saw nothing. Nonetheless, each remained still, waiting.

Gromov crested a low rise and was stunned. The Germans, backs toward him, were forty meters *in front*. He'd misjudged them. They'd moved even more swiftly than he. They were advancing rapidly, as if anticipating acquiring their target.

Gromov's jaw jutted with anger and determination. He wasn't going to let a few Germans thwart his victory.

Canidy held his breath so the sound of his breathing wouldn't interfere with his detection of movement. He heard nothing. He saw nothing.

Fulmar crawled next to him. "What do you see?"

"Nothing. I think something's back there, but whatever it is I can't see it, and we can't wait. We need to force the issue. We're close. The rest of you take Kapsky and go to the boat as fast as you can move. Matuszek, too. On my signal, sprint. Don't worry about making noise. Just run your asses off. Don't stop or look back, whatever you hear. I'll cover you until I think you've separated enough and then I'll follow. Since Kapsky and McDermott can't move very well, I should be able to get to the boat about the same time as you do."

"If it's there."

"If it's there," Canidy conceded. "If it isn't, we're all screwed anyway. But if it is, and I'm not right on your tail, don't wait for me. Tell the Thorisdottirs to get the hell out of there and into the open water. I'll find my own way back, somehow."

Fulmar said nothing.

"Go."

Fulmar crawled toward the others. "Listen to me. We think someone's behind us. When I say 'Go,' we all get up and run like hell to the boat. Canidy will cover. I don't know exactly how far, but the boat's close. Regardless, run harder than you've ever run. Hold nothing back.

"Professor, this is your Olympics. Give it everything you've got."

Fulmar turned back to Canidy, who was lying on the ground with his left hand raised, and said, "Get ready."

Canidy dropped his arm. Fulmar said, "Go" and the forest erupted in gunfire.

Gromov was alarmed. The Americans and Germans were exchanging fire and Kapsky was somewhere in the midst of it.

Gromov could hear the air snapping from bullets streaking over him. Leaves and branches were fluttering from the impact of stray rounds.

This was madness. Kapsky would be killed.

Eight Germans armed with Karabiners were charging toward Canidy with astonishing speed. He sighted the one in front and squeezed the trigger of his M1911. The round struck the lead German squarely in the chest and he dropped to the ground as if a trapdoor had opened beneath him. The others kept charging without a pause, firing as they ran.

Canidy fired four rounds to give himself cover, rose from the ground, and ran in the direction of the dock. The air snapped around him as the Germans fired a volley of rounds after him. Canidy broke through a bank of thornbushes into a clearing and saw Fulmar, Kapsky, Matuszek, and McDermott no more than seventy-five meters in front of him along the bank of the canal. Fifty meters north of them sat the *Njord*, the Thorisdottir twins standing on deck, fists on hips.

Canidy spun and fired three more rounds at the pursuing Germans, dropping one of them on his face. The other six stopped, aimed, and fired several rounds. One grazed Canidy's left shoulder, spinning him sixty degrees to the left. He grimaced, gathered himself, and fired a round that went wide but caused the pursuing Germans to dive to the ground.

Canidy catapulted himself off the ground and sprinted toward the dock, zigzagging as he went. He could see Fulmar, Matuszek, McDermott, and Kapsky at the dock beginning to board the boat and Kristin raising her Gevarm to her shoulder. Seeing a weapon raised in his direction, Canidy immediately dove to the ground as Kristin fired several blind rounds at the Germans, causing them to drop to the ground for cover once again.

Canidy instantly popped back up and resumed sprinting, the effort producing a piercing sensation in his wounded shoulder. He heard the air snap inches from his right ear and a millisecond later saw Matuszek pitch forward and disappear onto the deck of the *Njord*. Canidy turned, fired toward the Germans, striking one in the throat, but without slowing the charge of the remainder. He emptied his weapon firing at the five remaining Germans, turned, and resumed running toward the dock.

Again, the air snapped above him and his eyes locked on the dock and the boat, where Fulmar and McDermott were struggling to assist an exhausted professor onto the vessel—all three presenting prime targets to the Germans.

Canidy shouted, "Move! Move! Move!" and leapt onto the dock and turned just in time to see the five Germans slow to a halt forty meters from the dock. For Canidy, the next ten seconds seemed to grind almost to a standstill and unfold over minutes rather than seconds. As Fulmar and McDermott lifted Kapsky onto the deck, the Germans trained their rifles at the boat. Everyone but Matuszek and Katla Thorisdottir was exposed on either the dock or the deck. Kapsky, being held upright on the deck of the boat by Fulmar and McDermott, displayed his back to the Germans as if it were a bull's-eye.

Even as Canidy thrust himself toward Kapsky to knock him to the ground he knew it was too late. He and Kapsky, along with Fulmar and McDermott, would be shredded by Karabiner rounds.

As he drove himself against Kapsky, Canidy heard a rapid succession of gunshots. Crashing into Kapsky, Fulmar, and McDermott, he braced for the sickening impact of the rounds. All three fell to the deck of the *Njord* as Katla drove the boat away from the dock up the canal.

But there was no pain. No blood. Not even a moan.

Canidy and Fulmar, lying together on the foredeck of the boat, stared at each other in astonishment, astonishment that they were both alive, astonishment that Kapsky, though debilitated, was unharmed.

They remained prone on the deck waiting for another volley of shots. None came.

Major Taras Gromov emerged from the brush, lowered his rifle, and surveyed the scene fifty meters in front of him. Five German soldiers lay on the mossy banks of the canal. One hundred meters beyond them, the stern of the *Njord* was rapidly disappearing around a shallow bend in the canal.

Kapsky was on the boat with the Americans. They would reach the Baltic within minutes, and from there— if Gromov's intelligence was as accurate as it had been throughout this operation—they would proceed toward Gotland. They needed to avoid U-boats and Messerschmitts, of course, but from Gotland the Americans would take Kapsky to RAF East Moor Field in Britain. Most likely Kapsky would remain there for a few days while British physicians nursed him back to health. Then he would be flown to Gander, Newfoundland, on his way to Princeton, New Jersey, by way of New York.

After a short period of rest, Kapsky would be debriefed by scientific luminaries. Kapsky would be giving the West what would seem to be an insuperable advantage over Germany and any other rivals that might challenge them after the war. An edge that could exist for decades.

Gromov pulled a cigar from his breast pocket, lit it, and took his time stoking it. It was Turkish, not pure tobacco, but he savored it nonetheless, sitting on a smooth boulder next to the canal as he puffed.

When he'd seen the Americans scrambling to get Kapsky aboard the boat, it was clear that the Germans had no idea who Kapsky was. They were simply shooting at an enemy who they'd tracked through the forest to a boat on the canal. Thorough, efficient, and perhaps expecting commendations, they would have killed Kapsky, oblivious to who he was. Under the circumstances, Gromov made the only decision he could and killed every single one of the German soldiers before they killed Kapsky.

Belyanov, of course, would be furious. The Americans had won. Gromov hadn't killed them and they had Kapsky. Not only would Kapsky provide the science for superweapons, but he would tell them about Katyn Forest. Stalin now would have to somehow convince the Western Allies that despite Kapsky's allegations, the Wehrmacht, not the NKVD, was responsible for the massacre. But, after all, how difficult would it be to convince the Americans and British that the *Nazis* had committed atrocities? Besides, Churchill was already pressing Roosevelt to open a Western Front against Hitler. Churchill needed it as much as Stalin did. And it was becoming increasingly clear to Roosevelt that it was imperative for the United States to do it. Beyond that, Belyanov would have his own problems. As Gromov looked at Goncharov's corpse, he imagined how Stalin would react upon hearing that the assassin Belyanov had sent after Gromov interfered in his attempt to capture Kapsky, thereby letting the scientist escape.

Gromov permitted himself a faint smile. He would still receive the Order of Lenin, perhaps awarded by Joseph Vissarionovich himself.

He stabbed the cigar into the soil, rose, and began walking back toward the vehicle he'd left on the edge of the forest. He proceeded at a leisurely pace, stopping after approximately one hundred meters to squat and yank his NR-40 from Colonel Yevgeni Goncharov's still-warm corpse. The dead man had been a respectable assassin—talented—but had stepped on one twig too many. Gromov wished he could be present when Belyanov would be forced to explain to Beria why his favorite assassin had himself been marked for assassination by Goncharov.

Gromov wiped the blade against his right thigh before returning it to the sheath in the back of his collar. Then he trod cautiously back through the forest. He paused after a few steps, thought for a moment, and walked back to the corpses of the Germans lying along the canal. He chose one that most closely approximated his size and removed his clothing. Then Gromov undressed and donned the German uniform.

A careful assassin is a live assassin.

CHAPTER 64

Baltic Sea

1703, 15 August 1943

The galley of the *Njord* in some ways resembled a field hospital, except everyone's spirits were high.

Katla was dressing Matuszek's wound with iodine, adhesive tape, and gauze. McDermott was resting on a floor mat, his back propped against the hull. Despite having suffered the most—and most severe—wounds, he was smiling broadly, having consumed the missing half of the bottle of Mortlach cradled in his lap. By comparison, Canidy's and Fulmar's wounds were minor, but their grins were nearly as broad, courtesy of healthy gulps of the Luksusowa vodka that had once inhabited the empty bottle on the galley floor.

Kapsky was in a deep sleep on a cot. Kristin and Katla recognized that in addition to suffering from extreme exhaustion, he appeared dehydrated. They'd fed him copious amounts of herring and bread that he'd consumed with generous amounts of beer and water. Before he fell asleep, he lifted his shirt and gently peeled from his left side the tape holding his notebook and handed it to Canidy, who handed it to Kristin and said, "Please keep this in the most secure compartment on the vessel until we disembark."

None of the passengers gave any thought to a possible encounter with U-boats or Messerschmitts. They were too elated or too exhausted and had the fatalism of transient victors. Canidy and Fulmar in particular looked both contemplative and elated.

"Don't worry, Commander," Canidy said to Matuszek, who was complaining, albeit good-naturedly, about being away from the battlefield. "After Gotland, we'll get you to Britain, patch you up, and you can return to the fight."

Matuszek's eyes lit up. "Do you think that perhaps I might even meet Sikorski?"

Canidy grinned. "Hell, Commander, I'll bet he'll insist on meeting *you*."

Fulmar said to Canidy, "Can't wait until we see Donovan. I bet he gave us no more than a ten percent chance of coming back alive, let alone coming back alive with Kapsky."

"The minute we get to the London OSS office, this will be legendary. Dulles will inform Donovan; Donovan will inform Roosevelt and Stimson. As long as we're in London, we won't have to buy a drink. And for at least the first week after we get back to the United States, too."

Canidy rose to his feet and began ascending the steps to the deck.

"What are you doing?" Fulmar asked.

Candidy winked. "Gonna extend our gratitude to the captain."

He found Kristin standing on the bow, chin held high, scanning the northern horizon. The sky to the west was a mixture of crimson, gold, and violet as the sun's corona sank into the sea. The evening air had a chill, but Candidy was insulated by success and alcohol.

Without turning, Kristin sensed his presence. "Congratulations, Major."

Candidy came beside her. "How long did you wait?" Candidy asked.

"Longer than I promised myself."

Candidy smiled.

"You should know, Major, that we will reach Gotland in approximately three hours, but your plane to Britain will not be arriving for approximately twenty-four hours thereafter due to weather off the North Sea."

"How disappointing," Candidy said with mock earnestness.

"There is, however, an outpost in Gotland that will tend to your wounds and provide food and lodging. You should be quite comfortable. All of your immediate needs will be met."

"And where will you go?"

"Katla and I are to be debriefed in Gotland and will depart when your flight arrives."

Candidy drew closer. "Enough time to teach me how to fish?"

Kristin turned. Her lips brushed lightly against his cheek.

"Not nearly enough, I'm afraid."

Canidy turned at the sound of Katla coming onto the deck.

"All is secure below," she reported.

"It's been a challenging last couple of days," Canidy said. "If you don't mind, I need to get some rest before we arrive in Gotland."

Kristin smiled. Electric. "Of course."

Kristin and Katla watched as Canidy disappeared down the steps to the lower deck. Kristin said, "Keep an eye on the steps. This should only take a minute."

Katla stationed herself at the top of the stairs to the galley as Kristin locked the wheel and proceeded to the bow, where she removed the tarp from a three-by-five maple cabinet. She opened the double doors, flipped the transmitter on the RCA radio, and placed the microphone close to her mouth.

Gromov proceeded east along a desolate dirt road. He encountered no German patrols or checkpoints, although he'd seen Wehrmacht vehicles in the distance. He'd determined not, however, to press his luck. Even though he had the cover of the German uniform and the Kübelwagen, and he spoke German well, remaining on the roadways was a risk. The vehicle made him visible, and in this environment visibility, however camouflaged, was a risk.

He heard a raspy sound and immediately slowed and came to a stop on the side of the road. The sound erupted again and he reached into his bag on the seat next to him and pulled out a gray metal box the size of a large dictionary. A headset with earphones and microphone were attached.

Freed from the bag, the noise, while still raspy, became intelligible. It was a voice speaking in Russian.

Gromov arranged the earphones over his head and the raspiness disappeared.

"*Njord* to Bulba."

Gromov adjusted the microphone in front of his mouth and responded. "Bulba, *Njord*. Go."

"We have obtained the notebook."

"Repeat."

"We have obtained the notebook. And we have its author, who is likely to acquire a terminal illness and probably will not survive the journey. All is well."

Gromov nodded to himself in satisfaction. "Received. Good work. Proceed as planned. Bulba out."

Gromov got out, bashed the radio against the door of the vehicle until it was inoperable, and threw it into the brush alongside the road. Then he threw his bag over his shoulder and began walking east.

With her dying breath the redheaded woman had provided at least one piece of truthful information. And that information had secured Gromov's victory.

A look of satisfaction covered his face as he began the long journey back to the front.

November 1943. Stalin is pressing the Allies to open a second front in Europe in order to ease the pressure on the bloody grinding war in the East. Roosevelt and Churchill agree to meet the Soviet premier in Tehran.

Wild Bill Donovan, the charismatic leader of the OSS, has intelligence that someone is planning to assassinate either or both of the Western leaders at the conference. He sends his best agent, Dick Canidy, to thwart the plan, but how can he do that when he doesn't even know if the killer is a Nazi or an Ally?

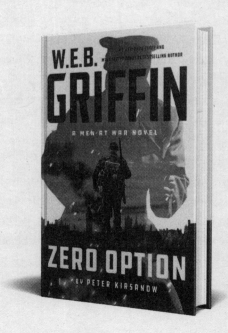

CHAPTER 1

76 Tirpitzufer, Berlin, Germany
August 17, 1943, 1:55 p.m.

The eyes of the Oberstleutnant stationed behind the desk in the anteroom to the office grew large with awe as the door opened.

The most important and imposing figures in all of the Wehrmacht had at some point during the war walked through that door: Guderian, Jodl, Keitel, Blomberg, Rommel—even Himmler and Göring. At some point during the war each had reason to meet with Vice Admiral Wilhelm Franz Canaris, chief of the Abwehr—The Genius. Each of the figures was powerful and impressive in his own right, commanding vast military or political resources. But none, save perhaps for Rommel, had a reputation as storied as the man who had just walked through the door.

SS Obersturmbannführer Otto Skorzeny would have been impressive even to those who were oblivious to his many exploits that had bedeviled the Allies since the advent of the war. The commando's muscular six-foot-four-inch frame conveyed the attitude and physicality of the superb natural athlete he'd been before the war, as did the four-inch scar that spanned his left cheek—the consequence of a fencing duel while at university in Vienna. So consequential had his covert missions been that it was claimed that when British General Bernard Law Montgomery was poring over the detailed maps of Operation Husky—the massive July invasion of Sicily that engaged nearly two hundred thousand Allied troops as well as more than seven thousand ships and aircraft—he scanned the German troop, tank, artillery, and aircraft positions and asked his staff one question:

"But where is Skorzeny?"

The Oberstleutnant glanced at the large black-and-white wall clock above the door. All visitors to Canaris's office were expected to arrive five minutes prior to the scheduled appointment. No exceptions, no matter the visitor's importance. In most cases those who were late were required to reschedule. Skorzeny, however, was precisely on time—five minutes early.

Skorzeny presented himself before the Oberstleutnant and said affably, but with standard Teutonic military decorum, "Obersturmbannführer Skorzeny at Herr Admiral Canaris's pleasure."

The Oberstleutnant gestured deferentially toward one of the two chairs to his right. "Yes. The Admiral awaits. Please be seated until the appointment time."

Skorzeny smiled and nodded. "I prefer to stand."

At precisely 2:00 p.m. the Oberstleutnant cleared his throat, rose from behind his desk, and opened the door to Canaris's office. Skorzeny proceeded through the door and saw Canaris seated behind a small, highly polished desk completely devoid of paper, pens, or memorabilia.

Skorzeny stood in front of Canaris's desk. Even at attention the commando looked relaxed and composed. Nazi Germany's intelligence chief placed the memorandum he was holding on the mirrorlike desktop and gestured for the commando to take a seat in one of the three high-backed mahogany chairs that formed a semicircle around the desk. Skorzeny bowed slightly and then sat in the middle chair. Canaris said nothing for several seconds, his thick white eyebrows forming a canopy over his penetrating eyes—a gaze that appeared to look through and beyond anything they were directed toward. Most found the gaze unnerving. Skorzeny simply smiled.

Canaris spoke softly and precisely.

"You have been briefed?"

"Only, Herr Admiral, that the mission concluded without obtaining the objective."

"That was an understatement. Were you informed of the nature of the objective?"

"I was told that its purpose was to obtain strategically critical scientific and mathematical data," Skorzeny replied.

Canaris nodded. "Again, quite an understatement. Who briefed you?"

"Oskar Brecht, Herr Admiral," Skorzeny replied. "It was clear he was being quite reserved in his description."

"As he should be," Canaris said appreciatively. "The item to which Brecht was referring was being sought by the British, Americans, and Soviets, as well as by us. Each power considered the item to be of paramount importance to the outcome of the war, as well as to the postwar balance of power."

"May I ask, Herr Admiral, who has obtained this item?"

Canaris's gaze became even more intense, almost searing. "You understand, Skorzeny, that this information and the manner in which we've obtained it is known only to the Führer, Reichsführer Himmler, Reichsmarschall Göring, and me?"

"Fully understood, Herr Admiral," Skorzeny nodded, his face relaxed. "Upon pain of death."

Canaris nodded. "Precisely. Even with your understanding and assurances I am constrained to tell you only *who* obtained the information, not *how we know* they obtained it." Canaris paused for several seconds. Although his office was the most secure location in all of Germany, he spoke in a hushed tone. "The Americans and British believe they have the information in the form of the professor who developed it, Sebastian Kapsky. But the Soviets actually have it." Canaris paused. "More precisely, the Soviets believe they *will* have custody of it imminently, in the form of the professor's notebook. Shortly after obtaining the information—the formulae—whoever has it will have strategic dominance during the balance of the war and for decades thereafter." Canaris's jaw tightened. "They will be the world hegemon."

Skorzeny straightened. "Forgive my presumptuousness, Herr Admiral . . ."

Canaris waved dismissively. "No, no. You are often two steps ahead. Go on . . ."

Flattered but sober, Skorzeny said, "Again, at the risk of being presumptuous, I conclude that you would like me to somehow retrieve the information from whomever possesses it"—Skorzeny paused and tilted his head—"either by seizing Kapsky from the Americans or his notebook of formulae from the Soviets. Or both."

The normally taciturn Genius permitted himself a barely perceptible smile at Skorzeny's confidence and nonchalance.

"That, Obersturmbannführer Skorzeny, would be the most audacious operation in the history of modern warfare. Perhaps the most spectacular since the Greeks breached the walls of Troy with a wooden horse."

Skorzeny nodded. "The difficulty, of course, is in the logistics," he noted clinically. "Finding and seizing the mathematician, presumably somewhere in Britain or America, and finding and seizing his notebook of formulae—and any copies that may have been made—presumably someplace in Eastern Europe . . ." Skorzeny seemed to concentrate on a spot on the ceiling. "Obviously, it will be difficult. Many will die. But it *can* be done. The most serious, and *perhaps* insuperable, problem is that we cannot control for any copies of the notebook that the Soviets may have made before we seize it."

Canaris nodded. "Your analysis is quite logical. But we calculate that the probability of copies having been made before acquisition of the notebook as low. Our information is that the notebook will be or already is being conveyed to Moscow by a Major Taras Gromov. Our sources do not have his precise location at this moment, but it is calculated that he should be within thirty kilometers of Tallinn. We estimate that it will take him three to four days to deliver the notebook to OKRNKVD Chief Aleksander Belyanov in the Kremlin. Once in Belyanov's possession it will likely take an indeterminate amount of time to make copies, even if each of the characters in the formulae is legible and decipherable. I am advised that their scientists will endeavor to render each and every character in the various formulae with painstaking precision so that there can be no error, not the slightest deviation or misinterpretation. It *must* be flawless."

"What is the estimate, Herr Admiral, for how long that will take?"

"As noted, given current battlefield deployments, we calculate it will take Gromov three to four days to arrive at the Kremlin and another fourteen days for their mathematicians—working twenty-four hours a day in shifts—to make and verify precise copies."

Skorzeny smiled. "Splendid. The logistical challenge remains daunting, but provided we are given accurate information regarding the whereabouts of the item, I assess the operation as feasible."

Canaris leaned forward. "You are exceptionally confident in your abilities, Skorzeny."

Without a hint of arrogance, the commando asked, "Forgive me, Herr Admiral, should I not be?"

No, you should not, Canaris conceded to himself. Skorzeny had proven himself capable of executing the most audacious of missions, all while making the British and Americans look like fools. The mission would be impossible for all *but* Skorzeny. "What of acquiring Kapsky? How do you assess the probability of accomplishing that?"

"Clearly that is far more problematic, both in terms of planning and actual execution. Kapsky likely is many thousands of kilometers—nearly a hemisphere—away from the notebook."

Skorzeny paused, gazed for a moment at the floor, and then shrugged. "Assuming reasonably reliable intelligence and planning, the execution will be difficult but feasible."

Canaris assessed Skorzeny's demeanor for several seconds. The commando appeared thoughtful and restrained, with no discernable trace of hubris. Canaris pressed a button on the underside of his desk and the Oberstleutnant immediately appeared at the door. Canaris gestured toward Skorzeny. "Provide Obersturmbannführer Skorzeny with the Washington briefing packet." The officer retreated and reappeared within seconds holding a dark brown expandable folder and handed it to Canaris. The Genius scanned the packet's contents and nodded to the Oberstleutnant, who turned and quickly left the office, closing the door behind him.

Canaris held up the packet. "You will study this on your way to Washington, DC."

Skorzeny nodded. "I assume I am to depart immediately."

"U-422 is at Danzig under the command of Oberleutnant zur See Poeschel. It will embark at 1:00 a.m. morning after next and will convey you to the coast of the American state of New Jersey. You will be met there by Ernst Haupt and Heinrich Thiel, two of our most effective agents, who will assist in every aspect of discharging your mission."

"Which is . . . ?"

"Bring Dr. Sebastian Kapsky here. Or, failing that, kill him."

The Battle For Quang Tri . . .

The battle plans were drawn in one hour: a lightning air assault into the middle of the North Vietnamese heavy weapons sites.

The helicopters skimmed low underneath the clouds and banked sharply to land the Skytroopers directly among the NVA mortars, recoiless rifles, and AA machine guns.

The North Vietnamese machine gunners frantically shifted their guns to fire directly into the descending helicopters, but were unable to stop the aerial assault from overwhelming the position. The cavalrymen leaped off the skids of the lowering helicopters as bullets peppered the doorframes. The Skytroopers jumped into action with their M16s blazing . . .

"Stanton has a special gift . . . he can cause an old familiar feeling in the pit of the stomach, recall a remembered sadness and reproduce a sensation of grim pride that a veteran would recognize. This book is a good read."

—Col. Rod Paschall, USA, Director U.S. Army Military History Institute for *Military Review*

"Clear . . . concise . . . an excellent book for the military reader interested in an in-depth review of the development of air mobility and in the history of the 1st Cavalry Division in Vietnam."

—Maj. Gen. John W. Barnes, U.S. Army, *New York City Tribune*

"Respected military historian Stanton knows the men of Vietnam, the issues, the battle strategies and tactics, and his numerous descriptions of helicopters in warfare are genuinely captivating."

—*The Book Reader* (San Francisco)

ANATOMY OF A DIVISION

The 1st Cav in Vietnam

SHELBY L. STANTON

WARNER BOOKS

A Warner Communications Company

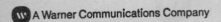

To the memory of my father,
Samuel Shelton Stanton
1914–1986

Contents

Maps

Preface

Historically, the majority of U.S. cavalry served as dragoons. They rode into battle but fought on foot. The airmobile 1st Cavalry Division continued this cavalry tradition by riding helicopters into battle. The division cavalrymen employed automatic weapons, and were supported by aerial rocket artillery—the airmobile equivalent of the famed horse artillery—but dismounted to fight.

This book is a critical analysis of the mechanism and composition of the airmobile cavalry division, from its inception through the end of the Vietnam conflict (when its airmobile status was terminated). How the airmobile cavalry division was raised, managed, functioned, performed, and was supported are the important themes of this work. The book compares the division's utilization of helicopters which gave vertical dimension to such cavalry missions as reconnaissance, pursuit, raids, screening, exploitation, and the flexible shock action of mounted attack.

The book is not intended as a conventional division history, and therefore does not attempt to recount every divisional encounter of the Vietnam war. Although the main course of the division's service in Vietnam is given as a necessary prelude to understanding its unique combat role, specific actions were chosen to represent certain cavalry techniques as applied in an airmobile environment. Since the book is arranged chronologically, with special topics treated last, the missions and organization of the division's various components are not addressed until Chapter 10. However, the reader is encouraged to read this chapter preparatory to the battle sections, if more clarity is desired in intradivisional unit relationships.

Throughout this volume's treatment of division performance in Vietnam, the reader should remember that the airmobile division was still being developed when thrust into combat. The tactical and operational warfare parameters which determined the airmobile division's employment were also in the experimental stage. The division was sent into a remote, geographically hostile environment, burdened with many political restrictions in an increasingly unpopular war against a strong and cunning enemy, and was expected to demonstrate the value of combat airmobility by securing battlefield victory. It reflects great credit upon the personnel of the 1st Cavalry Division that this airmobile doctrine was implemented successfully under such circumstances.

The author received encouragement and assistance from several people in the writing of this book. Of these, the author is especially grateful for the excellent guidance of Colonel Rod Paschall, Director of the U.S. Army Military History Institute, and he outstanding professional resources which this important facility offered. Special thanks are owed to my editor, Adele Horwitz, and my wife, Kathryn, for their dedicated support. The author must also pay tribute to the government military historians of the Vietnam era, who insured that a valuable record of the Army's role and internal action was available for future scholars.

Shelby L. Stanton
Captain, U.S. Army, Retired
Bethesda, Maryland

ANATOMY OF A DIVISION

"Cavalry, and I Don't Mean Horses!"

Aerial Cavalry Evolution

The 1st Cavalry Division's arrival on the battlefields of Vietnam was not presaged by the sound of trumpets or thundering hooves, but rather by the close suppressive fires of aerial gunships and fighter-bombers escorting waves of assault helicopters. After being transported over miles of normally inaccessible jungle terrain, the airmobile cavalrymen were inserted into their remote landing zones by dismounting from their troopship skids into the midst of enemy positions below. For the first time in military history, a combat organization was designed and structured to rely on the shock and fury of vertical helicopter attack to deliver its frontline soldiers. However, these bold airmobile strikes represented only the mailed fists of a larger Army machine. How this machine was conceived and created, the interrelationship of its component parts, and how it functioned and performed are the substance of this book.

The air assault itself represented the very *raison d'être* of the airmobile cavalry division and the culminated focus of its resources toward battlefield domination. The dangerous art of infantry attack from the sky demanded a carefully conceived and synchronized orchestration of all division elements of the greater body. Scout and reconnaissance aircraft and pathfinders served as the eyes which found and marked the landing fields and their approaches. Airlifted artillery howitzers and cannon, the muscle power manned by artillerymen but supplied and maintained by ammunition and ordnance teams, fired the necessary preparatory barrages.

The assault helicopter formations were an integral part of division aviation, the legs of the division, and the troops they carried were the hardened workhands with the essential tools of war. Fire support was continued during final helicopter descents by shifting artillery to one side, conducting simultaneous airstrikes with napalm, bombs, and 20-mm cannon strafing on the opposite flank, and using armed helicopters with rockets, miniguns, and automatic grenade launchers to cover the rest of the target area. Navigation for the airmobile columns had to be precise and tightly controlled in order to avoid Air Force flight paths and artillery shell trajectories. This rigid fire control was insured by commanders and observation officers, the directing brains, in control helicopters linked by signalmen with sophisticated radio and communications equipment.

Once on the ground, the air assaulted troops relied on the integrated efficiency of all other organizational segments for their survival and replenishment. If the hands were cut off and eliminated, the remainder of the divisional body was denuded of its main protection and directly threatened with destruction. The successful conduct of the air assault was the responsibility of the primary and special staffs, the heart of the division, which planned and coordinated offensive action with all constituent segments. Engineers provided the building muscle required to clear the ground, construct airstrips and helipads, and furnish defensive positions. Their skilled enterprise could cover body parts with a shell of protection or shield of defense. Discipline within the body of troops was enforced and regulated by an organic military police corps. The entire divisional structure was nourished by a host of supply troops, serviced by support technicians, and repaired by maintenance personnel.

Together, these diverse but integral elements composed the total division fighting machine. Without them the division lacked the fabric of life; without the fusion of their combined energy the division was crippled in its performance; without the direction offered by aggressive leadership the division remained blinded and handicapped in its ability. When properly led and interconnected, these components forged a powerful division that became a major instrument of national will.

Divisions are a recent development in the history of organized warfare, being initially employed by France in the late 1700s. They became an accepted part of peacetime European military establishments during the next century. In the United States, divisions were temporarily raised during the Civil War, but did not become primary formations within the army structure until the passage of the National Defense Act of 1916, just prior to America's entry into World War I. Divisions now constitute the basic framework of most world armies.

The division is essentially the modern equivalent of the ancient Roman legion. In both cases, infantry, engineer, artillery, signal, and service troops are combined into permanent organizations capable of independent and sustained combat operations. Divisions, like legions, are self-sufficient combat commands capable of influencing direction of battle with only normal support. As Rome safeguarded her empire with a vanguard of fighting legions, the modern United States protected its global interests with a number of combat divisions. In the post–World War II era, the United States usually fielded an average of sixteen Army and two Marine divisions.

In the mid-twentieth century, divisions were still landbound. Although marine divisions had amphibious ability, and airborne divisions could enter desired territory by parachute descent, actual battlefield maneuver was restricted to the timeless pace and terrain limitations of marching infantry. Mechanized and armored divisions were faster, but were confined by terrain restrictions. In the 1950 Korean War even vehicular speed, which promised to reset the clockwork of modern battle during previous lightning war campaigns, was effectively slowed by rugged landscape and improved antitank weapons to the step of escorting foot soldiers. Aerial transport of divisions was rare, since airlift was expensive and required assembly in secure airport staging areas at either end of the trip.

At the same time, helicopter technology was producing machines of increasing size and dependability. In the immediate post-Korean decade, the technical basis was built for a series of helicopters which could deliver hovering firepower and vertical lift dimensions to the battlefield. These newly introduced designs were improved and utilized to create an organization destined to radically alter forever both the mode and rate of ground combat.

Under the farsighted guidance of a few select leaders, the United States Army engineered a novel set of tactics based on newly developed weaponry and air assault principles. This effort was initiated during the summer of 1962, when a board of officers headed by Gen. Hamilton H. Howze studied the promise of tactical airmobility with a few trial units at the infantry school post of Fort Benning, Georgia. Following their recommendations for further formal testing, the Army raised the 11th Air Assault Division and its associated 10th Air Transport Brigade. After three years of testing, an entirely new type of division was created. This unit, the 1st Cavalry Division (Airmobile), represented the first airmobile combat force in history and "a landmark in the evolution of U.S. Army organization."[1]

In 1965 the 1st Cavalry Division was deployed to the war-torn highlands and jungles of Vietnam. There for the next seven years, this highly mobile and aggressive formation proved the validity of the airmobile concept. The division contained more than twenty thousand men at peak combat strength, but its real firepower was forged by fusing its manpower, weapons, and transportation with cavalry doctrine. Maximum shockpower was maintained by joining the division's light infantrymen and supporting artillery with an aerial armada of helicopters. A host of command ships following a vanguard of scout helicopters led the troop-filled utility helicopters into battle. They were escorted by waves of attack gunships and rocket helicopters, while medical evacuation and resupply helicopters stood ready to assist. From the smallest scout helicopters brazenly circling over enemy targets to the largest crane and cargo helicopters whirling howitzers and supplies into forward positions, the 1st Cavalry Division (Airmobile) represented the essence of modern, mobile Army striking power. From the field its wartime commander Maj. Gen. Harry W. O. Kinnard declared to *Newsweek* that he was "freed from the tyranny of terrain."[2]

The 1st Cavalry Division (Airmobile) was one of the most powerful war machines ever fielded, and certainly one of the best-trained and best-equipped American units sent into combat. The division successfully merged the infant doctrine of vertical aerial assault with traditional cavalry functions to produce a revolutionary new style of warfare. Its actual genesis, however, was conceived a decade earlier in the frozen hills of Korea as a result of one of the worst battlefield defeats suffered by American arms, a loss occasioned by the lack of cavalry.

1. Virgil Ney, *Evolution of the U.S. Army Division, 1939–1968*, CORG Memorandum M-365, Headquarters, United States Army Combat Developments Command, Fort Belvoir, Virginia, 1969, p. 92.
2. *Newsweek*, 13 December 1965, p. 28.

In the American tradition, cavalry had always signified the fast light cavalry: horse troopers capable of covering the wilderness distances of a vast continent. Light cavalry excelled in scouting and reconnaissance, providing a mobile screen for the slower infantry, and riding dispatches as messengers. Mounted militia volunteers, rangers, and light dragoons served a vital role in frontier warfare, tracking down and pursuing Indian marauders. During the Mexican War, horse soldiers performed important reconnaissance and pursuit missions. Later mass migration west into unexplored territory brought the need for mobile protection of the settlers, and mounted riflemen answered the call.

In the United States, cavalry became a force to be reckoned with during the Civil War. Cavalry activity often closely conformed to traditional experience. For instance, mounted riders gathered information about opposing forces, destroyed bridges and engaged in other harassing actions, and provided general messenger and mobile guard details. The dash and cunning of a few imaginative cavalry leaders also gave a new, expanded dimension to cavalry service. Their names rang like rattling sabers across the pages of history: Jeb Stuart, Custer, Sheridan, and Forrest. They grouped cavalrymen into independent formations equally capable of executing swift attacks or decisive delaying actions and sent reinforced units of riders patrolling through the broken eastern woodlands to cover the flanks of entire armies marching on campaign.

One of the most important tactical results of this heightened cavalry emphasis was the cavalry raid. Cavalry raids overran outposts and disrupted lines of communication, created havoc and confusion in the opponent's camp, captured or destroyed supplies, secured reliable long-range information about enemy dispositions, and shielded larger troop movements.

After the Civil War, cavalry was again fragmented as a result of the fluid warfare required in securing the Far West. Cavalry regiments were dispersed across the thinly garrisoned frontier. The end of the Indian Wars and the reduced need to police the western interior spelled the doom of the traditional American cavalry, although several later Mexican border incidents temporarily created a need for cavalry on mounted patrol duty. In the next few conflicts preceding World War II, American cavalry troops were generally limited to courier service or fighting as dismounted infantry.

Renewed bandit and other illegal activity along the desolate boundary between Mexico and the United States necessitated continuous patrolling of the region by horse soldiers. Under the new National Defense Act, the 1st Cavalry Division was formed on 12 September 1921 to safeguard the southwestern borders and to prevent gunrunning, cattle rustling, and the smuggling of narcotics, liquor, and other high-duty items. The economic depression of the 1930s spawned the Civilian Conservation Corps, and the division was soon relegated to providing logistical and administrative cadre for CCC companies in the Arizona–New Mexico district.

Prior to and during the Second World War, there was little agreement on the proper employment and function of Army cavalry on the armored-infantry battlefield, so the cavalry compromised, adopting a little of both. The basic problem was the advent of improved motorization in the scheme of modern warfare, and the resulting demise of the horse on which the cavalry was largely reliant and traditionally attached to. Cavalry adopted new doctrines premised on light mechanized reconnaissance, converted into infantry, or perished. This led to a postwar consensus that cavalry had either been misused altogether or lacked enough combat striking power to properly fulfill its assigned reconnaissance roles.

In 1941 the entire 1st Cavalry Division was assembled at Fort Bliss, Texas, for extensive field training. Its authorized personnel strength jumped from 3,575 to 10,110 troops. News of the Japanese attack on Pearl Harbor, which thrust the United States into active hostilities, found many members of the division on furlough or back in civilian life, but men poured into Fort Bliss from all over the country to rejoin their units. The cavalry troopers remained horse soldiers until February 1943, when the division received orders assigning it overseas. The changeover from horses to jeeps commenced. Since the division was intended for amphibious assault duty in the southwest Pacific, it was transformed by special equipment allowances and its cavalrymen retrained as foot soldiers. Finally, on 20 July 1945, in the Philippines, the division was completely reorganized as an infantry formation. At that point the division's only association with its proud cavalry heritage was the honorary retention of its cavalry designators.

While the 1st Cavalry Division fought as infantry, other smaller cavalry units struggled across Europe in armored cars and light tanks. Their tactical reconnaissance functions were lost in a war where big armored divisions were relied upon to punch through enemy lines, and strategic cavalry functions were replaced by aircraft. Even Lt. Gen. George S. Patton, Jr.'s, own Third Army "Household Cavalry," the 6th Cavalry Group, was relegated to messenger service between his speeding armored divisions; he officially redesignated the group as his Army Information Service.

Armor emerged from the conclusion of World War II as the decisive ground arm of mobility. The eminence of armor was sealed by the Army Organization Act of 1950, which combined armor and cavalry into one branch, designated as armor. The armor branch was technically to be a continuation of cavalry, but actual cavalry functions were quickly eroded by the mainstream armor philosophy that massed tank formations would dominate the atomic battlefield of the future. Many armor officers believed that future wars would witness the mailed fists of armored giants hammering each other into capitulation under a rain of nuclear warheads and held little regard for the traditional American cavalry mode of fast raids, light reconnaissance, and mobile security. In the immediate postwar years the only cavalry that existed was the U.S. Constabulary in occupied Europe and the 1st Cavalry Division, an infantry outfit stationed in Japan.

Cavalry was conceptually a different arm of mobility from armor. The cavalry mobility differential was based on shock effect through firepower, which also screened both time and information. Cavalry existed to deny the enemy that talisman of success—surprise—while providing friendly forces with the means to achieve the same result. Cavalry had ceased to be associated with horses, crossed sabres, crumpled wide-brimmed campaign hats, and carbines slung from the hip, but no one seemed to know where modern cavalry fitted. "Fighting Joe" Hooker's famous Civil War adage, "Who ever saw a dead cavalryman?" had been sadly shortened to simply "Who ever saw cavalry?" By June 1950, when invading North Korean armies surged over the 38th parallel into the south, the United States military had lost its real cavalry ability. The gallant arm of decision which Forrest had once described as arriving "fustest with the mostest" was now, in terms of mobility and firepower, "lastest with the leastest."

On 18 July 1950, fifteen years before entering Vietnam, the 1st Cavalry Division was sent to the rugged peninsula of South Korea to reinforce Lt. Gen. Walton H. Walker's Eighth Army. The division was one-third understrength and infantry in all but name. It was committed to the rapidly shrinking Pusan perimeter as Walker's allied contingents retreated farther south. Obviously, the tactical situation called for a cavalry force to be committed at once, to screen and delay while the heavier infantry and armored forces built up a more substantial defense. Neither Walker, United Nations Command General Douglas MacArthur, nor the United States military had any true cavalry available. In many cases Walker's infantry was outpaced by North Korean armored columns. The Eighth Army fell back with wide-open flanks, desperately trading space, weapons, and even lives for time. On Walker's left a gap of a hundred miles extending to the sea could have been readily penetrated, a situation begging for cavalry, but none was around. The "cavalry" division on hand was composed of foot soldiers in foxholes grimly defending the main road from Seoul to Pusan.

By mid-September Walker's army was compressed into a dangerously small pocket in the extreme southeastern portion of the Korean peninsula. General MacArthur broke this stalemate on 15 September with a daring amphibious assault behind North Korean lines at Inchon, just west of Seoul. The successful surprise landing left the North Korean army stunned and cut off. The return to fluid warfare on American terms of mobility promised both a rapid breakthrough to the north and a fast linkup between the invading X Corps and Walker's army advancing from the south. The situation was ripe for highly mobile cavalry forces which could exploit the opening, but none was forthcoming. The rear of the Naktong River line could have been seized in hours by daring cavalry, but instead nearly two weeks elapsed before the American forces linked up.

The move north to destroy the remnants of the North Korean army was not preceded by "flying columns" of swift cavalry, but advanced at the tortuous road-bound pace of a mechanized column twisting through the jagged Korean mountains. This column was composed of mixed tanks and trucks, all moving forward at the pace of foot soldiers groping blindly from road bend to road bend and from hill to hill. In October the entire Korean peninsula was wide open, but Walker's divisions were forced by the lack of adequate long-range cavalry reconnaissance to advance in ignorance of enemy dispositions.

The lack of cavalry prevented the scouting of likely enemy assembly areas throughout the advance. In late October the 6th Republic of Korea Division was surprised and broken by a sudden attack east of Unsan. On 1 November a battalion of the 1st Cavalry Division's 8th Cavalry Regiment was suddenly surrounded and smashed by another carefully prepared trap, leaving the Americans bewildered as the enemy melted into the mist-shrouded mountains. T. R. Fehrenbach aptly described the situation in his classic treatise on the Korean conflict, *This Kind of War:* "In the frightful terrain such patrolling was dangerous. It could not be supported by wheels, and where wheels could not go, neither could sizable units of Americans. And in such horrendous terrain a vast army could be—and was—hidden in a very small area, observing perfect camouflage discipline, waiting."[3]

During the last week of October, the Americans reached the Yalu River, but the absence of any properly balanced cavalry force continued to invite disaster. Adequate ground surveillance of the Yalu River crossings was manifestly impossible. The American divisions were struck with complete and overwhelming surprise by thirty Chinese divisions on 26 November 1950. Without cavalry to patrol or cover the steep maze of mountain peaks and razorback ridges, Walker was doomed to a crushing piecemeal defeat as unit after unit stumbled into Chinese ambush.

The question "Where was Walker's cavalry?" was answered bluntly four years later by Maj. Gen. James M. Gavin (West Point, 1929), an enthusiastic cavalry supporter and highly respected commander of the crack 82d Airborne Division during World War II, in his landmark *Armor* article, "Cavalry, and I Don't Mean Horses!" Gavin found that Walker simply had no adequate cavalry, since real cavalry had ceased to exist throughout the Army, and offered a startling but technically feasible solution to the tragic Yalu debacle. He stated, "Where was the cavalry? . . . and I don't mean horses. I mean helicopters and light aircraft, to lift soldiers armed with automatic weapons and hand-carried light antitank weapons, and also lightweight reconnaissance vehicles, mounting antitank weapons the equal of or better than the Russian T-34s [tanks]. . . . If ever in the history of our armed forces there was a need for the cavalry arm—airlifted in light planes, helicopters, and assault-type aircraft—this was it."[4]

---

3. T. R. Fehrenbach, *This Kind of War* (New York: Macmillan Company, 1963) p. 296.
4. Maj. Gen. James M. Gavin, "Cavalry, and I Don't Mean Horses!" *Armor*, Volume LXIII, No. 3, p. 18.

General Gavin was a paratrooper, a light infantryman well acquainted with the mobility potential of aircraft. Like many hardy World War II army parachute volunteers, he felt paratroopers were the modern heirs to the bold cavalrymen of yesteryear, since the emphasis on heavy armor excluded most tankers from the fast raiding and slashing agility of the old light dragoons. In the 1943 invasion of Sicily, Gavin's 505th Parachute Regimental Combat Team drew the tough assignment of parachuting between the German reserves and the allied assault beaches. Although their method of entry called for parachutes instead of saddles, their actual missions were all historically typical of cavalry—to screen larger troop movements (the landings), to delay enemy use of critical terrain, and to secure several crossroads.

Gavin considered most parachutist missions conducted during the war to be cavalry-style operations. For example, a battalion of the 509th Parachute Infantry jumped into Avellino, Italy, to secure a key road center leading to the allied landing site at Salerno. In the invasion of France, the 82d and 101st Airborne Divisions were directed to block all enemy attempts to reinforce the beaches and to attack from the rear, another classic cavalry mission. Gavin was convinced that "what we needed next was a closer integration with the inheritors of the cavalry role, the armored forces, without loss to the highly mobile and aggressive character of the airborne forces, the 'lean and mean' philosophy."[5]

Gavin felt that the armor branch was unresponsive. Instead of reducing the weight of mechanized equipment so that aircraft could be developed and produced to carry the new light armored forces into battle, vehicles got only heavier. He refused to give up, and when promoted to Army Assistant Chief of Staff for Operations, Gavin walked the halls of the Pentagon, pleading for the cause of airmobility. He had several staff studies prepared on the subject and summarized these in his article which first appeared in *Harper's* magazine, but it did not receive widespread professional military attention until reprinted in the May-June issue of *Armor* magazine, itself the retitled continuation of the older esteemed *Cavalry Journal*. Gavin wrote urgently, "Cavalry-type screening missions will have to be conducted at much greater distances, and with much greater rapidity, than have hitherto

5. Ibid., p. 21.

been considered acceptable. The mobility differential to make this possible *must* be achieved. It is within our grasp, fortunately, in the air vehicles now being developed—assault transports, light utility planes, helicopters, and convertaplanes. Forces so organized and equipped will have a predominant influence on future warfare."[6]

Gavin's article reflected the vision of a few cavalry and helicopter enthusiasts and proved to be the catalyst which sparked the imagination of several other forward-thinking officers. These capable men represented diverse backgrounds, ranging from old horsemen-turned-armor-commanders to light infantrymen who doubled as aviators, but they all shared Gavin's conviction that modern aerial cavalry was necessary. They eventually implemented the revolutionary air assault philosophy, but the realization of airmobility still faced the prospects of a long, uphill struggle through the restrained Army bureaucracy.

After the Korean War, in the mid-1950s, the Army was axed by budget cuts. Big bombs and massive retaliation were the rage in military thought. Maj. Edwin L. "Spec" Powell, who would later become the Director of Army Aviation, listened to many analysts proclaiming, "Well, the only purpose for an army in the future is to defend strategic air bases."[7] Within the Army there was widespread sentiment that the Korean War was the cause of current disfavor and that the conflict had been "fought on Asian soil on Asiatic terms," where restricted combat in the hellish mountain ranges forced the Army to trade rifleman for rifleman, without benefit of America's technical edge in mobility and supporting firepower.

The Army possessed airplanes and primitive helicopters, but had no conception of their true value. Many officers with Korean experience under their belts vividly remembered the fragile light observation helicopters darting up and down sheer mountainsides carrying litter patients and emergency supplies. Only a very few foresaw the future possibility of waves of sturdier helicopters ferrying whole battalions across such ranges. The natural inertia of the military

---

6. Ibid., p. 22. Emphasis cited in the original article.
7. U.S. Army Military History Institute, *Senior Officers Debriefing Program*, conversations between Brig. Gen. Edwin L. Powell and Col. Bryce R. Kramer and Col. Ralph J. Powell, Carlisle Barracks, Pennsylvania, 1978, p. 31. Hereafter cited as USAMHI, Powell Debriefing.

institution confined embryonic aviation development to practices everyone was used to, such as spotting artillery fire with light Cub observation planes.

The Director of Army Aviation in 1955 was a distinguished ex–horse cavalryman, Gen. Hamilton H. Howze, who became one of the driving forces in airmobile development. A West Point graduate who was qualified as both an airplane and helicopter pilot, Howze had seen World War II action with the 1st Armored Division in North Africa and Italy. He recalled that the "army hadn't grasped at all, from its experience in Korea, the real utility of the light aircraft and what could be done by really integrating them into the tactics and combat support of the army. There was really very little knowledge in the army that the Marines, during one very small operation in Korea, had lifted a small party of Marines to the top of an unoccupied mountain, and had found this to be a useful thing to do."[8] Still, the Korean conflict had produced a general awareness of the need to strengthen Army aviation.

In the absence of formal Army policy, officers in several scattered posts began experimenting with whatever material was available. They often worked without official guidance and in spite of high-echelon disapproval and even ridicule. In June 1956 Col. Jay D. Vanderpool, the energetic chief of the Army aviation school's combat development office at Fort Rucker, Alabama, assembled an armed helicopter platoon, mounting weapons and other hardware scrounged, borrowed, or stolen from junkyards and other units. Jay's "Sky-Cav" platoon soon gained a notorious reputation for jerry-rigged rockets and hair-raising treetop-level aerial firing demonstrations. Two years later this unlikely outfit was legitimized as the Army's provisional 7292d Aerial Combat Reconnaissance Company, but Vanderpool was already conceiving "armair" formations up to division in size. Col. John J. Tolson took over the Army infantry school's airborne department at Fort Benning, Georgia, and created an airmo-

---

8. U.S. Army Military History Institute Research Collection, *Senior Officer Debriefing Program: History of Army Aviation*, conversations between Gen. Hamilton Howze and Col. Glenn A. Smith and Lt. Col. August M. Cianciolo, Carlisle Barracks, Pennsylvania, p. 8. Hereafter cited as USAMHI, Howze Debriefing.

bility section which included a field experiment helicopter company.[9]

This formative stage of airmobility reflected the continuing disjointed nature of the Army aviation effort. In October 1959 the Army Chief of Research and Development, Lt. Gen. Arthur G. Trudeau, initiated the Army aircraft development plan to seek firm guidance in bridging the gap between Army and Air Force responsibilities and to permit aircraft development in harmony with projected Army requirements. Although Trudeau felt that light observation aircraft remained the "bread-and-butter" mission of Army aviation, Army expectation studies in two other areas (manned surveillance and tactical transport) were also presented to industry at Fort Monroe, Virginia, on 1 December 1959. These studies allowed exploration of technical approaches by the aircraft manufacturers, and two months later forty-five companies submitted 119 design concepts in response.[10]

The Army Chief of Staff, Gen. Lyman L. Lemnitzer, established a board of officers on 15 January 1960 to consider the Army aircraft development plan and to receive the industry proposals. The board was chaired by Lt. Gen. Gordon B. Rogers, the deputy commanding general of the Continental Army Command, and included several airmobility enthusiasts. The guiding genius behind the board was its secretary, Col. Robert R. "Bob" Williams, who was the first pilot to be designated Master Army Aviator. The Rogers Board advocated immediate development of a new helicopter capable of observation, target acquisition, reconnaissance, and command and control functions. Although the Rogers Board was primarily interested in deciding on aircraft types, it also recommended that a study be prepared "to determine whether the concept of air fighting units was practical and if an experimental unit should be activated to test feasibility and develop material requirements."[11]

The Rogers Board review was almost completely confined to development in aviation material. The board still suggested the possible

9. Lt. Gen. John J. Tolson, *Vietnam Studies: Airmobility, 1961–1971* (Washington, D.C.: Department of the Army, 1973), pp. 5–6.
10. Army Aircraft Requirements Review Board booklet, Fort Monroe, Virginia, dtd 29 February 1960.
11. Ltr, Army Aircraft Requirements Review Board to CofSA, dtd 10 March 1960. Subj: AACFT Rqr Rev Bd, commonly referred to as the Rogers Board Report.

aviation means needed to reposition fighting forces on the battlefield using aerial lift instead of relying solely on ground maneuver. The board was soon outpaced by events which gripped the Army and altered its aviation outlook after 1960: the reorganization of Army divisions (ROAD), the Berlin and Cuban emergencies and the reserve call-up, the rapid unit expansion in response to a multitude of international crises, and Military Advisory Group Army aircraft requirements in many countries—including the prospect of combat needs in Laos, Thailand, and Vietnam. Cols. John Norton, the chief of the Continental Army's aviation section, and Alexander J. Rankin of the aviation board at Fort Rucker, clearly recognized that a fresh approach was needed.

When Robert S. McNamara became Secretary of Defense in 1961, he ushered in sweeping changes aimed at completely reorganizing the Department of the Army and its methods of warfare. He was highly displeased with Army Secretary Elvis J. Stahr, Jr.'s, report on the status of Army aviation plans. McNamara realized that the current Army procurement program was hopelessly inadequate in every category of aircraft and considered it dangerously conservative. Furthermore, McNamara felt that the Army failed to exert any strong, unified aviation effort and was plagued by reticence and budgetary restraint which were blocking the adaptation of necessary aircraft and equipment. Most important, he believed that officers with progressive ideas about airmobility were not being heard.

McNamara's team of civilian experts in the Systems Analysis Office was determined to allow modern ideas to get to the secretary without being stifled by reactionary bureaucratic resistance. Several officials of that office arranged for McNamara to consult privately with Brig. Gen. Clifton F. von Kann, the Director of Army Aviation (who was a parachutist as well as a pilot and former Rogers Board member), and another Army airmobility enthusiast, Maj. James J. Brockmyer, the Army Aviation Action Officer, who was one of the original Cub pilots. McNamara was convinced that a breakthrough in airmobility was possible with the new Bell helicopter models. He was given a list of officers who also believed that Army aviation needed new direction, and the substance for letters which he sent to the Secretary of the Army.[12]

12. Alain C. Enthoven and K. Wayne Smith, *How Much Is Enough? Shaping the Defense Program, 1961–1969* (New York: Harper & Row) p. 100.

Defense Secretary McNamara sent two strong directives to Stahr on 19 April 1962, summarizing his extreme dissatisfaction with Army aviation posture. Furthermore, McNamara took the radical step of directly naming Lt. Gen. Hamilton H. Howze and other pro-airmobility officers to a task force to re-examine the Army's posture. In effect, McNamara ordered the Army to implement airmobility, told the Army how to do it, and who should run it. While both memorandums opened new horizons, the second proved to be the birthright of the new airmobile division, and is reproduced here in its entirety:[13]

THE SECRETARY OF DEFENSE
Washington, D.C.
April 19, 1962

MEMORANDUM FOR MR. STAHR

I have not been satisfied with Army program submissions for tactical mobility. I do not believe that the Army has fully explored the opportunities offered by aeronautical technology for making a revolutionary break with traditional surface mobility means. Air vehicles operating close to, but above, the ground appear to me to offer the possibility of a quantum increase in effectiveness. I think that every possibility in this area should be explored.

We have found that air transportation is cheaper than rail or ship transportation even in peacetime. The urgency of wartime operation makes air transportation even more important. By exploiting aeronautical potential, we should be able to achieve a major increase in effectiveness while spending on air mobility systems no more than we have been spending on systems oriented for ground transportation.

I therefore believe that the Army's re-examination of its aviation requirements should be a bold "new look" at land warfare mobility. It should be conducted in an atmosphere divorced from traditional viewpoints and past policies. The only objective the actual task force should be given is that of acquiring the maximum attainable mobility within alternative funding levels and technology. This necessitates a readiness to substitute air

13. Memo, SECDEF for SA, 19 Apr 62, Subj: AAVN, w/Incl, with comments from USAMHI; Powell Debriefing.

mobility systems for traditional ground systems wherever analysis shows the substitution to improve our capabilities or effectiveness. It also requires that bold, new ideas which the task force may recommend be protected from veto or dilution by conservative staff review.

In order to ensure the success of the re-examination I am requesting in my official memorandum, I urge you to give its implementation your close personal attention. More specifically, I suggest that you establish a managing group of selected individuals to direct the review and keep you advised of its progress. If you choose to appoint such a committee, I suggest the following individuals be considered as appropriate for service thereon: Lt. Gen. Hamilton H. Howze, Brig. Gen. Delk M. Oden, Brig. Gen. Walter B. Richardson, Col. Robert R. Williams, Col. John Norton, Col. A. J. Rankin, Mr. Frank A. Parker, Dr. Edwin W. Paxson, and Mr. Edward H. Heinemann.

Existing Army activities such as Fort Rucker, RAC, STAG (Strategic and Tactics Analysis Group, Washington, D.C.), CDEC (Combat Development Experimental Center, Ft. Ord), and CORG (Combat Operations Research Group, Ft. Monroe), combined with the troop units and military study headquarters of CONARC, and in cooperation with Air Force troop carrier elements, appear to provide the required capabilities to conduct the analyses, field tests and exercises, provided their efforts are properly directed.

The studies already made by the Army of air mobile divisions and their subordinate air mobile units, of air mobile reconnaissance regiments, and of aerial artillery indicate the type of doctrinal concepts which could be evolved, although there has been no action to carry these concepts into effect. Parallel studies are also needed to provide air vehicles of improved capabilities and to eliminate ground-surface equipment and forces whose duplicate but less effective capabilities can no longer be justified economically. Improved V/STOL (Vertical/Short Takeoff or Landing) air vehicles may also be required as optimized weapons platforms, command and communications vehicles, and as short-range prime movers of heavy loads up to 40 or 50 tons.

I shall be disappointed if the Army's re-examination merely produces logistics-oriented recommendations to procure more of the same, rather than a plan for implementing fresh and perhaps unorthodox concepts which will give us a significant increase in mobility.

(Signed) ROBERT S. McNAMARA

Gen. George H. Decker, the Army Chief of Staff, was infuriated that inside insurgents had circumvented proper channels. The memorandums caused consternation in the military staff, sending shock waves throughout the upper echelons of the Army establishment, but they allowed recommendations to reach the top without being watered down. Within a week Lieutenant General Howze, commander of the XVIII Airborne Corps at Fort Bragg, was directed to head the task force, formally called the U.S. Army Tactical Mobility Requirements Board. The Army accorded the undertaking the highest possible priority, second only to operations in active combat areas. The Army's new Director of Aviation, Brig. Gen. Delk M. Oden, a 2d Armored Division war-hero-turned-pilot, was very pleased, while Howze called McNamara's memorandum the "best directive ever written."[14]

McNamara was handing the Secretary of the Army deadlines so fast that there was little time to do anything but say yes. The Howze Board was instructed to submit its final report within four months of actual working time, and its dynamic officers were determined to make it a success. Some, like chairman of the security committee Brig. Gen. Frederic W. Boye, Jr., the assistant commandant of the armor school, had distinguished themselves as armor leaders in World War II and were sons of horse cavalry officers. Many, like Brig. Gen. Edward L. Rowny, who headed the critical field test committee, were paratrooper graduates of the Army airborne school. The administrative workhorse of the Howze Board was the Secretariat, composed of rising stars of airmobility such as Cols. Norton, Putnam, Rankin, and Beatty.

The board was headquartered in Fort Bragg's Erwin School building, since it was empty during summer vacation, where the lights

14. USAMHI, Howze Debriefing. It is important to remember that the Army's Combat Developments Command, which would normally conduct such a study, was not organized until June 1962; thus the need for a special board under Howze.

burned past midnight every night as officers argued, wrote, and struggled through files and reports. They worked at a feverish pace as committee members constantly shuttled all over the country, and brainstorming sessions lasted until all hours. One recalled, "Many of us just ran ourselves into the ground; we worked so darned hard we almost couldn't think straight." The documents were "roughly knee deep on the floor" of one large room, and staff sections had to be limited in generating paperwork. Even so, by September more than six hundred footlocker loads of paperwork were produced.[15]

There were precious few aviation assets to work with, and a dispute arose between staffs at Fort Rucker and Fort Knox concerning the constitution of the provisional 17th Air Cavalry Group, since General Howze insisted on having the best-qualified personnel and best equipment available. However, some units, like the 1st Aviation Company (Caribou transport), were already being sent overseas, where Army Secretary Stahr believed it could still be part of the study "in the operational laboratory of Vietnam." This proved impossible. A smattering of other units, like the 8305th Aerial Combat Reconnaissance Unit (Provisional) at Fort Rucker, were employed.[16]

The Howze Board studied the application of Army aircraft to the traditional cavalry role of mounted combat, especially in reconnaissance, security, and target acquisition. They examined possible Army operations in Southeast Asia, Europe, Northeast Asia, and the Middle East. One of the board's most innovative concepts was the proposal for an Air Cavalry Combat Brigade (ACCB) to fight from an aerial-mounted position and perform the historical role of cavalry in exploitation, pursuit, counterattack, delay, and flank protection. This brigade was designed for the offense, seeking out and destroying the enemy while carrying out traditional cavalry missions. An even larger Combined Arms Air Brigade was envisioned to "flesh out" the ACCB and provide the commander with a decisive combat tool.[17]

15. Frederic A. Bergerson, *The Army Gets an Air Force* (Baltimore and London: The Johns Hopkins University Press, 1980), p. 112.

16. U.S. Army Combat Developments Command, *The Origins, Deliberations, and Recommendations of the U.S. Army Tactical Mobility Requirements Board*, Fort Leavenworth, Kansas, 1969, pp. 19, 47, 60.

17. Ibid., pp. 50–51.

For divisional purposes the committees began with the simplest, lightest, and most airmobile force they could develop, looking first at Southeast Asia. For this purpose an Army Reorganized Airmobile Division (RAID) was proposed along with a corps task force, which was actually a small airmobile field army supported by a special support brigade. The RAID could provide enough aircraft to sustain combat by aerial reconnaissance and fire support, simultaneously airlifting one-third of itself for distances of more than sixty miles. Since three RAID divisions were claimed to be as effective in Southeast Asia as four Army and two Marine divisions combined, they needed to be fielded as quickly as possible. For European fighting the board developed an aviation-enhanced armored division, which was termed the Reorganized Universal Division.

General Howze felt that completely new organizations such as RAID were unrealistic, but in keeping with his directive to implement "bold, new ideas" had the board redesign the standard infantry division, replacing wheels with aviation wherever possible. This resulted in an airmobile division with slightly less manpower than a standard division, but with 2,751 fewer vehicles and some four hundred aircraft.[18] The board agreed that fast, hard-hitting troops were needed to destroy an enemy quickly, to seize an objective, and then to deploy to areas from which they could make the most of their gains. The organization needed to be light, but effective, in firepower, communications, and mobility.

The test force at the board's disposal included one battle group, engineers, and artillery from the 82d Airborne Division and 150 aircraft of the 6th Aviation Group (Provisional).[19] Forty field tests were

18. The Howze Board proposed airmobile division contained 14,678 personnel compared to the standard 15,799; 920 vehicles compared to 3,671; and 400 aircraft compared to 103 in the standard infantry division.
19. The 6th Aviation Group was board-generated and built around the 3d Transportation and the 82d Aviation Battalions, reinforced by the 31st Transportation Company (Light Helicopter), 61st Aviation Company (Light Fixed Wing), 123d Medical Company (Helicopter), 82d and 101st Aviation Companies (Airmobile), 54th Transportation Company (Medium Helicopter), 22d Special Warfare Aviation Detachment, and Troop C of the 17th Cavalry (Air). The 138th, 154th, 544th Transportation Detachments (Field Maintenance), 6th Aviation Operating Detachment, 25th Transportation

conducted, but only three were of week-long duration, pitting airmobile troops against mock irregulars in the Appalachian Mountains (which simulated Laotian territory), Fort Bragg, and Fort Stewart.

The board finally proposed several new organizations: an air assault division, a division with increased mobility through its 459 aircraft; an air cavalry combat brigade totaling 316 helicopters to destroy or neutralize mechanized enemy forces by aerial firepower; a corps aviation brigade (207 aircraft) to allow rapid movement of reserves; an air transport brigade (134 aircraft) to support the air assault division logistically; and a special warfare aviation brigade of 125 aircraft to render immediate aviation support to units in combat. The board also considered the future, where the air cavalry combat brigade would be succeeded by the armair brigade, a self-sustaining unit of all arms smaller than a division, which could be used for rapid strike, economy of force, mobile reserve, and fire brigade actions. A more lethal airmobile division was foreseen as the outgrowth of the air assault division.

The board recommended that the mix of forces best suited to modernize the Army would, within six years, give four infantry, four mechanized, and three armored divisions; five air assault divisions with their five associated air transport brigades; and three air cavalry combat brigades. One air assault division was to be based in Korea; another stationed in Hawaii with a brigade forward on Okinawa; and of the three envisioned for United States assignment, two would be additionally paratrooper-qualified. One air cavalry combat brigade was to be sent to Europe for availability in the Middle East or North Africa, and two brigades placed in the United States were to replace the armored cavalry regiments there. The special warfare brigade, which the board urgently recommended be activated the following year at Fort Bragg, would have five operational squadrons—four of them organized for Southeast Asia, the Middle East, Africa, and Latin America. Over $5.4 billion (in 1962 dollars) would have to be spent to procure the 10,565 total aircraft required.

General Howze knew that the Army would probably react nega-

Company (Direct Support), and Simmons Army Air Field Command were also involved. USATMRB, Annex O—Field Tests, and Howze Board correspondence.

tively toward the increased cost of airmobile units over conventional forces. The initial investment for more complex aircraft, as well as the higher costs for operation and maintenance, was quite high. The estimated $987 million cost of an air assault division was somewhat offset by its favorable ratio of effectiveness over a standard division, priced at $742 million. The frightfully expensive $366 million air cavalry combat brigade was considered absolutely necessary for Laotian and Vietnam duty, where indigenous troops could not secure overland supply routes. The board recommendations that the Army terminate development of both the main battle tank and rough-terrain vehicle, to allow financing of airmobility programs, were bound to cause hostility.[20]

Dr. Stockfisch, the Defense Secretary's representative, was very pleased with the way the Howze Board studies were progressing. He was particularly enthusiastic over the board's concept of the final presentation, which would include a two-page letter, a twenty-page summary, a two-inch-thick report, and a two-foot-thick backup in a foot locker. He believed Secretary McNamara should be furnished everything, including the footlocker.[21] In keeping with the 1 September 1962 deadline imposed by the Secretary of Defense, the board submitted its report to the Department of the Army on 20 August. General Howze's conclusion was direct and simple: "Adoption of the Army of the airmobile concept—however imperfectly it may be described and justified in this report—is necessary and desirable. In some respects the transition is inevitable, just as was that from animal mobility to motor."

The Howze Board was in operation from May through August 1962, working in five different U.S. locations. Consisting of 199 officers, 41 enlisted men, and 53 civilians, it involved more than 3,500

20. USCONARC/USARSTRIKE, *Annual Historical Summary, 1 July 1962–30 June 1963*, p.99. Costs are cited from U.S. Army Combat Developments Command, *The Origins, Deliberations, and Recommendations of the U.S. Army Tactical Mobility Requirements Board*, Fort Leavenworth, Kansas, 1969, p. 104. Comparative costs of other proposed organizations were the corps aviation brigade, $329 million; air transport brigade, $464 million; and the special warfare brigade, $149 million.

21. MFR, COL A. J. Rankin, 7 Jun 62, Subj: FONECON Between Mr. Fred Wolcott and COL Rankin, 7 June 62, 0930 hours. AJCG-AB.

personnel in direct support. The eight working committees had one purpose: to free the ground soldier from the restrictions of battlefield movement by replacing conventional ground transportation with aircraft. The study was conducted on a high-priority basis in an atmosphere divorced as far as possible from current viewpoints and doctrine.

Many of the board's conclusions were never acted upon. The Army never fielded a special warfare or corps aviation brigade. Only one air transport brigade was formed, to support one experimental, understrength air assault division. The Army formed only two airmobile divisions, both to fight in Vietnam, one—the 1st Cavalry—an outgrowth of the test air assault division in July 1965; the other—the 101st Airborne Division—three years later. No air cavalry combat brigade was officially organized, although an ad hoc formation was created temporarily on the Cambodian front during the Vietnam War by a former Howze Board officer.

The Howze Board charted new horizons in airmobility and represented the turning point in providing the Army with aerial cavalry. The board's recommendations led to further experimentation with the raising of the 11th Air Assault Division, but its ultimate legacy became the 1st Cavalry Division (Airmobile). This division was the major outcome of the board's hard work and deliberations. When the division was dispatched to Vietnam in 1965, it would ultimately change the conduct of land warfare. The division's bold air assault and sustained pursuit operations made it, six months after arriving in Vietnam, in Defense Secretary McNamara's words, "unique in the history of the American Army": there was "no other division in the world like it."

From Test to Battle

Progression from Air Assault to Cavalry Division

The new Secretary of the Army, Cyrus R. Vance, agreed with the Howze Board that helicoptered infantry offered unprecedented combat striking potential and that the Army should test airmobility at the earliest opportunity. He forwarded these recommendations to Defense Secretary McNamara on 15 September 1962. The Air Force was opposed to rapidly expanding Army aircraft utilization, especially in the armed helicopter and larger transport categories. However, McNamara wholeheartedly agreed that the Army required internal helicopter assets to make airmobility work and endorsed immediate field testing of the concept.[1]

When the final Howze report reached McNamara in September, the Army was escalating overseas operations and reorganizing its internal structure. Beginning that same month, Special Forces teams from the United States arrived in Vietnam to reinforce contingents from Okinawa. These increasing "Green Beret" troop commitments were at the forefront of additional aviation, combat support, and advisory elements. The situation in Vietnam was not the only factor causing the Army to endorse more flexible response. On 1 October racial troubles in the South required General Howze to leave his airmobile testing considerations and command ten paratrooper battle groups

---

1. Memo, SA to SECDEF, 15 Sep 62, Subj: Preliminary Army Review of the Report of the Army Tactical Mobility Requirements Board.

rapidly deployed to Mississippi and Tennessee. Just fifteen days later, major Army forces were alerted for a possible invasion of Cuba.

The Army ordered the new airmobile test force and evaluation group to be formed at the infantry school post of Fort Benning, Georgia, in the beginning of 1963. Although the project was given top priority, competing demands for aviation and personnel resources interfered with the trial airmobile unit throughout its existence. The programmed assembly and testing of the experimental unit continued to be affected adversely by Vietnam developments, domestic disturbances, and Cuban emergency contingencies, as well as the high level of activity at Fort Benning. The 2d Infantry Division stationed on post was planned for conversion to the new ROAD (Reorganization Objective Army Divisions) structure in January because of its planned rotation to Europe that April. The division's reorganization was already a year behind schedule because of the Berlin crisis.[2]

In accordance with McNamara's desires to commence airmobile testing in early 1963, Army Chief of Staff, Gen. Earle K. Wheeler, approved the activation of a reduced-strength air assault division and supporting air transport brigade just before the end of December. Maj. Gen. Harry W. O. Kinnard was handpicked to command the airmobile unit and summoned to the Pentagon. Kinnard was a vigorous and athletic paratroop commander, who served with particular esteem during World War II under Gen. Maxwell D. Taylor. Taylor later became President Kennedy's military advisor and was the current Chairman of the Joint Chiefs of Staff. Wheeler's guidance to Kinnard was straightforward: reconfigure the division so that all material could be flown by air, replacing as many wheels with helicopters as possible. Kinnard would have completely free reign, even in the selection of key personnel. Wheeler's final instructions were equally succinct: "You are going to run the organization. I want you to find out how far and fast the Army can go, and should go in the direction of air mobility."[3]

2. USCONARC/USARSTRIKE, *Annual Historical Summary, 1 July 1962–30 June 1963*, Fort Monroe, Virginia, dtd 1 Jan 65.
3. DCSUTR Avn Div, *Semiannual Hist Rept, 1 Jul–31 Jul 62*, pp. 1–3, and USAMHI, *Senior Officer Debriefing Program*, Lt. Gen. H. W. O. Kinnard, by Col. Glenn A. Smith and Lt. Col. August M. Cianciolo, Carlisle

Harry William Osborn Kinnard was born into an Army family on 7 May 1915 at Dallas, Texas. An avid sportsman and the captain of the fencing team at West Point, he graduated as an infantry lieutenant in 1939. Kinnard served initially with the Hawaiian Division and was sent to Fort Benning after America entered World War II. He completed jump school in late 1942 and joined the 501st Parachute Infantry Regiment, which was sent to Europe as part of the 101st Airborne Division. He parachuted into Normandy during the 6 June 1944 invasion of France and took over the regiment's 1st Battalion six days later. During the September 1944 airdrop into Holland, the division operations officer was severely wounded, and Major General Taylor promoted Kinnard to the job. At twenty-nine Kinnard was a full colonel. During the Battle of the Bulge, he served in the division's heroic defense of Bastogne. After the war, Kinnard held a succession of posts which included command of the 1st Airborne Battle Group, 501st Infantry (101st Airborne Division), and executive to the Secretary of the Army just prior to the assembly of the Howze Board. On 21 July 1962 he became assistant division commander of the 101st Airborne Division at Fort Campbell, Kentucky. In accordance with Wheeler's directive, Kinnard arrived at Fort Benning to take over the newly created 11th Air Assault Division (Test) on 1 February 1963 and received his aviator wings that July.

Kinnard knew that he faced a tough job. Part of the training scheme required joint testing with the Air Force, including long-range airlift support. The fact that the Air Force expressed open displeasure over "airmobility," which it considered an Army intrusion into the skies, was only one of his problems. The Army staff remained unconvinced that the frightfully expensive air assault division was actually worth the extra cost over a regular division. From that aspect alone Kinnard faced an uphill fight, since the military budget was being rapidly depleted by the global tempo of increased Army operations. Fortunately, for testing purposes at least, McNamara's blessing insured that enough money was available. As Col. George P. Seneff, who commanded the division's 11th Aviation Group, later summed up the situation, "For the first time in the history of the Army, a bunch of

---

Barracks, Pennsylvania: 1977, p. 12. Hereafter cited as USAMHI, Kinnard Debriefing.

people had been turned loose with high priority on personnel and equipment, given their own budget, and told, O.K., here's the dough, we'll get the people and equipment; [you] come up with a concept and prove it."[4]

General Kinnard was an infantryman with a solid airborne background who firmly believed that the airmobile division should conform to the light paratrooper infantry mold. He felt that the innovative science of airmobility must be linked to the flexible, tough airborne spirit rather than to the "old" Army aviation mentality, which he considered typified by Army aircraft liaison and cargo transport duty. Kinnard believed "air mobile parachute people were ideally suited to bring in the air mobile concept" since "airmobility required a frame of mind that paratroopers best adapted to," and emphasized that all combat arms of the test unit should be parachutist-qualified. As a result, the new formation was redesignated from the 11th Airborne Division, "The Blue Angels" of World War II fame in the Pacific.[5]

One of Major General Kinnard's first selections for his division staff was Col. John M. Wright, Jr., a distinguished soldier captured on Corregidor Island and held as a prisoner by the Japanese during World War II. Wright was assigned to Seventh Army at Stuttgart, Germany, when he received orders to the newly forming 11th Air Assault Division at Fort Benning, and remembered his assignment as a "bolt out of the blue." When Wright asked for information about the unit from his fellow operations officers, only a handful had even heard of it, and they guessed that it was some type of aviation outfit. The Seventh Army Chief of Staff told Wright, "It's an experimental division at Fort Benning, and you're lucky to be assigned there rather than anywhere else, because nobody knows anything about it, which means that you should know very quickly as much about it as anybody!"[6] Brigadier General Wright was appointed as Kinnard's Assis-

4. USAMHI, *Senior Officers Debriefing Program*, Lt. Gen. George P. Seneff, by Lt. Col. Ronald K. Anderson, Carlisle Barracks, Pennsylvania. Hereafter cited as USAMHI, Seneff Debriefing.

5. USAMHI, Kinnard Debriefing, p. 11.

6. USAMHI, *Senior Officers Oral History Program*, Project 83-5, Lt. Gen. John M. Wright, Jr., USA, Ret., interviewed by Lt. Col. David M. Fishback, Carlisle Barracks, Pennsylvania: 1983, p. 364. Hereafter cited as USAMHI, Wright Interview.

tant Division Commander-B responsible for the logistics and aviation side of the division. After repeated requests for the aviator training that he deemed necessary, Wright was finally permitted to attend aviation school.

Kinnard chose Brig. Gen. Richard "Dick" T. Knowles as Assistant Division Commander-A to control tactical employment and field operations. Kinnard's chief of staff was Col. Elvy B. Roberts, who commanded the 1st Cavalry Division in Vietnam six years later. In the meantime the Army nominated Brig. Gen. Robert R. "Bob" Williams to head the Test and Evaluation Group at Fort Benning, which was responsible for developing tests and for submitting progress reports. Williams's group reported directly to Lt. Gen. Charles W. G. Rich, who became overall test director for Project TEAM (Test and Evaluation of Air Mobility) on 1 August 1964 at Third Army headquarters, Fort McPherson. TEAM attempts to get hard data from Kinnard often led to acrimonious sessions, since the concept's rapid development often blurred distinctions between critical system flaws and simple training headaches. Kinnard was more interested in making the division go than in collecting statistics.

On 18 January 1963 the Army formally announced a three-phase testing program. Phase I would begin with Kinnard's infant air assault "division" at one-fourth strength, as available resources limited the force to one reinforced battalion and an equivalent small air transport "brigade" to support it. These elements would intensively train in airmobile operations and serve as a nucleus for progressive expansion in November. In Phase II, projected to last through most of 1964, the initial test unit would be expanded to a full brigade, still one-third the actual size of a division. Further training would culminate in a joint Army–Air Force testing program. During Phase III, starting in October 1964, the division would be brought up to full strength and undergo one year of advanced training. This phase would focus on the division's feasibility in all three levels of warfare: limited, medium, and all-out nuclear conflict. This final phase was never actually completed because of the need to expedite an airmobile force to Vietnam.[7]

7. Ltr OPS CDDC, DA dtd 7 Jan 63, Subj: Plans for the Initial Organization, Training, and Testing of Air Mobile Units.

Major General Kinnard's 11th Air Assault Division (Test) was activated along with its associated 10th Air Transport Brigade under Col. Delbert L. Bristol at Harmony Church, Fort Benning, Georgia, on 7 February 1963. The Phase I test force was initially authorized 291 officers, 187 warrant officers, and 3,114 enlisted men. The 1st Brigade under Col. George S. Beatty, Jr., consisted of a single battalion, Lt. Col. John T. "Jack" Hennessey's 3d Battalion, 187th Infantry, which was formed by levying officers and sergeants throughout the service and filling the ranks with soldiers from the 2d Infantry Division and paratrooper school on post. The 2d Battalion, 42d Artillery, was gathered from Fort Bragg, North Carolina, and Fort Sill, Oklahoma, and contained a battery each of howitzers, Little John missiles, and aerial rocket helicopters. Support, engineer, and maintenance units were created by gutting the 3d Missile Command at Fort Bragg. The aviation resources were created by stripping units scattered across the country from Fort Benning, Georgia, and Fort Riley, Kansas, to Fort Lewis, Washington. Factory production was stepped up in an effort to meet helicopter shortfalls.[8]

Fleshed out by this crusading cadre, who collectively referred to themselves as "Skysoldiers," the unit entered the field almost immediately in a series of grueling training and experimental exercises. Both ground troops and air crews forged a close-knit bond in their common zeal to prove that airmobility could work. Only limited heliports and training areas existed at Fort Benning, and the unit frequently went to Fort Stewart for more maneuver room. In September the reinforced infantry battalion moved there and began initial testing in Exercise AIR ASSAULT I. The command emphasis and continual observation that typified test force operations were already evident.

8. The 11th Air Assault Division (-) was initially composed of the 11th Aviation Group (Cos A and B of the 226th Avn Bn; Cos A and B of the 227th Avn Bn; Co A, 228th Avn Bn; 11th Avn Co; Co A, 611th Aircraft Maint & Support Bn; Tp B, 3d Sqdn, 17th Cav); 2d Bn of the 42d Artillery; 3d Bn of the 187th Infantry; Co A, 127th Engineer Bn; Co A, 511th Signal Bn; and the nucleus of the division general staff and support command (408th Supply & Service Co; Co A, 11th Medical Bn; and part of the 711th Maintenance Bn). On 1 October 1963 the 1st Bn, 187th Inf; Co A, 127th Eng Bn; and Co B, 6th Bn, 81st Arty, were officially designated as airborne units.

The scrutiny became so intense that Major General Kinnard retorted by punning Churchill's famous Battle of Britain tribute and quipped, "Never have so few been observed by so many so often." By October, when the exercise was completed, the bulk of personnel for the unit's Phase II expansion had been received.

The 11th Air Assault Division (Test) faced several serious problems, ranging from inadequate signal equipment to insufficient manning tables, but the most critical always remained aviation. Each aircraft type presented unique difficulties. The Air Force was very displeased about the Army's use of larger fixed-wing Caribou transport and Mohawk reconnaissance aircraft, which the division and air transport brigade considered essential. Kinnard's attempts to put machine guns on the OV1 Mohawk, a high-performance aircraft designed to seek out and provide immediate intelligence on the enemy regardless of terrain or weather conditions, caused a major interservice dispute. General Johnson finally withdrew the division's twenty-four armed Mohawks as "a sacrifice on the altar of accord with the Air Force." Later the Army was also forced to give up its valuable support CV2 Caribou transport planes.[9]

The UH-series Iroquois helicopters, popularly called Hueys by the soldiers, provided the majority of the unit's helicopter transport and gunship capability. The Huey carried eight combat-equipped soldiers along with a crew of two to four personnel, hauled equipment and supplies, and could be upgunned as an aerial weapons platform. Several production varieties insured better performance throughout the Vietnam era, and the Huey became the legendary mainstay of both the air assault test unit and its descendant, the 1st Cavalry Division.

The airmobile division depended on the twin-rotor CH47 Chinook helicopter, the principal Army air cargo transporter, to airlift its essential artillery and heavier supplies forward. Capable of carrying either forty-four troops or ten thousand pounds of cargo, the Chinook's importance was reflected in the division motto, "If you can't carry it in a Chinook, you're better off without it." Unfortunately, the Chinook was proving to be a first-rate disaster. Its producer, Vertol, had just sold out to Boeing, and extreme quality control and management problems plagued the entire Chinook program. The Chinook battalion

9. USAMHI, Kinnard Debriefing, p. 16.

skipper, Lt. Col. Benjamin S. Silver, considered it a sterling day if only half of his helicopters were flying. The Chinook was not only unreliable, but the division could not get spare parts. Rotor blades that spun off in flight caused an increasing number of fatal crashes. Colonel Seneff, the flight boss of the 11th Air Assault Division, considered the aircraft a nightmare.

The disastrous Chinook situation became so alarming that it endangered the entire test program, forcing Brigadier General Wright to meet face-to-face with Bob Tharrington of Boeing Company and its Vertol Division. Both agreed to do everything possible to correct the situation. Working in close cooperation, both division maintenance personnel and manufacturing employees struggled determinedly to improve CH47 helicopter performance. Finally, every Chinook could be put into the air at once, enabling Lieutenant Colonel Silver to begin formation exercises. Although the Chinook still faced problems, the division began to rely on this essential medium-size helicopter which served throughout the Vietnam War.

The Pentagon realigned the entire airmobility program in March 1964 to accelerate testing of the 11th Air Assault Division, so that separate Army and Air Force evaluations could be completed by the end of the year. The division continued to build as the training effort was redoubled. Aviation was stabilized at one aerial surveillance and escort (226th Avn) battalion, one Chinook assault support helicopter (228th Avn) battalion, and two Huey assault helicopter (227th, 229th Avn) battalions. The infantry brigade contained three battalions (1st Battalions of the 187th, 188th, and 511th Infantry), but Kinnard needed more riflemen and cannoneers. The following month Col. William R. Lynch's reinforced 2d Brigade of the Fort Benning–based 2d Infantry Division (2d Bn, 23d Inf, and 1st and 2d Bns, 38th Inf) was attached, allowing Kinnard to reorganize his division into three miniature brigades of two infantry battalions each, supported by one aerial rocket battalion (3d Bn, 377th Arty), one Little John missile battalion (2d Bn, 42d Arty), and three howitzer battalions (1st Bn, 15th Arty; 5th Bn, 38th Arty; and 6th Bn, 81st Arty). The division expanded its support components proportionately as preparation intensified for the important fall testing.

The main arguments brought against the Army's air assault unit were the supposed vulnerability of its helicopters in actual combat, under adverse weather conditions, and at night. To disprove these contentions, division flight operations needed to be as realistic as possible. Stateside safety considerations threatened to preclude the required experience, since night flying and aerial gunnery were severely restricted, and low-level, nap-of-the-earth helicopter techniques were only taught instead of practiced. Col. Jack Norton, the head aviator of Continental Army Command (CONARC), and Seneff threw away the book and "relaxed" safety standards.

Under such strenuous training, aircraft losses resulting from new-model teething problems or pilot error or plain bad luck were inevitable. On 22 April 1964 a low-flying 226th Aviation Battalion observation plane hit wires and crashed into Fort Benning's Juniper Lake, killing both pilot and copilot despite parachute-equipped ejection seats. One of the most frightful incidents, which transpired during a parachute jump, miraculously produced no injuries. On 21 July a light OH13 Sioux helicopter of the 3d Squadron, 17th Cavalry, became entangled with a descending canopy ten feet off the ground, immediately slamming both paratrooper and aircraft into the earth.

The division constantly rehearsed formation flying regardless of time or weather as it learned to deliver troops over long distances. Improved searchlights were used for group movements at night. Formation flight was emphasized to the point that the aviators began joking, "If two of you need to go to the can, be sure to fly in formation!" During one exercise, Lt. Col. John B. Stockton's 227th Aviation Battalion (Assault Helicopter) went from Camp Blanding, Florida, to Fort Benning despite a wall of thunderstorms. The massed helicopters pushed forward in the driving rain, but the formation was inevitably broken apart by the weather front. The whole battalion was forced to sit down its craft in ones, twos, and threes, scattered over four Georgia counties, where the hapless crews spent the night with their helicopters mired in muddy fields or along sandy farm lanes.

The continuous formation training, night flying, and weather flight practice demanded hard work, but produced promising results. At the same time, incessant Army demands for pilots and advisors in Vietnam threatened much of the progress. Priority activation of aviation units kept stripping elements out of Kinnard's command, and temporary-duty replacements could not make up for the loss of some of his best aircraft and well-trained people. Throughout the test period the division suffered from an acute shortage of helicopters and experienced pilots.

Major General Kinnard believed that the testing program was being severely jeopardized by the turbulence and tight scheduling, but the Pentagon insisted on staging the fall testing as planned. In September 1964 the division moved into North and South Carolina on Exercise HAWK BLADE, actually a dress rehearsal for the big test, Exercise AIR-ASSAULT II, to be conducted 14 October to 12 November across the same two states. The Joint Chiefs of Staff agreed to allow the Air Force to field-test its own alternate concept, GOLDFIRE I, at the same time (29 October to 13 November), using the 1st Infantry Division with the Ninth and Twelfth Air Forces in the Fort Leonard Wood, Missouri, area under the U.S. STRIKE Command. The requirement for additional joint testing would be determined after comparing results. Kinnard was keenly aware that the case for Army airmobility had to be successfully proven at this juncture.[10]

On the morning of 14 October 1964, the 11th Air Assault Division was scheduled to lift off in a massed 120-helicopter flight at 9:00 A.M. and assault objectives one hundred nautical miles away (the range of the Chinook). Hurricane Isbell offshore in the Atlantic blanketed the entire eastern seaboard with storms and low cloud ceilings, and the Air Force had already grounded most of its planes in that portion of the United States. Many distinguished visitors, in addition to the usual crowd of test observers, were present to witness the exercise. Those who wanted to see air cavalry defeated once and for all were rubbing their hands in anticipation.

Kinnard sent three aerial reconnaissance forces aloft, probing for holes in clouds laden with fierce winds and heavy rainstorms. John Stockton's assault helicopter battalion on the coast was flat on the ground, his Hueys awash in torrential rain, gusts snapping at the rotor blade tie-down ropes. The 229th Aviation Battalion (Assault Helicopter) under Earl Buchanan struggled through the middle route, while Seneff led his helicopters high on the hilltops. Skirting through towering thunderheads, the 120 troop-carrying helicopters followed his lead and planted a full battalion on the landing zones only one hour behind schedule.

10. ODSUTR Avn Div, *Semiannual Hist Rept, July–Dec 64*, pp. 2–3, and Hq TEC Gp, Fort Benning, *Final Report, Project Team*, dtd 15 Jan 65, Volume 1, p. ix.

The rash of predicted accidents failed to materialize during the next four weeks, although foul weather, pilot fatigue, and mechanical difficulties downed a number of aircraft. One of the worst losses occurred when two 10th Air Transport Brigade Caribou transports crashed head-on twelve miles from Fort Gordon over Hephzibah, Georgia, on the last day of October, killing all aboard. On 5 and 6 November two armed Hueys of the 3d Battalion, 377th Artillery, suffered engine compressor failures near Cheraw, South Carolina, resulting in either death or crippling vertebral fractures among all crew members. Power lines, terrain miscalculations, and futile attempts to switch over to instruments in sudden cloudbursts littered still more helicopters across the Carolina backcountry, but fortunately most injuries were not serious.

In one month the test division conclusively demonstrated that its elements could seek out the enemy over a wide area despite unfavorable weather conditions, find him, and then rapidly bring together the necessary firepower and troops to destroy him. Army airmobility passed its most crucial test. A month after AIR ASSAULT II was concluded, test director Lieutenant General Rich presented his final evaluation to Army Combat Developments Command, which forwarded it on 5 January 1965 with favorable comments to Army Chief of Staff Harold K. Johnson. Johnson recommended to the Joint Chiefs of Staff that no aspect of the Army airmobility concept warranted further joint testing by U.S. STRIKE Command.[11]

The Army's success with its test air assault division was a direct result of the innovative manner in which the unit was created and allowed to operate. Kinnard was given great latitude in making necessary changes in doctrine, techniques, and organization. In this manner the revolutionary airmobile concepts advanced by the Howze Board received continued vitality. Brigadier General Wright considered the experiment a brilliant exception to the usual bureaucratic path to Army modernization and adaptation. He later stated, "If you want to get someplace in a hurry with a new concept, new developments, or new ideas, then find a responsible individual, give him a mission, turn him loose, leave him alone, and let him report back when he is ready. And that's just what General Kinnard was permitted to do."[12]

Kinnard was immensely proud of his men and rewarded their hard training and sacrifice with a special air assault badge, designed to duplicate the esprit that the paratrooper and aviator wings achieved. The Army turned down all his attempts to make the badge official, but the test unit awarded it to all 1st Brigade members. On 3 December 1964 the badge was presented to the men of the 2d Brigade, formerly of the 2d Infantry Division, as a result of their performance in AIR ASSAULT II. Although the badge was terminated when the test unit was discontinued, it finally gained official sanction fifteen years later when revived for the airmobile infantrymen of the modern post-Vietnam Army.

In the spring of 1965, the general atmosphere within the 11th Air Assault Division was one of rueful resignation to expected disbandment rather than wartime preparation. No one visualized that in a few short months the division would be cranked up to combat strength and sent over to Vietnam. Most airmobile doctrinists actually predicted a dull period in Army aviation while reports of the test division were reviewed and torn apart, only to be ripped up again at Army and Defense Department level, all to be followed by a couple of years of debate.

The division originators felt there was ample evidence to support this gloomy conclusion, even though Lieutenant General Rich's report strongly recommended against losing two years of test effort experience and equipment by dissipating the personnel or fragmenting the tested units. Division members considered actual Army interest in the unit fairly low. Overall support for the test unit was spotty as a result of competing demands, and many important outsiders were still vocally adamant in their opposition to the airmobile force. Kinnard's division had been formed only for trial purposes in the first place and remained at cadre status.

Officially, of course, the 11th Air Assault Division was never specifically intended for the war that was heating up in Vietnam. The airmobility test was designed to cover the tactical usefulness of the unit in any region. In Vietnam the difficult terrain and elusive enemy presented a perfect opportunity for employing a division with rapid, integrated helicopter transport and firepower, but the Army budget and contingency plans were not programmed for an airmobile division. Brigadier General Powell recalled the general consensus of opinion as "we did what McNamara told us to do and tested the division, now we'd send people off to other assignments and file the reports."

A confluence of several events joined to send the division to Vietnam instead of disbandment. Foremost was the worsening military situation inside South Vietnam, where coups and battlefield defeats were giving the communist insurgency an upper hand against the Army of the Republic of Vietnam (ARVN). The United States decided to intervene with regular forces to prevent communist takeover of this allied country, but lacked light divisions capable of operating efficiently in the tropical wilderness and mountain hinterland. Both 82d and 101st Airborne Divisions had limited mobility once on the ground; normal infantry divisions were either mechanized or very reliant on motorized equipment; and armor divisions were too heavy. Another strategic consideration favored airmobile conversion. One of the most threatened areas in South Vietnam was its rugged central highlands, dominated by the politically important highland city of Pleiku. The road leading inland (Highway 19) to Pleiku had been closed for years, preventing the expeditious arrival of any conventional division.

After the Marines landed to safeguard South Vietnam's northernmost airfield, followed by an Army paratrooper brigade to secure the southern airfield near the capital, the decision was made to send the new helicopter formation into the central section of South Vietnam. Gen. Creighton W. Abrams, the Vice Chief of Staff, presided over a particularly bitter March Army policy council meeting concerning the deployment feasibility of such a move. Abrams, a staunch armor officer, had had initial misgivings about the airmobility concept, but these had been erased during an earlier visit to Kinnard's outfit at Fort Benning. Major General Kinnard had personally flown Abrams around in his helicopter, touring the dispersed, fast-paced test maneuvers and had shown him "exactly what the hell was going on." At the conclusion of the heliborne command briefing, Abrams had confided to him, "I have to say, I'm considerably impressed." After much discussion at the council meeting, Abrams flatly stated, "I feel it is extremely propitious that we happen to have this organization in existence at this point in time, and we will deploy it to Vietnam."[13]

Because of programming considerations, the 11th Air Assault Division (Test) would be inactivated and its assets merged into an already-budgeted regular Army division, which would be converted to airmobile status. Major General Kinnard felt that his own 101st Airborne Division should be the first converted to airmobile status and that another parachute division be used next. However, Army Chief of Staff General Johnson was a former 1st Cavalry Division trooper and had greater affinity for his own unit currently serving on border duty in Korea. General Johnson also believed that the cavalry title fitted better with swift, airmobile pursuit and was more suitable for counterinsurgency operations. The cavalry term appealed to many government officials who felt it very appropriate for an anti-insurgent campaign in Vietnam.

For low- to mid-intensity warfare operations, such as Vietnam, the new division was designed to provide stability and area control for both population and crop resources through the increased military advantages of aerial reconnaissance and heliborne security. After feverish preparation, the Army Combat Developments Command rushed brand-new test airmobile division tables of organization and equipment (TOE 67T) to Department of the Army (DA) headquarters on 1 May 1965, where they were approved before the end of the month. Out of respect for Kinnard's heartfelt desire for paratroopers, the Army Vice Chief of Staff directed that the 1st Brigade remain parachute-qualified.[14]

As a result of these recommendations, on 15 June 1965 Defense Secretary McNamara approved the incorporation of an airmobile division into the Army force structure with the designation of the 1st Cavalry Division (Airmobile). Since the present 1st Cavalry Division was serving as a standard ROAD infantry division at Tonggu, Korea, its assets were used to form a new Korea-based 2d Infantry Division. The cavalry colors were flown to Georgia for conversion beginning 1 July 1965. This swap of flags permitted the new division to draw

13. USAMHI, Kinnard Debriefing, p. 16, and Seneff Debriefing, p. 37.
14. Because of the nature of combat operations, paratrooper replacement difficulties, and the presence of other airborne units in Vietnam, the airborne capability of the 1st Cavalry Division was officially terminated on 1 September 1967.

on all resources at Fort Benning, but these provided only partial troop fill and material. Yet the newly formed division was ordered to be ready for combatant deployment, at full personnel manning and equipment levels, by 28 July 1965.[15]

Airmobile cavalry would be sent to war after years of conceptual and field testing. However, General Kinnard still faced one last seemingly impossible hurdle: to raise his air assault unit nucleus to wartime division status in less than one month. The deadline appeared especially unreasonable since it ignored the extent of needed reorganization and training. A minimum of three months' preparation was mandated if a division required major restructuring prior to movement into a combat zone. Resulting short-fuse time pressures, major equipment shortages, and personnel problems threatened to cripple the airmobile enterprise even before it departed the United States. The lack of firm national policy direction toward Vietnam was primarily responsible for such an arbitrary deadline, but the Army also deliberately disregarded the most elementary time allowances involved in accomplishing such a major task.

Organizationally, the division was authorized eight airmobile infantry cavalry battalions, three light artillery battalions, one aerial rocket artillery battalion, a cavalry reconnaissance squadron, an engineer battalion, and supporting units. Several battalions had to be raised from scratch. Additional equipment procurement in excess of $28 million was estimated to outfit the new division. All stateside depots and supply points were frantically combed to locate and deliver thousands of required major and secondary items in the compressed time remaining. The logistical burden and high cost of displacing emergency equipment resources throughout the country created great waste and multiplied expenditures. Fortunately, sufficient prewar stockage and material shortcuts, such as helicopter depot rebuilds, enabled the division to reach projected levels.

The division was authorized 15,890 men upon activation. Only 9,489 were assigned, and more than 50 percent of this original complement was ineligible for overseas deployment under peacetime service criteria. Replacements were brought into the division around the

15. USCONARC/USARSTRIKE, *Annual Historical Summary, 1 July 1965 to 30 June 1965*, p. 187.

clock, immediately fed a hot meal, processed, assigned, and transported to their units. Continual personnel turbulence effectively shut down most unit training, since indoctrination and basic soldiering consumed the limited time available. The impending division move to Vietnam was secret, and many reporting soldiers arrived at Fort Benning with their families. Civilian dependents were turned away, creating severe individual financial and dislocation hardships which further disrupted troop programming.[16]

There was an acute shortage of aviators, paratroopers, and support personnel. Entire aviation companies were sent to Fort Benning from other commands, but more than three hundred newly assigned aviators (most of whom arrived after 15 July) still required transition on entirely new models of aircraft. The division training capacity was hopelessly swamped and, despite the full help of the aviation school, more than fifty division pilots still sailed without completing transition. The division initially contained 900 paratroopers, but needed 3,470. To secure manpower, the airborne-designated 1st and 2d Battalions of the 8th Cavalry resorted to "extreme pressure for volunteers" and a flurry of abbreviated jump courses. Support components never received their proper allocation of maintenance and supply experts.[17]

The most serious problem remained the large number of troops ineligible for overseas duty. Both DA and CONARC anticipated an emergency presidential announcement permitting the Vietnam-bound division to retain all essential troops. Divisional strength might even be supplemented by calling up selected reserve components. CONARC received word of the "no call-up" decision during Saturday afternoon, 24 July. Four days later President Johnson publicly an-

---

16. 1st Cavalry Division, *Quarterly Command Report*, OACSFOR-OT-RD 6501101, 1 Dec 65. Until 31 December 1965 personnel deploying with a unit to Vietnam had to have sixty days remaining on active duty from the date of departure from the port of embarkation, in addition to other peacetime criteria.

17. 1st Cavalry Division, *Quarterly Command Report*, OACSFOR-OT-RD 650110, 1 Dec 65, pp. 8, 9. Aviation companies attached to the division included the 110th Avn Co; Co A, 4th Avn Bn; Co A, 5th Avn Bn; 6th SFG Avn Co; and 7th SFG Avn Co. See also Shelby L. Stanton, *Vietnam Order of Battle*, rev. ed. (Millwood, N.Y.: Kraus Reprints, 1986), p. 72.

nounced that he was sending the 1st Cavalry Division to Vietnam, but chose not to issue the emergency decree. Major General Kinnard was "glued to the television set" during the national broadcast and was horrified to realize that his division would lose hundreds of highly skilled pilots, crew chiefs, mechanics, and other essential people at the worst possible time.[18]

Major General Kinnard departed Fort Benning on 16 August 1965 to be briefed by Gen. William C. Westmoreland, the commander of Military Assistance Command Vietnam (MACV). Kinnard was fearful that Westmoreland, who was in Vietnam during the 11th Air Assault tests at Fort Benning, might be out of touch with airmobility developments. These fears were confirmed as General Westmoreland announced a new plan of divisional utilization and moved to a large wall map. Pointing to widely scattered areas of the chart, he stated that he was breaking up the 1st Cavalry Division into three brigades: "I am going to put one here, and one here, and all over the country." Kinnard was aghast that his division, which depended upon massing fire- and shockpower, might be scattered all over the nation. He responded, "Please, can't I discuss that?" and countered that the Army Chief of Staff had specified the division's main task was prevention of a military split of South Vietnam by an NVA/VC thrust across critical east-west Highway 19 from Pleiku to Qui Nhon. Kinnard added that he needed the greatest concentrated mobility to insure this goal and concluded, "If you penny pocket them all over the country, you've lost it."[19]

General Kinnard actually wanted to base his division in Thailand and operate up and down Laos and Cambodia, breaking into the North Vietnamese Ho Chi Minh Trail—logistical and reinforcement lifeline into South Vietnam—at will. While this course of action would have caused maximum disruption and destruction of enemy forces, the United States politically limited the war's boundaries to operations inside South Vietnam only. Under the circumstances, Kinnard felt the next best thing was to keep the division together with a definite objective.

18. USAMHI, *Senior Officers Oral History Program*, Interview of LTG Harry W. O. Kinnard by LTC Jacob B. Couch, Jr., 1983; USACONARC/USARSTRIKE, *Annual Historical Summary, 1 Jul 65–30 Jun 66*, Fort Monroe, Virginia, pp. 79–81, 136–37.
19. USAMHI, Kinnard Debriefing, p. 34.

Westmoreland relented, and the division was assigned intact to secure the main line of communications into the western highlands.

Brigadier General Wright was already at Qui Nhon with a small thirty-one-man contingent, acquainting the MACV staff with division support needs and scouting a site for the future main base camp. He wanted enough space for a sizable rectangular heliport and the protective infantry and artillery which would be positioned around it, all on terrain suitable for a strong perimeter barrier. Since the cavalry division helicopters were its most vital resource, Wright was very concerned about a possible North Vietnamese or Chinese fighter-bomber attack on such a lucrative target. The MACV operations officer, Maj. Gen. William "Bill" DePuy, assured him, "Don't worry about an air attack on your base. If you should get that, we'll just wipe Peking off the map!"[20] Enemy airstrikes against the airmobile division's sprawling airfield complex represented the primary threat, but true to DePuy's word this vulnerability was never exposed during the Vietnam War.

Wright's contingent wore civilian clothes and traveled across the highlands, visiting Special Forces camps, regional outposts, and valley hamlets. They finally selected a centrally located area with good flying weather along Highway 19 at An Khe, a Green Beret campsite near two critical mountain passes. The French lost an entire mobile group along this strategic stretch of winding road in 1954, and devastating Viet Cong ambushes still interdicted the route. The An Khe Special Forces garrison had been defeated in a bloody contest for control of the road near Mang Yang Pass in February.

The 1,030-man division advance element was airlifted from Robbins Air Force Base, Georgia, to Cam Ranh Bay beginning 14 August 1965. On 27 August they were flown by C130 aircraft to the Special Forces An Khe camp airstrip, where they pitched pup tents along the runway. Brigadier General Wright did not want heavy earth-moving machinery clearing the airfield site, since the scraped ground would create severe dust and wreak havoc on helicopter operations. He walked over to the tents, machete in hand, and selected twenty-five senior officers and sergeants to follow him into the adjacent scrub brush. Wright's experience as a Japanese prisoner had taught him that a lot

---

20. USAMHI, Wright Interview, p. 389.

could be accomplished if enough men worked with their bare hands. As the assembled group watched curiously, Wright cut a twenty-foot circle of short-cropped, green grass out of the foliage with his machete and stated, "If each of us swung a machete enough times, and if we cleared enough of those twenty- to twenty-five-foot circles, then they would all finally fit together, and we would have a rectangle two kilometers by three kilometers where there would be nothing but this beautiful green grass . . . like a fine golf course."[21]

Not long afterward, a staff officer trying to find Col. Allen M. Burdett, Jr., was told that the colonel was out working on the "Golf Course." The name stuck, and the airfield's title became official for the duration of American presence in Vietnam. Over the next few weeks, the division base camp slowly took shape. Several deep gullies and boulder-strewn outcrops crisscrossed the landscape, but the longest sections of the new runway were laid out perfectly straight to enable better gunship firing passes against attacking infantry. Although initial base camp construction commenced without the division engineer battalion, the determined work of the advance element and borrowed construction troops made An Khe's Golf Course the world's largest helipad by the end of September.

While the division's advance party staked out and cleared the main camp, the majority of the division outloaded at Mobile, Alabama, and Jacksonville, Florida. The division embarkation was complicated by overcrowding problems and last-minute accommodation transfers at dockside. Several vessels, such as the poorly rehabilitated MSTS *Kula Gulf* and *Card*, were rapidly pressed into service for the journey. Steam pipes were leaking, machinery was broken, and conditions aboard were extremely uncomfortable. When Kinnard insisted on moving his aviators from the hottest bowels of the vessels to unused portions of the shiphand billeting area, the uncooperative Military Sea Transportation crews refused to sail. After some last-minute high command intervention, he secured better quarters and the threatened strike was averted. On 28 July 1965 the 1st Cavalry Division began its main overseas movement.

The task of moving the division across the Pacific was almost as momentous as getting it combat-ready in the first place. Six passenger

21. Ibid., p. 391.

vessels, eleven cargo ships, and four aircraft carriers were required to move more than 15,000 soldiers, 3,100 vehicles, 470 aircraft, and 19,000 long tons of cargo to Vietnam. The division continued training hundreds of new recruits even as it sailed. For example, the soldiers conducted familiarization and marksmanship training with new M16 automatic rifles by firing at apple crates pitched over vessel fantails into the ocean.

The undeveloped midcountry port of Qui Nhon was chosen as the division's destination because of its relative proximity to An Khe. However, Qui Nhon's unsophisticated facilities and shortage of service personnel led to predictions of a tedious over-the-beach unloading process lasting more than a month. One brigade was originally slated for offloading at Cam Ranh Bay, but directives changing it to Qui Nhon were received en route. Amendatory instructions were received throughout the voyage. Consequently, the arrival of cargo, personnel, and aircraft was disjointed.

The unloading process was complicated and backbreaking as cargo was lightered ashore from a distance of two to five miles at sea. Viet Cong attacks interrupted traffic on the access road to the final delivery area, and bad weather intervened, but the actual debarkation of the division (including the forty-mile inland move to An Khe) was completed in a mere fifteen days. However, the logistical inefficiency surrounding division support arrangements incountry led the Army to abandon properly conceived airmobile supply channels and simply adopt the "dumping ground" resource conditions of Qui Nhon and An Khe. This not only led to chronic supply mismanagement, but also created a crucial aviation gasoline shortage in the division's fall Ia Drang Valley campaign. Strategically the mobile 1st Cavalry Division became pinned to base security of the "An Khe logistical hub."[22]

The supply and medical difficulties were secondary to the fact that a powerful, reinforced division capable of aerial assault was emplaced in Vietnam ready to assist the allied cause. Westmoreland had the flying cavalry that Walker lacked, and it was located along a vital

22. I Field Force Vietnam, *Operational Report: Lessons Learned, 1 Oct–31 Dec 65*, p. 24. Some of these problems are also highlighted in Lt. Gen. John J. Tolson, *Vietnam Studies: Airmobility, 1961–1971* (Washington, D.C.: Dept. of the Army, 1973), pp. 67–73.

communications zone in one of the most threatened and remote regions of the country. Despite all the obstacles to the rapid assembly of the 1st Cavalry Division and the massive scope of its cross-Pacific move, the first elements of the division were engaged in combat on 18 September 1965—just ninety-five days after the reorganization of the 11th Air Assault Division into the 1st Cavalry Division had been approved.[23]

In retrospect the formation and testing of the initial air assault division concept were successful because most normal bureaucratic service obstacles were removed at the insistence of Defense Secretary McNamara. However, even with the highest national priorities attached to the airmobile program, competing requirements almost defeated the project. Only the diligence and sustained faith of the testing cadre, coupled with all-out industrial support, enabled Kinnard's experimental unit to flourish. The upgrading of this formation to a full-fledged division and its movement to Vietnam were nothing short of miraculous in view of last-minute deployment decisions and actions.

Every Army command, from the top at DA through STRIKE Command down to the local Fort Benning post garrison, contributed to the extraordinary effort which succeeded in making the 1st Cavalry Division (Airmobile) a battlefield reality. The division enjoyed the great advantages of an adequate continental manpower base, a sufficiently experienced NCO cadre, and the necessary supply stockage that existed at this early stage of the Vietnam buildup. Even so, in the final analysis the mission was accomplished because the high morale, well-drilled cooperation, extremely good training, and leadership of the pre-Vietnam Army allowed the division to surmount the worst difficulties. The prevailing soldiers' attitude was that, regardless of the drastic time, manpower, and material limitations, they were going to make the division work. The spirit of the First Team began to take hold. In less than one month, the small band of air assault Skysoldiers was turned into an entire division of airmobile Skytroopers.

23. 1st Cavalry Division, *Quarterly Command Report*, dtd 1 Dec 1965, pp. 11–14.

CHAPTER 3

Air Assault

Techniques, Ia Drang Valley Campaign

The arrival of the 1st Cavalry Division (Airmobile) in South Vietnam was part of an increasing American combat role in the Second Indochina War. During the Vietnam era, the official mission of an airmobile division was to provide reconnaissance for larger field force commands, participate in stability operations short of all-out nuclear war ("low- and mid-intensity operations"), and provide security and control over the population and resources of an assigned area. In accordance with this general mission statement, the 1st Cavalry Division was assigned the responsibility of protecting its own base, Camp Radcliff at An Khe, reopening Highway 19 from the coast to Pleiku and safeguarding its traffic, and guarding specific coastal lowland rice harvests from Viet Cong disruption. These represented extremely limited geographical objectives of a static security nature.

The 1st Cavalry Division, however, was designed and destined for offensive action. Airmobility offered such great vertical maneuver and firepower advantages that events soon thrust the division into a predominate mode of aerial attack. The airmobile division entered the acrid crucible of combat in the Ia Drang Valley of Vietnam's western border, where it marshaled its air assault assets to locate and battle North Vietnamese Army regulars. There were grave blunders in the execution of this campaign, some of which led to decimation of entire cavalry companies and battalions, but the airmobility concept was still new and needed refinement. The basic air cavalry combination was sound and proved so during the next ten years of battlefield application in Vietnam. No single engagement demonstrated the basic validity of air assault as strikingly as the 1st Cavalry Division's Ia Drang Valley campaign.

To an Army largely ground oriented, the rapid and flexible response inherent in airmobile operations over the wide expanse of the Ia Drang Valley was almost beyond comprehension. In the thirty-seven-day period beginning late in October, divisional helicopters conducted twenty-two infantry battalion moves and sixty-six artillery battery displacements across distances as great as seventy-five miles at a time. While this new style of airmobile warfare used modern helicopters to overfly difficult terrain and leap beyond enemy defenses to strike deep into targeted objectives, its most successful application was in the traditional cavalry mode. The division excelled in assignments to reconnoiter, screen, delay, and conduct raids over wide fronts. By December 1965 division operations extended from the South China Sea to the Cambodian border along the axis of Highway 19, and from Bong Son to Tuy Hoa along the Vietnamese coast.[1]

The air assault reigned supreme in the attack phase of airmobility. Once contact was made, troops could be flexibly extracted by helicopter from less critical situations and quickly concentrated at the point of battle. Instant radio communications enabled commanders, who themselves were often aloft in helicopters, to monitor scoutship transmissions and to direct responsive airlandings in the midst of the most fluid situations. As the infantrymen poured out of helicopters with rifles and machine guns blazing, hovering gunships rendered immediate, close-in covering fire with rockets and other weapons. Rapid helicopter airlift of howitzers and ordnance assured that sustained artillery support was available for infantry fighting for remote and isolated landing zones. The NVA opposition was stunned and overwhelmed by this swiftly executed initial aerial onslaught, gaining the division an immediate reputation for tactical success.

When the North Vietnamese attacked the small Special Forces Plei Me camp near Cambodia on 19 October 1965, they were not anticipating any American airmobile response. Even from the allied standpoint, the encounter seemed to be an unlikely prelude for the most famous divisional airmobile retaliation in history. Camp Plei Me was located along the western highland border, an area outside direct 1st Cavalry Division responsibility, and the attack was disregarded as

1. 1st Cavalry Division, *Quarterly Command Report for Second Fiscal Quarter FY 66*, dtd 30 Nov 65, p. 1.

a mere regimental baptism-of-fire "shakedown" exercise. Such attacks of opportunity were not unusual as North Vietnamese formations traveled to permanent base areas inside South Vietnam. However, three days after Plei Me was besieged, allied intelligence estimated that at least two freshly infiltrated NVA regiments, spearheaded by VC shock troops, were involved in a determined bid to overrun the campsite. Since Plei Me guarded the southwestern approach to Pleiku, an enemy victory was a direct menace to Pleiku, which the 1st Cavalry Division had been sent to Vietnam to protect.[2]

The South Vietnamese II Corps commander gathered his available mechanized reserves within Pleiku City and began a road march to relieve Camp Plei Me. Usually NVA/VC attack plans included elaborate measures to entrap and destroy forces attempting to reach a besieged garrison, and the 1st Cavalry Division was requested to render artillery support in case of ambush. Col. Elvy B. Roberts's 1st Brigade was flown into the Pleiku vicinity on 23 October. The next day the South Vietnamese relief column was mauled by a major ambush which threatened to block further road movement. A divisional artillery control team was sent on one of the medical evacuation helicopters to the stranded convoy. The forward observers scrambled into the lead vehicles, and the advance resumed behind a rolling curtain of massed artillery fire.

The relief force reached Plei Me under this umbrella of shellfire at dusk on 25 October, breaking the siege. General Westmoreland believed that regimental-size NVA formations still endangered South Vietnam's entire central region. The intensity of the attack on Plei Me verified that the North Vietnamese might contest other critical locations, storm Pleiku, or even attempt to militarily slice the country across the middle. Westmoreland helicoptered to the 1st Brigade's forward command post at LZ (Landing Zone) Homecoming, where the howitzers of the 2d Battalion, 19th Artillery, were still shelling the jungles around Plei Me. The division already forestalled the NVA drive by helping to turn back enemy elements committed against Plei Me, but Westmoreland wanted the North Vietnamese decisively defeated. He ordered that the division "must now do more than merely

2. DA AGM-P(M) ACSFOR Report, *Operations Report 3-66—The Pleiku Campaign*, dtd 10 May 66, p. 10.

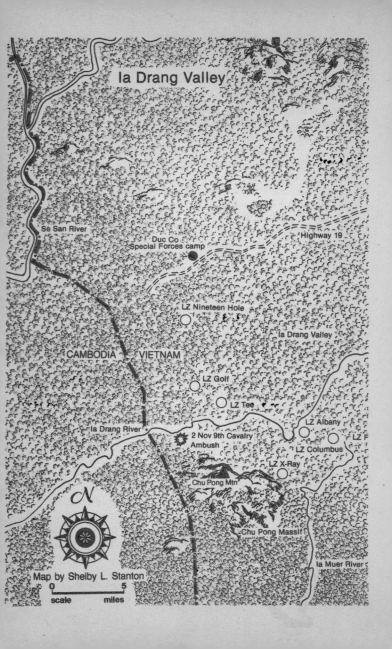

Ia Drang Valley

Se San River

Duc Co
Special Forces camp

Highway 19

LZ Nineteen Hole

Ia Drang Valley

CAMBODIA   VIETNAM

LZ Golf

LZ Tee

LZ Albany

Ia Drang River

2 Nov 9th Cavalry
Ambush

LZ F

LZ Columbus

LZ X-Ray

Chu Pong Mtn

Chu Pong Massif

Ia Muer River

Map by Shelby L. Stanton

0   5
scale   miles

contain the enemy; he must be sought out aggressively and destroyed."[3]

The NVA units which had participated in the Plei Me action were suspected to be regrouping in a 2,500-square kilometer area of rolling flatland between Plei Me and Cambodia. General Kinnard was confident that bold orchestration of his division's combined resources with air assault tactics would result in absolute domination of such a large battle arena. The region was not well mapped and contained few roads. The existing maze of trails could easily confuse normal ground orientation, but aerial observation promised accurate direction regardless. While a conventional division might be ineffective in seeking out and closing with the enemy in this vast and unfamiliar wilderness, the territory was ideal for long-range airmobile cavalry thrusts and flight operations.

Weather and terrain conditions were almost perfect. Only a few clouds were scattered high in the skies; night humidity was low; and temperatures ranged comfortably between 76 and 86 degrees Fahrenheit. Months of unrelenting heat had baked the red clay throughout the valleys and ridgelines into suitably hard earth for helicopter landings. Rivers and streams were seasonably dry. Only lush tropical vegetation and giant anthills protruded above the high elephant grass. The most thickly jungled sector existed on and around the prominent Chu Pong massif, which straddled the Cambodian border and loomed over the southwestern portion of the region's Ia Drang Valley.

The campaign, which existed under a series of operational code words (LONG REACH, SILVER BAYONET, GREEN HOUSE), but became historically designated after the main Ia Drang Valley west of Plei Me, began on 27 October 1965. The 1st Brigade—consisting of four infantry battalions, one light artillery battalion, most of the divisional cavalry reconnaissance squadron, and one aerial rocket artillery battery of gunship helicopters—fanned west of Pleiku toward Cambodia in classic cavalry pursuit of the enemy. Somewhere in the grasslands and forests below, bands of elusive *33d NVA Regiment* infantrymen were traveling back to their assembly areas. They were packing only light bedrolls, minimal personal gear, and sidearms as they dodged through woods and man-high grass.

3. Ibid., p. 42.

Lt. Col. John B. Stockton's reconnaissance 1st Squadron, 9th Cavalry, led the aerial drive. The small scoutships and armed gunships darted over the landscape, spotting and strafing small groups of fleeing North Vietnamese riflemen. The line battalions followed in dozens of Huey helicopters crammed with men and equipment. The first mission was to find the enemy. To effect the widest search as rapidly as possible, infantry battalions were fragmented into company-size increments. The troops were deposited over a multitude of selected landing sites; they cut their way out of the fields and into surrounding woodlines with machetes and axes and began patrolling their assigned sectors in the blistering sun. Fortunately, light leafy forests predominated, and foot movement was not unduly hampered by dense vegetation. Individual companies were deliberately placed in danger of clashing with larger enemy units, but the brigade was depending on its helicopters to speedily react and reinforce any contact which developed.

The brigade was soon dispersed over the entire area northwest of Plei Me, but the North Vietnamese had seemingly disappeared like phantoms. Nightly ambush positions and daily cloverleaf patrolling were exhausting and disappointing. Over the next few days Stockton's helicopters were reporting more fire passes and return automatic rifle fire, but there was no way to assess results. The various cavalry companies roaming the bush were inevitably trapping a few prisoners. These revealed that the North Vietnamese were growing tired and afraid of this unexpected helicopter harassment, but the main North Vietnamese contingents were still unlocated.

A band of enemy soldiers was observed by aerial scouts midway between Plei Me and Chu Pong mountain on the morning of 1 November. One of the reconnaissance squadron's three ground platoons, the Troop B Rifles, was already in flight and diverted to the scene. They skirmished across a small streambed and uncovered a fully stocked regimental hospital. The sweating cavalrymen spent most of the day dumping heaps of captured medical supplies aboard outgoing helicopters. Another squadron rifle platoon landed to help destroy the rest of the site. The squadron maintained a screen of scoutships overhead looking for more enemy soldiers, and that afternoon they detected hundreds of North Vietnamese soldiers approaching from the northeast. Gunships roared down to blast the advancing enemy with rockets and automatic weapons fire, but failed to slow down the counterattack on the hospital position. While aerial firepower rated high test scores with its appearance of utter devastation, the explosions and bullets seemed only to be tearing off tree limbs and killing a few clusters of men.

The defending ground cavalry force at the hospital was quickly compressed into a very small perimeter. The last rifle platoon was inserted at the height of this intense firefight and was forced to leave the bullet-riddled helicopters under a hailstorm of gunfire. The hospital was beyond the range of division artillery, and close-quarters combat soon rendered aerial support impractical. The North Vietnamese assault faltered under the volume of return automatic and grenade fire and was discontinued when additional reinforcements of the 2d Battalion, 12th Cavalry, were airlanded later that day. The cavalry scored an opening success in its first confrontation with the NVA, although the enemy had not pressed its counterattack once it became evident that the hospital's condition was no longer worth fighting for.

Two days later Stockton's squadron probed deeper into the Ia Drang River Valley, where numerous trails leading into Cambodia were disclosed by aircraft reconnaissance. The squadron's same trio of rifle platoons established a hasty overnight patrol point south of the river and set up ambushes along a major east-west trail. Troop C Rifles at the southernmost ambush position sighted a full NVA company carrying supplies down the trail at 7:30 that evening. The North Vietnamese were talking and laughing loudly. Just before they entered the actual ambush site, the enemy commander decided to take a rest break. The Americans froze into their positions, not making a sound. This ordeal lasted an hour and a half, during which time various unaware NVA soldiers strayed close to the hidden cavalrymen, but failed to detect them.

Finally, the North Vietnamese re-formed into a single file and resumed marching down the trail. The cavalrymen breathlessly waited until the lead platoon passed the prepared kill zone and sprung the trap against the following weapons carriers. A deafening explosion of claymore-mine and automatic-rifle fire ripped through the main portage party, which was carrying machine guns, mortars, and recoilless rifles. The lead enemy platoon, which had been allowed to pass the main ambush, was simultaneously annihilated by cross fire from the cavalry ambush flank security element and another string of preset claymore mines. The firing lasted only two minutes and was executed with such violence and precision that every enemy soldier was cut down without firing a shot in return.

The cavalry platoon leader wisely decided that the destroyed company might be the vanguard of a larger force. The Troop C Rifles immediately returned to the main patrol base without counting bodies or collecting captured equipment. The base was set up just inside the treeline which surrounded the landing zone and was occupied by the other two 9th Cavalry rifle platoons and a mortar section. Within an hour the entire *8th Battalion* of the *66th NVA Regiment* surrounded the cavalry perimeter. The first mass attack against the patrol base was shattered by concentrated defensive fire. Numerous NVA snipers climbed into the trees and began to pick off cavalrymen exposed by the bright moonlight flooding the forest.

The North Vietnamese mounted another major assault against the weakening American lines at 11:15 P.M. For the first time in division history, aerial rocket artillery was employed at night in a close support role. Gunships hovering overhead responded with volleys of rocket salvos which careened through the foliage and detonated with lethal precision a scant fifty yards from friendly positions. The situation was becoming desperate, and urgent calls were made for reinforcements and medical evacuation craft. Incoming helicopters were buffeted by NVA gunfire during their descent; seriously wounded troopers were rushed aboard, and the helicopters pulled away. One crashed just beyond the landing zone, but another helicopter quickly dipped down to rescue its crew and radios before the North Vietnamese could reach the wreckage. One helicopter was so riddled by shrapnel and bullets that it almost disintegrated upon touching down with its load of wounded at the Special Forces Duc Co camp airstrip.

Twenty minutes after midnight reinforcements began to arrive at the patrol perimeter, marking the first time that divisional heliborne infantry reinforced a nocturnal military engagement. The available landing field was so small that only thirty men at a time could be inserted, but Company A of the 1st Battalion, 8th Cavalry, was emplaced alongside the squadron riflemen when the third major North Vietnamese assault smashed into the American lines at 3:30 A.M. The cavalry grimly held their positions. Just before dawn they repulsed the final and most determined NVA attack. One of the most gallant heroes of the firefight was Troop C Rifles Platoon Sgt. Florendo S. Pascual, who was killed at his post during the thick of combat.

During the entire firefight an attached Special Forces–led Rhade tribal reaction platoon had manned a separate ambush position just outside the main patrol perimeter. However, this added support could not be effectively utilized during the night action. The Troop B Rifles commander was hesitant about recalling them from their ambush position to reinforce, lest they be caught in NVA cross fires or become mistaken by their own troops for the enemy. He radioed the Special Forces–led Rhade platoon to move carefully and slowly toward the fight and to prepare to infiltrate into the defensive perimeter before dawn. Throughout the war, such elementary difficulties as native and Special Forces attire (causing uniform complications), language problems, and different tactical methods often precluded effective teamwork between regular Army and irregular troops.

The last brigade clash in the Ia Drang campaign's opening rounds occurred on 6 November near LZ Wing. Company B of the 2d Battalion, 8th Cavalry, stumbled across trenchlines containing North Vietnamese infantry and immediately attacked with two platoons. The entrenched *6th Battalion, 33d NVA Regiment,* not only pinned both platoons, but countered by moving to surround the entire company. The battalion's Company C hacked through dense jungle to reach its stranded sister unit and smashed into the rear of the North Vietnamese force at a stream crossing. As the new company tried to press a flanking attack, it also became locked in heavy combat and stalled.

Although a profuse amount of supporting air and artillery strikes was delivered, the two companies were unable to crack the NVA positions. After dark the companies linked up to establish one defensive perimeter, which was raked by NVA automatic weapons fire for the remainder of the night. During darkness the North Vietnamese withdrew, leaving snipers behind to mask their departure. The firefight was the bloodiest division confrontation in Vietnam to date, costing the cavalry twenty-six dead and fifty-three wounded. More ominous to division staff was the disheartening realization that the North Vietnamese were excellent jungle fighters and masters of light infantry tactics. They maintained their aggressive spirit despite battlefield losses or sudden shifts in local advantage because of airmobile response.

For the next three days the 1st Brigade conducted company sweeps which netted only stragglers and evidence that the *33d NVA Regiment* had been split apart and chased from the area. By 9 November the region west of Plei Me was considered largely clear of enemy troops since the missing *32d NVA Regiment,* which had not been encountered, was now suspected of having slipped east of Plei Me. Col. Thomas W. Brown's 3d Brigade took over the 1st Brigade's search mission, but intended to move east toward the central highlands instead. However, field force command believed that the NVA were still concentrating along the western Cambodian border. Since Roberts's brigade had just completed twelve days of airmobile hopping through mostly empty territory, Brown decided to reinvestigate a sector where previous combat had flared up, but no follow-up ground sweep was conducted: the heavily jungled Ia Drang Valley. Although, "having drawn a blank up to this point, I wasn't sure what we would find or even if we'd find anything."[4] Colonel Brown possessed intelligence that an enemy base camp might exist there and thus give opportunity for decisive battle.

The North Vietnamese conveniently confirmed their continued presence west of Plei Me by mortaring Brown's 3d Brigade headquarters at the Cateckia Tea Plantation (southwest of Pleiku) just before midnight on 12 November. The brigade maneuvered its three fresh infantry and two artillery battalions westward, spearheaded by Stockton's ubiquitous 1st Squadron, 9th Cavalry. Lt. Col. Harold G. Moore's 1st Battalion of the 7th Cavalry was directed to begin searching the area around the Ia Drang near Chu Pong mountain on 14 November.

Lieutenant Colonel Moore was confident of NVA activity in the Ia Drang Valley. Suspecting possible trouble, Moore wanted his initial airlanded company to rapidly consolidate and the entire battalion landing expedited. He needed a field big enough to hold ten helicopters at once, and he personally conducted a reconnaissance flight over the rain forest canopy early on the designated morning of the air assault. Only two fields of that size existed, and one was full of jagged tree stumps. Moore quickly selected the other grassy clearing, coded LZ X-Ray, at the base of Chu Pong massif, and alerted supporting howitzers at nearby LZ Falcon to commence bombarding it.

Part of standard airmobile doctrine was breaking up possible enemy defenses around landing zones by firing artillery preparations on

4. Ltr, Col. Brown, Chief, CINCPAC J3 Current Ground Ops Branch, to Cpt Cash, DA Office of the Chief of Mil History, dtd 8 Aug 67, p. 2.

the chosen locations. To maintain a heavy volume of fire against the target, attack helicopters made rocket and machine gun runs across the LZ as the artillery fire was stopped or shifted. Troopships whirled in to land the infantry as the gunships made their final passes. Captain John Herren's Company B was air assaulted onto LZ X-Ray at 10:50 A.M. The cavalrymen did not meet immediate resistance as they moved through the grass and around the six-foot-high anthills to enter the woodline beyond. However, Lt. Al Deveny's 1st Platoon came under intense NVA fire in the scrub brush just after it crossed a dry creek.

Lt. Henry Herrick's 2d Platoon tried to link up with Deveny's pinned men, but was suddenly engulfed by intense fire from all sides and cut off. One four-man American machine gun team was wiped out, and North Vietnamese quickly turned the M60 weapon against the surrounded cavalrymen. Bullets clipped at grass-high level and slammed into the crumpled heaps of dead and wounded troops. The platoon survivors returned fire with their rifles flat against the dirt. Lieutenant Herrick and his platoon NCO, Sergeant First Class Palmer, were killed. By midafternoon, when squad leader Sgt. Clyde E. Savage assumed command after the other NCOs had been either killed or disabled, the original twenty-seven-man platoon had been reduced to only seven unwounded soldiers.

Within minutes after the Battle for LZ X-Ray began with the decimation of Herrick's platoon, it was apparent that Moore's battalion had tripped a hornet's nest. The majority of both *33d and 66th NVA Regiments* was located on the Chu Pong. Artillery and airstrikes pummeled the jungle with smoke-filled explosions, but failed to check the North Vietnamese infantrymen surging down the mountain slopes toward Company B's two platoons on the ridge. A steady rain of North Vietnamese mortar fires sent geysers of red dirt across the landing zone, and the thick pall of dust and smoke hindered fire support direction. Lieutenant Deal's reserve platoon was ordered to try to reach the trapped soldiers, even as Captain Herren heaved grenades at advancing NVA appearing in the high grass and streambeds on and around LZ X-Ray itself.

Lieutenant Colonel Moore set up his command post next to the emergency aid station at a large anthill in the center of the LZ and immediately called for the rest of his battalion. Helicopters darted in with Company C, doubling the number of Americans on the ground. When Capt. Ramon A. Nadal's Company A arrived next, Moore used them to reinforce the escalating firefight at the creekbed. Unfortunately, the situation deteriorated too fast to permit airlanding of Capt. Louis R. "Ray" Lefebvre's Company D. Accurate NVA automatic weapons fire swept the entire landing zone and even peppered the command anthill. Several Company D troopers were killed or wounded before their helicopters touched down, and Moore was forced to wave off further troopships.

Company B was embroiled in the most desperate fighting on the high ground just beyond the stream. Captain Nadal of Company A sent one of his platoons under Lt. Walter J. "Joe" Marm, Jr., to assist the breakthrough attempt by Deal's platoon of Company B, which was already advancing toward its isolated comrades. Lieutenant Marm formed his men in a line of skirmish to catch up, but the gap between him and Deal's platoon proved most fortuitous. By following behind Company B in the dense tropical vegetation, Marm's troops were able to mow down scores of fresh NVA soldiers who were moving around Company B's rear and unaware his platoon was closing the gap.

The North Vietnamese turned to charge Marm's platoon and flank his unit by scrambling past them into the creekbed, but succeeded only in running into the rest of Nadal's Company A, which was taking up positions in the gully. The sudden clash surprised both sides, and firing erupted at extremely close range. Lt. Bob Taft of the forward platoon was killed instantly, and radio communications silenced. The cavalrymen in the creekbed shoot-out reeled from the shock of the firefight, leaving Taft's body and a wounded trooper behind. Captain Nadal and his radioman, Sergeant Gill, jumped into the creek channel and pulled out the fallen men.

Farther uphill the violence of the North Vietnamese attack defeated all attempts to reach the shattered 2d Platoon. Increasing numbers of NVA reinforcements used frontal assaults and encircling movements to force the rest of Company B to fall back on Marm's platoon and retreat toward the creek. Both Companies A and B combined to form a defensive line facing the Chu Pong mountain, employing the waist-high creekbed as a trench. With these two depleted companies tied in to cover the LZ's western perimeter, Moore sent Capt. Robert H. Edward's Company C to defend the southern sector. His men had just assumed positions when they were charged by massed North Vietnamese infantry attempting to overrun the landing zone from a new direction. This attack was broken up, but another NVA group tried to penetrate between the two companies at the creek. Moore sent in his last reserves, the few troops of Company D under Captain LeFebvre, who had managed to land before the other helicopter insertions had been canceled. The NVA were blocked, but American losses were high. S. Sgt. George Gonzales took over the company remnants after LeFebvre was severely wounded.

Lieutenant Colonel Moore took advantage of a midafternoon respite to airland the rest of his battalion with the loss of only two helicopters. He reconstituted the emergency reserve and parceled out replacements throughout the perimeter. At the creek bottom Companies A and B took advantage of the slackening combat level to launch another counterattack aimed at reaching the isolated 2d Platoon. The cavalrymen surged forward at 4:20 P.M., but were fiercely opposed by well-camouflaged NVA soldiers occupying spider holes dug into the slope's dense tangle of shrubbery and bamboo thickets. Many troops were hit at point-blank range as they continued to struggle uphill.

Lieutenant Marm inspired his men forward by personal example, valiantly destroying one NVA machine gun nest with grenades (an act which earned him the first Medal of Honor awarded the division in Vietnam), but he was shot through the head and critically wounded. Several key forward observers were killed, and soon the entire artillery liaison radio frequency was swamped by undisciplined and frantic calls for urgent fire support. With crucial artillery direction hampered and casualties mounting in the face of more NVA crew-served weapons pits, the momentum of attack was lost. Lieutenant Colonel Moore resorted to an old Korean War trick, calling in white phosphorus rounds on top of the leading cavalrymen to enable the companies to break contact and regroup at the creek before twilight.

One of the foremost dangers of air assaulting infantry into unknown territory was the chance that units would be projected too close to larger enemy formations under unfavorable circumstances. This concern was counterbalanced by the division's need to force combat against an enemy reluctant to engage on other than his own terms. Therefore, airmobile commanders were trained to act boldly, even if such action meant risking adverse battle situations. Airmobile doctrine was to strike hard and fast, and reserves were counted on to redress the inevitable lack of proper but time-consuming battleground preparation. The trouble at LZ X-Ray resulted from the fact that Colonel Brown had insufficient reserves available to assist Moore's beleaguered battalion.

The rest of Colonel Brown's brigade was widely scattered in other ongoing sweep operations, and only one company was ready for rapid commitment to LZ X-Ray. This was the brigade's own base security element—Company B, 2d Battalion, 7th Cavalry, under Capt. Myron Diduryk. The company was airlifted to bolster Moore's battalion that evening, but this move only provided some extra manpower if battalion survival was jeopardized during the night. To provide enough strength to reverse the North Vietnamese battlefield initiative, other battalions were required. Beginning that afternoon, the rest of Lt. Col. Robert A. McDade's 2d Battalion, 7th Cavalry, was airmobiled west to LZ Macon, closer to X-Ray, but marshy ground there forced the helicopters to land on more-distant LZ Columbus instead.

In the meantime Lt. Col. Robert B. Tully's 2d Battalion of the 5th Cavalry was put back together at LZ Victor, but the assembly required time and led to other complications. The lack of helicopters, impending nightfall, and Brown's desire to avoid landing troops on a small LZ under fire after dark delayed Tully's departure until the next morning. The battalion was ordered to march overland to LZ X-Ray at first light, instead of using helicopter movement, because Brown "didn't relish the idea of moving a steady stream of helicopters into an LZ as hot as X-Ray," and he "was sure a foot move would be unobserved and the battalion might come in behind the enemy."[5]

Company C of Tully's battalion, under Capt. Edward A. Boyt, was searching through dense forest late that afternoon when word was received to cease operations and prepare the company for immediate helicopter extraction. Boyt was told they would be shuttled to LZ Victor overnight and form part of the relief expedition to X-Ray. His attached engineers frantically cleared a small landing zone out of the woods before sunset, using thirty pounds of explosives and breaking seventeen entrenching tools in the process. As the company was lifted out by helicopter, Boyt glimpsed the ongoing Battle of LZ X-Ray in the distance. It resembled a heavy ground fog with dancing splotches

5. Ibid., p. 3.

of colors, which he knew were produced by the discharge of dyed smoke grenades. He recalled thinking, "Oh hell, this is it!"[6]

Moore's men endured a restless but uneventful night on LZ X-Ray, and at dawn on 15 November patrols were sent forward beyond the foxholes. On the perimeter's southern side these cavalrymen were suddenly struck and overwhelmed by an NVA human-wave assault. The North Vietnamese soldiers charged across the elephant grass and through a series of multiple explosions as final defensive artillery shells and rockets pounded the earth. Cavalry grenadier and automatic rifle fire joined in hammering the NVA ranks, but the attack closed too fast to be defeated in front of the foxholes. The screaming North Vietnamese infantrymen bounded into the cavalry lines with bayonets fixed to their AK47 rifles. The melee of hand-to-hand combat was punctuated by rifle bursts fired from the hip. Individual struggles sometimes ended in mutual death as soldiers of both sides were sent spinning into the dirt. Captain Edwards was struck down as he radioed urgently for help.

A heavy cross fire ripped across the entire landing zone. Sergeant First Class McCawley led Company A's 2d Platoon out of the creekbed and tried to cross over the field to reinforce the southern side. His counterattack was stalled by a hail of gunfire near an anthill midway there. The North Vietnamese stormed the extended frontage held by Company D, an attack which threatened to overrun the nearby battalion mortars. Several perimeter sectors were under simultaneous attack, and the entire situation became chaotic. Supporting fires and airstrikes were brought in as close as possible and ordnance spilled into friendly lines. In many instances combatants were intermixed and any distinguishable edge of battle ceased to exist. The array of colored marking smoke mixed with thick clouds of powder and haze drifting over the battlefield.

Lieutenant Colonel Moore exerted a forceful, professional coolness in the midst of the confusion and near panic. One A1E Skyraider misdropped napalm close by his central command post, setting all the stacked rifle ammunition and grenade reserves on fire. Air Force F4C Phantoms and F100 fighter-bombers streaked in low over the horizon to hurl bomb clusters into the midst of massing North Vietnamese

6. Ltr, Capt. Boyt, Co D, USAINTS, dtd 20 Nov 67, p. 1.

infantry. The NVA attack waves disintegrated under this prompt air support, enabling the fatigued and hard-pressed cavalrymen to hold their positions during the most critical hours.

Just a mile and a half away, at LZ Victor, Tully's relief battalion began marching toward the din of battle at 8:00 A.M. Captain Boyt's company led one of the two columns as they advanced over a small ridgeline and brushed past a few sniper teams. Effective support fire was kept close by, and artillery rounds were lobbed into the woods around them. Tully's troops reached LZ X-Ray at noon. Although the movement failed in Brown's optimistic desire to trap NVA units between Moore's defending battalion and Tully's advancing one, the linkup relieved much of the danger. The North Vietnamese pulled back shortly after the reinforcing battalion arrived.

Lieutenant Colonel Moore's first task was to rescue the isolated platoon. The decimated unit was charged three times during the night, but each assault was defeated by the close-in shellfire directed by Sergeant Savage. The platoon position was reached and the wounded survivors and dead evacuated downslope. The rest of the day was spent consolidating positions, while Major General Kinnard dispatched another battalion, Lt. Col. Frederic Ackerson's 1st Battalion of the 5th Cavalry, to Colonel Brown's brigade base.

During the night, the NVA made two probes against LZ X-Ray positions. On the morning of 16 November, Diduryk's company became engaged in a firefight while searching the broken ground outside the perimeter. The company broke contact under covering artillery fire and called in airstrikes. A later sweep of the battlefield satisfied one of Moore's last major concerns, when the bodies of three missing battalion members were discovered. Although pesky North Vietnamese sniper fire continued, the Battle for LZ X-Ray was over. No attempt was made to go into the Chu Pong after the North Vietnamese, because B52 bombing strikes were now planned against the mountain. The men of Moore's battalion were airlifted to Pleiku for rest and reorganization. LZ X-Ray was occupied by both Tully's and Mc-Dade's battalions for another night and then abandoned on 17 November.[7]

---

7. U.S. units present at the Battle for LZ X-Ray were 1st Battalion, 7th Cavalry; Company A and B, 2d Battalion, 7th Cavalry; Company C, 8th

Tully's battalion went back to LZ Columbus while McDade's battalion moved overland to meet helicopters at a field coded LZ Albany, six miles away. McDade's order of march was led by Company A, followed by the battalion reconnaissance platoon, Company C, Company D, the battalion command group, and Company A from Ackerson's recently arrived battalion (this final company replaced McDade's own Company B, which fought hard at LZ X-Ray and was airlifted to Pleiku with Moore's personnel). The long, winding column pushed northwest through the tropical forest and high elephant grass.

The first elements had already reached LZ Albany when the *8th Battalion, 66th NVA Regiment*, attacked the length of the column. The ferocity and scale of the ambush split the battalion in two. Machine gun, grenade, and automatic rifle fire raked the cavalry ranks as snipers shot down leaders and radiomen. The middle of the column caved in under the force of the attack as North Vietnamese soldiers charged completely through the cavalry lines in several places. As the column was shattered, the battle disintegrated into a largely leaderless gel of individual melees and skirmishes between splintered groups.

Some soldiers were in a state of shock, running and firing at everything. Others were locked in a vortex of close-quarters fighting. Arriving North Vietnamese reinforcements were sent straight into battle without discarding their heavy combat packs. Dead and wounded men were strewn across fields littered with military accoutrements and smashed brushwood. There were hardly any field dressings, water, or transmission of orders. To many, it seemed that the air was filled with a sleet of bullets.

Throughout the action, groups of cavalrymen rushed toward nearby patches of open grassland, mistaking them for the landing zone and thereby actually running deeper into the ambush. The terrified troops were either frozen to the ground or crawled on their elbows, pistols and rifles propped up in wildly shaking hands. Slithering along the grass, they pushed aside clumps of foliage to fire directly into the

Engineer Battalion, and three demolitions teams; 229th Pathfinder Team (Provisional), 11th Aviation Group; artillery liaison and forward observer sections of the 1st Battalion, 21st Artillery. Losses were KIA: 79, WIA: 121. NVA killed by body count were 634 with more than 1,000 more casualties estimated; 6 were captured.

faces of enemy soldiers also wriggling through the same singed and cratered earth. Grenade explosions and the incessant rattle of small arms fire never drowned out the shrill cries for medics and the chilling screams of death. One veteran remembered the battle only as "a massacre."[8]

For hours the amorphous battle prevented artillery and tactical air support, but by midafternoon two large, ragged pockets of American resistance had formed. The stunned remnants of Company C joined McDade's command group, which combined to fight west toward the clearing where both Company A and the recon platoon were making their stands. Company D and the 5th Cavalry's Company A were separated and pushed to the east by the flow of battle. This gave enough semblance to the battlefield to enable rocket-firing helicopters to sweep across the front, followed by close-range napalm bombing. The roaring fireballs spewed across the burning grass and through onrushing NVA riflemen, although some Americans trapped outside the treeline were also burned to death.

Once again brigade reinforcing options were found wanting. Colonel Brown at the brigade's tea plantation base possessed only a single company available for immediate deployment. This was Company B of McDade's original command, already depleted at X-Ray and recuperating at Pleiku. At dusk the unit was flown into the main LZ Albany pocket of resistance. The tempo of fighting tapered off at nightfall, and Company B of Ackerson's battalion marched from LZ Columbus toward the other defensive pocket. The company reached the eastern perimeter, which was held by sister Company A (at the tail of McDade's original column), at 10:00 P.M. A continuous ring of artillery shellfire and aircraft flare illumination around the surrounded perimeters discouraged further mass NVA attacks.

The killing continued outside the perimeters as NVA soldiers combed the woods seeking out lost or wounded Americans. Automatic gunfire lashed through the forests, sending rounds ricocheting off darkened trees. Shadows crossed and wobbled under parachuted flares sinking to earth. Volunteers made repeated forays beyond the main lines into this eerie, artificial half-light to bring in wounded

8. Sp4 Jack P. Smith, "Death in the Ia Drang Valley," *Saturday Evening Post*.

comrades from the open. Sometimes the cavalry rescue parties and stretcher teams encountered so many wounded that only a few could be carried back. The wounded dragged themselves after full litters until they collapsed or lost consciousness.

The North Vietnamese retreated as daylight approached, and McDade's battalion was assembled around LZ Albany on 18 November. The other main pocket of soldiers, consisting mostly of 5th Cavalry troops, withdrew to LZ Columbus under Ackerson's control. McDade's troops spent the rest of the day searching the battlefield to find the wounded and missing, recover the dead, and collect equipment. Although an NVA attack was made against LZ Columbus that evening, the sanguinary Battle of LZ Albany was the last major action of the Ia Drang Valley campaign.[9]

On 20 November Col. William R. Lynch's 2d Brigade relieved Brown's brigade, but the fresh airmobile battalions made only meager contacts as the NVA retreated into Cambodia. North Vietnamese cohesion and battlefield staying power had been destroyed by weeks of unrelenting division air assault pressure and heavy losses. Below the division's wide-ranging Huey helicopters, the fields and patches of woodland were finally clear of North Vietnamese troops. A 9th Cavalry scoutship rescued Pfc. Toby Braveboy (Co A, 2d Bn, 7th Cavalry), who had been twice wounded in the LZ Albany battle on 17 November, when he was sighted waving his T-shirt from a jungle clearing on 24 November. Two days later Operation SILVER BAYONET was officially terminated. The Ia Drang Valley campaign was over.

During a month of sustained action, the 1st Cavalry Division (Airmobile) sought out, located, and met the regular NVA on the field of battle and won some of its fiercest Vietnam encounters. Helicopter-delivered infantry dominated the zone of operations, setting the future pace of wartime airmobility and validating the revolutionary role of aerial cavalry as originally perceived by General Gavin. Many suspected doctrinal truths about airmobility were verified. Airmobile operations had to be characterized by careful planning and followed by

---

9. Casualties in the Battle of LZ Albany on 17 November 1965 were KIA: 151, WIA: 121, and MIA: 4. NVA losses were 403 killed and confirmed by body count with many more losses suspected.

deliberate, bold, and violent execution. While the division could helicopter its troops throughout the battle zone, regardless of terrain restrictions, faster than any other organization and decisively engage distant enemy units by vertical air assault, this flexible striking power placed a very high premium on thorough preparation and the availability of sufficient reserves.

Numerous problems arose in the course of the bitterly fought campaign. Unexpected levels of combat outstripped division capability to reinforce adverse situations, especially in the Battles of LZs X-Ray and Albany, where the lack of properly assembled reserves almost resulted in disaster. The inability of aerial firepower alone to effectively stop NVA close assaults was manifested in the Battle of LZ Albany and a number of other firefights. The October division logistical crises produced severe shortages of essential supply stocks, such as aviation fuel, during the entire period. There were initial difficulties maintaining radio communications over the long distances involved, although orbiting CV2 radio relay aircraft offered a partial solution. The division spent the month of December rebuilding its logistical posture, extensively overhauling its overworked helicopters and equipment, and replacing personnel.

The frightful casualty levels seriously eroded division strength. In the two months of October and November the division suffered 334 killed, 736 wounded, 364 nonbattle injuries, and 2,828 cases of malaria, scrub typhus, and other serious diseases. This total represented more than 25 percent of the division's authorized strength (15,955). Even though many men were eventually returned to their units, the division used 5,211 replacements to complete rebuilding by the end of the year. Division assigned strength thus stood at 16,732 in December, but nearly a third (31 percent) were newly assigned. Such a high turnover rate invariably created turmoil and reduced overall efficiency.[10]

Despite the significant problems and high cost, the division's Ia Drang Valley campaign remained a magnificent military accomplishment. An initial North Vietnamese victory over Camp Plei Me was prevented by the 1st Cavalry Division's presence in the region. The

---

10. Personnel statistics from 1st Cavalry Division, *Quarterly Command Report for Second Fiscal Quarter FY 66*, pp. 5, 25.

strategic provincial capital of Pleiku was the key to the central highlands and could not be stripped of protection. No South Vietnamese force would have been spared to help Plei Me without divisional assurance that the city would be safeguarded in its absence. When the relief column was ambushed, division artillery coordination kept the advance moving and insured the breakthrough into Plei Me.

Once the siege was broken, MACV ordered Major General Kinnard's division to locate the NVA forces and render them ineffective. Three brigades were sent in close succession to search out a vast, normally inaccessible territorial wilderness. The North Vietnamese forces withdrawing from Plei Me were unprepared to cope with the division's new style of airmobile warfare. Nothing in NVA training or experience had taught its soldiers how to deal with close helicopter pursuit. The *33d NVA Regiment* was hounded from the area and routed from its normal hiding places. However, the largest enemy units were located through unintended meeting engagements.

The Battles of LZs X-Ray and Albany were both initiated by unexpected North Vietnamese troop concentrations in hostile terrain. The division's campaign losses in large part reflected the severity of such encounters. The ratio of killed to wounded was 334 to 736, or 1:2.2., considerably higher than the 1:4 experienced in World War II and Korea. Most of the battle wounds were caused by small arms fire, with a very large number of head and chest hits, and very few wounds resulted from shell fragments. Most of those killed suffered multiple bullet impacts. The outcome of both actions was decided by massive air and artillery support, as well as by the individual courage and fighting stamina of the division's ground troops.

In the final analysis the Ia Drang Valley campaign was military history's first division-scale air assault victory. The 1st Cavalry Division accomplished all of its assigned objectives. Airmobile reinforcement insured the survival of a remote but critical outpost; cavalry surveillance followed and found the enemy, and cavalry air assault brought the enemy into battle and pinpointed his strongpoints. Major General Kinnard resorted to strategic B52 bombing to shatter these jungled redoubts once they were identified, as in the Chu Pong after LZ X-Ray. In the process two regular North Vietnamese Army regiments were largely annihilated and had to be completely reformed in Cambodia.

The 1st Battalion of the 7th Cavalry returned to LZ X-Ray in April 1966. It wasn't a sentimental visit, as the battalion was providing security for two artillery batteries and preparing to air assault onto the Chu Pong massif. Most of the original battalion members had departed, but there were still quite a few veterans of the original X-Ray battle serving with the unit. Sgt. Steven Hansen had been a forward observer in Captain Nadal's Company A on that fateful day. Now he was a mortar sergeant in Company D.

Sergeant Hansen paced the old perimeter line and gently stepped across the open field. He still remained uneasy standing in the peaceful, grassy clearing where so many troopers had fallen under a hailstorm of bullets. Signs of the battle remained: lots of discarded gear from both sides, a set of American dog tags, and even bone fragments in front of the overgrown foxhole line. In contrast to later engagements, the North Vietnamese had not bothered to bury their dead at LZ X-Ray.

To Sergeant Hansen, the sight of so many howitzers pointing their muzzled tubes at the sky, with their crews lounging nearby, looked out of place on the curled grass of LZ X-Ray, almost as an affront to the sacred soil he stood upon. He remembered the heroism of his comrades, the bone weariness and mental fatigue of the heavy fighting, and how men's speech became halting and hardly audible, if anyone spoke at all. He gazed at the anthill used as Moore's command post; the same mound was being used by his new battalion commander, Lt. Col. Raymond Kampe. When Captain Coleman asked about his feelings, Hansen replied slowly, "It gives me a funny feeling to walk around a place where so many died. In a way I'm glad we came back, but I'd still just rather forget the whole thing."[11]

11. *Army Times*, 11 May 1966, p. 32.

CHAPTER 4

Sustained Pursuit

Techniques, 1966 Coastal Campaign

The 1st Cavalry Division's hard-won victory in the Ia Drang Valley was especially important to the allied cause. Before the introduction of the airmobile division to central South Vietnam, MACV was largely powerless to counteract growing Viet Cong influence in this critical region. In harmony with the 1966 allied buildup and burgeoning offensive activity, General Westmoreland ordered Major General Kinnard's division to help clear II Corps Tactical Zone from the border to the coast.

Throughout the new year the airmobile cavalry continued to sweep the rugged central highland interior and strike at North Vietnamese regiments venturing out of Cambodia. However, as the 4th Infantry Division became established in the Pleiku vicinity and took over responsibility for western II CTZ, the 1st Cavalry Division concentrated its major efforts against the Viet Cong–dominated ricelands and adjacent mountain strongholds of Connecticut-size Binh Dinh Province along the South China Sea. MACV's ultimate goal was to break the VC grip over the densely populated and agriculturally important eastern portion of the province and to return this National Priority Area to government control, but this was impossible as long as the region remained unsecure to South Vietnamese authorities.

The geography of the central highlands compressed the fertile, extensively cultivated lowlands into a series of valleys surrounded by jagged ridgelines crowding toward the ocean. Clearing the VC/NVA out of their maze of fortified hamlets and hidden jungle bases throughout the region required the continual application of multidirectional pressure. This style of area warfare differed radically from the linear frontline tactics of conflicts in other wars. Most objectives had to be reswept several times, and troops fought over familiar battlefields. The directionless nature of area warfare often frustrated conventional military solutions, but it offered ideal circumstances for an airmobile division to exercise a basic cavalry task. From late-January Tet-66 through mid-February Tet-67, the 1st Cavalry Division waged a relentless year-long drive against NVA/VC forces throughout eastern Binh Dinh Province. The succession of operations included MASHER/WHITE WING, JIM BOWIE, DAVY CROCKETT, CRAZY HORSE, THAYER I, IRVING, and THAYER II, and they represented the first airmobile application of sustained cavalry pursuit.

Pursuit is an offensive action against a retreating enemy. Rapid helicopter mobility favored fluid pursuit operations. Throughout the 1966 coastal campaign the 1st Cavalry Division sought to push NVA/VC units out of their areas of influence, using aerial reconnaissance to disclose enemy locations and then triggering their retreat with helicopter assaults and superior firepower. Ideally, airmobile infantry would envelop the retreating enemy and block escape routes. The division realized that terrain and distance presented serious obstacles, but counted on massive helicopter employment to minimize these problems. Airmobility enabled the attack to be carried into the remote tropical valleys and mist-shrouded canyons which served as the main Viet Cong bases. The division hoped to turn these previously impervious VC redoubts into chokepoints, where the retreating enemy could be finally entrapped and eliminated.

The opening blow of this campaign was Operation MASHER/WHITE WING, which commenced immediately after the Vietnamese Tet holidays on 25 January 1966. The 3d Brigade, commanded by newly promoted Col. Harold G. Moore, was directed to find and destroy a major enemy regimental recruiting and rice supply center near Bong Son. The cavalrymen became embroiled in heavy combat against a well-defended Viet Cong village at the outset, and this initial confrontation escalated into intense fighting across the brigade front. Airmobile pursuit was initiated, and within three weeks the majority of the 1st Cavalry Division was committed against a full NVA/VC division consisting of the *18th NVA, 22d NVA,* and *2d VC Regiments.*

On the misty foggy morning of 28 January, a phalanx of helicopters combat assaulted Lieutenant Colonel McDade's 2d Battalion, 7th Cavalry, onto the shoreline four miles north of Bong Son. McDade's battalion was having unusually bad luck. His battalion was largely rebuilt after the unfortunate battle at LZ Albany, but a C123 crash outside An Khe caused forty-two deaths in one line company being transported to the Bong Son area before the operation even started. The battalion's first air assault of MASHER was violently opposed as Viet Cong machine gunners hidden in the clusters of beachfront hootches fired into the low-flying aircraft. The helicopters broke formation to avoid the automatic weapons fire and scattered Capt. John Fesmire's Company C in small groups across one thousand yards of open sand in close proximity to Cu Nghi. The village, which surrounded much of the landing zone, was staunchly defended by VC entrenched in earthworks, palm groves, and bamboo thickets. This concealed network of VC mortars, snipers, and machine gun bunkers prevented the separated company from maneuvering.

McDade's other air assault element, understrength Company A commanded by Capt. Joel Sugdinis, landed some distance south of Fesmire. The unit moved overland through numerous hamlets to reach the isolated landing zone, but was stopped just short of its objective. Colonel Moore's brigade was soon mired in combat throughout its axis of advance. Within an hour four CH47 Chinooks were shot down and twelve UH1D Huey troopships badly damaged; by midafternoon twenty-eight helicopters were grounded. One Chinook sling-loading a 105mm howitzer was forced down, and Company B of Lieutenant Colonel Kampe's 1st Battalion, 7th Cavalry, contested the crash site with the Viet Cong. The company finally secured the location by manhandling the artillery piece into firing position, leveling its tube, and firing rounds directly into the charging VC.

At Cu Nghi, Fesmire's men grimly held their positions as the light rain turned into a cold, soaking drizzle. Artillery support was ordered stopped for fear of hitting friendly troops. Captain Sugdinis's advance to reach Fesmire was stalled by VC machine gun nests covering the wet rice paddy between the two companies. The leading troops of Company A could see colored signal smoke from Fesmire's command, but VC automatic weapons fire prevented them from linking up. After an extended firefight in the flat ricefield, both VC weapons positions were destroyed and the drenched American reinforcements reached the main battlefield. Lieutenant Colonel McDade attempted to bring in additional men from Company B late that afternoon, using an artillery barrage to seal off the LZ's eastern perimeter, but all six helicopters were hit by VC fire from positions not masked by the shellfire. He waited until after dark to bring in desperately needed ammunition and medical supplies, but another incoming helicopter was shot down. During the night the exhausted cavalrymen regrouped behind the village's sand burial mounds in the howling wind and rain as enemy grenadiers and snipers intensified their volume of fire.

The air cavalry's mainstay, tactical air support, became available after daybreak. The low overcast lifted enough to permit low-level bombing runs by jet aircraft. Air Force fighter-bombers napalmed village dwellings and trenches, detonating enemy ammunition stocks and causing large fires. Artillery bombarded the front throughout the rest of the morning as Colonel Moore arrived with Lieutenant Colonel Ingram's 2d Battalion, 12th Cavalry, and Kampe's battalion airmobiled into blocking positions north of the village. The cavalrymen overmastered some of the interlocking fortifications and tunnels, but spent another night under close-range fire from the uncleared village. The next day Colonel Moore's combined battalions forced the *7th and 9th Battalions, 22d NVA Regiment*, to retreat from the village. The three-day action in the Cu Nghi vicinity was costly and confused and generally marred by poor coordination between cavalry elements as a result of the weather and unanticipated ferocity of enemy resistance. The battle cost the cavalry 121 killed and another 220 wounded (660 enemy bodies were counted), but division pursuit operations could now be initiated.[1]

On 4 February 1966, as Colonel Moore's 3d Brigade prepared to press pursuit operations to the southwest into the An Lao Valley, the division reinforced the drive with Colonel Lynch's 2d Brigade. On the same day, the cavalry offensive was renamed WHITE WING after President Johnson angrily protested that the original operational title, MASHER, did not reflect "pacification emphasis." The An Lao Valley had been controlled by the Viet Cong since South Vietnam had been created. The valley was one of the most fertile agricultural basins of central South Vietnam, but also one of the most rugged and

---

1. 1st Cav Div, *Seven Month History and Briefing Data, September–March 1966*, dtd 9 June 67; 1st Cav Div, *Operational Report on Lessons Learned*, dtd 5 May 66.

dangerous. Several reconnaissance teams of Special Forces elite Project DELTA (Detachment B-52) were inserted into the valley in conjunction with the division's search pattern, but were quickly overwhelmed and destroyed.

The opening brigade airmobile assault was delayed two days by monsoon storms, marking the first time in division airmobile experience that a major cavalry operation was precluded by adverse weather. The NVA/VC forces used the opportunity to effect an unimpeded retreat as heavy clouds cloaked the densely forested mountainsides and disgorged torrential rains. Pursuing cavalry entered the valley only to find recently abandoned defensive positions.

Opponents of aerial cavalry most often cited its susceptibility to enemy anti-air weapons and weather conditions as valid reasons to discourage the concept. In Vietnam the absence of enemy aircraft and sophisticated antiair defenses meant that weather extremes represented the only real detriment to divisional mobility. However, these opponents considered Vietnam's tropical climate severe enough to undermine airmobile divisional effectiveness. During Operation MASHER/WHITE WING the division deliberately continued to rely on its helicopters and persevered with cavalry pursuit operations despite unfavorable wind and rain conditions. Major General Kinnard proved his division capable of maintaining pressure against an elusive, retreating enemy despite periods of forced inactivity.

Major General Kinnard used Colonel Lynch's newly introduced brigade to search the An Lao Valley mountains. He shifted the division's major pursuit effort farther south by diverting Colonel Moore's brigade into the Kim Son ("Crow's Foot") Valley region. The area was named the Crow's Foot after the shape of the surrounding valley hills on a military contour map. The eight twisting ridgelines around the Crow's Foot compress the bottomland into seven valleys which contain numerous streams and a fast-flowing river. Like the An Lao Valley, this secluded area was an ideal Viet Cong base. It provided concealment and innumerable hiding places for food and weapons caches, controlled entrances and numerous escape routes, excellent water and rice-growing resources, and complete absence of government control over the pro-VC local populace.

Colonel Moore altered his tactics upon entering the Kim Son, deliberately fragmenting his brigade and utilizing terrain in an attempt

to outmaneuver any Viet Cong evasion. Helicopters first searched out
the many natural valley avenues. Then, using deceptive landings and
other flight patterns to confuse enemy scouts, company-size forces
with two days' rations were carefully emplaced on the hills and ridges
dominating the valley exits. On 11 February the splintered brigade
began maneuvering from the hilltops toward the valley floor, while
supporting artillery pummeled ravines and trails. Many dead Viet Cong
were found downslope where they had been caught by the shower of
artillery and rocket fire. The brigade continued its pursuit mode
throughout the nights as patrols sortied under flare illumination, attempting to flush out the VC toward prepared ambush positions. The
fire missions and ambuscades netted 249 enemy dead at the cost of
only 6 cavalrymen killed. One VC battalion headquarters was located
through documents found on a fallen enemy soldier, and Captain Diduryk's company of McDade's battalion was airlifted near the Soui
Run River to pinpoint the unit before it could escape.

Captain Diduryk's company clashed against prepared VC positions along the densely jungled streambank on the morning of 15 February. Accurate defensive fire stalled two of his platoons, and decisive action was essential to prevent Viet Cong withdrawal before
airmobile reinforcements arrived. An airstrike was promptly called
for, and just before noon, as the last bombs were falling, the 3d Platoon fixed bayonets and charged the entrenched Viet Cong across the
stream. The fury of this frontal assault at bayonet point unnerved the
defenders, who fled their lines directly into the pathway of rocket-
firing helicopters and company machine guns. The élan and courage
of the cavalrymen carried the field, enabling Diduryk's men to thoroughly defeat two VC main force companies before evening. This
First Team spirit fused the dash of cavalry enterprise with modern
airmobile lethality to power the 1st Cavalry Division war engine
throughout the Vietnam conflict.

The persistent pace of pursuit was maintained the next day as
Colonel Moore's brigade was switched with Colonel Roberts's fresh
1st Brigade. The new brigade rapidly helicoptered into the virtually
inaccessible lower portion of the Kim Son Valley. Lt. Col. Edward
C. Meyer's 2d Battalion of the 5th Cavalry helicoptered into the narrow jungle river bottom between densely forested mountain crags,
and shortly afterward Company B was engulfed by devastating fire
from an upslope heavy weapons battalion of the *18th NVA Regiment*.

The intense recoilless rifle, mortar, and machine gun fire temporarily wiped out artillery liaison and locked the entire battalion into a grueling standoff. The engagement was decided that evening when airmobile reinforcements were flexibly inserted behind the enemy lines, and the NVA were driven from their commanding positions.

On the same day, interrogation of a captured NVA battalion commander by Colonel Lynch's brigade staff revealed the location of the *22d NVA Regiment* on the eastern edge of the Kim Son Valley. Lieutenant Colonel Ackerson's battalion (1/5th Cav) led the attack, but became deadlocked in combat against entrenched NVA defending the main camp. Frontal assaults against the formidable earthworks were mired in the thick tropical foliage as hidden machine gun bunkers built flush to the ground suddenly opened fire and cut apart the advancing platoons. Casualties had to be left where they fell, and fighting raged for days around the extensive jungle stronghold. The stalemate was punctuated by attacks and counterattacks on both sides. One of the most serious North Vietnamese sallies was defeated on 20 February after Company A's command post was nearly overrun by three different assault waves. During this period, thirty-three separate battalion attacks, each supported by massive artillery and rocket expenditures, failed to breach the enemy bastion.

North Vietnamese forces trapped in the Kim Son Valley by the sustained cavalry pursuit desperately defended their base, and MACV decided to employ strategic B52 bombers to finish the job. Ackerson's battalion was pulled back on 21 February as the objective area was subjected to high-altitude bombing and then saturated with riot gas. The battalion moved back unopposed into leveled forests and cratered remnants of the NVA position. They found shattered trees tossed through wooden blockhouse ruins, interconnecting tunnels, and even underground stove facilities. The encounter amply demonstrated the futility of defending territory against a determined aerial cavalry onslaught to the North Vietnamese. Contact became increasingly sporadic during the following week. The division terminated its Kim Son (Crow's Foot) Valley sweep at the end of the month. The valley claimed nearly a battalion's worth of American casualties (107 dead and 561 wounded compared to 710 NVA/VC bodies counted), but airmobile pursuit successfully penetrated and led to the elimination of a major enemy redoubt.

The division completed forty-one days of hard campaigning as

Colonel Lynch's brigade scoured the reputed VC stronghold of the seaside Cay Giep Mountains before coming full circle back into the Bong Son Plains. The troops were lowered onto the forested Cay Giep hillmass by CH47-dropped Jacob's ladders suspended through bomb-created clearings, but found few Viet Cong. Operation MASHER/WHITE WING, the harshest test of airmobile durability to date, ended on 6 March 1966.[2]

Major General Kinnard reaffirmed the airmobile division's staying power in a harsh environment, contrasting sharply with the gently rolling, uninhabited landscape and favorable climatic conditions of the fall 1965 Ia Drang Valley campaign. The 1st Cavalry Division pressed through monsoon rainstorms and fortified NVA/VC defenses to drive the enemy out of villages and mountain hideouts in four main base areas. The effectiveness of modern cavalry pursuit was verified as the division cut a wide circle through a formerly uncontested, densely populated swath of Viet Cong territory. During this time, division aviation flew 77,627 sorties, which included airlifting 120,585 cavalry troops (data includes multiple lifts of the same personnel).[3]

The 1st Cavalry Division's operations were less successful when conducted in response to faulty allied intelligence, a common problem throughout the Vietnam War. For instance, Major General Kinnard retaliated against a Viet Cong raid on the division's An Khe base camp by sending two brigades into the suspected 3,000-strong "Kon Truck" VC staging area during the rest of March (Operation JIM BOWIE). The expedition forced the 1st and 3d Brigades to conduct a fruitless search through very difficult tropical terrain containing few landing zones. Lt. Col. Robert J. Malley's 8th Engineer Battalion airlifted teams with minidozers to carve out fragile clearings on the edge of steep ridgelines and rocky pinnacles. Helicopters swarmed over the sun-baked valleys and deployed a multitude of ambush patrols, which only confirmed that the Viet Cong had executed an orderly withdrawal several days prior to the operation.

The division incurred a large number of losses in spite of the scant opposition. The brigades suffered 380 casualties, mostly from

2. 1st Cav Div, *Combat Operations After Action Report*, dtd 28 Apr 66.
3. 1st Cav Div, *Operational Report on Lessons Learned*, dtd 5 May 66, Appendix 4-3, Aviation Data.

punji-stake wounds and a series of fire-related mishaps. The elephant grass near one landing zone was set ablaze by aerial rocket fire, and the fire was almost extinguished when a hovering Chinook fanned the flames anew. The raging inferno raced two hundred yards through the grass and engulfed an entire mortar platoon. While Operation JIM BOWIE was a marked failure at finding the VC, claiming only 27 confirmed dead, it proved a valuable exercise in refining airmobile doctrine under adverse terrain conditions.[4]

The division was now firmly established in Vietnam, and its record of battlefield success was evident by Viet Cong avoidance of the unit wherever possible. Much of the division's success was directly due to Maj. Gen. Harry W. O. Kinnard, who created the first air assault force in military history and tranformed it into the Army's first airmobile fighting division. He relinquished command of the 1st Cavalry Division to Maj. Gen. John "Jack" Norton on 6 May 1966.

Major General Norton, the son of Col. Augustus Norton, was born 14 April 1918 at Fort Monroe, Virginia. He graduated as first captain of the Corps of Cadets at West Point in 1941 and joined the 505th Parachute Infantry Regiment after paratrooper school a year later. He fought through Europe with the 82d Airborne Division in World War II and served as Secretary of the Army Frank Pace, Jr.'s, military assistant during the Korean conflict. In 1955 Colonel Norton began a series of assignments in the Office of the Chief for Research and Development, which placed him in the forefront of airmobility development. As chief of the Air Mobility Division, Norton became qualified as both fixed-wing and helicopter pilot. He commanded the 2d Battle Group, 4th Cavalry, of the 1st Cavalry Division in Korea before returning to the United States in 1960 as the aviation officer of CONARC. He was on several high-level boards engaged in Army reorganization and airmobile doctrine, including the Howze Board. On 1 April 1963 Norton was promoted to brigadier general and became assistant commandant of the Army infantry school at Fort Benning. He was sent to Vietnam two years later, where General Westmoreland handpicked him to command the 1st Cavalry Division after

---

4. 1st Cav Div, *Combat Operations After Action Report (RCS: MACV J3-32)*, dtd 8 May 66; 1st Cav Div, *Critique of Operation JIM BOWIE*, dtd 15 April 66.

a stint of duty commanding U.S. Army Vietnam support troops. Major General Norton led the 1st Cavalry Division with a firm understanding of both airmobile development and the Army logistical structure in Vietnam, an important resource to the highly technical and equipment-dependent airmobile division.

Major General Norton continued resweeping Binh Dinh Province on 4 May 1966 in Operation DAVY CROCKETT. Colonel Moore's 3d Brigade reentered the Bong Son Plains during the seasonal weather transition, which brought clear weather and high humidity. Flight conditions were enhanced, but troops marched and fought under an unrelenting tropical sun with temperatures of 94 to 110 degrees Fahrenheit. Aerial pursuit was initiated by Lt. Col. James C. Smith's 1st Squadron, 9th Cavalry, which attacked northward, seeking a reported Viet Cong battalion. The chase led to skirmishing the next day at Bing Di, where two battalions of the 7th Cavalry airmobiled to encircle the rapidly moving VC force. A furious artillery barrage inflicted heavy losses, but the VC managed to elude the encirclement during the night. Contact was reestablished when a squadron helicopter was shot down at Than Son village on 6 May, and the division quickly implemented an airmobile response.

The 7th Cavalry's 2d Battalion air assaulted to seal off the village's southern exits while the 1st Battalion moved toward the hamlet from the other direction. Ground reconnaissance troops from the 9th Cavalry, reinforced with mechanized ARVN vehicles, blocked off the east. Twelve F4C Phantom sorties rained high explosives on the VC-occupied hamlet, and both 7th Cavalry battalions advanced toward the fortified VC trenchlines from two sides. At one point, with only three hundred yards separating the advancing cavalrymen, one VC company defensive position was demolished by well-placed 750-pound Air Force bombs, bringing Colonel Moore's accolade that it was "the most accurate display of tactical air precision bombing I have ever seen."[5] The 1st Cavalry Division was most effective when its air-ground teamwork was functioning smoothly throughout the pursuit and final entrapment of the enemy. The battalions made visual contact late in the afternoon, spent the night in vigilant encirclement, and

5. 1st Cav Div, *Seven Month History and Briefing Data: April–October 1966*, dtd 1 May 67, p. 79.

overran the VC battalion and village after a sharp skirmish the next day.

The brigade began searching the Kim Son (Crow's Foot) Valley on 11 May, but few contacts developed, and the mission was being terminated five days later when cavalrymen patrolling the nearby Vinh Thanh Valley clashed violently with the Viet Cong. A cavalry battalion had been dispatched to that area after evidence captured earlier revealed that the Special Forces Vinh Thanh camp might be attacked on 19 May, Ho Chi Minh's birthday. Many major operations in Vietnam were triggered by such small incidents, and the division was "backed into (Operation) CRAZY HORSE by the virtue of the unusual intelligence that was developed." The Viet Cong were discovered in force on the eastern rim of the Kim Son Valley, causing Colonel Moore to remark bluntly at a later operational critique, "How the hell did we finish DAVY CROCKETT without knowing that he [2d VC Regiment] was in the CRAZY HORSE area?"[6]

The clash occurred on the afternoon of 16 May 1966. Capt. John D. Coleman's Company B of the 2d Battalion, 8th Cavalry, landed one helicopter at a time on LZ Hereford near Camp Vinh Thanh, climbed a ridgeline, and encountered the VC in prepared positions. One squad moving forward was annihilated by a sudden Viet Cong counterattack. Attempts to retrieve American dead and wounded only increased casualties and disclosed further VC strongpoints in the dense undergrowth. An afternoon thunderstorm unleashed sheets of rain across the jungle canopy and dimmed the faint sunlight reaching the forest floor. The VC took advantage of the darkened conditions to make repeated attacks, which compressed Coleman's men into a small defensive perimeter under automatic weapons fire from all sides.

The fighting continued into early evening under conditions too close for tube artillery support. The rainstorm seemed to prevent aerial rocket assistance, which was the last-resort weapon available to save an isolated airmobile ground element in trouble. Two armed helicopters of the 2d Battalion, 20th Artillery, led by commander Lt. Col. Morris J. Brady, carefully edged up the ridgeline in the downpour. Guided by radio instructions from the beleaguered company,

6. 1st Cav Div, *Critique Summary—Operation CRAZY HORSE*, dtd 27 June 66, p. 16.

both helicopters loomed over the trees and fired rockets directly into the charging Viet Cong. The massed explosions from their closely delivered salvos shattered the VC assault.

Airmobile reinforcements were dispatched to LZ Hereford, and during the night Capt. John W. Cummings's Company A of the 1st Battalion, 12th Cavalry, reinforced Coleman's lines. The next morning both companies were attacked by a battalion of the *2d VC Regiment*. For two hours throngs of VC surged out of the jungle at intervals and rushed the foxholes, many being brought down and killed just outside the perimeter. Ammunition was so low that many troopers were down to their last rifle magazines and had already fixed bayonets. Another relief force from Lt. Col. William B. Ray's 1st Battalion of the 5th Cavalry airmobiled to the rescue, and these additional reinforcements prompted the Viet Cong to withdraw.

Col. John J. Hennessey's 1st Brigade commenced pursuit with Lieutenant Colonel Ray's battalion and the 2d Battalion of the 12th Cavalry under Lt. Col. Otis C. Lynn. Both units swept east into the mountains in an effort to cut off suspected VC escape routes. The jagged ridges were blanketed by triple-canopy jungle, which sloped into deep heavily vegetated ravines laced with cascading waterfalls and swift streams. Suitable spots for landing zones were so scarce that the Viet Cong were able to keep most under constant surveillance. Adverse skirmishes often erupted in close proximity to them, as Hill 766 (LZ Horse) and when a cavalry mortar platoon was overrun on 21 May (LZ Hereford). On the latter date elements of Lt. Col. Levin B. Broughton's 1st Battalion of the 8th Cavalry also fought a pitched engagement against hillside Viet Cong machine gun bunkers. The knoll's summit was stormed and the VC positions eliminated in an unusual American night assault. In some of these battles the thick jungle caused grenadiers to cease using their weapons, as the M79 projectiles bounded back to explode in friendly lines (later this deficiency was corrected by setting the rounds to arm at a distance from the firer).

By this time Major General Norton had committed the majority of his division to the operation. The bulk of the *2d VC Regiment* remained within the mountains between the Soui Ca and Vinh Thanh valleys, where the difficult terrain effectively masked its movement and location. The division adopted a new tactical methodology on 24 May, when helicopter troop insertions were replaced by massed fire-

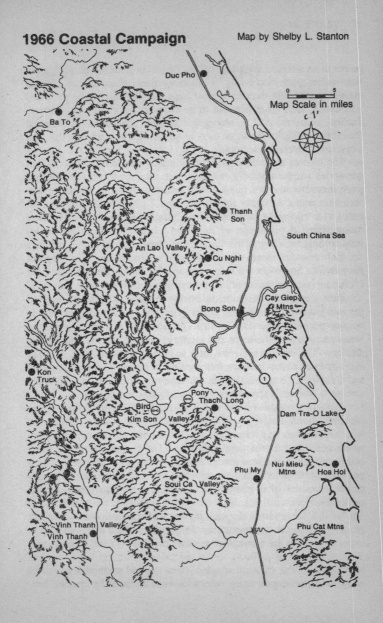

1966 Coastal Campaign

Map by Shelby L. Stanton

Duc Pho

Ba To

Thanh Son

An Lao Valley

Cu Nghi

South China Sea

Bong Son

Cay Giep Mtns

Kon Truck

Pony
Bird
Kim Son Valley

Thach Long

Dam Tra-O Lake

Soui Ca Valley

Phu My

Nui Mieu Mtns

Hoa Hoi

Vinh Thanh Valley

Vinh Thanh

Phu Cat Mtns

0 — 5
Map Scale in miles

power in an effort to drive the VC out of valley pockets. Ground units were pulled back into a ring of company-size ambush points outside the strike zone, but the area was so large that it could not be patrolled adequately. One large gap had to be covered with a CS gas barrier. Tactical airstrikes, B52 bombing, and artillery concentrations pounded the hillmass interior for three days in an attempt to stampede the Viet Cong out of targeted sectors.

The closest air-ground coordination was required. Flight pattern advisories were constantly radioed in an attempt to prevent aircraft from inadvertently intermixing with artillery shellfire, but the entire sector remained a "rather mad target area," characterized in the best terms as a "nip-and-tuck proposition." Major General Norton himself accompanied Army Secretary Resor on a helicopter from the battlefield to Saigon. During the flight "our chase ship said that artillery out there is awful close—we were lucky not to get hit. When we got back to Tan Son Nhut we found out another Huey had been shot out of the air just five minutes behind us by our own artillery."[7]

Such attempts to dislodge the enemy through firepower neglected the real value of dismounted cavalry (infantry) to the total airmobile cavalry package. The 1st Cavalry Division was a triad of powerful weapons systems—helicoptered infantry, armed aircraft, and mobile artillery. The enemy suffered little sustained damage from artillery and airpower unless infantry followed up to actually seize the ground and completed his destruction. In this case the infantry follow-up really consisted of mere exploratory sweeps to ascertain damage.

Airmobile pursuit efforts in CRAZY HORSE were stymied after the initial fierce firefights. Retreat was triggered, but the rugged terrain, severe heat and humidity, and heightened enemy activity elsewhere precluded a relentless follow-up. The remainder of the operation sputtered into a semisearch through the valley wilderness, which garnered only sporadic contact with the Viet Cong. Although considerable quantities of foodstuffs and supplies were uncovered, results were rapidly diminishing. Renewed NVA activity in the western portion of II CTZ required division presence elsewhere. Major General Norton was forced to decide how long such a large and logistically expensive effort in a rough area like the Vinh Thanh Valley was

7. Ibid., p. 11.

worthwhile. The division kept its aerial reconnaissance squadron and four rotating battalions in the area until 5 June 1966, when he ordered the operation terminated. Operation CRAZY HORSE, with its toll of 79 KIA, 1 MIA, and 356 WIA (compared to 350 enemy killed by body count and another 330 estimated), was a costly lesson in the limits of sustained pursuit.[8]

The 1st Cavalry Division turned its attention to enemy threats elsewhere for the next several months. Two operations were conducted around Tuy Hoa in Phu Yen Province, followed by engagements in the central highlands and a return to old division haunts in the western Ia Drang–Chu Pong region. In the meantime Binh Dinh Province remained only partially subdued by the Korean Capital Division, which occupied its southeastern portion. Reliable intelligence indicated that the *3d NVA Division* (also known as the *610th*) was still using the An Lao, Soui Ca, and Kim Son (Crow's Foot) valleys as important assembly and supply base areas. In mid-September 1966 the division returned to the coast from the Cambodian border to begin an extended seventeen-month campaign to pacify northeastern Binh Dinh Province. Major General Norton reinitiated cavalry pursuit by launching Operation THAYER I, the first stage of this renewed campaign.

For three days prior to the operation, numerous B52 bombing runs were made to separate the NVA/VC from their various havens and neutralize or drive them toward the Kim Son region. Colonel Smith's 1st Squadron of the 9th Cavalry provided aerial surveillance on all strikes, but was unable to render the necessary ground observation because of the lack of landing zones in six of the targeted areas. The exact dispositions of the North Vietnamese remained largely unknown.

On 13 September 1966 the division conducted its largest air assault to date as more than 120 Hueys and Chinooks lifted five battalions of Col. Archie K. Hyle's 1st Brigade and Col. Marvin J. Berenzweig's 2d Brigade into a circular configuration on the ridges around

---

8. 1st Cav Div, *Combat Operations After Action Report (RCS: MACV J3-32)*, dtd 10 Sep 66; 1st Cav Div, *Critique Summary—Operation CRAZY HORSE*, dtd 27 Jun 66; various 14 MH Det opns chronologies and summary fact sheets.

the Crow's Foot. The *18th NVA Regiment* quickly split up, side-stepped the advance, and slipped away. For the next two weeks the brigades made only scant contact as troop-laden helicopters leap-frogged battalions in airmobile pursuit of the fleeing enemy columns. Several food and clothing caches, a major hospital, and even a grenade and mine factory were uncovered, but the only significant personnel claim was one song-and-dance troupe specializing in musical propaganda, captured while traveling between villages.

Although progress seemed disheartening, an NVA regiment had been displaced from the Kim Son Valley base area and forced to retreat an even greater distance from its supply sources. The relentless cavalry drive apparently caused considerable consternation among the *7th* and *8th Battalions* of the *18th NVA Regiment*, which decided they had to fight their way out of the situation. The NVA force exposed its location by making an unsuccessful nighttime attack against an ARVN regimental command post on 23 September and then moved farther east onto the coastal plain. The division maintained its momentum of pursuit and entrapped both battalions there four days later.

The two identified NVA battalions were pocketed into an area bounded by the South China Sea, the Phu Cat Mountains to the south, and the Nui Mieu hillmass to the north. Aggressive airmobile cavalry maneuvering blocked all routes of egress back west into the valley regions. Major General Norton tightened his cavalry screen to make enemy exfiltration more difficult and exchanged the Berenzweig brigade for Col. Charles D. Daniel's fresh 3d Brigade. Additional South Vietnamese and Korean forces were brought in to complete the encirclement, and THAYER I was declared terminated as preparations for Operation IRVING began.[9]

Operation IRVING, actually an extension of THAYER I, commenced on 1 October 1966 as five battalions air assaulted into the seacoast pocket. Colonel Hyle's 1st Brigade fought an opening two-day battle at Hoa Hoi, which became a classic demonstration of combined airmobile tactics. In true cavalry fashion, aerial reconnaissance started the battle as 9th Cavalry "White" scoutships spotted several

9. Hq 1st Bde 1st Cav Div, *Combat Operations After Action Report*, dtd 29 Oct 66; Hq 2d Bde 1st Cav Div, *Combat Operations After Action Report*, dtd 28 Oct 66.

enemy soldiers on the sandy northern tip of the Hung Lac peninsula. Lt. Col. George W. McIlwain's Troop A of the 1st Squadron, 9th Cavalry, aggressively exploited the initial contact with "Red" gunships and its "Blue" rifle platoon to determine the size of the opposing forces. A sizable North Vietnamese contingent was confirmed occupying the hedgerows, dikes, and natural defensive bulwarks of beachside Hoa Hoi village.

Colonel Hyle's brigade responded with optimum airmobile flexibility. The situation was relayed to Lt. Col. James T. Root, commanding 1st Battalion, 12th Cavalry, who dispatched Company B under Capt. Frederick Mayer, already in flight to another mission, to the scene of action. Captain Mayer's men air assaulted onto the open beach and were mortared as they maneuvered into line formation. Two exploding rounds wounded Mayer, who, despite profuse bleeding, remained in charge and directed the company through the well-prepared enemy bunker and trench system crisscrossing in front of Hoa Hoi. The rest of the battalion was rapidly airmobiled into nearby blocking positions. The line companies then fought closer toward the village's main defenses in carefully phased and coordinated attacks.

One advancing platoon was momentarily stopped by intense fire, but the men quickly recovered, stood up with rifles blazing, and charged the first trench. The gallantry of two privates, one (Pfc. Roy Salazar) killed leading a squad to breach a strongpoint and the other (Pfc. Francis Royal) mortally wounded carrying a wounded comrade to safety, established the pace of action for the duration of the battle. Throughout the action the cavalrymen adhered to the Rules of Engagement, when the easier and safer course would have been to ignore them. Lt. Donald Grigg of 3d Platoon, Company A, was leading his men across an open field when he saw several civilians suddenly walk aimlessly onto the field in the direct line of fire between the two forces. Immediately Lieutenant Grigg threw down his weapon, web gear, and helmet and raced more than fifty yards through enemy automatic weapons fire to carry two small children back to his own lines, followed by the rest of the old men and women.

The fighting in the village outworks raged throughout the day. At dusk the battalion pulled back from the village to form a tight cordon, preventing enemy exfiltration during the night. A continuous naval and field artillery bombardment was conducted under flarelight. Several bands of NVA soldiers tried to probe and shoot their way out of the encirclement, but each attempt was repulsed. The battalion made its final assault against the village the next morning. Fighting was heaviest in the final trenches, but continued unabated through the bunker-studded hootches themselves. Several times the cavalrymen were temporarily halted by the desperate resistance of heavy weapons strongpoints, but each time the soldiers rallied and carried the attack forward, sometimes in hand-to-hand combat. Elements of the *7th and 8th Battalions, 18th NVA Regiment*, lost 233 killed by body count and 35 captured at Hoa Hoi, compared to the relatively slight cavalry casualties of 6 killed and 32 wounded.[10]

While the coastal pursuit continued, the division also realized that continual military presence was required to discourage enemy return to long-held base areas. By 13 October the division reconcentrated in the Soui Ca and Kim Son region, where fast reconnaissance sweeps were interspersed with artillery raids. These tactics yielded more significant cache discoveries and denied the NVA/VC any unimpeded opportunity to reconsolidate. When Operation IRVING was terminated at midnight on 24 October, the division's aviation had again rendered remarkable mobile service, airlifting the equivalent of forty-six infantry battalions and thirty-six artillery batteries during Operations THAYER I/IRVING.[11]

Operation THAYER II, which commenced 25 October 1966 with the return of the northeast monsoon season and continued into 1967, was a two-brigade sustained pursuit effort to exploit the success of the previous five weeks of almost continuous contact with the NVA/VC in the rich coastal plain and the Kim Son and Soui Ca valleys to the west. Strong surges of monsoon weather dominated the operation with turbulent, wind-driven rainstorms and excessive humidity. Division aviation struggled though the dense morning fogs and after-

10. 1st Cav Div Unit Historical Rpt #6, *The Battle of Hoa Hoi*; 1st Cav Div, *Report of Action 2–3 October 1966*. As a sidenote, the first platoon, under Lt. Joe Anderson, had a French film team attached under producer Pierre Schoendoerffer. The film later produced, *The Anderson Platoon*, devotes a significant portion to the Hoa Hoi battle.
11. 1st Cav Div, *Combat Operations After Action Report*, dtd 13 Jan 67; and *Operational Report on Lessons Learned*, dtd 22 Nov 66, Appendix 5-3.

noon thunderstorms to lift the equivalent of 142 infantry battalions and 70 artillery batteries during the operation.

The *18th NVA Regiment* was critically short of food because of the incessant cavalry offensive, since many rice-gathering details were destroyed, captured, or surrendered. Several firefights erupted in the flooded valleys as the fractured enemy battalions desperately sought to replenish their caches with the recently harvested lowland rice. While most encounters were cavalry victories, two large battles were fought under confusing and tactically unsound circumstances, partially reflecting the unfavorable impact on the division of personnel turbulence and the long strain of campaigning.

On 16 December 1966 Colonel Daniel's brigade was replaced by Col. James C. Smith's 1st Brigade, while Col. George W. Casey's 2d Brigade continued operating. The next day seven cavalry companies from the newly inserted brigade responded to a 9th Cavalry clash with two NVA companies in the Crow's Foot near Thach Long, but control difficulties between elements nullified the vital coordination required in all fast-moving airmobile operations. Poor scheduling led to helicoptered units arriving at the same time as airstrikes, so that reinforcements were kept circling while the battle was raging below. Some platoons sat idle for hours on pickup zones, and entire companies were fed piecemeal into the battle. Time and time again arriving forces walked straight into the killing fields of well-camouflaged enemy hedgerow bunker positions, some of which were previously detected, and were decimated in lethal cross fires. Only the courage of individual cavalrymen allowed units to push forward, but ironically this further locked depleted cavalry forces in adverse situations from which extrication was very difficult. The Viet Cong ended the battle by withdrawing virtually unhindered after dark. Lt. Col. George D. Eggers's 1st Battalion, 12th Cavalry, suffered heavy casualties, and its Company D ended the day with only thirty-five troops left.[12]

The division's supporting howitzers were concentrated on two large landing zones in the Crow's Foot, LZs Pony and Bird, which could fire supporting artillery anywhere in the Kim Son Valley. They were obviously prime targets for enemy action, and Division Artillery warned

12. 1st Cav Div, *The Battle in the 506 Valley, 17 Dec 66*, Unit Historical Rpt #15.

them to expect an attack immediately following the Christmas Truce on 26 December. Almost unbelievably, the *22d NVA Regiment* was able to emplace supporting fire weapons and stage a massive surprise close assault which nearly overran LZ Bird in the early morning darkness of 27 December 1966. Approximately 700 North Vietnamese regulars crawled to within fifteen feet of the landing zone perimeter without being discovered. Covered by well-placed machine guns and recoilless rifles, they surged forward with bayonets fixed, screaming, "GI, you die!" as a sudden mortar barrage swept through the American lines.

The perimeter cavalrymen of Company C, 1st Battalion, 12th Cavalry, were quickly overwhelmed, and the NVA charged through all five 155mm howitzer positions of Battery C, 6th Battalion, 16th Artillery, as well as half of the 105mm howitzers of Battery B, 2d Battalion, 19th Artillery. The waves of NVA soldiers became intermixed with retreating cavalrymen. Burning ammunition bunkers were exploding, communications were knocked out, and all cohesion disappeared under the weight of attack. Some of the most violent hand-to-hand fighting transpired as gun crews were killed making last stands around their howitzers.

The executive officer of the light howitzers, 1Lt. John D. Piper, frantically loaded a Bee Hive round into the lowered tube of one of his last remaining weapons and aimed it at hundreds of NVA swarming around an overrun 155mm howitzer. The Bee Hive round, composed of more than 8,500 steel flechettes, had been specifically designed to stop mass infantry assaults. Lieutenant Piper was unable to find the flare to alert possible friendly troops in its pathway and yelled, "Bee Hive!" repeatedly. Sergeant Graham, who had been forced out of the targeted position and was now in a drainage ditch out front, screamed back, "Shoot it!" He recalled that it sounded like "a million whips being whirled over my head." Piper could see the resulting carnage in the flarelight, yelled, "Tube left," quickly chambered another Bee Hive round, and pulled the lanyard. The North Vietnamese attack was stopped.[13]

The combination of Bee Hive rounds and overhead aerial artillery

13. 1st Cav Div, *The Attack on LZ Bird*, Unit Historical Rpt #2, p. 13.

rocket fire caused the North Vietnamese attack to falter, and the enemy withdrew before daylight. Landing Zone Bird was left in shambles, and the 266 dead North Vietnamese were interspersed with 58 dead and 77 wounded Americans. While the defending units were later awarded the Presidential Unit Citation in recognition of their valiant defense of LZ Bird and the individual valor exhibited there, disturbing questions over proper security were left unresolved. The 1st Cavalry Division immediately launched pursuit operations, which continued for the next several days as the *22d Regiment* attempted to withdraw north to the An Lao Valley, but meaningful contact was never regained. Even so, the division could justifiably point to the severe losses inflicted on the regiment, which temporarily knocked it out of action.

On 3 January 1967 the 3d Brigade of the 25th Infantry Division was placed under the operational control of the 1st Cavalry Division to support its own engaged six battalions oriented against the National Priority Area of eastern Binh Dinh Province. The continuous battering rendered the *18th NVA Regiment* mostly combat-ineffective. The unit suffered heavy losses, which included all original company commanders, and an intercepted message of 10 January revealed that the enemy division commander considered the unit unreliable because of its low morale. Scattered by several large engagements and uncounted bush contacts, the regiment fragmented into small groups which attempted to escape northwest into the An Lao Valley to reequip. Cavalry patrols continually brushed with these exfiltrating elements.[14]

Operation THAYER II, which ended after the Tet truce of 8 to 12 February 1967, was typified by long periods of relatively unopposed search operations punctuated by sharp contacts, and marked the final stage in the 1st Cavalry Division's year of sustained pursuit. There were negative aspects in the total campaign. It was uneven and often hampered by insufficient intelligence and competing requirements to reinforce other fronts, especially battles in the western highlands. In certain areas the high cost of continued search ruled out continued expenditure of effort for large blocks of time. Some battles

14. 1st Cav Div, *Operation THAYER II Combat After Action Report*, dtd 25 Jun 67.

were tactically mishandled, and a critical division artillery firebase was even surprised and almost destroyed. The highly proficient and elusive NVA/VC units were often able to take advantage of adverse weather and the rugged jungle to evade many airmobile thrusts and to avoid absolute annihilation. Above all, the division's human cost was staggering. From 31 January 1966 to the end of January 1967, the division suffered 19,512 casualties in all operations: 720 killed in action; 3,039 wounded; 2,304 nonbattle deaths and injuries; and 13,449 as a result of disease.[15]

Yet the positive military gains were most impressive. The cumulative effect of sustained cavalry pursuit greatly reduced NVA/VC control in most provincial sectors by wearing down effective resistance. The campaign disorganized the Viet Cong control structure, creating havoc among VC tax gathering, recruiting, medical services, and administration. Viet Cong government members evading death or capture were forced to work less openly and with much less effectiveness.

In summation the cavalry pursuit of the 1966 coastal campaign established the basis for the cavalry clearing operations of 1967. In many ways this campaign also marked the final evolution of Major General Kinnard's airmobile doctrine into a battlefield staple of the Vietnam War. The 1st Cavalry Division exerted persistent airmobile pressure, found and engaged strong enemy forces, maintained a steady pace of extended helicopter operations, and triumphed over weather and enemy adversity.

15. 1st Cav Div, *Operational Report on Lessons Learned*, dtd 5 May 66, p. 40; dtd 15 Aug 66, p. 8; dtd 22 Nov 66, pp. 8–9; dtd 15 Feb 67, p. 8.

CHAPTER 5

Clearing Operations
Techniques, 1967 Coastal Campaign

The 1st Cavalry Division began the campaign for military control of Binh Dinh Province's coastal plains, narrow valleys, and rugged mountains in 1966. During 1967 the division still had the job of finding and destroying the NVA/VC military and support network, but it emphasized pacification as a part of clearing operations as MACV expanded Major General Norton's priority list.

Great political emphasis was being placed on doing more than just killing Viet Cong. Ellsworth Bunker replaced Henry Cabot Lodge as ambassador and insisted that the military get more forcefully involved in pacification efforts. In May President Johnson's special ambassador for pacification, Robert Komer, created CORDS (Civil Operations and Revolutionary Development Support) directly under Westmoreland's chain of command to consolidate the previously disjointed Allied efforts. Komer was anxious to eliminate the VC infrastructure and tax-collection system, and recognized that divisions might serve as excellent vehicles for security duty.

The 1st Cavalry Division, designed as a swift and powerful formation able to influence battles by dint of its airmobility, was hardly formulated for occupation tasks. Its cannons, aircraft, and automatic weapons were in the hands of skilled personnel trained to seek out and annihilate NVA/VC main force units. Nevertheless, with a minimum of guidance, but a great deal of confusing high command directives, the 1st Cavalry Division found itself intimately involved in trying to help the South Vietnamese government assert administrative control over the rich agricultural eastern area of Vietnam's most populous province.

The 1st Cavalry Division's clearing offensive in the 1,600 square miles of Binh Dinh Province was labeled Operation PERSHING, and it would last from 11 February 1967 until 21 January 1968. It might have continued indefinitely, except that the regular North Vietnamese Army divisions, which the politicians consistently underrated or ignored (and which would actually blitzkrieg South Vietnam into destruction during 1975), forced the cavalry's redeployment to I CTZ. In the meantime, with his troops committed to endure another annual cycle of heavy northeast monsoon rains and dry southwest monsoon heat along the central coast, Major General Norton set up his command post at LZ English outside Bong Son.

The burden of implementing a pacification program that supplemented combat operations with meaningful civic action fell on the shoulders of the cavalry provost marshal, Lt. Col. James P. Oliver. As a military policeman, he simply combined the divisional 545th Military Police Company with the 816th South Vietnamese National Police Field Force (NPFF) to form an ad hoc cavalry-advised NPFF battalion which became operational the same day CORDS became official: 26 May 1967. The police battalion would seal off selected hamlets and search them for tunnels and caches while interrogating the residents. Colonel Oliver strictly enforced the Rules of Engagement, since everyone at least agreed that proper troop conduct was basic to winning the respect and cooperation of the local population.

Operation PERSHING was essentially a clearing operation emphasizing population control and area security. Most of it consisted of slow and tedious searches aimed at breaking VC village-level power. To the soldier's eye this part of the operation was deceptively unglamorous—consisting of searches day after day through homes and compost piles, often in pouring rain or searing heat—and tedious, since he was keenly aware that he was under constant observation by an enemy quick to capitalize on his slightest mistake. The innumerable, monotonous cordon-and-search missions could be marred by sudden and violent hamlet firefights, and the NVA/VC defended enough fortified villages and valley passes to kill and maim cavalrymen in numbers surpassing all division operational losses of 1966.

Regardless of allied pacification intentions, the fact was that the 1st Cavalry Division still faced a viable enemy main force threat in Binh Dinh Province and adjacent areas. Therefore, Operation PERSHING contained numerous platoon actions, brigade emergency displacements, long-range airmobile raids, and some of the hardest-fought engagements of the division's Vietnam service. The 1st Cavalry Division's massed helicopter airlift, vertical air assault muscle, and swift aerial and artillery firepower were all significant in subduing the province's pro–Viet Cong population and its armed units. To this air-oriented dimension, the 1st Cavalry Division added armor and mechanization for the first time. Tanks provided essential fortifications suppression and gave the psychological edge in ground attacks. The 1st Battalion of the 50th Infantry (Mechanized), attached to the division in September, was used either way. The armored personnel carriers were employed either as fighting vehicles in a mounted role or as mobile gun platforms with minimum crews as the companies were helicoptered into combat as airmobile infantry.

The division's 1st Squadron of the 9th Cavalry remained in the forefront of all coastal campaign action. The aerial recon squadron was the sole Army unit of this type at the time, but already its unique scout and gunship composition was proving a deadly effective combination over the battlefield. The squadron's mission was direct and simple: find the enemy. To avail the widely separated brigades of its valuable service, the squadron parceled out one air cav troop to each. The ground troop (Troop D) was composed of fast-riding gunjeeps backed up by attached M42 Duster self-propelled flak guns and was used as a mobile light infantry reserve that protected the engineers who were sweeping mines and replacing blown bridges along Highway 1.

The 9th Cavalry thrived on speed in the hunt and quick reaction to any contact. Typical of its utilization was the June action at An Quang near Dam Tra-O Lake, a tidewater basin connected to the South China Sea. Troop C of the squadron was scouting for Col. Fred E. Karhohs's 2d Brigade, and a pair of light H13 observation "White team" helicopter pilots buzzing An Quang at treetop level spotted suspiciously fresh diggings and field work but no farmers. The sector was normally quiet, but had seen action in the past, and the troop commander decided to investigate with his "Blue" rifle platoon. The ground cavalrymen landed, found a large boulder whitewashed with "Welcome to the VC and NVA" in Vietnamese, and were fired upon when approaching the village. They called for several aerial rocketing runs by armed "Red team" helicopters and withdrew to block the southern exit from the village.

Colonel Karhohs arrived overhead in his command helicopter and immediately ordered the 2d Brigade quick reaction force platoon, 1st Platoon of Company B from Lt. Col. Joseph C. McDonough's 2d Battalion, 5th Cavalry, to land in support. The company was air assaulted beyond the village to block the northern direction, and its helicopters were fired upon while descending. The 9th Cavalry squadron commander, Lt. Col. R. H. Nevins, Jr., kept a swarm of armed and scout helicopters circling over the lake to the west. Judging from the amount of enemy return fire, Colonel Karhohs estimated that elements of two NVA companies were in the village complex and radioed for reinforcements. Even the "Blue" platoon was bolstered by a platoon of riflemen from Troop D that was airlifted to its assistance. What had started as a scouting report by the Troop C leader was now an opportunity for decisive brigade action. When Lieutenant Colonel McDonough arrived to take charge on the ground less than two hours after the initial contact, he had four and a half cavalry battalions surrounding An Quang.

Preparatory to his ground attack, McDonough massed a liberal diversity of fire support to soften the village defenses. Working with several controllers and observers, he coordinated the firepower of artillery, aerial rocket helicopters, regular gunships, Navy and Air Force tactical airstrikes, naval gunfire, medium battle tanks, M42 Duster 40mm self-propelled guns, and even CH47 "Guns A-Go-Go" minigun-armed Chinooks. Despite the destruction wrought by this heavy explosive ordnance, both Companies B and D were hit midway through the smoldering village. Two Viet Cong suddenly dashed out from spider holes and heaved grenades into the cavalry ranks, and machine guns and snipers swept the companies with accurate close-in fire. Dead and wounded Americans littered the open ground where they had been cut down next to weapons in tunnel entrances. A pair of tanks moved forward to blast the treetops with canister Bee Hive discharges, allowing the cavalrymen to pull back their wounded and get out of the village. They left behind one burning M42 Duster which had been knocked out in the fighting.

With evening approaching and regular brigade troops in position, the aerial squadron would have normally extracted its elements to continue reconnoitering or block other possible exfiltration routes. In this case, however, it was necessary for the two squadron ground platoons to stay situated and help seal off the village complex. The

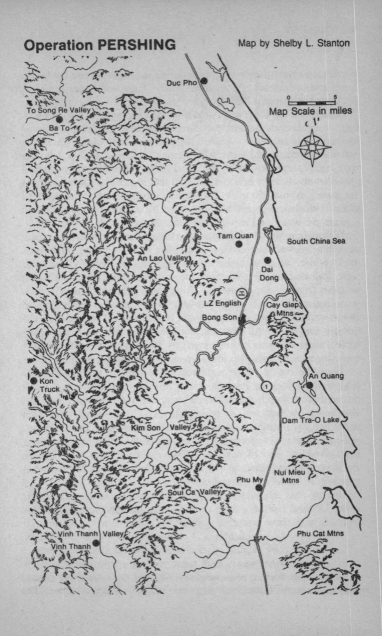

Operation PERSHING

Map by Shelby L. Stanton

Duc Pho

To Song Re Valley

Ba To

Tam Quan

South China Sea

An Lao Valley

Dai Dong

LZ English

Cay Giep Mtns

Bong Son

Kon Truck

An Quang

Dam Tra-O Lake

Kim Son Valley

Phu My

Nui Mieu Mtns

Soui Ca Valley

Vinh Thanh Valley

Phu Cat Mtns

Vinh Thanh

Map Scale in miles

0   5

1

North Vietnamese decided to evade during the night despite the bright moon and continuous illumination flares. They left a rear guard in An Quang which still had to be destroyed.

The following day thirty-three airstrikes and several artillery barrages were directed against the village complex. Lieutenant Colonel McDonough's battalion assaulted through the interlocking fire of the remaining bunkers and secured the hamlet. A total of 89 NVA bodies were found, and more were believed to be buried in the collapsed bunker ruins. Later a prisoner claimed that his *18th NVA Regiment's 9th Battalion* lost 150 of its 250-man complement in the action and that the survivors reached the Cay Giep Mountains only by slipping through the water and reeds around the northern edge of the lake.[1]

Throughout the 1967 coastal campaign, the aerial reconnaissance squadron sparked the majority of division contacts in the same fashion. "White" scout team helicopter sightings of NVA/VC activity were followed up by rocketing and strafing from the "Red" aero weapons teams and exploited by "Blue" aero rifle platoons. The contacts produced a variety of brigade-size battles, platoon firefights, and firings recorded only in flight logs, but the work was always extremely dangerous. All contacts, regardless of their length or significance, were likely to be challenged by some type of enemy antiaircraft fire with weapons up to 12.7mm AA machine guns in size.

Over the course of the squadron's 343 days in the PERSHING campaign, its forward reconnaissance role exacted such a heavy toll that its aircraft were replaced twice over. The 1st Squadron, 9th Cavalry, which operated with 88 helicopters and 770 personnel, was taken under fire 931 times, resulting in 250 helicopters being hit. Of these, 102 helicopters were so badly damaged that they had to be stricken from inventory, and 14 were shot down and fully destroyed. During this same time, the squadron lost 55 killed, 1 missing, and 264 wounded members in aerial and ground combat.[2]

Behind this advance umbrella of 9th Cavalry aerial scoutships, Major General Norton's three cavalry brigades and one attached infantry brigade from the 25th Infantry Division fanned out through

1. 1st Cav Div, *The Battle of Dam Tra-O*, Unit Historical Rpt #16.
2. Hq 1st Sqdn, 9th Cav, *Memorandum for Record, Operation PERSHING*, dtd Feb 68, pp. 6–7, 24.

Binh Dinh Province. Operation PERSHING began as Colonel Smith's 1st Brigade and Colonel Casey's 2d Brigade slashed into the Bong Son Plains in a wave of air assaults that took several hamlets by storm and flushed large numbers of hiding enemy soldiers from tunnels, wells, and concealed underground bunkers. Col. Jonathan R. Burton's 3d Brigade reconnoitered the forbidding An Lao Valley, and the attached 3d Brigade of the 25th Infantry Division covered area development chores of the ARVN 22d Division and Korean Capital Division as far south as the Soui Ca Valley and Phu My Plains.

Learning from its bitter lessons at Ia Drang and other early encounters, the division reserved one full battalion as a ready reaction force (RRF). The RRF conducted normal operations, but was prepared for swift consolidation and pickup by division helicopters specially earmarked for emergency utilization. The division RRF stood ready to land a company quick reaction force anywhere in the PERSHING area within just thirty minutes. This lead strike unit could be followed by the rest of the battalion RRF in three to four hours. Each brigade maintained a miniature company-size RRF, with one platoon designated as its quick reaction force. Throughout the upcoming campaign the airmobile reaction reserves offered the 1st Cavalry Division an unprecedented flexibility in dominating the battlefield.

The sister 1st and 2d Battalions of the 5th Cavalry battled across the village-studded Bong Son Plains through February as they wrestled more villages from the *22d NVA Regiment*. Two large engagements overshadowed a rash of platoon skirmishes and countless booby-trap and mechanical ambush device incidents. Engineer dozers were used to level any structures potentially useful as fortified strongpoints, but contact dwindled as search operations intensified. The division adopted a new stratagem to keep NVA/VC activity low in its old haunts of the mountains west of the coastal plains.

The 1st Cavalry Division instituted drastic clearing measures against the most troublesome VC base areas. The Kim Son (Crow's Foot), Soui Ca, and An Lao valleys were all written off as too remote and too hazardous to be effectively occupied. Classified as "denial areas," the division made final sweeps of them and forcibly removed the remaining inhabitants. Once depopulated, the valleys were smothered with Agent Orange by the Vietnamese Air Force, which flew repeated crop-destruction missions. The division hoped that liberal application of this toxic chemical would poison all future rice production in the valleys, ruining their usefulness as enemy havens. The mass roundups also denuded the land of VC labor and military recruits, but produced more than 93,000 refugees. The displacement problem became so acute that plans for other denial areas had to be dropped.[3]

The small sweeps and patrols became routine, but they always required a mastery of basic soldiering and leadership. Contact was normally light, but numerous mines, booby traps, snipers, and sudden firefights continued to decide the cavalrymen's survival. The fragmented division was waging a platoon-level war in its clearing campaign, which demanded the highest degree of judgment, discipline, and tactical expertise. Action on the Bong Son front simmered in March, but Colonel Casey's brigade engaged the *18th NVA Regiment* in several skirmishes around the Cay Giep Mountains and Dam Tra-O Lake. One encounter resulted in a brigade-size battle against well-defended NVA village defenses from 19 to 22 March near Tam Quan.

With Operation PERSHING well underway, and in keeping with MACV's annual rotation of division commands during the Vietnam War, Major General Norton relinquished command of the 1st Cavalry Division to Maj. Gen. John J. Tolson III on 1 April 1967. General Tolson, the Commandant of the U.S. Army Aviation School since 1965, fulfilled all the prerequisites shaping the airmobile division command ticket. He was a paratrooper veteran and a seasoned aviator, and he had long been in the forefront of airmobility development. Born 22 October 1915 in North Carolina, he graduated from West Point in 1937 and participated in the first tactical air movement of Army ground forces two years later. During World War II, Colonel Tolson served with the paratroopers in the Pacific, making combat jumps into New Guinea, Corregidor Island, and the Philippines with the 503d Parachute Infantry. In 1957 he became an aviator and later served as Director of Army Aviation.

Major General Tolson continued divisional searches in the coastal region and mountain valleys, but was also directed immediately to assist Marine Operation LEJEUNE in the Duc Pho region, just north of the Bong Son Plains. Major General Norton had been urging cav-

3. 1st Cav Div, *Combat After Action Report*, dtd 29 Jun 68, Tab 30; Ltr dtd 14 Jul 68, Incl. 7, Significant Contacts.

alry pursuit north of the Bong Son Plains for some time before his departure, and the division was anxious to explore the area. MACV commander General Westmoreland also deliberately slated this "fire brigade" reaction as a model exercise to test changes of operational direction with minimal advance warning. Assistant division commander Brig. Gen. George S. Blanchard was placed in charge of the sudden flurry of activity accompanying Colonel Karhohs's 2d Brigade airmobile expedition. Fortunately, April was a transition month of fair weather between the northeast and southwest monsoons, and the brigade enjoyed optimum atmospheric and sea conditions.

The entire brigade was airlifted into Duc Pho in a day and a half to permit rapid Marine redeployment. The rushed timetable and hectic helicopter shuffling caused some loss of air traffic control, mostly because of the lack of coordination between Marine and Army aircraft channels. Helicopters continually roared across unit boundaries in the confined beach area, dropped off gear and personnel in unsatisfactory locations, and then moved them around again. Rotor blades kicked up sand, knocked down tentage, and scattered equipment. The radio waves were cluttered with irate transmission outbursts typified by, "If you blow my tent down one more time, I'm going to shoot you out of the air!" but everything was soon in place without serious mishap.

The most impressive display of division capability during Operation LEJEUNE was the 8th Engineer Battalion's incredible airfield construction feat. More than two hundred tons of heavy equipment were airlifted by CH54 Flying Crane and CH47 Chinook helicopters to build a forward combat airfield in just twenty-four hours. The "Skybeaver" engineers worked around the clock for two more days making the field acceptable for C123 cargo transport aircraft. The Marines were awestruck by the lavish amounts of cavalry equipment and helicopter support, but expressed open concern about snipers as the airmobile engineers toiled nightly under floodlamps and vehicle headlights. Working with great skill in record time, Lt. Col. Charles G. Olentine's engineer battalion proved that the airmobile division could promptly build the airfield facilities necessary for its own support.

The 2d Brigade helped to build another airfield, secured the beach landing site as the Marines departed, conducted numerous search-and-destroy sweeps, and policed the Vietnamese as they harvested VC-planted rice.

The 1st Cavalry Division also touted a geographical first, since the move placed the division outside II CTZ for the first time since its arrival in Vietnam nineteen months before: Duc Pho was in Quang Ngai Province of I CTZ. On 19 April, with his mission accomplished, Colonel Karhohs turned over the Duc Pho sector and its recently constructed airfields to the 3d Brigade of the 25th Infantry Division, which was released from division control three days later. The excursion demonstrated the airmobile division's ability to transplant quickly a major task force into an unfamiliar area on short notice. This was one of the most valuable advantages of the aerial cavalry division to the MACV command.[4]

The 1st Cavalry Division's clearing operations began driving the NVA/VC main force units out of northeastern Binh Dinh Province and into the mountain ranges beyond the coastal valleys. To reach them, Major General Tolson mounted cavalry raids, which were time-honored cavalry tactics in a new airmobile mode. Fast and light, the cavalry battalions struck northwest of the An Lao Valley and stabbed into distant NVA/VC base areas. In early May, airmobile cavalry staged out of the remote Ba To Special Forces camp and searched for the suspected headquarters of the *3d NVA Division*. In August the 3d Brigade leapfrogged northward from the An Lao Valley in a series of airmobile thrusts which carried it into the long-suspected VC haven of the Quang Ngai Province's Song Re Valley. The twisting valley floor was suspiciously free of visible inhabitants, but filled with fertile ricefields between the jungle hillocks.

The 2d Battalion of the 8th Cavalry, under Lt. Col. John E. Stannard, had just completed a month's tour of duty guarding the division main base at Camp Radcliff. His battalion was attached to 3d Brigade and became part of a cavalry raid into the Song Re Valley. Once in the valley, Lieutenant Colonel Stannard planned to sweep his battalion toward blocking positions set up by one company airmobiled ahead onto a small ridge near the abandoned airstrip of Ta Ma, which would then move downslope and establish its positions.

On the morning of 9 August 1967, following five minutes of preparatory light artillery fire on the grassy ridgeline, Capt. Raymond K. Bluhm, Jr.'s, Company A was air assaulted into LZ Pat. The last helicopters were descending with the weapons platoon when heavy

4. 1st Cav Div, *Operation LEJEUNE*, Unit Historical Rpt #10.

North Vietnamese antiaircraft guns suddenly opened fire from two higher hills dominating the ridgeline on either side. Two 9th Cavalry helicopter gunships orbiting overhead were immediately shot down. An H13 observation helicopter and the brigade command and control ship were also quickly put out of action. The enemy flak guns turned to sweep the exposed ridge with intensely accurate fire, pinning Captain Bluhm's 120-man company close to the ground.

The company was unable to maneuver, and Viet Cong troops hidden in spiderholes and log bunkers on the ridgeline itself began firing into the cavalry lines. Several cavalrymen were killed in quick succession. One trooper was mortally wounded by a 12.7mm AA round that tossed him back five feet. Medical Sp5 Andrew Conrad became the first aidman killed when he was struck in the forehead by a bullet while trying to assist a wounded comrade. The increasing number of wounded could not be evacuated because the heavy antiaircraft fire blanketed the landing zone.

SSgt. John Stipes, the weapons platoon leader, quickly emplaced his 81mm mortar to fire against the muzzle flashes on the neighboring hillsides, but the tube stuck up like a stovepipe at such close range. The enemy returned a volley of mortar rounds against the obvious target, forcing Stipes to cease firing. Extra mortar ammunition was scattered in discarded packs, lying all over the LZ. Ammunition bearer Pfc. Prentice D. Leclair was shot through the head while trying to collect them.

With all recoilless rifle and mortar ammunition either expended or unreachable, the company's few M60 machine guns rattling defiantly at the adjacent jungled slopes constituted its main firepower. One by one they were knocked out. Gunner Sp4 Michael Hotchkiss had already lost several crew members when a mortar shell landed on his back and disintegrated the entire position. Platoon Sgt. Frank M. Theberge, who suffered a broken ankle after leaping eight feet from a helicopter when the firing started, crawled to a small knoll and took charge of the machine gun crew there. While trying to direct the gun, he was struck in the back of his head by a bullet and knocked unconscious.

A1E Skyraiders dived along the enemy-held ridges and spilled clusters of bombs directly against the enemy flak positions. Three medical evacuation helicopters braved concentrated fire to lift out the most seriously wounded. Close bombing passes by F4C Phantoms and F100 Supersabres blasted the surrounding hills. After forty-two sorties and an expenditure of 82,500 pounds of bombs, 28,500 pounds of napalm, and 22,600 pounds of 20mm cannon fire, enemy AA fire slackened enough to allow helicopter extraction of Bluhm's battered company before nightfall. The Battle of LZ Pat was a dour lesson in raiding a formidable enemy strongpoint with only light artillery and limited helicopter support. The Song Re Valley expedition served as a valuable dress rehearsal for stronger, division-size cavalry raids in the coming year.[5]

The 1st Cavalry Division continued to battle the NVA/VC across the Bong Son Plains and into the An Lao Valley during September. In early October the 3d Brigade was transferred to southern I CTZ to permit further Marine redeployments northward, and the division posted more emergency task forces to other fronts. By November, when Col. Donald V. Rattan's 1st Brigade was airlifted into the western highlands because of the raging Dak To campaign, Operation PERSHING had become essentially a holding action. I Field Force Vietnam commander Lt. Gen. Stanley R. Larsen expressed open concern over the worsening situation in the PERSHING area on 16 December 1967. While recognizing the fact that the 1st Cavalry Division had been assigned, for the time being, an economy of force role, he indicated that any further draw-down of his forces could have an adverse effect on the clearing operations in Binh Dinh Province. Whenever containing pressure weakened, the North Vietnamese slipped out of the hills and attempted to reestablish themselves in the coastal plains and ricelands. The NVA/VC resurfaced whenever the cavalry division dispatched fire brigades to Kontum Province or other locations.

The 1st Cavalry Division did not complete its clearing operations in Binh Dinh Province until 21 January 1968, but the coastal campaign culminated in the mid-December victory over a fortified seacoast village complex near Tam Quan. The action began on 6 December as a routine sighting in the midst of a dozen squad and platoon-size incidents throughout the PERSHING area. Aerial scoutships of the 9th Cavalry observed a communications antenna being pulled in near the village of Dai Dong, and shortly afterward enemy machine guns opened fire on an H13 observation helicopter.

5. 1st Cav Div, *The Battle of LZ Pat*, 14 MHD.

Troop A's rifle platoon was air assaulted into the vicinity late that afternoon, but became embroiled in combat and unable to disengage. A platoon of the squadron's Troop D inserted to assist became stranded as well. The North Vietnamese occupied an extensive network of spider holes and fortified strongpoints built into trenchlines around the terraced rice paddies and hamlets. The enemy positions were embedded in thick hedgerows formed by cacti and dense underbrush, and also interwoven into the numerous dwellings, bamboo thickets, and palm groves on a sandy barrier island.

Colonel Rattan dispatched several units to reinforce and rescue the isolated recon troops before dark from their untenable positions. One of the first in was his quick reaction force, Company B of Lt. Col. Christian Dubia's 1st Battalion, 8th Cavalry, which was air assaulted into the engagement. Shortly after landing, the reaction force was struck by extremely close-range automatic weapons and grenade fire erupting from positions concealed in the nearby hedgerows and shrubbery. The fighting was at such close range that the North Vietnamese surged out of their trenches to loot American wounded. The 2d Platoon clubbed its way out to prevent their mortally wounded lieutenant from being choked to death by NVA soldiers. In another area four armored personnel carriers sent from Company A, 1st Battalion of the 50th Infantry, were stopped by a dike at the edge of the barrier island. One of the mechanized vehicles became mired in paddy mud just short of the enemy trenchline and received a direct hit from a B40 rocket.

The battered reaction company pulled back and reorganized with the remaining three armored personnel carriers. After nightfall, as artillery and helicopter gunships pounded and rocketed the enemy defenses, one of the vehicles sped over to extract the trapped reconnaissance troops. The artillery bombardment was maintained throughout the night under aircraft searchlights and flare illumination. Colonel Rattan used the time to move the 40th ARVN Regiment into blocking positions around the general area and ordered in more mechanized support to include flamethrowing carriers. The rest of Lieutenant Colonel Dubia's battalion moved onto the battlefield.

Although the weather was cool and overcast, with intermittent rain showers and early morning ground haze, it never interfered with aerial support. In the morning helicopter gunships rocketed the village then doused it with riot gas. Four Duster self-propelled flak guns clanked into position to fire through the dense foliage covering the enemy lines. Dozers from the 8th Engineer Battalion pushed up a causeway across the muddy paddy water so that additional armored personnel carriers could fully support the renewed attack.

At 9:00 A.M. the cavalrymen started across the marshy ricefields, supported by several armored personnel carriers. They were met by a hail of machine gun, rifle, and grenade fire. Company A's advance was stopped in a heavily overgrown area, and on the left flank a platoon of Company B was pinned down by a heavy machine gun nest. Snipers were registering extremely accurate fire on the mechanized carriers, and many vehicle commanders and drivers were killed. This first assault was called off shortly after one of the mechanized vehicles was destroyed by a mine while carrying wounded to the rear. The units pulled back, allowing more artillery and airstrikes to be placed on the enemy fortifications.

The two companies assaulted the NVA lines later that morning with seven armored personnel carriers in front. The advancing cavalrymen had gained only one hundred yards when they were hit with a fusillade of devastating sniper, automatic weapons, and grenade fire. Almost instantly, one vehicle driver was killed and three armored vehicle commanders were severely wounded. Company A lost twenty men trying to cross over one low hedgerow, and the open field was covered with dead and wounded. The battalion was forced to retreat and reorganize under the cover of artillery fire, while twelve helicopter loads of wounded were medically evacuated.

That afternoon another attack was launched. As the cavalrymen moved forward, the armored personnel carriers slowly proceeded in front of them with shielded machine guns blazing. One armored flamethrowing carrier accompanied the advance. Although there were two mechanized flamethrowing carriers during the battle, only one could be used at a time. The other mechanized flamethrower was to the rear taking on a fresh mixture of napalm, and they rotated in this fashion throughout the action. As recoilless rifle fire and rocket-propelled grenades slammed into the advancing troops, one carrier exploded and stopped Company B's drive. The gush of smoke rising from the antitank weapon backblast revealed the enemy position, and it was scorched by the flamethrower.

Company A was also having difficulty, as one of the tracked vehicles in front of the unit threw a track and became immobilized. The enemy fire intensified, but the remaining three carriers suddenly put on a burst of speed fifty yards from the main trenchline. The engines sputtered from a walking rate to fifteen miles per hour, enabling the machines to smash into the trench. The unexpected violence of this maneuver completely disorganized the North Vietnamese, who tried to flee the onrushing vehicles. Several groups tried to climb the armored carriers only to be crushed under their steel tracks or shot down by the machine guns and rifles of the crew members. The infantry quickly caught up, and by evening the first trench was in cavalry hands. The limit of advance had been reached for the day.

Lieutenant Colonel Dubia airlifted Company C of his battalion into the line on the morning of 8 December to relieve Company B. The attack was continued, but opposition was already considerably weaker. The armored personnel carriers were followed by engineer dozers and demolition teams destroying emplacements and clearing lanes as the infantry pushed ahead. Hard fighting transpired in other nearby hamlets, and the entire engagement lasted several days. Every night the Americans pulled back to night laagers ringed with armored vehicles. The 1st Battalion of the 12th Cavalry was brought in as reinforcement from Dak To, and more NVA pockets of resistance were eradicated throughout the area. On 19 December 1967 the final action was fought by a company of Lieutenant Colonel Stannard's battalion against a Viet Cong force dug into the northern bank of the Bong Son River.

The Battle of Tam Quan was fought over a relatively large area on the Bong Son Plains between the towns of Tam Quan and Song Son from 6 to 20 December 1967. Colonel Rattan's brigade used its attached mechanized forces to optimum advantage in mauling both the *7th* and *8th Battalions, 22d NVA Regiment*. With the battle's conclusion, organized enemy regular forces were largely finished in northeastern Binh Dinh Province. The Battle of Tam Quan was costly to both sides. The 1st Cavalry Division lost 58 soldiers killed and 250 wounded, while more than 600 North Vietnamese bodies were found in the smashed trenches and charred strongpoints. The engagement was considered one of the most significant encounters fought during Operation PERSHING, and it represented the successful air cavalry utilization of mechanized support on a well-defended battlefield.

Operations in Vietnam placed the 1st Cavalry Division in the security business for the first time since its initial inception as a border patrol division in the southwestern United States. Clearing operations in Operation PERSHING brought a new dimension to airmobility as well. Traditionally favored air assaults, aerial surveillance, and rapid reaction capabilities were tailored to meet new division needs. The airmobile techniques most commonly used in PERSHING were either specifically innovated or refined for the clearing campaign: cordon and search, swooper, snatch and selective snatch, bushmaster, lightning bug, hunter-killer, minicav, artillery ambush, trail running, and artillery raids.

Cordon-and-search missions applied to temporary village occupation. Under the cover of early morning darkness, a cavalry rifle company marched to a selected hamlet and surrounded it before dawn. Just after first light a South Vietnamese field police platoon was airlifted in to thoroughly search the village. One police team set up a screening and collection point for the villagers while the rest of the platoon searched each home and questioned its inhabitants. Persons detained during the search were whisked out by helicopter to a separate collection center at brigade level. The other villagers were assembled and listened to a propaganda team explain the U.S. presence and South Vietnamese government aims, and were encouraged to give information about the Viet Cong. At the same time, division medical personnel established a MEDCAP medical clinic in the hamlet.

At division and brigade level the provost marshal established police operations centers jointly staffed by the division military police, NPFF, special branch police, and officers from the ARVN 22d Division G2 and G5 sections. Here village detainees were subjected to closer scrutiny, and division military intelligence experts produced the feared counterintelligence "Black Lists" in the division police operations center. The magnitude of this effort was reflected by the 10,407 detainees processed by the 545th Military Police Company's "dragnet" screening points at division and brigade level. They ranged from individual farmers scooped up while tilling rice in selective snatch missions to whole regional populations forcibly evacuated from zones such as the An Lao Valley. From 26 May 1967, when the joint cavalry-NPFF force conducted its first cordon and search, the division conducted 946 such missions, which checked 319,313 undetained "innocent" civilians.

Speed and surprise were essential in cordon-and-search missions because the Viet Cong quickly fled villages being approached by allied military units. The timing and methods of surrounding villages were constantly changed to avoid setting patterns. Companies were often airmobiled around villages on swooper missions. Considerable surprise could be achieved by sudden swooper airmobile insertions if the time of day was varied sufficiently to throw VC guards off balance. Sometimes the cavalry even amphibiously landed near seaside hamlets from naval craft covered by swift boats.

Snatch missions tried to capture Viet Cong among the people working in the fields outside the villages. Developed in late July, a typical snatch mission used a pair of scout helicopters and a third helicopter, which carried the battalion operations officer. He randomly surveyed the ricefields for large groups of people and called for a snatch mission by radioing the standby airmobile rifle platoon and Vietnamese police team. Escorted by two gunships, the troop helicopters corralled any selected group of people by landing around them. The platoon riflemen got out of the helicopters and compressed the surrounded farmers, who were usually men, women, and children of all ages, toward one spot for screening and inspection by the police. Since snatch missions could be conducted in one hour and netted many VC suspects, they were considered very successful.

Within a few weeks, however, people no longer gathered in groups large enough to make a snatch mission worthwhile. The division responded by developing the selective snatch. These missions normally involved two Huey troopships with three riflemen from battalion headquarters on each, escorted by two gunships and a pair of scout helicopters. The battalion operations officer flew above the ricefields looking for anybody who appeared suspicious and directed the two Hueys to descend swiftly on both sides of suspects to allow apprehension by the six cavalrymen. The selective snatch mission generally terminated when the lift ships were full of suspects.

Division bushmaster missions were night infantry ambushes along suspected NVA/VC infiltration routes, employed by platoon-size elements. Multiple ambush forces were usually fielded within reinforcing distance of their company forward base and were mutually supporting. During Operation RICE GRAIN, a suboperation guarding the October rice harvest, bushmaster missions were conducted to prevent night harvesting for possible VC consumption.

Lightning bug missions were another nighttime activity to detect and inhibit enemy travel, using special searchlight-fitted helicopters at division level. Since helicopter-mounted spotlights were almost useless if dense foliage existed, these "firefly" aircraft usually probed the darkened coastal region. A lightning bug team consisted of one searchlight helicopter, a team of two helicopter gunships, and a flare-dropping helicopter. The gunships fired on targets revealed by the powerful spotlight beams of the searchlight helicopter. Alternatively, the lights could be turned off and targets spotted with starlight scopes, in which case the flare-dropping helicopter provided target illumination for the gunships. Often a SLAR-equipped aircraft flew ahead of the lightning bug team to scan for likely searchlight targets such as sampans.

The hunter-killer missions were battalion-level night helicopter searches. One Huey helicopter carried a starlight scope operator, who was chosen by battalion headquarters, and he marked targets with tracer rounds for the two helicopter gunships which made up the rest of the hunter-killer team. All nightly surveillance was kept deliberately on an irregular basis.

Minicav missions were small airmobile search operations which normally air assaulted a rifle platoon onto an objective, with other airmobile reinforcements on standby in case of contact. The minicav mission differed somewhat from ordinary platoon sweep operations because the platoon was under the control of a flight leader overhead in an observation helicopter. He moved the platoon to check out his visual sightings and could rapidly extract and reinsert the platoon with great flexibility to search wide areas.

Artillery ambushes and trail-running missions were division artillery night firings. Artillery shelling was used in Vietnam for harassing and interdiction purposes on a nightly basis. To find targets automatically, artillery ambushes were triggered by seismic intrusion devices or field-expedient trip flares along trails and suspected pathways. An artillery section or battery was prepared to fire a barrage on signal and could switch to firing illumination rounds for helicopter surveillance or additional aerial rocketing if desired. Artillery ambush effectiveness was enhanced during 1967 by electronic Sandia Devices, miniature seis: graph sensors capable of detecting footsteps, which transmitted the signals to receiver sets. Trail running was simply the placement of artillery fire along the length of trails or ridgelines.

Artillery raids were conducted if worthwhile NVA/VC targets were reported beyond the range of normally positioned division artillery. Airmobile infantry secured a forward location, and CH47 Chinooks brought in an artillery battery to the new landing zone. Observers in scout helicopters spotted targets for the artillery raiding battery. Lucrative sightings could be engaged also by the infantry as the howitzers switched to a fire support role. The artillery raid was brief, usually being completed within six hours, and offered Division Artillery an ability to react rapidly to targets of opportunity.

Searching, swooping, and raiding across half a province for an entire year demanded large amounts of manpower. The 1st Cavalry Division was always up to strength, but there were critical shortages of infantry, aviation, artillery, and medical personnel during certain periods. These occurred because of Army-wide shortages, peak rotational times, and other personnel management problems. From October through December, for example, serious shortages of artillerymen and medical personnel developed. Since replacements in those fields were not forthcoming from the United States, the divisional artillery firepower was significantly diminished, while medical support was only hindered (medical service could be increased by cutting out hamlet MEDCAP clinics).[6]

The 1st Cavalry Division casualties in Operation PERSHING totalled 852 troopers killed in action, 22 missing in action, 286 killed in noncombat circumstances, and 4,119 wounded, which exceeded all division operational losses during 1966. With actual division strength averaging 19,571 personnel throughout Operation PERSHING, these casualties amounted to 27 percent of available manpower, not counting injuries or disease. Most losses were taken by the infantrymen, and USARV responded quickly to send infantry replacements, but loss rates were still too high to permit smooth transition in training and experience among division personnel.[7]

The success of the division's clearing campaign in Operation PERSHING was difficult to measure. There was no precise way to gauge whether the Viet Cong were being ferreted out of the hamlets

6. 1st Cav Div, *Combat After Action Report*, dtd 29 Jun 68, Tab 13: MOS Shortages.
7. Ibid., Tab 12, and Incl. 4 to cover ltr dtd 14 Jul 68, Subj: Recommendation for PUC.

or were simply lying low. The pacification effort's success in winning over the people in Binh Dinh Province to the South Vietnamese government was impossible to ascertain. The division offered considerable tangible evidence to show that its airmobility enhanced the security process. Highway 1 was opened for commercial traffic through Binh Dinh Province for the first time in years, and government-sponsored elections were held for the first time on 3 September. The division claimed 2,029 NVA killed and 3,367 VC killed in Operation PERSHING, with another 236 NVA and 2,123 Viet Cong captured. However, perhaps the most telling evidence supporting the 1st Cavalry Division's claim to victory was one inescapable military reality. During the major NVA/VC Tet-68 offensive, which engulfed the entire country only a week after PERSHING ended, the former communist stronghold of Binh Dinh Province was one of the least-affected regions in Vietnam.

CHAPTER 6

Flexible Response

Techniques, Tet-68

At the beginning of 1968, allied concerns about clearing Binh Dinh Province were cast aside as events worsened in the northernmost part of South Vietnam. While the 1st Cavalry Division was waging a slow-paced double war of search and pacification in the sandy hamlets and jungle valleys along the central coast, the Marines were combating entire North Vietnamese divisions driving across the DMZ. The major Marine border bastion at Khe Sanh was being challenged by freshly infiltrated NVA forces, and there were disturbing signs of increased NVA activity throughout northernmost Quang Tri and Thua Thien provinces. On 15 January 1968 MACV deputy commander Gen. Creighton W. Abrams ordered Major General Tolson to move his airmobile division northward to reinforce I Corps Tactical Zone at once.

When Tolson received notice to transplant his flag to Gia Le in upper I CTZ immediately, his division was still embroiled in Operation PERSHING. Although the bulk of the airmobile cavalry was concentrated in the central highlands on this major clearing operation, a number of secondary MACV missions had elements scattered from Phan Thiet, northeast of Saigon, to the Que Son Valley below Da Nang. The division had not been together under a single commander for nearly two years. As an airmobile formation, the 1st Cavalry Division was designed for flexible battlefield mobility, but it was sent to Vietnam before concept tests on such a vast scale could be conducted at Fort Benning.

The emergency movement north, coded Operation JEB STUART,

was the first actual test of rapid airmobile division displacement between combat theaters. This was also the first MACV undertaking of such magnitude, and the transfer would have been extremely difficult even in fair weather and the best of circumstances. Each zone had to be independently supplied in the absence of secure north-south communications lines. The overtaxed Navy supply system which governed I CTZ was woefully unprepared to cope with the arriving airmobile division's high rates of supply consumption. The incomplete logistical arrangements were further aggravated because the unprecedented relocation was made in direct response to a major battle zone crisis and had to be executed with great rapidity. Uprooting the 1st Cavalry Division and moving it two hundred miles to an entirely new military zone demanded optimum flexibility, quick reaction, and mastery of adverse weather conditions.

The 1st Cavalry Division, like all American formations in Vietnam, was an extremely large organization. It was tied to a huge, sophisticated main base complex which provided the vast amounts of necessary support and sustenance. Once emplaced, allied divisions rarely moved from their assigned geographical sector because of the expense and time required to shift the support base. This need to keep divisions within the logistical operating radius of their base camps inevitably transformed them into static security formations. Returning the 1st Cavalry Division to a flexible response posture meant cutting the An Khe umbilical cord. Such action would unfortunately reduce divisional combat power during the transition period.

Operation PERSHING was immediately curtailed as the division scaled down offensive activity in Binh Dinh Province to local patrolling. The widely separated units packed up their gear and streamed back to either the main An Khe garrison or Landing Zone English. Fleets of transport aircraft shuttled troops from An Khe in the central highlands and LZ English on the Bong Son Plains to Quang Tri and Hue–Phu Bai along the northern coast. Long truck convoys crowded the winding road from An Khe to the Qui Nhon docksides where the division cargo was transferred to Navy ships streaming toward Da Nang. Overhead, flights of division helicopters droned through overcast skies to their new helipads.

General Tolson moved his command post into a graveyard north of Phu Bai called LZ El Paso, but the barren landing zone was unsatisfactory for division headquarters. On 23 January General Abrams agreed that the 1st Cavalry Division should be relocated to Camp Evans, a former Marine regimental base. This move also fortuitously displaced Colonel Rattan's 1st Brigade to LZ Betty, just outside the key communications hub of Quang Tri, as the Marines withdrew on 25 January. The 3d Brigade under Col. Hubert S. Campbell was already in I CTZ, having spent four months fighting the *2d NVA Division* in the Que Son Valley, twenty-five miles south of Da Nang. Campbell's brigade was recalled to Quang Tri the same day, and the 2d Brigade was left in Binh Dinh Province to guard the old PERSHING area.

General Westmoreland wanted Tolson to have a full division of three working brigades in his new operational area. MACV attached Col. John H. Cushman's 2d Brigade of the 101st Airborne Division, which had just arrived in Vietnam, to the cavalry and transferred the new brigade from Cu Chi, west of Saigon, to Gia Le. General Tolson sent this brigade to LZ El Paso on 27 January, and it began transforming the innocuous site into Camp Eagle. The camp was destined to become one of the largest military field posts in the world after it became the main base of the 101st Airborne Division (Airmobile).

Operation JEB STUART I officially began on 21 January 1968. Unaware of the impending NVA/VC storm of Tet-68, which would sweep through Vietnam within a week, the division's original purpose was to help III Marine Amphibious Force (MAF) safeguard the stretch of territory between Quang Tri and Hue–Phu Bai. Colonel Rattan began helicoptering search parties west of the cities into the mountainous enemy base areas. These longstanding strongholds were known to be honeycombed with fortifications, supply bunkers, hospitals, training sites, and even recreation facilities. While the 1st Cavalry Division was preparing to thrust into the enemy-held jungles, the NVA/VC were making their own preparations for attack.

The NVA/VC targeted the city of Quang Tri, the capital of South Vietnam's northernmost province, as part of a country-wide wave of attacks aimed at capturing important population centers and provoking a general uprising against the Saigon regime. The enemy offensive was timed for the *Tet Nguyen Dan*, lunar new year, holiday celebrations to achieve as much surprise as possible. MACV's military forces were observing the Tet-68 truce period, and many ARVN soldiers were absent from their units. Allied intelligence was generally unaware of any unusual enemy plans or dispositions.

The original plans to capture Quang Tri were made long before the 1st Cavalry Division moved into I CTZ but never altered. Enemy planners knew that the division was present, but watched as its brigades engaged in mountain search efforts some distance to the west. The NVA/VC apparently discounted the airmobile cavalry's ability to reorient one of these brigades in time to affect the battle for Quang Tri.

The assumed inability of the 1st Cavalry Division quickly to shift internal resources was not unreasonable. The airmobile division's poor logistical posture was further impaired by the unexpected onslaught of Tet-68, engulfing the formation's new operational area just days after its arrival. Although many supplies for the division were pre-positioned in the new zone, they were placed in anticipation of allied directives prior to Tet and not where the division was actually sent. When the enemy offensive suddenly sliced the road networks, many essential logistical items—especially aviation fuel and artillery munitions—were reduced to fractional amounts delivered by C130 aircraft parachute drops.

The 1st Cavalry Division's logistical nightmare compounded itself in a vicious cycle. The troops were still building fuel storage revetments at Camp Evans when the Tet offensive started, and the limited containers on hand required daily refilling. The absence of a written requisition (an administrative error) prevented this resupply the day before Tet started, leaving the division with only ten thousand gallons of JP4 aviation fuel. A lack of helicopter fuel and the foul weather conditions limited available airlift to emergencies, so that stock levels remained dangerously low. This critical situation was aggravated by the marginal condition of overworked division aircraft trying to build up supplies and respond to tactical field missions, since insufficient maintenance elements accompanied them to I CTZ.

The cold northwest monsoon period of drizzling "crachin" rain presented the worst possible weather for airmobile operations. The low, misting clouds and dense ground fogs lasted for twenty-seven days straight, limiting aircraft-controlled airstrikes to five hours daily and forcing much artillery fire to be adjusted by sound alone. The bad flying weather frequently canceled helicopter gunship support and interrupted critical aerial replenishment, medical evacuation, and troop airlift.

The North Vietnamese and Viet Cong intended to take joint control of Quang Tri by infiltrating a sapper (engineer demolition) platoon of the *10th NVA Sapper Battalion* into the city before the main attack. The sappers would create as much confusion as possible with explosives and sabotage, weakening the town defenses for the primary assault by the *812th NVA Regiment* and two VC main force battalions from the outside. The battle began at 2:00 A.M. on 31 January 1968 as the sappers destroyed communications lines and attacked other critical points precisely on schedule. Fortunately for the allies, the North Vietnamese regimental advance was delayed more than two hours by rain-swollen streams and lack of terrain familiarity. This gap in timing later proved fatal, for the 1st ARVN Regiment in and around the city was quickly alerted once the sappers revealed themselves. The South Vietnamese battalion posted within Quang Tri eliminated most of the infiltrators before the main attack struck in the predawn darkness at 4:20 A.M.

The *814th VC Battalion* stormed through the outlying hamlet of Tri Buu, where the 9th ARVN Airborne Battalion was monitoring a revolutionary development program. The South Vietnamese paratroopers were pushed back into Quang Tri and desperately tried to shore up the inner defenses. The Viet Cong and North Vietnamese infantrymen rushed the city walls from several directions. The ARVN soldiers slowed the combined attack, but heavy fighting continued unabated throughout the morning. The *812th NVA Regiment* penetrated the city defenses at several points and advanced toward the sector headquarters. By noon on 31 January the outcome of the battle was still uncertain.

Shortly after noon the Quang Tri senior province advisor, Mr. Robert Brewer, urgently conferred with Colonel Rattan to assist the thin ARVN lines. Mr. Brewer briefed him that the situation at Quang Tri was "highly tenuous," with at least one enemy battalion already inside the city, and that the defenders might not be able to hold out. Since the NVA/VC firing positions were located on the eastern and southern fringes of the city, it appeared that he was reinforcing for the final blow from the east. Colonel Rattan hastily called division headquarters for authority to counterattack at once from the air, even though it was already late afternoon. General Tolson granted him the authority to use the limited division helicopters on hand.

The lead elements of Rattan's brigade had been in the Quang Tri area for only two weeks, and much of his command for only six days. Since then, he had tackled the southwestern approaches to Quang Tri by sending his brigade to a suspected enemy mountain base area nine miles away, with one firebase as far as twelve miles out. LZ Betty and the other fire support bases had been under rocket and mortar attack since dawn, as the North Vietnamese attempted to lock the cavalry in place. Despite the problems imposed by lack of advance reconnaissance, unfamiliar terrain, distance, and harassing fire, Rattan felt he could quickly airmobile two battalions to the aid of the city. The battle plans were drawn in one hour with the help of Mr. Brewer, who pointed out the most probable enemy infiltration and support routes. Selected assault areas were planned with the idea of blocking the enemy from reinforcing troops already engaged in the city, eliminating enemy fire support by landing on top of his supporting guns, and trapping whatever enemy forces were already in Quang Tri.

Additional helicopters were requested from Division Aviation, the aerial reconnaissance squadron and the aerial rocket artillery battalion were alerted, and the 1st Brigade issued its attack order at 1:45 P.M. Lt. Col. Daniel W. French's 1st Battalion of the 12th Cavalry, which was given priority on airlift, executed its lightning air assault into the middle of the North Vietnamese heavy weapons sites. The helicopters carrying Company C skimmed low underneath the clouds and banked sharply to land the Skytroopers among the mortars, recoilless rifles, and AA machine guns of the NVA fire support center for the *K-4 Battalion, 812th NVA Regiment*.

The North Vietnamese machine gunners frantically shifted their guns to fire directly into the descending helicopters, but were unable to stop the aerial assault from overwhelming the position. The cavalrymen leaped off the skids of the lowering helicopters as bullets peppered the doorframes and jumped into action with their M16s blazing. The cavalry squads quickly maneuvered forward as the enemy gunners turned more weapons against the surprise air assault. Company B also became engaged in heavy fighting as it landed on the other side of the enemy positions. After hours of bitter fighting, resistance tapered off after twilight as the North Vietnamese began abandoning the field. By landing two companies against the *K-4 Battalion's* heavy weapons support and destroying it, one-third of the

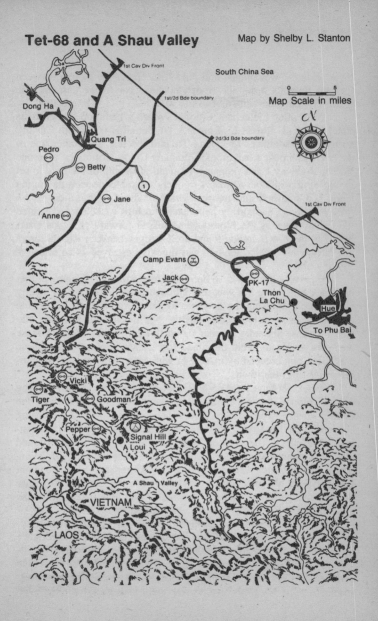

Tet-68 and A Shau Valley

Map by Shelby L. Stanton

1st Cav Div Front

South China Sea

1st/2d Bde boundary

Map Scale in miles

2d/3d Bde boundary

Dong Ha

Pedro

Quang Tri

Betty

1

Jane

Anne

1st Cav Div Front

Camp Evans

Jack

PK-17

Thon
La Chu

Hue

To Phu Bai

Vicki

Tiger

Goodman

Pepper

Signal Hill
A Loui

A Shau Valley

VIETNAM

LAOS

NVA regiment was pinned and rendered combat-ineffective between Colonel Rattan's airmobile troops in their rear to the east and the Quang Tri defenders in front to the west.

Shortly after Lieutenant Colonel French's battalion launched its attack, Lt. Col. Robert L. Runkle's 1st Battalion of the 5th Cavalry air assaulted southeast of Quang Tri into the rear of another one of the NVA regiment's battalions. Company C was airmobiled onto one side of Highway 1 as Company A landed just south of the road to set up blocking positions. Runkle's troopers scrambled toward the raging battle and smashed into the rear guard of the *K-6 Battalion, 812th NVA Regiment*. Supporting helicopter gunships rocketed and strafed the enemy lines as the Skytroopers pressed forward. Like its sister battalion, the *K-6 Battalion* found itself wedged between ARVN forces and advancing cavalrymen and was quickly destroyed as an effective fighting unit.

The cavalry thrust was so demoralizing to the NVA regiment that its attack on Quang Tri was discontinued after nightfall. All enemy efforts turned to using the darkness to get off the battlefield. Unable to conduct an orderly withdrawal, the North Vietnamese broke into small groups. Sporadic combat flared throughout the night as these elements sought to avoid the allied forces. Many North Vietnamese and Viet Cong escaped by mixing in with crowds of refugees streaming away from the town.

The next day the 1st ARVN Regiment completed clearing Quang Tri as Colonel Rattan's cavalrymen swept into close pursuit of the fleeing enemy. The cavalry forces helicoptered in ever-increasing concentric circles around the city, seeking to engage any NVA regimental remnants. The attached 1st Battalion of the 502d Infantry found a North Vietnamese contingent holed up in a cathedral south of Quang Tri. Aerial gunships were summoned, and Company D of Lieutenant Colonel French's battalion air assaulted into the firefight to insure numerical superiority. Similar but smaller firefights flared up for the next ten days, long after the city was cleared.

The North Vietnamese and Viet Cong were confident and superbly equipped when the battle opened, but their battle experience against the Marines had offered them only limited opportunity to witness airmobile tactics. Marine helicopters were comparatively rare and used as transports rather than as an integrated armada of aerial war machines. The NVA/VC were completely unprepared to cope with the dazzling pace and devastating firepower of air cavalry tactics. Not realizing their vulnerability if caught in the open, the North Vietnamese often "played dead" and seldom returned fire as helicopters approached. This primitive response cost them dearly as division helicopters swarmed over the fields and cut loose with rockets, cannons, machine guns, and grenade launchers into the prone enemy ranks.

The Battle for Quang Tri was a resounding allied victory which not only denied the NVA/VC an important Tet-68 objective, but also cost the enemy 914 killed along with 86 men and 331 weapons captured. The 1st Brigade, situated in the western highland foothills when the battle commenced, had wheeled its battalions around and helicoptered them to the rescue in the finest traditions of historic American cavalry.

For the first time in airmobile division history, vertical air assault was used to decide a major battle by conducting a classic surprise pincer counterattack. It was a "textbook" maneuver previously only dreamed of in military tactical planning sessions. The sudden airmobile blitz straddled the North Vietnamese heavy weapons positions and eradicated the fire support needed by the Quang Tri attackers. Trapped between the newly airlanded cavalrymen and the defending garrison of Quang Tri City, five enemy battalions were forced to quit the battlefield in complete disarray. The flexible response of modern aerial cavalry at Quang Tri gave MACV one of its most decisive successes during the long, discouraging weeks of Tet-68.

As Colonel Rattan's 1st Brigade was mopping up the last enemy resistance around Quang Tri, a much larger battle was shaping up in Hue. The enemy had over seven thousand troops in control of large portions of the ancient imperial capital when the Tet offensive started. The available airmobile cavalry in the area consisted of Colonel Campbell's 3d Brigade, which had just deployed around Camp Evans. Like Colonel Rattan's brigade, it was constructing firebases to the west, preparing to search out remote enemy base areas. Again a major city was attacked while the cavalrymen were carrying out assignments orienting them in the opposite direction. This failure of allied intelligence to appraise properly enemy intentions forced the cavalry brigade to make a complete turnabout with very limited helicopter resources in extremely poor weather conditions.

As the Marines and South Vietnamese struggled to recapture the city itself, Colonel Campbell's brigade attacked toward Hue from the northwest on 2 February. The brigade was assigned the mission of interdicting the northern and western approaches into Hue. If the brigade could cut off NVA/VC supply lines, further enemy access to the city would be denied, and his reinforcements would be prevented from reaching the raging battle. Estimates of the enemy situation were mostly guesswork, but it was suspected that five battalions were engaged in Hue, an unknown force probably occupied the hamlet of Thon La Chu just outside Hue, and other regiments or battalions were deployed to the west or southwest to protect enemy supply channels. Ambushes along Route 1 indicated that the enemy intended to block the main highway.

The 2d Battalion of the 12th Cavalry, commanded by Lt. Col. Richard S. Sweet, was given the mission of moving toward Hue, contacting the enemy, fixing his location, and destroying him. The battalion was helicoptered from Camp Evans, where it was providing base security, to a landing zone just outside PK-17, a South Vietnamese army camp six miles from Hue City. Early the next morning Sweet formed a diamond-shaped battalion formation with his line companies and began the advance parallel to and south of Highway 1 toward Hue. The low rural area consisted of continuous rice paddies, with slightly rolling hills and sparse scrub brush, interrupted only by scattered stone tombs and peasant houses composed of mud and straw.

At 10:30 A.M. Colonel Sweet halted his battalion after lead elements passed through a patch of woodland and spotted enemy soldiers milling about on the other side of a broad rice paddy in front of Thon La Chu. The hamlet had been captured at the outset of Tet-68 and was being used as the support and staging base of the *7th and 9th Battalions, 29th Regiment, 325C NVA Division,* which had just marched into the area from the Khe Sanh front. Thon La Chu was an elongated settlement surrounded by thick vegetation and, as a model Revolutionary Development project, contained sophisticated defenses designed by U.S. Army advisors.

During the next several hours, the battalion assaulted across the ricefield toward the far woodline. Capt. Robert L. Helvey's Company A led the attack, but the rolling ground fog and rainy haze prevented the usual helicopter support. Most division gunships were grounded. Two aerial rocket helicopters from the 2d Battalion, 20th Artillery, braved the dense fog to spew 2.75-inch rockets in front of the cavalrymen. This extra measure of support allowed some of Captain Helvey's men to reach the woodline and clear an area along the northern edge of the settlement. The formidable North Vietnamese machine gun, recoilless rifle, and mortar positions prevented any further advance. Helvey recalled, "In the Que Son [Valley] we fought the *2d NVA Division* in several knock-down, drag-out fights, so we knew what we were getting into. We reacted the way we should have reacted, but we were outnumbered and outgunned."[1]

Lieutenant Colonel Sweet pleaded for artillery support throughout the day, but the dismal weather prevented howitzers from being airlifted into range of the battle. Finally, two CH47 Chinook helicopters flew under the low overcast during the afternoon and brought two 105mm howitzers of the 1st Battalion, 77th Artillery, into PK-17. The cannoneers wrestled their artillery pieces into action despite enemy mortar fire, but the cavalrymen needed more than one section of two tubes in support.

As darkness fell, the 2d Battalion, 12th Cavalry, established a tight perimeter to better maintain control in close proximity to the enemy village because of the extremely low visibility. During the cold night of 3 February, the cavalrymen received only a few mortar rounds in their positions, but they were forced to sit miserably awake in fighting positions without packs, ponchos, or poncho liners to ward off the damp chill.

At dawn the North Vietnamese regiment launched a mass counterattack. Hundreds of mortar shells smothered the shrunken American perimeter, which measured only 150 yards across. It quickly became apparent that the enemy was making an all-out effort to eliminate the American force and regain his lost positions. The cavalry grenadiers and riflemen hurled back waves of NVA soldiers who were running at them firing AK47 automatic rifles from the hip as machine gunners laid down grazing cross fires in the fog. Enemy mortar rounds exploded through the compact battalion and scored several direct hits against crowded weapons pits and foxholes. By noon the 12th Cavalry lines were surrounded. Losses were heavy, and only a few medical evacuation helicopters were able to penetrate the intense, close-range fire to retrieve the seriously wounded.

1. 14th MHD Report on Tet-68, dtd 15 Apr 68, p. 17.

With an entire battalion isolated outside Hue, Colonel Campbell air assaulted Lt. Col. James B. Vaught's 5th Battalion, 7th Cavalry, into a landing zone south of PK-17 and astride Highway 1. The battalion prepared to move toward the stranded cavalrymen the following day, and more artillery was brought forward. However, Colonel Sweet realized that his men couldn't stay where they were another night. They had had less than six hours of sleep in the past forty-eight hours and were double fatigued by two days of desperate fighting for their survival. Ammunition, food, and canteen water were almost exhausted, and the troops were already skimming muddy rainwater from the wet clay to drink.

Late in the afternoon Sweet huddled with his battle-hardened officers and senior sergeants to devise a plan to extricate the battalion before it was annihilated. They decided to slip past the enemy after dark by going three miles deeper behind his lines to a hill overlooking the surrounding lowland, rather than pulling back as expected. It was a bold gamble and would require the entire night, but the poor visibility and misty cold conditions would assist the deception.

The troopers began gathering their equipment together singly at different times so that nothing unusual could be observed by the enemy. Loose gear was tied down and padded. Stretchers were improvised to carry wounded if action occurred during the march. Excess equipment belonging to the dead and injured was centrally collected in each company area and buried in a pit for timed detonation. Many of the troops rigged dummies in their foxholes, using sticks, spare clothing, and broken weapons.

The daring night march commenced at 8:00 P.M. Only six light howitzers were available to support the battalion, but their concentrated fire provided enough diversion to allow the battalion to assemble discreetly and start moving out. Smoke grenades were popped to create a smoke screen as the most reliable point man, Pfc. Hector L. Comacho, carefully led the battalion through the ankle-deep water of the rice paddies. "It was dark," Private Comacho said, "but I trust myself. The hardest part was finding some place where everyone could go, and making sure that everyone could keep up."[2]

The troopers were instructed not to fire under any circumstances,

2. 14th MHD, *The Battle for Hue*, undtd, 1st Cav Div files, p. 4.

and if fired upon to just drop to the ground and remain silent. Only company commanders could give the orders to return fire, and if this was necessary, only machine guns would be used. The battalion proceeded in a column of files with two companies abreast. The night was so dark that individuals moved within an arm's length of each other. The men trudged slowly west across the muddied ricefields. The enemy remained quiet and unaware of the escape. At one point the five-hundred-yard-long column froze when someone forward thought he heard an enemy rifle bolt slam forward, but when nothing happened, the cavalrymen began moving again. The battalion silently snaked through the quiet landscape.

As the battalion approached the river, the ground became boggy, and soon both files were sloshing noisily through the wet mud. The river was twenty feet wide and four to five feet deep, with a bottom of spongy mud. The troopers crossed individually, helping each other up the slippery far bank. As they were crossing the river, the equipment left behind and set for detonation exploded in a huge ball of fire. The cavalrymen at the rear of the column saw trip flares around the perimeter go off, and rifle fire started barking in the distance. An artillery barrage was used to discourage any North Vietnamese probing.

It was raining, and the bone-penetrating cold pierced the rolling ground fog. Everyone was extremely tired, and several wounded soldiers were trying to keep up. The battalion became noisier as the troops waded through the flooded ground, and sergeants occasionally lost contact with elements in front as they worked their squads around various obstacles. Whenever the lead element halted to let the column close, some of the exhausted men fell asleep on their feet, while others fell to the ground with a muddy splash. The sleeping soldiers were jostled awake as the column began moving again.

As soon as everyone was across the stream, the battalion swung south and traveled across the remaining two and a half miles of terraced paddies and rough pastureland. Along their route many noticed numerous combinations of signal lights flashing at them from woods and hamlets as they progressed southward. Later they surmised that these lights were part of some enemy regular route-marking system used on all passing NVA/VC units. The drowsiest soldiers were jarred awake stumbling across submerged dikes and looked up to see ghostly flares illuminating the skyline over Hue itself.

Finally, as full daylight flooded the landscape shortly after 7:00 A.M. the next morning, the ordeal ended. The weary, shivering cavalrymen climbed the hill which offered them defensible terrain and temporary respite from close-by NVA forces. Lieutenant Colonel Sweet stated, "We had men who had refused to be medevaced that afternoon. They hid their wounds so they could stay with the battalion. . . . And we found guys who were moving along; you'd see them limping; there was no talk. No noise at all. I've never seen such discipline in a unit. Little by little these guys started popping up—you'd find that the man up ahead of you who was dragging a foot had a bullet in his leg, and had it there for almost 24 hours. That's why the night march worked."[3]

By daybreak on 5 February, as Sweet's men safely reached their objective, Colonel Campbell realized that there was a multibattalion enemy force and perhaps a regimental headquarters at Thon La Chu. Radar-controlled bombs and naval gunfire pounded the North Vietnamese positions every day. The fresh troops of Lieutenant Colonel Vaught's reinforcing battalion moved against the northern edge of the village. In the meantime Sweet's men were rested and resupplied and then moved northwest through the sniper-filled hamlet of Thon Bon Tri to reach the enemy's southern flank. After attacking successive treelines on 9 February, the battalion was forced to halt in front of Thon La Chu's inner defenses that night. The actual extent of the enemy preparations in the fortified village was still unknown.

Captain Helvey led a fourteen-man volunteer patrol to scout the enemy positions that night. They crossed the darkened field between the enemy and cavalry lines until Helvey reached a graveyard with a deserted cement house. The patrol occupied the structure in the middle of no-man's-land, allowing him to scan the area with a starlight scope while the other patrol members fired M79 grenade launchers into the far treeline. There was no return fire, as the North Vietnamese refused to disclose their positions. The cavalry patrollers made two trips to the other side of the field past enemy lines.

On the second trip the patrol was spotted by a North Vietnamese soldier who unwittingly thought that Sp4 Michael Oberg, a short

3. 1st Cav Div Rpt on Tet-68, dtd 15 Apr 68, p. 19.

American, was a fellow Oriental. When the NVA soldier tried to engage him in conversation, Oberg shot him. About the same time, Sp4 David Dentinger stepped on something which started moving. He glanced down in horror to see the muzzle of an AK47 rifle and the firer frantically trying to pull it from underneath his foot. Dentinger emptied his M16 magazine into the soldier at point-blank range, and the patrollers scrambled back toward their own lines. A recoilless rifle shell slammed into the cement building as they moved past it, hastening their departure, but Captain Helvey's patrol arrived in friendly lines unscathed.

Lieutenant Colonel Sweet postponed a planned dawn attack based on the patrol's findings. Helvey's men discovered entrenched positions complete with 57mm recoilless rifles, B40 rocket launchers, and heavy machine guns in a double treeline, which meant that any attacking force reaching the first treeline would still have another to penetrate. The Company A executive officer, Tony Kalbli, remarked, "To attack would have been suicide. In that sense alone, the fourteen volunteers saved the battalion from almost complete destruction."[4]

Early that morning Lieutenant Colonel Vaught's battalion assaulted the northern side of the fortified hamlet. Company C poured flanking fire into one NVA company shifting positions to reinforce the main defensive line, dropping numerous bodies into the river. However, the battalion was forced to pull back as more mutually supporting bunkers opened up. Airstrikes throughout the rest of the day hit the village with sixteen tons of bombs and five tons of napalm.

Major General Tolson moved Col. Joseph C. McDonough's 2d Brigade north from Bong Son in II CTZ to rejoin the division. This additional reinforcement freed Colonel Campbell's brigade from all security duty and allowed him to concentrate it against Thon La Chu. Four battalions made the final attack on 21 February 1968. Lieutenant Colonel Vaught's battalion hit Thon La Chu from the north, with Lt. Col. Joseph E. Wasiak's 1st Battalion of the 7th Cavalry on the right flank, while the attached 2d Battalion, 501st Infantry, swung in from the west, and Lieutenant Colonel Sweet's battalion attacked northeast from their southern positions.

---

4. 1st Cav Div Rpt on the Battle for Hue, dtd 15 Apr 68, p. 6.

Lieutenant Colonel Vaught's men pushed into a fiercely defended treeline near the northwest corner of the hamlet. To destroy the NVA fortifications, the cavalrymen maneuvered troops with M72 antitank rocket launchers onto the berms. They fired just ahead of the advancing platoon point men, keeping the bunker occupants pinned down. Light H13 observation helicopters darted overhead, raking the backsides of the bunkers with machine gun fire to prevent enemy use of blind spots and to isolate entrances or adjacent earthworks. The ground point men coordinated with smoke grenades and radios and, on signal to cease supporting fire, rushed forward to push pole charges and satchel charges into bunker openings to explode and cave them in.

Two platoons were pinned down in a shallow ditch under mortar fire in front of one sniper-filled concrete bunker. Point man Pfc. Albert Rocha slowly crawled forward along the ditch toward the bunker as bullets clipped the dirt around him. One bullet smashed the handguard of his rifle. He reached the bunker and slithered on top of it, where he was joined by 1Lt. Frederick Krupa of Company D. While Rocha lowered his rifle to fire into the bunker aperture, Krupa jammed a ten-pound shaped pole charge into the bunker slit. The snipers inside frantically tried to push the charge back out, but the lieutenant kept it there until it exploded. One North Vietnamese soldier suddenly raced out the back exit, spotted Rocha, and broke into a broad grin as he aimed his rifle. Rocha quickly shot him.

Once the outer strongpoints were destroyed, the battalion swiftly continued its advance through the hamlet to the east and linked up with Lieutenant Colonel Wasiak's battalion as it drove south and Lieutenant Colonel Sweet's battalion advancing north. When the brigade consolidated, the fight for Thon La Chu was over. That night a soldier spotted a bypassed enemy tunnel position, grabbed a .38-caliber pistol and flashlight and went into the hole and returned with an NVA captive. The prisoner stated that throughout the battle the thousand North Vietnamese defenders rarely left their fighting positions. They were replenished with food, water, and ammunition in their bunkers by the Viet Cong, who suffered the bulk of the constant artillery and aerial pounding.

The action at Thon La Chu was the turning point in the division's battle at Hue. Colonel Campbell's brigade fanned out to scour the western approaches and sever NVA logistical lifelines into the city. At the same time, the 1st Cavalry Division's own supply difficulties were eased as supply convoys began rolling down Highway 1 from Quang Tri to Camp Evans. More Chinooks and Huey helicopters brought supplies to the field battalions. The Skytroopers were able to secure adequate rest and eat hot meals flown in each day at breakfast and supper. Morale peaked as the drive toward Hue resumed.

The cavalry brigade's determination was reinforced by a grim discovery made by an attacked battalion from Colonel Cushman's brigade. The soldiers found the bodies of fifteen women and children who had been savagely executed in a tiny hamlet only two miles west of Hue. The civilians had been herded into a trench by the North Vietnamese occupiers and shot at close range. Later a significantly larger NVA massacre inside Hue, involving thousands of slain civilians, would be uncovered.

On the night of 22–23 February, Sweet's battalion made another night march closer to Hue. This time they got within two miles of the city before the North Vietnamese opened up with automatic weapons, rockets, recoilless rifles, and mortars from solidly constructed ARVN positions captured at the beginning of the Tet offensive. The extensive fortifications and trench networks were over a mile long and nearly as deep and emplaced in thick jungle. The battalion spent three days clearing the well-defended obstruction.

Hue was attacked from the north by Lieutenant Colonel Vaught's battalion, which was stopped just a half-mile short of the city walls. A cleverly concealed NVA roadblock shattered the lead squad and engaged Capt. Michael S. Davison, Jr.'s, Company C in locked combat. When the firing started, Sp4 William Phifer edged his way through a cemetery on the right flank of the stranded company and tossed two grenades into a bunker. Both detonated, but had little effect. Phifer fired point-blank into the firing port with his pistol and pitched in another grenade. His grenade struck a Chicom grenade being thrown out at him, and they both exploded, lifting him about two feet off the ground. Miraculously, he was only shaken, but the four-man NVA heavy weapons crew was wiped out. The battalion fought past the roadblock and reached Hue's outer wall the next day.

On 23 February Lieutenant Colonel Wasiak's battalion, also advancing upon Hue from the north, ran into a mortar barrage just outside the city. NVA grenades and machine guns lashed the cavalrymen struggling forward through the waterlogged rice paddies. Sensing a slackening of enemy fire to the right, the lead company attacked in that direction. The North Vietnamese promptly shifted their troops and frantically began digging new positions. Rocket-firing helicopters darted through the low overhanging clouds to discharge volleys of rockets directly into the North Vietnamese soldiers. The intensive return automatic weapons fire still kept the cavalrymen flat on their stomachs in the freezing paddy water. Wounded were extracted by inflating air mattresses, rolling bloodied comrades over onto them, and then pulling the floating mattresses out behind crawling volunteers.

During the night the battalion spotted large numbers of North Vietnamese soldiers trying to exit Hue. They called in artillery bombardment on top of the enemy files and shelled the trails all night, producing terrific carnage. During the morning, Wasiak's men joined Vaught's battalion along the city walls. The North Vietnamese conducted one last-ditch counterattack against the 3d ARVN Regiment within the city, which was destroyed by concentrated artillery fire. At 5:00 A.M. on 24 February, the Viet Cong banner, which had flown over the Hue citadel since the beginning of the month, was torn down and the red-and-yellow flag of the Republic of Vietnam was hoisted.

On the morning of 25 February, Lieutenant Colonel Sweet's battered battalion reached the west wall and assaulted the final enemy trenchline. He chose his strongest companies to clear the last opposition in front of them, but each of the depleted companies sallying forward had been reduced since the drive started to a mere forty-eight men. The bloody battle for Hue was declared over, although mopping up continued for the next several days. Although the major brunt of the city combat was taken by U.S. Marines and South Vietnamese fighting block by block inside Hue, the 1st Cavalry Division brought tremendous pressure to bear against the NVA staging and reinforcement areas, stifling the enemy's capacity to hold out.[5]

After the Battles of Quang Tri and Hue, the NVA/VC forces sought to avoid contact and gain time to regroup their shattered forces by withdrawing far into mountain base areas. The 1st Cavalry Divi-

5. 1st Cav Div Rpt on the Battle for Hue, dtd 15 Apr 68; 2d Bn 12th Cav, *Battle for Hue: 2–5 Feb 68;* 3d Bde 1st Cav Div, *Operational Report— Lessons Learned,* dtd 11 Mar 68; 14th MHD, *Combat After Action Interview No. 5-68,* dtd 4 May 68; and Maj. Miles D. Waldron and Sp5 Richard W. Beavers, 14th MHD Study No. 2-68, *Operation Hue City,* dtd Aug 68.

sion maintained its flexible response through airmobility and pursued the enemy into their most remote strongholds. Actually, this penetration of enemy base areas was the original concept of Operation JEB STUART.

Colonel Campbell's brigade redeployed back through Camp Evans, reopened LZ Jack in the mountains, and began helicopter sweeps of the rugged jungle. During the month of March, the brigade conducted forty-eight reconnaissance missions and fourteen search-and-destroy operations in the region. Colonel Campbell's main clearing effort, however, was directed against the bunker-studded lowlands and rice cache areas of the northern coastal plains.

Colonel Rattan's brigade established LZ Pedro and swept into the mountains west of Quang Tri. The brigade used search-and-clear, cordon-and-search, and swooper operations to pursue the NVA/VC during the day and hunter-killer teams and night ambushes after dark. Like the 3d Brigade, the 1st Brigade also devoted considerable attention to the sandy coastal plains and cleaned out the remnants of the enemy units which attacked Quang Tri.

The last elements of Colonel McDonough's brigade arrived in I CTZ as the Battle of Hue was ending. The command post was set up at LZ Jane between the other two brigades, and on 1 March the fresh unit relieved the attached 2d Brigade of the 101st Airborne Division in the same sector. The two 2d Brigades had carried out ninety-nine reconnaissance missions and seventy-seven search-and-clear operations in the JEB STUART area by the time the operation was over at the end of the month.

Operation JEB STUART, which encompassed the division's hard-fought Tet-68 response, had lasted only forty-two days when it was cut short to enable the 1st Cavalry Division to relieve the beleaguered Marines at Khe Sanh. During this short time, the division lost 276 killed in action, 18 missing, and 1,498 wounded in I Corps Tactical Zone. The high casualty rates easily surpassed 1967 levels, and the personnel situation was worsened by great turnover in the ranks. Also, 2,484 division members were rotated routinely to the United States within this period; the division received 5,345 replacements from 22 January until the end of March alone.[6]

---

6. 1st Cav Div, *Combat Operations After Action Report*, dtd 2 Jul 68, Tab L (Adjutant General Services) and Tab T (Casualty and Medevac).

The tremendous toll on aviation resources was reflected in the fact that twenty-four helicopters were totally destroyed after being shot down and seventy-six aircraft were dropped from accountability, most of them as a result of battle damage, during Operation JEB STUART. The strain of combat, marginal weather, and lack of ready helicopter maintenance reduced aircraft availability to all-time lows.[7]

In exchange the 1st Cavalry Division's flexible response was instrumental in crushing several NVA/VC units, recapturing key cities and towns, and clearing critical territory during the large-scale enemy Tet-68 offensive. The airmobile division's success probably killed more than 3,200 NVA/VC troops (the actual body count was 313). The division secured a vital stretch of Vietnam's most valuable overland supply route, Highway 1. More important, the division assisted Marine and South Vietnamese forces engaged in battles of great political significance to the United States. For the first time in airmobile history, aerial cavalry proved its true worth as a national investment on a foreign battleground.

The 1st Brigade, miles from Quang Tri City when it was attacked on 31 January–1 February and moving in the opposite direction toward another objective, executed a complete turnabout and air assaulted troops into the battle within hours of notification. The Skytroopers landed between the enemy forces fighting inside Quang Tri and the enemy reserve, trapping considerable numbers of NVA and VC between the airmobile infantry and the South Vietnamese town garrison. The shock of this sudden countermove completely disrupted the enemy bid to overrun Quang Tri, enabling the city to be resecured within twenty-four hours. In the ensuing pursuit, cavalry artillery and helicopter gunships decimated the demoralized enemy and drove them into the mountains.

The 3d Brigade, advancing south along Highway 1 in February, fought a determined month-long battle for the critical northern and western approaches to Hue. Since the foggy, rainy weather impeded airmobile operations, the cavalrymen often switched to a conventional infantry foot advance. They defeated large enemy forces composed of elements of nineteen battalions, severed enemy reinforcement and supply lines, and insured the encirclement of the greater battlefield.

7. Ibid., Tab AE (Logistics).

The courage, adaptability, endurance, and fighting skill of this brigade underlined the highest expectations which MACV accorded the airmobile cavalry. Some of the most bitter Army fighting in Vietnam, under the most stressful conditions, was waged by the veteran battalions on this one prolonged drive.

Having seized the initiative, the 1st Cavalry Division relentlessly consolidated its gains and kept the enemy retreating from the population centers. The division pushed into the NVA/VC staging areas in the rugged mountains west of Hue and Quang Tri. Throughout March the airmobile battalions carved out firebases and prowled the dense jungles, uncovering vast quantities of weapons, ammunition, and food in formerly secret enemy sanctuaries. These operations were supplemented by division activity in the northern coastal plain, specifically designed to deny the enemy rice or recruits and to weed out the Viet Cong infrastructure. The division was called upon to deploy rapidly to another combat sector as the month ended and to undertake yet another highly critical mission: to reach the besieged Marine fortress of Khe Sanh in Operation PEGASUS.

Cavalry Raids

Techniques, Khe Sanh and A Shau

The cavalry raid has been one of the most valuable functions of mounted horsemen throughout history, and the 1st Cavalry Division brought this ability to Vietnam with helicopter-riding cavalrymen. Raids can be defined as rapid attacks into enemy territory to carry out specific missions. Without the intention of holding terrain, the raiding force promptly withdraws when its mission is accomplished. Like screening and scouting, fast raiding is a natural attribute of the airmobile cavalry.

Although most raids are carried out by small forces with very limited objectives, the 1st Cavalry Division executed two classic division-scale cavalry raids just after Tet-68. The first was the airmobile drive to raise the siege of Khe Sanh, and the second was the airmobile strike into the remote A Shau Valley enemy base area. Both cavalry raids were expedient attacks with precise objectives, completely divorced from terrain occupation, and involved expeditious withdrawals.

After reaching Khe Sanh, the division was immediately withdrawn to air assault into the A Shau Valley because long-range weather forecasts predicted April as the last month of favorable weather before monsoon rains would prevent helicopter flight in the valley. The division scheduled withdrawal accordingly. However, the most important cavalry raid in Vietnam was the division's attack to reach the isolated Marine fortress at Khe Sanh.

The Marine combat base at Khe Sanh was established in the far northwest corner of South Vietnam close to Laos as the most westerly strongpoint of the main Marine defensive lines facing North Vietnam.

Formerly a small Army Special Forces camp, the Marines built up the Khe Sanh bastion on the strategically located plateau and hills just north of Route 9 and garrisoned it with the reinforced 26th Marines. During January 1968, a series of violent hill fights around Khe Sanh disclosed that at least two NVA divisions had moved into the area and surrounded it. The battle for Khe Sanh mushroomed into a major confrontation between the United States and North Vietnam. Control of the citadel acquired overriding political importance as a test of national willpower under President Johnson.

Throughout the weeks that the 1st Cavalry Division was battling the NVA/VC Tet-68 offensive at Quang Tri and Hue, the besieged 26th Marines fought for Khe Sanh's survival under heavy bombardment and periodic ground attack. Enemy approach trenches extended to within a few yards of the outer wire, which was already breached in places by the bangalore torpedoes of NVA sappers. The few patrols sent out by the defenders were ambushed and destroyed. NVA heavy cannon, artillery, mortars, and recoilless rifles pounded Khe Sanh daily, and often more than a thousand rounds impacted within the perimeter every twenty-four hours. The airstrip was in shambles, and the Marines were soon cut off from both overland and airlanded supplies.

The North Vietnamese ringed the Marine lines with entrenched infantry and a multitude of antiaircraft weapons. Dense fogs and rain-swollen overcasts shrouded the jungled mountains. During February, 679 parachute drops were flown to keep the garrison alive. On the night of 7–8 February 1968, North Vietnamese tanks overran the outlying Special Forces fort at Lang Vei. On 23 February the beleaguered Marines endured their heaviest barrage of the siege and six days later hurled back a major North Vietnamese assault. Khe Sanh achieved paramount importance in American wartime direction because of President Johnson's fixation over its possible loss. He considered the situation completely desperate and demanded immediate MACV response. The Marines hung on through March as General Westmoreland mustered the powerful forces needed to achieve a breakthrough.

The MACV call for help went to Major General Tolson's 1st Cavalry Division as early as 25 January 1968, when the airmobile division was flown into I CTZ and prepared contingency plans for either the relief or reinforcement of Khe Sanh. The unexpected blows of Tet-68 interrupted the allied scheme as divisions and brigades were shifted to recapture and safeguard lowland cities and towns. The brunt of this enemy offensive in the northern zone was shattered by 2 March. At the same time, Hue was officially declared back in South Vietnamese hands. However, the Marines at Khe Sanh were still in danger, and Deputy MACV Commander General Abrams was anxious to send a relief expedition to their rescue at once.

On the second day in March, he summoned Tolson to Da Nang to brief III Marine Amphibious Force commander General Cushman on division concepts to break the siege. General Tolson suggested a lightning airmobile assault which would slash through enemy lines, over terrain and defensive obstacles, much like a division-size cavalry raid. The momentum of this aerial offensive would greatly assist the two Marine and ARVN divisions expected to advance on Khe Sanh up Route 9. After listening to Tolson's presentation, Generals Abrams and Cushman told him to commence final preparations for the attack. The operation would be labeled PEGASUS, named for the flying horse of mythology.

The 1st Cavalry Division began detailed planning on 11 March. Although the mission to strike into Khe Sanh, reopen Route 9, and destroy all enemy forces along the way was simple, the amount of coordination and meticulous planning involved was staggering. As division chief of staff, Col. George W. Putnam supervised the staff sections producing the tactical and logistical arrangements; Tolson helicoptered several times into surrounded Khe Sanh to confer directly with Marine defense commander Col. David E. Lownds.

Within three days of the division being alerted to orient toward Khe Sanh, the 8th Engineer Battalion was near Ca Lu, alongside Navy Seabees and Marine engineers, building the massive airfield and storage facilities required for the upcoming attack. Under the personal direction of Assistant Division Commander-B, Brig. Gen. Oscar E. Davis, Landing Zone Stud was transformed into a major airfield staging complex and supply depot. In only eleven days the construction included a 1,500-foot runway, ammunition storage bunkers, aircraft and vehicle refueling facilities, a communications center, and a sophisticated air terminal. Still retaining its landing zone designation, although larger than many bases, the compound became the advance operations center for PEGASUS.

On 25 March (D-Day minus six) the countdown to attack began.

For the next six days Lt. Col. Richard W. Diller's 1st Squadron of the 9th Cavalry was unleashed over the planned offensive axis of advance, along and on both sides of Route 9, toward Khe Sanh. Allied intelligence of enemy dispositions was vague and often unreliable, forcing the division to rely almost exclusively on its own 9th Cavalry scoutships to develop accurate data about actual ground conditions, find suitable landing zones, chart enemy defenses, and destroy potentially devastating AA positions.

The reconnaissance helicopters and gunships found the targets, destroyed what they could, and reported the rest. The division moved 8-inch and 105mm artillery batteries to Ca Lu and LZ Stud to supplement the 175mm-gun and howitzer units already pounding the newly located enemy. Tactical airstrikes by fighter-bombers, rocket and strafing runs by armed helicopters, and Arc Light heavy bombing by B52s blasted known and suspected enemy concentrations and fieldworks. Landing zones were selected and hit with tactical airstrikes using specially fused "Daisy-Cutter" bombs and other explosive ordnance to clear potential resistance.

As D-Day approached, division reconnaissance and construction efforts were stepped up. On D minus one, the day prior to the attack, Tolson moved his command post to LZ Stud, and Colonel Campbell's 3rd Brigade initial assault elements helicoptered to their final marshaling areas. On the morning of the attack, thick ground fog and low-hanging clouds merged to blanket the landscape in total overcast. The rows of helicopters lined up along the landing zone runway were shrouded in haze, but still the hub of activity as trooploads were sorted, instruments checked, and fuel topped off. However, they appeared idle to the Marines, whose reservations about airmobility seemed confirmed as their infantrymen stepped off the line of departure in full battle gear and began advancing toward Khe Sanh.

At noon the tropical sun began baking away the mists, the veteran cavalrymen clambered aboard their Hueys, and the shrill whine of starting helicopter engines surged into a deafening roar as hundreds of rotor blades whirled into life. At 1:00 P.M. sharp the first waves of dozens of troopships soared into the air as the largest cavalry raid in American history commenced. The Marines silently trudging along the road under the strain of their heavy packs heard an increasing drone in the distance over the clatter of their equipment. They lifted

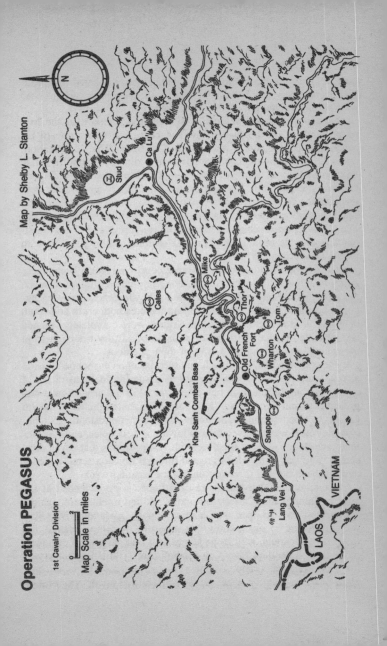

Operation PEGASUS

1st Cavalry Division

Map Scale in miles

0   2

Map by Shelby L. Stanton

N

Ca Lu

Stud

Mike

Cates

Thor

Khe Sanh Combat Base

Old French Fort

Wharton

Tom

Snapper

Lang Vei

LAOS

VIETNAM

their heads as the throbbing pitch of helicopters resonated overhead. The overcast sky was filled with swarms of helicopters racing ahead with all three battalions of the 7th Cavalry.

Lieutenant Colonel Wasiak's 1st Battalion roared over the Marines marching on the road below and continued flying toward LZ Mike, alongside Route 9 halfway to Khe Sanh. The 2d Battalion, under Lt. Col. Roscoe Robinson, Jr., came directly behind it, while Lieutenant Colonel Vaught's 5th Battalion airmobiled into LZ Cates two miles to the north. The spectacular 7th Cavalry air assaults were breathtaking to the aerial observation pilots, who circled their little scoutships out of the way as the troopship formations approached. The pilots reported seeing as many as thirty Hueys and Chinooks simultaneously descending onto an LZ, seemingly filling the air with machines and men.

The division's initial reconnaissance confirmed North Vietnamese Army intentions of blocking or delaying any allied attempt to reach the beleaguered Marine fortress at Khe Sanh. Elaborate enemy strongpoints occupied key hilltops and terrain features both north and south of Route 9. However, the NVA defenders were completely stunned and outwitted by the swift aerial intrusion of cavalry troops in front of, behind, and around the flanks of their positions.

The combined power, speed, and surprise of an airmobile division also became obvious to the Marines as a startling demonstration of combat accomplishment: in one afternoon a full infantry brigade was projected within five miles of Khe Sanh. The thoroughness of the 9th Cavalry's reconnaissance and target work became instantly evident. Not one round was received by any incoming helicopter, and this was in an area that had been bristling with AA positions just seven days earlier. The flak guns which greeted the first division scout helicopters had been put out of action during the ensuing week.

Operations escalated as more cavalrymen were airlanded at LZ Stud in Chinook and Caribou transports, shifted to Huey troopships, and air assaulted to open new landing zones. Operation PEGASUS was proceeding so successfully that schedules were accelerated, and Colonel McDonough's 2d Brigade was sent into the drive a day early on 3 April. Two days later Colonel Stannard's 1st Brigade was airlifted onto the battlefield. A South Vietnamese task force of three battalions was also air assaulted by the division south and west of

Khe Sanh. In one week Major General Tolson had deployed fifteen thousand combat soldiers into action.

The 1st Cavalry Division blasted open seven new landing zones in five days, each bringing the allies closer to Khe Sanh and driving more enemy soldiers from their defenses. Each air assault was prefaced with withering artillery fire, fighter-bomber passes, and final aerial rocketing against the field below, ending just seconds before the Skytroopers leaped from the open cabins and skids of their Hueys. The cavalrymen dashed out to form a quick perimeter. Within minutes Chinooks lumbered overhead with howitzers and slingloads of ammunition. The artillery was quickly unlimbered, ammunition crates were smashed open, and minutes later the sharp boom of howitzer fire echoed through the vegetation. The artillery tubes either shelled enemy defenses closer to Khe Sanh or sent final barrages into other fields chosen as LZs for the bounding infantry.

For the first time the cavalry artillery was answered by North Vietnamese artillery. As the fire support bases were set up on landing zones, artillery duels began. LZ Wharton was hit by twenty rounds from long-range 130mm cannon after it was established on 3 April. The division's quick-draw batteries lashed back by pumping out hundreds of rounds in counterbattery fire. The Chinooks of the 228th Aviation Battalion were soon hauling five hundred tons of ammunition a day to the forward tubes. LZ Stud was bombarded once by enemy artillery, but the forward observers were spotted on a nearby ridgeline and killed, and the base was not threatened again.

Typical of the fire support that paved the way for the cavalry advance were the exploits of 1st Battalion, 30th Artillery, forward observer 1Lt. Stephen Esh on 7 April. Lieutenant Esh flew in an OH6 Cayuse light observation helicopter. On the first mission of that day, he spotted four NVA soldiers and called in artillery, which resulted in two confirmed kills and two probables. His second mission took him over gently rolling hills two miles south of Khe Sanh and less than a mile from Laos. He spotted twenty NVA soldiers trekking through the elephant grass. The light helicopter made two passes over the enemy, coming in low and fast as the lieutenant hurriedly plotted the positions on his folded map and radioed for artillery. On the third pass he pinned down the enemy with M16 rifle bursts, lifting away just as the artillery shells began to hit the area.

While the artillery barrage swept the NVA, Esh scanned the vicinity further and spotted an NVA convoy of five trucks and one Russian-built tank on a nearby road. He immediately called for rocket-firing helicopters, and Cobra gunships swiftly arrived to demolish all six vehicles. Lieutenant Esh directed his helicopter low over the burning wreckage to count the clusters of dead North Vietnamese and noticed stenciled markings on some of the backpacks. Suspecting that they contained valuable intelligence, he ordered the pilot to land. The crew chief leaped out to get the packs as the lieutenant stood guard and shot down two North Vietnamese soldiers charging from the brush.

After stopping at LZ Stud and grabbing a quick meal, Lieutenant Esh picked up a fresh helicopter and crew and flew farther south. He directed the helicopter to circle an area only four hundred yards from the Laotian border and soon spotted another NVA truck convoy parked beside a road in a nearby valley. He directed artillery fire which destroyed seven trucks and killed large numbers of enemy troops. Secondary explosions rocked the jungle as a petroleum dump and two ammunition dumps suddenly detonated as well. The explosions and fires raged for hours, and Esh departed the burning target area as the helicopter fuel ran low. Such remarkably effective use of artillery observers in helicopters allowed the airmobile division to extend its artillery capability well beyond advancing ground troops.

As the advance continued and the enemy showed increasing signs of disorganization, General Tolson took advantage of the airmobile division's inherent flexibility to rapidly shift his battalions onto LZs and in directions not part of the original attack plan. On 2 April Lieutenant Colonel Robinson's battalion air assaulted into LZ Thor, a key position along Route 9 closer to Khe Sanh, and began moving west. Everywhere the cavalrymen went they were astonished to find huge piles of weapons and equipment littering the battlefield. This was unusual behavior for an enemy which just weeks earlier during JEB STUART had taken great risks to pick up any fallen man's weapon (where one weapon was retrieved for every five NVA killed). Around Khe Sanh the cavalry and Marines captured 763 individual and crew-served weapons that had been left on the ground, and it was apparent the North Vietnamese were in full retreat.

The next day Lieutenant Colonel Sweet's 2d Battalion, 12th Cavalry, seized LZ Wharton on a critical hilltop only four miles southwest of·the Marine fortress. Between LZ Wharton and Khe Sanh was an old French fort, and its defenses were upgraded and held by what was estimated to be an NVA battalion. Lieutenant Colonel Runkle's 1st Battalion, 5th Cavalry, was stopped below the fort by heavy mortar shelling which caused many casualties and mortally wounded the battalion commander. The battalion was extracted and replaced by the 2d Battalion of the 5th Cavalry under Lt. Col. Arthur J. Leary, which flanked the fort from the west. The North Vietnamese fled, and the fort was taken without resistance.

In the meantime Lieutenant Colonel Robinson's battalion was steadily pressing forward along Route 9, but was stopped 7 April by a final NVA defensive line. The enemy bunkers were on a ridge overlooking the road, only two miles short of the beleaguered Marine base. After bombarding the ridge with artillery and helicopter rockets, Robinson at once air assaulted four of his companies onto the enemy positions. Three companies touched down around the enemy position, while the fourth landed behind the blocking force like a hammer against an anvil. The North Vietnamese were routed from their positions in a sharp battle, and the road to Khe Sanh was finally opened.

At 8:00 A.M. on 8 April 1968, the cavalrymen linked up with the Marine garrison after walking the final two miles up the twisting narrow road into the Khe Sanh fortress. Pfc. Juan Fordoni, from Puerto Rico, was the first trooper to make contact as he clasped hands over the barbed wire with a Marine lance corporal, one of the defenders who had weathered the heaviest siege of the war. The simple handshake was sealed as Lt. Joe Abodeely blew a triumphant blast on a tarnished North Vietnamese bugle found during the final march along the roadside with other discarded NVA equipment. The siege of Khe Sanh was ended, exactly one week after the cavalry raid commenced.

Mopping up continued, and two days later the 1st Cavalry Division recaptured the overrun Lang Vei Special Forces camp against light rearguard resistance on 10 April. That same morning, General Tolson was suddenly ordered, without previous notification, to extract the entire division and prepare to air assault into the A Shau Valley. Operation PEGASUS formally terminated on 14 April 1968.

Tolson's swift and powerful cavalry raid had smashed through the enemy lines and broken the siege of Khe Sanh in the first division-scale air assault in history. Every line battalion was helicoptered directly onto the battlefield in the first airmobile division attack to use all three brigades. The raid's success can be attributed to many factors: the excellence of its aerial reconnaissance, the coordination of its elements, and the logistical improvement in division operations.

The cavalry raid was spearheaded throughout by the 1st Squadron of the 9th Cavalry. For a week prior to the upcoming division assault toward Khe Sanh, the dauntless squadron closely integrated its reconnaissance skills with the firepower of tactical airstrikes, artillery, and B52 strategic bombing to locate and destroy targets in the intervening enemy-held territory. The cavalry reconnaissance squadron brilliantly demonstrated its ability to prepare a divisional axis of advance despite the absence of higher command information about the enemy. The intelligence gathered by the division's aerial reconnaissance arm not only added immeasurably to the success of PEGASUS, but raised air cavalry to a new level of military acceptance.

The 1st Cavalry Division effectively coordinated an airmobile drive of eight cavalry battalions with a ground advance by seven Marine and four South Vietnamese infantry battalions. The pace of the division's aerial onslaught was set by waves of helicopters catapulting battalions of Skytroopers over successive enemy barriers. The multiple airmobile infantry prongs were both preceded and screened by rocket-firing Cobras and helicopter gunships directed by the reconnaissance squadron's observation craft. The combination of air assaulting infantry, aerial rocket attack, and scoutship harassment forced the NVA to abandon carefully prepared defenses and to retreat without regard to his planned directions of withdrawal. The hasty enemy departure was evidenced by the staggering amounts of munitions, emplaced weapons, and equipment left in defensive positions.

The division renewed emphasis on its supporting foundation, including the proper pre-positioning of supplies, as a result of lessons learned in the divisional transfer to I CTZ and Tet-68 battles during Operation JEB STUART. This favorable logistical posture enabled the division to increase the tempo of the drive despite continually unfavorable weather. Eleven complete battalions were helicoptered onto the battlefield by the seventh day of the raid (D plus six).

During Operation PEGASUS, the 1st Cavalry Division scored a decisive airmobile victory by quickly reaching the besieged Marine Khe Sanh bastion without setback or heavy losses, all within fifteen days. The careful planning and preparation preceding the raid was backed up by aggressive and innovative tactics during its execution.

At a cost of 315 casualties (including 59 KIA and 5 MIA), the division chased the North Vietnamese forces off the battlefield into Laos, forcing them to leave behind at least 638 dead soldiers and much valuable equipment.[1] Rarely has the potential of airmobile cavalry been more brilliantly applied.

Operation PEGASUS was summarily concluded in order to start Operation DELAWARE, the code name for General Tolson's next cavalry raid into the heart of the remote North Vietnamese–held A Shau Valley. The tropical valley was a mile-wide slash of flat bottomland covered by rain forest and elephant grass, wedged between mist-covered mountain ranges on the Laotian border. The North Vietnamese wrested control of the forbidding region from the allies by overrunning the A Shau Special Forces camp in 1966 and then turned the valley into their primary staging area for the assault on Hue during Tet-68. Because of its location and jagged topography, both Vietnam's northeast and southwest monsoons brought heavy rains, hail, and unpredictable storms raging through the valley's primeval jungle. This combination of terrain and weather made it inaccessible by road and difficult to navigate by air, but General Westmoreland was determined to strike deep after Tet-68 and eliminate the NVA bases located there.

General Westmoreland believed the 1st Cavalry Division was ideally suited to penetrate the A Shau for two simple reasons. First, the division was the only formation in the allied inventory that could airlift large numbers of troops into relatively inaccessible areas on short notice. Time was essential if the allies were to search the valley in 1968, because the brief transition period of mid-April to mid-May (between monsoons) offered the only respite in valley weather. (Unfortunately, this proved erroneous: as events were to prove, the premonsoon interval of fog and low clouds in the valley produced worse flying weather.) Secondly, no one knew what reception the NVA had prepared for allied intrusion. The 1st Cavalry Division was considered to be one of the toughest MACV divisions, able to triumph over whatever might be encountered.

Allied knowledge of enemy dispositions in the A Shau Valley was

1. 1st Cav Div, *Combat Operations After Action Report*, dtd 11 Jul 68, Tabs D and K.

even scantier than the intelligence provided prior to PEGASUS. Allied ground forces stayed out of the A Shau Valley, and aerial reconnaissance was nearly impossible. MACV could only guess at NVA dispositions inside the valley by judging the enemy forces which came out the south end. This estimate was very discouraging; whenever North Vietnamese units emerged from the valley, they were well organized, well equipped, and ready to fight. Although the extent of enemy fortifications inside the valley was unknown, aircraft overflights were challenged by extensive antiaircraft positions.

Lieutenant Colonel Diller's 9th Cavalry scouting squadron was sent into the valley to report all they could see or find, but almost immediately bad weather curtailed their activity. The raid was postponed two days to allow the reconnaissance craft more time to gather information. The light observation helicopters swept along the steep mountain slopes and rocky outcrops, using their nimble craft as bait to locate and chart the positions of dug-in batteries of heavy and light antiaircraft guns. The squadron paid a price—50 aircraft hit, of which 5 were destroyed and 18 damaged beyond repair, but fighter-bombers and strategic bombers responded by hitting the pinpointed targets with 209 tactical airstrikes and 21 B52 bombing runs preparatory to the raid.[2]

The cavalry raid into the A Shau Valley was much bolder than the PEGASUS expedition. The division would not only be raiding under marginal weather conditions, but also its forces would initially air assault beyond the supporting artillery fires of division howitzers. General Tolson wanted to achieve surprise and believed that this would more than offset the advantages of close artillery at the start of the raid. He gambled that aerial rocket artillery and other air support would suffice until the Chinooks airlifted howitzers in right behind the assaulting infantry.[3]

To conduct the raid, Tolson utilized seven of his nine line battalions (the 1st and 2d Battalions of the 5th Cavalry under 2d Brigade were temporarily attached to the Marines), but reinforced his division with a South Vietnamese brigade-size task force. All other division

2. 1st Sqdn 9th Cav, *Combat After Action Report*, dtd 4 Jun 68, p. 4.
3. 14th MHD Interview with MG John J Tolson by Cpt JWA Whitehorne, dtd 27 May 68, p. 4.

components were committed. The original plan envisioned Colonel Stannard's 1st Brigade making the initial assaults in the central A Shau Valley to secure the overgrown airfield of the lost Special Forces A Loui camp, which had been destroyed three years earlier. However, unsuppressed antiaircraft fire in this region led Tolson to open the raid instead by air assaulting Colonel Campbell's 3d Brigade into the extreme northern part of the valley. This switch destined Colonel Campbell's lead brigade of PEGASUS to be in the forefront of the second air cavalry division raid in history as well.

The cavalry raid commenced on 19 April 1968 as swarms of troopships and their gunship escorts lifted high into the clouds from Camp Evans. The helicopters crossed west over the highlands, bathed in a cloudy froth exposing only the highest peaks, and, once past the near mountain chain of the A Shau Valley, descended into the gloomy mists of the overcast valley. Capt. John Taylor, who commanded Company A of the 5th Battalion, 7th Cavalry, described the opening air assault: "The feeling the majority of the men had upon first coming into the valley was a sort of fear, distinctly different from that felt at Hue or Khe Sanh. We had heard so many stories about A Shau, like the possibilities of running into large concentrations [of flak]. We had a fear of the unknown. We thought that just around any corner we would run into a battalion of North Vietnamese."[4]

A wall of red antiaircraft tracers suddenly ripped through the lowering helicopter formation. Well-camouflaged mobile 37mm antiaircraft guns blazed continuously at thirty rounds every ten seconds. The shower of steel tore through twenty-three helicopters of two battalions and sent ten spiraling in flames to crash on the valley floor. The first two battalions air assaulted through the flak to establish landing zones on twin peaks overlooking the northern end of the valley. Lieutenant Colonel Vaught's battalion landed on LZ Tiger, but the unit suffered numerous casualties, including the battalion commander. Chinook helicopters managed to place a battery of light howitzers on LZ Tiger immediately following the assault. Lieutenant Colonel Wasiak's battalion landed on LZ Vicki, but deteriorating weather, the late hour of the assault, and intensified AA fire prevented artillery from being set down to reinforce them.

4. 1st Cav Div Ltr, Subj: Recommendation for PUC, dtd 15 Apr 69, p. 30.

In one of the most daring opening episodes of the attack, the division's Company E, 52d Infantry (Long Range Patrol), accompanied by combat engineers of the 8th Engineer Battalion and volunteers from the 13th Signal Battalion, rappelled from helicopters to establish a vital radio relay site on a five thousand-foot mountain peak which they dubbed Signal Hill. They worked frantically to complete the communications facility, which was needed to link the division communications at Camp Evans with its units on the valley floor. Bad weather set in, supplies stopped, and the North Vietnamese quickly used the opportunity to probe the defenses on the night of 20 April, killing four cavalrymen and wounding three others. The next day the clouds began to part, dozers and howitzers were lifted in by Flying Cranes, and Signal Hill was soon in full operation.

The thundering storm which masked Signal Hill swept through the entire valley for several days. The flashing lightning, severe wind gusts, and torrential rains confirmed the worst division apprehensions about A Shau weather. Visibility dropped to near zero and threatened logistical support of LZ Tiger. Despite the low cloud ceiling and almost blind flying conditions, division aviators were able to transport one company of Lieutenant Colonel Robinson's battalion farther south along the same ridgeline to LZ Pepper, to give the cavalrymen a better chance at resupply. Unfortunately, the lead Huey was shot down on the landing zone, and the wrecked helicopter blocked further lifts until engineers were able to cut out a larger clearing.

Wasiak's cavalrymen on LZ Vicki were in the worst predicament, as the battalion could not be lifted out, and attempts to sustain them on Vicki had to be abandoned. Their position was untenable, and Colonel Campbell was left with no choice but to direct Wasiak to march his men overland to LZ Goodman, a more favorable spot four miles south on the valley's eastern edge. Colonel Wasiak personally led the difficult trek for three days as the troopers struggled through the broken triple- and double-canopy jungle, following the ridge's tortuous terrain as it twisted and doubled back on itself. The drenched marchers became chilled and sick. They subsisted on ration tins and went without sufficient sleep. Late in the afternoon of 22 April they finally reached and secured the map location marked Goodman. Along the way they were amazed to find two Soviet-built dozers driven up into the hillside and carefully concealed. The equipment was the first significant find of the operation.

In spite of the marginal weather, the 5th Battalion, 7th Cavalry, began pushing downhill and crossed a major branch of the Ho Chi Minh Trail emptying into South Vietnam—Route 548 running through the middle of the A Shau Valley out of Laos. They found the NVA highway to be a hardened dirt road, reinforced by sections of corduroy logs and mud as well as steel planking, with trees along each side tied together at the top to form a concealing canopy overhead. Colonel Campbell's entire brigade was soon ranging throughout the northern valley, but the unsatisfactory weather continued.

Helicopter pilots were forced to leave Camp Evans by climbing individually through ceilings of nine thousand feet on instruments, reforming over the cloud layer broken only by the highest peaks, and fly into the valley through holes in the overcast. Switching back over to instruments, the young aviators probed through the murky gloom at near-zero visibility to find the cavalry positions. The normal ten-minute flight from Camp Evans in clear weather took at least an hour, and only the sheer flying heroics of the division's 11th Aviation Group made the raid possible.

On 24 April Colonel Stannard's brigade began air assaulting into the central valley around the abandoned A Loui airstrip, the original insertion area of the raid's planning. Despite intensive gunship preparation over LZ Stallion, the landings were opposed by considerable antiaircraft fire and a number of machine guns on the field itself. Lt. Col. John V. Gibney's 1st Battalion, 8th Cavalry—the first brigade battalion in—lost two CH47 Chinooks and a Huey, and only three howitzers could be landed the first day. The commander of the 8th Cavalry's 2d Battalion, Lt. Col. Christian Dubia, was medically evacuated during his unit's air assault the next day.

The seizure of A Loui permitted the 8th Engineer Battalion to begin airfield rehabilitation on 29 April. Flying Cranes lifted in the heavy construction equipment, and by 2 May the first C7 Caribou transport aircraft were landing. Logistical problems were greatly eased by the establishment of this division airhead. In the meantime the cavalry companies reconnoitering the valley found large quantities of abandoned trucks, wheeled 37mm AA guns, and other weapons. Contact remained light as Company D of Lieutenant Colonel Stockton's battalion brushed with an NVA platoon trying to evade the area on the night of 27 April.

The next day Company D of Lt. Col. George C. Horton's 1st

Battalion, 8th Cavalry, discovered a mile-long depressed corduroy road containing huge storage bunkers and defended by an entrenched NVA company with one tank in support. The cavalrymen pressed forward, wearing gas masks to ward off North Vietnamese chemical grenades, and Sgt. Hillery Craig wriggled forward to destroy the tank with two well-aimed M72 antitank rocket rounds. The North Vietnamese retaliated by trying to outflank the company, forcing it to withdraw. The cavalry reinforced, and the "Punchbowl" area was taken on 3 May after several days of fighting.

The Punchbowl turned out to be a large logistical center complete with hospitals and a headquarters site of a regiment-sized component of the *559th NVA Transportation Group*. During the first few days of May, the two cavalry brigades crisscrossed the valley and uncovered numerous well-stocked caches of tools and equipment. On 5 May the North Vietnamese began to strike back with increasing amounts of 122mm rocket, artillery, mortar, and recoilless rifle fire. The nearby border with Laos enabled the enemy to strike cavalry positions in the A Shau Valley by accurate indirect fire attacks with complete immunity from cavalry pursuit.

The cavalry raid was planned for termination in accordance with the northward advance of the monsoon. On 7 May, with the weather front fast approaching, Tolson decided to begin withdrawing his cavalry raiding force three days later. On 11 May the valley was deluged with torrential rains which quickly washed out the improved dirt A Loui airstrip. The division was forced to withdraw its raiding force by helicopters alone. As the last battalions were extracted under heavy rainstorms, Operation DELAWARE terminated on 17 May 1968.

Operation DELAWARE was conducted under far more arduous circumstances than PEGASUS; yet it was successfully confirmed that the large cavalry raid was a viable tactical role for employment of an airmobile division. The raid into the A Shau Valley achieved its objectives admirably. The raid determined enemy dispositions and area utilization, disrupted a principal supply area and infiltration route, and harassed NVA forces. The tangible success of this division cavalry raid was evidenced by the incredible amounts of enemy equipment captured, including 1 tank, 73 vehicles, 2 dozers, more than a dozen 37mm antiaircraft guns, 2,319 rifles and submachine guns, 31 flamethrowers, and 1,680 hand grenades. The cavalry raid was conducted under adverse weather and in the face of sophisticated antiaircraft defenses, and its casualties reflected these conditions: 86 killed, 47 missing, and 530 wounded troopers.[5]

Like the PEGASUS drive to relieve Khe Sanh, the division-scale cavalry raid to scour the A Shau Valley was a classic manifestation of the airmobile division's ability to conduct a traditional cavalry mission of great value to modern warfare. Both division-scale cavalry raids were further milestones in developing airmobile doctrine and further testaments to the proper wedding of airmobility and cavalry in the marriage of the cavalry division (airmobile) during the Vietnam War.

5. 1st Cav Div, *Combat Operations After Action Report*, dtd 11 Jul 68, Tab I.

Cavalry Screen

Safeguarding a Capital

The 1st Cavalry Division had completed three and a half months of unremitting combat by the time its helicopter-conveyed raiding forces departed the A Shau Valley on 17 May 1968. Fighting from Hue to Quang Tri into Khe Sanh and the A Shau, Major General Tolson's spectacular division had served as the backbone of the Army's versatile striking power in Vietnam. Airmobility was largely responsible for the allied spring victory in I Corps Tactical Zone.

The division regrouped and performed clearing operations through the rice-growing coastal lowlands and NVA/VC mountain strongholds in eastern Quang Tri Province until the last month of the year. The brigades opened new firebases, invaded the enemy jungle havens of Base Areas 101 and 114, and found large supply and food caches in Operations JEB STUART III and COMANCHE FALLS. Although sharp firefights and sudden clashes sparked throughout the summer and fall campaigns, the pace of these "rice and salt hunts" was slower, and the division needed the rest. The 1st Cavalry Division, deployed to I CTZ as an emergency mobile reaction force, was withdrawn from the northern region of the country after the situation stabilized and other Army formations were well emplaced in the area.

During its stay in I CTZ, the division's flexible response, raiding, and clearing operations cost combat casualties of 745 killed, 4,063 wounded, and 138 missing troopers in slightly more than eleven months. The incessant problem of personnel turbulence within division ranks was underlined by the loss of 18,681 veterans through rotation (in addition to combat casualties, injuries, disease, or nonbattle deaths) and the absorption of 23,202 new replacements. With an average assigned strength of 19,717 personnel during its service in I CTZ, the 1st Cavalry Division was completely refilled at least once within the span of less than a year.[1]

The Army temporarily retitled airmobile divisions as air cavalry divisions when the 101st Airborne Division was taken off paratrooper status and began conversion into an airmobile configuration. The air cavalry division was a term that the 1st Cavalry Division unofficially bestowed upon itself in Vietnam, especially by widespread use of the common abbreviation 1 ACD. On 27 June 1968 DA directed that the 1st Cavalry Division (Airmobile) and the 101st Airborne Division be redesignated as the 1st and 101st Air Cavalry Divisions (Airmobile). The directive provoked a great amount of dissatisfaction among the traditionalists, since both were proud divisions with independent heritage. As a result of extensive complaint, the Army officially revoked the terminology on 26 August 1968. The 1st Cavalry and 101st Airborne Divisions reverted to their original titles, using (Airmobile) as a mere cognomen.[2]

The leadership of the 1st Cavalry Division changed as well, as Major General Tolson departed on 15 July 1968, temporarily turning over the formation to his Assistant Division Commander-A, Brig. Gen. Richard "Dick" L. Irby. The new commander, Maj. Gen. George I. Forsythe, was already selected, but undergoing aviator training prior to assuming command. In fact, Forsythe actually expected to lead an infantry division because he lacked aviator wings. When Westmoreland told him that he was taking over a division, Forsythe was surprised because all the infantry divisions were filled. He replied, "Well, that's great news, sir. Which one?" Westmoreland smiled, "The First Cav."

---

1. Divisional averages assigned strengths determined by following total assigned strengths of the division: Opns JEB STUART I, 18,943; PEGASUS, 19,877; DELAWARE, 20,294; JEB STUART III, 19,757; Source: 1st Cav Div Recom for PUC, dtd 15 Apr 69, Incl 4; Casualties determined from figures in the following documents: 1st Cav Div COAAR dtd 15 Apr 69, Tab G; COAAR dtd 11 Jul 68 DELAWARE, Tab I; COAAR dtd 11 Jul 68 PEGASUS, Tab K; COAAR dtd 2 Jul 68, Tab L; ORLL dtd 26 Aug 68, Tab L.

2. MACV, *Command History*, 1968, Volume I, p. 245.

Forsythe was momentarily unable to respond because he knew that command of the elite airmobile division was considered one of the plum assignments within the Army and that the traditional ticket to the position included pilot qualification. He replied, "Well, that's great news, but I guess you know, sir, that I'm not an aviator." Westmoreland responded easily, "Oh, that's easy. We'll make you an aviator." With that authority, Maj. Gen. Forsythe dashed back stateside to complete a rush aviation course at Fort Rucker, Alabama, and returned to Vietnam to assume command of the 1st Cavalry Division on 19 August 1968 at Camp Evans.[3]

George I. Forsythe was born in Butte, Montana, on 21 July 1918 and graduated from the University of Montana with a degree in business administration in 1939. A reserve officer ordered to active duty with the 30th Infantry Regiment at the Presidio of San Francisco in 1940, he became a Regular Army officer in February 1942 and participated in the invasions of Aleutian Kiska Island and Kwajalein Atoll in 1943 and 1944. Promoted to lieutenant colonel in March 1944, Forsythe spent the rest of the war as the operations officer with XIX Corps in Europe. In 1954 he was promoted to colonel, later became paratrooper-qualified, and took over the reactivated 502d Airborne Infantry. After graduation from the Air War College in 1958, Colonel Forsythe was posted to Vietnam as the first senior advisor to the South Vietnamese Army's Field Command. Returning to Vietnam as a major general in June 1967, he served as General Westmoreland's deputy for CORDS until chosen to lead the 1st Cavalry Division.

While the NVA/VC menace decreased in I CTZ, substantial enemy force developments inside Cambodia threatened the South Vietnamese capital of Saigon in late 1968. Earlier that year Saigon was penetrated by sizable Viet Cong units in both February (Tet) and May (mini-Tet), resulting in great political embarrassment to the American government. The new MACV commander, General Abrams, was determined to block future enemy stabs into the capital. Allied intelligence reported at least four North Vietnamese divisions building up strength along the Cambodian border of northern III CTZ during October and estimated that a major attack against Saigon was imminent.

3. USAMHI, *Senior Officers Oral History Program*, Lt. Gen. George I. Forsythe Interview, Carlisle Barracks, Pennsylvania, p. 435. Hereafter cited as USAMHI, Forsythe Interview.

The 1st and 25th Infantry Divisions normally covered the enemy approaches between Cambodia and Saigon by guarding War Zones D and C, respectively. However, as part of General Abrams's emphasis on increased pacification efforts, both divisions were being pulled back from the frontier wilderness to support South Vietnamese military units and to assist pacification in more heavily populated regions. Since Abrams did not want to upset the progressive stability that this arrangement brought to his "One War Plan," he decided to shift the 1st Cavalry Division south and to use it as a corps covering force for II Field Force Vietnam which would screen and safeguard the capital.

On the afternoon of 26 October 1968, General Abrams ordered the cavalry moved into northern III CTZ immediately. General Abrams was keenly aware of the division's past record of air assault, sustained pursuit, clearing operations, flexible response, and cavalry raids. He now wanted the airmobile division in a screening role to meet the North Vietnamese on the border if they came across. Military screening missions are assigned to provide timely warning of enemy approach, maintain visual contact and report on enemy movement, destroy or repel small enemy forces, and impede the advance of larger enemy forces.

General Abrams did not expect that one division spread over such a vast area could stop a determined multidivisional NVA attack, but he knew that the cavalry's airmobile infantry and firepower could chew it up. He ordered Forsythe to get his cavalry into position on the Cambodian front at once and if the North Vietnamese came across, to "ride them with your spurs all the way down, down to the point where, if and when they do get to the populated areas, they will be a relatively ineffective fighting force!"[4]

Ninety minutes after notification that the move would start within twenty-four hours, Forsythe and selected staff members flew south to Long Binh. The U.S. Army Southeast Asia Signal Training Facility was placed at their disposal and became the advance command post. Continuous communication would have to be maintained between all units, as the division would be participating in three major operations on two fronts simultaneously.

When Forsythe inquired about special precautions to keep the move

---

4. USAMHI, Forsythe Interview, p. 443.

secret, such as taking off cloth insignia, reinforcing NVA/VC uncertainty about the extent of division redeployment, Abrams would have none of that. He told Forsythe that he specifically wanted to show the North Vietnamese that "you could move a division 600 miles overnight," and to "leave the cav patch painted on their [helicopter] noses to show them" the tremendous flexibility the airmobile division afforded the MACV command.

The task of moving the 1st Cavalry Division, coded Operation LIBERTY CANYON, represented the largest allied intratheater combat deployment of the Second Indochina War. The division withdrew its scattered battalions from the jungled mountains at one end of the country and moved them more than 570 miles by air, land, and sea for commitment into flat territory against an unfamiliar enemy at the other end. Operation LIBERTY CANYON commenced 27 October 1968 as Brigadier General Irby began sending the cavalry battalions south at the rate of one per day.

Lt. Col. Frank L. Henry's 2d Battalion of the 8th Cavalry "Mountain Boys" began packing on 27 October. After stashing all their equipment into CONEX containers, which were trucked to the docksides in Hue for shipment by sea, the troops camped on the Quang Tri airstrip with only their combat gear. Two days later C130 transport aircraft ferried them into Quan Loi, where they spent two days preparing to air assault into LZ Joe on Halloween, the last day of the month. Rocket-firing gunships and artillery pounded the woodlines as the battalion conducted the first cavalry division air assault in III CTZ. Waves of supply helicopters followed with materials as a new fire support base was hastily constructed.

Lt. Col. Addison Davis's 2d Battalion of the 7th Cavalry was flown to Quan Loi, paused for breath, and airmobiled onto LZ Billy in the forested borderland on 1 November. The order of the day was simply "Dig down or build up, but hurry." Reinforced by a battery from the 2d Battalion, 19th Artillery, and two squads of engineers, the troops felled trees with chain saws, cleared fields of fire with explosives, dug foxholes in the swampy soil, set up observation posts, and started building bunkers with steel planking, sandbags, logs, and sod. The bunker walls were stacked with hundreds of dirt-filled ammunition crates, quickly rendered excess as the light howitzers pumped shells into the nearby forest. In two days 181 helicopter sorties lifted in food, ammunition, fortification materials, light vehicles, radios, tents, and other equipment to establish the new fire support base. Rockets slammed nightly into the perimeter, and local patrols were already clashing with the Viet Cong. Company D's probe of a nearby woodline embroiled the battalion on its first southern firefight against a VC battalion just days later, on 6–7 November 1968.

On 27 October Lt. Col. James W. Dingeman learned that he would be moving his 2d Battalion of the 12th Cavalry south in approximately a day and a half and began planning to pull his companies in from the mountains. By noon on 29 October, his troops were assembled. Whipped by dust and pebbles from the twin rotors of descending Chinooks, they clambered aboard and were whisked to the Quang Tri airport for transport by C130 cargo planes into their new territory.

With three battalions locked into III CTZ, the 3d Brigade relocation was complete, and Col. Robert J. Baer's 1st Brigade began arriving to take over the southeastern portion of the former brigade's area. The inherent airmobile division flexibility allowed the screen to be adjusted wherever needed. For instance, Lt. Col. John F. McGraw, Jr.'s, 5th Battalion, 7th Cavalry, was originally ordered to Phuoc Vinh, but was shifted to "The Fishhook" area, a sharp bend in the border, where Lieutenant Colonel Henry's battalion encountered the enemy. The 2d Brigade lingered in I CTZ on COMANCHE FALLS until the operation was terminated 7 November and moved south the next day, where it was taken over by Col. Conrad L. Stansberry before the end of the month.

The 11th Aviation Group flew its own four hundred aircraft and 2,164 men down the coast from Da Nang to Bear Cat. From there the helicopters were flown to helipads and fire support bases being built near Army Special Forces campsites along the border. This arrangement provided some mutual security, allowed aircraft to operate out of prepared airstrips, and enabled battalions to be briefed on their individual areas by Special Forces teams. The 1st Cavalry Division headquarters deployed to its new main camp at Phuoc Vinh, a former 1st Infantry Division brigade base, on 7 November. Operation LIBERTY CANYON was concluded as the last essential combat equipment of the division arrived in III CTZ on 15 November 1968.

The amount of personnel and material moved during the transfer was staggering. During sixteen days of frantic Air Force aircraft shuttling, the 834th Air Division's 437 C130 transport sorties carried 11,550 troops and 3,399 tons of cargo from Quang Tri, Camp Evans, and

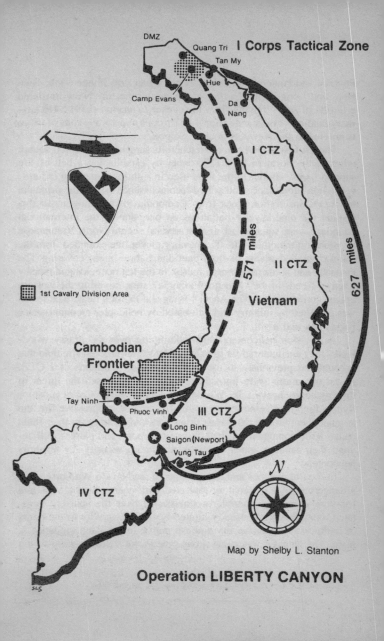

DMZ

Quang Tri

I Corps Tactical Zone

Tan My

Hue

Camp Evans

Da Nang

I CTZ

571 miles

627 miles

II CTZ

Vietnam

■ 1st Cavalry Division Area

Cambodian Frontier

Tay Ninh

Phuoc Vinh

III CTZ

Long Binh

Saigon (Newport)

Vung Tau

IV CTZ

N

Map by Shelby L. Stanton

Operation LIBERTY CANYON

Phu Bai and landed them at Tay Ninh, Quan Loi, Phuoc Vinh, Bien Hoa, and Long Thanh North. At the same time, the Navy mustered a flotilla of ships ranging from the carrier *Princeton* (LPH-5) to auxiliary landing vessels and sailed 4,037 troops and 16,593 tons of cargo from Hue to the Newport dock at Saigon.[5]

The 1st Cavalry Division stretched its screen across 4,800 square miles of the northern III CTZ frontier by establishing a belt of fire support bases, similar to the forts used in fighting American Indians, to provide surveillance and armed reconnaissance astride the principal NVA/VC infiltration lanes from Cambodia toward Saigon. In this fashion the nine cavalry battalions on one side of the international boundary were squared off against several secure North Vietnamese divisions on the other side. The cavalry picket line extended from the rolling, jungled plains of the "Sheridan Sabre" area, covering The Fishhook and northern approach routes, to the flat ricefields and marshy Plain of Reeds in the "Navajo Warhorse" area, covering the western Saigon corridor facing The Angel's Wing and Parrot's Beak. The screen was patrolled by infantry and buttressed by helicopter reconnaissance flights day and night.

As division helicopters began skimming over the grassy woodlands, they encountered far greater NVA/VC antiaircraft fire than that encountered previously in the northern coastal lowlands of I CTZ. Aerial operations were immediately adjusted to lessen the threat of this frequently heavy flak. Whenever possible, attack Cobra gunships flying "high bird" escorted scoutships to provide suppressive fire and to guide them around dangerous firing sites and clearings in their flight paths. Rifle companies pushed observation posts and patrols well beyond their landing zones to insure maximum security for resupply helicopters.

In the flat marshes and rice paddies of the Navajo Warhorse area, a dangerous slice of territory saturated with enemy booby traps and trip-wire explosives, aerial reconnaissance over the sparsely vegetated, open landscape usually limited NVA/VC activity to the hours of darkness. Roving cavalry ambush patrols maintained vigilance at night. The plentiful waterways around the Parrot's Beak, jutting within

5. 14th MHD, *Operation Liberty Canyon*, dtd 30 Jan 69.

thirty miles of Saigon, were screened with cavalrymen on Navy river patrol boats in joint "Nav-Cav" operations. The Nav-Cav search patrols swept through the Plain of Reeds and often crossed into the adjacent IV Corps Tactical Zone of South Vietnam's delta region. The 1st Cavalry Division became the only Army division to serve in all four Vietnam corps tactical zones.

Search operations in War Zone C's tropical rain forests pitted the cavalry against well-fortified, superbly camouflaged bunkers built for mutually interlocking fire and always designed in unique arrangements. Fields-of-fire, invisible to the advancing cavalrymen, were cut in the thick overgrowth only a few feet off the ground. Caught in such killing zones, entire platoons could be wiped out in a matter of seconds. The lethal bunker complexes could be mastered only by using carefully coordinated, overwhelming fire support and airpower. Even in the absence of such fieldworks, maneuvering cavalry was targeted by increased use of close-range enemy B40 rocket launchers. The companies reduced this danger by changing locations daily, aggressively sweeping the flanks of moving units, staking out night ambush sites, and establishing listening posts around perimeters at night.

The cavalrymen, accustomed to combating NVA entrenched into the monsoon-laden mountains who concealed their signal lines, found enemy communications wire simply strung along the trails. In one instance the wire was tapped as the enemy was relaying traffic. However, the troops quickly learned that following the wire often led to disaster for the point unit. Safe wire tracking required that units move in arcs every fifty yards, relocating the wire farther down the trail, then repeating the procedure until the wire's source was discovered.

The joint aerial cavalry reconnaissance and fire support base patrolling screen inhibited the flow of enemy supplies. At midnight on 14 November 1968, the enemy made its first determined bid to smash the cavalry screen in the corner of War Zone C. The *95C Regiment* struck Fire Support Base Dot, held by the ARVN 36th Ranger Battalion under the division's operational control and backed up by 2d Brigade gunships, artillery, and scout helicopters. Preceded by a heavy mortar and rocket barrage, thousands of NVA infantrymen surged forward, trying to overrun the base. The South Vietnamese rangers lowered their artillery tubes to fire point-blank into the massed charges, which were also mauled by defensive artillery, helicopters, and F100 fighter-bombers. The attackers retreated with heavy losses, and division gunships rocketed and strafed the defeated remnants for four miles as they streamed back to Cambodia.

During the month of December, the allies gained evidence that the North Vietnamese were planning a multidivision repeat attack against Saigon during the Tet-69 period. The *5th VC Division* was assigned the task of moving down Adams Road (the Song Be corridor) to eliminate the allied command's strategic Bien Hoa–Long Binh complex outside Saigon. This division's movement was the linchpin of the enemy's battle plan. The closer *1st*, *7th*, and *9th Divisions* would continue to reconnoiter and stash forward caches, but would not move toward Saigon until the *5th VC Division* was in position on the eastern flank. The *1st NVA Division* was given the diversionary mission of marching out of War Zone C to draw the allied reserves from their positions. The two other divisions would then advance on the capital itself, the *7th NVA Division* from the north down the Saigon corridor and the *9th VC Division* from the west directly out of The Angel's Wing.

All NVA/VC offensives required high levels of supplies prestocked in advance depots. In anticipation of the upcoming offensive against Saigon, the enemy increased his flow of materials into Vietnam. Supply lines such as the X-Cache Route, Saigon corridor, Serge's Jungle Highway, Adams Road, and Jolley Trail were shifted or strengthened to pierce the airmobile screen. Although December was generally a period of light, sporadic contact, the 1st Cavalry Division's battalions opened and closed fire support bases in rapid succession as they tried to remain ahead of the NVA forces infiltrating into attack positions.

Col. Karl R. Morton took over the 3d Brigade on 15 November and shifted brigade efforts to cover Serge's Jungle Highway, a critical enemy midzone infiltration lane, on 1 December 1968. That same day, Lt. Col. George D. Hardesty, Jr., assumed command of the 2d Battalion, 7th Cavalry. Captain Fitzsimmons's Company D had been moving northwest of Quan Loi for several days, engaging only small pockets of resistance and occasional sniper fire. The field first sergeant, Sfc. John Allison, a veteran of the same company during his previous Vietnam tour in 1966–67, noticed that the scant contact was making the troops restless and that they were becoming lax. On the night of 2 December, Captain Fitzsimmons announced that the company would be air assaulted into a new area. He turned to Sergeant Allison and said, "Six Mike (Allison's call sign), we are going in without a prep or chopper gunships working over the LZ prior to the troops coming in on helicopters." Sergeant Allison was aghast. Fitzsimmons quickly replied that he was only joking, and everyone sighed with relief.

On the following morning the 116-men company airmobiled by increments into LZ Eleanor. Artillery and armed helicopters ceased pounding the horseshoe-shaped woodline around the landing zone as the first troopships glided toward the LZ. Helicopter door gunners raking the trees and dense undergrowth were not challenged during the final descent, and the signal "LZ Green!" (meaning safe or secured) was given. The first troopers nonchalantly moved through the waist-high grass and around small anthills on the two-hundred-yard-wide field. An hour before noon the helicopters returned with the rest of the troops, and the company began final preparation to consolidate the perimeter.

The cavalrymen were unaware that their landing zone was ringed by bunkers set twenty-five yards or less into the treeline and surrounded by four hundred North Vietnamese soldiers. The enemy troops were silently watching and waiting with automatic weapons, heavy machine guns, mortars, and B40 rockets at the ready. Dozens of snipers were tied into the trees to prevent their falling, even if hit. The North Vietnamese leaders quietly observed the Americans begin organizing search teams to probe the woodline, but held their fire as a single Huey descended into the clearing.

Lieutenant Colonel Hardesty stepped out of his command helicopter, briefly conferred with Captain Fitzsimmons, then returned to the Huey. As the command ship was clearing the treetops, the NVA suddenly opened fire. The landing zone was swept by a devastating hailstorm of bullets, mortar explosions, and rocket detonations. Dead and wounded cavalrymen fell everywhere, and the majority of the company never had a chance. The surviving troopers desperately tried to dig in, but the ground was like rock underneath the parched cracked crust, leaving them completely exposed.

The first B40 rocket burst into a raging grass fire on the field. The troops frantically attempted to beat out the blazing grass with their tunics as they returned fire into the trees, and many were killed or wounded in the effort. Some men were wounded so badly that they were unable to crawl away, and the fire burned them alive as their ammunition pouches discharged from the heat.

Sergeant Allison considered the scene a nightmare where everything was going wrong, and foolish heroism was compounding the slaughter. The artillery forward observer, who had celebrated his twentieth birthday on the eve of the assault, stood up and began calling in artillery fire as everyone shouted, "Get down, Thirty!" (his call sign). He was killed almost instantly. The dead lieutenant observer slumped over the radioman, who struggled to push the body off and use the radio. Finally, the radio operator was able to start directing fire support through the smoke into the forest.

Captain Fitzsimmons's radioman, "Buzz," dropped his radio, grabbed a machine gun, and disappeared into the grass as he moved all over the field firing bursts of return fire. Sergeant Allison furiously grabbed the abandoned radio and tried to stay in contact with battalion, but communications kept fading. Each time he set the radio upright, the North Vietnamese concentrated their fire on the antenna, so Allison laid the backpack radio flat on the ground and put the whip antenna over his shoulder to keep it off the ground. A sniper round slapped dirt in the sergeant's face, but miraculously he wasn't hit. He called for immediate resupply of water, ammunition, and medical evacuation support.

The medical helicopter whirled onto the burning, fire-swept field, but was riddled with machine gun bullets as it landed. The pilot, door gunner, and all the medical aidmen on board were shot, and the co-pilot lifted the stricken helicopter out of the maelstrom at once. Other helicopters darted overhead as their crews tossed out ammunition containers, but they were dropped too high and landed beyond reach. A number of troopers tried to secure the precious cargo, only to be killed or wounded in the process. Men were lying all over the landing zone, crying for water and help, and three medics were killed trying to treat the growing number of casualties.

After five hours of combat, the enemy fire ceased in volume and Sergeant Allison reasoned that the enemy was preparing to overrun the field. He shouted for everyone to gather what ammunition and grenades he could and crawl to his position, thus forming a small perimeter with the thirty-six cavalrymen who were still able to fight.

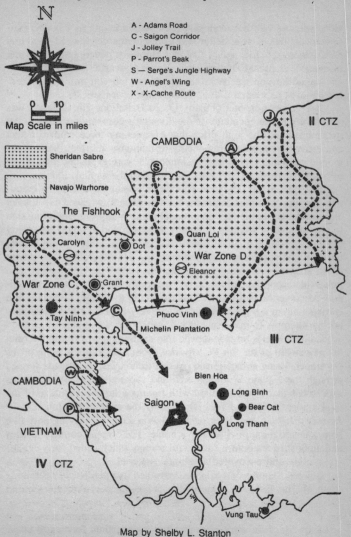

Cavalry Screen in III Corps Tactical Zone

A - Adams Road
C - Saigon Corridor
J - Jolley Trail
P - Parrot's Beak
S — Serge's Jungle Highway
W - Angel's Wing
X - X-Cache Route

Map Scale in miles

Sheridan Sabre

Navajo Warhorse

CAMBODIA

II CTZ

The Fishhook

Carolyn
Dot
Quan Loi
War Zone D
Eleanor
War Zone C
Grant
Phuoc Vinh
Tay Ninh
Michelin Plantation
III CTZ

CAMBODIA
VIETNAM
Saigon
Bien Hoa
Long Binh
Bear Cat
Long Thanh

IV CTZ

Vung Tau

Map by Shelby L. Stanton

However, the North Vietnamese were withdrawing as cavalry reinforcements reached the battlefield to rescue the dehydrated survivors of Company D. Lieutenant Colonel Hardesty helicoptered onto the blackened, shattered landing zone. He went over to Sergeant Allison and patted him on the back, saying, "Fine job you did, Six Mike," but his eyes expressed only, "What a hell of a mess."[6]

The decimation of Company D, 2d Battalion, 7th Cavalry, was a relatively minor encounter in the division's covering operations, but it demonstrated the high price that a screening force paid to detect and harass large, advancing enemy formations. In effect, valiant airmobile companies such as Fitzsimmons's were exposing themselves to North Vietnamese divisions to safeguard the capital, Saigon.

The 1st Cavalry Division was flexible enough to send its battalions hopping over great distances, but they often fragmented into smaller elements to cover the vast operational area. With a screening mission to provide timely warning of enemy approach and to report on enemy movement, these small airmobile forces often landed in unsecured territory and sometimes suffered reverses. However, the total power of an airmobile division was greater than the sum of its parts, and powerful responsive forces could be rapidly shifted to battle the enemy wherever he was found. This capability to change directions and skirmish along a wide front was effectively impeding and frustrating enemy attempts to make headway through the war zones.

Colonel Baer's brigade moved into the Saigon corridor to interdict the movement of the *9th VC Division* from The Angel's Wing on 15 December. Using airmobile and riverine techniques, the brigade slashed through the Navajo Warhorse area and captured so many munitions and caches that it was credited with finding a large percentage of the total amount infiltrated into III CTZ by the enemy division. On 19 January 1969 Colonel Baer reentered War Zone C, leaving only two companies to monitor Navajo Warhorse. The brigade combed jungles and ambushed trails in a successful screen which killed forty NVA/VC a night and uncovered additional material.

Colonel Stansberry's brigade continued its interdictory operations south of The Fishhook. One of the largest caches was found by its

---

6. Ltr fm Sfc. John Allison in ref to Div investigation, undtd, frm Elizabethtown, Ky, contained in 1st Cav Div Opn TOAN THANG II files.

attached South Vietnamese 3d Marine Battalion. Containing 250 large rockets, 324 assault rifles, 22 crew-served weapons, and a ton of munitions, the cache could have supplied an entire NVA battalion for a sizable attack. In the meantime Colonel Morton's brigade air assaulted into War Zone D to head off the *5th VC Division*. This mobile screening increased the distance from the border on the western flank, giving the air cavalry reconnaissance squadron more time to detect the enemy approach and use long-range division artillery against it.

The NVA/VC were forced to break their units into smaller components to pass through the screen and to divert combat troops to move additional supplies in order to replace critical material losses. The cavalry continued to batter enemy rear service elements struggling to protect and move their caches, and these support units took the actual brunt of casualties. The main enemy divisions inexorably worked their way forward: the *1st* and *7th NVA Divisions* into the area just north of Michelin Rubber Plantation, and the *5th* and *9th VC Divisions* on both sides of Saigon in The Angel's Wing and southwestern War Zone D, respectively.[7]

The enemy offensive began on 23 February 1969 after the conclusion of the Tet-69 truce, as firefights and rocket or mortar barrages erupted over a wide front. The strength of the *5th VC Division* pushing toward Saigon was steadily eroded. One regiment of the *5th VC Division*, repeatedly hit by ambushes and artillery, aborted its mission and returned to War Zone D. By the time the weakened division attacked the allied gates and bunker line at Bien Hoa airbase, it was stopped cold by the 199th Infantry Brigade. The 1st Infantry Division repelled a regimental assault of the other weakened enemy prong at Dau Tieng and counterattacked through the Michelin Rubber Plantation to finish off the attackers.

In War Zone C the *1st NVA Division* had been bottled up by the 1st Brigade, under the command of Col. Joseph P. Kingston since 3 March 1969. Cavalry operating out of Fire Support Base Grant, occupied by Lt. Col. Peter Gorvard's 2d Battalion of the 12th Cavalry, kept interdicting the enemy division's lines of communication and prevented it from conducting the assigned diversion mission. Shortly after midnight on 8 March 1969, the base was hit by intense rocket

7. 1st Cav Div, *Combat Operations After Action Report*, dtd 2 Sep 69.

and mortar fire and stormed by the *95C Regiment*. The battalion head-quarters bunker was destroyed by two 120mm rockets in the opening bombardment, killing Colonel Gorvad and numerous other key personnel.

The massed enemy attack on Fire Support Base Grant was smashed by concentrated defensive fires and airstrikes. Quad .50-caliber machine guns sliced through the onrushing NVA soldiers with four-barreled ribbons of fire. Capt. Bill Capshaw of Battery C, 1st Battalion, 77th Artillery, directed his troops as they manhandled a 105mm howitzer forward to rake the North Vietnamese with Bee Hive rounds. While the main assault was finally destroyed in the perimeter wire, enemy regimental reserves were smothered by artillery concentrations. The shattered remnants fled the battlefield only two hours after the attack commenced.

Two battalions of the *101D Regiment* tried to overrun Fire Support Base Grant in the predawn hours of 11 March 1969, but were quickly repulsed. Fast pursuit by 1st Squadron, 9th Cavalry, helicopters further diminished the retreating enemy. The successful defense of Fire Support Base Grant insured the continuity of the cavalry screen in War Zone C, and Colonel Baer shifted his brigade flag to take over the Navajo Warhorse area. During March the Navajo Warhorse area also flared with action as the cavalry intercepted elements of the *9th VC Division* attempting to drive east into Saigon.[8] The 2d Brigade became responsible for War Zone C, while Colonel Morton's brigade continued hunting expeditions in War Zone D.

With the NVA/VC offensive timetable wrecked and its combat formations in obviously depleted condition, II Field Force Vietnam went over to the offensive in Operation ATLAS WEDGE during mid-March. The 11th Armored Cavalry Regiment fought through the Michelin Rubber Plantation and pushed the *7th NVA Division* out of its staging area. By the end of March 1969, it was apparent that the North Vietnamese threat to Saigon was over. The airmobile division accomplished its screening objectives by impeding the advance of four

8. A detailed account of a particularly bitter night firefight by the 1st Cavalry Division in The Angel's Wing sector can be found in the author's *The Rise and Fall of an American Army*, (Novato, Calif.: Presidio Press, 1985), pp. 308–13.

NVA/VC divisions, causing large enemy cache and material losses throughout northern III CTZ, and breaking the core of the projected enemy sweep into Saigon during the enemy post-Tet 1969 spring offensive.

Cavalry screening was largely uneventful during April. The division initiated the MONTANA SCOUT/MONTANA RAIDER series of operations, seeking the NVA/VC forces which were refitting in III CTZ. Colonel Morton's brigade screened War Zone D to locate and intercept the *5th VC Division*. In early May the *9th VC Division* initiated an attack toward Tay Ninh in coordination with the *1st NVA Division*, while the *7th Division* held the Saigon corridor open. With all four enemy divisions once again on the move, the 1st Cavalry Division retracted its mobile screening net to assume an interdictory posture, typified by small patrols and ambushes, across the southern portion of War Zone C.

Maj. Gen. Elvy Benton Roberts brought a wealth of veteran airmobile knowledge and combat paratrooper background when he took command of the 1st Cavalry Division on 5 May 1969. Roberts was born in Manchester, Kentucky, on 21 August 1917. He graduated from West Point in January 1943, then completed infantry, parachute, and airborne school demolitions courses before joining the 501st Parachute Infantry Regiment of the famous 101st Airborne Division at the end of the year. He jumped into Normandy during D-Day, 6 June 1944, and served with the regiment throughout the rest of World War II, participating in five major campaigns, including the parachute assault of Holland and the defense of Bastogne.

After the war, Roberts served on various assignments in the United States, Germany, and Iran, including the command of the 1st Airborne Battle Group, 506th Infantry, at Fort Campbell, Kentucky, from June 1961 through January 1963. At that point Colonel Roberts was assigned as Chief of Staff of the 11th Air Assault Division and became one of the prime developers of the modern airmobile division concept. He brought the 1st Cavalry Division's 1st Airborne Brigade to Vietnam and led it through the central highlands until March 1966, when he was assigned to MACV and promoted to brigadier general that September. Returning to Vietnam as deputy commander of the 9th Infantry Division in June 1968, Roberts moved up to USARV Deputy Chief of Staff for Plans and Operations before taking command of the 1st Cavalry Division. Possessing an intimate knowledge of airmobile application, Major General Roberts acted aggressively and without hesitation in shifting division forces to interdict and destroy enemy elements throughout northern III CTZ.

The day after Roberts assumed command, the 1st Cavalry Division scored one of its hardest-fought screening victories during the battle of Landing Zone Carolyn. Lt. Col. Richard W. Wood's 2d Battalion of the 8th Cavalry had opened LZ Carolyn two weeks earlier in a large open area near the abandoned Prek Klok Special Forces camp as a forward command and firebase inside War Zone C. Two batteries of artillery were located inside the perimeter: Battery B of the 1st Battalion, 30th Artillery (155mm), on the northern side; and Battery A of the 2d Battalion, 19th Artillery (105mm), along the western perimeter. The cavalry operating out of LZ Carolyn quickly became a thorn in the side of enemy forces, engaging NVA/VC forces in sixty-two separate contacts within the period of twenty-four days. The North Vietnamese decided to annihilate the post because of its pressure on X-Cache Trail traffic.

In the early morning darkness of 6 May, the North Vietnamese retaliated with an intensive rocket and mortar barrage, followed by a massive *95th Regiment* pincer ground assault against two sides of the base an hour later. LZ Carolyn's garrison was reduced by the absence of several line companies on patrol, and the withering defensive fires of the battalion's Company C and E were unable to prevent the onrushing battalions from storming through the wire and into the landing zone from both directions. Six perimeter bunkers were overrun, one of the medium howitzers was captured, and the enemy threatened to slice through the center of the base.

The Americans counterattacked with all available personnel, the officers involved being killed at the head of their troops. Artillerymen, supply and signal personnel, and engineers fought and died as emergency infantry reserves. The counterattacks were hurled against both enemy penetrations, but the most violent fighting occurred on the northern side, where a seesaw battle raged for possession of the 155mm howitzer position. During the course of the battle, this weapon exchanged hands three times in hand-to-hand fighting decided at close range with rifles and entrenching tools.

Overhead, rocket-firing AH1G Cobra helicopters rolled in, ignoring heavy flak, and blasted the NVA with rockets and miniguns. Air Force AC47 "Spooky" and AC119 "Shadow" aircraft, supported by fighter-bombers, were employed against the numerous enemy antiaircraft weapons ringing the perimeter.

Controlled and uncontrolled fires were raging everywhere, and it seemed that LZ Carolyn was ablaze throughout its entire length. Waves of North Vietnamese infantry charging into the southern lines were met by defending troops who took advantage of the aviation gasoline storage area. They shot holes in the fuel drums and ignited them to create a flaming barrier, which effectively blocked further enemy penetration. In the LZ's opposite sector, a medium howitzer gun pit received three direct hits which touched off a fire in its powder bunker, yet the crew calmly stood by its weapon and employed it throughout the night.

Both 105mm artillery ammunition points were exploded by enemy fire around 3:30 A.M., and shrapnel from more than six hundred disintegrating rounds in the two dumps sprayed the entire landing zone continuously for four hours. LZ Carolyn appeared threatened with total destruction as the thundering conflagration tossed detonating artillery projectiles to shower men and equipment with flying rounds and burning shell fragments.

The defending artillerymen and mortar crews fought in desperation heightened by the loss of communications between most weapons and their fire direction centers (FDC). The initial enemy barrage destroyed communications from the 155mm gun sections to their FDC, forcing crews to individually engage targets on their own volition by leveling tubes full of Bee Hive or high-explosive charges. When telephone lines from the mortar tubes to their FDC were severed, the direction personnel switched to a bullhorn to relay fire commands across the deafening noise of the battlefield. The battalion mortar platoon's four tubes fired fifteen hundred rounds, ranging from critical illumination to searing white phosphorus. In all cases effective fire support was maintained.

Ammunition shortages quickly developed. As on-hand mortar ammunition beside the weapons was exhausted, volunteers dashed through fire-swept open areas to retrieve more rounds from storage bunkers. The destruction of the 105mm ammunition points caused an immediate crisis in the light howitzer pits. The cannoneers were forced to redistribute remaining ammunition by crawling from one gun section to another under a hail of enemy direct fire and spinning shrapnel from the exploding dump. The crews continued rendering direct fire, even though they were often embroiled in defending their own weapons. One light howitzer section was caught in an enemy cross fire between a heavy machine gun and rifles, until the artillerymen managed to turn their lowered muzzle and pump Bee Hive flechettes into the enemy. All automatic weapons fire against the howitzer was instantly silenced. Cavalry counterattacks reestablished the perimeter, and the enemy force began withdrawing, breaking contact at 6:00 A.M.[9]

The NVA/VC forces increased their activity throughout the war zone, but the high point was reached between 12 and 14 May 1969 as Fire Support Bases Grant, Jamie, and Phyllis were hit by ground attacks. Action tapered off almost immediately afterward as the cavalry screen effectively disrupted the flow of enemy logistical traffic needed to sustain the enemy's advance. Now General Roberts airmobiled his division into the attack as he resumed its offensive role, striking enemy formations and their assembly areas throughout central War Zone C. Division forces conducted air assaults throughout the thick jungles in the wake of massed B52 bombing runs. Extensive use was made of large amounts of chemical gas crystal to channel enemy movement and contaminate his supplies.

Division search operations and difficult "bunker busting" tasks continued through the humid summer, reducing the next round of NVA/VC attacks in August to feeble one-battalion thrusts against remote provincial capitals near Cambodia. These attacks could be staged directly across the border from The Fishhook and other adjacent territory without having attacking units run the gauntlet of cavalry interception or relying on forward depots subject to destruction by cavalry patrolling.

The 1st Cavalry Division screen was stretched across northern III CTZ from 15 November 1968, when Operation LIBERTY CANYON ended, until 23 June 1969, the official termination date of the Operation MONTANA SCOUT/MONTANA RAIDER series. During this time the cavalry screening effort cost the lives of 567 troopers killed in action and another 3,555 wounded.[10] In exchange, the di-

9. Hq 2d Bn, 8th Cav, Ltr dtd 1 Jun 69, Subj: Recomm for Awd of the VUA w/spt papers.
10. 1st Cav Div, *Operational Report*, dtd 15 Feb 69, Tab J; and 14th MHD, *The Shield and the Hammer: The 1st Cav Div in War Zone C and Western III Corps*, undtd, p. 28.

vision whittled down the offensive momentum of four NVA/VC divisions in the heart of war zone country and rendered them incapable of inflicting damage on Saigon. For the 1st Cavalry Division, the successful conclusion of this mission represented the airmobile fulfillment of a quintessential cavalry function throughout military history: the cavalry screen.

CHAPTER 9

Cavalry Exploitation

The Cambodian Invasion

Maj. Gen. E. B. Roberts's 1st Cavalry Division paired up its brigades with ARVN airborne brigades in late 1969 to assist South Vietnam to develop its Airborne Division into an airmobile strike force. The cavalry conducted extensive joint field exercises to impart technical airmobile doctrine and helicopter expertise to the South Vietnamese units. This posture temporarily reduced division field screening, but by early 1970 the division and its mated Vietnamese airborne brigades were leapfrogging closer to the Cambodian border, giving the Vietnamese practical combat experience in airmobile cavalry techniques.

The cavalry was traveling fast and light to actively interdict the sparse enemy foot, cart, and truck traffic. The advance was preceded by division ranger teams weaving and ambushing their way deep into uncharted territory to scout out the trail networks and bunker complexes for NVA/VC troops and to report rapidly on enemy movements. Behind the rangers the airmobile companies and platoons fanned out through the maze of forest trails, being resupplied twice a week and using temporary firebases closed out every few days. An umbrella of B52 bombers, helicopters, fighter-bombers, and aerial artillery remained overhead.

This dangerous business was being pushed steadily forward in northwestern War Zone C by Col. William V. Ochs, Jr.'s, 1st Brigade and attached 3d ARVN Airborne Brigade. His command consisted of two cavalry battalions, the 2d Battalions of the 7th and 8th Cavalry (later replaced by the 5th Battalion, 7th Cavalry), and the

5th, 9th, and 11th ARVN airborne battalions, all reinforced by the 1st Squadron of the 11th Armored Cavalry Regiment.[1]

Fire Support Base (FSB) Illingworth was among a dozen hasty forts built by the brigade, but it was placed extremely close to Cambodia in the corner pocket of War Zone C, a rough patch of no-man's-land that the troops rancorously called the "Dog's Head." Lt. Col. Michael J. Conrad's 2d Battalion, 8th Cavalry, occupied FSB Illingworth on 18 March 1970. The command post, one line cavalry company, and the support company were placed alongside eleven howitzers and five combat vehicles. The rest of the battalion began scouring the nearby jungle.

Company A performed the garrison duty until a close-range B40 rocket and machine gun attack cut into the fire support base perimeter in the evening ten days later, causing thirty-five casualties and the company's withdrawal to rest and absorb replacements. That same night in the "Dog's Throat" sector four miles directly south, a massed NVA attack nearly overran FSB Jay of Lt. Col. Robert Hannas's 2d Battalion, 7th Cavalry. The garrison of FSB Illingworth were told to brace for assault next, and Company C became the perimeter company. Since it mustered only thirty-nine troops, the battalion recon platoon was added so that three officers and seventy-four enlisted men manned the berm.[2]

FSB Illingworth was a typical late-war forward base on the Cambodian front. The oval-shaped fort contained twenty squad sandbag bunkers, each containing six or nine men, roofed with steel culvert sections and three sandbag layers, built into the four-foot-high earth berm. Foxholes were dug between bunkers. The company placed a dozen claymore antipersonnel mines in front of each bunker, but only set two machine guns on the perimeter because of recent losses. Four armored personnel carriers and one Sheridan light tank backed up the line, but the Sheridan was inoperative except for its .50-caliber machine gun. This weapon was pulled off and dug in beside the single quadruple .50-caliber antiaircraft gun on the southwest berm corner.

---

1. 1st Cav Div, *Operational Report*, dtd 15 May 70.
2. Exact organization of FSB Illingworth was Battalion CP and Companies C and E of the 2d Bn, 8th Cav; Btry A, 1st Bn, 30th Arty; Btry A, 2d Bn, 32d Arty; Btry B, 1st Bn, 77th Arty; part of Tp A, 1st Sqdn, 11th Arm Cav Regt.

One 8-inch (another was unserviceable), three 155mm medium, and six 105mm light howitzers were prepared with "killer junior" and other antiinfantry rounds.

No barbed wire was placed around FSB Illingworth because it was not intended as a permanent firebase, but rather one that could be dismantled in a day. Barbed wire was ineffective in slowing enemy sappers unless it was staked down and included tanglefoot, and the battalion did not have sufficient personnel to build elaborate wire barriers nor the airlift needed to backhaul it. For the same reasons, all relating to the temporary nature of the position and its hasty assembly, chemical gas projectors, fougasse flame barrels, and other weapons were not emplaced. The field first sergeant of Company C, Sfc. Charles H. Beauchamp, was distressed about the condition of Company A's previous fighting bunkers, which were not well constructed.

At precisely 2:18 A.M., 1 April 1970, the NVA/VC opened their attack on the fort with a blistering rocket and mortar barrage, knocking out the communications antennas. Groups of NVA troops charged out of the woodline toward the firebase parapets. A heavy pall of choking dust, raised by weapons firing on both sides, dropped visibility to nearly zero and fouled many weapons. The cavalry defenders were unable to see the North Vietnamese infantrymen until they were nearly on top of them. The enemy soldiers, clad in shorts and sandals and, sometimes, shirts, ran forward firing assault rifles and tossing satchel charges, as the cavalry riflemen returned fire with M16s until their weapons jammed (between 2 and 3 magazines) and then threw hand grenades. In seconds the NVA were up and over the berm in a welter of hand-to-hand combat. Sp4 Gordon A. Flessner stabbed his way through several enemy soldiers with a bowie knife, Sp4 Frederick L. Sporar and SSgt. James L. Taylor strangled NVA with their bare hands, and Sp4 Peter C. Lemon (later awarded the Medal of Honor) used his rifle as a club.

The mortar platoon leader, 1Lt. Michael H. Russell, could hear the screaming and firing, but it was impossible to see even muzzle flashes through the cloud of dust enveloping the battle area. He fired his mortars based on sound, but suddenly one mortar tube disintegrated as a satchel charge was heaved into it. Within minutes another crew started shouting and dived behind the blast wall as their mortar was detonated by a sapper. The ammunition stocks in both destroyed mortar pits began burning and exploding intermittently.

The reconnaissance platoon members under 1Lt. Gregory J. Peters made a fighting withdrawal to a secondary defensive line, where they stopped the North Vietnamese who had broken through. The howitzers were starting to fire, although one was destroyed by a direct hit, and the 8-inch ammunition dump was on fire. The situation seemed to improve as the berm was recaptured and cleared of the enemy. Overhead, AC47 "Spooky" aircraft, tactical fighters, and armed helicopters were gaining firepower ascendancy.

Shortly after 3:00 A.M. the fires started to worsen at the 8-inch ammunition point, which had not been dug in. The excessive amount of projectiles, cannisters, and powder bags were heaped together in ammunition carriers and on the ground.[3] The point's controlling artillerymen of the 2d Battalion, 32d Artillery (attached to the division), had witnessed their previous 175mm cannon ammunition dump explode with catastrophic results at FSB St. Barbara and shouted to warn the recon troops and other cavalry to get away.

Lieutenant Peters and his men elected to stay at their positions to prevent another breach of the line. Within ten minutes the entire ammunition dump detonated in a single fiery blast which completely demolished part of the fort, destroyed two full-tracked M548 ammo carriers, ripped apart one 8-inch howitzer, and leveled much of the berm line. Troops were hurled through the air (including Lieutenant Peters, who survived), and flying shrapnel sliced through men and material. All artillery stopped firing as the crews dropped, wounded or stunned by ruptured eardrums. However, the tremendous explosion stopped an enemy company—the NVA fled from the field.

The attack on FSB Illingworth repeated many circumstances at FSB Jay. In both cases the first enemy volley struck down the antenna array and a heavy curtain of dust made observation nearly impossible. Defensive deficiencies inherent in such hasty fortifications abounded. The defending garrison lost twenty-four killed and fifty-four wounded in the action, while seventy-four complete enemy bodies were counted, although doubtless many more were carried away by comrades retreating into Cambodia. In the final analysis it was probably the valor of a few cavalrymen that saved the tiny fort from certain destruction. As Sp4 Richard Whittier, a platoon radioman of Conrad's battalion,

3. 1st Cav Div, *Operational Report*, dtd 15 May 70, p. 49.

stated, "I had never seen so many enemy in the open. . . . It is my profound belief that Illingworth wasn't overrun because these people stayed, probably in the knowledge of certain death and knowing that the 8-inch ammo dump was about to go up. They held their positions."[4]

Prior to 1970 the North Vietnamese were able freely to occupy and use parts of two neutral countries, Laos and Cambodia, adjacent to South Vietnam for massive material and reinforcement routes and division staging bases. MACV was politically restricted from maneuvering against these enemy trail networks and base camps. The NVA/VC developed increasingly sophisticated sanctuaries close to Vietnam, in which supplies could be stockpiled and armies refurbished with immunity from allied intervention.

The 1st Cavalry Division troopers were understandably frustrated by their inability to pursue North Vietnamese marauders into Cambodian territory, but permission would be forthcoming shortly. The communist military use of Cambodian sanctuaries had become so blatantly menacing by the spring of 1970 that military action against them was urgently required. President Richard M. Nixon wanted the safety of both the Saigon area and the remaining American troops guaranteed as U.S. troop withdrawals accelerated. Once the politically sensitive decision was made to conduct a limited spoiling offensive, the tropical Cambodian environment mandated that action be quickly taken during the brief April–May seasonal transition between the northeast and southwest monsoons.

Detailed MACV combined planning for a multidivision Cambodian attack was initiated on 27 March 1970, a day previous to the FSB Jay attack. Lt. Gen. Michael S. Davison, the commander of II Field Force Vietnam, received instructions from MACV to begin preparations for a drive into The Fishhook area of Cambodia on 24 April. Two days later Major General Roberts was given the task of planning and directing the major II Field Force Vietnam thrust into The Fishhook area to disrupt the suspected enemy headquarters for the Viet Cong Liberation Front and to eradicate his major depots.

The allied spring invasion of Cambodia would be the most dramatic and significant utilization of the division during 1970 and placed

4. 14th MHD, *Combat After Action Interview Report*, dtd 3 Jan 71, p. 15.

a capstone on its service in the Second Indochina War. At this stage of the conflict, the 1st Cavalry Division (Airmobile) was the un-questioned premier attack division of the allied command, and it would spearhead the main Cambodian offensive. The division personnel pre-pared for revenge after years of command-imposed restraint from challenging the North Vietnamese in foreign base territory.

The 1st Cavalry Division's Cambodian operations exemplified the essence of another historically vital cavalry function: mobile cavalry exploitation. The 1st Cavalry Division was selected as the main ex-ploitation force of the entire Cambodian operation. Military exploi-tation is a role historically undertaken by cavalry to follow up success in the attack. Cavalry formations exercising this mode of attack rely on two overriding considerations: speed and violence. The attackers bypass pockets of resistance to concentrate on the destruction of the more vulnerable headquarters, combat support, and service support units. They disrupt the enemy's command and control structure and his flow of fuel, ammunition, repair parts, food, and other necessities. This weakens or destroys the enemy defenses and makes it possible for smaller (or less proficient, as was the ARVN) forces to overpower a larger enemy.

The main assault on The Fishhook was coded TOAN THANG (ROCKCRUSHER) 43. The Cambodian Fishhook was a raised hilly area of rugged jungle and swamps which melted into the flat, wet riceland plain to either side. As the rolling terrain faded both east and west into the lowland, the dense patches of jungle became intermixed with light, leafy forests and grassy fields, and finally with upland rice and rubber plantations. Allied intelligence believed that the Com-munist Supreme Command for the liberation of South Vietnam (COSVN) lurked somewhere in the jungled morass of The Fishhook, defended by the *7th NVA Division*, recently withdrawn from War Zone C, and supported by various artillery and service regiments. Addi-tionally, the *5th VC Division*'s right flank was tied in to the eastern flank of The Fishhook region.

Brig. Gen. Robert M. Shoemaker, the brilliant airmobile tactician and veteran of the 11th Air Assault Division, was given command and control over The Fishhook drive. He arrived as Chief of Staff of the 1st Cavalry Division on 21 April 1969, but the high point of his tenure came on 12 August 1969, when the enemy launched an attack

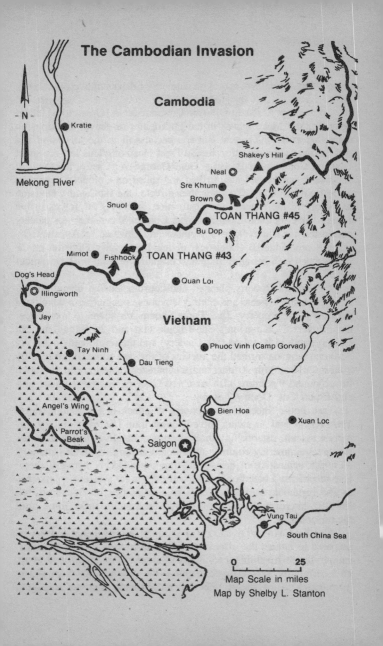

The Cambodian Invasion

Cambodia

Kratie

Mekong River

Shakey's Hill

Neal

Sre Khtum

Brown

TOAN THANG #45

Snuol

Bu Dop

TOAN THANG #43

Mimot

Fishhook

Quan Loi

Dog's Head

Illingworth

Jay

Vietnam

Tay Ninh

Dau Tieng

Phuoc Vinh (Camp Gorvad)

Angel's Wing

Parrot's Beak

Bien Hoa

Xuan Loc

Saigon

Vung Tau

South China Sea

0   25

Map Scale in miles

Map by Shelby L. Stanton

against Binh Long Province with supporting drives in two other provinces.

On that day Assistant Division Commander-A (Operations), Brigadier General Meszar, was in the Philippines on leave, and division commander Major General Roberts became ill in the afternoon and was medically evacuated to the 3d Field Hospital. This left Assistant Division Commander-B, Brig. Gen. George W. Casey, in technical command, but he had just arrived and relied on Colonel Shoemaker as his right-hand man. Together they directed the 1st Cavalry Division to victory in the repulse and destruction of NVA/VC forces in the August battle for Binh Long Province. Colonel Shoemaker was quickly nominated for star rank in September and elevated to Assistant Division Commander-B (Logistics) of the 1st Cavalry Division on 22 November 1969, being promoted to brigadier general on 1 December 1969.

As General Roberts planned and coordinated the operation, insuring that his officers and their Vietnamese counterparts developed the final plans properly, Task Force Shoemaker began to take shape. Col. Robert C. Kingston's 3d Brigade (1st and 2d Battalions, 7th Cavalry, and 2d Battalion, 5th Cavalry) and the reinforced 3d ARVN Airborne Brigade formed the nucleus of the task force, reinforced by a tank (2d Bn, 34th Armor) and mechanized battalion (2d Bn, 47th Infantry) and the entire 11th Armored Cavalry Regiment under cavalry expert Col. Donn A. Starry.

Task Force Shoemaker's concept of attack in Operation TOAN THANG 43 was to swing directly west into The Fishhook by airmobile assault, establishing three deep penetration airheads as anvils for three hammering columns of armored cavalry and tank battalions to smash against from the south, trapping COSVN between them. One mechanized battalion would seal off the far western approaches to The Fishhook, while the aerial reconnaissance 1st Squadron, 9th Cavalry, intercepted any threat behind the cavalry strike force from the far north.

The 1st Cavalry Division was initially informed that it must be prepared to launch the offensive within seventy-two hours of notification. On 28 April this lead time was shortened to forty-eight hours after permission was received to extend the planning down to brigade level. On 30 April, the original date for initiation of operations, Task

Force Shoemaker was established at Quan Loi as the control headquarters for the first U.S. cross-border operation. However, President Nixon delayed the attack twenty-four hours, so that U.S. forces actually crossed the border on 1 May 1970.

The allied Cambodian invasion commenced in the predawn darkness, as 6 heavy B52 strategic bomber serials pummeled Cambodia's thick jungle in front of the cavalry's lines. At 6:00 A.M., as the last high-level bombs were exploding through the layers of rain forest, a massive preparatory artillery bombardment thundered across the border. For the next six hours, the 94 long-range cannon and heavy howitzers of II Field Force Vietnam Artillery, placed in direct support of Task Force Shoemaker, boomed incessantly and fired 2,436 shells into preselected targets. Fighter-bombers roared through the morning sky to deliver 48 tactical airstrikes. On the invasion day a total of 5,460 II FFV artillery rounds, 36 strategic B52 bombing strikes, and 185 tactical airstrikes supported the attack.[5]

The South Vietnamese airborne battalions helicoptered into two landing zones, LZ East and LZ Center, which were carved out of thick jungle by detonating Air Force Commando Vault fifteen thousand-pound bombs seven feet off the ground. The scout helicopters of Lt. Col. Clark A. Burnett's 1st Squadron, 9th Cavalry, dashed above the rolling jungle and through drifting plumes of smoke to strafe surprised NVA truck drivers and soldiers unexpectedly caught in the cyclone of the airmobile advance. The Vietnamese 5th Airborne Battalion helicoptered into LZ Center and immediately engaged a North Vietnamese battalion. The twenty-two supporting Cobra gunships furiously raked the NVA lines with rocket volleys and minigun fire, shattering the enemy ranks and sending them fleeing from the aerial onslaught.

Complete tactical surprise was achieved as the stunned NVA/VC elements milled in confusion, then scattered in full retreat, pursued by division armed helicopters and observation craft. More cavalry battalions joined the attack as the cavalry penetration deepened. The Cambodian offensive was politically limited to a depth of twenty miles,

5. Maj. Gen. David E. Ott, *Vietnam Studies: Field Artillery* (Washington, D.C.: Dept. of the Army, 1975), p. 212.

but numerous enemy depots and astonishing quantities of weapons, ammunition, vehicles, and foodstuffs were discovered within this zone during the first five days of the operation. At that point in the drive, with more than six hundred enemy soldiers eliminated and the discovery of several large storage and training areas, Task Force Shoemaker was dissolved.

On 5 May 1970 the 1st Cavalry Division headquarters assumed direct control of the Cambodian drive, now consisting of thirteen allied maneuver battalions. The division's 1st and 3d Brigades and 1st ARVN Airborne Brigade drove deeper into the NVA/VC base areas as the 11th Armored Cavalry Regiment sped north to seize Snoul in a series of sharp skirmishes. Col. Carter W. Clarke, Jr.'s, 2d Brigade initiated the division's second cross-border drive, TOAN THANG 45, by air assaulting two battalions into Cambodia northeast of Bu Dop on 6 May. At the outset resistance was light and scattered. An early evening contact on 7 May led to the discovery of a very large ammunition and weapons storage area the next day by Lt. Col. Francis A. Ianni's 2d Battalion, 12th Cavalry. The area was nicknamed "Rock Island East," after a major U.S. arsenal located at Rock Island, Illinois. Supporting engineers opened a road into the massive depot to haul out the vast amount of seized material. Removing the contents of the Rock Island East complex required nine days.

The largest enemy depot was discovered by Troop B of the 1st Squadron, 9th Cavalry, on 4 May 1970. The scoutships detected several field positions and structures in dense jungle, complete with paths matted with bamboo between complexes. The next day elements of Lt. Col. James L. Anderson's 1st Battalion, 5th Cavalry, airmobiled into the area and found 182 large storage bunkers, 18 mess halls, and a training area complete with an animal farm. One of the troopers remarked that the enemy storage complex looked like a small city. The depot, which supported the *7th NVA Division* with provisions and supplies, was promptly nicknamed "The City." Supporting engineers constructed a connecting road into Vietnam to facilitate overland evacuation of the large quantities of new weapons, quartermaster supplies, material, and rice.

Beginning on 6 May 1970, the 1st Cavalry Division commenced its exploitation of the NVA/VC warehouse areas and supply marshaling areas. Air cavalry elements were employed against small vehicle convoys and enemy troop movements, while the cavalrymen continued removing materials from the various caches and logistical complexes. On 11 May 1970 the 5th Battalion of the 7th Cavalry vacated FSB Brown in the TOAN THANG 45 sector, and the attached 5th Battalion of the 12th Infantry moved into the fort. The next night FSB Brown was attacked by a large enemy force, marking one of the first NVA counterattacks.

With the Cambodian invasion well underway, Maj. Gen. George W. Casey took command of the 1st Cavalry Division on 12 May 1970. A former brigade commander and chief of staff of the division from 1966 to 1968, Casey possessed experience as an airmobile wartime leader and comprehended clearly both the unique missions and capabilities of the airmobile division. He was born 9 March 1922 in Maine and graduated from West Point in 1945, served as a paratrooper officer with the 11th Airborne Division until 1948, and earned the Silver Star in heavy combat with the 7th Infantry Division in 1952 during the Korean War.

The 1st Cavalry Division continued to uncover more weapons and food storage areas, but by 29 May every battalion was reporting contact with the enemy. The cache discoveries in the meantime had grown in number faster than the committed units could evacuate or destroy their contents. On 5 June 1970 Major General Casey air assaulted his last remaining maneuver battalion into Cambodia. Aerial cavalry struck lucrative personnel and material targets throughout this period, but weather conditions were rapidly worsening. On 20 June the division started a phased withdrawal from Cambodia as fog and rain increased. B52 bombing runs were used to hinder enemy forces from interfering with the cavalry withdrawal and to destroy the multitude of supply sites found but not fully searched. The last cavalry elements withdrew from Cambodia on 29 June 1970.[6]

The pace of the Cambodian offensive and exploitation can be best judged by following one battalion into Cambodia. The 5th Battalion of the 7th Cavalry under Lt. Col. Maurice O. Edmonds was flown to Bu Dop on 5 May 1970, and the next morning Company B spearheaded the battalion air assault into Cambodia. Contact remained light as the advancing cavalrymen fired on small teams of North Vietnamese evading the area. An air assault by Company A on 7 May, to

6. 1st Cav Div, *1st Cav Div, Operational Report*, dtd 14 Aug 70.

establish Fire Support Base Neal, was challenged by scattered anti-aircraft fire, but the enemy quickly dispersed. The cavalrymen began finding increasing amounts of rice and weapons in their sweeps around FSB Neal. Within ten days combat started to increase as the enemy recovered and tried to defend his larger cache sites. Two days later Company A fought for six hours to advance up one hill and found a hospital complex on the summit.

Late in the afternoon of 23 May, Company B fought past stubborn rearguard resistance on a small hill to find rows of ammunition bunkers. The rising ground was called "Shakey's Hill," in honor of the first man killed on the hill, Pfc. Chris Keffalos of Albuquerque, New Mexico, who was nicknamed "Shakey." Company D was inserted to help empty the multitude of enemy munitions bunkers and tunnels full of mortar rounds, B40 and B41 rockets, recoilless rifle shells, and antiaircraft ammunition. The North Vietnamese tried to salvage part of the stockpile, but avoided further combat. On the morning of 30 May, a platoon from Company D, moving forward to clear a bunker, was engaged by enemy fire. Capt. Glenn Colvin moved the platoon on line and swept into the attack, but the enemy force fled, leaving behind a pistol belt, a small bag of rice, and two Chinese grenades. The month ended as Company C found a motor pool containing ten jeeps, twelve bicycles, and a maintenance shop.

In June ambush activity escalated throughout the battalion sector as Company D continued the back-breaking chore of emptying out the bunkers on Shakey's Hill. They were forced laboriously to haul the boxes of munitions from the ammunition point back uphill, but there was little complaint, as the troops explained. "Better to haul it out of the bunkers and up the damn hill than to have Charlie shoot it at us!" The troops began calling the depot simply "Charlie's Rod and Gun Club."

Their work was not only hard, but it was also extremely dangerous. Cache sites were normally booby-trapped, and the NVA implanted mechanical ambush devices in several of the bunkers at Shakey's Hill. One bunker was rigged with a Chinese grenade pull-string tied to a stack of mortar boxes, with the grenade itself buried deep in flamethrower fuel thickener. Fortunately for the cavalrymen, the moisture had rotted the string, and it simply broke two inches above the grenade when a trooper inadvertently tripped it. In another bunker a blasting cap was set to detonate a mortar round and explode the entire structure, but the trap was detected and disarmed. On 2 June Company D turned over the task of completing the depot clearance to another battalion.

The monsoon rains began in earnest the following day, and daily thunderstorms intensified. The North Vietnamese were also reorganizing, and combat became more frequent. On 7 June FSB Neal started receiving ground probes. Two bodies of 199th Infantrymen reported earlier as missing in action were found by Company C and carried to the 5th Battalion of the 12th Infantry at FSB Myron. In the meantime Company D suffered a small ambush by four enemy soldiers armed with B40 rockets and machine guns while moving into their night defensive positions. Enemy hit-and-run raids increased, and American casualties started to escalate. For example, a single B40 rocket round exploded inside Company B's perimeter on 10 June, wounding three cavalrymen. The company engaged the suspected enemy firing position with defensive fires, artillery, and rocket-firing helicopters, but reported "negative enemy assessment."

The next day Company A reached Hill 315 and found a sixty-ton rice cache. The battalion supply helicopter crashed on the afternoon of 13 June, wounding the pilot. The crew was extracted, but the helicopter was stripped and burned as a total loss by the cavalrymen before they left the area. The battalion continued to probe the general area around FSB Neal, freely giving captured rice to Cambodian natives who approached them riding elephants. After continued light skirmishing and discovery of other scattered caches, the battalion prepared to leave Cambodia. Several more members were seriously wounded by an ammunition supply point fire at FSB Barry (when a trip flare ignited in a box of mixed ammunition), and another battalion supply helicopter crashed. Led by Company B, Lieutenant Colonel Edmonds's battalion helicoptered out of Cambodia at noon on 29 June for a three-day rest at Bien Hoa, outside Saigon.[7]

The Cambodian invasion became the supreme test of the cavalry division's ability to maintain fast-paced communication, but the operation outstripped its signal capacity. For example, Task Force Shoemaker in its jump-off position at Quan Loi was supported by elements of the single division tactical signal battalion. Communications was

7. Hq 1st Bn 5th Cav, *Unit History*, 1970.

barely adequate to support the division equivalent of one cavalry brigade, one Vietnamese airborne brigade, and the armored cavalry regiment. On the final day preparatory to the attack, this force expanded with the addition of a tank battalion and a mechanized battalion, another infantry battalion (5th Battalion, 12th Infantry, from the 199th Infantry Brigade), and the division's 2d Brigade.

Signal difficulties quickly developed as the offensive began, especially among the frequency modulated (FM) radios which were the primary means of communication. The scope and diversity of the offensive overwhelmed FM radio communications, as radio interference, channel duplication, and congested airwaves swamped signal efforts. At least one hundred FM radio nets existed within the task force headquarters, and one signal tower belonging to the 3d Brigade contained more than fifty antennas. The desire for secrecy greatly hampered communication exchange between rapidly moving elements, which tightly guarded their signal operating instructions, cipher keylists, code material, and channel frequencies.

By the fifth day of the Cambodian incursion, when the task force increased to the equivalent of two divisions and reverted to direct 1st Cavalry Division control, communications was a signal nightmare. The overworked divisional 13th Signal Battalion was operating well beyond its intended capacity, and operations were simply "hand to mouth" on an emergency basis. Near-impossible feats of communications were performed by innovative cavalry communications specialists. However, the division suffered from an absence of required signal resources because MACV apparently underestimated communication levels and requirements for such a large maneuver.

Throughout this period enemy action aggravated the adverse communications situation. For example, on 14 June 1970 the North Vietnamese hit Fire Support Base David from three directions, destroying critical forward signal transmissions equipment and severely wounding the brigade signal officer and dozens of other signalmen. Acting Sergeant Goldsworthy, who was in charge of the variable high frequency (VHF) equipment, valiantly maintained communications throughout the battle and earned the Silver Star for gallantry in action.[8]

8. Lt. Gen. Charles R. Meyer, *Vietnam Studies: Division-Level Communications* (Washington, D.C.: Dept. of the Army, 1982), pp. 55–59.

Despite such problems, the Cambodian invasion was an overwhelming material success. While COSVN escaped destruction, the NVA base depots suffered heavy damage and stock depletion. The strategic cavalry exploitation in Cambodia stymied enemy offensive capability and allowed South Vietnam to enjoy a prolonged respite from NVA/VC Cambodian-launched activity into III CTZ for several years afterward.

The overall invasion success was verified by the vast quantities of foodstuffs and weapons captured by the allied forces. The NVA/VC lost enough rice to feed more than twenty-five thousand soldiers for one year, or nearly thirty-eight thousand soldiers on reduced rations for a year. Enough individual weapons were taken to equip fifty-five full-strength Viet Cong infantry battalions, and enough machine guns and other crew-served weapons were seized to outfit thirty-three full-strength Viet Cong infantry battalions.[9]

Comparative statistics show that the 1st Cavalry Division (Airmobile) was responsible for the bulk of exploitive damage inflicted on the NVA/VC in Cambodia. During Operation TOAN THANG 43 (the largest operation involving U.S. forces), the 1st Cavalry Division killed 1,336 enemy, captured 3,009 individual weapons, and took 167 vehicles, compared to 664 enemy dead, 382 individual weapons, and 54 vehicles credited to the 25th Infantry Division. The differences in ammunition stocks is even more revealing. The 1st Cavalry Division seized 1,779,720 rounds of 7.62mm machine gun ammunition and 2,630 grenades, compared to 17,316 MG rounds and 1,040 grenades taken by the 25th Infantry Division, out of a total of 2,211,836 rounds and 4,230 grenades captured by the allies (the ARVN found 414,800 rounds and 560 grenades).[10]

The Cambodian invasion offers a convenient set-piece battle, rare in Vietnam, for mathematically assessing whether the 1st Cavalry Division was employing "unbridled firepower" in the Second Indochina War. The tremendous amount of ordnance utilized to support the division's Cambodian offensive is displayed by category in Table A. During this time the 1st Cavalry Division claimed a total of 2,574

9. MACV, *Command History*, 1970, Volume I, p. C-106.
10. Ibid., pp. C-73, C-74.

TABLE A

1st Cavalry Division Ammunition Expenditures, Cambodian Offensive
1 May to 30 June 1970[1]

Rifle and machine gun ammunition (M16 and M60)	6,167,645 rounds
Mortar ammunition (81mm)	119,127 rounds
Light artillery ammunition (105mm)	241,294 rounds
Medium artillery ammunition (155mm)	65,028 rounds
Aerial rocket artillery ammunition (2.75-inch)	92,016 rounds
C-4 explosive demolition compound	75,418 pounds
Detonation cord	152,200 feet
TNT explosive compound	1,736 pounds

1. 1st Cav Div, *Combat After Action Report for the Cambodian Campaign*, Annex B-IV, Logistical Operations in Support of Operations in Cambodia (d) Class V Expenditures, p. B-13.

enemy personnel killed inside Cambodia. Additionally, 31 enemy soldiers were taken prisoner and 18 voluntarily surrendered (Hoi Chanh).[11] The division used an average of 2,396 bullets and 201 shells or rockets for every enemy soldier known to be killed, which reflected the prodigious expenditures of ammunition in Vietnam, even by elite formations.

The 1st Cavalry Division's exploitation mission exacted the highest price of any U.S. formation involved in the Cambodian operations. The division suffered 122 killed in action, 964 wounded, 10 taken prisoner, and 6 missing in action in the territory of Cambodia. This represented nearly half of all U.S. casualties incurred in Cambodia (284 KIA, 2,339 WIA, 29 POW, 13 MIA), despite the fact that nearly three other division equivalents participated: 25th Infantry Division, 3d Brigade of the 9th Infantry Division, 199th Infantry Brigade, 11th Armored Cavalry Regiment, 12th Aviation Group, II Field Force Vietnam Artillery, and various other II Field Force Vietnam units.[12]

11. 1st Cav Div, *Combat After Action Report for Cambodian Campaign*, dtd 15 Feb 71, p. 63-A.
12. MACV, *Command History*, 1970, Volume I, p. C-51.

The division casualty losses during the May–June 1970 period were actually higher, since personnel (such as Major General Casey) were killed inside Vietnam on Cambodia-related missions and there was a considerable degree of incomplete casualty reporting. In fact, this serious problem was addressed in the division operational report of this period and was found to stem from subordinate unit noncompliance with follow-up paperwork after casualties were sustained, as well as missing casualty reports from lack of communication. Medical evacuation helicopters from other aviation units simply whisked patients to the nearest field station or hospital, and the division relied on input from internal units to keep posted.

Disregarding the unknown quantity of missing data, the total division losses for May and June were reported as 157 killed in action, 9 missing, and 1,124 wounded troopers. In addition, according to personnel reports for May and June, the division sustained 32 deaths and 247 injuries from noncombat causes. The division surgeon, again acknowledging incomplete information, reported 1,530 cases of disease (1,167 from malaria or fevers of unknown origin). The increase in serious disease rates was traced to increased exposure because of "the higher number of troops in the field" and their "operations in the hyperendemic malaria areas which were recently NVA sanctuaries,"[13] and seasonal increases associated with the monsoon shift.

Given the certainty that the lightly wounded (about 200 according to the 15th Medical Battalion records) and many ill patients returned to their units, the division still suffered high personnel losses during two months' time. Of course, none of these loss statistics counts the thousands of personnel departing the division on normal end-of-tour rotation or those temporarily absent on R&R (Rest and Recreation). In the latter category alone, 1,937 troops were absent in May and another 1,877 during June, taking them to Hawaii, Sydney, Hong Kong, Bangkok, Toyko, Taipei, and Manila. Perhaps the most telling indicators of actual manpower drain are the replacement reports, which show that the division had to absorb 1,762 replacements in May, 1,955 in June, and 2,101 in July—a total of 5,818 new personnel in one-quarter of a year.[14]

13. 1st Cav Div, *Operational Report*, dtd 14 Aug 70, p. 93.
14. Ibid., Tab I (G1 Activities), Tab M (Surgeon Activities).

Another salient aspect of the personnel situation, common to all Army divisions serving in Vietnam, was the tremendous size of the division rear echelon support base compared to line fighting strength. In this regard the 1st Cavalry Division was no exception. A graphic illustration of who was actually bearing the burden of field service and risk exposure is presented by the division's personnel daily summary for the evening of the Cambodian invasion on 1 May 1970 (Table B). On that date both the division assigned strength and numbers deployed in frontline capacity were maximized, because of its offensive stance as well as close command scrutiny by II FFV. On 1 May 1970, the critical opening day of the only major U.S. cross-border attack in the Second Indochina War, the spearhead 1st Cavalry Division was assigned 20,211 personnel, but only 7,822 troops were engaged in firebases and forward combat locations both in Vietnam and Cambodia (as defined by the division itself, and separately categorized on the division report form).

This personnel situation report shows the large overhead which sapped division "foxhole strength" throughout the war. The 1st Cavalry Division, with an assigned level of 20,211, was close to its authorized strength of 20,154,[15] confirming that the division was in fact fielding as many troops as possible for the opening of the Cambodian attack. However, as Table B demonstrates, only a third of this number was actually somewhere close to combat, and nearly 80 percent of this one-third slice is in the cavalry maneuver (infantry) battalions. In fact, the only unit totally committed to the frontline was the division ranger company! Thus, whatever losses occurred in the 1st Cavalry Division must have come out of the thin crust of riflemen or artillerymen actually doing the fighting, with some modification for aviators discussed below.

Table B does not reflect aviation personnel exposed to combat, since helicopters are staged out of helipads, LZs, or airstrips and only spent transitory time over the combat area before returning. However, the division possessed a total of 426 helicopters and 8 fixed-wing aircraft on 1 May 1970,[16] and if we multiply this by three for the average crew of each (assuming that all aircraft are flying), then we can safely estimate that perhaps 1,302 more personnel were routinely

15. Ibid., Tab I-1.
16. 1st Cav Div, *Combat After Action Report*, dtd 6 Jul 70, Annex L-1.

exposed to frontline service on a daily basis. Obviously, their exposure would be of shorter duration than ground troops. The "Blue" riflemen of the 9th Cavalry reconnaissance squadron (about 90 men) should also be added, as these reaction troops on standby were often in the thick of combat. Even counting these additional estimates, the imbalance between rear and frontline allocation remains striking.

The division's Cambodian drive represented the only period when the formation mustered as many troops as possible for a major offensive involving a defined frontline on a conventional axis of advance. This time frame provides one of the few opportunities to compare objectively the ratio between division frontline and support manpower in the Vietnam War. The frontline ratio did not vary appreciably throughout the length of the campaign, but casualties were making inroads on frontline numbers by June, despite constant infusion of replacements. A close scrutiny of daily personnel summaries shows the following division distribution between total assigned strength/personnel at firebases and in forward combat locations: 20,211/7,822 (1 May 1970); 20,270/7,386 (15 May 1970); 20,003/6,813 (1 Jun 1970); 19,638/6,952 (15 Jun 1970); 19,417/6,674 (28 Jun 1970). In the final analysis the airmobile riflemen were the most endangered troopers who shouldered the crushing weight of most division losses.

No one realized their sacrifice more than division commander Maj. Gen. George W. Casey, who decided to fly across country into Cam Ranh Bay to visit the wounded Skytroopers in the coastal hospital on the morning of 7 July 1970. The general was proud of these men and the jobs they had done during the Cambodian campaign. Extremely heavy monsoon weather precluded normal flight operations, and his staff urged him to express his written congratulations already prepared for the division. However, Casey knew that some of the most seriously wounded were either dying or were already scheduled for medical evacuation to the United States and Japan. He insisted on giving them a personal report on their success.

The only way to reach Cam Ranh Bay from III CTZ in the monsoon front was by flying on instruments, using the notoriously unreliable DECCA low-level navigation system. DECCA was installed and maintained by the Army, but rarely used because of nonacceptance by the Air Force. Casey accepted the risk. Flying over the storm-laden, rugged mountains of the central highlands, his helicopter entered a thick cloud bank and disappeared. Search operations began

TABLE B

1st Cavalry Division Personnel Strengths, 1 May 1970 (Cambodian Incursion)[1]

Division Organization	Assigned			At Firebases and in Forward Combat Locations		
	Officer	Warrant	Enlisted	Officer	Warrant	Enlisted
A. Maneuver Battalions						
1st Bn, 5th Cavalry	41	2	798	29	0	625
2d Bn, 5th Cavalry	44	2	823	34	0	631
1st Bn, 7th Cavalry	39	2	796	26	0	608
2d Bn, 7th Cavalry	39	2	818	26	0	591
5th Bn, 7th Cavalry	42	3	833	30	0	609
1st Bn, 8th Cavalry	39	2	802	36	2	689
2d Bn, 8th Cavalry	42	2	838	36	2	681
1st Bn, 12th Cavalry	40	2	826	36	2	713
2d Bn, 12th Cavalry	42	2	831	38	2	740
Total in Maneuver Battalions	368	19	7,365	291	8	5,887

TABLE B
(continued)

B. Division Support

1st Sqdn, 9th Cavalry (Air)	63	95	890	3	0	104
11th Aviation Group	214	322	2,261	0	0	74
Division Headquarters	109	5	364	0	0	0
1st Brigade Headquarters	27	18	230	0	0	0
2d Brigade Headquarters	40	18	209	0	0	0
3d Brigade Headquarters	34	15	243	0	0	0
Division Artillery	273	86	2,273	103	1	1,002
Support Command	137	51	1,707	0	0	0
8th Engineer Battalion	38	2	627	11	0	218
13th Signal Battalion	17	4	386	0	0	16
Company H, 75th Infantry[2]	4	0	98	4	0	98
15th Administration Company	82	9	688	0	0	0
545th Military Police Company	8	2	201	0	0	0
Miscellaneous Assigned Units	13	9	127	0	0	0
Division Rear	33	1	426	0	0	2
Total in Division Support	1,092	637	10,730	121	1	1,514
Totals for Division	1,460	656	18,095	412	9	7,401

1. 1st Cavalry Division Personnel Daily Summary for the 24-Hour Period Ending 011800 May 70, Cav Form 68 Revised.
2. Ranger reconnaissance company.

immediately to comb the cloud-wrapped peaks and triple-canopied jungles. In the late afternoon of 9 July 1970, the wreckage of the general's command helicopter was found. Maj. Gen. George W. Casey and all those aboard had been killed instantly in the crash.

George W. Casey's final testament happened to be the congratulatory letter he drafted on the evening of his departure, 6 July 1970, addressed "To the SKYTROOPERS of the 1st Air Cavalry Division" about their accomplishments in Cambodia. After explaining that the operations exceeded all expectations, citing results and examples of team spirit, he closed by humbly honoring his men and expressing a special tribute to them:

> This is your achievement. This is yet another demonstration that you of the 1st Air Cavalry Division deserve—and have earned again—the accolade of the FIRST TEAM. It is my honor to have served alongside you during this crucial and historic period. Congratulations and best wishes to each of you![17]

Both Major General Casey and Major General Roberts, who planned the operation and led the division during the first two weeks of the cross-border invasion, were among those rare officers who are truly qualified to lead airmobile cavalry divisions. They possessed a combination of the brilliance and professionalism that wins battles, coupled with the deep love and respect for the division troopers who won their devotion. Their leadership ability insured that the 1st Cavalry Division excelled in meeting one of its most important challenges in airmobile development: aerial cavalry exploitation during a strategic offensive.

17. Hq 1st Cav Div AVDACG, Subj: The FIRST TEAM in Cambodia, dtd 6 Jul 70.

The First Team

Division Structure in Vietnam

In the Vietnam-era United States Army, a division represented the basic combat instrument capable of conducting large-scale independent missions with its own resources and which contained all necessary basic fighting and support components organically assigned. The 1st Cavalry Division (Airmobile) was designed to concentrate firepower and shock action on the battlefield while maintaining a high degree of responsive vertical mobility to maneuver rapidly over large areas. Theoretically "lean and light," wartime demands to sustain airmobile striking power over considerable distances transformed the organization into one similar to infantry divisions, with the addition of an aviation group.

The 1st Cavalry Division was composed of eight (later nine) cavalry ground maneuver battalions of infantry, five battalions of artillery, three assault helicopter battalions, four support-type battalions, one aerial reconnaissance squadron, one engineer battalion, one signal battalion, and a host of independent specialized companies and detachments. All division elements were usually attached to one of six principal intermediary headquarters which the division commander used to control his subordinate units: the 1st, 2d, and 3d Brigades, Division Artillery ("Divarty"); Division Support Command ("Discom"); and the 11th Aviation Group. The division commander and his immediate staff sometimes retained direct control over certain units.

The 1st Cavalry Division was commanded by a major general with an average of 25 years' regular Army service. His immediate retinue included two assistant division commanders (A and B), brigadier generals who respectively directed operations and logistics/

aviation. The division headquarters provided the command, staff planning, and supervision needed to administer and direct the division and all its functions. Division headquarters gradually increased in size during the war until it contained more than five hundred men, including the attached 14th Military History Detachment.

The chief of staff, a colonel, presided over the division general staff and division special staff. The general staff, as in other divisions, included the personnel, intelligence, operations/training, logistics, and civil affairs/psychological operations sections serialized as G1, G2, G3, G4, and G5, respectively. The special staff included the surgeon, inspector general, staff judge advocate, chaplain, adjutant general, information office, finance, chemical, provost marshal, and headquarters commandant sections. Each G-section was headed by an assistant chief of staff, a lieutenant colonel, who coordinated certain special staff sections. For instance, sections such as finance, chaplain, inspector general, judge advocate, provost marshal, and the information office were usually under the assistant chief of staff, G1.

The 1st, 2d, and 3d Brigades were the primary subordinate headquarters which normally controlled the nine maneuver cavalry battalions, and thus made up the tactical heart of the division. Commanded by colonels, these brigades flexibly attached cavalry battalions and other units as needed, depending on the task at hand and battlefield situation. Like a miniature division, the brigade contained a headquarters and headquarters company which contained special staffs, sequenced like division's but prefixed by "S" instead of "G." S-sections were often supplemented by subordinated units. For example, the commander of an attached engineer company would also become the brigade engineer. Brigade headquarters were ever-expanding, finally averaging 250 to 300 personnel.

The brigade usually contained three cavalry battalions and one of the division's three light artillery battalions in direct support. This match in turn enabled each cavalry battalion to have one firing battery in direct support. Each brigade also received a "slice" of the total combat support division "pie." In this fashion the engineer and medical battalions lent one company to each brigade, while Division Support Command provided forward supply platoons and other components.

Although brigades freely exchanged cavalry battalions among them, traditional associations developed over the course of the war. Thus, the 1st Brigade usually contained the 1st and 2d Battalions of the "Jumping Mustangs" 8th Cavalry and the 1st Battalion of the "Chargers" 12th Cavalry. The 2d Brigade normally contained the 1st and 2d Battalions of the "Black Knights" 5th Cavalry and the 2d Battalion of the 12th Cavalry. The 3d Brigade contained the 1st, 2d, and later 5th Battalions of the "Garry Owen" 7th Cavalry (which joined the division 20 August 1966 as its ninth maneuver battalion).

The nine maneuver cavalry battalions, organized as infantry, formed the division's fighting edge. These battalions were composed of the hardened infantrymen—riflemen, machine gunners, grenadiers, and mortarmen—who carried the main burden of the war. The battalions were sent to Vietnam as heliborne components with less manpower than infantry battalions in other divisions. In August 1967 DA initiated a phased program of standardization between all line battalions in the war zone, which brought cavalry battalion organization in line with other infantry battalions serving in Vietnam. The 767-man cavalry battalions were boosted to 920-man levels, giving each battalion a headquarters and headquarters company, four rifle companies, and a combat support company.[1]

As in all military formations, manpower tended to dwindle where the fighting was thickest, and battalions were hard-pressed to keep up to strength. Speaking at a MACV conference in Nha Trang on 2 April 1966, Major General Norton bluntly stated, "We haven't been doing well in keeping our strength in platoon leaders, key noncommissioned officers, and riflemen. Companies of 130 men and battalions of 550 men are common, and this strength is too low."[2]

The ordinary squad rifleman was the backbone of the division. He was armed with the lightweight M16, a highly effective jungle fighting weapon capable of spewing out rounds with such velocity that even a shoulder hit could cause fatal heartbeat reversal. Universally referred to as "grunts," riflemen might be airlifted onto the battlefield, but then "humped" through dense jungle, jagged mountains, broken ricefields, or brackish swamps. Commonly dressed in sweat-soaked rip-stop tropical fatigues, with camouflaged helmet covers colorfully inked over with slogans and short calendars, these dismounted

1. Shelby L. Stanton, *Vietnam Order of Battle* (Millwood, N.Y.: Kraus Reprints, 1986), Chapter 3.
2. MACV, *Command History*, 1967, Volume I, pp. 141–42.

cavalrymen displayed the tactical fire and movement expertise which gave the division a near-perfect record of battlefield success.

The riflemen often carried sixty-five pounds of equipment, munitions, and weaponry. These were stuffed into packs, rucksacks, and pouches suspended from front and back straps, wrapped around waists, and passed over shoulders. An individual's combat load consisted of several days' rations, five to six quarts of water in plastic bladders and canteens, two claymore mines, extra mortar rounds, two or three bandoliers of bullets, an entrenching tool, and a machete. Little room remained for personal items, and even a pair of spare socks found interim utility full of C-ration tins suspended from aluminum ruck frames.

Machine gunners carried the M60 "pig" slung from the shoulder by bunji straps, with one starter belt of 7.62mm ammunition locked in the weapon—ready to spit out that most vital burst of either opening or return fire. Other men in the company carried spare belts of more linked ammunition. The twenty-three-pound M60 machine gun was heavy and its auto-gas operation required continual care and cleaning. However, the handful of M60s in a line company represented more than half of its available firepower, and machine gunners occupied an important and privileged position. As a rule, they were excluded from walking point or checking bunkers.

Grenadiers were armed with the light, compact, and dependable 40mm M79 grenade launcher. This weapon allowed the infantrymen to cover the area between the longest reach of a hand grenade and the shortest range of a mortar. The M79 was popular and handy, being both thoroughly reliable and virtually maintenance-free. The soft, muffled thump of its round being discharged contrasted sharply with the loud explosion of impact. Besides its considerable psychological benefit, the explosion produced a shower of shrapnel often used to shake sniper teams out of trees. Although the grenadier carried a heavy load of ammo, about fifty rounds in vest pouches, he was a most welcome companion. A grenadier routinely walked just behind the point man with a buckshot round chambered in his break-open "thump gun." In case of contact, the grenadier snapped his weapon shut and blasted out "a fistful of ball bearings the size of early June peas."[3]

3. Sp5 George Vindedzis, "Grenadier," *The First Team,* Winter 1970, p. 9.

In Vietnam, where a cunning elusive enemy and difficult tropical terrain placed a premium on division scouting, the division soon raised special patrol units. The volunteer infantrymen of these small, six-man long-range patrols were rangers dedicated to finding the enemy under the most dangerous circumstances, in unknown territory far from friendly columns. Their effectiveness was so great that in March 1968 a MACV study of Vietnam-wide Long Range Patrol (LRP) efforts concluded that the division combination of ample helicopter support "facilitated deception techniques for insertion, assured rapid reaction to enemy contact, and provided an immediate responsive extraction capability. The result was that the 1st Cav Div LRP Company had a higher percentage of patrols lasting over 72 hours than any other division or separate brigade except the 4th Inf Div unit."[4]

Division long-range reconnaissance patrols (LRRP) were first officially organized on 2 February 1967, when two patrols of six men each were formed under the jurisdiction of the 191st Military Intelligence Company. That April the LRRPs were placed under the control of the division G2 section, completed the tough Special Forces–run MACV Recondo School, and expanded. Before the end of the year, on 20 December, this division recon element was formalized as the 118-man Company E of the 52d Infantry "Ready Rifles." The company became the basis of Company H, 75th Infantry (Ranger), created by the division in conformity with DA directives placing all ranger-type units throughout the Army in one parent regiment.

The 1st Cavalry Division increased its scouting capability by employing Kit Carson scouts (KCS), the appellation given former NVA/VC who defected to the allies under the Chieu Hoi "open arms" program and assisted in patrolling and intelligence work. The first Kit Carson scouts used by the division in April 1967 were former local Viet Cong familiar with the terrain in Binh Dinh Province. The 191st Military Intelligence Detachment formally initiated the Kit Carson program in February 1968, and that November the division G5 took control after all Kit Carson scouts were placed under the U.S. Army local national direct hire program. The 1st Cavalry Division employed 72 KCS personnel at the end of 1968 and a year later possessed 161 Kit Carson scouts out of 219 spaces allocated.

War dogs also played their part in division operations. The division had three infantry platoons of scout dogs (25th, 34th, and 37th)

4. MACV, *Command History*, 1968 Volume I, p. 244.

normally attached one per brigade, and one combat tracker infantry platoon (62d) attached to the 1st Squadron, 9th Cavalry. Scout dogs were skilled at detecting mechanical ambush devices, tunnel systems, enemy caches, and humans. Tracker dogs were Black Labradors specially trained for scent which followed retreating or evading enemy groups to reestablish contact. Platoons normally consisted of at least three teams, each having a team leader, a dog and his handler, a scout or tracker, and two covering riflemen.

The main reconnaissance arm of the division was its crack 1st Squadron of the 9th Cavalry, the "cav of the cav," which carried out the first stage of the division operating maxim that "aerial reconnaissance found the enemy, gunships fixed him, and airmobile infantry and artillery finished him." Widely considered the finest air scouting unit in the Army, these modern descendants of the all-Black "Buffalo" cavalrymen of the Indian Wars produced most division contacts in Vietnam. The thousand-member squadron had eighty-eight helicopters in three air troops (A–C), each organized into an aero scout "White" platoon, an aero weapons "Red" gunship platoon, and an aero rifle "Blue" platoon. The squadron also contained a ground reconnaissance Troop D, outfitted with gunjeeps and upgunned 3/4-ton vehicles.

Division aircraft totals remained rather constant. Comparing January 1969 aircraft strengths after division 1965 Vietnam arrivals, the only big changes were replacements of Huey-model gunships with improved Cobras and OH13 light observation helicopters with improved OH6A LOH models as follows: 272/193 UH-series Huey utility helicopters; 0/78 AH1G Cobra attack helicopters; 57/47 CH47 Chinook cargo helicopters, 107/86 light observation helicopters, 6/6 OV1 Mohawks, 0/6 O1 Bird Dogs, and O/2 U6 Beaver fixed-wing aircraft.

The bulk of this aerial armada was under the wing of the 11th Aviation Group, which airlifted the division's supplies, equipment, and troops. The group was commanded by a colonel, and was chiefly responsible for assigning support aircraft to operations ranging from combat assault missions to logistical resupply. The group also provided division with its aviation special staff personnel. The permanent integration of an aviation group into the division cemented air-ground working relationships, bolstering airmobile efficiency well beyond divisions with only temporarily attached helicopters.

The group was designed to provide enough internal aircraft capability to simultaneously airlift the assault elements of two airmobile infantry battalions and three light howitzer batteries. To perform this task, the group contained two assault helicopter battalions, one assault support helicopter battalion, one general support aviation company, and usually one heavy helicopter company attached. The group used internal assets to form such special task elements as the An Khe Airfield Command and was bolstered by various other units like the Air Force detachment of the 5th Weather Squadron which gave twelve- and twenty-four-hour forecast service, weather warnings and watch advisories, and flight briefings.

The 227th and 229th Aviation Battalions (Assault Helicopter) contained the 120 Huey lift helicopters which constituted the prime vehicles of airmobility. The UH1D Huey helicopter, later replaced by the UH1H model, was built to lift one infantry squad, but in Vietnam the added necessity for a door gunner and extra armor reduced this capacity to six or eight men. Each battalion was divided into three lift companies (A–C) of 20 Hueys each and a Company D devoted to armed aerial escort. The latter company was composed of 12 armed UH1B Hueys, later exchanged for AH1G Cobras, and shepherded the lift companies, providing suppressive fire on the LZ immediately prior to air assaults.

The 228th Aviation Battalion (Assault Support Helicopter) was the division's heavy lift workhorse battalion and contained all forty-eight divisional CH47 Chinooks, divided sixteen per company. Described by the troops as a "big green school bus with no class," these twin-rotored Chinooks were the prime movers of light artillery crews and their howitzers and ammunition. The Chinooks were also used extensively in logistical resupply and large troop movements, but required inordinate labor to keep them flying; about ten hours of work for each hour of flight time.

The 11th Aviation Company (General Support) provided command and liaison helicopters for division headquarters. This meant that the company cranked up at least seven Hueys daily to ferry around the division commander and his two assistant commanders, the aviation group commander, the division support commander, and the division's chief of staff. The light observation pilots carried liaison officers and transported visitors for the protocol and information offices. The Aerial Target and Surveillance Acquisition (ASTA) Platoon of the company contained three side-looking radar (SLAR) and three infrared-equipped OV1 Mohawk aircraft.

The largest helicopter within the division was the heavy cargo CH54 Flying Crane, which could transport twice as much weight as the Chinook. The priority roles for division Flying Cranes were airlifting medium artillery and recovery of aircraft, followed by heavy cargo lift. Flying Cranes were provided by the attached "Hurricane" 478th Aviation Company, which was replaced in 1969 by the "Skycrane" 273d Aviation Company.

Modern airmobility required rugged infantry scouts who doubled as air traffic controllers, known as pathfinders or "Blackhats" because of their headwear. The group controlled a pathfinder company which dropped or airlanded teams at objectives to determine the best helicopter approach and withdrawal lanes, scout out sites for heliborne forces, and establish landing zones. Division pathfinders were also air traffic controllers, as an average of two hundred helicopters used any new landing zone during its first forty-eight hours of operation.

By the spring of 1968, the 11th Pathfinder Company (Provisional) conducted thirteen combat parachute jumps in Vietnam. These jumps involved the infiltration of small teams into unsecured areas to provide navigational assistance and aircraft guidance in support of airmobile operations. The first was Capt. Richard D. Gillem's four-man-team jump on a moonless night into the trees of a secret VC base area near Kong Nhou Mountain southwest of Pleiku in December of 1965. Another eight-man pathfinder team was raked by VC machine gun fire as it descended on an objective ten miles southeast of Bong Son on the night of 25 January 1967. Afterward, the division changed its jump altitudes from 950 feet to 600 feet to lessen exposure in the air. These jumps accomplished great surprise in Vietnam because the NVA/VC were accustomed to preparatory artillery fires or helicopter noise prior to American movements.[5]

While aviation moved the division, artillery was relied on to provide most of the division's destructive power. The role of Division Artillery (Divarty), commanded by a colonel, was coordinating tube artillery, aerial rocket artillery, and airstrikes with artillery forward observers to provide accurate, fast, and massive firepower. The mobile artillery forward command post facilitated clearance procedures

5. 1st Cavalry Division, *Airborne Operations of the 11th Pathfinder Company (Airborne)*, dtd 5 Apr 68.

and quick fire channels, insuring that prompt artillery support was available to the fast-paced airmobile infantry. Since howitzers in transit could not support maneuver forces, artillery had to be displaced rapidly to minimize loss of fire support. The swift tempo of artillery operations was highlighted during 1966 Operation MASHER/WHITE WING (discussed in Chapter 4), where artillery battery displacements totaled 57 by air and 109 by road in just forty-one days.

The "Blue Max" 2d Battalion of the 20th Artillery was an aerial rocket battalion intended to substitute for the normally missing divisional medium howitzer battalion. The battalion rendered immediate and devastating fire support, especially for units operating beyond the range of ground artillery, and became the usual savior of isolated airmobile elements in trouble. Initially the battalion was equipped with 2.75-inch rockets and antibunker SS-11 missiles mounted on thirty-six UH1B Huey helicopters, but during 1968 transitioned to thirty-six AH1G Cobra helicopters, each with nineteen-tube 2.75-inch rocket launchers and 7.62mm miniguns. Unlike the Hueys, the Cobras were specifically designed for fire support and carried the firepower equivalent to three conventional artillery batteries.

The three direct support 105mm light howitzer battalions were the mainstay of division firepower, providing the bulk of artillery preparations, time-on-target missions, and enemy contact responses. The advantages of uninterrupted working relationships soon solidified specific artillery battalion assignments to certain brigades. The 2d Battalion of the 19th Artillery usually provided direct support to 1st Brigade. The 1st Battalion of the 21st Artillery normally served with the 3d Brigade. The 1st Battalion of the 77th Artillery rendered direct support to 2d Brigade.

The 1st Battalion of the 30th Artillery, a general support 155mm medium howitzer battalion, was assigned to the division as combat theater augmentation. When operational planning precluded medium artillery support because airlift was impossible, Col. John J. Hennessey's Division Support Command fabricated special slings so the 155mm howitzers could be flown forward by Flying Crane helicopters. After February 1966, the division was able to displace the battalion in the same manner as the rest of its artillery.[6]

The "artillery's air wing" was Battery E of the 82d Artillery, which

6. Maj. Gen. David E. Ott, *Vietnam Studies: Field Artillery* (Washington, D.C.: Dept. of the Army, 1975), p. 104.

used an assortment of light fixed-wing O1 Bird Dogs and utility U6 Beavers as well as Huey and light observation helicopters to adjust artillery fire and provide command liaison for Division Artillery. The flying battery conducted visual reconnaissance, registered artillery fire, relayed radio transmissions, and dropped flares and psychological operations ("psyops") leaflets. Most cavalrymen warmly recalled their constant overhead nighttime surveillance of division base camps and firebases, watching the woodlines for mortar flashes.

Armor was generally a scarce commodity in the 1st Cavalry Division. The small assigned mechanized complement, Troop D of the reconnaissance squadron (1st Sqdn/9th Cav) was known collectively as the "Rat Patrol." By the fall of 1970, it contained twenty-seven combat vehicles, ranging from turreted V100 security vehicles with three machine guns to gunjeeps and armor-plated 3/4-ton trucks with field-expedient machine gun pedestals. Rat Patrol platoons were used extensively for convoy escort, protection of road checkpoints, and limited ambush duties.[7]

General Westmoreland denied repeated division requests for tank support during operations in 1966, exemplified by denial of a tank company attachment even after the THAYER area revealed extensive fortified bunkers which offered excellent tank targets. Reasons cited for refusal of this request included the perceived insufficiency of the area roads and the crop damage and other loss to civilian property which might react unfavorably on civil affairs programs.[8] Finally, in 1967, needed armor reinforcement was permitted, and the mechanized 1st Battalion, 50th Infantry, arrived in Qui Nhon for divisional employment in II CTZ, becoming operational on 29 September 1967. The division was later reinforced with the entire 11th Armored Cavalry Regiment for extended periods beginning in 1969, and it invaded Cambodia alongside the division a year later.

The division's "own private construction firm" was the 8th Engineer Battalion, which averaged just over 650 men in Vietnam. The unit was smaller than most division engineer battalions because it lacked the bridging company and its equipment was lighter for airlift purposes. The battalion spent most of its time building firebases, airstrips, and upgrading landing zones. CH54 Flying Cranes normally

7. Sp5 Jerry Norton, "Rat Patrol," *The First Team*, Fall 1970, pp. 23–26.
8. MACV, *Command History*, 1966, Volume I, p. 378.

transported larger construction equipment such as graders and tractor-scrapers disassembled into several loads and also carried the Chinook-liftable dozers. CH47 Chinooks were used by the engineers to lift the critical International-series of dozers and frontloader/backhoes, which could be brought in under Chinooks complete and ready to work. As a result, these machines were essential to most air assaults and did the lion's share of early LZ clearance, artillery position construction, and bunker building.

The communications required to coordinate all these division activities was rendered by the "Voice of Command" 13th Signal Battalion, which averaged about four hundred men. In Vietnam, FM command nets were the lifeline of battle, and the battalion furnished its vital FM communications with airborne FM radio relay in fixed-wing aircraft. The system was expensive to maintain in manpower and material, but necessary to keep fast-moving elements "on the air." The high frequency communications systems were used almost entirely for radio teletypewriter operation and gave maneuver battalions their only means of secure printed communications. At brigade and division levels multichannel secure teletypewriter circuits were used instead. The battalion also included very high frequency (VHF) systems, tactical operations center switchboards, telephone operations, and multichannel trunking and switching systems.

Unfortunately, the far-flung mobile nature of airmobile division operations in Vietnam quickly disclosed the inadequacy of the signal organization provided. Personnel and equipment were simply insufficient to meet the division's need for responsive, sophisticated communications. Numerous complaints were received by DA throughout the war expressing the need for a stronger airmobile signal battalion. During extended operations, the signal battalion's shortfalls became especially pronounced, and only extensive supplementation by the 1st Signal Brigade kept the division communicating. The wide dispersion of the 1st Cavalry Division made it very difficult for the signal battalion to maintain proper supervision and control.[9]

One unique battalion signal mode seeking to partially remedy signal deficiencies was unfortunately of short duration. In 1966 division

9. 1st Cav Div, *Operational Report—Lessons Learned*, dtd 14 Nov 70, p. 37, with commentary by U.S. Army Pacific at p. 54.

commander Maj. Gen. John Norton directed the reintroduction of carrier pigeons with two birds, Ralph and Spuzy, under CWO James S. Steven, Jr. One of Spuzy's first combat missions involved bringing a message capsule to 2d Brigade during Operation THAYER II, where the bird was spotted on the wire by the brigade intelligence officer. He mistakenly identified the pigeon as a probable Viet Cong messenger and summoned a soldier, who shot it dead, ending the experiment ingloriously.[10]

The soldier who shot Spuzy promptly went AWOL (absent without leave) and became another case for the division's 545th Military Police Company. This company of just over two hundred men provided basic police work to the division community of eighteen thousand to twenty-one thousand people spread over an area as large as four thousand square miles. The unit provided the provost marshal section to headquarters; maintained traffic control and convoy protection; entered villages and checked identification; and insured internal security by enforcing military laws through checkpoints and patrols, crime investigation, and custodial control over offenders. The military police also escorted high-priority shipments, guarded military payment currency and sensitive items, and were used as infantry in emergency situations.

The only support task more difficult than policing and providing signal and construction service to such a large and scattered division with more than 450 aircraft was supplying and maintaining it. This was a job of Division Support Command (Discom), commanded by a colonel, which had a supply and service battalion, two maintenance battalions, and a medical battalion, as well as a headquarters company and the Skytrooper Band. The command fulfilled its mobile battlefield role by dividing assets into mobile logistical depots known as Forward Support Elements (FSE). Each directly supported one brigade at distances averaging twenty-five miles. These contained Forward Support Points, which were usually established along roads and stocked by trucks. Flying supplies from such points lessened the strain of logistical airlift.

---

10. Lt. Gen. Charles R. Myer, *Vietnam Studies: Division-Level Communications* (Washington, D.C.: Dept. of the Army, 1982), p. 45.

The division used an average of 1.6 million pounds of supplies every day in Vietnam. Everything that the Skytroopers ate, wore, built, or shot involved the 15th Supply & Service Battalion. The battalion furnished almost anything in the division that moved or needed moving, or that the division consumed or expended. This diversity of activity was mirrored by the unit's dazzling array of subordinated elements, from "Redhat" riggers hooking cargo slings underneath helicopters to stock controllers filling normally routine requests which always included the bizarre—such as antifreeze and snow chains. The battalion also supplied all foodstuffs. In Vietnam, military-issue rations were only a small part of the soldiers' diet. Most food was imported, mostly from the mainland United States through such firms as International Marketing, but the battalion also supervised procurement of bananas from local plantations, tomatoes from Japan, fresh fruit from Hawaii, and bread from the Long Binh bakery.

Maintaining the 1st Cavalry Division and its complex aviation inventory required two battalions, which divided their workload according to the division maintenance logo: "If it doesn't fly, the 27th Maintenance Battalion handles it; if it does fly, the 15th Transportation Battalion keeps it that way." The smaller 27th Maintenance Battalion had a headquarters and Company A, a main support detachment, and three lettered detachments. These provided a range of automotive, engineer, electronics, and artillery–small arms and instrument maintenance, but also completed jobs involving everything from glass cutting to canvas repair. The battalion additionally supplied most ground repair parts to the division.

The 15th Transportation Battalion (Aircraft Maintenance) had the unenviable reputation of being perhaps the most overworked unit in the division and had more than thirteen hundred personnel assigned. In mid-1969 the battalion was reorganized and streamlined under the decentralized maintenance concept into a headquarters company, two lettered support companies, and nineteen independent forward detachments with individual aviation units. These detachments maintained the aircraft, effected minor repairs, and generally kept the division flying. Heavier jobs were sent to Companies A and B, which contained the flight line chiefs, mechanics, and shopmen who repaired the difficult cases. Company A handled 60 percent of the helicopters, including the troublesome Chinooks, while Company B maintained the others. The battalion avionics section provided service for aircraft electronics systems involving communications, stabilization, and navigation instrumentation. The biggest headache was non-availability of parts, forcing itinerant battalion personnel to expedite critical item deliveries throughout Vietnam.

Division-level medical support was provided by the 15th Medical Battalion. Specifically tailored for airmobile operations, its twelve medical helicopters allowed aeromedical and air crash rescue support over wide areas. The battalion also provided limited ground evacuation of wounded personnel, medical treatment to include emergency surgery, divisional medical supply and medical equipment maintenance, and complete optometry service. A major part of unit efforts was spent working in medical civic action programs (MEDCAPS), visiting hamlets to treat local Vietnamese villagers. The battalion consisted of a headquarters and support company and three lettered companies, which usually operated in direct support of the brigades. Each company contained a clearing aid station platoon, a ground evacuation platoon, and two supporting air ambulance helicopters.

Installations of hoists on division medical evacuation craft allowed the extraction of casualties from triple-canopy jungle and other inaccessible areas, using either forest penetrators or rigid canvas litters with steel ribbing. The 250-foot hoist cables were color coded to mark length of cable extensions, and detonator charges at the top of the hoist cable permitted instant severing of the steel cord from the ship in case the hovering rescue helicopter was forced to quickly exit the area. The dangers involved in hoist missions were demonstrated during the Cambodian incursion of May 1970, when such missions accounted for only 7.6 percent of the total division flights, but accounted for 53 percent of the helicopters hit.[11]

The 15th Administration Company, which comprised the division headquarters rear echelon, was probably one of the largest companies in the Army. Authorized 380 personnel, the company mushroomed to nearly 800 by the time of the Cambodian invasion in May 1970. The company provided personnel for various staff sections throughout the division, such as finance clerks, legal counsels, postal workers,

---

11. 1st Cavalry Division, *The First Team in Cambodia*, dtd 6 Jul 70, App. L-3.

1st Cavalry Division

20,346 soldiers

418 aircraft

1969 Average Monthly Issues

 Foodstuffs   1,005 tons

 Rations   597,311 meals

 Milk   944,780 pints

 Ice Cream   11,430 gallons

 Ice   2,777 tons

 Clothing & Equipment   1,082 tons

 Barrier Materials   749 tons

 Fuel   4,010,700 gallons

 Ammunition   4,609 tons

by Shelby L. Stanton

personnel specialists, and information managers, and even the division's 24 chaplains. The company became so large that it created the 1st Personnel Service Battalion (Provisional) out of its own resources, to which it also attached the 41st and 42d Public Information Detachments.

The divisional Replacement Training Center was formed on 1 October 1966 to consolidate training of replacements at division level. The center conducted a four-day replacement training course (RTC) and a combat leaders course (CLC) in facilities including booby-trapped pathways and a complete mock fortified village. The center became the basis of the First Team Academy stationed at Bien Hoa after the division moved south in 1968. The academy instituted a division sniper program and graduated its first snipers on 31 July 1969.

Combat intelligence and counterintelligence were handled by the division's 191st Military Intelligence Company and its attached 583d MI Detachment, which also supported the Deputy G2's combat intelligence center in the Division Tactical Operations Center. The company was compartmentalized into sections devoted to enemy order of battle, prisoner interrogation, aerial imagery interpretation, and counterintelligence. The local intelligence service provided by the company's screening of NVA/VC prisoners, detainees, and ralliers (Hoi Chanhs) was often significant; for instance, in July 1969 the debriefing of a Hoi Chanh furnished timely information on enemy attack plans against a fire support base at Quan Loi.

The 184th Chemical Platoon and its attached 26th Chemical Detachment were responsible for all chemical material within the division, and its tasks ranged from delivery of riot gas and use of flame weapons to spraying of insecticides and inspection of protective masks. Chemical weapons included flamethrowers, incendiary fire drums filled with jellied gasoline (fougasse barrels), and persistent gas "Bunker Use Restriction Bombs" (BURBs), invented by division M. Sgt. Jack Watts. Division Chemical also operated the helicopter-mounted "people sniffer" personnel detectors and was extensively engaged in defoliation operations with Agent Orange and other agents, relying primarily on four-hundred-gallon metal tanks fabricated for CH47 helicopters and one-hundred-gallon spray apparatus on UH-series Hueys.

The combination of assigned components made the division quite strong in manpower, not including all the attachments. In a normal stateside mode an airmobile division was authorized 15,818 personnel (as of 31 December 1968). This compared very favorably with the 14,253 total present in a standard infantry division of World War II in June 1944, and with the 14,843 men permitted the 1st Cavalry Division in the Korean conflict in July 1951. In comparison, a modern cavalry division enjoyed a higher allowance of enlisted cavalrymen than the entire U.S. Army of fifteen cavalry regiments at the turn of the century (12,240 in 1902).[12]

The actual strength of the 1st Cavalry Division in Vietnam fluctuated during the war, but always exceeded its standard authorizations by wide margins. The division's assigned strength of 16,732 at the end of December 1965 steadily increased to 17,405 by mid-1966 to over 18,000 during the crucial years of 1967 and 1968 (18,194 on 31 January 1967; 18,309 on 31 January 1968–Tet). During its last two years of full Vietnam service, in 1969 and 1970, the division expanded to more than 20,000 assigned personnel, containing 20,346 at the end of January 1969 and 20,211 on 1 May 1970, the start of the Cambodian offensive.[13]

Comparison of personnel statistics at the end of 1968, chosen as the high point in American Vietnam participation as well as division overseas service, renders a typical summary of manpower allocations. On 31 December 1968 the 1st Cavalry Division was authorized 15,818 men by TOE 67-Test, but was modified upward by MACV combat augmentation to 19,465 men. On that date the division had 20,271 personnel actually assigned. This represented a 28 percent increase in actual division strength over TOE authorization. While warrant officer spaces reflected little variation and the number of pilots remained about even, officers increased 22 percent (1,442 actual compared to 1,179 by TOE) and enlisted strength jumped 30 percent (18,168

---

12. TOE 7 (adjusted to Jun 44); DA Rpt CSCAP-13-R2, *Strength in Troop Program Sequence by Organization and Type of Personnel,* Sec 1-A (31 Jul 51); TOE 67-T w/Change 1 (adjusted to 31 Dec 68); Hq of the Army General Orders No. 108, *Organization of the Army as directed by the President,* dtd 24 Oct 1902.
13. 1st Cav Div, *Operational Report on Lessons Learned,* dtd 5 May 66, p. 6; Shelby L. Stanton, *Vietnam Order of Battle* (Millwood, N.Y.: Kraus Reprints, 1986), p. 7; 1st Cav Div, *Operational Reports—Lessons Learned,* dtd 15 Feb 69, App. I-1; 1st Cav Div, *Personnel Daily Summary,* dtd 1 May 70.

actual compared to 13,965 by TOE). Not counting aviators, the division officer-enlisted ratio was actually 1:12, compared to 1:15 in Korea and 1:17 in World War II. While increased officer proportions partially mirrored increased technology, the division's Vietnam ratio was still top-heavy.

The division was handicapped throughout the war by the DA-imposed individual rotation system, which required all soldiers to serve only one year in the combat zone. This policy constantly refilled the formation with green troops and caused severe personnel turbulence. The resulting instability was particularly disruptive in late 1966 operations, because most division members were lost in a single block of time as their twelve-month combat tours expired. MACV replacement inexperience at this early juncture of the war could not properly counterbalance such "hump periods." The division lacked leverage over higher command's belated and insufficient infusion policies, and devastating imbalances occurred in such key categories as aviation. As the war continued, the Army adopted better methods of insuring division refill with phased programs.

The enormity of the one-year combat tour problem was illustrated by the numbers involved. From the beginning of 1966 through January 1967, the division absorbed 19,837 new enlisted replacements and lost 16,173 enlisted veterans to outprocessing, injuries, or death.[14] Since officer turnover also exceeded 100 percent the division underwent complete recycling which actually accelerated in later years (after the casualties of Tet-68, for example). However, morale was most threatened in the first "hump crisis," which the division command took stern steps to counteract. Brigadier General Wright, then Assistant Division Commander-A under Major General Norton, was aghast to hear new division troops being referred to as the "Second Team" as the initial "First Team" headed home. Internal command emphasis stamped out such derogatory references, and instilled collective pride of accomplishment as the First Team (actually a World War II term) for all serving members.

Rampant personnel turbulence had the potential of greatly diminishing the combat proficiency of any unit. The 1st Cavalry Division

---

14. 1st Cavalry Division, *Operational Reports—Lessons Learned*, dtd 5 May 66, p. 6; 15 Aug 66, p. 6; 22 Nov 66, p. 5, and 15 Feb 67, pp. 4, 5.

was fortunate in that pride of heritage and dedicated teamwork provided much wartime stiffening which lessened adverse turnover impact. Both the spirit of the predecessor 11th Air Assault Division and determined sense of mission displayed by the airmobile 1st Cavalry Division forged a strong bond of individual and unit identity. The dash and daring which typified division operations in Vietnam directly resulted from the unusually high confidence and appreciation that division members expressed for their teammates. Soldiers worked hard and competently to earn the trust of their comrades and implicitly felt that the whole division was behind their efforts. While teamwork was the goal of any military organization, the 1st Cavalry Division excelled in creating a special aura of cooperation and teamwork reflected in a favorite motto, "Anyone who isn't engaged is in reserve."

The members of the 1st Cavalry Division were very proud of and identified closely with their large shoulder sleeve insignia containing a black horsehead and diagonal bar on a golden shield. This patch was worn by assigned troops on their uniform's right shoulder sleeve, and wartime division service was signified by its wear on the left. Veterans returning for additional duty could display their patches "sandwiched." The insignia was designed in response to an official directive after the War Department authorized the division's establishment in September 1921. The message outlined the design criteria: that it bind men together in a common devotion, be an easily recognizable sign by which men could reassemble after battle, and be a symbol of inspiration to division members.

The resulting patch was designed by Mrs. Ben Dorcy, the wife of the 7th Cavalry Regiment's commanding colonel. She used the bright yellow inner liner of one of her husband's old dress capes as the cloth on which the design was first drawn. The choice of the horse's head was made by the Dorcys after they observed a mounted trooper ride by their home on a beautiful shining black thoroughbred. The shape of the patch represented the shield carried by knights in battle, and the bar, or slash, represented a scaling ladder used to breach castle walls. (On 7 January 1969 Mrs. Dorcy wrote the division a letter suggesting that the ladder also represented the Chinook-dropped Jacob's ladders of the Vietnam period.) Because of economic concerns, the Army specified that only two colors be used, and Mrs. Dorcy chose blue and yellow, the traditional colors of the cavalry. Over time the blue was changed to black. The patch was purposely oversize compared to other division insignia, according to Mrs. Dorcy, because "the patch had to be large enough to be seen through the dust and sand at Fort Bliss." The 1st Cavalry Division shoulder sleeve patch insignia remains the largest in the Army.

The First Team mystique was evident at all levels, from its Army-wide reputation of success to individual deeds of selfless team spirit known only within the division. At the higher level the division quickly gained an unsurpassed record of operational skill at finding and defeating NVA/VC forces. There were accounts of lightning airmobile assaults so sudden that the Viet Cong were caught firing unarmed mortar shells, the shipping plugs still inserted, at cavalrymen spilling out of their helicopters. While MACV expressed open delight at the uncanny willingness of division elements to search out and knock heads with the enemy, division members were more impressed with the unflinching reliability of their fellow soldiers.

Maj. Gen. George I. Forsythe, who commanded the division from August 1968 until April 1969, recounted an incident which exemplified the internal First Team spirit. The last platoon of the 1st Battalion, 12th Cavalry, was being picked up from a typical jungle landing zone. The platoon radio-telephone operator (RTO) had already been ordered aboard one of the helicopters lifting out. Suddenly four NVA machine guns in the treeline raked the LZ, and the pilots pulled pitch to clear the area. The young RTO took only an instant to realize his platoon was being left without radio communications; grabbed his radio backboard from the helicopter cabin floor; and, forty feet from the ground, jumped out. He broke both legs, but crawled back through the fire-swept elephant grass, enabling his lieutenant to call in gunships. When his actions were later rewarded with the Silver Star, he stated that his dedication to the team had been an automatic response.[15]

The 1st Cavalry Division encouraged high morale in every way possible. Communications call signs were not changed because over time they became trusted bywords. The division was intensely proud of its field living conditions and did not relish other commands with air-conditioned bunkers and velvet curtains over mapboards. The

15. USAMHI, *Senior Officers Oral History Program*, Lt. Gen. George I. Forsythe Interview, p. 448.

division helicoptered slingloads of freshly laundered fatigues into remote sectors to give troops clean clothes regardless of size or markings and dismissed complaints from higher headquarters about mixed-up or missing name tags. While this emphasis on morale undoubtedly reinforced division standards, the 1st Cavalry Division also enjoyed many real advantages over other American formations in Vietnam.

The MACV commanders, Generals Westmoreland and Abrams, displayed unabashed admiration for the division. This favoritism was reflected in May 1967 when MACV force requirements were adjusted to place the 1st Cavalry Division in the role of a special exploiting force designed to penetrate and neutralize major NVA/VC base areas. All other MACV divisions except the 1st Infantry Division (the other exploiting force) were linked to specific provinces. In September 1967, in view of increased NVA activity in northern I CTZ, General Westmoreland revised the force structure of MACV to establish the 1st Cavalry Division as the sole "countrywide offensive force." These heightened responsibilities were invariably matched by special MACV command emphasis. In addition to priority on equipment, informal guidance was issued to the 22d and, later, 90th Replacement Battalions so that the division received the pick of nonparatrooper arrivals. This MACV effort lavished the division with high-quality personnel and equipment to insure levels of performance excellence.[16]

It is important to remember, however, that although the 1st Cavalry Division appeared magnificently endowed with aviation and personnel assets, the reality of Southeast Asian warfare greatly diminished its airmobile strike capability. Vietnam's higher air density and the combat necessity to add the weight of armor, emergency supplies, and larger armament systems onto helicopters greatly reduced aircraft power. Even if all its aircraft were flying, the division normally worked with one-third less lift capacity than that projected by the airmobile developers at Fort Benning.

Insufficient numbers of mission-ready aircraft further eroded airmobile potential. During 1966 aircraft availability averaged only 68 percent for UH-series Hueys, 63 percent for CH54 Sky Cranes, and a mere 43 percent for CH47 Chinooks, attributed mostly to lack of

16. MACV, *Command History*, 1967, Volume I, pp. 144–45, 152.

spare parts beyond effective MACV influence. By late 1968 the mission readiness of Huey helicopters had dropped to 60 percent and Chinooks to 40 percent. Instead of the practically unlimited aerial response that most people believed the airmobile division possessed, the 1st Cavalry Division was continually forced to modify its tactical operations with great economy and innovation.[17]

17. 1st Cav Div, *Operational Reports on Lessons Learned*, dtd 5 May 66, App. 4-9; dtd 15 Aug 66, App. 4-8; dtd 22 Nov 66, App. 5-4; dtd 15 Feb 67, p. 75; dtd 15 Feb 69, p. 68.

The Skytroopers

Division Performance in Vietnam

More than 150,000 troops served in the 1st Cavalry Division during eighty-two months of combat in the Second Indochina War.[1] These division personnel were primarily responsible for the wartime development of the airmobile concept and for the aerial cavalry's success or failure as a viable military instrument. How these troops fought and behaved is an essential aspect of division operations in Vietnam and an integral ingredient of the mobile cavalry's capability.

The hallmark of ground maneuver which dominated Army tactics in Vietnam was the fire support base, often referred to simply as firebase. Conceptually, the fire support base functioned simply to provide a secure but mobile artillery position capable of rendering fire support to infantry operating in areas beyond the normal range of their main base camp cannon and howitzers. This concept afforded infantry a greater degree of flexibility without sacrificing artillery protection. However, firebases quickly became targets for enemy counterattacks and bombardments, and increased defensive measures were undertaken. More sophistication meant less mobility. Over the course of the war, firebases developed to the point where ground maneuver was

1. 1st Cavalry Division service credited as commencing in Vietnam in September 1965 and ending with the withdrawal of its 3d Brigade in June 1972; personnel total taken from 1st Cav Div Vietnam Departure Ceremony brochure dtd 26 Mar 71, p. 5. Considering that the separate 3d Brigade remained in Vietnam another fifteen months, the totals of personnel were doubtless much higher.

hampered because of their size, elaborate construction, demand on supply and protective resources, and troop reluctance to leave their comforts and safety, a condition called "firebase psychosis."

The 1st Cavalry Division (Airmobile), as the most tactically mobile formation in Vietnam, gave priority to rapid firebase deployment and construction. In order adequately to cover its large areas of operation, the division was constantly opening, closing, and reopening firebases throughout the war. The first division firebase was designated as Bill, built during October 1965 in Pleiku Province. However, by 1969 they had blossomed from jungle clearings with unsophisticated defenses into formidable semipermanent fortresses.

The typical cavalry fire support base was a defensive area roughly 250 yards in diameter with an 800-yard perimeter, which contained howitzers and enough equipment and supplies to support the infantry with artillery fire around the clock. The firebase also supplied logistics, communications, medical, and rest facilities for the cavalrymen within its area. The division's 8th Engineer Battalion was responsible for initiating firebase construction. The engineer line companies, assigned one to a brigade, cleared the initial area, performed demolitions work, established water points, and provided the supervisory expertise, equipment, and manpower to build sophisticated fieldworks.

Once the fire support base site was selected, usually by aerial photographic reconnaissance at division level, the brigade and battalion responsible for its sector began detailed construction planning. Terrain and weather information were used to determine its size, shape, and required facilities. Construction priorities were then issued, hopefully in a timely fashion. It was proven repeatedly that minutes spent in coordinated planning by all concerned units saved hours in actual construction time. The normal order of construction was: temporary helicopter pad for delivery of supplies, howitzer positions, perimeter berm, artillery fire direction center (FDC), infantry tactical operations center (TOC, the command post), ammunition supply point, "VIP" helicopter pad, garbage sump, defensive wire barrier, and, finally, medium artillery positions if applicable.

The division prepared basic firebase kits, each designed for a battalion-level fire support base and its supporting six light howitzers, which contained all the necessary materials for construction. Nails, spikes, metal culverts, chain-link fence rolls, tar paper, sandbags, pickets, and lumber were all prepalletized or arranged in slingloads for rapid helicopter delivery. The firebase kit required about twenty-five CH47 Chinook cargo helicopter sorties to deliver to the field.

The amount of equipment needed to clear the area of the firebase varied depending upon terrain. In dense jungle large Air Force bombs were used to demolish enough vegetation to blast out a landing zone. The more common bomb of this type was the 750-pound "Daisy Cutter" that detonated about ten feet above the ground, effectively destroying all foliage for ten feet around and knocking down trees over a considerably larger radius. The 10,000-pound "Instant LZ" opened up larger swaths of demolished jungle, while late-war 15,000-pound "Commando Vault" bombs offered the most destructive power. Napalm was a useful supplement if tropical forests were clogged with bamboo or additional thick jungle growth.

The air assault to secure and establish the firebase site was the riskiest part of the construction task. If the site was not large enough to accommodate the landing of a single helicopter, combat engineers with axes and explosives rappelled from a helicopter hovering fifty to one hundred feet above the ground. They were escorted by small parties of volunteer infantry which provided security while the engineers cleared an area large enough for the CH47 Chinook and CH54 Flying Crane cargo helicopters. Using demolitions and chain saws, the assault engineers could clear a landing zone for the larger helicopters within three hours. Of course, in most instances the selection of open fields demanded only a small amount of advance clearing.

The foremost task of any firebase construction effort was to produce a tenable tactical position by nightfall on the first day, with overhead cover for every man. This "tactical phase" was a time of heavy helicopter traffic bringing in more engineers and their equipment, the infantry and artillerymen, ammunition, barrier and bunker materials, rations, fuel, water, and howitzers and other weapons. As soon as the perimeter trace was cut out, defensive positions were started.

The normal construction site required the use of one engineer platoon under the direction of a "project engineer" with two medium D6B dozers, two Case light dozers, and one backhoe. As engineers worked with explosive charges, bangalore torpedoes, and chain saws to expand the perimeter, the first vehicular machines were being flown to the area. The invaluable light dozers could be airlifted in one piece underneath Chinooks and were the first equipment in. They were used to clear fields of small trees and stumps and to level artillery positions. The backhoe dug emplacements for the TOC, FDC, medical bunker, and perimeter bunker. Heavy dozers were lifted in two pieces, the blades and tracks by Chinook and the tractor body by Flying Crane. Once hauled in, the dozer had to be assembled, which required at least thirty minutes (more if the pilot did not set the machine down on its tracks); then it was immediately put to work pushing up earth to create a four-foot berm completely around the perimeter.

As engineer dozers and backhoes carved out the main firebase defenses, the infantry and artillerymen began emplacing wire entanglements, digging perimeter fighting holes, and emplacing perimeter bunkers in backhoe excavations. "Quick Fix" combat bunkers were simply five-foot-by-eight-foot shoulder-high holes covered with lumber or natural timber and sandbags. Standard perimeter bunkers provided better protection because they were covered by wooden stringers and steel mat decking. The simplest fighting positions were the two-man foxholes, each covered by three sections of sixty-inch metal culverts and topped by sandbags. In the meantime, once the first strand of tactical wire was emplaced, the artillerymen returned to build ammo storage bunkers and parapets around their weapons.

The final defensive phase of construction began when the Chinooks had delivered enough kit material to permit the engineers to build the main infantry TOC, artillery FDC, and medical bunker. These were built using large dimensional timbers, precut to anticipated firebase requirements. The main bunkers were started at the end of the first day or the beginning of the second day and finished by the end of the fourth day. Construction time was often shortened by employing reusable TOC and FDC bunker modules. Bunker modules were composed of two CONEX containers emplaced facing each other, with the overhead gap between them covered by steel matting. Two modules (four containers) sufficed for a battalion command center. Using these containers allowed an operational TOC/FDC complex to be completed within eight hours, including pushing earth fill around the sides and sandbagging the tops.

The infantry and artillerymen continued improving the wire barriers with tanglefoot and a second perimeter strand. Individual sleeping positions were built using metal seventy-two-inch half-culvert sections. The improvement of firebases was a never-ending job, as all structures were continually reinforced, surface drainage improved, and fields-of-fire constantly maintained by additional clearance. One squad of engineers was normally kept on any fire support base.

The life span of a fire support base depended on the tactical situation in its area. Since firebases were normally established to give a battalion and its direct support howitzer battery a pivot of operations to patrol the immediate vicinity, the firebase was closed when the battalion relocated. When the decision was made to close out a firebase, the brigade engineer usually provided one platoon to assist the infantry company tasked with dismantling it. Structural removal was aimed at salvaging the timbers, culverts, steel matting, and chain-link fencing in order to reconstitute division firebase kits, but holes were filled and berms leveled at command discretion.[2]

The 1st Cavalry Division's fire support bases were another example of adopting traditional frontier cavalry forts to the Vietnam environment, fusing airmobility to enhance the process. The advent of helicopter support and better material resources allowed these forts to be established more quickly and more often and projected cavalry battalions into hostile territory with greater assured safety. Once emplaced, however, they effectively limited cavalry movement to the radius of their guns. More substantial firebases of a semipermanent nature mushroomed into major camps with recreation areas, snack shops, mess halls, and elaborate living facilities, which actively hindered field operations because of their large garrison requirements.

The infantry which swept through the trackless, arboreal wilderness within range of fire support bases, usually found the NVA/VC entrenched in well-constructed, mutually supporting bunker positions. One outgoing battalion intelligence officer briefed his replacement on enemy fortifications within his area of operations by merely flattening his hands against the tactical wall map and saying, "Place your hand anywhere on the map and you've got a thousand bunkers in the palm of your hand." The myriad NVA/VC infiltration and supply trails were randomly connected to base camps of various sizes which were guarded by bunker complexes.

Reduction of fortified positions in World War II and Korea was a matter of deliberate attack against a deliberate defense. Elimination

2. 1st Cav Div Document, Subj: The Construction of a Fire Base in the 1st Cav Div, 7-69, dtd 10 Oct 69.

of sophisticated enemy defense lines was accomplished by using heavy concentrations of naval gunfire, artillery, and aerial bombing, followed by mixed teams of infantry, armor, and engineers to destroy successive enemy positions. After the initial fire support preparation, artillery was fired as the assault teams approached in order to drive the enemy soldiers out of lightly protected supporting positions and back into their larger shelters. Then tanks, tank destroyers, and assault guns fired armor-defeating rounds at the bunker embrasures to suppress enemy defensive fires. Under the cover of these armored vehicles, infantry and engineers moved up and used flamethrowers, rocket launchers, and explosives to eliminate the enemy defensive works. This method required large ground forces well versed in demolition techniques.

In Vietnam the 1st Cavalry Division encountered enemy bunkers in sudden clashes, usually when enemy machine gun and rocket crews occupying perfectly camouflaged bunkers opened fire on advancing infantry at close quarters. The bunkers were built in mutually supporting arrangements in dense bamboo groves or thick jungle undergrowth and constructed from locally available material. Although the division encountered some concrete bunkers, these were the exception. NVA/VC fortifications were not designed for deliberate defense, but only to disorganize and delay the attackers until withdrawal could be effected. The enemy bunkers and spider holes ringed base camps which contained living quarters, workshops, logistical depots, rest areas, and other facilities. The base camps were constructed in a circular pattern for all-around defense until prompt evacuation of supplies could be effected.

The bunkers themselves were so well camouflaged that they remained undetected until the enemy initiated fire on the unsuspecting cavalrymen. Usually, the advancing troopers were allowed to approach within five or ten feet of bunkers before the enemy positions cut loose with devastating cross fires. When the battle started, the cavalry was often mired in confused fighting, with a number of casualties.

Immediate retreat was required to save the seriously wounded, but intensely accurate automatic weapons fire ripped into troops trying to reach and drag their comrades out of the hail of enemy bullets. Leading platoons were often able to pull back only by using helicopter-dropped bangalore torpedoes. Once delivered, these exploded enough vegetation to allow accurate counterfire with machine guns and light antitank weapons. Positions were marked with smoke and white phosphorus to create smoke screens, which both covered the withdrawal and enabled aircraft to spot the forward edge of the battlefield.

One of the best ways to break close contact was by dropping chemical gas canister clusters out of helicopters. The troops donned gas masks as the command and control helicopter raced low overhead, and crew members kicked riot gas bomblets directly on top of the enemy positions. The 1st Battalion, 12th Cavalry, experienced several hard bunker contests, but reported that the enemy was never able to place effective fire on friendly troops after the gas was dropped.

At the outset of the action, the enemy usually not only blocked further infantry advance, but forced a tactical retreat. However, the enemy situation was extremely precarious. The cavalry had located his positions, and by breaking contact the troops could call in airstrikes and artillery to pound the base camp and prevent successful evacuation. Sometimes cavalry units were fortunate enough to know their exact positions and were able to bring accurate artillery fire on the rear and flanks of bunker complexes within minutes. Aerial scout helicopter teams often sealed off exits by calling in artillery and aerial rockets while they strafed escape routes. Physically blocking routes of egress with additional infantry was not preferred because of fire support coordination difficulties and the chance of encountering more bunkers in masking positions.

The "bunker busting" phase of the battle commenced as the Air Force dropped 500- and 750-pound bombs to clear the jungle canopy and to blast large holes in the foliage. The explosive power of direct bomb hits crushed many field positions and drove dazed enemy troops into the impact areas. After enough of the overhead canopy was blown away, aerial observers and forward air controllers could direct precision fires on the bunkers and installations within the base camp. The enemy bunkers were usually so solid that only 17-pound helicopter rockets and heavy bombs were effective against them. Light 105mm howitzer fire was ineffective against bunkers, while medium 155mm artillery fire could achieve only a low rate of destruction. The heavy 8-inch howitzer was both accurate and destructive, but the time and ammunition expenditures required made it impractical to use this weapon against a cluster of only sixty bunkers.

Artillery and aircraft saturated the target area with a cloud of riot gas to force the enemy out of remaining defensive positions. After giving time for the gas to take effect, cluster bomb units, light and medium artillery barrages, and aerial rockets were used to annihilate enemy soldiers in the open. In one instance, where the 1st Battalion, 77th Artillery, employed "firecracker" munitions mixed with quick-fused high explosives in this manner, the helicopter pilot adjusting artillery fire described the target as looking like an anthill that had been kicked.

When the ground commander estimated that the bunker complex was adequately "softened up," he directed that supporting firepower be shifted to cover enemy withdrawal and reinforcement routes. The cavalry troops then proceeded back into the area to finish the bunkers at rifle point. If heavy enemy return fire was encountered, another retreat was ordered and the preparatory fires resumed. Artillery and tactical airstrikes were applied until the enemy defenses were sufficiently weakened to allow the infantry to get into the bunker complex and mop up individual pockets of resistance. In this final phase of bunker destruction, the cavalrymen relied on .50-caliber machine guns, M72 light antitank weapons, 90mm recoilless rifles, and lightweight XM191 multishot flame projectors (FLASH). Regular flamethrowers were used infrequently because of their weight and refilling problems. The 1st Cavalry Division rarely used tanks because of mine hazards and poor avenues of approach. Tanks could not crash through dense jungle for long distances without considerable drain on the vehicles and crews.[3]

The whole complexion of fighting fortifications in Vietnam was totally different from previous conventional conflicts. Instead of a deliberately planned attack to get within range of enemy fieldworks, the infantry was subjected to an unexpected clash at very short ranges. Instead of a deliberate defense, the enemy tried to stay in action only long enough to permit his base garrison to escape with supplies. Instead of using artillery and bombers to fix the enemy in place and infantry-armor-engineer assault groups to destroy him, the cavalry used infantry to fix enemy defenses and artillery and airpower to destroy him. These tactical differences partially reflected area warfare attrition versus linear warfare territorial advance, but both placed an equally high premium on courage, tactical expertise, and calm leadership.

3. 1st Cav Div, *Bunker Busting: Attack on Fortified Areas*, dtd 18 Jan 71.

"Bunker busting" became the norm of offensive cavalry combat after 1968, and this style of fighting proved to be one of the most difficult tests of combat fortitude in Vietnam.

Throughout the mobile and fragmented war in Vietnam, a premium was placed on intelligence gathering to locate elusive enemy forces, base areas, and trail networks. The 1st Cavalry Division's long-range patrol (LRP) company, later designated as ranger infantry, provided much of this dangerous work. Each patrol platoon was commanded by a lieutenant, who had eight six-man teams under him. Each team was authorized a staff sergeant team leader, a sergeant assistant team leader, a front scout, a rear scout, a radioman, and a medic. However, most teams were led by buck sergeants or Specialists 4th Class during the war. All long-range patrol members were volunteers, and the majority were parachutists.

Each long-range patrol mission was unique, and the experience of one patrol of Company E, 52d Infantry, on 17 August 1968 is presented as an example of the dangers and accomplishments of this elite force. On that day SSgt. Stephen Tefft was told that his LRP Team 32 would be inserted in the southern portion of Enemy Base Area 101, a jungled mountain area of I CTZ. Staff Sergeant Tefft and his assistant team leader, Sgt. George Kennedy, were taken on a helicopter reconnaissance over their area of operations that afternoon. They familiarized themselves with the prominent terrain features that could be used later as reference points should they become disoriented or have need of an emergency extraction pickup zone. Upon their return to the team's rear base location, Tefft called his men together and gave them the patrol order.

In a small patrol, operating deep in enemy territory, it was necessary that all team members clearly understood their mission, the terrain, and the enemy situation. Since the mission entailed a two-day patrol, no rucksacks were carried. All ammunition and basic necessities were placed in pouches on their combat harnasses or in their bedrolls, which consisted of half a poncho per man. Full rubber ponchos reflected too much light and made too much noise, but the half-poncho was lightweight and kept the upper part of the body warm. Also, if the team was hit at night, a man could quickly discard the poncho half and be ready for action. Only two dehydrated LRP ration meals were carried per man, and since the weather was cool no need existed for water beyond the five quarts that each man carried.

The insertion was scheduled for 6:30 P.M. the next evening, so Sergeant Tefft gave his men time off until noon the following day. This helped to counterbalance the high tension they would face during the patrol. On the afternoon of 18 August, the team assembled again. This time they were dressed in camouflaged fatigues and bush hats, and their faces were streaked and darkened by charcoal sticks. They were briefed once more, then they rehearsed immediate action and contact drills for the rest of the day. These were automatic procedures used in case of sudden contact with the enemy and were practiced over and over until performance became instinctive. Since the patrol was so small, they faced superior numbers in virtually any expected encounter. Survival depended on teamwork and the instant, coordinated reaction of the entire patrol.

At 6:30 P.M. the team was aboard the helicopter, part of a three-troopship formation with two gunships flying escort, en route to its landing zone. The insertion was made in an old bomb crater in the middle of triple-canopy jungle at last light. The lift helicopters approached the landing zone in file with the patrol in the first troopship. The control helicopter was second, and an empty helicopter was last in file. The first helicopter sat down quickly, and the team dashed out, while the other two helicopters continued to fly at low level overhead. At precisely the right moment, the team helicopter lifted off to become third in file. By executing a number of hops in this fashion, the NVA/VC remained unaware of the exact drop-off point for any patrol.

Everything was quiet on the ground, and the team quickly left the bomb crater and moved one hundred yards directly south into the jungle, where they made their initial communications check with the long-range patrol control headquarters. It was becoming very dark as the patrol moved a little farther and discovered a trail. The front scout, Sp4 Clare Michlin, checked the pathway for signs of recent use. The front scout fulfilled both point and tracking duties, looking for signs such as recently broken brush or discarded material. After determining that the trail was probably cold, the team moved away from the path and up a small hill. They set out claymore mines and prepared an overnight position. Usually, after 9:00 P.M. Sergeant Tefft kept one man awake, on half-hour shifts, but on occasion, depending on the enemy situation, the whole patrol stayed awake.

Early the next morning the team moved farther south and traveled down the hill into a valley. At 8:00 A.M. they tried another communications check, but could not establish radio communication because of the low ground. Finally, they made contact with a friendly station which acted as relay. The team continued its cautious movement through the jungle until 11:00 A.M., when they sat down for "Pak time." This interval lasted until 2:00 P.M. and was observed to conform patrol movement to enemy travel habits. The NVA/VC frequently took a midday break during these hours.

At 7:00 P.M. that evening, the patrol trekked south into a gully containing a stream. The men refilled their canteens and then silently listened for any sounds of possible enemy presence. After waiting for a while and hearing nothing unusual, the patrol continued. About two-hundred years downstream they found a trail which ended at the bank, and Staff Sergeant Tefft believed that this might be an enemy water point. The patrol moved up the trail, but had proceeded only a few feet when they saw a group of twenty North Vietnamese soldiers walking directly toward them. Before the team could jump off the trail, the enemy opened fire with automatic rifles.

The patrol responded automatically with their reaction drill. Specialist Michlin, the point man closest to the enemy group, threw a white phosphorous grenade in front of the North Vietnamese soldiers, who were also taking evasive action. The patrol quickly maneuvered back to the stream, the men giving covering fire to each other as they bounded backward. This leapfrogging retreat soon placed the rear scout closest to the advancing enemy troops, and he also tossed a white phosphorous grenade in an attempt to discourage pursuit. The patrol was equipped with claymore mines and time-capsule fuses, which it usually carried for emergencies when contact had to be broken, but the charges had a fifteen-minute delay period. The enemy was too close.

The team ran across the stream and clambered up a steep slope into a treeline along an upland rice paddy where they reassembled into a hasty perimeter. Sp4 Plisch frantically called for aerial support on his radio. Since they had been spotted, Staff Sergeant Tefft decided to try for an emergency extraction under the covering fire of helicopter gunships. During Plisch's radio transmissions for help, the other team members saw another eight enemy soldiers moving across a clearing to surround them. They fired on this new NVA element with silencer-equipped M16 rifles. The enemy squad, unsure of the exact location of return fire, stopped forward movement and became pinned down.

A Cobra gunship and a scout helicopter from the 1st Squadron, 9th Cavalry, were quickly overhead. The Cobra was diverted from another mission, and its low ammunition and fuel status allowed the pilot to make only one firing pass. The light observation helicopter remained at the scene, firing its M60 defiantly in support and guiding the team to a suitable pickup point. The team used fire and movement tactics to relocate for extraction. Two more Cobra gunships and a second light helicopter appeared within minutes, and their rockets and miniguns caused the North Vietnamese to retreat. A Huey troopship quickly swooped down, and when it was three feet off the ground, the team jumped aboard. Although their primary mission, reconnoitering for enemy movement, was compromised, the patrol was credited with finding the enemy and directing aerial rocket fire on his positions.

The long-range patrol members received no extra pay or privileges for their work. Their satisfaction came from pride of comradeship and the special contribution they made to the effectiveness of the First Team. Throughout the Vietnam War the rifle scouts of the 9th Cavalry, battalion and brigade recon forces, and the long-range/ranger infantry of the division patrol company served the 1st Cavalry Division with confidence and valor. Their exploits more than made up for their small numbers, because they operated over a wide area to find the NVA/VC, report on his movements, disrupt his activities, and pioneer areas for large-scale action by the airmobile battalions.[4]

While the combat performance of elite and line battalion components of the 1st Cavalry Division was beyond reproach, the general personal conduct of all personnel within the division was quite high. Accurate assessments of such intangibles as morale and esprit de corps are probably impossible, but quantitative evaluation can be made in determining troop discipline and obedience to orders. Division troop performance in these areas is examined by surveying general crime rates, grenade incidents ("fragging"), and war crimes in Vietnam.

The personnel of the division demonstrated exemplary behavior

---

4. 1st Cav Div AVDAMH Doc, Subj: Long Range Patrols of the 1st Air Cav Div, dtd 26 Dec 68.

compared to other formations stationed in Vietnam. The USARV provost marshal quarterly summary reports for all major Army commands confirm the high esteem in which the division was held. Two sample quarters are statistically cited here, as they represent the final three-month figures for 1969 and 1970, the most troubled period of American troop service when all units were still incountry and before strengths were eroded by major withdrawals.

During the period of October through December 1969, the 1st Cavalry Division had only 37 persons confined in the USARV Long Binh stockade, a rate of 1.85 per thousand, and the lowest of any division or equivalent command. In crimes against persons and property, where there was a 7.2 percent rise in other division crime rates to include murder, manslaughter, and rape, the 1st Cavalry Division's most serious crimes from October through December 1969 were six aggravated assaults, eleven simple assaults, one robbery, and twelve larcenies (most under fifty dollars). One year later, during the period of October through December 1970, the 1st Cavalry Division had 96 persons in the USARV prisoner population at Long Binh, a rate of 4.68 per thousand, which resulted largely from increased division crackdowns on drug offenders. The true measure of division troop behavior again focuses on serious crimes against persons and property, which at this point in the war had escalated to alarming levels throughout USARV. However, the 1st Cavalry Division had only one case of murder, twenty simple assaults, and fifteen petty larcenies. These statistics are astonishingly low, even for a peacetime garrison division in Europe or the United States, and a tribute to the leadership and men of the division.[5]

In Vietnam, "fragging" was a slang expression originally referring to the use of a fragmentation grenade to kill or injure another person, usually as a measure taken against unpopular officers or sergeants. However, a great deal of fragging was directed toward fellow enlisted men as a result of grievances and drug trafficking. Common Army usage expanded the meaning of the term to encompass the use of other varied explosive devices. The crux of the problem in Vietnam was found in control and leadership at the company and battalion

5. USARV, *Command Progress Reports*, 2d Qtr FY-69, pp. 60.02, 60.08; 2d Qtr FY-70, pp. 70.05, 70.08.

level. Most commanders and senior sergeants were rarely able to see their entire unit at one time, because of widespread base camp elements and dispersed units in the field.

Fragging incidents rose sharply throughout Army divisions and separate brigades in 1970, which represented the peak year for this type of criminal activity. A close scrutiny of fraggings and shootings during the second half of the year gives a good picture of how the 1st Cavalry Division compared in troop discontent. During these six months, the division had only five incidents of grenade fraggings and twenty-two cases of shootings. At the same time there was a total of thirty-eight grenade fraggings and ninety-seven shootings among the five Army divisions and five separate combat brigades from July through December 1970 (with two brigades departing country during this period). Again, the 1st Cavalry Division has a conspicuously low rate of grenade incidents, despite having the highest number of assigned personnel and the largest area of operations with scattered firebases in Vietnam.[6]

The 1st Cavalry Division was also remarkably free from the taint of war crime accusation during its service in Vietnam. This fact reflects great credit upon an organization that waged a very difficult war in the midst of an often hostile civilian population.

There were only three main allegations of improper wartime activity brought against units of the 1st Cavalry Division in Vietnam. The first complaint stemmed from the alleged mistreatment of a Viet Cong prisoner following the appearance of an Associated Press photograph in the 30 December 1965 issues of *The Chicago Daily News* and *Milwaukee Journal*. The photo showed a seemingly nonchalant cavalry major looking on while "a Vietnamese Popular Forces militiaman kicks a Viet Cong prisoner in the head at an interrogation point . . . after being captured by U.S. troops of the 1st Cavalry (Air Mobile) Division." The Army ordered a full investigation with the following results.

The 1st Cavalry Division received a report in December 1965 that some VC were hiding in caves in the Binh Khe district. The Binh Khe district chief appointed one of his policemen as a guide for a

---

6. DCS P&A DF TO C/OS Dept. of the Army, fm Maj. Woodbeck AVHDP-MMW, DF, Subj: Grenade Incidents, dtd 14 Mar 71, w/supporting papers.

search expedition by the 1st Squadron, 9th Cavalry. No caves were found, but a VC suspect was captured by Troop C of the squadron and evacuated to the landing zone for immediate interrogation by the 3d Brigade intelligence officer (a major) prior to evacuation as a prisoner of war. About the same time that the helicopter arrived with the major and AP photographer Mr. Huet, the Binh Khe policeman saw the prisoner and recognized him as a fellow villager. The policeman accused him of being a known Viet Cong responsible for trouble in the hamlet and ran over and kicked him before the cavalrymen could react. The major rushed over and immediately stopped the civilian policeman from kicking the prone VC suspect.

Mr. Huet later stated that he had already had his camera focused; otherwise, he would have been unable to take the picture, since the incident happened so quickly. He also agreed that the photo was misleading because the major was about to rush over to stop the mistreatment. Unfortunately, the major seemed to be permitting, or merely observing, the kicking at the instant the shutter clicked. The photograph was that of an isolated incident whereby a civilian guide was inadvertently allowed to get close enough to a village adversary to vent his rage upon him. The situation was quickly remedied, but not before a chance photograph gave a completely erroneous impression of the incident. The 1st Cavalry Division, which prided itself on according prisoners proper treatment, ironically became associated with harsh retribution by a national press eager for dramatic photographs.[7]

The next untoward division incident, the "Brooks Incident," did not arise until 18 May 1971, when a "hunter-killer" team of three helicopters from Troop A, 1st Squadron, 9th Cavalry, performed a visual reconnaissance mission over a small Cambodian village. The scoutship crew observed a number of motorcycles and bicycles with packs near the hamlet, which they suspected was an enemy convoy. The villagers were signaled from the air to open the packs, and machine gun fire was used to force the inhabitants into the open after the instructions were ignored. On another pass over the area, the pilot of the observation helicopter heard gunfire behind his craft and notified the Cobra gunship that he was taking fire. The mission commander in the third helicopter saw automatic weapon muzzle flashes

7. MACJI Ltr Serial No. 3844 1st Ind, Subj: Complaint, Alleged Mistreatment of a Viet Cong Prisoner, dtd 1 Mar 66, w/ investig papers.

from a dike one hundred yards south of the village and so advised the Cobra pilot. The attack helicopter rocketed the dike and adjacent buildings, while the gunner aboard the scoutship sprayed the rest of the village.

An ARVN platoon led by cavalry Capt. Arnold H. Brooks was airmobiled into the contact area under the cover of gunship support fires (this was a technical violation of standing orders not to enter Cambodia at the time). The South Vietnamese raced into the village with weapons blazing, gunning down several people, including children, then looted the hamlet. The platoon was not fired on, did not search for enemy positions, and did not treat any of the wounded civilians. The Vietnamese troops left the area, taking large quantities of tobacco, poultry, radios, and other booty, while Captain Brooks helped himself to a motorcycle which he later presented to Lt. Col. Carl C. Putnam, the squadron commander, as a war trophy. Several days later Lieutenant Colonel Putnam decided to investigate.

The Army concluded that the 9th Cavalry had engaged in excessive bombardment and pillage of a Cambodian village and had violated several rules of engagement. Letters of reprimand were issued to Lieutenant Colonel Putnam and others, but court-martial charges against Captain Brooks were dismissed at Fort Knox, Kentucky, on 21 April 1972. Division members felt that the cavalry actions were appropriate, that the South Vietnamese were responsible for the actual problems, and that the investigation was unfair. Air cavalrymen functioned in a very dangerous flight pattern. A "low bird" light observation helicopter was flown at slow speed as a carrot to make the enemy reveal his location. The "high bird," an armed helicopter, circled the bait scoutship to render immediate protective response. To stay alive, these aviators had to react instantly with deadly effective firepower. This incident transpired in a "hot area" full of enemy traffic, where it was common NVA/VC practice to use motorcycles and bicycles for transporting war materials and supplies.[8]

The final war crime incident involving a 1st Cavalry Division unit was commonly known as the "Woodcutters Incident," since it allegedly involved the murder of two Vietnamese woodcutters. On 7 Jan-

8. CG Third Regional Assistance Cmd Ltr AVDACG, Subj: Report of Investigation: Firing Incident in Cambodia, dtd 12 Dec 71, and related paperwork; DA Investigation summary #219, dtd 1 May 72.

uary 1972 a Mr. Nguyen Xuan Tuyet from Binh Son hamlet near the village of Long An reported that three days earlier an unidentified helicopter fired upon some woodcutters in his district, hitting two of them. He stated that the helicopter then landed, at which time Army soldiers got out and finished the woodcutters off with pistols, took their cnain saw and bicycle, and departed. MACV immediately initiated a full investigation.

The investigation revealed that the Vietnamese were actually killed in a ground action by Ranger Team 73 of Company H, 75th Infantry (Ranger) of the 3d Brigade, 1st Cavalry Division, and that no helicopter weapons were fired during that mission. The ranger team was in a special strike zone on a reconnaissance patrol when two armed Vietnamese were spotted sitting beside a pile of brush. Both were immediately ambushed and killed. The rangers stripped the bodies of clothing, an AK47 assault rifle, two grenades, and some small tools, but no identification was found on either. The rangers found a bicycle twenty-five yards away and placed it aboard their helicopter. A small, inoperative chain saw was sighted but not taken.

The Vietnamese officials were using a pass system for woodcutters in the area. The Vietnamese in the hamlet insisted that the victims had such passes and reiterated that the victims were merely innocent woodcutters. However, the hamlet was rated as 70 percent VC sympathetic in the latest MACV Hamlet Evaluation System rating report. The MACV investigation concluded that there was insufficient evidence to refute the ranger team's testimony, but concluded that they violated the laws of war by taking the bicycle. This result was so ludicrous, however, that after the brigade commander "took appropriate action to preclude recurrence of such an act as the taking of the bicycle," the Army dismissed the complaint.[9]

The excellent combat and personal performance of the 1st Cavalry Division troopers during its long service in Vietnam reflects very favorably on a formation which experienced great personal turbulence and heavy action. The remarkable ability of this highly mobile division to retain its characteristic élan and combat spirit is especially noteworthy in the final war years, when the rest of the Army had entered a marked state of decline in morale, fighting efficiency, and individual behavior.

9. DA Investigation Summary #214 dtd 7 Aug 72.

The Total Battlefield

From Airmobility to Armor

After the summer of 1970, when contingents of the 1st Cavalry Division returned from Cambodia to Vietnamese soil, the American withdrawal from Southeast Asia began escalating sharply. Pentagon war plans were revised to hasten the extrication of remaining U.S. ground forces and to turn the war's conduct over entirely to the South Vietnamese regime. Partially in deference to these larger plans, Maj. Gen. George W. Putnam, Jr., was selected to command the 1st Cavalry Division in the wake of Major General Casey's tragic death on 7 July. At that time Major General Putnam was in charge of the 1st Aviation Brigade, which was heavily engaged in direct support of ARVN operations against Cambodia and thoroughly familiar with both airmobile doctrine and Vietnamese requirements.

George W. Putnam, Jr., was born in Fort Fairfield, Maine, on 5 May 1920 and was commissioned in the field artillery from officer candidate school during May 1942. During World War II, he was a gunnery instructor and battalion operations officer, arriving in Europe early in 1945. He transferred to the Regular Army in August 1946, served in the occupation forces of Japan, and became aviator-qualified ten years later. Appointed to the crucial airmobility development Howze Board, Colonel Putnam served as executive to the Secretariat, which was the administrative workhorse of the board. He was Deputy Director of Army Aviation until May 1965, when he was named the Assistant Commandant of the Army Aviation School at Fort Rucker, Alabama. His next assignment took him to Vietnam, where he served successively as the 1st Cavalry Division artillery commander, acting assistant division commander, and division chief of staff. In 1968

General Putnam became the Director of Officer Personnel in the Pentagon and returned to Vietnam in January 1970 as the commanding officer of the 1st Aviation Brigade and the chief aviation officer of USARV.

Major General Putnam was anxious to implement one important concept of the Howze Board that had not been tested because of lack of funding and the events of the Vietnam War, the Air Cavalry Combat Brigade (ACCB). The Howze Board's final report of 21 June 1962 had specified that the ACCB was one of the most original and decisive combat tools of projected airmobile force structuring. The air cavalry combat brigade was to be predominantly an offensive machine in the true spirit of swiftly mobile cavalry, designed to "seek out and destroy the enemy and carry out traditional cavalry missions." Two or more attack helicopter squadrons were to be grouped under a tactical headquarters to form a brigade in the Howze Board scheme.[1]

The 1st Cavalry Division was given a new operational area to fill the gap created by redeploying American units such as the 199th Infantry Brigade after the Cambodian incursion. The division was tasked to cover an immense region of 4,536 square miles east of Saigon, spanning the width of the entire country from the Cambodian border through War Zone D all the way to the South China Sea. This increased territorial responsibility presented Major General Putnam with the need to stretch air cavalry assets and a reason to create his de facto air cavalry combat brigade. In August 1970 he directed a divisional aircraft productivity analysis which found that the attack Cobra gunship platoons escorting the aviation lift battalions were not being used correctly and that many light observation helicopters could be freed from general support duties.

Based on the findings of this internal aircraft resource investigation, the assault weapons companies (Company D) were withdrawn from both the 227th and 229th Aviation Battalions beginning on 1 September and transferred to the control of the 1st Squadron, 9th Cavalry, as lettered air cavalry troops. Combined with a sudden infusion

1. U.S. Army Combat Developments Command Combat Arms Group, *The Origins, Deliberations, and Recommendations of the U.S. Army Tactical Mobility Requirements Board*, Fort Leavenworth, Kansas, April 1969, p. 51.

of light observation helicopters garnered from other division elements, the 9th Cavalry's aerial reconnaissance squadron (with air Troops A, B, and C) blossomed overnight into a reinforced five-troop (A, B, C, E, F) search-and-attack cavalry squadron. Several squadron scout helicopters were even outfitted with miniguns. While this represented a powerful helicopter squadron, it constituted only half of any projected air cavalry combat brigade.[2]

On 26 October 1970 Putnam secured the 3d Squadron of the 17th Cavalry, an independent aerial reconnaissance unit from his former 1st Aviation Brigade, and attached it to the division. This squadron was bolstered by an additional air cavalry Troop E (Provisional), created by temporarily redesignating the separate 334th Aviation Company on 5 December. The reinforced 1st Squadron of the 9th Cavalry and 3d Squadron of the 17th Cavalry under division control gave Major General Putnam the two search-and-attack helicopter squadrons needed to form a provisional ACCB. The air cavalry combat brigade's effectiveness was increased by assigning two elite airmobile ground reconnaissance companies to help locate enemy forces and material: Troop D of the 9th Cavalry's 1st Squadron and ranger Company H, 75th Infantry, with the 62d Infantry Platoon (Combat Tracker) thrown in for good measure. Finally, the division's sole aerial rocket artillery battalion, the Cobra-equipped "Blue Max" 2d Battalion of the 20th Artillery, was placed in direct support. The 9th Air Cavalry Brigade (Combat) was officially announced as a reality by division General Orders on 5 December 1970.

The 9th Cavalry Brigade had a rather brief and confusing existence and was mostly scattered in support of various divisional and ARVN parachutist or ranger elements. Each air cavalry troop was assigned a zone of responsibility coinciding with a division or ARVN airborne brigade sector. During the month of December alone, it restructured its task organization three times and conducted only one independent operation.

On 29 December 1970 the brigade received a warning order to locate and free allied prisoners supposedly located in the Razorback vicinity of War Zone C. ACCB Task Force Nevins arrived at the

---

2. 1st Cav Div, *Operational Report*, dtd 14 Nov 70, p. 21.

abandoned Special Forces Camp Dau Tieng airstrip and on the morning of 31 December established a forward operating base with refueling and rearming points. Task Force Nevins consisted of one infantry battalion and two air cavalry troops. Although the mission started with heavy action, a promising sign that the NVA/VC were guarding something worth defending, the operation was abruptly terminated that afternoon because MACV insisted on strictly observing the holiday cease-fire. All elements of Task Force Nevins were pulled back from Dau Tieng airstrip by 7:30 that evening.[3]

The provisional air cavalry combat brigade was sent into Cambodia to support four ARVN task forces along the Kampong Cham–Snoul front on 22 February 1971. Two days later it was augmented further by the addition of the air cavalry troop from the 11th Armored Cavalry Regiment. Adverse modifications to normal air cavalry maneuver were immediately imposed because of the stringent rules of engagement concerning Cambodian operations. The results were generally unsatisfactory. Tortuous clearances for fire support rendered the ACCB incapable of responding effectively with the prompt, devastating firepower it was designed to deliver. ARVN airmobile ground forces called "Browns" replaced the experienced U.S. infantry "Blues" employed by the brigade as quick reaction forces, since American combatants were not allowed on the ground. The "Browns" not only lacked rudimentary knowledge of helicopter tactics, but often were not responsive to American control.

The exact date of disbandment of the 9th Cavalry Brigade is hard to pinpoint. The ACCB was actually whittled away over a period of months as components left to reinforce the Laotian battlefront during Operation LAM SON 719, rejoin parent units, or depart Vietnam. The provisional brigade's final report gives its own closure as 15 February, but the quarterly division operation report (mentioning the unauthorized ACCB under the guise of the 1/9 Cav TF) claims reassignment to the 12th Aviation Group of 1st Aviation Brigade on 10 April 1971. General Putnam's air cavalry force was inside Cambodia with at least six troops and an aerial rocket artillery battery at the beginning of April.

The experimental air cavalry combat brigade was created as an

3. 1st Cav Div, *Operational Report*, dtd 13 May 71, p. 36.

ad hoc enterprise to field-test Howze Board findings under combat conditions. Its mission in Vietnam as stated was to: (1) perform reconnaissance and security for the division or its major subordinated elements, (2) engage in combat "as an economy-of-force unit," and (3) provide a limited air and ground antitank capability. Additionally, the brigade was tasked to receive and employ other combat units, such as the composite infantry and rocket artillery battalion later assigned. The brigade was to serve as a senior command and control headquarters for a specific area of operations.[4]

The ACCB concept as outlined above was actually tailored to European- and Middle Eastern–style warfare and could not be adequately demonstrated in Vietnam or Cambodia because of political constraints in the form of unique rules of engagement. General Putnam had the right idea, to create a true cavalry force by taking the gunships out of the lift battalions and giving their escort mission to the aerial artillery battalion. His ACCB harmonized with enlightened Howze Board recommendations about creating special corps cavalry reserves, but was still too advanced to be grasped adequately by the Army. In the Vietnam theater the experiment was stifled. He merely proved that the ACCB initiated 67 percent of all division actions against hostile forces during the period of its existence, that an infantry battalion would be a useful adjunct to the air cavalry combat brigade, and that further testing was needed. Even the contact initiation statistic was suspect, since it was only slightly better than the performance of the aerial reconnaissance squadron used as intended, but the ACCB possessed twice the aerial capacity. Again, the most serious and vexing problem was the lack of qualified maintenance personnel to keep the air cavalry combat brigade flying.

Further experimentation with lingering Howze Board ideas or tactical innovations was given lower priority after 20 December 1970, when the men of the 1st Cavalry Division (Airmobile) were notified of divisional selection as part of the sixth redeployment increment from Vietnam, coded KEYSTONE ROBIN CHARLIE. From the beginning of 1971 until the main division withdrawal at the end of April, the division staff was occupied primarily with planning, coordinating,

---

4. 9th Cav Bde (Prov) ADVARS-3, *Combat After Action Report*, dtd 23 Mar 71, with attached ltr dtd 24 Oct 70.

and implementing retrograde procedures. Fortunately, NVA/VC activity within the region actually decreased during this period, enabling the division to phase out smoothly with minimal enemy interference. Small roving platoon and squad-size airmobile cavalry forces were able to patrol their defensive sectors without difficulty.

Composite or split artillery batteries were used to provide adequate coverage, but these configurations were disadvantageous since they increased helicopter support requirements and logistical problems. The lack of meaningful North Vietnamese confrontations enabled the 1st Cavalry Division to boast of using strike infantry flexibly outside the range of tube artillery, armed only instead with Huey-transportable 81mm mortars as close defense. This was largely a hollow doctrinal improvement because the intensity of the "big battle years" in Vietnam (for the American Army, from 1966 to 1968) relegated support weapons like 81mm medium mortars to either idle storage or supplementary support in base camps. The intensity of the Ia Drang Valley campaign of late 1965 offered early demonstrable proof of mortar insufficiency compared to heavier artillery. Only the lowered level of NVA/VC combat, coupled with the lack of continuous frontline experience institutionalized by the Army rotation system, allowed the 1st Cavalry Division to rely on and claim the advantages of mortar substitution.

Beginning in February, the division's operational area was reduced as more Vietnamese territorial forces were summoned to perform guardianship over roads and hamlets and line ARVN units were moved into former cavalry firebases. The 1st Cavalry Division continued to function with high esprit throughout this difficult withdrawal period. For example, the 1st Battalion of the 5th Cavalry fought fifteen skirmishes with the North Vietnamese during its last nine days in the field, with every member of the battalion keenly aware of the exact day scheduled for extraction from the jungle. The two-battalion 2d Brigade, charged with interdiction of NVA/VC supply channels between Cambodia and War Zone D, completed its disengagement by turning over Fire Support Base Buttons to the South Vietnamese on 11 March 1971. The 1st Brigade with four battalions scoured War Zone D until 24 March, when it commenced stand-down. These events left the three-battalion 3d Brigade, slated to remain as a separate entity in Vietnam after the rest of the division departed, with defense of the central region just east of Bien Hoa and Saigon, protecting the most crucial military installations from rocket barrage.[5]

On 29 April 1971 the 1st Cavalry Division (Airmobile) furled its guidons and left Vietnam for Fort Hood, Texas. Sixteen days previously, former Assistant Division Commander-A, Brig. Gen. Jonathan R. Burton, took over the separate 3d Brigade "Garry Owen" Task Force. His separate brigade was assigned a very large area encompassing thirty-five hundred square miles and defensive responsibility for the eastern approaches toward vital Saigon and Long Binh. As a result, the brigade was reconstituted with seven recycled battalions as well as sixteen additional companies and platoons. The brigade contained four infantry battalions (2/5 Cav, 1/7 Cav, 2/8 Cav, 1/12 Cav), one reinforced artillery battalion (1/21 Arty), one composite 229th Aviation Battalion, and the 215th Support Battalion. The eight separate companies or batteries included rangers (Co H/75 Inf), aerial rocket artillery (F/79 Arty), howitzers (Prov F/26 Arty), aviation target acquisition (F/77 Arty), signal (525th), engineers (501st), military intelligence (191st), and aviation (362d). The 362d Aviation Company was effectively converted into an air cav reconnaissance troop to supplement the brigade's intrinsic Troop F, 9th Cavalry. The brigade's platoons and detachments, ranging from chemical to military police, gave the task force all the trappings of a miniature division. This formidable cavalry contingent had an assigned strength of 7,632 men at the end of 1971.

General Burton had two concurrent main concerns, finding the enemy and personnel management within the brigade. The NVA/VC routinely avoided confrontation with the cavalry, and increased emphasis was placed on remaining abreast of enemy activity. The brigade's two air cavalry troops gained the most information on enemy dispositions and discovered new base camps or resupply routes. Air cavalry missions were accomplished normally by using OH6A scout "white bird" in a visual reconnaissance role to draw fire under the covering support of an AH1G Cobra "red bird," which also provided suppressive fire, navigational control, and a communications

---

5. 1st Cav Div, *KEYSTONE ROBIN CHARLIE After Action Report*, dtd 15 Apr 71, Appendix 3 to Annex C.

link to higher headquarters. Together, these "pink team" combinations rendered 44 percent of all credited brigade kills from April through December 1971.[6]

The outstanding success of the ranger company was attributed to its extensive training, as well as individual ranger team knowledge that the entire brigade stood ready to react rapidly in case of adverse hostile contact. The strength of Company H, 75th Infantry (Ranger), had been reduced to conform with 3d Brigade size, but Burton doubled the number of teams from four to eight based on its battlefield performance. All ranger volunteers were trained by the company staff, and the rigorous training standards washed out three-fourths of all candidates each training cycle. Qualified rangers became skilled in rappelling and the use of McQuire rigs, which were Special Forces–developed hoisting devices for penetration of difficult tropical terrain. Brigade ranger teams were inserted into enemy-dominated territory on missions of five-day duration primarily to gather intelligence, but their skill at ambush accounted for approximately 30 percent of all brigade kills from April through December.[7]

The brigade's internal military intelligence posture was enhanced by close coordination between the Vietnamese Counterintelligence Service and the dreaded Military Security Service (MSS) beginning in September 1971. When four MSS agents were added to the brigade, it marked the first time that MSS personnel were assigned to a U.S. combat unit in Vietnam. Several female MSS agents were hired in a drug-suppression role. General Burton implemented a strong drug abuse intervention program centered around the special Brigade Drug Rehabilitation Center. From 1 May to 31 October, 633 brigade personnel underwent detoxification and treatment at the center. Unannounced urinalysis testing was conducted frequently, and often identified drug users were sent to the Drug Abuser Holding Center (DAHC) for administrative and judicial action.[8]

Troop welfare was also maintained through positive rewards, primarily by the introduction of a rifle company rotation program. The

6. DAAG-PAP-A (M), *Senior Officer Debriefing Report: BG Jonathan R. Burton*, dtd 3 May 72, p. 7.

7. Ibid., pp. 6–7.

8. Ibid., p. 13.

infantry companies operated independently to cover the wide expanse of the brigade's area of responsibility, but each remained within the artillery fan of at least one firebase. The general pattern kept companies in the field for fifteen days, where they received helicopter resupply of ammunition, rations, and water every three or four days. If the landing zone conditions permitted, a hot meal and ice cream, change of clothing, mail, and other comfort items were delivered. When the company completed its fifteen-day field duty, it was rotated to a fire support base to provide security for another five days. During this time, the company was refitted, underwent bunker assault and marksmanship training, and took care of personnel affairs. Every forty-five days, on a rotational basis, each rifle company and recon platoon was sent to the First Team R&R Center, opened at the beach resort of Vung Tau in March 1971, for three days of rest and recreation. The troops were given considerable latitude to unwind after six weeks in the field. The maintenance of the center was a drain on brigade material, personnel, and monetary assets, but the high effect on morale was considered worthwhile.

Brig. Gen. James F. Hamlet, another former Assistant Division Commander-A, took over the separate 3d Brigade on 14 December 1971. The formation was infused with a rash of transferred soldiers from other redeploying divisions, such as the 101st Airborne (Airmobile), at the rate of five hundred a week. Regardless of "bush time," these new arrivals were sent through the brigade Combat Training Center. The cavalry brigade continued its fourfold mission of defending the Saigon–Long Binh military complex, training Vietnamese territorial forces, remaining ready to move into other military regions as a security fire brigade, and preparing to execute various late-war contingency plans.[9]

The separate 3d Brigade was still involved occasionally in heavy combat, despite continuing readjustment of operational areas to bring it closer into the defensive arc of the Bien Hoa–Long Binh–Saigon rocket belt (that area within range of NVA rocket attacks). The brigade's former forward operating base at FOB Mace, beside Nui Chua Chan, was closed, and a new rearmament and refueling facility was

9. 3d Bde (Sep) 1st Cav Div, *Operational Report*, dtd 1 May 72, p. 1 (Mission) and Tab I-1 (Brigade Strength Report).

opened at Xuan Loc airfield. On 3 January 1972 the 2d Battalion of the 5th Cavalry was displaced to FSB Charger in conjunction with this rearward move. A platoon of Company C was attacked by elements of the *33d NVA Regiment* using a hasty U-shaped ambush. The company maneuvered to link up with its trapped platoon and to attack the ambush site from another direction. The North Vietnamese fled the field after a fierce two-hour skirmish, during which the airmobile cavalry reaction force, gunships, and medical evacuation helicopters all suffered heavy return fire.

On 1 April 1972 the generally slow pace of the war in Military Region 3 suddenly changed. Three NVA divisions attacked from the Cambodian Fishhook vicinity after staging a diversionary assault north of Tay Ninh. The enemy quickly overran Loc Ninh and besieged An Loc. The 3d Brigade ground troops were not members of this fighting force, but the two brigade air troops (F/9 Cav and D/229 Avn Bn) and the aerial rocket artillery battery (F/79 Arty) were involved in constant combat to stem the North Vietnamese advance. Despite intense antiaircraft fire from 23mm, 37mm, and even some 85mm AA guns, the brigade's AH1G Cobra gunships destroyed twenty-nine trucks and five tanks and damaged a sixth.

Attempts to rescue American advisors at Loc Ninh were unsuccessful, but several advisors were lifted by brigade helicopters from the Cam Lo Bridge after being cut off and surrounded for three days. The brigade aviators also evacuated ARVN soldiers and civilians from Bu Dop and Song Be, helped repulse an NVA attack against the Nui Ba Den radio relay site, and supported several South Vietnamese counterattacks into An Loc.[10]

The American withdrawal from Vietnam continued unabated even though such renewed NVA/VC onslaughts threatened to destroy the Saigon government without continued U.S. military presence. The 3d Brigade (Separate) of the 1st Cavalry Division was redeployed from South Vietnam as part of Increment XII KEYSTONE PHEASANT on 26 June 1972 and returned to rejoin the rest of the 1st Cavalry Division at Fort Hood, Texas. The division had been located there since its own KEYSTONE ROBIN CHARLIE arrival the previous year.

10. 3d Bde 1st Cav Div, *Operational Report*, dtd 1 May 72.

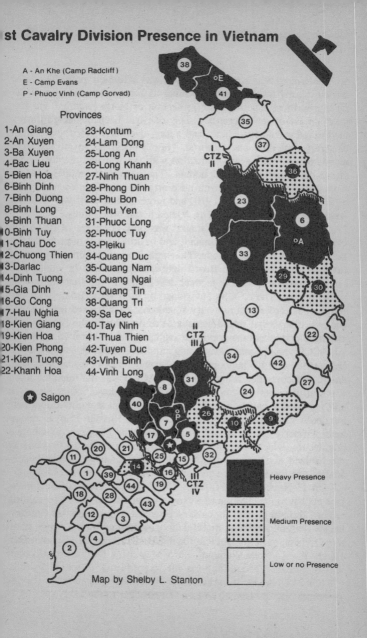

st Cavalry Division Presence in Vietnam

A - An Khe (Camp Radcliff)
E - Camp Evans
P - Phuoc Vinh (Camp Gorvad)

Provinces

1-An Giang
2-An Xuyen
3-Ba Xuyen
4-Bac Lieu
5-Bien Hoa
6-Binh Dinh
7-Binh Duong
8-Binh Long
9-Binh Thuan
10-Binh Tuy
11-Chau Doc
12-Chuong Thien
13-Darlac
14-Dinh Tuong
15-Gia Dinh
16-Go Cong
17-Hau Nghia
18-Kien Giang
19-Kien Hoa
20-Kien Phong
21-Kien Tuong
22-Khanh Hoa

23-Kontum
24-Lam Dong
25-Long An
26-Long Khanh
27-Ninh Thuan
28-Phong Dinh
29-Phu Bon
30-Phu Yen
31-Phuoc Long
32-Phuoc Tuy
33-Pleiku
34-Quang Duc
35-Quang Nam
36-Quang Ngai
37-Quang Tin
38-Quang Tri
39-Sa Dec
40-Tay Ninh
41-Thua Thien
42-Tuyen Duc
43-Vinh Binh
44-Vinh Long

⭐ Saigon

Heavy Presence

Medium Presence

Low or no Presence

Map by Shelby L. Stanton

The United States military posture was extremely poor. The most difficult Army task was reconforming its forces to meet national defense priorities, especially the protection of North America and Europe in case of major conflict. This risk had been neglected during the limited war in Indochina, and a long-overdue major reorientation of Army structure was required. New tactical organizations were mandated, but public dissatisfaction with the war had drastically reduced the Army's size and budget. The seemingly radical Modern Volunteer Army Program with no draft was implemented-with great difficulty past 13 October 1970, and large quantities of war material were still being siphoned off to Vietnam and other allies.

Lt. Gen. Harry W. O. Kinnard was now in charge of the Army Combat Developments Command, and he still wanted to properly test the air cavalry combat brigade. This organization remained a personal favorite from the Howze Board deliberations, which he considered one step further down the tactical development road than the air assault division. The ACCBs envisioned by the Howze Board were homogeneous forces of air cavalry squadrons, each backed up by aerial rocket artillery, that would be capable of performing the Army's cavalry mission (except the armored cavalry regimental ground mission). An ACCB would contain everything required—firing helicopters, scout helicopters, and lift helicopters—to provide each corps with its own small, self-contained army. While the ACCB was not intended to be a powerful group of shooting helicopters to block Soviet armor, it still provided a swiftly mobile and balanced unit that could dominate hundreds of square miles of Iranian desert or Russian Pripyat marshland. Properly balanced and commanded, the brigade could harass and destroy widespread enemy forces by using scouts to find enemy mechanized and infantry forces, airmobile infantry to furnish ambushes and local security, and gunships to attack selected targets.

On 23 November 1970 Army Chief of Staff General Westmoreland approved the creation of a "triple capability" division combining armor, airmobile, and air cavalry brigades to test possible high-intensity-warfare structural modifications. He programmed the 1st Cavalry Division to be the vehicle for this project upon its arrival at Fort Hood, Texas, from Vietnam. On 5 May 1971 the cavalry division was reorganized accordingly as the experimental Triple Capability (TRICAP) Division. It used the personnel and equipment of the 1st Armored Division, which in turn sent its flag to Germany.

The potential of the TRICAP and allied ACCB enterprise was suffocated from the start by Army bureaucratic imcompetence. The test division was placed at Fort Hood, an entrenched armor post full of officers convinced that tanks would dominate future battlefields and that aircraft were only supplementary to tracked steel. Furthermore, both TRICAP and ACCB were buried in an institutional morass under the unlikely direction of Project MASSTER (Mobile Army Sensor Systems Test, Evaluation, and Review).

Project MASSTER was established in 1969 to manage the development of surveillance, target acquisition, and night observation (STANO) equipment and doctrine. The task apparently engendered so little respect that the Army's Vice Chief of Staff was forced to direct that "CONARC, USACDC (Combat Developments Command), USAMC (Material Command), and USASA (Security Agency) establish visible STANO offices within their headquarters to serve as points of contact for the coordination of STANO matters in intercommand and Department of the Army Staff–command activities."[11] Nestled at Fort Hood since 1 October 1969, MASSTER provided an already funded but suitably vague bureaucratic instrument available to incorporate TRICAP.

The method that produced the highly successful 11th Air Assault and airmobile 1st Cavalry Divisions had been the appointment of a young brigadier "tiger" with open directives and wide latitude to report back with results. In this case, however, the Army followed its usual nonprogressive path of testing and analysis, reports and more reports. TRICAP was incorporated into the unwieldy MASSTER management structure, which was expanded to oversee sensor and night surveillance equipment development, the integrated battlefield control system (IBCS), and, last, TRICAP/ACCB. On 25 June 1971 the MASSTER acronym was conveniently retained by changing the organizational title to Modern Army Selected Systems Test, Evaluation, and Review. The revised MASSTER charter was published on 2 September, designating the commanding general of III Corps and Fort Hood to be the commanding general of MASSTER as an additional duty.[12]

11. USCONARC, *Annual Historical Summary: FY 71*, p. 121–22.
12. III Corps and Fort Hood GO 275, dtd 25 Jun 71, and CONARC, *Annual Historical Summary*, dtd 15 Jul 72, p. 122.

The charter's objectives were so hopelessly diversified as to be almost ludicrous. MASSTER (nicknamed the "Mass Management Structure") was charged—in this exact order—with testing to improve the Army's combat intelligence/reconnaissance and STANO capabilities, improving the Army's tactical command and control capability within the IBCS framework, evaluating the air cavalry combat brigade and the TRICAP division concept, and supporting the development of other selected concepts, organizations, and material systems which might be assigned for evaluation.

Confusion reigned supreme. The serious shortage of helicopters initially prevented the air cavalry combat brigade from either conforming to the organization envisioned by the Army Combat Developments Command or commencing meaningful training. Although one air cavalry squadron was present, the other envisioned attack helicopter squadron was instead a battalion of medium tanks.

Even more detrimental to evaluation of either ACCB or the TRICAP testing was the fact that the resource-starved Army suddenly decided to redress emergency war plans for Europe. The Army ordered the entire TRICAP/ACCB test package to be made potentially available as a combat-ready division. During the same month that the 1st Cavalry Division was redesignated as TRICAP, instructions were received to fashion the new structure to facilitate quick conversion into a standard armored division which, by using reserve components, could replace the already-departed armored division at Fort Hood. So many variations on the possible employment of the 1st Cavalry Division began appearing that frustrated staff officers, drafting long-range stationing alternatives for Army units, simply labeled it the "Experimental Division"—with no particular numbering, title, or imagined composition—under Fort Hood entries.[13]

The 1st Cavalry Division, with its 3d Brigade still separated in Vietnam, lost most of its airmobility under TRICAP. A 4th Brigade was formed, and the armored commanders at Fort Hood brought over their tanks and armored personnel carriers. The Johnny-come-lately battalion to Vietnam (5th Bn, 7th Cav) was inactivated, and the howitzer battalion picked up overseas (1st Bn, 30th Arty) sent to Fort

---

13. CONARC/ARSTRIKE, *Annual Historical Summary—FY 1971*, dtd 15 Jul 72, Table 8.

Sill, Oklahoma. This left the 1st Cavalry Division (TRICAP) with four mechanized cavalry battalions from each of its traditional regiments (1st Bn, 5th Cav; 2d Bn, 7th Cav; 1st Bn, 8th Cav; 2d Bn, 12th Cav); two aviation units newly formed at Fort Hood (170th Avn Co and 230th Avn Bn, later retitled as the 227th to preserve Vietnam heritage); three tank battalions transferred from the armored division (1st and 2d Bns, 13th Armor, and 1st Bn, 81st Armor); three artillery battalions (the 1st Bn, 6th Arty, and 3d Bn, 19th Arty, arrived from the armored division; the 1st Bn, 77th Arty, remained; and both 2d Bn, 19th Arty, and 2d Bn, 20th Arty, were inactivated); and one cavalry reconnaissance squadron (4th Sqdn, 9th Cav, previously the armored division's 3d Sqdn, 1st Cav, which became the 1st Sqdn, 9th Cav, when the latter returned from Vietnam on 28 June 1971). The support structure was revised as well.[14]

Numerous MASSTER tests were undertaken during the year. As predicted by the airmobile pessimists, battalion organizational and tactical development models were jointly tested with such things as STANO border surveillance/anti-infiltration devices, unattended ground sensors, and battle information control centers. An attack helicopter squadron was finally activated for both TRICAP and ACCB testing at the end of February 1972, when the 4th Squadron, 9th Cavalry, was reformed at Fort Hood. The unit was raised by folding down the 170th Aviation Company and inactivating Company C, 2d Battalion, 13th Armor, on temporary duty supporting tests at Hunter-Liggett Military Reservation in California, and bringing back its personnel and equipment. Only the personal intervention of Lt. Gen. George P. Seneff, Jr., now the III Corps commander, forced the Army to rescind the attack helicopter title and authorize reorganization of the unit as an air cavalry squadron on 22 March 1972.[15]

14. The 1st Cavalry Division (TRICAP) support base contained the 8th Engineer Bn, 13th Signal Bn, 15th Medical Bn, 15th Supply & Transport Bn, 27th Maint Bn, 315th Support Bn, 545th MP Co, 15th Admin Co, 15th Finance Co, and 15th Data Processing Unit. Note the loss of the 15th Trans Bn and 15th Supply & Service Bn, but the addition of two new battalions (15th S&T Bn, 315th Spt Bn) in their places. Source of 1st Cav Div reorganization from DA Msg 091810Z Apr 71, Subj: Reorg and Inactiv of Armored Div; and DA Msg 091930Z Mar 71, Subj: Reorg to TRICAP Div.
15. ODCSFOR, *Semi-Annual Hist Report, January–June 1972*, p. 4.

While air cavalry proponents became more frustrated over the miring of TRICAP and ACCB in the bureaucratic quagmire at Fort Hood, the 101st Airborne Division (Airmobile) was completely reorganized and rebuilt at Fort Campbell, Kentucky, during 1972. The 101st Airborne Division was the second airmobile division raised by the Army for Vietnam duty. On 4 October 1974 the division dropped its parenthetical airmobile identifier in exchange for air assault and became the Army's second air assault formation. Although the "unique capability of its air assault resources" was not recognized as an official part of its mission statement until 31 August 1977, the division's modern rendezvous with destiny was clear. On that date the division's 477 helicopters and 16,600 well-trained light infantrymen and women, replete with their silver air assault badges, placed the 101st Airborne Division (Air Assault) in the dynamic future of airmobility forfeited by the 1st Cavalry Division.[16]

TRICAP and ACCB failed because their real purpose was simply to justify as many troops in the force structure as possible, while revitalizing the old Howze Board dream of an air cavalry combat brigade in the early 1970s. The resulting division mix consisted of an infantry brigade, an armor brigade, and an air cavalry brigade, each of which was too vastly different to form an integrated whole.[17]

The overriding demand to conform scant Army resources to projected war plans forced the experimental division into an emergency armored division mode for European contingencies. This was perhaps a foreseeable result of placing cavalry units in the backyard of heavy armor advocates at Fort Hood. Light and swift air cavalry could not be nurtured in such an environment. Finally, the experiment was doomed by its subjugation to the bureaucratic MASSTER beast. Throughout the rest of the decade, the triplex surveillance-cavalry-target acquisition relationship was solidified by the Armor and Military Intelligence Centers. By 1 August 1980 this latter development inevitably transformed the 1st Cavalry into a heavy armored division with a target servicing air cavalry attack brigade.

Airmobile firepower relied not on tanks linked to target-seeking

16. 101st Abn Div, *1975 Historical Summary*, p. 31; *Fiscal 1977 Historical Summary*, pp. 9, 12.
17. USAMHI, Seneff Debriefing.

aircraft, but on fusing manpower, weapons, and aerial transport with cavalry doctrine. Air assault integrates attack, transport, and observation aircraft with the fighting elements of a division. By maintaining intrinsic helicopter and other aircraft resources, the air assault division insures the continuous availability of proficient aviation responsive to its unique tactical requirements. Even an air assault aviation cadre subjected to heavy battle loss and fatigue on a nuclear battlefield will sustain this advantage. While the 1st Cavalry Division performed this role, it was officially termed airmobile. The 101st Airborne Division (Air Assault) now wears the crown, and in many historical respects this is proper, given the original preferences of General Howze and other paratroopers who formulated modern Army airmobility principles. As long as the 101st represents a lean, light infantry organization, the forward thinking and spirit that General Kinnard considered essential for dashing airmobile operations will be preserved.

The Army's cavalry normally consisted of either ground or aerial reconnaissance units. Armored cavalry was used much like standard armor in Vietnam. It was in the air that cavalry played such a unique role. The 1st Cavalry Division, endowed with the great mobility and flexible response offered by its organic aircraft, was the first organization to combine light infantry and artillery howitzer forces with vertical assault, aerial firepower, and air reconnaissance capabilities in combat. Deployed to Vietnam as early as was practical, the division quickly demonstrated its skill and determination in finding and eliminating the enemy through air assault and clearing operations. Unleashed throughout the country as MACV's premier fighting formation to locate and destroy the elusive NVA/VC, the First Team insured battlefield domination with a dazzling array of cavalry techniques ranging from sustained pursuit and cavalry raids to screening and cavalry exploitation.

Unfortunately, the United States Army ultimately failed to grasp the permanent bond between fast raiding and other cavalry techniques with modern airmobile and air assault doctrine. The fusion of the Vietnam-era 1st Cavalry Division with helicopter mobility and firepower forged a powerful war machine, naturally attuned to optimum performance of military tasks in the rich tradition of American light cavalry. By allowing the 1st Cavalry Division to be retreaded into a conventional armored division, the United States Army forsook the original foresight of Lieutenant General Gavin, the prophet of airmobility.

General Gavin's vision of modern aerial cavalry freed the Army from the tyranny of terrain and sent Skytroopers over the cloud-banked rim of Southeast Asia to battle the enemy from the air. His plea still echoes through the vaults of the Pentagon, the grassy fields of Fort Benning, the concrete helicopter pads of Fort Rucker, and the overgrown foxholes of the lush Ia Drang Valley with a resounding, "Cavalry, and I don't mean horses! I mean helicopters and light aircraft to lift soldiers armed with automatic weapons and hand-carried light antitank weapons, and also lightweight reconnaissance vehicles, mounting antitank weapons the equal of or better than the Russian [tanks]. . . . If ever in the history of our armed forces there was a need for a cavalry arm—airlifted in light planes, helicopters, and assault-type aircraft—this was it!" The legacy of the 1st Cavalry Division remains, and the need still exists.

1st Cavalry Division (Airmobile)

Assigned Units

Command

Headquarters & Headquarters Company, 1st Cavalry Division
Headquarters & Headquarters Company, 1st Brigade
Headquarters & Headquarters Company, 2d Brigade
Headquarters & Headquarters Company, 3d Brigade
Headquarters & Headquarters Company and Band, Support
  Command
Headquarters & Headquarters Company, Rear (Provisional)

Infantry

1st Battalion, 5th Cavalry
2d Battalion, 5th Cavalry
1st Battalion, 7th Cavalry
2d Battalion, 7th Cavalry
5th Battalion, 7th Cavalry
1st Battalion, 8th Cavalry
2d Battalion, 8th Cavalry
1st Battalion, 12th Cavalry
2d Battalion, 12th Cavalry

Aviation

Headquarters & Headquarters Company, 11th Aviation Group
227th Aviation Battalion (Assault Helicopter)
228th Aviation Battalion (Assault Support Helicopter)
229th Aviation Battalion (Assault Helicopter)

11th Aviation Company (General Support)
Air Traffic Control Platoon (Provisional)

Division Artillery

2d Battalion, 19th Artillery (105mm Howitzer)
2d Battalion, 20th Artillery (Aerial Rocket)
1st Battalion, 21st Artillery (105mm Howitzer)
1st Battalion, 30th Artillery (155mm Howitzer)[1]
1st Battalion, 77th Artillery (105mm Howitzer)
Battery E, 82d Artillery (Aviation)

Division Reconnaissance

1st Squadron, 9th Cavalry (Aerial Reconnaissance)
11th Pathfinder Company/Platoon (Provisional)
Company E, 52d Infantry (Long Range Patrol)[2]
Company H, 75th Infantry (Ranger)[2]

Division Support

1st Forward Service Support Element
2d Forward Service Support Element
3d Forward Service Support Element
8th Engineer Battalion
13th Signal Battalion
15th Medical Battalion
15th Supply & Service Battalion
15th Transportation Battalion (Aircraft Maintenance & Supply)
27th Maintenance Battalion
15th Administrative Company
371st Army Security Agency Company
545th Military Police Company

1. The 1st Battalion, 30th Artillery, was attached to division 1 Jul 66 and assigned 1 Jun 68–6 Apr 71.
2. Company E of the 52d Infantry was formed as the long-range patrol company of the division on 20 Dec 67; on 1 Feb 69 it was inactivated and its assets were used to create Company H, 75th Infantry (Ranger).

1st Personnel Services Battalion (Provisional)[3]
An Khe Airfield Command (Provisional)[4]
Replacement Training School/FIRST TEAM Academy
    (Provisional)[5]
U.S. Army Special Security Detachment

Attached Units

Armored Cavalry and Infantry

1st Battalion, 50th Infantry (Mechanized)	22 Sep 67–15 Mar 68
11th Armored Cavalry Regiment, elements	12 Apr 69–April 71
25th Infantry Platoon (Scout Dog)	20 June 66–20 Mar 71
34th Infantry Platoon (Scout Dog)	21 Nov 66–20 Aug 72
37th Infantry Platoon (Scout Dog)	15 Nov 69–7 Mar 71
54th Infantry Detachment (Ground Radar)	27 May 66–17 Jan 68
62d Infantry Platoon (Combat Tracker)	15 Feb 68–15 Aug 72

Aviation

3d Squadron, 17th Cavalry (Air)	26 Oct 70–April 71
Troop F, 3d Squadron, 4th Cavalry	April 71
Air Cavalry Troop, 11th Arm Cavalry	24 Feb 71–Mar 71
17th Aviation Company (Fixed-Wing CV-2)	15 Sep 65–1 Jan 67
53d Aviation Detachment (Provisional)	1 Sep 66–30 Oct 66
273d Aviation Company (Heavy Helicopter)	Nov 68–Mar 71
334th Aviation Company (Aerial Weapons) on temporary duty as Troop E (Prov), 3d Sqdn, 17th Cavalry	5 Dec 70–17 Jan 71
478th Aviation Company (Heavy Helicopter)	Mar 66–28 Feb 69

3. The provisional 1st Personnel Services Battalion was formed by the division on 26 Jan 68 and was disestablished on 1 Jul 69, when it became a company in size.
4. The An Khe Airfield Command was created by internal division resources on 15 Dec 65 and was under division control until Oct 67.
5. The Replacement Training School, later termed the FIRST TEAM Academy, was a provisional organization formed on 1 Oct 66, lasting until the division left Vietnam.

Aircraft Maintenance Transportation Detachments

1st Squadron, 9th Cavalry	98th, 151st, 166th, 545th
2d Battalion, 20th Artillery	80th, 171st, 329th
Battery E, 82d Artillery	564th
11th Aviation Company	150th
227th Aviation Battalion	166th, 390th, 394th, 400th
228th Aviation Battalion	51st, 165th, 255th
229th Aviation Battalion	391st, 392d, 393d, 571st
3d Squadron, 17th Cavalry	369th, 575th, 576th
273d Aviation Company	652d
478th Aviation Company	382d

Artillery

Btry A, 5th Bn, 2d Artillery (40mm)	Jan 69–Mar 71
6th Bn, 14th Artillery (175mm Gun)	29 Oct 65–1 Feb 66
2d Bn, 17th Artillery (105mm Howitzer)	25 Oct 65–1966
3d Bn, 18th Artillery (8-inch Howitzer)	26 Oct 65–1 Oct 66
Btry B, 29th Artillery (Searchlight)	23 Oct 65–6 Oct 66
268th Artillery Detachment (Radar)	14 Apr 69–2 Jan 71
273d Artillery Detachment (Radar)	5 May 69–15 Apr 71

Support

14th Military History Detachment	27 Dec 65–20 Mar 72
26th Chemical Platoon (CBR Center)	16 Oct 65–26 Mar 72
41st Public Information Detachment	21 Mar 67–30 Jun 71
42d Public Information Detachment	21 Mar 67–29 Apr 71
184th Chemical Platoon (Direct Support)	16 Oct 65–1 Mar 71
191st Military Intelligence Company	25 Aug 65–29 Mar 71
583d Military Intelligence Detachment (Interrogation)	20 Jul 67–16 Feb 70
American Red Cross Female Contingent	

Air Force Weather Squadron Detachments

5th Weather Squadron, Dets 24 and 31	Dec 66–Mar 71
30th Weather Squadron elements	Oct 65–Nov 66

1st Cavalry Division (Airmobile) Formation*

Division Unit	Source
Headquarters & Headquarters Company, 1st Cavalry Division (Airmobile)	Headquarters & Headquarters Company, 11th Air Assault Division (Test)
HHC, 1st Brigade	**HHC, 1st Brigade, 11th Air Assault Division**
1st Battalion (Airborne), 8th Cavalry	1st Battalion (Airborne), 188th Infantry
2d Battalion (Airborne), 8th Cavalry	1st Battalion (Airborne), 511th Infantry
1st Battalion (Airborne), 12th Cavalry	1st Battalion (Airborne), 187th Infantry
HHC, 2d Brigade	**HHC, 2d Brigade, 2d Infantry Division**
1st Battalion, 5th Cavalry	1st Battalion, 38th Infantry
2d Battalion, 5th Cavalry	2d Battalion, 38th Infantry
2d Battalion, 12th Cavalry	1st Battalion, 23d Infantry

* Source: Hq 11th AAD AJVGT Ltr dtd 30 Jun 65, Subj: Reorganization of Units, w/Incl 1, and USARPAC GO 325, dtd 22 Nov 65 (inactivation and activation of aviation units).

257

Division Unit	Source
HHC, 3d Brigade	**HHC, 3d Brigade, 2d Infantry Division**
1st Battalion, 7th Cavalry	2d Battalion, 23d Infantry
2d Battalion, 7th Cavalry	2d Battalion, 9th Infantry
5th Battalion, 7th Cavalry**	1st Battalion, 11th Infantry**
HHB, Division Artillery	**HHB, 11th Air Assault Division Artillery**
2d Battalion, 19th Artillery (105mm)	6th Battalion, 81st Artillery (105mm)
2d Battalion, 20th Artillery (Aer Rocket)	3d Battalion, 377th Artillery (Aer Rocket)
1st Battalion, 21st Artillery (105mm)	5th Battalion, 38th Artillery (105mm)
1st Battalion, 77th Artillery (105mm)	1st Battalion, 15th Artillery (105mm)
HHC & Band, Support Command	**HHC & Band, 11th Air Assault Division Spt Cmd**
8th Engineer Battalion	127th Engineer Battalion
13th Signal Battalion	511th Signal Battalion
15th Medical Battalion	11th Medical Battalion
15th Supply & Service Battalion	408th Supply & Service Battalion
15th Transportation Battalion	611th Aircraft Maintenance & Supply Battalion
27th Maintenance Battalion	711th Maintenance Battalion
15th Administrative Company	11th Administrative Company
15th Supply & Service Battalion Aerial Equipment Support Company (Airborne)	165th Aerial Equipment Support Detachment

** 5th Battalion, 7th Cavalry, was activated 1 April 1966 at Fort Carson, Colorado, and joined the 1st Cavalry Division in Vietnam. Source of unit derived from *Army Times*, dtd 25 May 1966, "Carson Greets Airmobile Unit."

Division Unit	Source
545th Military Police Company	11th Military Police Company
191st Military Intelligence Detachment	11th Millitary Intelligence Detachment
371st Army Security Agency Company	Company C, 313th Army Security Agency Battalion
HHC, 11th Aviation Group (Airmobile)	**HHC, 11th Aviation Group (Test)**
HHC, 227th Aviation Battalion	HHC, 227th Aviation Battalion
Company A, 227th Aviation Battalion	Company A, 227th Aviation Battalion
Company B, 227th Aviation Battalion	Aviation Company, 6th Special Forces Group
Company C, 227th Aviation Battalion	Aviation Company, 7th Special Forces Group
Company D, 227th Aviation Battalion	110th Aviation Company (Aerial Weapons)
HHC, 228th Aviation Battalion	HHC, 228th Aviation Battalion
Company A, 228th Aviation Battalion	132d Aviation Company (Assault Support Hel)
Company B, 228th Aviation Battalion	133d Aviation Company (Assault Support Hel)
Company C, 228th Aviation Battalion	202d Aviation Company (Assault Support Hel)
HHC, 229th Aviation Battalion	HHC, 229th Aviation Battalion
Company A, 229th Aviation Battalion	Company A, 4th Aviation Battalion
Company B, 229th Aviation Battalion	Company A, 5th Aviation Battalion
Company C, 229th Aviation Battalion	194th Aviation Company (Assault Helicopter)
Company D, 229th Aviation Battalion	131st Aviation Company (Aerial Weapons)
11th Aviation Company	11th Aviation Company (General Support)
1st Squadron, 9th Cavalry	3d Squadron, 17th Cavalry

SOURCES AND BIBLIOGRAPHY

The research for this book was primarily based on division documents prepared during the Vietnam conflict, especially the quarterly operational reports, as supplemented by higher command histories issued on an annual basis. The internal division combat after action reports issued at the conclusion of most operations were very useful, as were the wartime division magazine issues of the *The First Team*. Annual historical summaries of the U.S. Continental Army Command and the reports of various Army testing boards provided much information on the stateside service of both the 11th Air Assault and 1st Cavalry Divisions before and after Vietnam service. One important postwar source was the senior officer oral history program conducted by the Oral History Branch, U.S. Army History Institute, Carlisle Barracks, Pennsylvania. The author also interviewed key participants with the 1st Cavalry Division during the Vietnam era, and made extensive utilization of the materials assembled for his earlier *Vietnam Order of Battle* project.

The following is a listing of the more readily available resources, although many reports and articles not listed below are cited for reader convenience in text footnotes.

The Air Cavalry Division, Vietnam: 1st Cavalry Division, 1969.

1st Cavalry Division, *Quarterly Command Report*, dtd 1 Dec 65, OACSFOR-OT-RD 650110.

1st Cavalry Division, *Quarterly Command Report*, dtd 10 Jan 66, OACSFOR-OT-RD 650109.

1st Cavalry Division, *Operational Report*, dtd 5 May 66, OACSFOR-OT-RD 660119.

1st Cavalry Division, *Operational Report*, dtd 15 Aug 66, OACSFOR-OT-RD 660292.

1st Cavalry Division, *Operational Report*, dtd 22 Nov 66, OACSFOR-OT-RD 660505.

1st Cavalry Division, *Operational Report*, dtd 15 Feb 67, OACSFOR-OT-RD 670226.

1st Cavalry Division, *Operational Report*, dtd 23 May 67, OACSFOR-OT-RD 670473.

1st Cavalry Division, *Operational Report*, dtd 15 Aug 67, OACSFOR-OT-RD 670798.

1st Cavalry Division, *Operational Report*, dtd 15 Nov 67, OACSFOR-OT-RD 674236.

1st Cavalry Division, *Operational Report*, dtd 17 Mar 68, OACSFOR-OT-RD 681288.

1st Cavalry Division, *Operational Report*, dtd 13 Jun 68, OACSFOR-OT-RD 682337.

1st Cavalry Division, *Operational Report*, dtd 20 Aug 68, OACSFOR-OT-RD 683305.

1st Cavalry Division, *Operational Report*, dtd 6 Dec 68, OACSFOR-OT-UT 684268.

1st Cavalry Division, *Operational Report*, dtd 15 Feb 69, OACSFOR-OT-UT 691115.

1st Cavalry Division, *Operational Report*, dtd 15 Apr 69, OACSFOR-OT-UT 692094.

1st Cavalry Division, *Operational Report*, dtd 15 Aug 69, OACSFOR-OT-UT 693030.

1st Cavalry Division, *Operational Report*, dtd 15 Nov 69, OACSFOR-OT-UT 694007.

1st Cavalry Division, *Operational Report*, dtd 15 Feb 70, OACSFOR-OT-UT 701072.

1st Cavalry Division, *Operational Report*, dtd 15 May 70, OACSFOR-OT-UT 702040.

1st Cavalry Division, *Operational Report*, dtd 14 Aug 70, OACSFOR-OT-UT 703016.

1st Cavalry Division, *Operational Report*, dtd 14 Nov 70, OACSFOR-OT-UT 704030.

1st Cavalry Division, *Keystone Robin Charlie Redeployment Report*, dtd 15 Apr 71, OACSFOR-OT-UT 71XOO6.

3d Brigade (Separate), *Operational Report*, dtd 13 Nov 71.

3d Brigade (Separate), *Operational Report*, dtd 1 May 72.

3d Brigade (Separate), *Operational Report*, dtd 20 Jun 72.

14th Military History Detachment, *The First Team in Cambodia*, dtd 15 Feb 71.

14th Military History Detachment, *The Construction of a Fire Base in the 1st Cavalry Division*, dtd 10 Oct 69.

14th Military History Detachment, *Bunker Busting: Attack on Fortified Areas*, dtd 18 Jan 71.

Albright, John, John A. Cash, and Allan W. Sandsrum, *Seven Firefights in Vietnam*, Washington, D.C.: U.S. Government Printing Office, 1970.

Bergerson, Frederic A., *The Army Gets an Air Force*, Baltimore and London: The Johns Hopkins University Press, 1980.

Brennan, Matthew, *Brennan's War*, Novato, California: Presidio Press, 1985.

Coleman, J. D., *Memories of the First Team in Vietnam*, 1st Cavalry Division Information Office: Vietnam, 1969.

Enthovan, Alain C. and K. Wayne Smith, *How Much is Enough: Shaping the Defense Program, 1961–1969*, New York: Harper & Row, 1961.

Fehrenbach, T. R., *This Kind of War*, New York: Macmillan Company, 1963.

Gavin, Maj. Gen. James M., "Cavalry and I Don't Mean Horses!", *Armor*, Volume LXIII, No. 3.

Hymoff, Edward, *The First Air Cavalry Division: Vietnam*, New York: M. W. Ladd Publishing Co., 1966.

Kinnard, Douglas, *The War Managers*, University of New England Press, 1977.

Marshall, S.L.A., *Battles in the Monsoon*, New York: Morrow, 1967.

———, *Bird: The Christmastide Battle*, New York: Cowles Book Co., 1968. 1968.

Mason, Robert, *Chickenhawk*, New York: Viking Press, 1978.

Ney, Virgil, *Evolution of the U.S. Army Division, 1939–1968*, CORG Memorandum M-365, Fort Belvoir, Virginia: U.S. Army Combat Developments Command, 1969.

Palmer, Gen. Bruce, Jr., *The 25-year War: America's Military Role In Vietnam*, University Press of Kentucky, 1984.

Palmer, Brig. Gen. Dave R., *Summons of the Trumpet*, Novato, California: Presidio Press, 1978.

Sharp, Adm. U.S.G. and Gen. W. C. Westmoreland, *Report on the War in Vietnam (as of 30 Jun 68)*, Washington, D.C.: U.S. Government Printing Office, 1968.

Stanton, Shelby L., *The Rise and Fall of an American Army*, Novato, California: Presidio Press, 1985.

Summers, Col. Harry G., *Vietnam War Almanac*, New York: Facts on File Publications, 1985.

Tolson, Lt. Gen. John J., *Vietnam Studies: Airmobility, 1961–1971*, Washington, D.C.: Department of the Army, 1973.

U.S. Army Training and Doctrine Command, *A History of Army 86*, Volumes I and II, Fort Monroe, Virginia: TRADOC Historical Monograph Series.

U.S. Army Combat Developments Command, *The Origins, Deliberations, and Recommendations of the U.S. Army Tactical Mobility Requirements Board*, Fort Leavenworth, Kansas, 1969.

Westmoreland, Gen. William C., *A Soldier Reports*, New York: Doubleday & Company, 1976.

INDEX